ALSO BY ELAINE T. PARTNOW

BOOKS

The New Quotable Woman
The Quotable Woman: 1800–1981
The Quotable Woman: Eve–1799
Breaking the Age Barrier
Everyday Speaking on All Occasions for Women, with Susan Partnow
Photographic Artists and Innovators, with Turner Browne

PLAYS AND PERFORMANCE WORKS

Hear Us Roar, A Woman's Connection
Hispanic Women Speak
Movers & Shakers: Living History Portraits of Women
A Visit with Emily Dickinson

THE FEMALE DRAMATIST

THE FEMALE DRAMATIST

*Profiles of Women Playwrights from the
Middle Ages to Contemporary Times*

ELAINE T. PARTNOW

WITH
LESLEY ANNE HYATT

Facts On File, Inc.

THE FEMALE DRAMATIST

Facts On File, Inc.
11 Penn Plaza
New York, NY 10001

Library of Congress Cataloging-in-Publication Data

Partnow, Elaine T.
    The female dramatist : profiles of women playwrights from
    the middle ages to contemporary times / by Elaine T.
    Partnow with Lesley Anne Hyatt.
        p. cm.
    Includes bibliographical references and index.
    ISBN 0-8160-3015-4
    1. Women dramatists—20th century—Interviews. 2. Playwrighting.
    I. Hyatt, Lesley Anne. II. Title.
PN471.P37 1998
809.2′082—dc21   97-26501

Facts On File books are available at special discounts when purchased in bulk quantities for businesses, associations, institutions or sales promotions. Please call our Special Sales Department in New York at (212) 967-8800 or (800) 322-8755.

You can find Facts On File on the World Wide Web at http://www.factsonfile.com

Text design by Cathy Rincon
Cover design by Nora Wertz

Printed in the United States of America

FOF VB 10 9 8 7 6 5 4 3 2 1

This book is printed on acid-free paper.

*T*o my father, Al Partnow—

You loved to see me perform
but were hesitant about my acting career;
yet you gifted me
with the joy of performing,
and for this gift I am wholeheartedly grateful.

CONTENTS

FOREWORD BY KAREN MALPEDE
IX

PREFACE BY ELAINE PARTNOW
XI

LIST OF ILLUSTRATIONS
XVII

TIME LINE
XIX

HOW TO USE THIS BOOK
XXIX

PROFILES
1

APPENDIX: SUPPLEMENTAL INDEX
231

BIBLIOGRAPHY
241

INDEX
243

FOREWORD

by Karen Malpede

This book is a vast compendium of information about women playwrights. The lives and works of more than 200 women from ten centuries are profiled here: a nun who defied the Catholic hierarchy to write; freedom fighters censored and jailed for their words; Renaissance women who had their character impugned for revealing the truth about the marriage market; Victorian women who dressed and lived as men to write; contemporary women who founded major experimental theaters and whose own plays are seminal works of the avant-garde; women who had great popular success, who won Pulitzer Prizes and Academy Awards; women called mad, who perished in obscurity, their life's work lost. Many of the lives sketched here read like modern myths—women born of their own desire to speak true, writing words to set actors in motion on the stage.

Here are women whose work I have long admired for its sheer excellence, and women whose life stories I have often turned to for the sustenance bold example gives. Some are women I know personally, with whom I've shared a piece of the century, but there are many, many others whose lives and works I was introduced to for the first time. The experience was dizzying, as if stepping suddenly out of a dank, dark cave where for years I had busily been making up my own half-truths from the shadows on the walls, and walking into the hot sun, I found the ground alive with women. "A lovely sight to see; all as one,/the old women and the young and the unmarried girls . . . they fastened their skins of fawn with writhing snakes/that licked their cheeks," as Euripedes' Messenger dares report in *The Bacchae*. After all, we exist. The Earth does vibrate to the rhythms of our speech. Only out of fear of our powers have women been silenced and ignored. No writer has been kept more invisible or isolate, has been more denigrated or despised than the female dramatist, whose matrilineage is suddenly rendered plain thanks to these brief incisive portraits by Elaine Partnow.

Now, I am sitting in the company of my sisters, thinking as I have thought before, that if women's plays were produced with the frequency, financial backing, and critical understanding accorded the plays of men, would this change the culture, or would it herald a culture already changed? And how do women envision culture? Is there any commonality among our diversities of history, style, vision, craft, class, country, ethnicity, and race? Indeed, over and over, one reads in this book, how one writer after another has sought to write the lives of women, to bring them into history, to explore a woman's interior self, to tell the story of the universe in a woman's voice. If we have something in common besides our rebellious natures, for one cannot escape the feeling that we have been rebels, each and every one, our commonality lies in our flesh. We are writing from within a female body, writing the stories of women's bodies, bodies subject to a culture's rage. We are writing our own desire, knowledge, shame, and strength.

The woman playwright listens, and her ear to the self, her "I" a tuning fork, she takes the measure of her time. Then, because she is a playwright, she makes forbidden knowledge public. She exteriorizes the inner life, speaks the hidden truths, exposes nightmare doubts of the culture in which she lives. Because she is a playwright, what she knows cannot remain hidden between the covers of a book, to be picked up surreptitiously, and read under the sheets as many women have learned to read. Because she is a playwright, her voice must live inside actors and reach up from their bellies through their voices to the ears of many people. Language spoken to an audience fuses them with a common knowledge and instant experience. They live together through events they can both contemplate and share. The theater offers space to reflect upon lived experience, to find that you are suddenly not alone, but bound together in community. When women's plays are staged, women's truth becomes universal.

Women's plays have not often fared well with critics; women playwrights have often been vilified, their works willfully misunderstood. The weakest most predictable plays by women have frequently been most highly praised. Comfortable plays that depict woman's frustrations, that show her inner life as limited, that watch her settling or solving her struggle through romance, or plays that show women killing, committing suicide, or being killed, plays that support the violence of our culture, are most likely to win awards. A woman who experiments with form, who expresses dense, unruly feeling, who glories in sexuality, who attempts to write of history, philosophy, or make a social protest, a woman who sets her characters on a culture-changing mission, may often find herself the most outcast and ignored. Even a woman who does these things with undisputed brilliance—Marguerite Duras, for example, whose theater poetry is as rich as Samuel Beckett's, or Gertrude Stein, as funny and fine as anyone—will be revered by only a small coterie, staged and taught relatively rarely, and often denied her historical role.

If women's plays were produced in numbers equal to the plays of men, human beings would be suddenly advantaged by a fuller vision. Though an individual never has full knowledge of where she came from, who she is, all drama is about the search against the odds for such self-knowledge and the need to act in the world despite not knowing who we are. Women dramatists inhabit the realm of the unfinished. We don't know what our lives would be if we had lived them fully, without terror, without disrespect. We struggle to imagine wholeness—an earth undefiled; a strikingly new balance between nature and culture; a greater tolerance for difference; a spiritual renewal untouched by fundamentalist violence and cant; and personal relationships based upon mutual respect. Women playwrights struggling to invent the female character equally are culture-changing agents, imagining beyond the known. Their plays attempt to tell us not only who we are, but what we might become.

PREFACE

Today's women playwrights have become a force to be reckoned with, both in the United States and Canada and in Europe. Though this may seem a new phenomenon, it is not: The same occurred during the Restoration in England and again during the suffrage movements in both England and the United States. What is also not new, despite these recurring booms, is how few women have emerged as members of the canon of dramatic literature. What is also not new is the same old neglect and dismissiveness with which women of talent in so many pursuits have been treated. Of the seventy-eight Pulitzer Prizes for drama awarded since the inception of the prize in 1910, eight have gone to women (ZONA GALE, 1921; SUSAN GLASPELL, 1931; ZOË AKINS, 1935; MARY CHASE, 1945; KETTI FRINGS, 1958; BETH HENLEY, 1981; MARSHA NORMAN, 1983; WENDY WASSERSTEIN, 1989). It is interesting to note that the longest gap between Pulitzer Prizes to women playwrights was 1958 to 1981—from the late fifties through the rise of feminism and the arrival of this century's "new woman."

Susan Faludi maintains in *Backlash*, her watershed 1991 book, "It has not been unusual that during periods when women have made great social strides they have been ignored or vilified." Looking back to the first great period of women playwrights, the Restoration, when, between 1660 and 1720, some sixty plays by women were staged, talented and popular playwrights such as APHRA BEHN, SUSANNA CENTLIVRE, HANNAH COWLEY, and DELARIVIERE MANLEY were scathingly abused by the press. There was an expression in that day, the "Salic law of wit," which derived from an ancient penal code, the Salic law. It contained, among other things, some civil law enactments, one of which declared that daughters could not inherit land. The Salic law took on critical importance under the French Valois dynasty in the sixteenth century when it was incorrectly cited as authority for the existing assumption that women should not succeed to the crown. Its derivative, the unwritten Salic law of wit, was, according to Nancy Cotton,

"sometimes enforced by audiences who heckled women's plays because of the author's sex."[1] This helps to explain why so many prologues and epilogues by women playwrights of the day were filled with a defense of the author's sex. Play writing was a threat to women's reputations in that day because of its very public aspect: Playwrights had to attend rehearsals, readings, performances, benefits. The backstage atmosphere of theater at that time was not as we now know it. It was often an unruly place filled with drunkenness, fisticuffs, even an occasional murder. Long banned from the boards in Great Britain, actresses began to appear on English stages at about the same time as women playwrights began their ascent in the 1660s. The actresses were inexperienced performers who were assigned roles as objects of beauty or sexuality, regardless of talent. Often, with all the resulting male attention, they took on lovers; some, like Nell Gwynne, became famous courtesans. The reputation of actresses became tarnished; women playwrights were guilty by association. (Some of this attitude has carried over right into this century: I can remember when, as a teenager, I stated my desire to become an actress. My father was disgusted. They were all prostitutes, as far as he was concerned. It took my own struggling career, with its concurrent friendships, to demonstrate to him that this was not so.) The historic connections harken back to the late Middle Ages when, as noted by Susan Case, "the Church had secured the notion that such immoral sexual conduct was the province of women: that is, that prostitutes caused prostitution. Therefore the control of prostitutes would control prostitution, or, more specifically, banning women from the stage would prevent the stage from becoming the site for immoral sexual conduct."[2] Such association was sometimes spoofed by the playwrights themselves in their plays. In the epilogue of Aphra Behn's *Sir Patient Fancy*, she quips, "Quickest in finding all the

---

[1] Cotton.
[2] Case (1).

subtlest ways/To make your Joys, why not to make your Plays?"

If female dramatists were not shunned as whores, they were accused of plagiarism, insinuating that women had no ideas of their own. In the preface to MARY DAVYS's *The Northern Heiress*, she writes, "As a Child born of a common Woman, has many Fathers, so my poor Offspring has been laid at a great many Doors . . . I am proud they think it deserves a better Author." When a woman's works were praised to be of exceptional quality, comments abounded as to how she wrote "like a man." Patronizing to today's ears, these remarks must be heard in the context of a time of strict patriarchy: Even the few women critics of the day made similar allusions.

The next great surge of women playwrights came between 1900 and 1920, when about 400 women wrote plays. Many of these works were concerned with the campaign for female suffrage, as well as the growing crusade for women's inclusion in higher education and the professions. Some of the propaganda plays were written by women such as Mary Shaw, the actress, Charlotte Perkins Gilman, the noted sociologist and writer, MERCY OTIS WARREN, RACHEL CROTHERS, RIDA JOHNSON YOUNG, and SUSAN GLASPELL. The majority of these plays, however, were written by women who were neither writers nor theater professionals, but were active in the women's movement. Because most of these 400 women did not consider themselves playwrights and did not build any body of theatrical work, they have been excluded from this book. Bettina Friedl, in her fascinating and comprehensive collection *On to Victory: Propaganda Plays of the Woman Suffrage Movement*[3], gives voice to this unique phenomenon that theatrically documents the rise of the women's movement from 1848 through 1920.

Although plays about women have existed since the origins of drama, and plays by women have been written and performed in the western world at least since the time of Sappho,[4] only in the last fifteen years or so have playwrights in significant numbers become self-consciously concerned about the presence—or absence—of women as women on stage. "Every time a woman writes a play about women, then, she is implicitly challenging the men still at center-stage," writes MICHELENE WANDOR. "She may not be a conscious feminist, she may want to take no part in changing things for other women in the theatrical profession, but she will still in some way be justifying her existence as a woman playwright, and justifying the existence of her subject matter as valid."[5] The author of *Understudies*, pub-

lished in 1981, which took an intriguing look at sexual politics in the theater, Wandor goes on to note that while women playwrights may tend to write about their own sex, so do male writers. "It is just that they rarely see that that is what they are doing," she remarks. I might add, the public does not usually see it either.

Wandor, an avid anthologizer of plays by women, asks "Why an anthology of plays by women? If one looks at the contents page of any play anthology, one is already halfway to the answer."[6]

The 1992 edition of the *International Directory of Theater* contains "the greatest and most performed plays in the world": 350 works are documented, including all thirty-seven of Shakespeare's plays, thirteen by Ibsen, nine each from Molière and Brecht, and one by a woman—Lillian Hellman, a white, American, middle-class woman. An investigation of other anthologies that embody what is considered the "dramatic canon" yields similar results: In John Gassner's *A Treasury of the Theatre*, the anthology used when I was a student of theater arts at UCLA in the late 1950s, early 1960s, thirty-nine plays are anthologized, two of which are by women (LADY GREGORY and LILLIAN HELLMAN); in a supplemental index, "A List of Modern Plays" cites 425 plays worldwide, of which seventeen are authored by women. Two decades later, when I was teaching theater history at a private school, Haskell M. Block and Robert G. Shedd's *Masters of Modern Drama* was the Baedeker of the day. In it, forty-five plays by thirty-five playwrights are anthologized; none is by a woman. Women have been writing plays since the time of Sappho; their contributions to the commedia del l'arte troupes in sixteenth-century Italy were an essential part of the evolution of classic comedy; some of the most beloved comedies of the Restoration were written by women; eight American women have received Pulitzer Prizes (Hellman is not among them)—however, these facts are grossly overlooked by the scholars who collect and critique these anthologies. And it is anthologies such as these that shape public perception of who the world's major playwrights have been. "The very concept of the 'writer' implies maleness, so that the sub-category 'woman writer' had to be developed in the nineteenth century to cover a species of creativity that challenged the dominant image. To a great extent we still live under the cloud of gender-confusion in our image of the 'writer,' especially in the theater."[7] This book is one response to Wandor's observation. By eliminating the choice of one gender over another, the biographical profiles assembled here offer readers the opportunity to examine the lives and works of playwrights whose stoutness in the body of theater demands their inclusion.

---

[3] Boston: Northeastern University Press, 1987.

[4] While it is known that Sappho wrote dramas as well as poetry, all that remains of her works are scattered fragments; thus, she has not been included among these profiles.

[5] Wandor (1).

---

[6] Wandor (2).

[7] Ibid.

Critics, too, have had their part in the repression of the works of women playwrights. For decades male drama critics—from George Jean Nathan to Heywood Broun, from Norris Houghton to Whitney Bolton—have been railing against women playwrights, either for portraying men as ineffectual, or women as too strong, too melodramatic, or too absolutist. In the seventeenth century, JUANA INÉS DE LA CRUZ penned, "Critics: in your sight/no woman can win:/keep you out, and she's too tight;/she's too loose if you get in." Yet so-called "feminist" plays, more often than not, merely "attempt to pay attention to the lives of women—as individuals, in relation to each other, and in relation to men."[8]

Lastly, even though there has been an influx of production and publication of women's plays in the last two decades, the networks of money and power that bring drama to the public remain primarily in the hands of men: That glass ceiling has yet to be shattered.

My goal has been to simply allow women playwrights throughout history to resurface, as well as to introduce some of the great female dramatists writing in other languages. My basis for inclusion encompassed a broad range of criteria: Some playwrights, for example, were part of the maturation of the theater of their day; others brought an original approach, pioneering a form or setting a precedent. Certainly, the entrants had to be playwrights of note. To be included, a playwright need not have been prolific, but her work must have made a significant contribution to the theater of her day. Almost without exception her plays must have been produced professionally and, with rare exception (see KATHERINE OF SUTTON, the 14th-century English baroness), published, and must still be available (even if only in archives), preferably in English. It was also preferable that her work had been considered critically, and that there was some body of work about her and her plays. If her plays addressed some feminist issues of her day, that, too, was desirable, but not necessary.

Although American and English dramatists comprise the bulk of this English-language anthology, a special effort was made to include foreign playwrights. Some of their works are available in English translation, which was preferable, but not in all instances possible. This book includes a smattering of playwrights from such countries as Germany, France, Finland, Israel, Italy, Ghana, Mexico, and Chile; in no way, however, is the work intended to be representative of the contributions made by women playwrights in those countries.

Playwrights from the Middle Ages—from whence derived the first extant dramas by a woman playwright, HROTSVITHA VON GANDERSHEIM—through the Restoration to the twentieth century are represented. Receipt of an award, such as the Antoinette Perry or the Obie (off-Broadway) Award in the United States or the Olivier in England, for example, was a strong consideration, though not a necessary criterion for inclusion.

Asked to define "major playwright" by an editor of *People* magazine, playwright VELINA HASU HOUSTON could only reply how subjective that definition must be, with the exception of such contemporary giants as Arthur Miller and Tennessee Williams, Stephen Sondheim and Andrew Lloyd Webber (the latter of whom may be considered "major" due to box office receipts rather than critical reception). Perhaps we must rid ourselves of this desire to consider major playwrights, and instead consider major plays (after all, not all plays by major playwrights are in themselves major). One might ask oneself, as Houston has, what makes a play important? She says,

> The kinds of plays that are important to me are plays that give something to the world in which we live, that recycle our emotions, spirits, and intellect to refuel and improve the world—not destroy it. Important plays are rich with cultural and political substance. They reflect a social consciousness without losing a sense of the personal. Their vision remains inextricably tied to the never-ending exploration and excavation of the human condition. For theater should not only entertain but also enlighten.[9]

Theater is a democratic art form—it speaks to the myriad complexities of mood, intellect, station, age, and social status that make up an audience. If it succeeds in moving that amorphous body, whether to laughter, tears, reflection, or anger, it is good theater. If it happens to speak particularly to the members of "the ruling class"—upper class, white, powerful—it may garner the reputation of great theater. But greatness is mostly personal. Although Shakespeare consistently created many great plays, it is rare that a play, even by a great playwright, is so great that it moves those beyond its evident ken. Arthur Miller's *Death of a Salesman* and LORRAINE HANSBERRY's *A Raisin in the Sun* come to mind as rare exceptions.

Success in theater is most often measured by box office receipts. The relationship of feminist drama to commerce and public attention in many ways follows a predictable pattern. While some of the most innovative and challenging plays by feminists are produced in obscure venues and are heralded by a relatively small group of supporters, the dramas by women that have achieved commercial success in the West End or Broadway tend to take fewer theatrical risks and to be less threatening to middle-class audiences than those performed on the fringe of the theater establishment. Thus we juxtapose the better-known Wendy Wasserstein and Beth Henley against the lesser-known

---

[8] Keyssar.

[9] Houston.

Maria Irene Fornés and Megan Terry. A rare exception to this rule of risk is Caryl Churchill, whose cutting-edge works have actually achieved a modicum of commercial success.

Many talented and important women were left out of this collection because, though they were intrinsically involved with the creation of many plays—such as those of the many collaborative feminist theaters begun in the 1970s—they had not specifically authored a play. The one exception I have made is JOAN LITTLEWOOD, who was instrumental in helping to create a number of plays by heralded male and female dramatists.

A brief note with regards to my use of the word *theatrician*. There are some members of the theatrical community so multitalented, so accomplished that hyphenates describing their contributions might be endless: to wit, playwright-director-actor-designer-producer . . ., etc. This became apparent to me many years ago when I was doing research for my first book, *The Quotable Woman,* originally published in 1977 and now in its fifth edition (New York: Facts On File, 1992). I coined the word at the time, making conservative use of it in the biographical index. Since that time I have noted its use elsewhere on occasion, as in Jack Kroll's introduction to *Transients Welcome,* a collection of ROSALYN DREXLER's plays (New York: Broadway Play Pub., 1984). Language is a living, breathing element in our lives and if my use of "theatarician" causes some eyebrows to rise, I ask that you recall the words of the great Emily Dickinson: "A word is dead when it is said, some say/I say it just begins to live that day."

The trouble with creating a work of this nature is knowing when and how to place boundaries on it. It could just continue and continue, there are so many talented and worthy women playwrights in the world. Perhaps to assuage my distress more than anything else, I have created a Supplemental Index listing 140 playwrights: that they were not profiled in the body of the text has to do with the fact that either I was unable to find sufficient information to write a meaningful sketch or the entrant has not yet created a sufficiently significant body of dramatic works to warrant inclusion, or the entrant's foray into theater has been an insignificant part of her career.

Even with the inclusion of the Supplemental Index, I am fully cogent of the many omissions that are bound to surface in relation to a work of this nature, and I fully assume all responsibility for such. Were it not for the help and support of many individuals and the theater-rich community of Seattle, however, there would have been far more oversights. I should like to specifically thank staff members at the Intiman, The Empty Space, Seattle Repertory Theater, A Contemporary Theatre, Seattle Children's Theater, and The Group for supplying me with program notes. Individuals associated with these theaters who were especially helpful were Gary Tucker, Richard Menna, Barry Alar, and Janet Berkow. My old high school friend Michael Krieger supplied me with fascinating information, and my good friend, stage director and theater maven Aaron Levin contributed a careful eye and expertise. Gary Krebbs, my former editor, launched me on this fascinating journey and provided much needed encouragement and support. Several editors were subsequently assigned to the project, but Hilary Poole, who made many useful suggestions, and James Chambers, who saw it to its conclusion, have been especially helpful. My agent, Faith Hamlin, as always, patiently answered my questions and concerns and buoyed me up when I felt I was sinking.

Several publishers were kind enough to send me vital reference works that enhanced my research: Facts On File, New York; Cambridge University Press, New York branch; University of Michigan Press, Ann Arbor.

A special note of appreciation goes to Michelle Ishshalom, who read and then wrote synopses of many of the plays noted throughout this text. Her careful consideration and insightful interpretations of these works have been invaluable to me, and I have made great use of them. Michelle has worked as a teacher, a workshop leader in self-development, and an arbiter of black-white relations in the business world; she has followed a unique and varied path in life, and I am proud to call her my friend. She has returned to her native South Africa to continue the much-needed healing in that land; I shall miss her.

Also of great assistance was Selah Brown, my secretary in 1994. Without her organizational skills, her enthusiasm, and her sympathy (I was writing much of this book under great personal duress), I could not have completed the work in anything even approaching a timely manner. Alexandra Saperstein, a recent Mills College graduate, did much to help organize my notes and brought her special brand of humor to brighten up several gray Seattle days.

Since 1995, Gina Hicks has been the secretary and office manager for the small business run by me and my husband. She has done "yowoman's" duty in helping piece together this work. Specifically, she created the time line and organized the supplemental index; she masterfully managed the computer aspects of this large and cumbersome manuscript. Most important, her calm and expertise kept me from going mad when the computer acted up.

Last goes a note of tremendous gratitude and respect to my beloved niece, Lesley Anne Hyatt, who worked with me on this project. She displayed an excellent eye for detail and a gift for extracting the most unique aspect of a woman's life or work. Her way with words in putting the final polish on these profiles certainly impressed me. I am so proud to have such a talented niece, and thrilled at this opportunity to have worked with her. I also must thank, as always, my dear husband, Turner. First of all, he did a masterful job as the photographic editor on this work, making a special effort to find images rarely seen. But even more important to me, his supportiveness and forbearance created the windows of time in which I could work. He always seemed to know when to tear me away from the computer for a break—and he always made sure I ate something!

It is my sincere wish that this book will inspire and encourage those in a position to do so to produce the unknown yet laudable plays of some of the incredibly talented but unsung playwrights in this book.

—Elaine Partnow
Seattle

LIST OF ILLUSTRATIONS

Enid Bagnold	7
Joanna Baillie	9
Vicki Baum	12
Aphra Behn	13
Gertrude Berg	16
Julie Bovasso	21
Vinette Carroll	27
Susanna Centlivre	31
Drury Lane Theatre	34
Alice Childress	37
Agatha Christie	39
Caryl Churchill	41
Catherine Clive	46
Betty Comden	48
Hannah Cowley	50
Rachel Crothers	52
Alma De Groen	60
Dorothy Fields	73
Maria Irene Fornés	77
Zona Gale	81
Susan Glaspell	92
Ruth Gordon	94
Lorraine Hansberry	99
Lillian Hellman	102
Beth Henley	104
Tina Howe	110
Ann Jellicoe	119
Sor Juana Inés de la Cruz	122
Jean Kerr	127
Joan Littlewood	136

Anita Loos   137
Clare Boothe Luce   138
Emily Mann   145
Carson McCullers   148
Edna St. Vincent Millay   152
Hannah More   154
Marsha Norman   160
Rochelle Owens   165
Louise Page   168
Franca Rame   176
Ntozake Shange   189
Anna Deavere Smith   191
Bella Spewack   194
Gertrude Stein   195
Megan Terry   200
Sophie Treadwell   203
Jane Wagner   211
Wendy Wasserstein   214
Mae West   219
Hella Wuolijoki   220

TIME LINE

Name	Nationality	Life Span
Hrotsvitha von Gandersheim	German	935?–1000?
Katherine of Sutton	English	1363–1376 (fl.)
Mary Sidney Herbert	English	1561–1621
Christopher Marlowe	English	1564–1593
William Shakespeare	English	1564–1616
Ben Jonson	English	1572–1637
Lope de Vega	Spanish	1582–1635
Elizabeth Tanfield Cary	English	1585/6–1639
Caldéron	Spanish	1600–1681
Pierre Corneille	French	1606–1684
Henrietta Maria of France (queen of England)	French-English	1609–1669
Molière	French	1622–1673
Margaret Cavendish	English-French	1623–1673
Katherine Fowler Philips	English-Irish	1631–1664
Jean-Baptiste Racine	French	1639–1699
Aphra Behn	English	1640–1689
Sor Juana Inés de la Cruz	Mexican	1651–1695
Anne Kingsmill Finch	English	1661–1720
Mary Griffith Pix	English	1666–1709/20?
Delariviere Manley	English	1667/72–1724
Frances Boothby	English	1669 (fl.)

Name	Nationality	Life Span
Susanna Centlivre	Irish-English	1667/9–1723
William Congreve	English	1670–1729
Mary Davys	Irish-English	1674–1732
Catherine Trotter	English	1679–1749
Eliza Fowler Haywood	English	1689/93–1756
Ariadne	English	1695 (fl.)
Charlotte Charke	English	1710–1760
Catherine Clive	English	1711–1785
Mary Leapor	English	1722–1746
Frances Brooke	English	1724–1789
Mercy Otis Warren	American	1728–1814
Gotthold Ephraim Lessing	German	1729–1781
Oliver Goldsmith	Irish	1730–1774
Hannah Cowley	English	1743–1809
Hannah More	English	1745–1833
Johann Wolfgang von Goethe	German	1749–1832
Richard Sheridan	Irish	1751–1816
Frances Burney	English	1752–1840
Elizabeth Inchbald	English	1753–1821
Susanna Haswell Rowson	English-American	1762–1824
Joanna Baillie	Scottish-English	1762–1851
Hannah Brand	English	1794–98 (fl.)
Nikolai Gogol	Russian	1809–1852
Gertrudis Gomez de Avellaneda	Cuban-Spanish	1814–1873
Ivan Turgenev	Russian	1818–1883
Anna Cora Mowatt	French-American	1819–1870
Dion Boucicault	Irish-American	1820–1890
Alexandre Dumas	French	1824–1895
Henrik Ibsen	Norwegian	1828–1906
Leo N. Tolstoy	Russian	1828–1910
Henry Becque	French	1837–1899

Name	Nationality	Life Span
Lydia Koidula	Estonian	1843–1886
Minna Canth	Finnish	1844–1897
August Strindberg	Swedish	1849–1912
Augusta Gregory	Irish	1852–1932
Oscar Wilde	Irish	1854–1900
Gabriela Zapolska	Polish	1857–1921
Anton Chekhov	Russian	1860–1904
James Barrie	Scottish	1860–1937
Anna Brigadere	Latvian	1861–1933
Arthur Schnitzler	Austrian	1862–1931
Gerhart Hauptmann	German	1862–1946
Maurice Maeterlinck	Belgian	1862–1949
Frank Wedekind	German	1864–1918
Martha Morton	American	1865–1925
W. B. Yeats	Irish	1865–1939
George Bernard Shaw	Irish	1865–1950
Luigi Pirandello	Italian	1867–1936
Edmond Rostand	French	1868–1918
Maxim Gorky	Russian	1868–1936
Aspazija	Latvian	1868–1943
Zinaida Gippius	Russian	1869–1945
Else Lasker-Schüler	German	1869–1945
John M. Synge	Irish	1871–1909
Josephine Preston Peabody	American	1874–1922
Hugo von Hofmannsthal	Austrian	1874–1929
Zona Gale	American	1874–1938
Gertrude Stein	American-French	1874–1946
Anne Crawford Flexner	American	1874–1955
María Martínez Sierra	Spanish-Argentinian	1874–1974
Rida Johnson Young	American	1875–1926
Susan Glaspell	American	1876/82–1948
May Roberts Rinehart	American	1876–1958
Elizabeth Baker	English	1876–1962

Name	Nationality	Life Span
Georg Kaiser	German	1878–1945
Ferenc Molnár	Hungarian	1878–1952
Rachel Crothers	American	1878–1958
Christopher (Marie) St. John	English	188?–1960
Maria Jotuni	Finnish	1880–1943
Sean O'Casey	Irish	1880–1964
Jean Giraudoux	French	1882–1944
Sofija Čiurlionienė Kymantaitė	Lithuanian	1885–1958
Edna Ferber	American	1885–1968
Alice Gerstenberg	American	1885–1972
Sophie Treadwell	American	1885/90–1970
Hella Wuolijoki	Finnish	1886–1954
Zoë Akins	American	1886–1958
Georgia Douglas Johnson	African-American	1886–1966
Clemence Dane	English	1887/8–1965
Clare Kummer	American	1888?–1948
Eugene O'Neill	American	1888–1953
Maxwell Anderson	American	1888–1959
Vicki Baum	Austrian-American	1888–1960
T. S. Eliot	American-English	1888–1965
Anita Loos	American	1888–1981
Jean Cocteau	French	1889–1963
Enid Bagnold	English	1889–1981
Karel Čapek	Czechoslovakian	1890–1938
Agatha Christie	English	1890–1976
Marc Connelly	American	1890–1980
Zora Neale Hurston	African-American	1891–1960
Anne Nichols	American	1891/6–1966
Marina Tsvetayeva	Russian	1892–1941
Edna St. Vincent Millay	American	1892–1952
Ugo Betti	Italian	1892–1953
Djuna Barnes	American	1892–1982
Mae West	American	1893–1980

Name	Nationality	Life Span
Dorothy L. Sayers	English	1893–1957
Jean Devanny	New Zealand-Australian	1894–1962
Oscar Hammerstein II	American	1895–1960
Rose Franken	American	1895–1988
Gordon Daviot	Scottish	1896–1952
Robert Sherwood	American	1896–1955
Carl Zuckmayer	German	1896–1977
Ruth Gordon	American	1896–1985
Dodie Smith	English	1896–1990
Thornton Wilder	American	1897–1975
Frederico Garcia Lorca	Spanish	1898–1936
Antonin Artaud	French	1898–1948
Elina Zālīte	Latvian	1898–1955
Bertolt Brecht	German	1898–1956
Gertrude Berg	American	1899–1966
Noel Coward	English	1899–1973
Bella Spewack	American	1899–1990
Marieluise Fleißer	German	1901–1974
Clare Boothe Luce	American	1903–1987
Vera Fyodorovna Panova	Soviet Russian	1905–1973
Dorothy Fields	American	1905–1974
Jean-Paul Sartre	French	1905–1980
Lillian Hellman	American	1905–1984
Clifford Odets	American	1906–1963
Samuel Beckett	Irish-French	1906–1989
Mary Chase	American	1907–1981
Daphne du Maurier	English	1907–1989
William Saroyan	American	1908–1981
Eugene Ionesco	Rumanian-French	1909–
Jean Anouilh	French	1910–1987
Tennessee Williams	American	1911–1983
Max Frisch	Swiss	1911–1991
Yang Chiang	Chinese	1911–

Name	Nationality	Life Span
Anne Ridler	English	1912–
Albert Camus	Algerian-French	1913–1960
William Inge	American	1913–1973
Bridget Boland	English	1913–1988
Marguerite Duras	French	1914–1996
Joan Littlewood	English	1914–
Ketti Frings	American	1915–1981
Aldona Liobytė	Lithuanian	1915–
Arthur Miller	American	1915–
Natalia Ginzburg	Italian	1916–1991
Fay Kanin	American	1916?–
Eve Merriam	American	1916–
Carson McCullers	American	1917–1967
Isadora Aguirre	Chilean	1919–
Ellen Bergman	Swedish	1919–
Betty Comden	American	1919–
Doris Lessing	English	1919–
Alice Childress	African-American	1920–1994
Eeva-Liisa Manner	Finnish	1921–
Vinette Carroll	African-American	1922–
Paddy Chayefsky	American	1923–
Dorothy Hewett	Australian	1923–
Jean Kerr	American	1923–
Efua Sutherland	Ghanian	1924–
Wakako Yamauchi	Asian-American	1924–
Rosario Castellanos	Mexican	1925–1974
Pam Gems	English	1925–
Beah Richards	American	1925/8–
Rosalyn Drexler	American	1926–
Dario Fo	Italian	1926–
Gerline Reinshagen	German	1926–
Ann Jellicoe	English	1927–
Neil Simon	American	1927–
Jane Wagner	American	1927/35–

Name	Nationality	Life Span
Edward Albee	American	1928–
Griselda Gambaro	Argentinian	1928–
Adalet Ağaoğlu	Turkish	1929–
Brian Friel	Irish	1929–
Elaine Jackson	African-American	1929–
John Osborne	English	1929–
Denis Bonal	Algerian-French	193?–
Franca Rame	Italian	193?–
Lorraine Hansberry	American	1930–1965
Julie Bovasso	American	1930–1991
Maria Irene Fornés	Cuban-American	1930–
Harold Pinter	English	1930–
Stephen Sondheim	American	1930–
Kathleen Collins	African-American	1931–1988
Thomas Bernhard	Austrian	1931–1989
Adrienne Kennedy	American	1931–
Athol Fugard	South African	1932–
Shirley Gee	English	1932–
Megan Terry	American	1932–
Maruxa Vilalta	Mexican	1932–
Maureen Duffy	English	1933–
Corinne Jacker	American	1933–
Fay Weldon	English	1933–
Margaretta D'Arcy	Irish	1934–
Gretchen Cryer	American	1935–
Myrna Lamb	American	1935–
Dacia Maraini	Italian	1935/6–
Françoise Sagan	French	1935–
Zulu Sofola	Nigerian	1935–
Martha Gross Boesing	American	1936–
Nell Dunn	English	1936–
Rochelle Owens	American	1936–
Sharon Pollock	Canadian	1936–
Jane Chambers	American	1937–1983

Name	Nationality	Life Span
JoAnne Akalaitis	American	1937–
Hélène Cixous	Algerian-French	1937–
Tina Howe	American	1937–
Tom Stoppard	Czechoslovakian-English	1937–
Simone Benmussa	French	1938?–
Caryl Churchill	English	1938–
Lyudmila Petrushevskaya	Russian	1938–
Alena Vostrá	Czechoslovakian	1938–
Alan Ayckbourn	English	1939?–
Shelagh Delaney	English	1939–
Anne Commire	American	1940?–
Wendy Kesselman	American	1940–
Michelene Wandor	English	1940–
Carol Bolt	Canadian	1941–
Alma De Groen	New Zealand-Australian	1941–
Barbara Garson	American	1941–
Mary O'Malley	English	1941–
Susan Yankowitz	American	1941–
Ama Ata Aidoo	Ghanian	1942–
Bilgesu Erenus	Turkish	1943–
Sam Shepard	American	1943–
Fatima Gallaire-Bourega	Algerian-French	1944–
Susan Miller	American	1944–
Suzanne Osten	Swedish	1944–
Abla Farhoud	Lebanese	1945–
Karen Malpede	American	1945–
Honor Moore	American	1945–
August Wilson	American	1945–
Genny Lim	Asian-American	1946–
Sue Townsend	English	1946–
Timberlake Wertenbaker	American-English	1946?–
Mary Gallagher	American	1947–

Name	Nationality	Life Span
David Mamet	American	1947–
Marsha Norman	American	1947–
Pearl Cleage	American-English	1948–
Doris Baizley	American	1948?–
Ludmila Razumovskaya	Lithuanian	1948–
Erika Ritter	Canadian	1948–
Friederike Roth	German	1948–
Ntozake Shange	American	1948–
Andrew Lloyd Webber	English	1948–
Jessica Tarahata Hagedorn	Filipino-American	1949–
P. J. Gibson	American	195?–
Irene Hause	Swedish	1950–
Aishah Rahman	African-American	1950–
Anna Deavere Smith	African-American	1950–
Wendy Wasserstein	American	1950–
Sharman MacDonald	Scottish	1951–
Marlane Meyer	American	1951–
Paula Vogel	American	1951–
Beth Henley	American	1952–
Emily Mann	American	1952–
Milcha Sanchez-Scott	Balinese-American	1954/5–
Darrah Cloud	American	1955–
Debbie Horsfield	English	1955–
Louise Page	English	1955–
Sarah Daniels	English	1957–
Velina Hasu Houston	Native American- African-Asian	1957–
Mia Tornqvist	Swedish	1957–
Christina Herrström	Swedish	1959–
Rona Munro	Scottish	1959–
Cheryl L. West	African-American	1959–
Suzan-Lori Parks	African-American	1963–
Charlotte Keatley	English	1960–

Name	Nationality	Life Span
Andrea Dunbar	English	1961–1991
Marina Carr	Irish	1965–
Michele Fabien	Belgian	1970 (fl.)

HOW TO USE THIS BOOK

As often as possible, the year following each play in the bibliographical listing of each woman's work refer to the first year of production, not publication, which often came later. Unknown dates are indicated by *n.d.* (no date). Most, but not all, of the plays listed are published, though some may exist only in manuscript form in an archive. While several of the bibliographies are complete, many are "selected," deliberately leaving out some works; this is particularly the case with those giants of literature whose output has been prodigious. Under "Works About," while there are often myriad articles in magazines, journals, and newspapers, and while the playwright may be included in works focusing on a broader spectrum of the theatrical scene that includes her, only books specifically devoted to the particular playwright are listed. Where neither "selected" nor "complete" appears, every effort was made to make a full listing, but this may not have been accomplished.

Footnotes referencing works listed in the general bibliography found at the back of this work use only the author's or first listed editor's last name; where more than one work by the same author is utilized, each is assigned a number; thus, Case (1) and Case (2). A name appearing in small capital letters in a profile indicates that there is a separate profile on that woman.

The order in the "Time Line" is dictated by the year of birth. When it is not known, the year of death, if known, or the first year of a range of years designated "flourish" (fl.) dictates placement. In those few instances when the year of birth and the year of death are the same for more than one playwright, they are alphabetized.

All entrants in the "Supplemental Index" are playwrights and so only additional professions are noted. The index uses a few abbreviations that are spelled out in the body of the text. They are:

AUDELCO—Audience Development Committee, sponsored by AT&T and the Apollo Theatre Foundation
BBC—British Broadcasting Corporation
CAPS—Creative Arts Public Service award
NEW—National Endowment for the Arts
OBIE—Off-Broadway Award
PEN—Poets, Playwrights, Editors, Essayists, and Novelists (P.E.N. Club)
Tony—Antoinette Perry Award

Because the dates of so many publications were not able to be ascertained, the term *n.d.* (no date) has been dispensed with in this index.

The bibliography at the end of the text includes only those works that were repeatedly used throughout the body of the text and are footnoted only with the author or editor's last name. All other works are footnoted thoroughly within each profile that cited from it.

THE FEMALE DRAMATIST

A

Adalet Ağaoğlu
(1929–)

Turkish novelist, translator, and dramatist Adalet Ağaoğlu is one of the founders of the Meydan Sahnesi (Arena Theatre). After graduating from Ankara University, she worked at the Turkish Radio and TV Corporation for more than twenty years. Although she began writing plays in the early 1950s, her first important work, *Çatidaki çatlak* (The Crack in the Structure), was not staged until 1965. Metin And calls the play "a bitter denunciation of the prevalent social and economic system in Turkey . . ."[1] All of Ağaoğlu's work focuses on the political in some capacity. She has addressed isolationism and xenophobia in *Kozalar* (Cocoons; 1969) and *Çikiş* (Exit; 1969), as well as peace and social justice in *Sinirlada* (At the Borders; 1969) and *Kendin yazan şarki* (Song Written by Itself; 1973).

In addition to her prodigious work as a playwright, Ağaoğlu has translated into Turkish many works by Jean-Paul Sartre and Bertolt Brecht, among others. She has written several novels and short stories and has won several major literary awards.

PLAYS

Bir kahramanin ölümü (Death of a Hero), 1969; *Bir piyes yazalim* (Let's Write a Play), w/Sevim Uzgörim, 1953; *Bir sessiz adam* (A Quiet Man), 1973; *Çatidaki çatlak* (The Crack in the Structure), 1965; *Çikiş* (Exit), 1969; *Evcilik oyunu* (Playing House), 1964; *Kendin yazan şarki* (Song Written by Itself), 1973; *Kozalar* (Cocoons), 1969; *Sinirlada* (At the Borders), 1969; *Tombala* (Bingo), 1969

1. Hochman.

Isadora Aguirre
(MARCH 22, 1919–)

CAROLINA. Besides when I say "nothing," what I mean is: everything.

—from *Carolina*

Isadora Aguirre, along with other members of the so-called "Generation of the 1950s," was a pivotal figure in the move away from the naturalistic theater that had dominated the Chilean stage for decades.[1] Her works are filled with experiments in expressionism and realism, and they reflect her firm belief that social themes in drama and literature "are a living testimony which obligates the audience to become aware of the problems."[2] Aguirre distinguished herself early on as a writer who boldly broke the traditional mold of the passive, ineffective female character: Her women are passionate warriors, willing to fight for freedom and justice.

Interestingly, Aguirre's family was hardly working class. She enjoyed a privileged childhood, attended a private French high school, Jeanne D'Arc, and continued her education at a French university for two years. In France she changed her course of study according to her whim: first social services, then drawing, ballet, drama, and cinematography, each at a different educational institution. Upon returning to Chile, she began writing novels and children's books, which she also illustrated. She also began to study play writing at the Chilean Academy of the Ministry of Education. By 1954 Aguirre was focused completely on creating works for the stage.

Some of her earliest plays were light comedies, but with *Las tres pascualas** (1957), she established herself as a serious sociopolitical dramatist, intent on dealing with Chilean society and, later, those of other Latin American countries. Many believe *Pascualas* to be Aguirre's most important work. The play tells the story of three women who drown themselves for the love of a stranger. Based on a true incident that occurred around the turn of the century in the Chilean lakes regions, the tale was already a national legend. But Aguirre uses it as a structure in which to illustrate the differences in the way the upper and lower classes perceive and experience the power and wisdom of the tale.

Aguirre's fifth play, the musical comedy *Le pérgola de las flores* (The Flower Stand; 1959) brought her great fame and fortune. It became the most popular musical comedy in Chilean history, and has been produced in Mexico, Cuba, Spain, Bolivia, and Argentina, where it was adapted for film. Set in the 1920s, *Le pérgola* satirizes Santiago's upper crust while it sympathizes with the common folk. Her other 1959 work, *La población Esperanza* (A Suburb Named Hope), is a much darker drama that depicts the miserable life of the slums. It won the Golden Laurel Prize in 1960.

Not surprisingly, while Aguirre cites Anton Chekhov, Arthur Miller, Eugene O'Neill, Shakespeare, Armand Gatty, and Jean Genet as primary influences on her work, she singles out Bertolt Brecht for the role of mentor. His impact is evidenced in her 1964 play *Los papeleros* (The Newsboys), in which she incorporates Brecht's ideas of epic theater. "Aguirre tries . . . to appeal to the audience's sense of reason," writes Elba Andrade, "rather than to their emotions in order to present convincingly her social message."[3] This work also marks Aguirre's first effort to subvert the stereotypical Chilean image of women: Romilia, a leader of the garbage collectors, displays a great combative spirit.

Los que van quedando en el camino (Left Behind in the Streets; 1969) utilizes real-life stories in its depiction of a peasant rebellion. Much as CARYL CHURCHILL did for her play *Mad Forest*, Aguirre interviewed survivors and researched the uprising in order to present an accurate portrayal of the event. Again, there is a strong woman at the play's core: Lorenza is courageous and spirited, and bears a high moral tone. *Quedando* is also noteworthy in that, for the first time in one of her dramas, Aguirre offers solutions rather than simply presenting a problem. And,

contrary to Brecht's intent, this work most decidedly leads the audience to an emotional, rather than reasoned, conclusion.

Like her women characters, Aguirre has "a lively spirit and an abundance of energy."[4] From 1959 to 1973 she taught drama at the University of Chile and at the State Technical University. During this period she also developed workshops in play writing techniques and dramatic improvisation. She has served on various national and international panels for theater conventions and festivals and has led workshops in Ecuador, Peru, and Colombia. She has received many national and international awards. Aguirre has also written screenplays and adapted classical dramas such as Lope de Vega Carpio's *The Sheep-well* and Shakespeare's *Richard III*.

PLAYS

Anacleto chin, chin, 1956; *Los cabezones de la feria*, 1972; *Carolina* (a.k.a. *Express for Santiago*), 1955; *La dama del canasto*, 1965; *Dos y dos son cinco* (Two and Two Are Five), 1956; *En Aquellos locos años veinte*, 1974; *Entre dos trenes*, 1956; *Lautaro*, 1982; *Maggy ante el espejo*, 1968; *La micro*, 1956; *Pacto de medianoche* (A Midnight Pact), 1954; *Los papeleros* (The Newsboys), 1964; *Le pérgola de las flores* (The Flower Stand), book for musical comedy, 1959; *La población Esperanza* (A Suburb Named Hope), w/Manuel Rojas, 1959; *Los que van quedando en el camino* (Left Behind in the Streets), 1969; *Quien tuvo la culpa de la muerte de la María*, 1970; *Las sardinas: O, La supresión de amanda*, 1956; *Las tres pascualas* (The Three Pascualas)*, 1957

OTHER WORKS

Alsino and the Condor, w/Miguel Littin, 1982; *Ocho cuentos*, 1945; *Waikii*, 1948

1. Essay by Elba Andrade in Magill.
2. Ibid.
3. Ibid.
4. Ibid.

*Author's note: The literal translation of this title—"the three *pascualas*"—bears metaphorical meaning. *Pascua* means "feast" and is often connected to Pascua de Resurección, which refers to Easter or Passover. It is not illogical to assume, given the circumstances of the story, that the title refers to some sort of resurrection, perhaps of the spirit or the love they bore, of the three women.

(Christina) Ama Ata Aidoo
(MARCH 23, 1942–   )

ANOWA. I hear in other lands a woman is nothing. And they let her know this from the day of her birth. But here, O my spirit mother, they let a girl grow up as she pleases until she is married. And then she is like any woman anywhere: in order for her man to be a man, she must not think, she must not talk.

—from *Anowa*

One of Africa's most gifted and creative writers, Ama Ata Aidoo (née Abeadzi Kyiakor) was born near Saltpond, Gold Coast, in the central region of what is now Ghana. Most of Aidoo's work, which includes novels, short stories, and verse, as well as plays, addresses the conflict between indigenous ways and Western influence, particularly with respect to women. Despite the serious nature of her work, Aidoo manages to fuse her writing with wry humor and lively characters.

Anowa, her second dramatic work, takes place in the nineteenth century, yet its thematic turf ventures into contemporary territory. It deals with how willfulness and ambition in a young woman of tremendous potential make her an outcast, unaccepted by her parents, her husband, or her community. The play cries out for African women to attain a more liberated role in society—this, Aidoo suggests, is the greatest hope for both women *and* men. Suppressing the minds and bodies of women can only be detrimental to both sexes in a society that kills those it cannot confine. This concept is reflected in the play by the suicide of both Anowa and her weak, bewildered, and ultimately emasculated husband, Kofi. *Anowa* is, without doubt, one of the major plays to come out of contemporary African theater.[1]

Like Kofi, Ato, the central male character in *The Dilemma of a Ghost* (1964), is also a weak man, unable to make a decision about the direction of his life. Educated in America, Ato is a "been to" (an African educated abroad), thanks to the hard work and sacrifices of his mother, Esi. He returns to his native land with an American wife, Eulalie. Esi's family is mortified that Eulalie is descended from slaves—she has no tribe. As for Eulalie, she is thrilled to be in Africa, but finds acculturation not without its difficulties: She refuses to cook the snails her mother-in-law has brought! Although Ato's family expects him and Eulalie to have a child immediately, Ato convinces his wife that they should wait. The couple continue to practice birth control, yet Ato offers his family members no explanation as to why they have not conceived. He even refuses the fertility herbs they bring him. Soon it becomes clear that Ato is deceiving everyone: Eulalie, Esi, even himself. Haunted by the childhood game he used to play about a ghost who cannot decide which direction to go in ("Shall I go to Cape Coast, Shall I go to Elmina? I can't tell . . ."), Ato takes out his frustration on Eulalie and strikes her. Eulalie cannot abide this behavior. She leaves Ato, who goes to his mother and confesses to the violence, the birth control, everything. Esi is furious with him for not having been candid with her, and when Eulalie later arrives at her

door, Esi takes her in. The play ends with Ato torn between returning to his mother's door or his own.

Like *Anowa*, *Dilemma of a Ghost* addresses the thematic heart of all Aidoo's work: the contemporary African family's cultural and historical purgatory. In Aidoo's world, men and women cannot resolve their differences with respect to power and society, nor can they make peace with their pasts.

An educator as well as a writer, Aidoo was a lecturer from 1970–82 at the University of Ghana, Cape Coast, where she received her B.A. with honors in 1964. She was also appointed Research Fellow of the Institute of African Studies at the university. She attended the Advanced Creative Writing Program at Stanford University, California, and she was writer in residence at the University of Richmond, Virginia, in 1989, following the award of a Fulbright scholarship. From 1982–83 Aidoo served as the Minister of Education for her country. She currently resides in Zimbabwe.

PLAYS

Anowa, 1970; *The Dilemma of a Ghost*, 1964

OTHER WORKS

Birds and Other Poems, 1987; *Changes—A Love Story* (novel), 1991; *Dancing Out Doubts* (essays), 1982; *The Eagle and the Chickens and Other Stories* (children's stories), 1986; *No Sweetness Here* (short stories), 1970; *Our Sister Killjoy, or Reflections from a Black-eyed Squint* (novel), 1979; *Someone Talking to Sometime* (poems), 1985

WORKS ABOUT

Azodo, Ada Uzomaka, *Emerging Perspectives on Ama Ata Aidoo*, 1997; Odmatlen, Vincento, *The Art of Ama Ata Aidoo*, 1994

1. Essay by Martin Banham in Hawkins-Dady (2).

JoAnne Akalaitis
(JUNE 29, 1937–   )

JESSICA. One evening, I asked my evening school teacher to tell me the real difference between "I was writing" and "I have written." . . . "Well," he said grandly, "The imperfect tense refers to what WAS, while the present perfect tense refers to what HAS BEEN."

—from *Green Card*, Act I, "English"

In *Green Card*, JoAnne Akalaitis's 1986 play, the Ellis Island experience is presented in the format of a TV game show. Amidst a collage of historical images and spoken testimonials, immigrant contestants vie for the privilege of residency by struggling to define the vagaries of the English language. As in all of Akalaitis's work, *Green Card* dazzles the audience with its rapid-fire, multimedia, nonlinear approach to some of society's cruelest ills: the corruption of idealism and the ruthlessness of human behavior. Even her earliest efforts reflect this arresting form and content. *Dead End Kids* (1980), called an "impassioned repudiation of nuclear ineptitude"[1] by the playwright, anachronistically draws on the alchemical traditions of physics, layering historical events upon each other in the context of, for example, a 1960s TV variety show and a science fair. Roxana Petzold has written that "to experience Akalaitis's theater is to sit in at the atomic level."[2]

A native of Chicago, Akalaitis earned her B.A. in philosophy at the University of Chicago (1960). Known primarily as a director, in 1970 she became a founding member of Mabou Mimes, and has been active with the company ever since, not only as a director, but also as a performer, designer, and, of course, playwright. Additionally, she served as playwright in residence at the Mark Taper Forum in Los Angeles (1984–85), artistic associate for the Joseph Papp Public Theater in New York (1990–91), and artistic director for the New York Shakespeare Festival (1991–94). She has traveled the world, presenting her works and teaching play writing. Among her many awards are four Obies, the Drama Desk Award, a Guggenheim Fellowship, a National Endowment for the Arts grant, and a Rockefeller Foundation play writing grant for *Green Card*, which was produced at the Mark Taper Forum in Los Angeles.

PLAYS

Dead End Kids: A History of Nuclear Power, w/music by David Byrne (also screenplay, 1986), 1980; *Green Card*, 1986; *Southern Exposure* (also screenplay, 1986), 1979; *The Voyage of the Beagle* (opera), w/music by Jon Gibson, 1986

1. Essay by Roxana Petzold in Berney (2).
2. Ibid.

Zoë Akins
(OCTOBER 30, 1886–OCTOBER 29, 1958)

CHARLOTTE. (*Interrupting*) Tina, Tina, why must you always think that people are interested in you?
TINA. (*Challengingly*) Why shouldn't I? Aren't they?
DELIA. (*Indulgently*) My dear! What will people think of you if you talk like that?

CHARLOTTE. (*Gravely; busy with her knitting again*) Just what she deserves, probably.

—from *The Old Maid*, 4th episode

Zoë Akins's interest in theater dates back to her days at Hosmer Hall, her St. Louis high school, where classmates staged the young writer's work. She helped establish the Juvenile Theater of St. Louis in 1908, just before she left for New York, where she hoped to make a name for herself as an actress and playwright. She found work writing short pieces for *McClure's* magazine, a job that provided her an auspicious connection: Her editor, Willa Cather, took a kindly interest in Akins and encouraged her more creative pursuits.

By 1911, *Interpretations*, her first collection of poetry, appeared; two years later *Papa*, her first play, was published, although it was not staged until 1916 in Los Angeles. Critics did not love *Papa*, which was tagged an "amorality play": *Town and Country* magazine reported it as "a play in which the characters are depicted as being unaware of the decencies of the real world."[1] Fortunately, also in 1916, the Washington Square Players in New York performed Akins's *The Magical City*, a very popular one-act that launched the playwright's long and successful career.

Akins went on to write over two dozen plays, both serious dramas and light-hearted, romantic comedies. Many critics considered her best work to be *Greatness*, a 1922 comedy about a temperamental opera singer; however, it was her stage adaptation of Edith Wharton's story "The Old Maid" that won her the Pulitzer Prize in 1935. The play spans twenty years in the life of Charlotte Lovell, the title character, who struggles to win the affections of her illegitimate daughter.

Akins bore her own struggles in her personal life. Her marriage in 1932 (when she was forty-six) to Captain Hugo Cecil Levings Rumbold, a British painter and set designer, ended tragically when Rumbold died from war injuries that same year. Akins continued to write in spite of her misfortune, penning screenplays in addition to her poetry and stage plays. Her most famous big-screen work was *Camille* (1937), based on the Alexandre Dumas novel and starring Greta Garbo.

Although many of Akins's characters seem somewhat dated today, contemporary audiences may still appreciate how, as Felicia Hardison Londré of the University of Missouri puts it, "her dialogue often sparkles, and her all-too-humanly frail characters are still capable of capturing one's interest and sympathy."[2]

PLAYS

Another Darling, 1950; *The Crown Prince*, 1927; *Déclassé*, 1919; *Daddy's Gone A-Hunting*, 1921; *Did It Really Hap-*

pen?, 1917; *First Love*, 1926; *Foot Loose*, 1920; *The Furies*, 1928; *Greatness* (a.k.a. *The Texas Nightingale*), 1922; *The Greeks Had a Word for It* (also screenplay, *The Golddiggers*), 1929; *The Happy Days*, 1942; *I Am Different*, 1938; *The Little Miracle*, 1935; *The Love Duel*, 1929; *The Magical City*, 1916; *The Moon-Flower*, 1924; *Mrs. January and Mr. Ex*, 1944; *O Evening Star!*, 1936; *The Old Maid* (adapt. of story by Edith Wharton), 1935; *Papa*, 1916; *Pardon My Glove*, 1926; *A Royal Fandango*, 1923; *Such a Charming Young Man*, 1916; *The Swallow's Next*, 1950; *Thou Desperate Pilot*, 1927; *The Varying Shore*, 1921

OTHER WORKS

Cake Upon the Waters (novel), 1919; *Camille* (screenplay), 1936; *Desire Me* (screenplay), 1947; *Eve's Secret* (screenplay), 1925; *The Hills Grow Smaller* (poetry), 1937; *Interpretations* (poetry), 1911; *Morning Glory* (screenplay), 1932; *Showboat* (screenplay), 1931

1. *Town & Country*, December 1, 1916.
2. Essay by Felicia Hardison Londré in Robinson.

Ariadne
(FL. 1695)

(*Enter* CHARLOTTE *and* JULIANA *in men's clothes.*)
JULIANA. Faith, Charlotte, the breeches become you so well 'tis almost pity you should ever part with 'em.
CHARLOTTE. Nor will I, till I can find one can make better use of them to bestow 'em on, and then I'll resign my title to 'em for ever.
JULIANA. 'Tis well if you find it so easy for a woman once vested in authority though 'tis by no other than her own making, does not willingly part with it. But, prithee child, what is thy design? For I am yet to learn.
CHARLOTTE. Why, to ramble the town till I can meet with the man I can find in my heart to take for better or for worse. . . . Should I meet with the man whose outside pleased me, 'twill be impossible by any other means to discover his humour; for they are so used to flatter and deceive our sex, that there's nothing but the angel appears, though the devil lies lurking within, and never so much as shows his paw till he has got his prey fast in his clutches.

—from *She Ventures and He Wins*, Act I, Scene 1

The first of four new women playwrights introduced in the 1695–96 London season, Ariadne's true identity is a mystery. For her only known play, *She Ventures and He Wins*, she signed herself "Ariadne, a young lady." Speculations have abounded as to whom she really was. Some believe her to have been MARY GRIFFITH PIX[1]; Germiane Greer hypothesized that she was a man.[2] (Considering the bias against women writers, one wonders why a man

would choose so detrimental a deception.) A possible reason for Ariadne's reticence in publicizing herself and her work is referred to in the play's prologue. Evidently, she was unwilling to submit her play for production due to her idolization of APHRA BEHN. She wrote, "Our author hopes indeed,/You will not think, though charming Aphra's dead,/All Wit with her, and Orinda's fled." She went on to say that since Behn's death, she "has claim'd a kind of Privilege; and, in spite of me, broke from her Confinement." One imagines Behn would have approved of *She Ventures,* which was the first play by a woman to have been produced in the six years since Behn's death.

She Ventures opened at Lincoln's Inn Fields Theatre in September 1695 with a sterling cast of players and was received enthusiastically. The plot is a comedy of intrigue about women's efforts to test the virtue of men. Charlotte, a rich heiress, longs to find a husband who loves her for herself and not for her money. The aptly named Lovewell captures her affection, but Charlotte is unsure of the authenticity of his feelings for her. Using a set of disguises, she dupes Lovewell into believing she is a whore. When he cannot renounce his love for her, even under those dire circumstances, Charlotte is satisfied that he is a man of integrity. She reveals herself to him, and they are united in bliss. The subplot revolves around Urania and Freeman, a husband and wife determined to expose Squire Wouldbe as the unfaithful fool he is to his wife Dowdy. The women in the play are effective, cunning, and witty, gleefully wrapping the men around their fingers.

PLAYS

She Ventures and He Wins, 1695.

1. Lyons, Paddy, and Fidelis Morgan, eds., *Female Playwrights of the Restoration* (London: J. M. Dent, 1991).
2. Greer, Germaine, ed., *Kissing the Rod: an anthology of seventeenth-century women's verse* (New York: Farrar Strauss Giroux, 1989).

Aspāzija
(MARCH 16, 1868–NOVEMBER 5, 1943)

To the great dismay of her parents, the Latvian dramatist Elza Rozenberga chose to study poetry and literature, rather than learning "the art of gracious living," the more expected and acceptable route for young, affluent ladies such as herself. The boldness of Rozenberga's decision led one of her classics instructors to dub her "Aspāzija," after the independently minded wife of Pericles of Athens, the ancient Greek statesman and patron of the arts.

Rozenberga found herself perfectly suited to her new name. Throughout her life she fought for the political and social emancipation of all subjugated peoples, particularly women. In 1891 she embarked on a career as a poet and tutor; over the course of her life she published ten volumes of poetry, which became her primary genre in her last years.

In 1893 she became dramaturg for the Theater of the Latvian Association of Riga. Within a year she had penned two plays, *Vaidelote* (The Vestal), a tragedy based on fourteenth-century Lithuanian legends, and *Zaudētas tiesības*, a realistic melodrama that stirred up a heated public debate and earned her the reputation of a staunch women's rights advocate. Her 1895 play *Ragana* (The Witch) offered a more palatable tale for most critics. A musical fantasy, *Ragana* portrays Liesma, the witch, who, unlike her sisters, yearns to live in the sun and be human. Yet, as in the more familiar folk tale "Beauty and the Beast," until Liesma understands the nature of true love, she will remain a witch. When Almars, the object of her affection, rejects Liesma, she lies to the king in order to get Almars imprisoned. It is only after his execution that she comprehends the extent of her own doom: She will never reach the sun, never become human, because she did not learn the meaning of love.

Although Aspāzija continued to create dramatic works, her desire to serve humanity led her to medical school in Zurich in 1896. However, she returned to Latvia a year later to become editor of *Dienas lapa* (The Daily Bulletin) and to participate in *Jauna strava* (The New Current), a nationalist and socialist movement. One of the movement's more charismatic leaders was Jānis Pliekšāns, known to his followers as Rainis. Aspāzija and Rainis were married in 1897.

In 1888 Aspāzija's play *Atriebēja* (The Avengeress) won first prize in the play writing contest sponsored by the Theater of the Latvian Association of Riga. Despite its potboiler tendencies (including baby swapping, kidnapping, and vengeance-seeking women), *Atriebēja* took such a strong stand against classism that censors forbade production of the play claiming it was anti-German; it remained unpublished until 1904. No amount of censorship, however, could silence Aspāzija. In 1905, just before she and her husband were forced to flee to Switzerland because of the Latvian political climate, she wrote *Sidraba šķidrauts* (The Silver Veil), a highly symbolic play that utilizes mythology to deal with such concepts as love versus duty, the loss of innocence, and the power of an oppressive tyranny that contains the seeds of its own destruction.

Much like their Russian contemporaries, ZINAIDA GIPPIUS and Dimitri Merezhkovsky, Aspāzija and Rainis were not able to return to their homeland until 1920. Interestingly, Aspāzija completed only one play, *Laime* (Fortune), during her exile. After her homecoming, she penned the ironically eponymous *Aspāzija*, which is set in the ancient Athenian court of Pericles. In the play the title character fools her husband and his erudite colleagues (Sophocles, Phidias, and Socrates, among them) by disguising herself as a man and impressing the other men with her sensitive manner and speech. When Aspāzija reveals her true identity, the men are shocked and outraged. She incurs the jealous wrath of their wives, in spite of her demand that society reexamine its disrespectful attitudes toward women. She dramatically tears down the statues of the male gods and unveils a new statue of Athena, carved in her own image. The women and religious leaders bring charges of heresy and corruption against Aspāzija, and when Pericles defends her, he too is accused of treason. Ultimately, the lots are cast in court, and both are found innocent. The Athenians unite and welcome the new age. At about this time Aspāzija also wrote a loosely autobiographical drama *Neaizsniegts mērkis* (Unattained Goal), which zeros in on the suspicion people place on women who thirst for knowledge, and the consequential lack of education suffered by women. It is surely no accident, persecuted as she and her husband were, that the returning Aspāzija would pen two works that focus on redemption.

In addition to her plays, poetry, and humanitarian work, Aspāzija translated a variety of Russian and German literature, including works by Goethe and Sienkiewicz. She received the Nation's Award for Poetry in 1934. In all of her writings she managed to balance herself on the fine line between romanticism and realism, marking her efforts with her stamp as a progressive romantic who continually fought for the rights of women and of all individuals.[1]

PLAYS

Aspāzija, 1923; *Atriebēja* (The Avengeress, Astrid Barbina-Stahnke, tr., 1975), 1888; *Boass un Rute* (Boaz and Ruth), 1925; *Laime* (Fortune), 1913; *Neaizsniegts mērkis* (Unattained Goal), 1920; ; *Pūcesspieģelis* (The Clown), 1932; *Ragana* (The Witch), 1895; *Sidraba šķidrauts* (The Silver Veil, A. B-S., tr., 1977), 1905; *Sokrāts un Bakhante* (Socrates and Bacchante), n.d.; *Torna cēlējs* (The Tower Builder), 1927; *Vaidelote* (The Vestal), 1894; *Velna nauda* (Devil's Money), 1933; *Zalkša līgava* (The Sea Serpent's Bride, A. B-S., tr., 1978), n.d.; *Zaudētas tiesības*, 1894; *Zeltīte* (Goldie; a.k.a *Spoku dīķis* [Pond of Ghosts]), 1901

1. Straumanis.

Enid Bagnold
(OCTOBER 27, 1889–MARCH 31, 1981)

JUDGE. A judge does not always get to the bottom of a case.
MADRIGAL. No. It takes the pity of God to get to the bottom of things.

—from *The Chalk Garden*

Although English writer Enid Bagnold may be remembered best for the quintessential classic screenplay *National Velvet*, her stage plays are equally impressive and socially pertinent. They consistently and cleverly present the difficulties encountered by intelligent women in modern society, and Bagnold's women are anything but simple. For example, Madrigal, the heroine of *The Chalk Garden*, is a recently released murderer who, after surviving a terrible trial and fifteen years in prison, finds a position as guardian to Laurel, a bright, manipulative girl. As Laurel gathers snippets of suspicious information about Madrigal, tensions and innuendos fly. But Madrigal perseveres with her strong character, wit, and bravery intact. "One can lie," she says, "but truth is more interesting." Despite the horrors of her incarceration, she is wise, perceptive, and ultimately compassionate. Through Madrigal, Bagnold encourages the audience to accept the life one has been dealt and have the courage to live.

Bagnold enjoyed a privileged upbringing. She was the first child of Arthur Bagnold, a commissioner in the Royal Engineers, who made the first telephones in England, and Ethel Alger, whose family held a high social position in the west country of England.

Although Bagnold's mother spoiled and indulged her, her father was a strict disciplinarian who did not refrain from the occasional whipping. Bagnold was a quick and precocious child who read by age four, showing an early interest in and aptitude for language. She began her professional life as a cub reporter for *Hearth and Home*, a

Enid Bagnold
COURTESY OF THE BILLY ROSE THEATRE COLLECTION

publication run by Frank Harris. Despite Harris's physical unattractiveness, he was extremely charismatic. Bagnold was quite infatuated with him, and pursued him romantically even though she knew he was married: their clandestine affair lasted until it was discovered and publicized. Harris was accustomed to scandal and went about his business, but Bagnold's career as a reporter ended abruptly. She returned to her family's home, where she remained until she met and married Sir Roderick Jones many years later.

Throughout her life, Bagnold struggled with a fractured identity. She aligned herself with two incompatible worlds: the "smart set," as the upper class was called, and the realm of artists. Among her acquaintances were Virginia and Leonard Woolf, Prince Antoine Bibesco, H. G. Wells, and Vita Sackville-West. It was Lady Sackville, Vita's mother, who introduced Bagnold to Sir Roderick. Titled, but not an aristocrat, the forty-two-year-old bachelor had purposefully avoided marriage. "I had always been fearful of being permanently tied up to another human being whom I might find incompatible and want to escape from," he revealed in his autobiography.[1] Yet he was smitten by Bagnold and proposed to her three weeks after their first meeting. She was thirty-one when they married in 1921.

During World War II, she volunteered with the Red Cross. Unlike other writers, Bagnold found little inspiration in the war. In her journal she wrote, "I am sick, sick of the war, sick of the unending misery in these hospitals here . . . I am unable to turn pain and loss to an account . . . I am not inspired to any turn of thought. I find nothing provocative, nothing suggestive." The particular demands of wartime life affected even families of Bagnold's position, and she found herself facing the difficult challenge of feeding her family. Bagnold turned the three-and-a-half-acre patch of grass attached to North End House into a small farm. She maintained a variety of livestock: hens, geese, chickens, ducks, rabbits, a goat, and a cow, and began to make her own cheese. According to her biographer Anne Sebba, Bagnold once proclaimed that cheese-making was "a sort of science and a sort of legend, evolved from man's necessities and from the empirical advices and observations of women long dead and gone—a mixture today of higher mathematics and decimals of acidity, mixed with witchcraft and a sort of rough luck. Now and then you throw up a good cheese like a good poem."

Bagnold's personal struggle with balancing her domestic and artistic needs, and her willingness to meet life's challenges, reflects the strength and courage of many of her female characters. In *The Chinese Prime Minister*, SHE, an actress with two married adult sons, wrestles with the confines of her professional and personal life, and the shaky terrain ventured upon by men and women. She remarks, "Women are so dutiful and the best men make them work so hard for them. I have yet to find out what a day is like when I'm not planning the next one!" Later, SHE articulates the crux of Bagnold's own dilemma: "I want the whole of myself—and not half again!" "You were meant to be a single woman," says her butler, Bent. "Women of individuality are damned uncomfortable for men." SHE's daughter-in-law, Alice, whom SHE resents, asks her own anxious questions: "What is this ghastly difference between men and women? What is this closeness that works—and doesn't work! That boils, that burns and blisters, and is so near love!" *The Chinese Prime Minister* demonstrates how hard yet necessary it is for women to choose their own lives, and to become their "sheroes," as Maya Angelou has coined.

The issues of relationships and compromise, and love and loneliness, are evidenced as well in Bagnold's last play, *A Matter of Gravity*. Here Bagnold adds the class struggle to her recipe. The play covers eight years at an old English country manse, where a cast of quirky, engaging characters grapple with Bagnold's familiar themes. Mrs. Basil, the pivotal character, and the people in her life—her alcoholic cook Dubois, who can fly, her grandson Nick and his wife Elizabeth, her friend Herbert, and others—meet and talk and reveal themselves. Mrs. Basil, the pivotal character, is a generous, zany, and honest woman. Regarding class consciousness and racism, Mrs. Basil says, "I think it's snobbery and a sort of outrage to despise people for the way they were born." To her bright and materialistic daughter-in-law Elizabeth (of whom Mrs. Basil comments, "There is no end of an end of an end—to her discontent."), she says, "Intelligence is such an easy thing—one knows at once. But the stuff that shoulders a life and a wife is harder to discern."

Enid Bagnold's choices are a testament to Mrs. Basil's remark. Above all else in her life, Bagnold prized her three sons most, and believed they, not her literary accomplishments, were "her most enduring memorial." Had she not been so devoted to her children, she might have written more. "By refusing to shun either social delights or the pleasures of sharing her children's lives," Sebba writes, "she failed to concentrate fully on intellectual pursuits. By refusing, as she did, to put her writing first, to the exclusion of all else, she laid herself open to charges of amateurism, irrespective of how hard she might have worked." Nevertheless, Bagnold's writing reveals "a talent for the use of words, a fondness for aphorisms and elliptical utterances, and a flair for wit and humor."

PLAYS

A Matter of Gravity, 1978; *Call Me Jacky*, 1968; *The Chalk Garden*, 1955; *The Chinese Prime Minister*, 1964; *Four Plays*, 1970; *Gertie*, 1952; *The Last Joke*, 1960; *Lottie Dundass*, 1941; *National Velvet* (screenplay, 1944), 1946; *Poor Judas*, 1946; *Two Plays*, 1951

OTHER WORKS

A Diary Without Dates, 1918; *Alexander of Asia* (*Alexandre asiatique*, tr. by Marthe Bibesco), 1935; *Alice and Thomas and Jane*, 1930; *A Matter of Gravity*, 1978; *Enid Bagnold's Autobiography*, 1969; *The Girl's Journey* (repr. of *The Happy Foreigner and The Squire*), 1954; *The Happy Foreigner*, 1920; *Letters to Frank Harris and Others*, 1980; *The Loved and Envied*, 1951; *National Velvet*, 1935; *Poems*, 1978; *The Sailing Ships and Other Poems*, 1918; *Serena Blandish, or The Difficulty of Getting Married*, 1924 *The Squire*, 1938

WORKS ABOUT

Friedman, Lenemaja, *Enid Bagnold*, 1986; Sebba, Anne, *Enid Bagnold, The Authorized Biography*, 1986.

1. All quotations from Anne Sebba, *Enid Bagnold, The Authorized Biography* (New York: Taplinger, 1986).

Joanna Baillie
(SEPTEMBER 11, 1762–FEBRUARY 23, 1851)

COUNTESS OF ALBINI. For she who only finds her self-esteem
In other's admiration, begs in alms;
Depends on others for her daily food,
And is the very servant of her slaves . . .

—from *Count Basil*, Act 1, Scene 4

Although more than sixteen of Joanna Baillie's plays were successfully produced in her lifetime, very little is known about her life. She was born in Hamilton, Lanark, near Bothwell, Scotland, to Reverend James Baillie; he died when his daughter was sixteen, leaving her and his wife, Dorothea, to carry on alone. Eventually, Baillie relocated to London, where she found success as a playwright and remained for the rest of her days.

Of her many plays, Baillie's tragedies merit special distinction. Stephen Jones writes in his *Biographia Dramatica* that these reflect "a strong conception of character, an accurate delineation of the various feelings and passions, vivid imagery, and a great command of poetical diction."[1] At a time when serious drama was in a sad state of decline in England, Baillie's works stood out like a beacon. Despite the fame she enjoyed in her lifetime, Baillie has been remembered for having been the friend of Sir Walter Scott and for her single volume of verse rather than for her dramatic works.

In a preface to her two-volume *Series of Plays*, Baillie states that she "attempted to delineate the stronger passions of the mind, each passion being the subject of a tragedy and a comedy." Indeed, her works reveal an in-

Joanna Baillie
COURTESY OF CORBIS-BETTMANN

herent wisdom about human nature and an undeniable yearning to illustrate men's and women's best qualities. Her understanding of the dialectic of social ambition and spiritual passion is evidenced in *The Election* (1802) when Charlotte wails, "I wish I were with some of the wild people that run in the woods, and know nothing about accomplishments!"

PLAYS

The Alienated Manor, 1836; *The Beacon*, 1802; *The Bride*, 1836; *Constantine Paleologus*, 1804; *Count Basil*, 1798; *The Country Inn*, 1804; *De Monfrot*, 1798; *The Election*, 1802; *Ethwald, Parts First and Second*, 1802; *The Family Legend*, 1810; *Miscellaneous Plays*, n.d.; *Orra*, 1812; *The Phantom*, 1836; *Plays on the Passions* (3 vols.), 1798–1812; *Rayner*, 1804; *The Second Marriage*, 1802; *A Series of Plays* (2 vols.) n.d.; *The Trial*, 1798.

OTHER WORKS

Fugitive Verses, 1790

1. Jones

Doris Baizley
(1948?–   )

DOT. This isn't a contest I'm in up here, it's every day of my life and I'm so damned good at it I can't stop.

—from *Mrs. California*

Doris Baizley has been highly active in the regional theater scene in the United States; her works have been produced by dozens of the major regional playhouses in the country, including A Contemporary Theatre in Seattle, the Cleveland Playhouse, the Mark Taper Forum in Los Angeles, and the National Theater of the Deaf. Many of her works have also been performed abroad: Her adaptation of *A Christmas Carol* has been produced annually at the Semafor Theatre in Prague, and *Daniel in Babylon* opened the Icon Theatre at the National Theatre of Taiwan in 1993. For seven years Baizley was resident playwright for the Mark Taper Forum's Improvisational Theatre Project. There her work *Ph*reaks*, cowritten with Victoria Ann Lewis, was performed at the 1993 New Play Festival as part of the Disability History Project.

Mrs. California (1986) takes place in the 1950s and addresses the changing roles of women in America. "By 1955, the year in which Doris Baizley's *Mrs. California* takes place," writes Robert Meiksins, literary manager of the Capital Repertory Company, "the image of the American woman was shifting, or perhaps had already shifted, from Rosie the Riveter to Suzie Homemaker."[1] The play centers on a contest to find the perfect housewife. We meet Mrs. San Francisco, Mrs. San Bernardino, and Mrs. Modesto, all vying to be chosen as Mrs. California.

For Baizley these ladies are not intended to be silly, two-dimensional caricatures: she cautions the four actors playing the contestants to "believe in their presentation. Find any way you can not to condescend to these women. . . . Remember this isn't about the cuteness or stupidity of the '50s, it's about the danger of the 'housewife state.' " Lee Shallat, who directed a production of *Mrs. California* at A Contemporary Theatre, said, "There's an atmosphere of paranoia in the play that I think is characteristic of the paranoia that existed in the '50s. . . . There was a certain fear about what one did and didn't do . . . What the judges in the Mrs. California contest say and do is what one was supposed to say and do at the time."[2]

Most of Baizley's work tackles the dilemmas faced by contemporary American women. *Tears of Rage*, (1985) the title of which is taken from a Bob Dylan song, takes place during the 1960s, a time when the women's movement was coming of age. Through the eyes of the women in the play, we are given a fresh and original perspective on the Vietnam era, much of which is drawn from Baizley's personal experiences.

Currently, Doris Baizley lives in Los Angeles, where she is a founding member of LA Theatreworks and has led their Writer's Dialogue workshop for women playwrights.

PLAYS

Agnes Smedley: Our American Friend, 1993; *Beowulf and the Tapes*, 1980; *Bugs*, 1976; *Catholic Girls*, 1979; *A Christmas Carol* (coadaptation w/Victoria Ann Lewis), 1977; *Concrete Dreams*, 1978; *Daniel in Babylon*, 1982; *Darkest Africa: A Ladies' Guide to the Nile*, 1972; *Dolls: An Evening with the Women of Jacqueline Susann*, 1985; *Guns*, 1975; *Lines*, 1977; *Mary Dyer Hanged in Boston*, 1971; *Mrs. California*, 1986; *Nevada 62*, 1981; *Orange Trees*, 1976; *Ph*reaks*, w/Victoria Ann Lewis, 1993; *Tears of Rage*, 1985

OTHER WORKS

Land of Little Rain (teleplay), 1987; *Until She Talks* (teleplay), 1984

1. "A Contemporary Theatre," *Playbill* 1:2 (1988).
2. Ibid.

Elizabeth Baker
(1876–MARCH 8, 1962)

MAGGIE. Office work is awf'lly monotonous.
MRS. MASSEY. Of course it is. So is all work. Do you expect work to be pleasant? Does anybody ever like work? The idea is absurd. Anyone would think work was to be pleasant. You don't come into the world to have pleasure. We've got to do our duty, and the more cheerfully we can do it, the better for ourselves and everybody else.

—from *Chains*, Act III

Although Elizabeth Baker's plays were dismissed by many critics as "mere journalism," this London-born playwright attempted to depict the lives of working-class women at a time when such themes were less than popular. Indeed, although she completed a great deal of her oeuvre in the 1910s, her work was not staged until the 1931 production of *Chains* by the Play Actors at the Royal Court Theater in London.

Chains portrays the grim world of three women who are inextricably bound to the roles dictated to them by social and economic norms. In the end, only Maggie breaks from what she knows is expected of her. By deciding to keep her hated sales job and reject the dull Mr. Foster's marriage proposal, she "chooses chains she knows she can later reject, rather than the ones of marriage which she knows she won't be able to break."[1] In another play,

Miss Tassey, a spinster of forty-five is dismissed from her position at a drapery store due to her age and an infirmity caused by her work. Having nothing and no one in her life, she commits suicide.

Baker's own life was strangely opposite to those of her characters. She was married to James E. Allaway and enjoyed a leisurely lifestyle, favoring country walks and literature. Yet her politics concerning women's issues were conveyed loudly and clearly in the more than fifteen plays she wrote, published, and produced in her lifetime, earning her a due place alongside the other playwrights of her era.

PLAYS

Beastly Pride, 1914; *Bert's Girl*, 1925; *Chains*, 1909; *Cupid in Clapham*, 1910; *Edith*, 1912; *One of the Spicers*, 1931; *Over a Garden Wall*, 1915; *Partnership*, 1917; *Penelope Forgives*, 1930; *The Picture*, 1929; *The Price of Thomas Scott*, 1913; *Miss Robinson*, 1918; *Miss Tassey*, 1910; *Umbrellas*, 1928

1. Fitzsimmons, Linda, and Viv Gardner, ed. and intro. *New Woman Plays* (London: Methuen Drama, 1991).

Djuna Barnes
(JUNE 12, 1892–JUNE 18, 1982)

After Djuna Barnes died, her ashes were scattered over Storm King Mountain at Cornwall-on-Hudson in New York, her birthplace and the place of creative importance to some of this century's great writers, among them Anaïs Nin, William Faulkner, Isak Dinesen, and Truman Capote. Though she was more recognized for her literary contributions as a writer of modern fiction, Barnes wrote a dozen plays. Erlene Hendrix writes that "her unique exploration of character relationships and her emphasis on sound and rhythm are qualities that drama has increasingly embodied. Moreover, women are central characters in all of Barnes's writing . . . there is a revival of interest, influenced largely by feminists, in her plays."[1]

Barnes began as an actress for the Washington Square Players and Provincetown Players in New York. Under the pseudonym Lydia Steptoe, she wrote a series of "Ten-Minute" plays. Her first three-act drama, *The Antiphon*, was originally produced by Stockholm's Royal Dramatic Theater in 1961, with a translation by Dag Hammarskjöld and Karl Ragner Gierow. Interestingly, *The Antiphon*, generally considered the defining mark of Barnes's work as a playwright, has yet to be staged in English. Critic Edwin Muir called the verse drama "one of the greatest things . . . written in our time."[2]

The drama of Barnes's life tends to upstage even her most popular work. Born in New York to Elizabeth Chappell and Waldo Barnes, an amateur artist and musician who composed operas, the young Djuna learned to play the banjo, violin, and French horn. Her grandmother was a teacher and suffragist. Though never formally educated, she began writing and drawing while still in her teens and published her first poem in a 1911 issue of *Harper's Weekly* before she reached twenty. Later she studied at the Pratt Institute and the Art Students' League. As a girl, she was evidently influenced by the writings of Marie Bashkirtseff.

Barnes's early years as a professional writer were spent as a journalist for a number of New York City newspapers and magazines. After World War I, she left for Paris, where, throughout the 1920s and '30s, she wrote prolifically as a poet, novelist, and playwright. She also established herself as a graphic artist. She remained an important figure among expatriate artists in Europe, and counted playwright Samuel Beckett, photographer Berenice Abbott, as well as James Joyce and T. S. Eliot, as close friends. In Eliot's introduction to Barnes's novel *Nightwood*, Eliot admired the book's "quality of horror and doom very nearly related to that of Elizabethan tragedy." She achieved immediate fame following its publication in 1936.

Beautiful, sharp-witted, and outspoken, Barnes cultivated a controversial reputation for her sexual exploits over the years, which included liaisons with women as well as men. However, in 1936 she embarked on a sudden, self-imposed exile. She published very little after that and spent the last forty-odd years of her life in relative seclusion. A member of the American Academy of Arts and Letters, Barnes died in New York in 1982.

PLAYS

The Antiphon, 1958; *The Dove*, n.d.; *An Irish Triangle*, 1919; *Kurzy of the Sea*, 1919; *A Passion Play*, n.d.; *She Tells Her Daughter*, n.d.; *Three From the Earth*, 1919; *To the Dogs*, n.d.

OTHER WORKS (SELECTED)

A Book (various writings; rev. 1929, *A Night Among the Horses*), 1923; *The Book of Repulsive Women* (poems and drawings), 1915; *Ladies' Almanack* (novel), 1928; *Nightwood* (novel), 1936; *Ryder* (novel), 1928; *Selected Works*, 1962; *Smoke and Other Early Stories*, 1982

WORKS ABOUT

Barry, Alyce, ed., *Djuna Barnes Interviews*, 1985; Field, Andrew, *Djuna: The Formidable Miss Barnes*, 1985; Herring, Phillip, *Djuna: the life and work of Djuna Barnes*,

1995; Kannenstine, Louis F., *The Art of Djuna Barnes*, 1977; Messerli, Douglas, *Djuna Barnes: A Bibliography*, 1975; O'Neal, Hank, *Life Is Painful, Nasty and Short: An Informal Memoir of Djuna Barnes*, 1990; Plumb, Cheryl J., *Fancy's Craft: Art and Identity in the Early Works of Djuna Barnes*, 1986

1. Essay by Erlene Hendrix in Robinson.

2. Quoted in Kinsman, Clare D., and Mary Ann Tennanhouse, eds., *Contemporary Authors* (Detroit, Mich.: Gale Research, 1974).

Vicki Baum
(JANUARY 24, 1888–AUGUST 29, 1960)

GRUSINSKAYA. I want to be alone.

—from *Grand Hotel*

Grand Hotel, Vicki Baum's most renowned play, has lived more lives than the characters who people it. Long before Hollywood made it legendary with Greta Garbo, Joan Crawford, and John and Lionel Barrymore, *Grand Hotel* made its first appearance in Berlin as a humble magazine serial entitled *Menshen im Hotel* (People at the Hotel). It proved so popular that even before the serial ended, a the-

atrical agent asked Baum to adapt it into a play. *Grand Hotel* was first produced in Berlin by Max Reinhardt in 1929. It was an enormous hit. The play subsequently appeared on 146 European stages. The novel of *Grand Hotel* (which Baum also adapted from the magazine serial) became a best-seller in Germany and, in its translated form, in Great Britain and the United States. The play opened on Broadway in 1930 and ran for fifty-nine weeks, grossing more than $1,250,000. Then came the film versions: first the Academy Award–winning film in 1932, then the film musical, *Weekend at the Waldorf*, in 1945, which later became a stage musical.

The play centers on the crisscrossing lives of a myriad of characters: a dancer, a baron, a hotel clerk, a secretary, a businessman. Through these people, Baum adeptly weaves together the epic themes of destiny, love, and death, with the universal angst each individual faces upon encountering life's great obstacles: debts, dreams, deals.

> It is a model of speedy action, driving on with the tideless torrent of time; it presents a series of neatly drawn character studies, catching each person in a moment of hang-fire decision; and it weaves the several lives into one multiplex pattern. Its persons and their problems pass swiftly through the Grand Hotel of life. Insignificant and little known beyond the narrow borders of their concerns, they are the sort that, like us that watch them, make up the world.[1]

The success of *Grand Hotel* eventually beckoned Vienna-born Baum to emigrate to the United States. She became a Hollywood screenwriter in 1932 and, in 1938, became an American citizen. Although she continued to work, little else that Baum wrote rivaled the acclaim of *Grand Hotel*. Nevertheless, to create one work with the capacity to touch the lives of so many audiences is no small feat. As critic James Agate exclaimed at the London opening of *Grand Hotel*: "*Veni, vidi*, Vicki!"

PLAYS

Divine Drudge, 1934; *Grand Hotel* (also novel, 1929, and screenplay, 1932), 1930; *Summer Night*, w/Benjamin F. Glazer, 1939

NOVELS (SELECTED)

Danger from Deer, 1951; *Grand Opera*, 1942; *Helene*, Zda Zeitlin, tr., 1933; *Hotel Berlin '43* (also screenplay), 1944; *It Was All Quite Different* (memoirs), 1964; *Men Never Know*, 1935; *Mortgage on Life*, 1946; *Shanghai '37*, 1938; *The Mustard Seed*, 1953; *Tale of Bali*, 1938; *Theme for Ballet*, 1958; *Written on Water*, 1956

Vicki Baum
COURTESY OF THE BILLY ROSE THEATRE COLLECTION

1. Shipley.

Aphra Behn
(JULY 10, 1640–APRIL 16, 1689)

PROLOGUE: . . . I have heard the most of that which bears the name of learning, and which has abused such quantities of ink and paper, and continually employs so many ignorant, unhappy souls for ten, twelve, twenty years in the university—(who yet, poor wretches, think they are doing something all the while)—as logic, et cetera, and several other things which are much more absolutely nothing than the errantist play that e'er was writ.

—from "An Epistle to the Reader," *The Dutch Lover*, 1673

In Virginia Woolf's classic essay collection *A Room of One's Own*, she writes, "Here begins the freedom of the mind . . . For now that Aphra Behn had done it, girls could say . . . I can make money by my pen." Aphra Behn distinguished herself as the first woman in history to have earned a living as a writer. A prolific iconoclast, she was blasted by the critics of her day—and called a harlot by at least one—for the scandalous behavior presented in her dramas and in her own life. Nevertheless, her work enjoyed great popularity. Behn's penchant for bawdy intrigue comedies merely reflects the colorfulness of her own life.

Born Aphra Amis, when still a toddler she traveled with her family from her native England to the nation of Suriname, tucked between what we now think of as Guyana and French Guiana. Her father, John Amis, planned to assume an important post there, but he died during the voyage. However, upon arriving at their destination (probably Paramaribo, the capital), Aphra's mother chose to stay and raise her children in the new country. They did not return to London until around 1663.

By then a charming, clever young woman, Aphra soon married a wealthy Dutch merchant named Behn. The couple circulated in the most elite social circles, at least once appearing at the court of Charles II, where she managed to delight the king himself with her witty anecdotes.[1] But soon Behn found herself in a rather dire circumstance: Her husband died in 1665, quite likely from the plague. Without any means of support, she applied to the court for assistance. The Dutch derivation of her married name led to a position in Holland, where she was ordered to spy in the name of the English crown. She signed her dispatches "Astrea," the same name that appears on her early poetry. Yet she received little financial compensation for her efforts, and was soon in desperate straits. She managed to obtain a loan from a wealthy acquaintance, but upon returning to England, she was thrown into debtors' prison. A letter to the King ultimately freed her; her debts were paid, and she was awarded a small compensation for her trouble.

At this point, Behn decided to put her cleverness to a more practical use: She began writing for the stage. Her

Aphra Behn
COURTESY OF THE BILLY ROSE THEATRE COLLECTION

first three efforts, *The Forc'd Marriage* (1670), *The Amorous Prince* (1671), and *The Dutch Lover* (1673) brought her fame, fortune, and influential friends, John Dryden among them. With *The Dutch Lover*, Behn established her ability to pen formulaic comedies of intrigue that featured snappy colloquial dialogue. Her plots typically entail a number of couples who, in attempting to elude unwanted arranged marriages, according to Nancy Cotton, "meet, bed and/or wed after innumerable intrigues, mistaken identities, duels, disguises, and practical jokes . . . Her scenes of comic lowlife are delightful, full of landladies, bawds, buffoons, and prostitutes."[2]

The Amazon was a favorite female character of Behn's, and came to represent the role she gradually assumed herself as she continuously battled the ardent sexism she faced as a female dramatist. Initially, Behn's gender was fancied as a sort of novelty, but soon it became clear to the theatrical world that this woman would be a serious contender for money and prestige. Resistance set in, as Cotton has averred, and "a cabal formed against her," culminating with the critical flaying of *The Dutch Lover*. Deeply scarred by the experience, Behn did not write a play for another three years. Yet by 1678, having securely resurfaced, she had become righteously outspoken about what she considered to be the egregious behavior of the critics. In an epistle to the reader in *Sir Patient Fancy*, she revisited her *Dutch Lover* experience with this comment: "The play had no other Misfortune but that of coming out for a Womans: had it been owned by a Man, though the most Dull Unthinking Rascally Scribler in Town, it had been a most admirable Play."

All of Behn's plays reflect her firm attitude about the fine line between the role of a wife and the role of a prostitute, the courtesan being another traditional character of which she was clearly fond. In *The Rover*, Parts I and II (1677 and 1681), she goes so far as to suggest that "prostitution is the more candid, less hypocritical way for a woman to earn a living."[3] Upon being chastised by a man for selling love for money, Angellica Bianca retorts, "Pray, tell me, Sir, are not you guilty of the same mercenary Crime? When a Lady is proposed to you for a Wife, you never ask, how fair, discreet, or virtuous she is; but what's her Fortune—" (Act II, Scene 2). Angellica also decries, "Who made the laws by which you judge me? Men! Men who would rove and ramble, but require that women must be nice."

Although her cohorts described Behn as a social and convivial woman, a brilliant conversationalist, and a loyal friend, she remained a controversial figure throughout her life, and even through the nineteenth century, as when a Dr. Doranis wrote, "No one equaled this woman in downright nastiness save Ravenscroft and Wycherly. . . . She was a mere harlot . . ."[4] In the mid-Victorian era, Julia Kavanagh wrote in *English Women of Letters* (1863), "Even if her life remained pure, it is amply evident her mind was tainted to the very core. Grossness was congenial to her. . . . Mrs. Behn's indelicacy was useless and worse than useless, the superfluous addition of a corrupt mind and vitiated taste."[5]

Behn's work, however, has the last word. Even her novels enjoyed almost as much fame and popularity as did her plays, particularly *Oroonoko, or the History of the Royal Slave* (1688). Often called the first abolitionist novel, this romantic fiction contains realistic details about the oppression and rebellion of slaves brought to the New World; *Oroonoko* is set in Suriname, where Behn spent her youth. By the time of her death at age forty-nine, Behn had completed over two dozen plays, plus numerous novels, poetry collections, and translations. She is buried in the east cloisters of Westminster Abbey; a black marble slab marks the spot. On it are graven the words:

> "Here lies a Proof that Wit can never be
> Defence enough against Morality."

PLAYS

Abdelazer, or The Moor's Revenge, 1676; *The Amorous Prince, or The Curious Husband*, 1671; *The City Heiress, or Sir Timothy Treat-all*, 1682; *The Counterfeit Bridegroom, or The Defeated Widow* (attr.), 1677; *The Debauchee, or The Credulous Cuckold* (attr.), 1677; *The Dutch Lover*, 1673; *The Emperor of the Moon*, 1687; *The False Count, or A New Way to Play an Old Game*, 1681; *The Feign'd Courtezans, or A Night's Intrigue*, 1679; *The Forc'd Marriage, or The Jealous Bridegroom*, 1670; *Like Father Like Son, or The Mistaken Brothers*, 1682; *The Lucky Chance, or An Alderman's Bargain*, 1686; *The Revenge, or A Match in Newgate* (attr.) 1680; *Romulus and Hersila* (prologue, epilogue, and song "Where are thou"), 1682; *The Round-Heads, or The Good Old Cause*, 1682; *The Rover, or The Banished Cavaliers* (Part I), 1677, (Part II), 1681; *Sir Patient Fancy*, 1678; *The Town-Fop, or Sir Timothy Tawdrey*, 1676; *The Wavering Nymph, or Mad Amyntas*, 1684; *The Widow Ranter, or The History of Bacon in Virginia*, 1689; *The Woman Turned Bully*, 1675; *The Younger Brother, or The Amorous Jilt*, 1696; *The Young King, or The Mistake*, 1679 (pup. in 1683)

OTHER WORKS

The Adventure of the Black Lady (novel), 1683/4 (pub. posthumously, 1997); *Aesop's Fables* (tr.), 1687; *Agnes de Castro, or The Force of Generous Love* (tr. from Mme. de Brilhac), 1688; *A Discovery of New Worlds* (tr. from Fontanelle), 1688; *The Dumb Virgin* (novel), 1687; *The Fair Jilt*, 1688; *Floriana, a Pastoral*, 1681; *The History of the Nun, or The Fair Vow-Breaker*, 1688; *History of the Oracles and Cheats of the Pagan Priests* (tr. from Fontanelle), 1688; *The King of Bantam*, 1997; *The Lives of Sundry and Notorious Villains*, 1678; *Love Letters between a Nobleman and his Sister*, 1684; *Love Letters to a Gentleman* (attr.), 1696; *Love of the Plants, book VI: Of Trees*, 1689; *The Lucky Mistake*, 1689; *Lycidus, a Voyage from the Island of Love*, 1684; *Memoirs of the Court of the King of Bantam*, 1696; *Memoirs on the Life of Mrs. Behn*, 1696; *Miscellany* (poems), 1685; *La Montre, or the Lover's Watch*, 1685; *Oroonoko, or The History of a Royal Slave* (novel), 1688; *Paraphrase on the . . . 'Epistle of Oenone to Paris' in Ovid's 'Epistoles,'* 1727; *Perplexed Prince*, 1682; *Poems*, n.d.; *Three Histories*, 1688; *The Unfortunate Bride* (novel), 1687; *The Unfortunate Happy Lady; a True History*, 1698; *The Unhappy Mistake* (novel), 1687; *The Wandering Beauty* (novel), 1687

WORKS ABOUT

Duffy, M., *The Passionate Shepherdess*, 1989; Gildon, Charles, *An Account of the Life of the Incomparable Mrs.*

Behn, 1700?; Sackville-West, Victoria, *Aphra Behn, the incomparable Astrea,* 1928; Summers, Montague, ed., *The Works of Aphra Behn,* (1915; reprint, 1967); Todd, Janet, *The Secret Life of Aphra Behn,* 1996; Woodcock, George, *The Incomparable Aphra,* (1948)

1. According to Summers, Montague, ed., *The Works of Aphra Behn* (1915; reprint, New York: Benjamin Blom, 1967).

2. Cotton.

3. Ibid.

4. Op. cit., Summers.

5. Ibid.

Simone Benmussa
(1938?–)

ALBERT NOBBS. I thought that regrets had passed away with the petticoats. But you've awakened the woman in me. You've brought it all up again. But I mustn't let on like this; it's very foolish of an old perhapser like me, neither man nor woman. But I can't help it. You understand . . . the loneliness . . .

—from *The Singular Life of Albert Nobbs,*
"Albert Nobbs' Tale"

Born in Tunisia to a Jewish-French family, Simone Benmussa enrolled at the University of Paris in 1955 and still resides in the French capital. Although she began her work in theater by typing and editing scripts, eventually she allied herself with the famed Compagnie Renaud-Barrault and became editor of their journal, the *Cahiers Renaud-Barrault,* a position she held for twenty years. In 1958 she began broadcasting the prophetically titled "In the Wings of the Theatre of France," which was heard on French radio for ten years.

Despite the tremendous responsibility she shouldered for the Compagnie as its literary manager, Benmussa did not receive her first titled appointment until the mid-1970s: artistic director of the Petit Rond Point Theatre, an offshoot of the Rond Point Theatre complex—home of the Compagnie. Around 1976 she began creating and directing her own stage plays, primarily adapting from literary works such as Irish writer George Moore's *The Singular Life of Albert Nobbs* and Edna O'Brien's *Virginia,* and the works of Virginia Woolf and Nathalie Sarraute.

Thanks to the last-minute cancellation of a dance troupe, Benmussa's career as a playwright debuted on a week's notice, with *The Portrait of Dora,* which was based on the novel *Portrait de Dora* by the French feminist theorist/poet HÉLÈNE CIXOUS. Benmussa and Cixous worked together closely on the adaptation. *Dora* is based on a Freudian case study of female homosexuality. Benmussa's production was extremely well received, and subsequently traveled to Geneva, Zurich, and Vienna.

Dora was followed by *The Singular Life of Albert Nobbs,* Benmussa's most notable English-language work (due primarily to Barbara Wright's translation and the productions by London's New End Theater, 1978, and the Manhattan Theatre Club, 1982). *Nobbs* pushed the playwright's feminist sensibilities into a new direction, addressing head-on the politics of class and the privileges of the male gender.

Set in a nineteenth-century Dublin hotel, the play tells the story of the perfect waiter. Albert Nobbs is a man who never drinks, smokes, or flirts with the chambermaids. He is also a man with a secret: He is actually a woman, compelled to dress as a man in order to earn a living. In the play's pivotal scene, Nobbs must reluctantly reveal herself to a sensitive painter who has invited her to bed. Here, Benmussa throws her trump card: the painter is disguised as well! *Nobbs,* as Marilyn Stasio writes in a *New York Post* review, is "a singular work of searing beauty . . . [that] tells the story of a woman who lives her entire lifetime disguised as man—not from any sexual motive, but from the economic necessity of finding decent work in Victorian working society."[1] According to Benmussa herself, "*Albert Nobbs* is not a play about transvestites. Their male dress comes from dire necessity, and necessity lends itself no more to laughter than to pleasure. That a woman must cease to be a woman in order to assert her right to work is a fact too often forgotten in the class struggle, a fact which appears in a different form today, but which is still as tenacious."[2]

Benmussa favors an improvisational style in shaping her plays, and she works closely with actors. Case observes that the playwright "makes no division between playwright, housekeeper,* and director in her professional identity." Benmussa truly believes that the creation of a play is wholly collaborative. Not surprisingly, she has been recognized for her meticulous attention to her plays' presentations. Stasio wrote, "Benmussa has made masterful use of her lighting and set designs to communicate the physical fragmentation and spiritual isolation of women's lives within the period."[3]

In addition to her work with the Compagnie Renaud-Barrault, Benmussa has served as theater editor for Gallimard Publishers, written for French radio, translated Edward Bond's *Lear* into French, and written a biography of playwright Eugene Ionesco.

---

*Sue-Ellen Case (in *Feminism and Theatre*) applies this term as the way in which many women have learned theater craft, i.e., by doing the "dirty work" around the theater, from typing to tidying up.

PLADYS

Appearances, n.d.; *The Death of Ivan Illich*, n.d.; *Portrait of Dora*, 1976; *The Revolt*, n.d.; *La vie singulière d'Albert Nobbs* (adapt. of George Moore short story "The Singular Life of Albert Nobbs," Barbara Wright, tr.), 1977; *Virginia* (from Edna O'Brien's work), n.d.

1. Marilyn Stasio, *New York Post*, June 18, 1982.
2. Case (1).
3. Op. cit., Stasio.

Gertrude Berg
(OCTOBER 3, 1899–SEPTEMBER 14, 1966)

MOLLY GOLDBERG. So who's to know?

—from *Me and Molly*

Born in Harlem at a time when its primary residents were middle-class immigrants, Gertrude Berg expressed an interest in writing radio plays even as a little girl. She learned how to entertain audiences early on with skits she wrote and performed at the various Catskills hotels run at one time or another by her entrepreneurial father, Jacob Edelstein. After graduating from Wadleigh High School, she married Lewis W. Berg, a successful chemical engineer, and studied play writing at Columbia University. Her own

Gertrude Berg
COURTESY OF THE BILLY ROSE THEATRE COLLECTION

success did not come quickly, however. When she submitted her first radio piece to a local station, the manager rejected it, but he offered her five dollars to translate into Yiddish and record a gasoline commercial. Soon after this experience, the Bergs relocated for a time to a Louisiana plantation where Lewis was hired as an expert in sugar technology. After they returned to New York, they had two children, Robert (1922) and Harriet (1926).

Berg continued to pen scripts for her father's resorts and for the Jewish Art Theater, but it was not until her husband's business ran into trouble that she decided to try again for a career as a radio dramatist. Her script *Effie and Laurie* (1920) was originally snatched up by one station, but was canceled after only four months because the management disagreed with its progressive stance on love and marriage. Yet this small success encouraged Berg. She began to fashion a new work using her own large family as a model. Her father's self-important, larger-than-life personality suited itself perfectly for characterization. Both he and Berg's mother, Diana Goldstein, were the children of immigrant parents.

Upon completing the script, Berg knew her only chance to sell it would be to perform it herself—a performance would reveal all the clever nuances of the characters and dialogue. Therefore, she cleverly submitted the work in an illegible handwritten copy. Her plan worked like a charm: The producers asked her to read it, and thus began the long life of "The Rise of the Goldbergs" (note the fusion of her mother's and her own surnames), which ran uninterrupted from 1929 to 1946 for a total of 4,500 broadcasts (not all penned by Berg). In 1934 the series was adapted as a vaudeville act. The show was also turned into an NBC television series in 1949, but ran into trouble when one of the lead actors, Philip Loeb, Molly's husband in the show, was targeted by McCarthyists as a suspected Communist. General Foods, the show's sponsor, panicked and pulled out its support. The network canceled the show temporarily, though it returned briefly on another network in 1954 for one final season. Sadly, Loeb committed suicide the following year.

The appeal of "Goldbergs," the top rated show during radio's golden age, was multifaceted. Audiences responded to its idiosyncratic Jewish colloquialisms and its comic approach to family problems. But the show's greatest strength came from "Berg's tart recognition of human frailties and her blunt but understanding sense of humor."[1] Berg herself recognized the importance of injecting authentic experiences into her drama. "It is impossible to improve on reality," she wrote. "The good radio story should never escape reality and the problems of real people." Berg starred in all the scripts she crafted, making popular "the ultimate 'Jewish mother' in the days when the term meant warmth, affection, and only slight 'noodging'."[2]

After "The Goldbergs" left the radio airwaves, Berg's Broadway career began. She appeared in her own Broadway play, *Me and Molly*. She acted in the plays of others, too, most notably *A Majority of One*, written by her one-time coauthor Leonard Spigelgass, and for which her portrayal of the widowed Mrs. Jacoby won her an Antoinette Perry Award in 1959. She also won an Emmy for her portrayal of Molly Goldberg on "The Goldbergs" television series.

For several years Gertrude Berg was considered to be the most popular dramatist in America. According to essayist Donald Ray Schwartz, "Without question she advanced the art of popular American play writing and paved the way for women in the field."[3]

PLAYS

Dear Me, the Sky Is Falling, w/Leonard Spigelgass, 1963; *Me and Molly*, 1948

OTHER WORKS

Effie and Laurie (radio series), 1920; *House of Glass* (radio series), 1934; *How to Be a Jewish Mother* (album), 1966; *Molly and Me*, w/Cherney Robert Berg (autobio.), 1961; *The Rise of the Goldbergs* (radio series), 1929–46

1. *Time* magazine article, n.d.

2. Smith, Ronald L., *Who's Who in Comedy* (New York: Facts On File, 1992).

3. Essay by Donald Ray Schwartz in Robinson.

Ellen Bergman
(1919–)

Like many creative women who marry famous men, Ellen Bergman's marriage to renowned Swedish filmmaker and theatrician Ingmar Bergman often upstages the examination of her own works. A native of Gothenburg, Bergman was born to Gunnar Hollender and Inger Lindman. She attended school in Dresden. She married twice before her twenty-sixth birthday, first, briefly, to then-unknown photographer Christopher Strömholm, and shortly after to Bergman (1945). The second marriage for both, they had been introduced by Ingmar's first wife, Else Fisher! In Bergman's autobiography, he describes Ellen as "a strikingly beautiful girl who radiated erotic appeal, was talented, original and highly emotional." In 1948, Ellen's stepfather killed himself, leaving large debts. Ellen's mother and her small son moved in with Ellen, Ingmar, and their three children (they were to have one more). Also living with them was Ingmar's eldest daughter from his previous marriage to Else, who was ill at the time. Ten people in a five room apartment. Neither Ellen nor Ingmar, who had not yet found success as a filmmaker, had the discipline to live within their means, and the bills produced bitter quarrels, not to mention the numerous infidelities and lies to which Bergman himself readily admits. The marriage did not survive, but Bergman has said Ellen was "a good and strong friend." Although he remarried within a year, she did not, choosing instead to concentrate on raising their children and working in theater.

Bergman has written over a half dozen dramas for children's and adult theater. Almost invariably, her plays address the lives and experiences of women. *Maria,* her adaptation of August Strindberg's *Pariah,* alters the original by turning what had been a play about two men into a controversial drama about Jesus's mother and her lover, Pantera, Jesus's real father. This kind of feminist revisionism is evidenced in many of Bergman's works. She tackles Islam in *Fatima's Hand*, which shows the illiterate Mohammed dictating the Koran to his daughter Fatima, a forthright woman who does not always share her father's opinions. In *Selma* she reveals how the famous writer Selma Lagerlöf* broke from a father who expected his daughter to serve as his housekeeper. *Urtida Kvinnor* reexamines the old island history of Eddan, illustrating the suffering of the strong, brave women rather than the traditionally depicted men.

PLAYS

En Afton 1783, n.d.; *Fatima's Hand,* n.d.; *Maria,* n.d.; *Samvaro,* n.d.; *Selma,* n.d.; *Shoppingvagnen,* n.d.; *Urtida Kvinnor,* n.d

---

Martha Gross Boesing
(JANUARY 24, 1936–)

ABIGAIL. I have this malady: I try to make sense out of everything that happens to me. I cling to the neurotic belief that if I could understand what events mean, then I could stop obsessing about them.

—from *The Web*, Act 1

As a fifteen-year-old growing up in Providence, Rhode Island, Martha Gross Boesing spent her summers in summer stock theaters. She trained as an actor, director, and stage technician—a diverse apprenticeship that served to inform her dynamic approach to theater as a collaborative

---

*Lagerlöf was the first woman to receive the Nobel Prize for literature (1909).

art form, one which occurs in the dimension of time, as she has said, not space.

Boesing has been an active presence in regional theater since her teenage years. She has founded numerous theatrical enterprises, such as the Fourth Street Players and the Moppet Players (which became the acclaimed Minneapolis Children's Theater). In 1974 she originated the Minneapolis feminist theater collective At the Foot of the Mountain, for which she has served as playwright in residence. Along with earning two college degrees, raising four children, and surviving two marriages and divorces, Boesing has penned over seventeen works for the stage. With her second husband, composer/musician/actor Paul Boesing, she created several musical theater pieces.

Boesing's work leans toward a nonlinear, psychologically rich aesthetic that, thematically, concentrates on women's needs, imaginings, and apprehensions. Some of her more recent efforts are *Junkie!*, about all kinds of addictions—food, sex, work, violence; *Song for Johanna*, about a woman's decision to leave her family; and *The Web*, an experimental piece that takes place entirely in the mind, memory, and imagination of Abigail, the protagonist. She has received numerous awards, including a McKnight Fellowship (1983), a National Endowment for the Arts fellowship (1979), a Bush Foundation Fellowship (1984), and a Ford Foundation grant (1983).

PLAYS (SELECTED)

Accent on Fools, 1956; *Ashes, Ashes, We All Fall Down*, 1982; *The Business at Hand*, 1988; *The Chameleons*, w/ Paul Boesing, 1971; *Earth Song*, w/P.B., 1970; *The Gelding*, 1974; *Journey to Canaan*, 1974; *Junkie!*, 1981; *Las Gringas*, 1984; *Pimp*, 1973; *Raped: A Look at Brecht's The Exception and the Rule*, 1976; *River Journal*, 1975; *Shadows: A Dream Opera*, w/P.B., 1972; *Song for Johanna* (radio play), 1981; *The Story of a Mother*, 1977; *The Wanderer*, w/P.B., 1966; *The Web*, 1981

Bridget Boland
(MARCH 13, 1913–JANUARY 19, 1988)

Bridget Boland once said that most of her work reflects the theme "belief is dangerous."[1] Skeptics need only to look at her 1948 play *Cockpit* to understand what she means. *Cockpit* stunned viewers by transforming the theater into a "defamiliarized" zone. Audiences arrived to find notices warning them not to bear arms; "guards" took up stations at all the exits, shouting at patrons militaristically; actors planted in the audience quarreled. Later, the possible exposure to an infectious disease carried by one of the characters caused the theater to be "quarantined." Al-

though it ran only fifty-eight performances, *Cockpit* caused quite a stir; it is a forerunner in the advent of environmental theater—and perhaps guerrilla theater, too.

Boland was born in London to Irish parents; her father had been an Irish politician. While she has written "frothy comedy," as she puts it, she acknowledges that her strength lies in her political dramas. Freelance writer/director Ronald Hayman calls *The Prisoner* her best play. Inspired in part by the trial of Hungarian Cardinal Mindszenty, and, according to Hayman, in part by the novel *Darkness at Noon*, by Arthur Koestler, *Prisoner* takes a microscopic look at the development between its two main adversaries: the Interrogator, a clever aristocrat, and the Cardinal, a proletarian. Despite its tendency to lapse into sentimentality, some "highly theatrical climaxes"[2] make it a worthy effort.

Although Boland was known more for her screenplays (particularly *Anne of a Thousand Days* and *Gaslight*), she also wrote drama and fiction, and was an ardent gardener. The 20-by-20-foot backyard garden in London that she shared with her sister Maureen, a bookseller who died in 1976, was often photographed for books and magazines and was even open to the public. When the sisters moved to Hampshire, they eventually published two books on country gardening lore.

PLAYS

A Juan by Degrees (adapt. of Pierre Humblot play), 1965; *The Arabian Nights*, 1948; *Cockpit*, 1948; *The Damascus Blade*, 1950; *The Prisoner* (also screenplay, 1955), 1954; *The Return* (a.k.a. *Journey to Earth*), 1952; *The Zodiac in the Establishment* (a.k.a. *Time out of Mind*), 1963

SCREENPLAYS (SELECTED)

Anne of a Thousand Days, w/John Hale, 1970; *Damon and Pythias*, 1962; *Gaslight* (a.k.a. *Angel Street*), w/A. R. Rawlinson, 1940; *This England*, w/A.R.R. and Emlyn Williams, 1941; *War and Peace*, w/others, 1956

OTHER WORKS

At My Mother's Knee, 1978; *Caterina* (novel), 1975; *Forever Beautiful* (teleplay), 1965; *Old Wives' Lore for Gardeners*, w/Maureen Boland, 1976; *Portrait of a Lady in Love* (novel), 1942; *Sheba* (radio play), 1954; *The Wild Geese* (novel), 1942

1. Essay by Ronald Hayman in Berney (1).
2. Ibid.

Carol Bolt
(AUGUST 25, 1941–)

EMMA. . . . freeing herself from the fear of public opinion and public condemnation will set a woman free, will make her a force hitherto unknown in the world.

—from *Red Emma*

In the words of theater historians Souchotte and Brissenden, the plays of Carol Bolt involve "a unique form of social documentary using factual reference material to gain access to an imaginative Canadian mythology."[1] Bolt's 1972 work *Buffalo Jump* illustrates this perfectly. In depicting the effects of the Great Depression on the unemployed in Vancouver, British Columbia, Bolt combined two actual Canadian heroes from the period, "Red" Walsh and "Slim" Evans, into a single character: Red Evans. Even though most of her dramas venture into political territory, Bolt has stated that her interests lie in the realm of "adventure, rather than the polemics of politics."[2] She goes so far as to say that her play *Red Emma, Queen of the Anarchists* (1974), which centers on the life of the young revolutionary Emma Goldman, "is about as political as *The Prisoner of Zenda*."[3] Occasionally she departs from historical adventure, as in *One Night Stand*, a 1977 award-winning murder drama about a tryst between an engaging country-and-western singer and a forlorn young woman.

Born Carol Johnson, she originally hails from Winnipeg, but grew up in Vancouver. Eight years after earning her B.A. at the University of British Columbia in 1969, she married David Bolt; they have one son. Prior to her theater career, Bolt worked as a researcher for a variety of demographic organizations. She was appointed dramaturg for the Playwrights Co-op in Toronto in 1972 and, later, for the Toronto Free Theatre. Among her awards and honors are a Canada Council grant and an Ontario Arts Council grant, as well as a writing residency at the University of Toronto. She has created several pieces expressly for young people. Bolt's minimalist style, solid craftsmanship, and highly entertaining characters have made her one of Canada's best-known playwrights.

PLAYS

The Bluebird (adapt. of Marie d'Aulnoy story), 1973; *Buffalo Jump* (a.k.a. *Next Year Country*), 1972; *Cyclone Jack*, 1972; *Daganawida*, 1970; *Deadline*, 1979; *Desperadoes*, 1977; *Escape Entertainment*, 1982; *Finding Bumble*, 1975; *Gabe*, 1973; *I Wish*, 1966; *Love or Money*, 1981; *Maurice*, 1975; *My Best Friend Is Twelve Feet High*, w/music by Jane Vasey, 1972; *Norman Bethune: On Board the S.S. Empress of Asia*, 1976; *Okey Doke*, 1976; *One Night Stand* (also screenplay), 1977; *Pauline*, 1973; *Red Emma, Queen of the Anarchists*, 1974; *Shelter*, 1975; *Star Quality*, 1980; *Tangleflags*, 1973; *TV Lounge*, 1977

OTHER WORKS

Distance (teleplay), 1974; *Fast Forward* (radio play),1976; *A Nice Girl Like You* (teleplay), 1974; *Talk Him Down* (teleplay), 1975

1. Eassy by Souchotte and Brissenden in Berney (2).
2. Ibid.
3. Ibid.

Denis Bonal
(193?–)

VINCENT. Yeah, being forty isn't so easy . . .
MOTHER. True, it was pretty hard for me, too, at forty. I had a shop with bills to pay, curly hair, voted for the left, went out with my girls, scrimped and saved, frequent chest colds, had my nails done, geraniums on the balcony . . . but my body was gone. No wonder I forgot. Forty years old when Charles died! No man ever slept beside me since. Winter nights are the worst. Summer nights are violent. You keep cats. And you learn never to look at a couple kissing again.

—from *A Picture Perfect Sky*

Algerian-born playwright Denis Bonal moved with her family to Paris at the age of twelve. Within a few years she was performing and touring with French regional theater companies, an occupation she continued from 1951–71. During this time, Bonal wrote short stories and adapted novels for radio, sometimes using the pseudonym Luis Aftel.

Currently, only her most recent work has been translated into English; both *A Picture Perfect Sky* and *Family Portrait* reveal the author's interest in the difficult dynamics of family relationships. *A Picture Perfect Sky*, set in contemporary France, revolves around three married sisters struggling to cope with their mother, whom they consider to be unfit to live alone. The sisters and their husbands gather to watch a solar eclipse and to discuss their mother's dilemma. It becomes evident that each is unhappy in her marriage and her life, and none wants to take responsibility for the mother, preferring to place her in an old age home. But when the matriarch enters, she proclaims that old age homes bore her; she has no intention of spending the rest of her life in one of them. Then she announces her shocking plan to adopt her tenant, a Canadian, as her son. They have developed a close relationship and plan to travel together. The daughters, worried about their inheritance, become seriously distraught. After several confrontations and revelations, the tenant arrives and waves to the mother. The eclipse begins. When it ends, mother and tenant have disappeared, leaving the unhappy offspring and their spouses behind. Bonal's message is clear: The possibility of contentment comes only to those courageous enough to defy social expectation and to take risks.

Some of the characters in *Family Portrait* (1985) echo those in *A Picture Perfect Sky*. *Portrait* focuses on a working-class French family in a border town. According to Sy Syna, it "is a devastating indictment of an utterly amoral generation. . . . Each character, for whatever reasons, is unfeeling where others are concerned; all are motivated only by what they perceive to be best for themselves."[1]

All Bonal's plays have been successfully produced. She has won several awards and has taught on the faculty of the Paris Conservatoire National d'Art Dramatique (French National School of Dramatic Art). She lives in Paris, and since 1972 has divided her time between acting, writing, and teaching.

PLAYS

Beware the Heart (Richard Miller, tr.), n.d.; *Honorée par un petit monument*, 1978; *Légère en août*, 1974; *Lit vers le thé*, 1983; *Les moutons de la nuit*, 1976; *Passions et prairie* (*A Picture Perfect Sky*, Timothy Johns, tr.), 1987; *Portrait de famille* (*Family Portrait*, Timothy Johns, tr.), 1985

1. Review by Sy Syna in *Backstage*, June 5, 1992.

Frances Boothby
(FL. 1669)

Frances Boothby's *Marcelia* has earned the dramatist the distinction of being the first Englishwoman to have an original play produced on the *public* stage. It appeared at the Theatre Royal in London eighteen months after KATHERINE FOWLER PHILIPS's *Horace* was performed privately at the court of King Charles II in 1671, and about sixteen months before APHRA BEHN's first production, *The Forced Marriage*. However, according to Fidelis Morgan, "the play itself [was] unremarkable."[1] There is no record of any further writings by Boothby, and little is known of her other than that she was a relative of Lady Yate of Harvington, in Worcestershire.

PLAYS

Marcelia, or The Treacherous Friend, 1670

1. Morgan.

Julie Bovasso
(AUGUST 1, 1930–SEPTEMBER 14, 1991)

BEBE. I didn't take it all back: I simply adjusted my initial reaction.

—from *Schubert's Last Serenade*

Seduced by the stage at the age of thirteen, Brooklyn-born Julie Bovasso made her acting debut on August 3, 1943, as a maid in *The Bells* at New York's Davenport Free Theatre. At seventeen she began a two-year stint with the Rolling Players, portraying diverse roles in plays by Oscar Wilde, Henrik Ibsen, and others. She studied theater at the High School of Music and Art in New York City and City College of New York (1948–51), and received her acting training from Uta Hagen, Herbert Berghof, Mira Rostova, and Harold Clurman. Bovasso's busy acting career took her to major American regional theaters throughout the 1950s and '60s including Provincetown Players; Living Theater; San Francisco Repertory Theater; American Shakespeare Festival Theater in Stratford, Connecticut; and Chelsea Theater Centre in Brooklyn.

By 1953, Bovasso was no longer content with just acting. Eager to find a conduit for the absurdist theater she had come to love, she established the Tempo in New York City, where she introduced American audiences to the works of Jean Genet, Eugène Ionesco, and Michel de Ghelderode. It was, as Carolyn Karis notes, "a daring enterprise for a young woman, [and] represented a pioneering movement in the development of Off-Broadway theater and an early arena in the United States for absurdist plays by European playwrights."[1] The Tempo won the *Village Voice* off-Broadway award for best experimental theater in 1956, the same year Bovasso won for her performances as Claire and Solange in her theater's production of Genet's *The Maids*.

While continuing to serve as actor-manager at the Tempo, Bovasso juggled television performances (e.g., a featured role in *The Iceman Cometh*), and an extensive teaching career, conducting classes at the High School for Performing Arts, Brooklyn College Graduate School, the New School for Social Research, and Sarah Lawrence College. It was only in the late 1960s that Bovasso finally began to write plays. Naturally, her work throbs with an absurdist pulse.

Her first produced play, *The Moondreamers*, was mounted in 1968 at Ellen Stewart's off-Broadway La MaMa Experimental Theater Club. The play's positive reception encouraged Bovasso. *Gloria and Esperanza*, her next endeavor, "takes us with her on an epic journey from underground hip culture to the sixties to the fantasy world of one of [the play's] central characters, the poet Julius

Esperanza . . ."[2] It is Esperanza's down-to-earth, funny, meddlesome girlfriend, Gloria B. Gilbert (originally portrayed by Bovasso herself), who holds together the disparate cast of madcaps. Bovasso received three Obies for the play: best play, best actress, and best direction. Brendan Gill of *The New Yorker* hailed *Gloria and Esperanza* as "a calculatedly incoherent phantasmagoria that always threatens to make our flesh creep but chooses to make us laugh instead—a collision, at once comic and murderous, between the author and the many aspects of our society that arouse her contempt" (February 14, 1970). In *Schubert's Last Serenade*, which Tish Dace called ". . . a bauble, but a bauble with class,"[3] Bovasso repeated her triple play, once again writing, directing, and acting.

Bovasso never strayed far from her love of the absurd. As Karis writes, " 'Camp collage' aptly describes a Bovasso play with its mixture of whimsy, fairy tale, parody, stereotypical characters, and stock situations . . . [Her] plays have a story line or a plot ornamented by nightmarish events and bizarre images. But, however sprawling the plays may seem, Bovasso maintains her control, and the plays issue as daydreams with sunny moods."[4]

Bovasso was a great supporter of new works by women playwrights and helped to organize the Women's Theater Council, along with ROCHELLE OWENS, ROSALYN DREXLER, MEGAN TERRY, MARIE IRENE FORNES, and ADRIENNE KENNEDY. The council eventually became the New York Theater Strategy, a larger group that included several male playwrights, Sam Shepard and Lanford Wilson among them.

In addition to her five Obies, Bovasso was awarded a Rockefeller Foundation playwriting grant and a Guggenheim Fellowship, and was playwright in residence at the Circle Repertory Company in 1976. Active in theater until her untimely death from cancer, just after her sixty-first birthday in 1991, Bovasso always lived up to Dace's 1977 proclamation: "She just might be—as actress, director, and playwright—the most valuable creative intelligence in the New York theater."[5]

PLAYS

Angelo's Wedding, 1983; *Down by the River Where Waterlilies Are Disfigured Every Day*, 1971; *The Final Analysis*, 1975; *Gloria and Esperanza*, 1969; *Monday on the Way to Mercury Island*, 1971; *The Moondreamers*, 1968; *The Nothing Kid*, 1975; *Schubert's Last Serenade*, 1975; *Standard Safety*, 1975; *Super Lover*, 1975

1. Essay by Carolyn Karis in Robinson.

2. Keyssar.

3. Review by Tish Dace in the *Soho Weekly News*, September 15, 1977.

Julie Bovasso
COURTESY OF THE BILLY ROSE THEATRE COLLECTION

4. Op. cit., Karis.

5. Op. cit., Dace.

Hannah Brand
(FL. 1794–98)

"A lady of talents and learning, who conducted a respectable seminary for French education at Norwich, with great success and respectability," wrote an unknown reviewer of Brand's play *Huniades*, produced in 1796.[1] An actress and dramatist, she appeared in *Huniades*, a performance noted for its "force and spirit." Not much is recorded about Brand's life, though; she was described as very sensible, but too learned, by Tate Wilkinson in his *Wandering Patentee*. In answer to a question inquiring what farce she would approve of attending, Wilkinson quotes her as replying, "Why, Sir, should I strike the anvil of my brain, when there is nothing to hammer out?" Brand considered farces inconsequential and "degrading to taste." In his *Bio-*

graphia Dramatica, Stephen Jones points out that "she seldom went or came from the theatre at York but in a chair, so dreadfully fearful was she in that quiet city of the insulter."[2]

Huniades is a tragedy that takes place in Belgrade, which was besieged by the Turks in 1456; they brought an immense artillery yet were defeated by the heroine, who is poisoned and dies at the play's end. The eighteenth-century critic writes that "The whole of this Tragedy is written with strong marks of genius and a feeling mind. . . . but its extreme length rendered it not so acceptable at the conclusion." Not only did critics impugn Brand's work, they took it upon themselves to berate the portly woman's propensity for dressing in an overly romantic style. Despite these admonishments from the press, Brand applied herself with all seriousness to her work.

PLAYS

Adelinda, 1796; *Agmunda* (variant of *Huniades*), 1794; *The Conflict*, 1798; *Huniades*, 1796

1. Stead Collection, New York Public Library.

2. Jones.

Anna Brigadere
(OCTOBER 1, 1861–JUNE 25, 1933)

According to Alfreds Straumanis, the plays of Latvian dramatist Anna Brigadere blend "masterful craftsmanship [with] acute observations about little recognized realities of human relations distilling a wisdom that is at the same time profound and commonplace."[1] Brigadere's ability to create complex fairy tale dramas, such as *Sprīdītis* (1903), a spirited retelling of the Tom Thumb story, made her one of the most well-loved playwrights of her time.

Unlike ASPAZIJA, Brigadere was born to a family of humble origins in Tervete. She was deeply influenced by her father, an itinerant farm worker. While striving to earn her teaching degree, she worked as a seamstress and a shop girl. For many years she was employed as a governess. Later, she edited literary supplements of various magazines. She did not turn exclusively to creative writing until her early forties.

Straumanis writes, "In most of her plays Brigadere reflects her belief in traditional and ethical values: reverence towards one's elders, piety, exaltation in physical labor, the moral superiority of the poor, and the degrading effect of wealth."[2] *Raudupiete* (Raudup's Widow; 1914), a psychological study of love, hate, guilt, and remorse, is executed with such honesty, it rises above mere melodrama, em-

bodying traces of real tragedy. *Lielais loms* (The Big Haul; 1925) is a five-act folk comedy set in rural Latvia during the 1920s. Two enthusiastic and enterprising young men form an amateur theater group and put on a traditional melodrama. As rehearsals progress, more and more people see themselves in the play's characters and, ultimately, roles are played out offstage as well as on.

By the end of her life, Brigadere had accomplished careers as a teacher, editor, novelist, poet, and playwright. Her prose works include several short story collections and two volumes of poetry in which themes of love for her nation and land predominate, as well as an autobiographical trilogy: *Dievs, daba, darbs* (Wide World of Wonder, literally translated as God, Nature, Work; 1926), *Skarbos vējos* (In Harsh Winds; 1920), and *Akmens sprostā* (The Stone Cage; 1933). The latter became one of the most popular works in Latvian literature.

Before she died Brigadere established a fund for a triennial prize that would be awarded to the best Latvian literary work expounding the love of the author's homeland. She died in Sprēīdīši in her country home, which was a gift from her nation as their gratitude for her contributions to Latvian literature.

PLAYS (SELECTED)

Aiz līdzcietības (Out of Pity; one-act), 1897; *Atkalredzēšanās* (The Reunion; one-act), 1901; *Ausmā*, 1905; *Čaukstenes* (Tattle-Tales; one-act), 1907; *Dieviškā seja* (The Divine Face), 1926; *Izredzētais* (The Chosen One), 1901; *Kad sievas spēkojas* (War of the Wives), 1929; *Karaliene Jāna* (Empress Jana), 1932; *Kvēlošā lokā* (In the Burning Arc), 1937; *Lielais loms* (The Big Haul), 1925; *Lolitas brīnumputns* (Lolita's Wonderbird, or Magic Bird), 1926; *Maija und Paija* (Maija and Paija, Alfreds Straumanis tr., 1979[3]), 1921; *Pastari* (The Last Born), 1931; *Pie latviešu miljonāra* (The Latvian Millionaire), 1909; *Princese Gundega un karālis Brusubārda* (Princess Buttercup and King Bristlebeard), 1912; *Raudupiete* (Raudup's Widow), 1914; *Sievu kari ar Belcebulu* (Women Against Beelzebub, 1925; *Sprīdītis* (*Tom Thumb Grows Up*, Margrieta Ēdels, tr., 1976), 1903; *Šuvējas sapnis* (Dream of a Seamstress), 1930; *Zvanu meitenes* (Girls of the Bells; one-act), 1934

OTHER WORKS

Akmens sprostā (The Stone Cage; autobio. trilogy, pt. 3), 1933; *Dievs, daba, darbs* (Wide World of Wonder; autobio. trilogy, pt. 2), 1926; *Dzejas* (Poems), 1913; *Kvēlošā lokā* (The Flaming Circle; novel), 1928; *Paisums* (Tide; poetry), 1922; *Skarbos vējos* (In Harsh Winds; autobio. trilogy, pt. 1), 1920; *Slimnīcā* (In the Hospital), 1896

1. Silenieks, Juris and Alfreds Straumanis, "Latvian Dramatists," in *Baltic Drama*, Alfreds Straumanis, ed. (Prospect Heights, Ill.: Waveland Press, 1981).

2. Ibid.

3. Included in English in *The Golden Steed*, Alfreds Straumanis, ed. (Prospect Heights, Ill.: Waveland Press, 1979.)

Frances Brooke
(1724–1789)

ROSINA. Why should I repine? Heaven, which deprived me of my parents and my fortune, left me health, content, and innocence. Or is it certain that riches lead to happiness? Think the nightingale sings the sweeter for being in a gilded cage?

—from *Rosina*, Act I, Scene 1

RUSTIC. . . . I hate money when it is not my own.

—Ibid., Act II, Scene 1

In addition to her plays and opera, English writer Frances Brooke, known professionally as Mary Singleton, wrote fictions, histories, and translations. In Stephen Jones's *Biographia Dramatica*, he wrote that Brooke was "a lady of first-rate abilities, and as remarkable for gentleness and suavity of manners as for her literary talents."[1]

Brooke's pastoral opera *Rosina* was warmly received. Adapted from a French folk tale, it tells the story of a young orphan girl who is saved by her brother from the designs of a lurid suitor. One critic remarked, "[Rosina's] dialogue is easy and agreeable, and the airs in general are not destitute of poetical merit."

Born Frances Moore, she married Rev. John Brooke, who died on January 21, 1789. Frances passed on five days later at the house of her son.

PLAYS

Marian, 1788; *Rosina: A Comic Opera*, 1783; *Siege of Sinope*, 1781; *Virginia*, 1756

OTHER WORKS

The History of Emily Montague, n.d.; *The Excursion*, n.d.; *Lady Julia Mandeville*, n.d.; *Marquis of St. Forlaix*, n.d.; *The Old Maid* (periodical), n.d.; *Milot's Elements of the History of England*, tr., n.d.

1. Jones.

Frances Burney
(1752–1840)

CECILIA. Oh how unequally are we affected by the progress of time! winged with the gay plumage of hope, how rapid seems its flight,—oppressed with the burden of misery, how tedious its motion!—yet it varies not,—insensible to smiles and callous to tears, its acceleration and its tardiness are mere phantasms of our disordered imaginations.

—from *The Witlings*, Act V, Scene 1

Born at King's Lynn, Norfolk, Fanny Burney was the daughter of Charles Burney, a self-taught musicologist who published several respected books on music. Her family moved to London in 1760, and Fanny was educated at home. Her father had taught her well, so that she might make copies of his manuscripts. In so doing, she began making early attempts at her own writing, producing stories and a diary that evolved into journal-letters that circulated among her appreciative family circle. The Burney home was frequently the center of scintillating and star-studded company, and the likes of David Garrick and Richard Sheridan were known to stop by regularly.

The tremendous reception enjoyed by her first novel, *Evelina*, owed much to her early journal writing, which taught her how to develop character and dialogue, as well as the sense of comic interplay for which she became known. The intelligentsia courted her; Elizabeth Montagu, the leading Bluestocking hostess, made much of her.

Burney crossed over into play writing because she thought it to be a more lucrative field; she had made precious little money with her novel. But her first dramatic effort, *The Witlings*, was suppressed at the advice of family members and friends: In this satire, Burney had focused her ridicule on the Bluestockings, with Lady Smatter, the lead character, so strongly suggesting Elizabeth Montagu, a powerful society broker, that no one who knew her could have escaped the realization. The play was not published until recently.

Still single and unable to make a living at writing, despite another successful novel, Burney reluctantly accepted an appointment as Second Keeper of the Robes to Queen Charlotte, a post at which she remained for five stifling years (1786–91). Shortly after returning to private life, she met and fell in love with a French officer and émigré, Alexandre d'Arblay. They married and she was thenceforth known as Mme. d'Arblay. Alexandre was penniless, without prospects. She bore him a son. They were in difficult straits. When Mme. d'Arblay negotiated for her third novel, she drove a hard bargain and managed to reap 2,000 francs for it, which must have been particularly difficult, as she had been a shy child. According to her sister Susan,

Fanny was noted in her family for her "sense, sensibility, and bashfulness, and even a degree of prudery."[1]

Despite having written another three comedies, now lost, her only play to reach the stage was *Edwy and Elgiva*, "a dreary tragedy, written during her most unhappy time at Court."[2] It was a flop.

PLAYS

Edwy and Elgiva, 1795; *The Witlings*, 1779?

OTHER WORKS

Camilla, 1796; *Cecilia*, 1782; *Diary and Letters of Madame D'Arblay, 1778–1840*, Barrett, Charlotte, ed., 8 vols., 1904; *Evelina*, 1778

WORKS ABOUT

Delery, Clayton J., *The Witlings*, 1993; Doody, Margaret Anne, *Frances Burney: The Life in the Works*, 1988; Rogers, Katharine M., "Britain's First Woman Drama Critic: Elizabeth Inchbald," in *Curtain Calls: British and American Women and the Theatre, 1660–1820*, 1991

1. Introduction by Lewis Gibbs from *The Diary of Fanny Burney* (1940; reprint, New York: Dutton, 1971).
2. Feder.

Minna Canth
(1844–1897)

HOMSANTUU. Your law and justice . . . These are what I ought to have shot.

—from *The Working Man's Wife*

Born Ulrika Wilhelmina Johnsson in Tampere, Finland, the young Minna Canth benefited from her father's professional resourcefulness. A foreman at Finlayson's textile mills, he acquired a shop that sold the mill's yarns. The subsequent income from this business coup enabled him to send Canth to an elite girls' school in the capital. Canth exhibited a real passion for learning and language. After mastering Swedish, she entered the teachers' seminary at Jyväskylä, even though her father disapproved of her continuing education. Canth thrived under the influence of Uno Cyganeus, an erstwhile Lutheran pastor and the school's founder and principal. Her studies ended after one year, however, when she fell in love with and married J. Ferdinand Canth, a teacher.

Canth and her husband worked as a team: He edited *Keski-Suomi*, a weekly paper; she did most of the writing. She also wrote for the journal *Päijäne*. Yet Canth was not destined for a life of domestic and professional bliss. In 1878 Ferdinand died, leaving his thirty-four-year-old wife with six children and a seventh on the way.

Unable to keep afloat above the financial demands, Canth and her children returned to Kuopio, where she took charge of her father's failing business. Clever and energetic, she soon turned around the shop's fortunes. Canth prospered intellectually in Kuopio, as well. The town, albeit small, thrived with a rich cultural life because it housed a bishop's seat. Before long Canth was at the center of the intelligentsia. Her home became a salon filled with young intellectuals discussing the works of great Scandinavian and European thinkers. Here, Canth wrote translations, kept up her journalism, and finally began writing plays.

Murtovarkaus and *Roinilan talossa*, her first staged plays, were quite successful. Canth had never shied away from the political arena; she identified strongly with the struggles of women and workers. According to Virpi Zuck, Canth was particularly affected by the work of Leo Tolstoy, whose "ideas of pacifism, love, faith, and humility"[1] are evidenced in many of her works. Her plays tackled such problematic social issues as economic imbalance, the double standards endured by women, the plight of the working class, and the church's blind complicity in the face of these injustices. The central characters in Canth's plays were usually strong women of the middle and lower classes who persevered in spite of their gender. Yet Canth's rage against the bourgeois stung both men and women, and at times her popularity suffered. *Kovan onnen* brought her ridicule from even her former supporters, mostly young, male intellectuals.

G. C. Schoolfield suggests that Canth's plays come "dangerously close to melodrama; she does not have the manifold meanings of an Ibsen . . . [but] resembles, rather, Ibsen's contemporary Bjørnson . . ."[*2] Nonetheless, Canth remains one of Finland's foremost playwrights.

---

*Bjørnstjerne Martinues (1832–1920), a Norwegian writer, editor, playwright, and theater director, was one of the most prominent public figures of his day. He won the Nobel Prize for literature in 1903. Martinues was Henrik Ibsen's successor as artistic director at the Bergen Theater and later director of the Christiania Theater.

PLAYS

Anna Liisa, 1895; *Hän on Sysmästä,* 1893; *Kotoa pois,* 1895; *Kovan onnen lapsia* (The Children of Misfortune), 1888; *Murtovarkaus* (The Burglary), 1882; *Papin perhe* (The Pastor's Family), 1891; *Roinilan talossa* (At the Farm of Roinila), 1883; *Spiritistinen istunto,* 1894; *Sylvi,* 1893; *Työmiehen vaimo* (The Working Man's Wife), 1885

OTHER WORKS

Agnes, 1892; *Hanna,* 1886; *Kauppa-Lopo,* 1889; *Köyhää kansaa,* 1886; *Lain mukaan,* 1889; *Novelleja ja kertomuksia,* n.d.

1. Essay by Virpi Zuck in Magill.
2. Essay by G. C. Schoolfield in Hochman.

Marina Carr
(1965–   )

GRANDMOTHER. There's two types of people in this world, from what I can make out: them that puts their children first and them that puts their lover first. And for what it is worth, the nine-fingered fisherman and myself belongs to the latter of these. I would gladly have hurled all seven of you down the slopes of hell for one more night with the nine-fingered fisherman and may I rot eternally for such unmotherly feelings.

—from *The Mai*

Marina Carr, one of Ireland's most newly celebrated young playwrights, composes all of her work with a black felt-tipped pen, shunning technology with a blunt "There's the word, and there's the word processor."[1] At the age of nine she was staging her plays in the garage of her home near Pallas Lake, deep in the Irish Midlands. Her father, a playwright himself, and her mother, a Gaelic poet, encouraged their daughter, who was already well known locally for the barnyard humor she contributed to school Christmas plays. "The nuns loved it," Carr has said.

After graduating from University College in Dublin, she briefly worked as an elementary school teacher in Brooklyn, New York. Back in Ireland, Carr began to apply herself to the creation of dramatic works. Her first efforts, written during what the author calls her "Beckett stage," "generally left their audiences puzzled," according to James F. Clarity of the *New York Times.* But she rose to acclaim with her 1994 play *The Mai,* which played to standing-room-only crowds when it was first produced at the Abbey Theater. *The Mai* presents four generations of women from one Irish family who discuss, rant, and joke about their relationships to each other and to the men in their lives. Characters include a 100-year-old, opium-smoking grandmother, and a cellist who literally plays his wife with a bow. "The play is as deft as it is daft," wrote Finian O'Toole in the *Irish Times,* "with its head screwed on as well as screwed up." The play won first prize in the 1994 Dublin Theater Festival.

Carr attributes some of *The Mai*'s success to her own dramatic sensibility, which changed from Beckett-like absurdity to a more "Greek sense of destiny and fate and little escape." She cites Shakespeare's *King Lear* and Tennessee Williams's *The Glass Menagerie* as stalwart influences. Her most recent work is *Portia Coughlan,* a gothic tale of a woman haunted by her dead twin brother.

PLAYS (SELECTED)

Low in the Dark, n.d.; *The Mai,* 1994; *Portia Coughlan,* 1995

1. All quotations from "A Playwright's Post-Beckett Period" by James F. Clarity, *New York Times,* November 3, 1994.

Vinette Carroll
(MARCH 11, 1922–   )

Vinette Carroll was one of the first African-Americans to enter the one-person show arena (BEAH RICHARDS had begun touring her one-woman show, *A Black Woman Speaks,* in 1950, two years before Carroll began touring hers). While it was her aim to be an actor, the paucity of roles for women of color was such that she was impelled to create works for herself. This presented Carroll with unsought opportunity, and soon she found herself directing plays and organizing theater companies, all the while continuing to perform and create new works. All of which seems a highly unlikely career for a New York City–born daughter of a dentist who earned her master's degree in clinical and industrial psychology (Long Island University, B.A., 1944; New York University, M.A., 1946). Yet, barely two years after completing those studies, she was studying acting with Lee Strasberg (1945–46), Erwin Piscator (1948), and, later, Stella Adler (1954–55), and became a member of the directing unit at the Actor's Studio in New York. For several years, while pursuing her theater studies at night, she worked for the New York City Board of Education's Bureau of Child Guidance; in 1955 she gave up social work and began teaching at New York's High School of Performing Arts.

Carroll's acting career began traditionally enough; she worked her way through summer stock, initially playing such roles as "a Christian" in George Bernard Shaw's *Androcles and the Lion,* and Addie in LILLIAN HELLMAN's *The Little Foxes* (1948). A touring company production of

Shaw's *Caesar and Cleopatra* cast her as Ftatateeta (1959)—the first to employ a black woman in that role, according to Jo A. Tunner of City University of New York: Carroll received glowing notices for her part.[1]

In the 1950s she began putting together a one-woman show to countermand the dearth of challenging roles for black actresses. Carroll compiled a series of excerpts from theatrical works ranging from the classics to contemporary Broadway shows, and from the works of authors such as Dorothy Parker, Langston Hughes, and Edgar Allan Poe; the show toured for years throughout the United States and in the West Indies (1952–57). Carroll did not make her directorial debut until 1960, when she mounted the Equity Library Theatre (New York) production of the eerie Howard Richardson-William Berney musical fable *Dark of the Moon*, with an all-black cast. The next year, for the same group, she directed Langston Hughes's *Black Nativity*; she repeated that assignment for a Westinghouse Theater TV production in 1962.

Carroll's awards include the Drama Critics Circle Award for distinguished directing in 1972, a Ford Foundation grant for directing (1960–61), and an Obie for her portrayal of Sophia Adams in *Moon on a Rainbow Shawl* (1961). Her acting career has spanned the media, moving from the stage to films and television: including, for example, her work in the television productions of "Sojourner Truth" and CARSON MCCULLERS's "The Member of the Wedding"; series such as "All in the Family"; and films such as *One Potato Two Potato, Up the Down Staircase, Alice's Restaurant*, and *The Reivers*. In 1964, for CBS's prestigious "Stage 2," Carroll conceived, adapted, and supervised the production of "Beyond the Blues," for which she won an Emmy.

The difficulty of finding suitable material for black actors drove Carroll to create more and more of her own material: for example, *Trumpets of the Lord*, a musical adaptation of James Weldon Johnson's *God's Trombones*, which ran for 161 performances at the off-Broadway Astor Playhouse.

In 1967 she became associate director of the Inner City Repertory Company in Los Angeles. After six months, however, she was back in her beloved New York, where she organized the Urban Arts Corps (1967), a program designed to train young Puerto Ricans and blacks as performers and to develop opportunities for professionals using materials by black playwrights and composers. Concurrent with this project, she founded the Vinette Carroll Repertory Company in Fort Lauderdale, Florida. This was the beginning of a new era of creativity for Carroll.

In collaboration with Micki Grant she created the musical *Don't Bother Me, I Can't Cope* (1972), a huge success that toured the United States. Her landmark work, *Your Arms Too Short to Box with God*, received two Antoinette

Vinette Carroll
COURTESY OF THE BILLY ROSE THEATRE COLLECTION

Perry Award nominations and, with it, Carroll became Broadway's first black female director. These musicals and others created by the Grant-Carroll team draw upon the gospel-soul-jazz tradition.

It might not be typical to think of a sports car enthusiast who enjoys horseback riding, building furniture, and playing with her Great Dane as a pioneer in carving out a theater tradition for black artists in contemporary America, but Carroll has done just that. In a newspaper article, Carroll once stated, "They told me that I had one-third less chance because I was a woman and a third less chance again because I was black, but I tell you, I'm going to do one hell of a lot with that remaining one third."[2]

PLAYS

The Boogie-Woogie Rumble of a Dream Deferred (a.k.a. *Step Lively, Boy*), w/Micki Grant, 1982; *Bury the Dead*, w/M.G. (adapt. Irwin Shaw's work), n.d.; *But Never Jam Today*, w/M.G., n.d.; *Croesus and the Witch*, w/M.G., 1973; *Don't Bother Me, I Can't Cope*, w/M.G., 1972; *The Ups and Downs of Theophilus Maitland*, w/M.G., 1985; *What You Gonna Name that Pretty Little Baby?*, 1985; *When Hell Freezes I'll Skate*, 1984; *Your Arms Too Short to Box with God*, w/M.G. and Alex Bradford, 1975

1. Essay by Jo A. Tunner in Robinson.

2. Undated article by S. Patterson found in the Billy Rose Theatre Collection at the New York Public Library Performing Arts Research Center.

Elizabeth Tanfield Cary
a.k.a. Lady Falkland
(1585/6–1639)

CHORUS. Tis not enough for one that is a wife
To keep her spotless from an act of ill:
but from suspicion she should free her life,
And bare herself of power as well as will.
Tis not so glorious for her to be free,
As by her proper self restrained to be.

—from *Mariam, the Fair Queen*, Act III

Thanks to a detailed biography written by one of her daughters, Lady Fullerton, colorful stories about Elizabeth Cary's childhood abound. Young Elizabeth Cary, the first known female playwright of the English language, bribed the household maids to smuggle candles to her room because her parents had forbidden her to sit up all night reading. By the time her debts were paid prior to her marriage, she owed 100 pounds for the candles and 200 more for bribery fees.

Cary's sharp mind made an impact on the world, even at the age of ten. When she accompanied her father, Lawrence Tanfield, a wealthy Oxford lawyer, to court one day, her keen observations provoked questions that helped acquit a woman, who had been accused of witchcraft, in spite of her earlier coerced confession.[1]

With her immense and idiosyncratic hunger for knowledge, Cary refused to study under a tutor, insisting instead on a self-taught path. At the age of twelve she could offer a critical analysis of Calvin's *Institutes*. Deft with foreign languages, she developed fluency in French, Spanish, Italian, Latin, and Hebrew. Her gifts transcended the intellectual realm: She excelled in the art of needlework.

At seventeen she met and married Henry Cary (or Carew), who almost immediately returned abroad to finish his military service; he was twenty-five. Left alone, Cary began to write plays. Her second effort, *The Tragedie of Mariam, the Fair Queen of Jewry*, became quite well known. The play's central characters, Mariam, the dutiful and obedient wife, and Salome, the independent woman ahead of her time, personify the opposing halves of the playwright's own life: the deferential lady and the feisty, brilliant thinker. It is "a carefully researched and constructed" play, "attentive to historical details but also . . . sensitive to dramatic effectiveness."[2] When *Mariam* was published in 1613, it was considered "a landmark: this was the first play in English known to have been written by a woman."[3]

The next chapter of Cary's life more closely resembled the plight of Mariam; thus, she focused on her wifely responsibilities. Henry returned home after having been captured and subsequently ransomed for most of the family fortune. In 1620 he was raised to the Scottish peerage as Viscount Falkland, County of Fife, and shortly thereafter was appointed Lord Deputy of Ireland, where he and Elizabeth relocated with their many children (nine "born alive" by 1624).

In Ireland Cary converted to Catholicism, a decision that adversely affected her relationships with her father and her husband. For her father, who strongly disapproved when Cary included her inheritance as part of her marriage contract, the conversion was the last straw. Although she was his only child, he disowned her. She and Henry, who remained staunchly Protestant, became estranged; he took both her inheritance and the children. Eventually they did reconcile, just before Henry died from a fall off a horse. Despite Cary's reputation as a theologian and scholar, the rest of her life was spent in poverty. She reputedly generated many works that have since been lost.

PLAYS

The Tragedie of Mariam, the Fair Queen of Jewry, 1613

OTHER WORKS

The Reply of the Most Illustrious Cardinal Perron (tr.), 1630

WORKS ABOUT

Dolman, Charles, ed., *The Lady Falkland: Her Life*, 1861; Fullerton, Lady Georgiana Charlotte, *The Life of Elizabeth Lady Falkland* 1585–1639, Quarterly Series, vol. 6, 1883; Murdock, Kenneth B., *The Sun at Noon*, 1939

1. Mahl.

2. Cotton.

3. Op. cit., Mahl.

Rosario Castellanos
(1925–1974)

When the life of Mexican poet, dramatist, and political activist Rosario Castellanos was cut tragically short in an electrical accident in Tel Aviv, her body was flown home and buried in the Rotunda of Illustrious Men in the Palace of Fine Arts in Mexico City. She is the only woman to receive such an honor. Known primarily for her poetry,

Castellanos also wrote several plays, all of which convey strong feminist sensibilities. Her pair of verse dramas, *Salome* and *Judith*, are revisionist works that relocate the traditional tales of these women historically and geographically: *Salome* occurs during the Porfiriato* in San Cristobal and *Judith* amid the revolutionary war in Chiapas. A third play, *El eterno feminino* (The Eternal Feminine; 1975), attempts to examine and subvert the various mechanisms of the culturally constructed feminine mystique.

Castellanos spent a privileged childhood traveling among her father's vast land holdings. The young Rosario was often transported by hand-chairs that sat upon the shoulders of indigenous Mexicans. Uncomfortable with what she understood to be an unjust social system, she came to reject her father's world completely. When she eventually inherited his land, she made a gift of it to those who had worked for her family. These early experiences became the foundation for her creative and political work. Nevertheless, a quote noted by Myralyn Allgood suggests that Castellanos could not completely free herself from the lessons imposed on her in her early childhood. While defending the indigenous peoples ("Indians are human beings no different from whites. They simply live in very different—and unfavorable—circumstances"), Castellanos inadvertently reveals what may be construed as her own racist beliefs: "Since [Indians] are weaker, they have more potential for evil—violence, treachery, and hypocrisy—than whites."[1] Still, Castellanos fought for Indian rights throughout her life.

In 1958 she married Ricardo Guerra, a philosophy professor, with whom she had one son before they divorced. In addition to her plays, poems, fiction, and essays, she held several political posts, including that of cultural ambassador to Israel.

PLAYS

Album de familia, 1971; *El eterno feminino* (The Eternal Feminine), 1975; *Judith*, n.d.; *Salome*, n.d.

OTHER WORKS

Another Way to Be: Selected Works, Allgood, Myralyn F., ed. and tr., 1990; *Book of Lamentations*, 1996; *Cartas a Ricardo*, 1994; *City of Kings*, 1993; *Los convidados de augusto* (The August Guests), 1975; *Meditation on the Threshold*, Julian Palley, tr., 1996?; *The Nine Guardians* (novel), 1992; *Oficio de tinieblas* (The Black Market), 1977; *Poesia no eres tu: obra poetica, 1948–1971*, 1972; *A*

Rosario Castellanos Reader: An Anthology of Her Poetry, Short Fiction, Essays, and Drama, Maureen Ahern, ed., 1988; *The Selected Poems of Rosario Castellanos*, Cecilia Vicuña & Magda Bogin, eds. & trs., 1988

1. From introduction to *Selected Works of Rosario Castellanos* by Myralyn F. Allgood (Athens, Georgia: University of Georgia Press, 1990).

Margaret Cavendish
(1623–1673)

LADY SANSPAREILLE. . . . some men are so inconsiderately wise, gravely foolish and lowly base, as they had rather be thought cuckolds, than their wives should be thought wits, for fear the world should think their wife the wiser of the two . . .

—from *In Youth's Glory and Earth's Banquet*

Although Margaret Cavendish, the Duchess of Newcastle, may have lacked artistic and literary talent, she compensated by immortalizing herself as England's first feminist playwright and first woman to publish a collection of plays, to publish her autobiography and a biography of her husband, and to write about science. Wealthy and eccentric, Cavendish was unabashed about her motives: "I am very ambitious, yet 'tis neither for beauty, wit, titles, wealth, or power, but as they are steps to raise me to Fame's tower, which is to live by remembrance in after ages."[1] In her lifetime she published a dozen books, including poetry, fiction, drama, and social essays, among other genres. She has been the subject of more writings than any other early English female playwright—possibly because of the twenty-six plays she penned, but as likely, as Nancy Cotton puts it, "because she fulfills the popular fantasy that a woman writer is necessarily slightly demented."[2] Cotton goes on to say that Cavendish's dramas are ". . . structurally incoherent . . . [but] historically significant as early feminist statements."[3]

Margaret Lucas was the youngest of eight children; her father died when she was two. The eccentricity that eventually brought her notoriety began during her childhood when she began designing her own flamboyant clothes, a habit she maintained throughout her life. Although she was tutored in dancing, music, needlework, and French, her education was sorely lacking with respect to more serious academic subjects; hence, the absence of proper grammar in her works. Not surprisingly, she became a lifelong advocate for the education of women.

In 1645, at the age of twenty-two, Margaret followed the exiled Queen Henrietta, to whom she was in attendance as maid of honor, to France. There she met Sir William Cavendish, an amateur poet and playwright, and a generous patron of writers, philosophers, and artists.

*The Porfiriato refers to the period 1877–1911, during which Porfirio Díaz ruled as president of Mexico.

Margaret and William wed, though he was thirty years older than she; throughout their childless marriage, William supported Margaret in her writing. The couple lived abroad until the Restoration. Upon their return to England, her title and her eccentricity brought her some fame, but her writing did not, as it was neither particularly good nor entertaining. However, negative criticism did little to hinder her steady flow of work or stop her from addressing feminist themes. In *Bell in Campo (Plays)*, Lady Victoria raises a female army so that she may go off to battle with her husband:

> LADY VICTORIA. Now or never is the time to prove the courage of our Sex, to get liberty and freedome from the Female Slavery, and to make our selves equal with men: for shall Men only sit in Honours chair, and Women stand as waiters by? shall only Men in Triumphant Chariots ride, and Women run as Captives by? shall only men be Conquerors, and women Slaves? shall only men live by Fame, and women dy in Oblivion?

Despite Cavendish's firm belief in women's rights, she did not shirk from reproaching her own sex. She once wrote that women were "fools, uneducated, and that by entrusting the care of each generation of women to the last, this foolishness was being perpetuated."[4]

Evidently, none of her plays were ever performed, unless *The Humorous Lovers*, performed at the Duke's Theatre in 1667, was not, "as credited, by the Duke of Newcastle, but by his wife." This was the presumption of Samuel Pepys (*Diary*, May 30, 1667), who also noted the play was "the most silly thing that ever come upon a stage." Cavendish died in January 1673 and was buried in Westminster Abbey. In *A Room of One's Own* Virginia Woolf describes the proliferator: "What a vision of loneliness and riot the thought of Margaret Cavendish brings to mind! as if some giant cucumber had spread itself over all the roses and carnations in the garden and choked them to death . . . the Duchess became a bogey to frighten clever girls with."[5]

PLAYS

Kingdom's Intelligencer (14 plays), 1662; *Playes Written* (a collection of fourteen closet* dramas), 1662; *Plays Never Before Printed* (a collection of five plays plus dramatic fragments), 1668

OTHER WORKS

De Vita et Rebus Gestis, 1668; *The Description of a New World*, 1666; *Grounds of Natural Philosophy*, 1668; *Letters*,

---

*Closet dramas are written to be read rather than staged.

1676; *Life of . . . William Cavendish*, 1667; *Nature's Pictures*, 1656; *Observations upon Experimental Philosophy*, 1666; *Orations of Divers Sorts*, 1662; *The Philosophical and Physical Opinions*, 1655; *Philosophical Fancies*, 1653; *Philosophical Letters*, 1664; *Poems and Fancies*, 1653; *CCXI Sociable Letters*, 1664; *The World's Olio*, 1655; *A True Relation*, 1814

WORKS ABOUT

Brydges, Sir Samuel Egerton, ed., *A True Relation of the Life of Margaret Cavendish, Duchess of Newcastle*, 1814; Goulding, Richard William, ed., *Letters of Margaret Lucas to her Future Husband . . . 1645*, 1909; Grant, Douglas, *Margaret the First*, 1957; Lower, Mark Antony, ed., *The Lives of William Cavendish, Duke of Newcastle and of his wife, Margaret, Duchess of Newcastle*, 1872

1. Firth, C. H. "A True Relation of My Birth, Breeding, and Life." Originally the last section of *Nature's Pictures* (1656), included in *Life of William Cavendish, Duke of Newcastle*, 1886.
2. Cotton.
3. Ibid.
4. Mahl.
5. Woolf, Virginia, *A Room of One's Own* (New York: Harcourt Brace Jovanovich, 1929).

Susanna Centlivre
(CA.1667/9–DECEMBER 1, 1723)

> LADY REVELLER. Will you never be weary of these whimsies?
> VALERIA. Whimsies! Natural philosophy a whimsy! Oh! The unlearned world.
> LADY REVELLER. Ridiculous learning!
> MRS ALPIEW. Ridiculous indeed, for women. Philosophy suits our sex as jack-boots would do.
> VALERIA. Custom would bring them as much in fashion as furbelows, and practice would make us as valiant as e'er a hero of them all, the resolution is in the mind—Nothing can enslave that.
>
> —from *The Basset Table*, Act II, Scene 1

Although most of Susanna Centlivre's plays have remained intact throughout the centuries, the history of her early years has not. Indeed, contradictory stories abound about this prolific English dramatist, who has been called "perhaps the best comic playwright between [William] Congreve and [Henry] Fielding."[1] One legend avers that she was the daughter of a Parliamentarian; another asserts that her childhood was a common one. Either her father died when she was an infant, or she survived her mother's early death and her father remarried a woman who drove Susanna to run away from home at age fourteen. Some reports claim she joined a band of strolling players. Others state that Anthony Hammond, a gentleman studying at Cambridge, found her weeping at the side of the road, homeless. According to this tale, Hammond took Susanna with him to Cambridge, where she dressed as a boy and was introduced as his cousin. There she allegedly learned fencing and studied grammar, logic, rhetoric, and ethics before moving to London. Whatever the truth may be, she managed to learn to read and write, compose songs, and become fluent in French. She reportedly was married and widowed twice before meeting her last husband; her second husband was an army officer who was killed in a duel eighteen months after they were wed. Susanna took to the stage as an actor at the end of the Restoration to earn a living; she also began to write for the theater. Her epistles, or letters, which suggest an affair with George Farquhar,* appeared in print under the name Susanna Carroll (the surname of her dead second husband) just prior to the first production of her first play. Nancy Cotton remarks, "Her letters and incidental verses show her [to be] a woman of charm—lively, frank, affectionate and affable."[2]

With *Love's Contrivance* (1703), loosely based on Molière's *Le médecin malgré lui*, her formula for successful comedic intrigue dramas began its long ascent. In the preface to the printed edition of the play, Centlivre wrote that "writing is a kind of lottery in this fickle age, and dependence on the stage as precarious as the cast of a die." *Contrivance* followed the structure of a Molière play, and featured several plum comic roles. Enjoying moderate success, she followed it with *The Gamester* in 1705, a smash hit that continued to be staged over the next fifty years. She emulated *The Gamester* in her next several works, a series of farces that centered on gambling, a major eighteenth-century preoccupation. Also in 1705 she produced *The Basset Table*, which featured Valeria, a young lady interested in philosophy and science. She dissects frogs, fish, and flies, and responds to her suitor, Lovely, because he brings her objects for her experiments. As with most of Centlivre's comedic intrigues, the play's theme is the pursuit of love and all the tricks one can use to obtain it.

Despite the popularity of these plays, Centlivre's career was rocky at best during these early years—partially due to several unremarkable productions, but also because of the strong prejudice that existed against women writers. This bias inspired a feminist consciousness in Centlivre: In the dedication to *The Platonic Lady* in 1707, she wrote, "And why this Wrath against the Women's Works? Perhaps you'll answer, because they meddle with things out of their Sphere: But I say, no; for since the Poet is born, why not a Woman as well as a Man?"

The most accurate documented history about Centlivre's personal life begins in 1707 with the advent of her third marriage to Joseph Centlivre, Yeoman of the Mouth to Queen Anne (in other words, the cook!). Joseph had witnessed Susanna's performance as Alexander the Great in a touring production of *The Rival Queen* at Windsor Castle. He wasted little time in betrothing her and bringing her to live at Buckingham Court, where they remained for the rest of their lives. After marrying Joseph, Susanna stopped acting and, for a couple of years, ceased to write as well. However, soon she took up her pen again, primarily, it seems, for the income it brought her. In *The Man's Bewitched* (1710) this humorous verse appears: ". . . my Spouse who understands/Nought to be good, but Bills and Bonds, The ready Cash, or fruitful Lands,/Begins new Quarrels ev'ry Day,/And frights my dear lov'd Muse away . . ."

In 1709 Centlivre made a triumphant comeback with *The Busie Body*, in which the virtue of men is tested repeatedly by amorous young women. However, it becomes

Susanna Centlivre
COURTESY OF THE BILLY ROSE THEATRE COLLECTION

---

*Farquhar (1678–1707) was an Irish dramatist whose comedies are still performed.

clear that the fathers and guardians of the young women are the real culprits, as they withhold freedom from their charges. "The world cannot be more savage than our parents," claims one of the daughters. Not only did this play inaugurate a new beginning for Centlivre's career, but she commenced once again to sign her own name to her works, a custom she had sometimes avoided previously in an attempt to circumvent the prejudice against female authors.

Not noted for her wit or linguistic distinction, she nonetheless had a good ear for colloquialism and a great sense of the comedic situation. The setting of *A Bickerstaff's Burying* (1710), one of the few one-acts she wrote, is an island where divorce does not exist, and custom demands the burial of the whole married couple when only one partner dies. The play's humor derives from the married characters who would prefer to be single but not dead. In *A Bold Stroke for a Wife* (1719), one of her most acclaimed comedies, she introduced the phrase "Simon Pure," meaning "the real or genuine person or article." The juicy comic roles she created were perennial favorites of the great actors of the day—Charles Kemble and Kitty Clive among them. *The Busie Body* and *The Wonder!* (1714), which has been called "a masterpiece of comic theater . . . ,"[3] became staples of the distinguished actor David Garrick's repertoire. For his farewell performance he appeared as Don Felix in *The Wonder!*

While Centlivre's comedies provoked great laughter, the moral tone was somewhat elevated above that of APHRA BEHN. In many of Centlivre's works there is an air of realism to the characters not often found in the comedies of the age: Centlivre's men and women are both weak and strong; their bickering is over meaningless matters; their attempts at reconciliation awkward. Her plays have "emotion as well as motion, and as a result delighted theater goers for generations."[4]

Political references in Centlivre's prologues and epilogues were not unusual, but with *A Gotham Election* (1715) she met political controversy head on, as she did with *A Wife Well Manag'd* (1715). These works were ahead of their time; they were suppressed and were not staged until after Centlivre's death. Yet she herself led a proprietary life and enjoyed a wide circle of friends in the literary arena. Of course, she was not without her enemies: Her ardent support of the Whig party rendered her a traitor to Tories such as Jonathan Swift and Alexander Pope. Fortunately she suffered few personal attacks during her lifetime, although after she died, aspersions were cast on the lewdness of her life and her works.

Even though William Wycherley's *The Country Wife* and Congreve's *The Way of the World* are more remembered today, neither of these plays enjoyed the continual stagings of Centlivre's works. The celebrated dramatist became seriously ill in the early 1720s and died December 1, 1723, at her home in Buckingham Court. She is buried at St. Paul's, Covent Garden, yet no monument marks her grave. A proper epitaph might be her own words: "I think the main design of Comedy is to make us laugh."[5]

PLAYS

The Artifice, 1723; *The Basset Table*, 1705; *The Beau's Duel, or A Soldier for the Ladies*, 1702; *A Bickerstaff's Burying, or Work for the Upholders*, 1710; *A Bold Stroke for a Wife*, 1719; *The Busie Body*, 1709; *The Cruel Gift, or The Royal Resentment*, 1717; *The Gamester*, 1705; *The Gotham Election/The Humours of Elections* (one-act), 1715; *Love at a Venture*, 1706; *Love's Contrivance, or Le Médecin Malgré Lui*, 1703; *The Man's Bewitched, or The Devil to Do about Her*, 1710; *Mar-plot, or The Second Part of 'The Busy Body'*, 1711; *The Perjured Husband, or The Adventures of Venice*, 1700; *The Perplex'd Lovers*, 1712; *The Platonic Lady*, 1707; *The Stolen Heiress, or The Salamanca Doctor Outplotted*, 1703; *A Wife Well Manag'd* (one-act), 1715; *The Wonder! A Woman Keeps a Secret*, 1714

OTHER WORKS

Abelard to Heloise, 1755; *An Epistle to the King of Sweden*, 1717; *Letters of Wit*, ca. 1702; *A Poem Humbly Presented to George, His Most Sacred Majesty*, 1715

WORKS ABOUT

Bowyer, John Wilson, *The Celebrated Mrs. Centlivre*, 1952; Frushell, Richard, ed., *The Plays*, 3 vols., 1981

1. Cotton.
2. Ibid.
3. Ibid.
4. Ibid.
5. *Letters of Wit*, ca. 1702.

Jane Chambers
(MARCH 27, 1937–FEBRUARY 15, 1983)

ELLIE. When I was your age, "lesbian" was a dictionary word used only to frighten teenage girls and parents. Mothers fainted, fathers became violent, landlords evicted you, and nobody would hire you. A Lesbian was like a vampire: she looked in the mirror and there was no reflection.

—from *A Late Snow*

Carolyn Jane Chambers, a pioneer in bringing the gay experience to the stage, traveled many roads in her life, but she always used the same vehicle: the pen. Born in Columbia, South Carolina, she spent most of her childhood in Orlando, Florida. The teenaged Chambers created radio scripts for high school performances and local public stations. As an undergraduate at Florida's Rollins College in Winter Park, she produced, wrote, and starred in the television show "Youth Pops a Question." Dissatisfied with what she felt were limited opportunities in Florida, she relocated to California in 1956 and studied at the Pasadena Playhouse. A year later she moved to New York City, where she joined the Poet's Theater, performed in off-Broadway plays and coffeehouses, and worked as a reporter, first for theatrical trade papers and, later, for the *New York Times* and *Harper's*. In 1957 her first play, *The Marvelous Metropolis*, was produced at New York City's 41st Street Theatre.

After *Metropolis*, however, Chambers grew restless. She moved to Poland Springs, Maine, where she wrote program copy and developed material for Jack Paar on WMTW-TV. There she also starred in her own children's show, "The Merry Witch." Chambers also worked as a teacher and counselor for Job Corps in Maine. Until the late 1960s, she hustled between Maine and New York, bolstering her work in theater and with Job Corps. Even though, by the age of thirty-one, Chambers had managed to pack her life full, her most important work was still to come.

At Goddard College in 1968 Chambers met and fell in love with Beth Allen, the woman who would become her lifelong companion and manager. Allen encouraged Chambers to speak personally and professionally about her homosexuality. *A Late Snow* was Chambers's first attempt to illustrate the complexities of lesbian life. The play's characters, all openly gay women, are stranded in a cabin during a snowfall. Jill Dolan calls *A Late Snow* "a lesbian identity play inflected with the complementary demands of gay liberation as civil rights and early feminism's notion that the personal is political but not sexual for lesbians."[1]

In 1980 Chambers joined The Glines, a New York–based theater company dedicated to works that explored the gay experience. She wrote *Last Summer at Bluefish Cove*, considered by many to be her finest work, for The Glines's First Gay American Arts Festival. *Bluefish Cove* broadened the territory Chambers first tackled with *A Late Snow*. While still exploring the interpersonal relationships of lesbians, Chambers added a new ingredient to her recipe: a heterosexual woman who unwittingly rents a nearby cabin at a gay women's summer resort. The simultaneous seriousness and humor of the play garnered it a Dramalogue Critics Circle Award in 1980.

Not all of Chambers's plays specifically address the lesbian experience. In *Common Garden Variety*, Grandma, a strong-willed Southern woman who has lived on a remote Georgia hilltop all her life, is expected to raise wild, unruly, fourteen-year-old Sari, her own daughter Rachel's illegitimate child. When Rachel returns to reclaim Sari, these three powerful women, despite their love for each other, become mutually antagonistic, each fighting for her life by destroying the others' dreams and hopes.

In 1983 Chambers wrote *The Quintessential Image*, a sophisticated drama that examines "the dialectic of the reality of lesbian experience and the social perception of her."[2] The central character, a famous lesbian photographer, is being interviewed on a television talk show. As her photographs of women she has loved are projected on studio monitors, she recognizes how her work is obscured or made irrelevant by the TV cameramen who capture them on screen. *The Quintessential Image* reveals the truth behind the idea that "the camera never lies": the power lies not in the image itself, but in the hands of the powerful (read *men*) who control the presentation of the image.

Chambers's many awards and recognitions include the 1972 Eugene O'Neill Prize for *Tales of the Revolution and Other American Fables*, the 1973 Writers' Guild of American Award for her work on "Search for Tomorrow," and a CAPS grant in 1977. She also won the 1971 Rosenthal Award for Poetry, and CT TV Award for Best Religious Drama for her civil rights play *Christ in a Treehouse*. A fervent activist, Chambers helped found the New Jersey Women's Political Caucus and the Women's Interart Center in Manhattan, served on the board of the off-off Broadway Alliance, and was active with the Women's Program of the American Theatre Association.

On May 10, 1982, less than a year before her death from cancer, Chambers accepted the Fifth Annual Award of the Fund for Human Dignity, which honors persons who, by "their work or by the example of their lives, have made a major contribution to public understanding and acceptance of lesbians and gay men."

In that same year Women in Theatre established the Jane Chambers Playwriting Award for new plays that portray women's experiences and feature women in principal roles.

PLAYS (SELECTED)

A Late Snow, 1974; *Christ in a Treehouse*, 1971; *Common Garden Variety*, 1976; *Kudzu*, 1981; *Last Summer at Bluefish Cove*, 1980; *The Marvelous Metropolis*, 1957; *Mine!*, 1973; *My Blue Heaven*, 1981; *The Quintessential Image*, 1983; *Random Violence*, 1973; *Tales of the Revolution and Other American Fables*, 1972; *The Wife*, 1973

OTHER WORKS (SELECTED)

Burning (novel), 1978; *Chasin' Jason* (unpub. novel), n.d.; *Warrior at Rest* (poetry), 1984

1. Dolan.
2. Case. (1).

Charlotte Charke
(1710–1760)

An excellent Demonstration of the Humanity of those low-lived Wretches! who have no farther Regard to the Persons they employ, but while they are immediately serving 'em; and look upon Players like Pack-horses, though they live by 'em.

—from *A Narrative of the Life of Mrs. Charlotte Charke*

Charlotte Charke shuddered at the idea of becoming a proper eighteenth-century lady. Encouraged by her father, Colley Cibber, manager of London's renowned Theatre Royal Drury Lane, popularly referred to as the Drury Lane Theatre, and a poet laureate, Charlotte lived a tomboy youth: hunting, riding, gardening, and grooming horses to her heart's content. Even at boarding school, her unconventionality prevailed. She studied the female-appropriate fields of art and language, but eschewed needle crafts (her sisters' beloved pastime) in favor of medical sciences. When Charlotte began, like many little girls, to "play dress-up" at age four, she donned her father's clothes; to the great dismay of her father, her preference for men's clothing lasted until the end of her life. The sum of Charlotte's strange habits eventually caused her father to disown her.

Her early marriage to Richard Charke, an opportunist theater musician, ended shortly after she gave birth to their daughter. Faced with the task of raising her child alone, she followed in the footsteps of her father and beloved brother Theophilus and began working as an actress at the Drury Lane Theatre then managed by Charles Fleetwood, her retired father's successor. Not surprisingly, she fancied male roles but was reproved by her family and Fleetwood, who dismissed Charke from the Drury Lane.

In 1735 at the age of twenty-five, Charke began writing plays. Her second effort, *The Art of Management*, is essentially a morality play derived from her Drury Lane experiences. Fleetwood is represented by the character Brainless, who exploits and abuses Mrs. Tragic, based on Charke herself. Other characters of interest include Headpiece (Theophilus), who plans to lead an actors' revolt, and Bloodbolt, a thinly veiled Charles Macklin, another

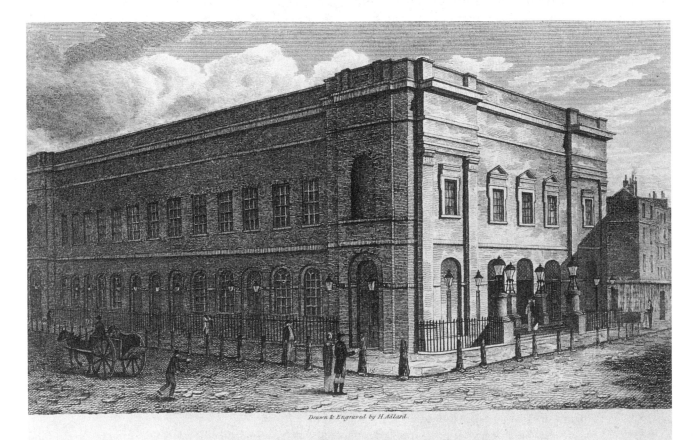

THEATRE ROYAL DRURY LANE.

The Drury Lane Theatre
COURTESY OF THE BILLY ROSE THEATRE COLLECTION

Drury Lane actor who had recently murdered a colleague in a dispute over a wig; unlike Charke, he was not fired! Subtextually, the play addressed the unresolved family rift that opened when Colley Cibber appointed Fleetwood manager, rather than one of his own children. Charke's stance on this decision is evidenced by Mrs. Tragic's assertion, " 'Tis every Parent's Duty to breed their Children with every Advantage their Fortunes will admit of . . ."

Ironically, at the bequest of Colley Cibber, Fleetwood rehired Charke after *The Art of Management* was performed. But the disgruntled Charke left London and embarked on a series of remarkable adventures, which she recorded in her autobiography. In the guise of a man, she worked as "a grocer, valet, waiter, sausage-seller, public house keeper, farmer, pastry cook, proofreader, prompter, and theater manager," as well as a strolling player named "Mr. Brown." Charke's resourcefulness seemed endless; however, her autobiography conveys her exhaustion as she was ". . . forced again to . . . find fresh means of Subsistence . . . 'till even the last thread of invention was worn out." Eventually she developed a disdain for provincial theater and returned to London, where she wrote several novels (now lost) and continued to act from 1754 until shortly before her death.

PLAYS

The Art of Management, or Tragedy Expelled, 1735; *The Carnival, or Harlequin Blunderer,* 1735; *Tit for Tat* (possibly a puppet show), 1743

OTHER WORKS

A Narrative of the Life of Mrs. Charlotte Charke, Youngest Daughter of Colley Cibber, 1755

WORKS ABOUT

Morgan, Fidelis, *The Well-Known Troublemaker: A Life of Charlotte Charke* (London: Faber, 1988)

Mary Chase
(FEBRUARY, 25, 1907–1981)

VETA. It's our dreams that keep us going. That separate us from the beasts. I wouldn't even want to live if I thought it was all just eating and sleeping and taking off my clothes.

—from *Harvey*

In the film version of *Harvey* the title character is portrayed as a six-foot white rabbit. However, as conceived by the work's author, Mary Coyle Chase, Harvey is a "pooka," a legendary Irish creature capable of changing shape at will. Chase was something of a shape-changer herself; she lived a diverse, productive life in which she juggled a successful career, marriage, motherhood, and a social conscience. She was born in Denver, Colorado, the youngest child of Frank Bernard Coyle and Mary McDonough, Irish immigrants. The Irish tales and legends told her by her mother and uncles entranced young Mary, whose imagination filled with stories of leprechauns, banshees, and pookas. Her mother instilled in her an Irish tolerance for the extraordinary.

Chase read voraciously. A precocious child, she left the following inscription on the flyleaf of a copy of Dickens's *A Tale of Two Cities*: "My name is Mary Coyle. I am eight years old. I have just read this book. Don't you think that I am smart?"[1] At eleven she sneaked into a performance of *Macbeth*, and her love affair with theater began.

A seminal event occurred in Chase's childhood when her brother was caught breaking the law and became wounded while trying to escape. Neighbors who had always been respectful toward the Coyles now snubbed them. Chase's response to the situation was to cultivate a combative and audacious attitude, which lasted the rest of her life.

While still in her teens, she began working as a daredevil reporter for the *Rocky Mountain News*, a job she took after dropping out of the University of Colorado. "She quickly gained a reputation for the reckless abandon with which she pursued her stories; she crash-landed in an airplane, tested 'truth serum' (which made her ill for a week), disguised herself as a man and was even accused of breaking and entering."[2] Ultimately her hot-headedness got her fired, but not before she met and married Robert Chase, a colleague at the paper.

The city editor tried to hire her back; however, Chase had already found new pursuits. She involved herself with social issues, particularly labor disputes and the rights of Mexican-Americans, raised three sons, and worked freelance for a wire service. She also wrote plays.

Several of Chase's dramatic works clearly draw from her personal experience and knowledge: The protagonist of *Colorado Dateline* is a young female reporter, *The Banshee* introduces an Irish fairy, and the mythological Irish pooka (originally portrayed as a parakeet) appears in *Harvey,* Chase's most famous play.

Harvey opened on Broadway in 1944 and closed four and a half years later: it is one of the four longest-running shows on Broadway. Elwood P. Dowd, the play's central character, is a wise, likable inebriate who alarms his upwardly mobile family when he is befriended by the questionably real Harvey. Elwood's sister Veta schemes to commit her brother to a sanatorium, but the plan backfires, and she is committed instead—but not before she meets Harvey herself. By the end, even head doctor Chumley has made Harvey's fantastic acquaintance.

The play endorsed what Chase's mother had asserted many years before: "Never be unkind or indifferent to a person others say is crazy. Often they have a deep wisdom. We pay them a great respect in the old country, and we call them fairy people, and, it could be, they are sometimes."[3]

Harvey won the New York Drama Critics Circle Award and the Pulitzer Prize for drama. Howard Barnes, writing of it in the *New York Herald Tribune*, sang, "One of those blessed theatrical events which occur all too rarely on Broadway. It is strange sorcery at its whimsical best." An American classic, the play has been translated and produced worldwide. The popular film version, for which Chase was paid an unprecedented one million dollars to adapt, was released in 1950. Although Chase would never again achieve the success she attained with *Harvey*, she continued to write. Still active in community affairs, she founded and operated the House of Hope, a home for alcoholic women (Chase herself was a recovering alcoholic) until her death from a heart attack in 1981.

Douglas Hughes of the Seattle Repertory Theatre wrote, "Mary Chase was a forceful, humane and witty woman whose creation tempts us to consider a crazy world where eternity is prized more highly than the passing moment, a world run by imagination, not by lies; a mad alternative universe where all men and women are not only created equal, but treated equally, and where they are encouraged to pursue peace and freedom, not wealth and status."[4]

Always an adventurer, Chase wrote in the introduction to her play *Bernardine*, "It's quite possible to leave your home for a walk in the early morning air and return a different person—beguiled, enchanted."

PLAYS

The Banshee, n.d.; *Bernardine* (also screenplay, 1957), 1952; *Cocktails with Mimi*, 1973; *Colorado Dateline*, n.d.; *The Dog Sitters*, 1963; *Harvey* (also screenplay, 1951), 1943; *Lolita*, 1954; *Me Third* (a.k.a *Now You've Done It*), 1936; *Mickey*, 1953; *Midgie Purvis*, 1961; *Mrs. McThing*, 1952; *The Next Half Hour*, 1945; *The Prize Play*, 1961; *A Slip of A Girl*, 1941; *Sorority House* (screenplay), 1938; *Too Much Business*, 1938

1. "Mary Chase vs. The Rabbit," by M. Mark Bocek. *Encore*, Seattle Repertory Theatre program notes. Vol. 13, no. 2. 1994.

2. Ibid.

3. Interview in *Saturday Evening Post*, ca. 1954.

4. Op. cit., Seattle Repertory Theatre.

Yang Chiang
(1911–)

SHEN. In the spring the flower blooms in the sun, the spring breeze blows it away where it will—ideals, love: they're nothing more than spring sunlight and spring breeze. Tomorrow that blossom will fall to earth, sprout, grow roots, nothing more than seed—if the environment lets it live. . . . There are botanical types that don't know their place. Here they fly, there they fly, thinking they have as much strength, that they're in charge! The law-abiding ones, like rice and wheat, have already quietly let themselves rot in the soil and turn into fertilizer for the next generation.

—from *Feng hsü* (Windswept Blossoms), Act I

Feng hsü (Windswept Blossoms), Chinese dramatist Yang Chiang's 1946 play, portrays the sad plight of a group of idealistic northern Chinese architects who, in the course of the piece, succumb to the same injustices they have sought to subvert. Their tragedy is invoked even in the play's title, which refers to the fallen flowers of the willow tree in spring. Like these blossoms, the central characters fall from their own idealism, although they are in the "spring" of their lives. Edward M. Gunn writes that although this is a common theme in social drama, "Windswept Blossoms is unusual for its concentration on the psychology of its characters."[1] Gunn, who avers that the work echoes Henrik Ibsen's *Hedda Gabler* and *The Wild Duck*, also comments on the irony of the play's dialogue and action, noting that Yang herself has remarked on the "potboiler" qualities of the drama, which include a torrid love triangle and a suicide. The play succeeds as a work of social commentary in spite of its melodramatic tendencies, attesting to Yang's skill as a playwright.

Yang Chiang was born Yang Chi-k'ang. She received a solid education, focusing on the study of foreign languages, in Soochow, Shanghai, and Beijing at Tsinghua University. At Tsinghua she met her husband, writer Ch'ien Chung-shu, perhaps best known for the 1970s film adaptation of his 1947 novel *Weicheng* (Fortress Besieged). The couple studied in Europe in the early 1930s and returned to China in 1937, settling in Shanghai. Yang took a position at Aurora Women's College, and began to turn her attention toward literary pursuits. From 1942–1947 she penned essays, short stories, and at least four dramas. Since the People's Republic of China has been established, she has held successive memberships with the Institute of Literature and the Institute of Foreign Literature of the Academy of Social Sciences. Yang has translated several classical works, including *Don Quixote*. More recently she has published *Ch'un ni chi* (Spring Soil; 1979), a collection of critical essays, and *Kan-hsiao liu-chi*

(Six Chapters from a Cadre School; 1981), about life during the Cultural Revolution.

PLAYS

Feng hsü (Windswept Blossoms), 1946

OTHER WORKS

Ch'un ni chi (Spring Soil; critical essays), 1979; *Kan-hsiao liu-chi* (Six Chapters from a Cadre School), 1981

1. Gunn, Edward M., ed. *Twentieth-Century Chinese Drama, An Anthology* (Bloomington: Indiana University Press, 1983).

Alice Childress
(OCTOBER 12, 1920–1994)

TOMMY. Accessories. Something you add on or take off. The real thing is takin' place on the inside . . . that's where the action is.

—from *Wine in the Wilderness*

As a high school student in Harlem, Alice Childress's (pronounced *chill-dress*) composition teachers urged her to write about successful black people, "those who win prizes and honors by overcoming cruel odds to inspire the

Alice Childress

reader/audience . . ."[1] But Childress disagreed: "I write about those who come in second, or not at all—the four hundred and ninety-nine and the intricate and magnificent patterns of a loser's life. No matter how many celebrities we may accrue, they cannot substitute for the masses of human beings."[2] Indeed, the enormous body of work Childress produced—plays, novels, nonfiction—steadily represented the plight of ordinary black women and men.

The storytelling grandmother who raised her inspired Childress's interests in performance and narrative. She left high school after two years in order to study acting with Vanzella Jones and Nadja Romanov. At nineteen, with her social conscience well-fueled, she helped found the American Negro Theater and initiated Harlem's first all-union off-Broadway contracts, which recognized both the Actors Equity Association and Harlem Stage Hand Local. Childress acted in American Negro Theater productions for the next eleven years.

In 1949 Childress wrote her first play. *Florence*, a one-act drama, drew heavily on the frustration and prejudice Childress encountered as a black actress. Florence suffers unemployment and penury as she struggles in a difficult profession made more difficult due to the scarcity of roles for black actors. When she is finally cast in a Broadway play, she is relegated to the part of a maid—a marginalized role that Florence herself plays in the real world. Sue-Ellen Case writes that the maid role ensures "relative invisibility and [brings] paltry financial reward. Florence's other option for work is to be ghettoized, separated from the dominant culture—she can find some work in all-black productions."[3]

First performed in a tiny Harlem loft, *Florence* brought Childress enormous critical acclaim and launched her playwriting career. Helene Keyssar notes that she became the first black woman playwright to have her work professionally produced off Broadway.[4] Childress's plays of the 1950s include *Just a Little Simple* (an adaptation of Langston Hughes's short story "Simple Speaks His Mind"), *Gold Through the Trees*, and the Obie-winning *Trouble in Mind*, a play that thematically echoes *Florence* in that it "exposes the historical racism of the American theater"[5] while raising the feminist ante. Wilmetta, a middle-aged black actress, is cast in the play-within-the-play as a servant for a white Southern family. Recognizing the parallel, Wilmetta rebels against the stereotype of her on-stage character. Helene Keyssar suggests that while *Trouble in Mind* is "a black social protest play whose context and inspiration is the racial integration movement of the fifties, it is also a play about roles in which female stereotypes are acknowledged and jarred."[6]

Some of Childress's later works address women's issues even more explicitly. *Let's Hear It for the Queen*, a young people's play that dramatized the Queen of Hearts nursery rhyme, "happily explodes stereotyped sex roles when the Queen's serving maid steps in as defense attorney for the knave accused of tart thievery. In her children's plays as well as her adult plays, Childress shows girls and women to be brave and creative in solving problems," cheers Rosemary Curb.[7]

Although Childress continued to enjoy her theatrical success, she often remarked on her preference for writing prose, the advantage of which was no interference by producers and directors. (Eventually, she produced and directed her own plays.) She wrote a regular column, "A Conversation from Life," for *Freedom*, the progressive Harlem newspaper founded by Paul Robeson, as well as other articles and stories for *Freedomway* and *Essence* magazines.

Her acclaimed novel *A Hero Ain't Nothin' but a Sandwich*, which sensitively and unsentimentally portrays the lives of teenage heroin addicts, was published in 1973. In *Hero*, according to Miguel Ortiz, "the portrait of whites is more realistic . . . more compassionate, and at the same time, because it is believable, more scathing."[8] Banned by the Savannah, Georgia, school libraries (the first work banned there since J. D. Salinger's *Catcher in the Rye* in the 1950s), the book became the center of several legal obscenity trials. The book received many distinctions, among them nominations for both the Newberry Medal and the National Book Award, the Jane Addams Honor Award for a young adult novel (1974), and the Lewis Carroll Shelf Award from the University of Wisconsin (1975). The film adaptation was released in 1978.

Despite her lack of formal education, Childress received many academic honors, such as appointment as playwright-scholar at the Radcliffe Institute for Independent Study (1966–68), where she was awarded the Alumni Graduate Medal for distinguished achievement in 1984. That same year she served as artist in residence at the University of Massachusetts at Amherst.

Other honors include the Paul Robeson Award from Actors Equity Association, bestowed to those who have shown respect for individual dignity and universal brotherhood, and who have made outstanding contributions to the performing arts; the Langston Hughes Medal; and an honorary doctorate in fine arts from New York State University (1990). She received a Rockfeller Foundation grant in 1967, and served on councils for the Dramatists Guild, the Writers Guild of America, and the Harlem Writers Guild. In 1975 the City of Atlanta, Georgia, named Childress an honorary citizen at the opening of her play *Wedding Band*. Like *Wine in the Wilderness, Wedding Band* was banned by several area stations when it was telecast. Childress has also been inducted in the Black Filmmakers Hall of Fame.

Never one to dodge a controversial topic, Childress exposed the pretentiousness and hypocrisy writhing in the black community in her play *Wine in the Wilderness*. Bill, an artist, and his friends discover a "poor, dumb chick" Bill can use for his new art work. But Tommy, a thirty-year-old lesbian factory worker, is anything but dumb. She effortlessly exposes Bill and his friends as their true selves: a shallow, elitist trio who merely pay lip service to the terms "brother" and "sister"; men who cannot identify real people such as Tommy and the Oldtimer, whose names they have never bothered to learn.

As exemplified in the characters of Florence, Wilmetta, and Tommy, Childress's female protagonists are strong and courageous women, in spite of their seeming ordinariness. Yet even her male characters remain remarkably believable and authentic. The accomplishments of Childress's characters reflect what ordinary people can achieve. Childress once remarked that she created "characters who feel rejected and have to painfully learn how to deal with other people, because I believe all human beings can be magnificent once they realize their full importance."[9]

Childress's willingness to "constantly battle against the negatives of life"[10] by exposing racism and hypocrisy among blacks and whites, women and men, may have inhibited her popularity. Rosemary Curb argues that Childress's controversial subject matter kept her works from reaching a larger audience, and denied the playwright the recognition she so richly deserved.[11]

PLAYS

The African Garden, w/music by Woodard, (unpub. and unprod.), 1971; *Florence*, 1949; *Gold through the Trees*, 1952; *Just a Little Simple* (adapt. of Langston Hughes's short story "Simple Speaks His Mind"), 1950; *Let's Hear It for the Queen*, 1976; *A Man Bearing a Pitcher*, 1969; *Mojo: A Black Love Story*, 1970; *MLK at Montgomery, Alabama*, w/music by Woodard, 1969; *Moms*, 1987; *Sea Island Song*, 1977; *String* (adapt. of Guy de Maupassant's "A Piece of String") (also teleplay), 1969; *Trouble in Mind*, 1955; *Vashti's Magic Mirror*, n.d.; *Wedding Band: A Love/Hate Story in Black and White* (also teleplay), 1966; *When the Rattlesnake Sounds: A Play about Harriet Tubman*, 1975; *Wine in the Wilderness* (radio and teleplay, 1969), 1978; *The World on a Hill*, 1968; *Young Martin Luther King* (a.k.a. *The Freedom Drum*), w/music by Woodard, 1969

OTHER WORKS

Black Scenes, A Collection of Scenes for Training of Black Actors (first collection of selections for black actors), 1971; "A Conversation from Life," *Freedom* (column), n.d.; *A Hero Ain't Nothin' but a Sandwich* (novel; also film, 1978), 1973; *Like One of the Family: Conversations from a Do-*

mestic's Life, 1956; *Many Closets,* 1987; *Portrait of Fannie Lou Hammer* (screenplay), 1986; *Rainbow Jordan* (novel), 1981; *A Short Walk* (novel), 1979; *Those Other People,* 1989

1. Wilkerson.

2. Alice Childress, "A Candle in a Gale Wind," in Mari Evans, ed., *Black Women Writers (1950–1980): A Critical Evaluation* (Garden City, New York: Anchor Books, 1984) p. 112.

3. Case (1).

4. Keyssar.

5. Op. cit., Wilkerson.

6. Op. cit., Keyssar.

7. Essay by Rosemary Curb in MacNicholas.

8. Essay by Miguel Ortiz in *Black Writers,* Linda Metzger, ed. (Detroit: Gale Research, 1989).

9. Gallo, Donald R., ed., *Speaking for Ourselves: Autobiographical Sketches by Notable Authors of Books for Young Adults* (National Council Teachers of English, 1990).

10. Ibid.

11. Op. cit., MacNicholas.

Agatha Christie
COURTESY OF CORBIS-BETTMANN

Agatha Christie
(SEPTEMBER 15, 1890–JANUARY 12, 1976)

TREVES. If one sticks too rigidly to one's principles one would hardly see anybody.

—from *Towards Zero,* Act 1

The prodigious oeuvre of Agatha Christie has kept readers and audiences at the edge of their seats for over seventy years. Her work has been translated internationally, and her most famous creations, the Belgian detective Hercule Poirot and the wise, practical Miss Jane Marple, have solved countless murders.

Born Agatha Mary Clarissa Miller in Torquay, Devon, a fashionable seaside resort on the southern coast of England, she was the youngest of three children, all educated at home and raised in the conventional upper middle-class world of tea parties and tennis clubs that eventually became the setting for so many of her mysteries. In 1912 she met Archie Christie. After a two-year engagement, they married just as Archie, a member of the Royal Flying Corps, was called for duty. They did not see each other again for four years.

During the war Christie worked as a pharmacist, an occupation that educated her about the many devious possibilities for poisoning. When her sister challenged her to write a detective story like those they had enjoyed as youngsters, Christie produced the novel *The Mysterious Affair at Styles,* and her new career began.

She continued writing even after Archie returned from the war. *The Murder of Roger Ackroyd,* which followed *Styles,* created quite a stir among mystery fans due to its unorthodox finale. The Christies lived a rather subdued, quiet life with their daughter until 1926, when Archie announced he had fallen in love with another woman. Agatha Christie's legendary, mysterious ten-day disappearance occurred after Archie's confession. An intense nationwide search was conducted by the press, the police, and amateur detectives (among them DOROTHY SAYERS): Christie finally appeared in a small provincial hotel, registered under the name of Archie's lover. She never revealed what transpired during that period of time.

The divorce was finalized in 1928, and the traumatized Christie turned to writing for sanctuary and salvation. Her output astonished readers and critics alike. In addition to her popular murder mysteries, she wrote several romantic novels under the name Mary Westmacott, such as *Absent in the Spring.* She also began writing plays.

Black Coffee, her first work written expressly for the stage, was successfully produced in 1930. That same year, Christie married archaeologist Max Mallowea, with whom she shared the happiest and most productive period of her life. She often traveled as Mallowea's assistant on Middle Eastern excavations, experiences that inspired her books *Death on the Nile, Murder in Mesopotamia,* and *Appointment with Death.*

Christie continued to pen new plays and novels throughout the 1930s and '40s. Then in 1952 *The Mousetrap* opened in London's West End. The play broke box office records and ran continuously for more than twenty-one years, setting a world record (8,862 performances at the Ambassadors Theatre). Despite its enormous popularity, *The Mousetrap* did not deliver the complexity of some of Christie's other work. Whereas *Mousetrap*, with its cast of deceivers, is quite simply a play about revenge, *Witness for the Prosecution*, written in 1950, which won the New York Drama Critics' Circle Award (1954–55), offers a thoroughly Machiavellian villain in a terse courtroom drama.

The signature twists that pepper Agatha Christie's work, "her old obsessions: disguise; people who actually are who they say they are, mixed up with people who are not; the hiding of people in the obvious place for them to be . . . ; the international conspiracy idea; the advertisement in the newspaper device,"[1] reveal the author's keen sense of observation. Christie also appreciated the importance of realistic characterization. For example, amidst the many strange occurrences in *The Hollow* is pragmatic Midge's first reaction to innocent Edward's marriage proposal: that she won't have to return to work at a horrid dress shop.

By the time of her death in 1976, Christie had completed twenty-two plays and more than a hundred novels. Several of her works became successful films as well, such as *Ten Little Indians (And Then There Were None), Death on the Nile, Murder on the Orient Express,* and *Witness for the Prosecution.* In spite of her popularity, Christie lived a reclusive, private life.

PLAYS

Akhnaton, 1937; *And Then There Were None* (a.k.a. *Ten Little Niggers*), 1942; *Black Coffee,* 1930; *Butter in a Lordly Dish* (radio play), 1955; *A Daughter's a Daughter* (also a novel), 1951; *Fiddlers Three,* 1972; *Go Back for Murder* (adapt. of *Five Little Pigs,* a.k.a. *Murder in Retrospect*), 1960; *The Hollow,* 1951; *Love from a Stranger* (adapt. from "Philomel Cottage"), 1944; *The Mousetrap* (adapt. from *Three Blind Mice,* also a film), 1952; *Murder on the Nile* (also a film, 1978), 1946; *Rule of Three,* a trilogy (*Afternoon at the Seaside, The Patient, The Rats*), 1962; *Spider's Web,* 1950; *Ten Little Indians (And Then There Were None)* (also a novel, 1939; also films, 1945, 1965, and 1975), 1946; *This Mortal Coil,* 1971; *Towards Zero,* 1957; *The Unexpected Guest,* 1957; *Verdict,* 1956; *Witness for the Prosecution* (also a film, 1958), 1953

NOVELS (SELECTED)

Absent in the Spring, 1944; *Appointment with Death,* 1938; *Curtain,* 1975; *Death on the Nile,* 1937; *Murder at the Vicarage,* 1930; *Murder in Mesopotamia,* 1936; *The Murder of Roger Ackroyd,* 1926; *Murder on the Orient Express* (also a film, 1974), 1934; *The Mysterious Affair at Styles,* 1920

WORKS ABOUT

Behre, Frank, *Agatha Christie's Writings,* 1967; Christie, Agatha, *Autobiography,* 1977; Keating, H. R., ed., *Agatha Christie: First Lady of Crime,* 1977; Robyns, Gwen, *The Mystery of Agatha Christie,* 1978

1. Morgan, Janet. *Agatha Christie* (New York: Knopf, 1985).

Caryl Churchill
(1938–   )

WIFE. But women can't preach. We bear children in pain, that's why. And they die. For our sin. Eve's sin. That's why we have pain. We're not clean. We have to obey. The man, whatever he's like. If he beats us that's why. We have blood, we're shameful, our bodies are worse than a man's. All bodies are evil but ours is worst. That's why we can't speak [in church].

—from *Light Shining in Buckinghamshire*

Caryl Churchill built her reputation with highly theatrical works that focus on class struggle and sexual politics. Her plays are consistently controversial and utterly unique. She has been hailed as "our finest living playwright, possessed of a genuinely innovative theatrical imagination. She defies categorization . . ."[1] Churchill's work crosses international and historical boundaries, molding fact-based raw materials into sensitive articulations of modern social concerns. Her subject matter runs the gamut: competition and success (*Top Girls*), rural deprivation (*Fen*), social control (*Softcops*), city life (*Serious Money*), the dynamic between the United Kingdom and the United States (*Icecream*), or the overthrow of Romanian President Nicolae Ceausescu (*Mad Forest,* a 1990 Obie winner).

Churchill spent her first ten years in London. In 1948 her family moved to Montreal, Canada, where they remained for seven years before returning to the city of her youth. As a student at Oxford University, Churchill first received attention for her dramatic works. Upon graduating, she married David Harter, a barrister, and began writing radio plays. Her first, *The Ants,* aired on Radio 3 in 1962. Already, Churchill was staking her thematic turf: "As in many of her later works, the insects in [*The Ants*] are a resonant image of the oppressions of the individual in a capitalist society."[2] Churchill's radio work includes *Lovesick,* a black comedy about the misadventures of a manipulative, inept psychologist; *Abortive,* which explores the dark, violent side of human nature; the spooky sci-fi drama *Not Not Not Not Not Enough Oxygen*; and *The After Dinner Joke*, an exploration of the uselessness of charity in the face of the social power structure.

As a young mother, Churchill struggled with balancing her domestic life with her writing life. She hired a nanny to help care for her three young sons, but felt unresolved about "paying someone else to take care of my children, about the feeling that I could do it better."[3] Nevertheless, during this period she penned several radio plays. When her youngest son turned two, Churchill assumed full responsibility for her children. Her already heightened awareness of society's ills intensified; she began weaving sharper feminist themes into her work.

In 1972 the Royal Court Theatre Upstairs staged *Owners*, Churchill's first professionally produced play. The play deftly lays bare a man's inability to cope with his wife's success—he cannot bear to have his "property" supersede him financially. When the man, Clegg, must close the butcher shop he has owned for twenty-five years, he decides to have his successful real estate agent wife, Marion, murdered. He rationalizes his plan to Worsely, the hired thug:

> It's very like having a talking dog, and it's on the front page at breakfast, the radio at dinner, the television at night— that's mine, look, that's my clever dog. But a time comes when you say, Heel. Home. Lie down.

In *Owners* Churchill shakes the bonds of marriage and parenthood like a dog does a rag, exposing the holes, the dirt, and the frayed edges. As the doors to Clegg's shop are closed for the last time, Marion says, "I know very well it's a sad moment. I can't be a failure just to help." After its London run, the play was mounted in New York. It brought Churchill attention and notoriety.

Churchill's affiliation with the alternative Joint Stock Company in the mid-1970s marked a new departure in her work. Joint Stock's mission was to create political theater in a Brechtian ensemble setting. Nonhierarchically, everyone worked together—directors, designers, actors, and playwrights. *Light Shining in Buckinghamshire*, Churchill's first effort with the company, premiered at the Traverse Theatre in Edinburgh in 1976. The playwright described her experience with *Light*:

> It is hard to explain exactly the relationship between the workshop and the text. The play is not improvised: it is a written text and the actors did not make up its lines. But many of the characters and scenes were based on ideas that came from improvisation at the workshop and during rehearsal. . . . Just as important, though harder to define, was the effect on the writing of the way the actors worked, their accuracy and commitment.[4]

Light Shining in Buckinghamshire is based on England's seventeenth-century civil war. While six actors portray dozens of characters, an episodic chronicle unfolds about the Levelers, Diggers, and Ranters who groped toward de-

mocracy when King Charles was defeated. Alisa Solomon wrote in the *Village Voice* that "Churchill writes like a new Isaiah, one who speaks not of how the world will break into pieces, but of how it might, just might, be reconstructed."[5] Mel Gussow of the *New York Times* said, "The playwright seeks to give a comprehensive picture of the passions—and paradoxes—at the root of a rebellion that proved to be so consequential in English history. . . . One feels especially the plight of women at home and men recruited to be killed in battle without ever knowing what they are fighting for. Injustice replaces the law of the land. . . . It is a play that commands one's attention and that can lead to enlightenment."[6]

Churchill's work with Joint Stock paved the way to Monstrous Regiment, another collaborative theater company, but one with a more hard-line feminist socialist leaning. *Vinegar Tom*, the result of Churchill's affiliation with Monstrous Regiment, pushes further the territory she claimed with *Light*. Again the time is seventeenth-century England, but instead of focusing on a war between men, *Tom* explodes the war between men and women, using the European burning of witches as its landscape.

> [I] rapidly left aside the interesting theory that witchcraft had existed as a survival of suppressed pre-Christian religions and went instead for the theory that witchcraft existed in the minds of its persecutors, that 'witches' were a scapegoat in

Caryl Churchill
COURTESY OF THE PLAYWRIGHT, PHOTO BY VAL RYLANDS

times of stress like Jews and blacks. I discovered for the first time the extent of Christian teaching against women and saw the connections between medieval attitudes to witches and continuing attitudes to women in general. . . . I wanted to write a play about witches with no witches in it; a play not about evil, hysteria and possession by the devil but about poverty, humiliation and prejudice, and how the women accused of witchcraft saw themselves.[7]

A sort of Brechtian musical with an all-female cast, the play interlaces musically modern songs (written in collaboration with Helen Glavin) with weighty, ideological dialogue. The effect of this combination emotionally connects the contemporary audience to the historical events of the play. Churchill suggests that, as the songs in the play are delivered in a modern manner, they suggest "that times may not be that different. In other words, the historical representation of witches actually represents the misogyny of the patriarchy."[8] Although *Vinegar Tom* was a triumph in London, other productions (in Northampton and San Francisco) were not as well produced or received.

Churchill's most commercially successful work to date is *Cloud Nine*, another Joint Stock production. *Cloud Nine* "dramatises [the] patriarchal colonisation of female experience by allowing the audience to see the man behind the image."[9] Through its bizarre cross-gender, cross-racial, and cross-generational casting, the play subverts the traditional sexual and political ideals imposed by the character Clive on his African-based, nineteenth-century British household. The off-Broadway production of *Cloud Nine*, directed by choreographer Tommy Tune, won Churchill an Obie.

Top Girls followed *Cloud Nine* from London to New York. Here, Churchill returns to examining the complex choices women must make between motherhood and a professional life. Particularly inventive is the first act, in which Churchill sets up paradigms that model different decisions (and the repercussions of those decisions) made by historical women. These historical characters are then paired with their contemporary equivalents. One historical figure, Pope Joan, who allegedly ruled from 845–856, tells the others how she became pregnant and was stoned to death while giving birth during a procession. "Women, children, and lunatics can't be Pope," she says.

Churchill commented that *Top Girls* is "about the unpleasantness of the sort of careers a capitalistic society offers to both men and women. Mrs. Thatcher, for instance, has succeeded because she has taken on male values and has not, by her success, done anything for the oppressed women of Britain. Women achieving things isn't success if it entails the exploitation of men and women."[10] The contemporary setting in *Top Girls* places a thirteenth-century Japanese courtesan, a figure from a Brueghel painting, a Victorian traveler, and Chaucer's Patient Griselda around the formal dinner table of Marlene, the owner of an employment agency. The fracture in Marlene's life is exposed when we learn that this prosperous businesswoman has convinced her sister to raise Marlene's child as her own; in other words, she has achieved her success only by the "colonisation of her own sister," as Case puts it. "The economic situation has created two choices for women: the relative economic poverty of child-rearing, or the emotional alienation of success within the structures of capitalism."[11]

Churchill's work continues to be controversial and ground-breaking. "Among contemporary British dramatists, Caryl Churchill must be the most truly, most bracingly modern," wrote Jim Hiley in *London's Listener*. "It's no longer enough to see her as a feminist playwright of exceptional imagination. Her grasp of the hottest philosophical issues is all-embracing, the nimbleness with which she invokes them unmatched in our theatre."[12]

PLAYS (SELECTED)

A Mouthful of Birds, w/David Lan, 1986; *Cloud Nine*, 1979; *Fen*, 1983; *Floorshow*, 1977; *Icecream*, 1989; *Light Shining in Buckinghamshire*, 1976; *Mad Forest* (Obie), 1990; *Moving Clocks*, 1975; *Objections to Sex and Violence*, 1975; *Owners*, 1972; *Serious Money*, 1987; *The Skriker*, 1994; *Softcops*, 1984; *Three More Sleepless Nights*, 1980; *Top Girls*, 1982; *Traps*, 1977; *Vinegar Tom*, 1976

RADIO PLAYS AND ONE-ACTS (SELECTED)

Abortive, n.d.; *The After Dinner Joke*, n.d.; *The Ants*, 1962; *Henry's Past*, 1972; *Identical Twins*, 1968; *Lovesick*, 1966; *Not Not Not Not Not Enough Oxygen*, 1971; *Perfect Happiness*, 1973; *Schreber's Nervous Illness*, 1971

TELEPLAYS (SELECTED)

The After Dinner Joke, n.d.; *The Judge's Wife*, n.d.; *Turkish Delight*, 1973

WORKS ABOUT

Cousins, Geraldine, *Churchill the Playwright*, 1989; Fitzsimmons, Linda, *Files on Churchill*, 1989

1. Remnant.

2. Keyssar.

3. Ibid., interview with author, March 1982.

4. Churchill, Caryl, "A Note on the Production," *Light Shining in Buckinghamshire* (London: Pluto Plays, 1978).

5. February 26, 1991.

6. February 17, 1991.

7. Cited in Wandor.

8. Ibid.

9. Ibid.

10. Play notes in American Conservatory Theatre (A.C.T.) program, June 1984, Seattle, Washington.

11. Case (1).

12. Review of *A Mouthful of Birds*, November 27, 1986.

Sofija Čiurlionienė-Kymantaitė
(MARCH 13, 1885–DECEMBER 1, 1958)

Born in Joniškis (Šiauliai County), Lithuania, Sofija Čiurlionienė-Kymantaitė spent her childhood at her priest-uncle's parish rectory, where her mother served as a housekeeper. She attended high school in Riga and then enrolled at Cracow University from 1904–07, studying philosophy and literature. After graduating, she worked on the editorial staff of *Viltis* (Hope), a newspaper based in the Lithuanian capital of Vilnius. In 1909 Kymantaitė married the artist-composer M. K. Čiurlionienė. During the next nine years she taught the Lithuanian language at schools in Kaunas and Voronezh. When Lithuania became an independent country in 1918, Čiurlionienė-Kymantaitė worked for its Ministry of Education. Although she had, by this time, written only one play, *Kalinys* (A Prisoner) in 1911, after Lithuania achieved independence Čiurlionienė-Kymantaitė began to apply herself more fervently to the business of penning dramas.

Of her early works, the comedic *Pinigėliai* (Money; 1918) is especially notable for its satirical characters, sharp conflicts, and political agenda.[1] The play features Mrs. Normantas, a wealthy woman who has acquired her riches by exploiting the poor and the disadvantaged. As her family and cohorts gather at her deathbed, awaiting news of her will, we discover the great rift between Mrs. Normantas and her only son, Jonas. He despises his mother's ways, and though he is the prime beneficiary of his mother's fortune, he refuses it because she has placed upon his inheritance the condition that he continue her unethical legacy. The wily Mrs. Normantas, however, has predicted such a rejection, and has arranged her will so that the young Birute, Jonas's lover, will inherit all if she promises never to see Jonas again. The lovers' commitment to their beliefs wins out, however. They resist Mrs. Normantas's greedy plan and, after she dies, go off to live and love by their own principles.

Many of Čiurlionienė-Kymantaitė's plays reflect a similar trend toward socio-political satire. One of her greatest successes was *Aušros sūnūs* (The Sons of Dawn; 1923), about Lithuanian book smugglers struggling with the Russian police during a great press ban prior to Lithuania's independence. *Vilos Puošmena* (The Villa's Adornment; 1932) also deals with books, but in an entirely different manner. A comedy, it pokes fun at writers of vulgar literature. *Dolpelis ministerijoj tarnauja* is actually a monologue spoken by a "country bumpkin" who, with the wisdom of the innocent, looks incisively at governmental work from the inside.

Young people were a favorite audience of Čiurlionienė-Kymantaitė. Among her works written specifically for youth are *Kuprotas oželis* (The Humpbacked He-Goat; 1920), which lays bare the greediness of employers, and *Dylika brolių juodvarniais laksčiusių* (The Twelve Brothers Turned into Ravens; 1932), a dramatized folktale that has been performed repeatedly on stage and radio and is one of the most popular pieces of work in Lithuanian drama. Čiurlionienė-Kymantaitė spoke out in favor of symbolic expression and of exploring folklore as a source of inspiration. In fact, she condemned realism as a harmful trend in Lithuanian literature. In order to propagate these ideas, in 1927 she began a literary salon in her home known as "Čiurlionienės šeštadieniai" (Čiurlionienė's Saturdays), where intellectuals would gather to discuss their work and current events.

From 1925–38 she was a lecturer of Lithuanian at the University of Kaunas, and from 1929–39 served as a member of the Lithuanian delegation to the League of Nations, representing Lithuanian women at international conventions. Although she gained recognition primarily with books of literary criticism, theory, and history, she was also a formidable playwright, journalist, poet, teacher, and translator.

PLAYS

Aušros sūnūs (The Sons of Dawn), 1923; *Barbutė piemenaitė* (Barbara the Shepherdess), 1918; *Cyp . . . cyp . . . cyp . . . miau . . . miau . . . miau . . .* (Cheep . . . cheep . . . cheep . . . meow . . . meow . . . meow . . .), 1918; *Didžioji mugė* (The Great Fair), 1939; *Dolpelis ministerijoj tarnuaja* (Dolpelis Works at the Ministry), 1920; *Dvylika brolių juodvarniais laksčiusių* (The Twelve Brothers Turned into Ravens), 1932; *Gegužis* (May), 1920; *Grybų barnis* (Mushrooms' Quarrel), 1918; *Kalinys* (A Prisoner), 1911; *Karalaitė tikroji teisybė* (The Princess Is the Real Truth), 1920; *Kuprotas oželis* (The Humpbacked He-Goat), 1920; *Mūsų jauja* (Our Corn Kiln), 1956; *Pasiutusi veidmainystė* (Frantic Acting), 1932; *Pinigėliai* (Money), 1920; *Riteris budėtojas* (The Knight on Duty), 1925; *Vaiva* (Vaiva), 1946; *Vilos puošmena* (The Villa's Adornment), 1932

1. Segel.

Hélène Cixous
(JUNE 5, 1937–   )

Much of the work by the French feminist Hélène Cixous addresses themes of boundaries—physical, cultural, linguistic, sexual—which does not, at first, appear unusual. However, unlike many writers who have tackled these ideas, Cixous has managed to address them brilliantly in both the creative and academic arenas. Whereas many theoreticians of Cixous's caliber have been content with merely thrusting their ideas out into the world, Cixous has given her theories life through her poetry, fiction, and plays. In this way, her work perfectly illustrates the balance between the personal and the political. In her groundbreaking manifesto "The Laugh of the Medusa," she wrote:

> Woman must write her self: must write about women and bring women to writing, from which they have been driven away as violently as from their bodies . . . Woman must put herself into the text—as into the world and into history— by her own movement.[1]

Rallying for her own cause, with SIMONE BENMUSSA she cowrote the 1976 drama *Portrait of Dora*, which is based on a Freudian case study of female homosexuality. As Sue-Ellen Case writes, "Reversing the Freudian mandate, Cixous shows Dora to have developed, rather than repressed, her sexuality, and in the end the inference is that it is Freud who made a transference onto the patient, rather than the other way around."[2] The play presents "a new kind of representation of women on stage, reversing the patriarchal order of desire determined by Freudian theories and the male gaze."[3]

Cixous was born in Oran, Algeria, and emigrated to France in 1955. Her first language was German. She has recounted that her will to fight human injustice and indignities was wrought by what she saw all around her during her formative years in North Africa. Cixous taught at the University of Bordeaux and at the Sorbonne. In 1968 she helped found the literary review *Poetique*. She established and is head of the Centre de Recherche en Études Féminin (Center of Research in Feminine Studies) in Paris. In several of the more than thirty works of fiction, drama, and essays she has published, Cixous reinterprets myths and analyzes the representation of women in Western culture. Her theoretical and creative works have been translated into Dutch, German, and English.

PLAYS

L'Indiade, ou L'Inde de leurs rêve (The Indiade, or India of their Dreams), 1987; *L'histoire (qu on ne connaîtra jamais)*, 1994; *La prise de l'école de Madhubai* (The Capture of the School of Madhubai), 1986; *Le nom d'Oedipe* (libretto), 1978; *On ne part pas, on ne revient pas* (Don't Leave, Don't Come Back), n.d.; *Portrait de Dora* (Portrait of Dora), 1976; *The Terrible but Unfinished Story of Norodam Sihanouk, King of Cambodia*, 1994; *Voile noire voile blanche*,

(*Black Mask, White Mask*, Catherine A. F. MacGillivray, tr.), 1994

OTHER WORKS (SELECTED)

Angst, 1985; *Coming to Writing and Other Essays*, 1991; *Dedans* (Inside: novel), 1969; *The Exile of James Joyce*, 1972; *Hélène Cixous lit preparatifs de noces au-dela de l'abîme* (sound recording), 1981; *La jeune née* (The Newly Born Woman; essays), w/Catherine Clément, 1975; *Le livre de Promethea* (The Book of Promethea; essays), 1991; *L'ange au secret* (The Secret Angel; novel), 1991; *L'heure de Clarice Lispector* (Reading with Clarice Lispector; novel), 1989; *Manne: For the Mandelstams for the Mandelas*, 1993; *Neutre* (Neuter), 1970–72; *Prénoms de personne* (Nobody's Name; essays), 1974; *Readings: The Poetics of Blanchot, Joyce, Kafka, Kleist, Lispector, and Tsvetayeva*, 1991; *Three Steps on the Ladder of Writing*, 1993; *Trilogy: Le troisième corps* (The Third Body), *Les commencements* (Beginnings), n.d.

1. "The Laugh of the Medusa," from Marks, Elaine and Isabelle de Courtivron, eds., *New French Feminisms*.

2. Case (2).

3. Ibid.

Pearl Cleage
(DECEMBER 7, 1948–)

> MISS LEAH. I needed to be someplace big enough for all my sons and all my ghost grandbabies to roam around. Big enough for me to think about all that sweetness they had stole from me and just holler about it as loud as I want to holler.
>
> —from *Flyin' West*

"The theater is for me—a hollering place. A place to talk about our black female lives, defined by our specific black female reality to each other first and then to others of good will who will take the time to listen and to understand,"[1] declares Pearl Cleage, who identifies herself as "a black nationalist who believes strongly in self-determination."[2]

Cleage's plays combine the theatricality of her minister father's sermons at the Shrine of the Black Madonna in Springfield, Massachusetts, with the firm lessons of her teacher mother. Along with her parents, she cites Langston Hughes, Alice Walker, NTOZAKE SHANGE, Henrik Ibsen, Tennessee Williams, the Temptations, Aretha Franklin, Bessie Smith, and LORRAINE HANSBERRY as her major influences. Cleage stresses that she writes "out of a strong sense of commitment to the African American community. My focus is on black women, but I'm not a separatist so there are often black men in my work . . . I am also a black feminist."[3] She did undergraduate work at Howard University (1966–69), the University of the West Indies (1971), and Spelman College, where she earned her B.A. in drama and is currently playwright in residence.

When Cleage was twenty-five she had a crucial experience: Working as press secretary to the mayor of Atlanta, she found the sexism of the political world utterly infuriating and unbearable. Cleage fought back by embracing feminism and incorporating feminist themes into her work. "My work is focused on making black women see themselves clearly as a first step toward fighting for their freedom." Even her more recent plays sustain this message.

Cleage's dramas incorporate both traditional and experimental sensibilities. *Flyin' West* follows the lives of a family of hardy black women farmers who live in a nineteenth-century Kentucky farming community settled largely by freed black slaves. When a family member returns from the East Coast with an arrogant, abusive husband, the other women show him the meaning of real power.

A less conventional play, *Late Bus to Mecca*, illustrates how the absence of mutual communication threatens to undermine black women's power. While waiting for a bus, Ava, a prostitute-cum-hairdresser, jabbers away at Another Black Woman, who remains silent throughout the thirteen scenes. Cleage says her silence represents "every physically battered, spirit-bruised black woman whose words have been ignored or used against her so often they seem beside the point."

Cleage is not a playwright who shirks from heated, unsettling issues. Rosa Jenkins, the sixteen-year-old protagonist of *Chains*, has been chained to the radiator by her parents, their only hope of alleviating her crack addiction. For seven days Rosa rails against a world from which she is wholly disconnected. Finally, the chain is cut, but by then Rosa's faith in everything familiar has been severed. She values nothing: not the love of her parents or boyfriend, not prayer or even God. Incapable of living in such a world, she opens the closet and retrieves the chain.

In *Blues for an Alabama Sky* Cleage demonstrates the sense of community that converged in Harlem during its Renaissance in the 1920s after the Great Migration, when a lot of African Americans had come north and were separated from their families. Partial to creating strong female characters who triumph at the end, Cleage says she had to come to terms with the failure of Angel, the central character in *Blues*, when she realized that by taking her usual route, she was forcing Angel to do something that was out of character. In keeping with her self-centeredness, Angel could not triumph. In an interview with Douglas Langworthy, Cleage divulges, "As a playwright I don't want to spend all my time fussing at white racism, but as a feminist, I don't want to spend all my time fussing at men . . .

The responsibility is to tell the complete truth, and if you do that, the whole question of role models is really moot."[4]

In addition to play writing, Cleage has created several performance art pieces for herself, such as "The Jean Harris Reading" (1981), "The Pearl and the Brood of Vipers" (1981), "Nothin' but a Movie" (1982), and "My Father Has a Son" (1986). She was playwright in residence at Atlanta's Just Us Theater Company until 1987, when she became Artistic Director. From 1970–71 she cohosted "Black Viewpoints," produced by Clark College and broadcast at WETV, Atlanta. Also in the early 1970s, she was very active with *Ebony Beat Journal*, where her several roles included staff writer and interviewer. Her pen has generated several works of fiction, poetry, and essays.

Cleage's many awards and grants include five years of National Endowment for the Arts residency grants for the Just Us Theater Company (1983–87) and five Audience Development Committee Awards in 1983 for her off-Broadway show *Hospice*, now anthologized in *New Plays for Black Theater*. Currently at work on her first novel, Cleage is also a regular columnist for the *Atlanta Tribune*, a contributing editor of *Ms.* magazine, and a regular contributor to *Essence* magazine.

PLAYS

Banana Bread (video; PBS), 1985; *Blues for an Alabama Sky*, 1996; *Chain* (one-act), 1992; *Come and Get These Memories*, 1988; *Duet for Three Voices* (one-act), 1969; *Essentials*, 1985; *Flyin' West*, 1992; *Good News*, 1984; *Hospice*, 1983; *Hymn for the Rebels* (one-act), 1968; *Late Bus to Mecca* (one-act), 1992; *Porch Songs*, 1985; *PR: A Political Romance*, w/Walter J. Huntley, 1985; *puppetplay*, 1983; *The Sale* (one-act), 1972

OTHER WORKS

The Brass Bed and Other Stories (young adult), 1991; *Christmas 1967* (short fiction), 1968; *Christmas 1981* (short fiction), 1982; *Deals with the Devil: And Other Reasons to Riot* (essays), 1993; *Dear Dark Faces: Portraits of a People* (poetry), 1980; *Mad at Miles: A Blackwoman's Guide to Truth* (essays), 1990; *One for the Brothers* (chapbook), 1983; *We Don't Need No Music* (poetry), 1971; *What Looks Like Crazy on an Ordinary Day*, 1997

WORKS ABOUT

In Black and White, 1980, 1985; Peterson, Bernard L., *Contemporary Black American Playwrights and Their Plays*, 1988

1. "A Hollering Place," speech given at the Literary Managers & Dramaturgs of the Americas (LMDA) conference in June 1994. Printed in *LMDA Review*. Vol. 6, no. 1.

2. Correspondence with author, 1994.

3. Ibid.

4. "Making Our History," *American Theater*. July/August 1996.

Catherine Clive
(1711–1785)

SIR ALBANY ODELOVE. If Men, who are properly graduated in Learning, who have swallow'd the Tincture of a polite Education, who, as I may say, are hand and glove with the Classics, if such Genius's as I'm describing, fail of Success in Dramatical Occurrences, or Performances, ('tis the same Sense in the Latin) what must a poor lady expect, who is ignorant as the Dirt.

—from *The Rehearsal*

Catherine Clive
COURTESY OF THE BILLY ROSE THEATRE COLLECTION

At the age of seventeen, Catherine "Kitty" Clive gave a Drury Lane performance that ushered in an illustrious forty-year stage acting career. Throughout the mid-1700s, Clive delighted audiences with her sharp comic timing and melodious singing voice, while off-stage, she built her reputation for having a hot temper. She is known to have quarreled with such luminous colleagues as Susanna Cibber and David Garrick, a close personal friend.

In 1750 Clive wrote *The Rehearsal, or Bays in Petticoats*, a clever satire about a woman playwright, in which she lampoons even herself. The play centers on Mrs. Hazard (played by the author), an imperious woman writer attempting to pen a showcase piece for Mrs. Clive: "I wish she don't spoil it," says Mrs. Hazard, "for she's so conceited, and insolent, that she won't let me teach it her." Nancy Cotton remarks that the play "puts the criticism of the female playwright into the mouths of fools . . . [It] simultaneously spoofs and exploits some of the clichés about women playwrights that had been current since APHRA BEHN's day, and even before."[1] *The Rehearsal* closely follows the plot from *The Female Wits*, the anonymously written 1696 satire about DELARIVIERE MANLEY, MARY PIX, and CATHERINE TROTTER.

Evidently, *The Rehearsal* was Clive's only play writing endeavor. After its production, she returned to acting, giving her farewell performance in 1769 as Flora, one of her most popular roles, in SUSANNA CENTLIVRE's *The Wonder*.

PLAYS

The Rehearsal, or Bays in Petticoats, 1750

1. Cotton.

Darrah Cloud
(FEBRUARY 11, 1955–   )

SONG. Those who love and understand this country are the only ones who ever really own it.

—from *O Pioneers!*

Alexandra, the courageous heroine of Willa Cather's *O Pioneers!*, which Darrah Cloud adapted for the stage in 1990, endures and prospers on her beloved land, trusting her own instincts, refusing to be bullied by the men in her life. Similarly, Cloud has remained true to her own internal voice and sensibilities. "I have found a language writing my own gender that is secret and which I want to reveal, so that it becomes part of the norm. For in language is perspective, and in perspective is a whole new way of looking at things."[1]

Cloud's plays, according to editor-playwright John Istel, "explore the means by which the violence at the heart of American society reflects itself in the dysfunction of family life—and vice versa." Istel also points out how Cloud's work questions "the poverty of American lower- and middle-class life."[2] *The House Across the Street*, Cloud's first produced play, is a farcical black comedy. While thirteen-year-old Donald gleefully watches police unearth mass-murdered bodies from the house across the street, his mother Lillian continually closes the blinds, attempting to shut out reality.

In *The Stick Wife* Cloud again manages to tackle serious issues—both racism and sexism—while maintaining a sense of humor. When the wife of a Ku Klux Klan member realizes her husband is responsible for a bomb that killed four black girls, she informs the FBI. The play's subtle humor is derived from the wife's reluctance to become a hero. *The Stick Wife* reinforces Cloud's conviction that in a patriarchal society, women "must deny their true feelings much like slaves once did, forced to hide their vibrant, inner life behind the 'Yes, Master' pose."[3]

The bulk of Cloud's most recent plays focus on the manifestation, fear, and power of female sexuality. Cloud incorporates brutally real characters along with fantastic ones in conveying her ideas: the five battered women in *The Sirens*; Shadow, the talking horse in *The Mud Angels*, the haunted newlywed couple in *The Braille Garden*. Cloud, who cites her major influences to be LORRAINE HANSBERRY, Bertolt Brecht, GERTRUDE STEIN, Virginia Woolf, William Faulkner, and F. Scott Fitzgerald, as well as her grandmother, claims, "All my themes are feminist because I am a woman." The playwright is bent on chronicling the behavior of women, with a viewpoint of spirituality in America.[4]

Originally from Evanston, Illinois, Cloud earned a B.A. from Goddard College in 1978 and two M.F.A. degrees in poetry and play writing from the University of Iowa's acclaimed Writers' Workshop. A recipient of National Endowment for the Arts and Rockefeller Foundation grants, she also won a Drama League award. For two years she was playwright in residence at the Perseverance Theatre in Juneau, Alaska. Cloud also writes for television and film. She enjoys horsemanship and, with her actor/director husband Dave Owens, the challenges of parenting their two children.

PLAYS

Braille Garden, 1990; *Dream House* (also screenplay), n.d.; *Genesis*, 1992; *Honor Song for Crazy Horse*, 1994; *The House Across the Street* (also screenplay), 1982; *The Mud Angel*, 1990; *The Obscene Bird of Night* (adapt. of Jose Donoso novel), 1989; *O Pioneers!* (adapt. of Willa Cather novel, also teleplay, 1992) w/music by Kim D. Sherman,

1990; *The Sirens*, 1992; *The Stick Wife*, 1987; *The Waking*, n.d.

SCREENPLAYS AND TELEPLAYS

A Christmas Romance, 1994; *The Haunted*, 1991

1. Quoted by John Istel in Berney (2).
2. Op. cit., essay by John Istel.
3. Op. cit., quoted by Istel.
4. Correspondence with author, 1995.

Kathleen Collins
(JANUARY 30, 1931–1988)

MARIETTA. Dear Pop, always so full of fire, the need to be different . . . First colored to get a job with the Post Office, first colored to own property in Riverview . . . Kept us all in an uproar . . . "Now Lawrence . . . I will not tolerate from my boys any scrawny colored lives . . ." . . . Isn't that him to a tee, all his stern benevolence reaching out to hold us, till we were pumped full to overflowing with his fire and dreams. . . . He had such dreams, saw each of us living in angry defiance of all Negro rules, always standing tall and sturdy as the first of the first of the first of the coloreds . . . Dear Pop, he was so full of fire, none of us could breathe . . .

—from *The Brothers*, Act III, Scene 2

Kathleen Collins's 1982 drama *The Brothers* offers an unapologetic depiction of a black family's existence in a racist society. The play manages to reveal the experiences of the men, who essentially must shed their black skins in order to pursue their dreams, as well as the women who buffer them and, as Frank Rich says, "pick up the pieces."[1] Unlike many of the earlier black playwrights of the radical 1960s who were concerned about characters being perceived as "too white, or not black enough . . . Collins's characters may try to escape the burden of blackness, but their lives are nevertheless framed by the color of their skins and their consciousness of its influence."[2] *The Brothers* earned Collins a National Endowment for the Arts playwriting grant and a nomination for the Susan Smith Blackburn Prize.

Collins comes from a film background; she made her feature film debut as writer/director/producer of *Losing Ground* in 1982. Already she had produced and directed *The Cruz Brothers and Miss Malloy*, a short film. She continues to create works for both the stage and screen, and is an associate professor of film at City College of New York. She has received numerous awards, including grants from the American Film Institute and the New York State Council on the Arts.

PLAYS

The Brothers, 1982; *In the Midnight Hour*, 1982; *Only the Sky Is Free*, 1986; *Remembrance*, 1985

OTHER WORKS

Summer Diary, (screenplay) 1986

1. *New York Times*, April 6, 1982
2. Wilkerson.

Betty Comden
(MAY 3, 1919–   )

ELLA (singing). The party's over—
It's time to call it a day—
No matter how you pretend
You knew it would end this way.
It's time to wind up the masquerade—
Just make your mind up—
The piper must be paid.

—from *Bells Are Ringing*, Act II, Scene 4

Born Elizabeth Cohen, Betty Comden, along with her lifetime friend and partner Adolph Green, created some of America's best-loved stage and film musicals. From *On*

Betty Comden
COURTESY OF THE BILLY ROSE THEATRE COLLECTION

the Town to *Singin' in the Rain* to *The Will Rogers Follies*, Comden has been a powerful force in American theater since the 1940s.

After receiving her B.S. in drama from New York University in 1938, Comden and her college buddy Green created The Revuers, a cabaret group. Aided by their friend Judy Tuvin, they landed a gig at the Village Vanguard. They were a terrific hit, soon selling out shows at numerous venues, including the Rainbow Room and the Blue Angel. With Tuvin performing with them, Comden and Green headed for Hollywood, where they hoped to gain success writing for the popular variety shows of the early 1940s. There only Tuvin was pursued by the entertainment industry; she received many film offers, which Comden and Green encouraged her to take. A quick name change transformed Judy Tuvin into Judy Holliday, and a star was born. Ever faithful to her old friends, Holliday agreed to appear in Comden and Green's *Bells Are Ringing*, which, with Jules Styne, they wrote especially for her. It was a giant Broadway hit.

Betty Comden and Adolph Green have been recognized with innumerable honors and awards for over fifty years: the Theater World Award (1944) and the Screenwriters Guild Award (1949) for *On the Town*; Antoinette Perry Awards for best musical play for *Wonderful Town* (1953), best score, best lyrics, and best musical for *Hallelujah, Baby!* (1968), and for the book of *Applause* (1970) to name just a few. Comden also received New York City's Mayor Award of Art and Culture in 1978 and the Kennedy Center Honor in 1991, and has been inducted into both the Songwriters Hall of Fame and the Theater Hall of Fame. The film *Singin' in the Rain*, for which she wrote book and lyrics (1952), enjoyed a stage adaptation in 1985, with Comden and Green adding new material to this universal classic. The pair's shows have been nominated for several Grammys, winning in 1992 for best musical show album and best soundtrack album with *The Will Rogers Follies*.

A thoroughly modern woman, Comden remained married to the same man, Steve Kyle, a textile and industrial designer, until his death ended their thirty-seven-year union. They had two children. Of her marriage, Comden said, "I have had a career all my life. . . . My husband was a totally enlightened man, interested in what I did and a supporter of Adolph and me. But the fact that I had that wonderful thing didn't mean I wasn't aware of what it's like for others."[1]

PLAYS (SELECTED; ALL WITH ADOLPH GREEN, UNLESS OTHERWISE NOTED)

STAGE AND BOOK LYRICS

Applause (also TV special), 1971; *Bells Are Ringing* (also screenplay, 1960) 1956; *Billion Dollar Baby*, 1945; *Bo-*

nanza Bound, 1947; *A Doll's Life*, 1982; *Fade Out–Fade In*, 1964; *On the Town* (also screenplay, 1949), 1944; *On the Twentieth Century*, 1981; *A Party with Betty Comden and Adolph Green* (revue), 1958; *Subways Are for Sleeping*, 1961/62; *Two on the Aisle*, 1951

LYRICS ONLY

By Bernstein, (w/others), 1975; *Diamonds* (w/others), 1984–85; *Do Re Mi*, 1960; *Hallelujah, Baby!*, 1967; *Leonard Bernstein's Theater Songs* (w/others), 1965; *Lorelei*, 1973; *The Madwoman of Central Park West* (and music; w/others), 1979; *Peter Pan* (addl. lyrics; also TV special), 1954; *Say, Darling*, 1958; *Two on the Aisle*, 1951; *The Will Rogers Follies*, 1991; *Wonderful Town* (also TV special), 1953

SCREENPLAYS (INC. LYRICS)

Auntie Mame (adapt. from Patrick Dennis's *Travels with My Aunt* and the play by Jerome Lawrence and Robert E. Lee), 1958; *The Band Wagon*, 1953; *The Barkleys of Broadway*, n.d.; *Good News*, 1947; *It's Always Fair Weather*, 1955; *Singin' in the Rain* (also stage play, 1985), 1952; *Take Me out to the Ballgame* (lyrics only), 1949; *What a Way to Go* (based on a story by Gwen Davis), 1964

1. Quoted by Jeremy Gerard in the *New York Times*, September 19, 1982; cited by Alice McDonnell Robinson in Robinson.

Anne Commire
(1940?–   )

SHAY. I finally learned when I'm alone—I'm total. I'm not rude, boring, or stupid. In fact, I become a very nice person. I like me and I don't hurt anyone. I don't like what's in here when I'm with people: jealousy, anger, boredom . . . That's why I shouldn't be allowed to run around loose. I'm sealing myself off for society's sake.

—from *Shay*, Act I

In an interview with Kathleen Betsko and Rachel Koenig, American playwright Anne Commire said, "When I was younger there were always two voices bumping around inside me. One said I'd conquer Kilimanjaro; the other was right behind it, a little giggle that said, 'Who, you?' "[1] Both these voices assert themselves loudly and clearly via Commire's characters: suburban women, mostly, who bravely face mountains of difficulty and disillusionment in their lives with good-natured humor and irony. As Lynne in *Starting Monday* (1990) articulates, "I've always been a bit stiff; afraid to be seen having fun.

Some ride roller coasters, some wait below, holding the coats. Now, there's a T-shirt if I ever heard one."

Commire's work leans toward tragedy, but her "gift for imagining theatrical characters and for crafting sharp comic dialogue"[2] renders her plays ultimately comedic. Her 1978 drama *Shay*, features, as Clive Barnes describes her, "an all-American cheerleader twenty years or so after the last cheer."[3] By all appearances Shay enjoys a typical middle-class existence with her husband, son, and daughter. But Commire deftly reveals that the seeming stability of Shay's life is utterly illusory. Pregnant at fifteen, forced into marriage, Shay has suffered a loss of self so all-encompassing that she has become agoraphobic. *Put Them All Together* (1979) ventures into the life of Maggie, who, like Shay, suffers from isolation and neglect in her suburban housewife existence. Her husband ignores her, her doctor patronizes her, and her young son is hyperactive. However, whereas Shay retreats into herself, Maggie's inability to cope manifests itself violently: She expresses her rage by striking her son.

Commire received her B.S. in 1961 at Eastern Michigan University. She also studied at New York University and Wayne State University. Her plays have been produced at American Conservatory Theatre in San Francisco, Playwrights Horizons, the Works Projects Administration in New York City, the McCarter Theatre in Princeton, and the L.A. Public Theatre, among others. She has been awarded both Creative Artists Public Service and Rockefeller Foundation grants and has held several playwright in residence posts. In 1984 she won ABC's Television Theater Award for her play *Melody Sisters*. She is a member of the Writers' Guild of America and the Dramatists Guild.

In spite of her good press, Commire believes vehemently that a serious gender bias exists in theater criticism: "We're being reviewed through male eyes or women with male-oriented eyes—women who want to 'write like a man.' It's not some great conspiracy. Most men are uncomfortable with a woman's mind . . . We like to pretend it's not an issue between (man) critic and (woman) writer. Check out the male critic's relationship with Mom and you'll see a direct connection to his receptivity toward women's themes."[4]

PLAYS

Melody Sisters, 1983; *Put Them All Together*, 1979; *Shay*, 1978; *Starting Monday*, 1990

OTHER WORKS

Breaking the Silence, w/Mariette Hartley, 1990; *Yesterday's Authors of Books for Children*, ed., 1978; *World Leaders: People Who Shaped the World*, ed. w/Rob Nagel, 1994

1. Betsko.
2. Review by Mel Gussow in the *New York Times*, March 8, 1978.
3. Review in the *New York Post*, March 8, 1978.
4. Op. cit., Betsko.

Hannah Cowley
(1743–1809)

OLIVIA. But no gentle Katharine will he find me, believe it. Katharine!—Why, she had not the spirit of a roasted chestnut! A few big words, an empty oath, and a scanty dinner, made her as submissive as a spaniel. My fire will not be so soon extinguished; it shall resist big words, oaths, and starving!

—from *A Bold Stroke for a Husband*

Daughter of a bookseller, wife of a businessman, and mother of four, Hannah Cowley surprised herself and everyone who knew her when she picked up a pen at age thirty-six and began a career that would make her one of the most successful women playwrights of the London stage. Born in Tiverton, Devonshire, Cowley was the daughter of Philip Parkhouse, a pillar of the community and a respected scholar who gladly encouraged a healthy intellect in his witty and talented daughter. Cowley's grat-

Hannah Cowley
COURTESY OF THE BILLY ROSE THEATRE COLLECTION

itude toward her father is evidenced in one of her early poems: "You gave my youthful Fancy wings to soar." It was poetry, not drama, that she first aspired to write, but though she penned poems throughout her life—often conveying her love of the English countryside—they are not particularly memorable. In 1772 she married Thomas Cowley, an employee of the East India Company, who was considerably younger than she. They settled in London, where they raised four children.

A few years after her marriage, Cowley began to concentrate her energies on writing for the theater. Whether she turned to drama due to financial concerns or an underlying need to write is unclear. In the preface to her 1779 play *Albina*, she wrote that the success of *The Runaway* "opened a new prospect of advantage to my Family, which I have since pursued with alacrity." Ultimately, Cowley's career proved essential to the well-being of her family when, in 1782, Thomas traveled to India and died the following year.

Between 1776 and 1801, Hannah Cowley wrote nine comedies, two tragedies, and a farce, as well as a considerable number of poems. Despite her literary bent, she was not an intellectual and had no formal training: She never studied classical scholarship and did not involve herself in either literary conversation or correspondence. Perhaps this very lack of formal education kept her more in touch with the theatergoing public. She appeared only marginally interested in her own success and never even attended opening nights of her plays. Nonetheless, she was integrally involved in the productions of her plays and had more than one argument with theater managers.

Cowley's work was noted for its lively wit, spontaneity, and naturalness. Her first play, *The Runaway* (1776), was a conventional comedy that borrowed a bit from the more farcical work of Oliver Goldsmith, but it is well crafted and clever. The noted actor-manager David Garrick produced it for Drury Lane, the only new piece he staged during his last season at the theater. Garrick encouraged Cowley in her rewrites, offering advice and suggestions. *The Runaway* was a terrific hit, but Cowley's success was squelched by playwright Richard Sheridan, who, with Garrick's retirement, took over the Drury Lane and proceeded to produce his own plays: *The School for Scandal*, *A Trip to Scarborough*, and *The Rivals*.

Before her next production, the 1779 comedy *Who's the Dupe?*, appeared, Cowley found herself embroiled in other troubles. For three years she and playwright HANNAH MORE engaged in a bitter legal battle: Cowley accused More of plagiarizing material from *Albina*, which had been rejected by Thomas Harris of Covent Garden. Harris subsequently mounted More's *Percy* and *Fatal Falsehood*, both of which, in Cowley's opinion, stole from *Albina*. To some degree, the Drury Lane staging of *Who's the Dupe?* helped smooth over these difficulties. *Dupe* established Cowley as a solid writer of comedies, and remains one of her most enduring pieces. In 1780 Cowley found an unlikely ally in Thomas Harris, who, perhaps as recompense for their earlier dispute, staged *The Belle's Stratagem* at Covent Garden; it became Cowley's most popular play.

By the time *A Bold Stroke for a Husband* was first mounted in 1783, Cowley's plays were standard fare in the London theater scene. Her firm reputation may have been what encouraged her to take some risks with *Bold Stroke*. First, she set the drama in Spain, hoping that this distant setting might allow her heroines to behave in a way thought highly unsuitable to contemporary English manners. The lively, resourceful women in *Bold Stroke* articulate, at times quite explicitly, their feelings and beliefs about men, marriage, and women's place in society. In the main plot Don Carlos, tired of his wife, Victoria, has settled his wife's estate on his mistress. By the end, Don Carlos is righteously duped by his wife. In the subplot Olivia, having set her marital sights on Julio, must divert the many suitors her father, Don Caesar, brings before her. Says Olivia of one such suitor: "He has a very pretty kind of conversation; 'tis like a parenthesis." "Like a parenthesis!" exclaims Don Caesar. "Yes," replies Olivia, "it might be all left out, and never missed." A stylistic diversity between the main plot and the subplot renders the play somewhat weaker than Cowley's best works, and in truth, the subplot of *Bold Stroke* proved far more popular with actors of the day, many of whom vied for these smaller yet richer roles. Olivia, in particular, speaks some of the most clever and controversial lines: "Dost think my husband shall contradict my will? Oh! I long to set a pattern to those milky wives, whose mean compliances degrade the sex!"

Although Cowley tended to stick to her tried-and-true comedic formulas, with *A Day in Turkey* (1792) she created a quite different sort of stage work. *Turkey*, a comic opera, lacks a substantial plot but boasts a demand for spectacle that superseded its weak story line. It was first produced at Covent Garden; the singers, comic figures, fanfare, and music overshadowed the serious actors.

Hannah Cowley's ability with character made her plays highly appealing to actors and actresses, and her natural and often witty dialogue delighted audiences. *The Town Before You* was the last of her plays to be produced while she lived, in 1794. Although Cowley was never quite able to repeat the commercial successes of either *The Belle's Stratagem* or *Who's the Dupe?*, she left a substantial body of work, much of which holds its own beside the plays of Oliver Goldsmith and Richard Sheridan.

PLAYS

Albina, 1779; *The Belle's Stratagem*, 1782; *A Bold Stroke for a Husband*, 1784; *A Day In Turkey*, 1792; *The Fate of Sparta*, 1788; *More Ways than One*, 1784; *The Runaway*, 1776; *A School for Graybeards*, 1786; *The Town Before You*, 1795; *Which is the Man?* 1782; *Who's the Dupe?*, 1779

WORKS ABOUT

Cowley, Hannah, *The Works of Mrs. Cowley, Dramas and Poems, in Three Volumes*, 1813; Link, Frederick M, "Introduction," *The Plays of Hannah Cowley*, 2 vols., 1979; Norton, Jane E., "Some Uncollected Authors, XVI: Hannah Cowley, 1743–1809," *Book Collector*, Vol. 7, 1958

Rachel Crothers
(DECEMBER 12, 1878–JULY 6, 1958)

WELLS (reading a book review). Her first work attracted wide attention when we thought Frank Ware was a man, but now that we know she is a woman we are more than ever impressed by the strength and scope of her work.

—from *A Man's World*, Act I

By the time of her death in 1958, Rachel Crothers had left an indelible mark on the stages of New York City. Playwright, actress, director, and community activist, Crothers arrived in New York at the age of sixteen. Her gift for theater was immediately evident: After completing a single term at the Stanhoope-Wheatcroft School of Acting, she was promoted to instructor.

Although Crothers debuted on the New York stage in 1897, it was her one-act plays, written for her drama students, that garnered her serious attention two years later. In 1906 *The Three of Us*, her first professionally produced play, opened at the Madison Square Theater; a hit, it ran for 227 performances. The play addresses social concerns and the struggle of the modern woman—themes that would soon dominate Crothers's life and work.

Interestingly, Crothers herself enjoyed a privileged upbringing in Bloomington, Illinois. Her parents, both physicians, were acquainted with President Lincoln: her maternal grandfather was a close friend of the President's, who appointed her father medical examiner of Civil War soldiers. Crothers's parents noticed their daughter's propensity for the theater, and they enrolled her in Boston's New England School of Dramatic Instruction. Perhaps due to her parents' involvement with the plight of ordinary people, Crothers also cultivated a lifelong commitment to social service work. She founded and led the Stage Relief Fund in 1932 and, in 1940, the American Theater Wing for War Relief, for which Crothers helped mobilize more than 3,000 women nationwide. She also organized the Stage Door Canteen for servicemen in New York in 1945,

Rachel Crothers
COURTESY OF THE BILLY ROSE THEATRE COLLECTION

The plight of the creative woman first surfaced in *A Man's World*, Crothers's first success, produced in 1910. The play's heroine is writer Frank Ware, a woman of great heart and courage, who has just enjoyed her first flush of success with the publication of a well-received book. Frank devotes time and energy to helping women on the poor side of town, going so far as to adopt Kiddie, the son of a young woman who was abandoned by her lover. Frank fights her affections for her own lover, Gaskell, because he does not share her views on women. Gaskell believes he must protect and take care of Frank; he sees her as helpless. As the play unfolds, Frank discovers that Gaskell is the man who deserted Kiddie's mother. He defends himself, playing down his responsibility: "We don't live under the same laws," Gaskell tells her. Yet, had be been the woman, his life would have been ruined. Frank's commitment to her internal laws and principles compel her to leave Gaskell. Frank Ware illustrates Judith Olauson's claim that "Crothers's women are able to resolve their separate predicaments because they become aware that they are ultimately responsible for the choices they make and that the rightness or wrongness of those choices is of their own devising."[2]

By 1918 Crothers had directed productions of all of her plays. She staged her final drama, *Susan and God*, with Gertrude Lawrence in the lead role, in 1937. *Susan and God* centers around the idle life of an unhappy housewife. When she latches on to a "newly found religion," she brags to her friends that her troubles are over, despite her alcoholic husband and miserable, neglected daughter. Susan's desperate grasp at the "gold ring" on the merry-go-round of life is as insubstantial as cotton candy. Finally, acknowledging the importance of an open, caring relationship with her husband and daughter, she learns that only through a good, hard look at one's values and honest, open communication with those one loves can one transform one's life. Crothers's play "proposes that human beings are frail but can be reclaimed . . ."[3]

Although *Susan and God* was her last production, Crothers remained active in theater—producing, directing, supporting new talent—until the mid-1940s. Crothers was elected to the National Institute of Arts and Letters in 1933, and the Theater Club cited *Susan and God* the season's most outstanding play of 1937. She received a 1938 National Achievement Award, and in 1941 the Drama Study Club honored her for the year's most distinguished service to the theater. Crothers died in her comfortable Connecticut farmhouse, "Roadside," on July 6, 1958; she was eighty years old.

which was staffed by volunteers from the theater community.

Complex female characters permeate Crothers's plays. *He and She*, which was revised several times before its first successful production in 1919, is arguably Crothers's most powerful, complex work: The playwright explores the cost of women's independence, particularly in light of its effect on marriage and family. Ann Hereford, a sculptor like her husband, is faced with a dilemma: As she nears completion of her most important sculpture, one which promises to confirm her genius in the art world, her teenage daughter has an emotional crisis. Without the devotion and guidance of her mother, the girl's life might turn toward disaster. Not without difficulty, Ann chooses to tend to her daughter. By revealing the truth behind the supposed equality of the husband-wife sculptor team, Crothers suggests that Ann's decision is informed by her desire to save both her daughter and her marriage: When Ann wins a competition in which they are both contenders, Tom accuses her of excessive ambition and selfishness. *He and She* predicts "the great distance still to be traveled before America would provide a hospitable climate for women's freedom, and before American women would defeat the fears and guilt about freedom that lurked in their natures."[1]

PLAYS (SELECTED)

As Husbands Go, 1930; *The Coming of Mrs. Patrick*, 1907; *Criss-Cross*, 1899; *Expressing Willie*, 1924; *The Heart of*

Paddy Whack, 1914; *He and She* (a.k.a. *The Herfords*), 1920; *Let Us Be Gay*, 1929; *A Man's World*, 1910; *Mary the Third*, 1923; *Mother Carey's Chickens*, w/Kate Douglas Wiggin, 1917; *Myself, Bettina*, 1908; *Nice People*, 1921; *Nora*, 1903; *Once Upon a Time*, 1917; *Ourselves*, 1913; *Pollyanna*, 1902; *The Rector*, 1902; *Six One-Act Plays*, 1925; *Susan and God*, 1937; *The Three of Us*, 1906; *39 East (Expressing Willie; Nice People; 39 East)*, 1919; *Venus*, 1927; *When Ladies Meet*, 1932; *Young Wisdom*, 1914

OTHER WORKS

Quinn, Arthur H., foreword, "The Construction of a Play" (1928) in *The Art of Playwriting*, 1967

WORKS ABOUT

Gottlieb, Lois C., *Rachel Crothers*, 1979

1. Undated clipping from Boston, in Crothers's scrapbook. Special collections, Illinois State University. Cited in Gottlieb, Lois, C., *Rachel Crothers* (Boston: Twayne Publishers, 1979).

2. Olauson.

3. Ibid.

Gretchen Cryer
(OCTOBER 17, 1935–   )

TRIO. If you smile in just the right way
You'll make a pretty wife
And someone will take care of you
For all your pretty life
If you smile, smile, smile
If you smile

—from *I'm Getting My Act Together and Taking It on the Road*

The intimate, autobiographical play has become such a sturdy mainstay for so many theater artists, most theater-goers today are unaware that this phenomenon originated quite recently: BEAH RICHARDS regaled audiences with her one-person show *A Black Woman Speaks* in 1950. In 1978, four years after NTOZAKE SHANGE's self-confessional choreopoem *for colored girls . . .* was first mounted, Gretchen Cryer's *I'm Getting My Act Together and Taking It on the Road* was produced by the New York Shakespeare Festival. *Getting My Act* pushed the form further by adding music and song. In the musical Cryer and her cohorts speak and sing of the lessons she has learned about love and life thus far. The whole show takes place on the stage of a cabaret music house, where a band, consisting of five players and two backup singers, sing, play various musical instruments, and act out the various characters in the life of the woman who is, well . . . getting her act together. At one point in the play, Cryer quotes her own mother's words, which she heard as a child in Dunreith, Indiana, "The woman has to go 75% of the way because the man will only go 25%, if that much." Cryer had to learn that lesson herself. She married, and later divorced, actor/producer/singer David Cryer, with whom she had a son, actor Jon Cryer.

She was educated at DePauw University in Indiana, and is not only a playwright, but an actress, singer, and lyricist as well. She made her Broadway acting debut in 1962 as Miss Kepplewhite in *Little Me*, and has appeared in other Broadway productions such as *110 in the Shade* and *Now Is the Time for All Good Men*, a musical that she coauthored with her longtime collaborator, Nancy Ford, with whom she formed an alliance while still in college in the 1950s. Their play *The Last Sweet Days of Isaac* won four major awards: an Obie, a Drama Desk, an Outer Critics Circle, and *Variety*'s Poll.

PLAYS (ALL W/MUSIC BY NANCY FORD, UNLESS OTHERWISE NOTED)

Hang Onto the Good Times, 1985; *I'm Getting My Act Together and Taking It on the Road*, 1978; *The Last Sweet Days of Isaac*, 1970; *Now Is the Time for All Good Men*, 1967; *Shelter*, 1973; *The Wedding of Iphigenia*, w/Doug Dyer and Peter Link, 1971

Clemence Dane
(1887/8–MARCH 28, 1965)

DOCTOR. The war taught what peace couldn't teach us—
that when conditions are evil, your duty, in spite of protests,
in spite of sentiment, your duty . . . is to see that these conditions are changed . . . Grow or perish—it's the law of life.

—from *A Bill of Divorcement*

St. John Ervine, an important critic and playwright of his
day, called Dane "the most distinguished woman dramatist in the theatre." However, he also called women
" 'oncers' at best and unlikely ever to offer serious rivalry
to men."[1] It is certainly likely that Dane, whose works
often depicted the plight of women, was bemused by the
irony embedded in Ervine's remarks.

Born Winifred Ashton in Blackheath, England, she led
a rather peripatetic youth. At age sixteen she left for Geneva, where she worked as a French tutor; then she studied
art in Dresden and at the Slade School in London, and
then went to Ireland, where she taught school and drew
theater posters. Finally, in 1913, Ashton began working
as an actress. Under the stage name Diane Cortis, she
made her debut in *Eliza Comes to Stay*.

Not completely satisfied with her new career, she assumed the pen name Clemence Dane (which she appro-
priated from a London church) and wrote a novel. Her
first book, *Regiment of Women* (1917), was a best-seller.
Inevitably, the combination of theater and literature
prompted Dane toward play writing. In 1921 Dane
penned *A Bill of Divorcement*, which starred Katherine
Cornell and opened to great acclaim. The play's title refers

to a parliamentary bill under consideration at the time that
would enable women to obtain a divorce only if their
spouses were drunkards, habitual criminals, or insane (evidently, physical abuse was not sufficient cause). Dane
chose to contextualize the divorce issue within one family's
struggle to cope with the effects of modern warfare. Margaret's husband, a victim of shell shock, has been institutionalized for fifteen years. She finally decides to divorce
him and remarry another, when, astonishingly, he completely recovers. Under the bill, Margaret would have no
choice but to return to her old life, since she would still
be legally married to her first husband (and illegally married to her second!). Her dilemma, whether to obey the
law and return to her old life, or defy the law and move
forward with her new one, exemplified the bill's controversy.

Also well received in 1921 was *Will Shakespeare*, a
clever portrait of the Bard written in blank verse. Dane's
"invention" domesticates the great poet, setting him
among his family and friends. Critics loved it; many called
it the most feasible account of Shakespeare to be seen on
the stage. Dane continued to turn to the literary world for
inspiration. Her *Wild Decembers* revolves around the lives
of the Brontës, and she adapted several classical works,
such as Edmond Rostand's *L'Aiglon*, Friedrich von Schiller's *Don Carlos*, and Friedrich Hebbel's *Herod and Mariamne*.

In the late 1920s Dane began a long-standing collaboration with composer Richard Addinsell. Together, they
wrote *Adam's Opera*, a social satire loosely based on "Sleeping Beauty"; *Come of Age*, about the life of English poet
Thomas Chatterton; and *Alice's Adventures in Wonderland
and Through the Looking Glass*, adapted from Lewis Car-

roll's classic books. Dane also wrote many screenplays, notably *Anna Karenina,* her first, and *Vacation from Marriage,* for which she received an Academy Award in 1946.

All told, the prolific Dane wrote thirty stage plays, sixteen works of fiction, and numerous screenplays and radio plays, as well as her memoir, *London Has a Garden.* Additionally, she was an active painter and journalist, serving as president of the Society of Women Journalists in 1941. In 1953 she was bestowed with the Order of the Commander of the British Empire.

PLAYS (SELECTED)

Adam's Opera, 1928; *L'Aiglon* (adapt. of Rostand's work), 1934; *Alice's Adventures in Wonderland and Through the Looking Glass* (adapt. of Lewis Carroll's work), w/music by Richard Addinsell, 1943; *A Bill of Divorcement,* 1921; *Call Home the Heart,* 1947; *Cathedral Steps,* 1942; *Come of Age,* w/music by R. A., 1934; *Cousin Muriel,* 1940; *Eighty in the Shade,* 1959; *England's Darling,* 1934; *The Golden Reign of Queen Elizabeth,* 1941; *Gooseberry Fool,* w/Helen Simpson, 1929; *Granite,* 1926; *The Happy Hypocrite,* 1936; *Herod and Mariamne* (based on Hebbel's play), 1938; *Legend* (also novel), 1919; *The Lion and the Unicorn,* 1952; *Mariners,* 1927; *Moonlight Is Silver,* 1934; *Naboth's Vineyard,* 1925; *The Saviours, Seven Plays on One Theme,* 1942; *The Terror,* 1921; *The Way Things Happen,* 1924; *Wild Decembers,* 1932; *Will Shakespeare: An Invention,* 1921

OTHER WORKS (SELECTED; NOVELS, UNLESS OTHERWISE NOTED)

Anna Karenina (screenplay), 1935; *The Arrogant History of White Ben,* 1939; *Broome Stages,* 1931; *Fate Cries Out: Nine Tales,* 1935; *The Flower Girls,* 1955; *He Brings Great News,* 1945; *London has a Garden* (memoir), 1964; *Regiment of Women,* 1917; *Tradition and Hugh Walpole* (history), 1928; *The Women's Side,* 1927

1. Essay by Erica Beth Weintraub in Weintraub.

Sarah Daniels
(1957–)

MARY (suicide note to her husband). Your dinner and my head are in the oven.

—from *Ripen Our Darkness*

By 1984 Sarah Daniels's plays were routinely raising the blood pressure of London's theater critics. "[*Masterpieces*] makes Strindberg look like Crossroads: it could crack a relationship wide open," wrote *The Guardian's* Irene McManus. Daniels's feminist fury has incited vitriolic criticism from many male theatergoers, who Daniels asserts are "not equipped to judge" the works of women; however, she is frequently championed by women critics. Carol Woddis applauded Daniels in London's *City Limits* (July 10, 1986), remarking on how the playwright's "lacerating wit subversively [exposes] how, under patriarchy, women are pushed to the very edge of lunatic behavior . . . Daniels is overtly political and has taken on issues that challenge some of the most sensitive areas of the patriarchal society, as she sees it."

The Royal Court Theatre has staged four of Daniels's plays, including her first, *Ripen Our Darkness,* in 1981. *Darkness,* which addresses the drudgery imposed on the working-class woman, ruffled audiences when the central character, after committing suicide, has a celestial encounter with what Michael Coveney of the *Financial Times* tagged a "wholly feminist trinity." Daniels returned to the life of the working-class woman for her 1983 play *The Devil's Gateway,* which Lyn Gardner called in *City Limits* "a gloriously funny . . . moving and true account of the consciousness raising of a working-class woman in Bethnal Green who has spent a lifetime mopping up after redundancy, unemployment and children." Carol Woddis posits, also in *City Limits* (1983), that *Gateway* provides an example "of the women's movement's adage that the personal *is* political which Daniels combines with a sure comic touch."

The controversial themes of Daniels' work continued to draw barbs from critics. *Masterpieces,* her best known play and considered by some to be a feminist classic, explores the connection between pornography and male violence. Obliterating the lines between soft and hard pornography, it is seen by many to be a persuasive argument for banning such material.

Neaptide, which deals with the legal and social prejudices towards lesbians in child custody cases, was received with mixed reviews. Critics appreciated her passion and earnestness but, as John Barber put it in the *Daily Telegraph,* "the real courage the play required" was some deft pruning.[1] Utilizing the myth of Demeter and Persephone, Daniels illustrates a woman's struggle to reconcile integrity, compromise, and love in the face of prejudice and injustice.

Daniels got a serious lashing from the press with *Byrthrite:* "The one original and exciting idea in Sara Daniels's dour and humourless new play is voiced towards the end when a 17th century feminist playwright buries the text of her unproduced play. The unspoken words will, she says, come to life when she is dead. This is a fascinating alternative to full theatrical production and one which Ms Daniels and the Royal Court might in future pursue."[2]

Daniels's most recent work, *Beside Herself,* highlights the denial and silence resulting from sexual abuse, while questioning the social controls imposed on those labeled "mad." *Beside Herself* portrays a woman possessed by a rage so intense and so silenced by society, her mind turns in on itself.

Despite the derision from male critics, "her plays have filled theatres again and again, with audiences reacting to the vitality, humour, and honesty of her work with just about every emotion one can imagine (including fear, it would seem)—but never boredom. This is what theatre is all about," writes Mary Remnant in *Plays by Women*.[3] Daniels has professed a desire to write for television, a medium that, she feels, can help widen her audience. Whether her work will appear on the small screen is currently unclear: Daniels is skeptical of the compromises she may have to make.

PLAYS

Beside Herself, 1990; *Byrthrite*, 1986; *The Devil's Gateway*, 1983; *The Gut Girls*, 1988; *Ma's Flesh Is Grass*, 1981; *Masterpieces*, 1983/4; *Neaptide*, 1984; *Penumbra*, 1981; *Ripen Our Darkness*, 1981

1. John Barber, *Daily Telegraph*, March 7, 1986.

2. Mark Lawson, *Independent*, November 28, 1986.

3. Remnant, vol. 5. 1986.

Margaretta (Ruth) D'Arcy
(JUNE 14, 1934–   )

SINGER (to the air: 'Long Lankin').
The cold rain of Ireland blows over the water
To furrow the face of fair England's proud daughter.

How long will it fall, O as sharp as a knife?
Till the dogteeth of England let go of our life.

Let go of our heart and the voice in our throat.
Till the day of that good-morning, no end to the fight . . .

—from *Vandaleur's Folly*, Prologue

Margaretta D'Arcy's plays extend the reach of drama beyond the confines of conventional theater. She and her husband, John Arden, have produced a body of work that incorporates a serious political agenda with music, song, verse, mime, and audience involvement. To D'Arcy and Arden, "playful" and "a play" are inextricably bound.

D'Arcy came of age in post–World War II Dublin, the daughter of an Irish nationalist (her father served in the Irish Republican Army during the War of Independence) and a staunch Zionist (some members of her mother's family actively participated in the campaign to create the state of Israel). "As a result," she writes, "I was, from an early age, heavily saturated with illusory nationalism and realistic anti-imperialism. Hence my distaste for British

official culture. (I knew nothing of British popular culture.)"[1]

Until the age of thirteen, D'Arcy lived among an enclosed order of nuns in Dublin. She described the atmosphere as "one of extreme nationalism mixed with a keen awareness of money."[2] Most of the nuns, who were largely from rural farm families, had grown up in the early part of the century, when anti-British sentiment and religious sectarianism prevailed; they had been almost completely shielded from the social changes that occurred after World War II. Even though D'Arcy herself was raised in this cloistered environment, on holidays she mixed with suffragists, pacifists, trade unionists, and even Protestants.

As a young woman in the 1950s, D'Arcy worked as an actress in Dublin's improvisational fringe theaters. Her play writing began after she married Arden, himself a noted author and playwright, in 1957.* In their collaborative work, D'Arcy and Arden have frequently addressed the complex history and contemporary issues surrounding Irish nationalism: The life and death of the great Irish revolutionary hero James Connolly is the subject of *The Non-Stop Connolly Show*, a cycle play in six parts written in verse; *The Hero Rises Up* explores the professional and personal unorthodoxies of Lord Horatio Nelson and Lady Hamilton; *The Little Gray Home in the West*, *The Ballygombeen Bequest*, and *Vandaleur's Folly* all examine "the furious contradiction of Ireland" by means of satire and melodrama; and the 1977 Irish general election is surrealistically portrayed in *A Pinprick of History*.

The Royal Shakespeare Company (RSC) staged D'Arcy and Arden's *The Island of the Mighty* in 1972. *Island* uses the story of Merlin and King Arthur to convey the relationship of the poet to society. By emphasizing the struggles of Arthur's subjects as much as the king's own personal crisis, the playwrights intended, according to Elaine Turner, to provoke "discussions regarding historical perspectives, national myth, patriotism, and storytelling." However, D'Arcy and Arden felt that the RSC's production reduced the play's complexity to a romantic tale about a failing hero, and the couple actually picketed the Company's rehearsals at the Aldwych Theater: it was the couple's last production in the West End. RSC officials dismissed D'Arcy as a "difficult woman," a label that, again according to Turner, "explicitly illustrates the necessity and urgency in this talented, tireless woman's energetic fight against the patriarchal hierarchy."

Margaretta D'Arcy has remained true to her notion of "play" (influenced, in part, by Neva L. Boyd, a pioneer in the field of creative group play and mentor to the more widely known Viola Spolin: see MEGAN TERRY). Her work rises above the ordinariness of so many contempo-

---

*Elaine Turner points out that the work of John Arden is different in form and intent from the collaborative work he did with D'Arcy.

rary commercial productions. "I am not sure whether there is a connection between the loss of the concept of 'play,' " commented D'Arcy, "and our present-day mechanistic bums-on-seats 'task-profit' syndrome where the finished commodity off the cultural production-line is all that matters and to hell with the personal growth and vision of the workers."

PLAYS (SELECTED, ALL W/JOHN ARDEN)

Ars Longa, Vita Brevis, 1963; *The Ballygombeen Bequest*, 1972; *The Business of Good Government*, 1962; *Friday's Hiding*, 1965; *The Happy Haven*, 1960; *The Hero Rises Up*, 1968; *The Island of the Mighty*, 1972; *Keep the People Moving* (radio play), 1972; *The Little Gray Home in the West*, 1978; *Muggins Is a Martyr*, 1968; *The Non-Stop Connolly Show*, 1975; *A Pinprick of History*, 1977; *The Royal Pardon*, 1966; *Vandaleur's Folly*, 1978

1. All D'Arcy's comments and quotations, unless otherwise noted, cited in an essay by Elaine Turner in Berney (2).

2. Preface to *The Island of the Mighty*, 1972.

Gordon Daviot
(1896–FEBRUARY 13, 1952)

JOHN OF GAUNT. He holds England in his two hands and laughs like a wicked child and men pause and hold their breath.

—from *Richard Bordeaux*

Born Elizabeth Mackintosh in Inverness, this Scotswoman was educated at the Royal Academy there. She furthered her studies at Anstey Physical Training College in Birmingham, after which she taught physical training. Before her success as a playwright, Daviot wrote most of her fiction under the name Josephine Tey. When she entered her first novel, *The Man in the Queue*, in a competition, she took the pseudonym Gordon Daviot (undoubtedly a wily consideration to increase her chances of winning).

Richard Bordeaux is generally considered her best theatrical work. John Gielgud both directed and starred in its first production at London's Arts Theatre Club in 1932. Following the history of Richard II, it is a more accurate account than Shakespeare's of the king's character and provides an incredibly challenging role for its portrayer. It made Gielgud, heretofore known as a Shakespearean actor, a West End celebrity. Daviot's fine characterizations, the use of modern speech, and the parallel relevance of contemporary events (Hitler had recently come to power and England was a-jitter) all conspired to make *Richard Bor-*

deaux, according to critics, "the finest drama since Shaw's *Saint Joan*; not without reason for like Shaw's play it was written with wit [and] political irony . . ."[1]

Her next work, *The Laughing Woman*, is also one of her best. Loosely based on the lives of Henri Gaudier and Sophie Brzeska, it is about the platonic relationship between a brilliant young French sculptor and an older woman who models for him and lives with him. It is a fascinating study of the chains that bind two people, and of genius.

PLAYS

Dickon, 1955; *The Laughing Woman*, 1934; *Leith Sands and Other Short Plays*, 1946; *The Little Dry Thorn*, 1947; *Queen of Scots* (also book, 1934), 1934; *Richard of Bordeaux* (also book, 1933), 1932; *The Stars Bow Down* (also book, 1939), 1949; *Valerius*, 1948

OTHER WORKS (SELECTED)

Brat Farrar, 1950; *Claverhouse*, 1937; *The Daughter of Time*, 1941; *Kif*, 1929; *The Man in the Queue*, 1929; *The Privateer*, 1952; *To Love and Be Wise*, 1951

1. Essay by Audrey Williamson in Weintraub.

Mary Davys
(1674–1732)

PROLOGUE. When Women write, the Criticks, now-a-days,
Are ready, e'er they see, to damn their Plays:
Wit, as the Men's Prerogative, they claim,
And with one Voice, the bold Invader blame.
Tell me the Cause, ye Gallants of the Pit,
Did Phoebus e'er the Salique Law* admit?

—from *The Self Rival*

Dublin-born Mary Davys married well, but her husband, Reverend Peter Davys, headmaster of the free school at St. Patrick's, died in 1698 when she was but twenty-four. Without any means of support, she moved to York and tried her hand at writing. Jonathan Swift, who had been a friend of her husband's, evidently lent her a helping hand. She opened a coffeehouse in Cambridge in 1713, where she remained for the balance of her life. At forty-one she wrote her first play, *The Northern Heiress*, and took it to London, where she found a venue for it at Lincoln's

---

*Code of laws first compiled early in the sixth century by the Salians, a Frankish people. Among its civil statutes was one prohibiting daughters from inheriting land. It is this aspect of the law to which the term "Salic law" is most often applied.

Inn Fields. An intrigue comedy, it spotlights three hilarious and unique country wives who drink strong beer together. The belching, stinking, and perfectly named Lady Greasy manages to come up with the most outrageous articulations: "Love is like a bug, the longer it sticks in the skin, the harder it is to pluck out." Bursting with malapropisms, she warns her daughter's suitor "to come no more salivating [serenading] under our windows."

Davys's strength lay in her dialogue, which was always peppered with truisms about the relationship between men and women. In *The Self Rival* (1725), Mrs. Fallow remarks, "So many Men and Women go together, that, in all probability, could never have met." Quite aware of her society's narrow-minded attitude toward women writers, Davys once glibly commented that a heckling male audience member "would have shewn a greater Contempt, had he said, This is a Woman's Play, and consequently below my Resentment."[1]

In addition to her stage works, Davys wrote six novels, including the highly popular *The Reformed Coquet* (1724), a favorite throughout the eighteenth and nineteenth centuries. Of her plays Davys wrote in her collected *Works* (1: vii): "I never was so vain, as to think they deserv'd a Place in the first Rank, or so humble, as to resign them to the last."

PLAYS

The Northern Heiress, or The Humours of York, 1716; *The Self Rival*, 1725

OTHER WORKS

The Accomplished Rake, or The Modern Fine Gentleman . . . repr. 1756; *The Cousins*, 1725; *Familiar Letters Between a Gentleman and a Lady*, 1725; *The Lady's Tale*, 1725; *The Merry Wanderer*, 1725; *The Modern Poet*, 1725; *The Reformed Coquet . . .* , 1724; *Works*, 1725

1. Cotton.

Alma De Groen
(SEPTEMBER 5, 1941–   )

WAYNE. I live in a room—and it isn't home. I live on earth—and it isn't home.

—from *Rivers of China*

The societal alienation of women is thematically woven into a great many of Alma De Groen's plays. De Groen pushes the limits of the conventional narrative, and has incorporated into her plays everything from the pop cul-ture conceit of a TV game show to the transplanted mind of a literary icon. "Her best works," writes theater historian Helen Gilbert, "achieve a fluidity of form that characterizes the feminist aesthetic in its ability to break down boundaries and challenge conventional expectations."[1]

The New Zealand-born De Groen began writing for the stage in the late 1960s. Her earliest play, *The Joss Adams Show*, throws the title character into a nightmarish version of the TV game show "This is Your Life." In De Groen's version, however, the title character's husband and relatives are asked to witness and judge her life. They watch as Joss beats her baby, who eventually dies, yet they fail to comprehend her desperation and misery. The family accuses Joss, yet De Groen indicts them, the representatives of a society that cares little about women's lives and is unable to deal with violence and neglect. De Groen handles the severity of her subject matter with compassion, wit, and humor.

De Groen "frequently foregrounds art as the contested ideological space on and through which male/female conflicts are enacted. She is deeply concerned with the role of the female artist in patriarchal society."[2] This is particularly evident in *Vocations*, in which two artist couples juggle careers and relationships, as well as in *Rivers of China*, perhaps De Groen's most successful work.

Rivers tells two seemingly unrelated stories: the final months in the life of short story master Katherine Mansfield, who died of tuberculosis at the age of thirty-five, and the contemporary tale of a young male psychiatric patient in Sydney. The two lives converge when, after the young man unsuccessfully attempts suicide, his female doctor transplants Mansfield's mind into his own through hypnosis. His new world inverts Mansfield's old one—it is a world in which men have no history and few rights. "You can give anybody a history that never happened and they'll believe it," says the doctor. De Groen's point is not to advocate this reversal, but to reveal what it means to be without history.

Critics hailed *Rivers* as the "crowning glory" of Sydney theater in 1987, calling it "Innovative, thought-provoking and beautifully crafted . . . [it is] an engrossing, profound experience."[3] Paul McGillick wrote that the play came "close to achieving [De Groen's] often-stated ambition to fuse form and content—in other words, to have the audience experience directly, through the play's form, the thematic concerns of the play."[4]

De Groen was appointed writer in residence at the West Australian Institute of Technology in Perth (1986), the University of Queensland at St. Lucia (1989), and Rollins College in Florida (1989). She also served as dramaturg at the Griffin Theatre Company in Sydney (1987). Her honors and awards include a Canada Council grant (1970) and the Australian Writers Guild Award (1985). She also writes for television.

Alma De Groen
COURTESY OF THE PLAYWRIGHT

PLAYS

The After-Life of Arthur Cravan, 1973; *Chidley,* 1977; *The Girl Who Saw Everything,* 1991; *Going Home* (also teleplay, 1980), 1976; *The Joss Adams Show,* 1970; *Perfectly All Right,* 1973; *Rivers of China,* 1987; *The Sweatproof Boy,* 1972; *Vocations,* 1981

TELEVISION PLAYS

After Marcuse, 1986; *Available Light* (radio play), 1991; *Man of Letters* (adapt. of Glen Tomasatti novel), 1986

1. Essay by Helen Gilbert in Berney (2).

2. Ibid.

3. *Variety,* p. 132, 1987.

4. Essay by Paul McGillick in Hawkins-Dady (1).

Shelagh Delaney
(NOVEMBER 25, 1939–   )

HELEN. The only consolation I can find in your immediate presence is your ultimate absence.

—from *A Taste of Honey,* Act I, Scene 1

At the age of nineteen, Shelagh Delaney earned the distinction of being one of the youngest authors ever to have a hit show on the West End. *A Taste of Honey* enjoyed a long run in London before it opened to enthusiastic audiences in New York. Delaney, the undereducated daughter of a Lancashire bus driver, worked at a variety of insignificant jobs before catching a glimpse of Sir Terence Rattigan's *Variation on a Theme.* Rattigan's play changed Delaney's life, but not because she appreciated the work. Instead, convinced she could improve upon the theatrical form, Delaney transformed her in-progress novel into a play: *A Taste of Honey* was born.

Honey tells the unsentimental story of Helen and Jo, a mother/daughter team for whom there is little bond. When Helen abandons her daughter in order to marry Peter, Jo finds comfort in the arms of Jimmy, a young black sailor on a brief shore leave. Soon Jo is pregnant and trying to make ends meet. She befriends Geoff, a kind, gay art student, who becomes her platonic roommate and surrogate husband/mother: He busily prepares for the baby's arrival, knitting baby clothes, tidying up—until Helen, jilted by Peter, returns to live with Jo and Geoff, wreaking havoc on the household.

In spite of the play's grim plot, the *New York Times'* Howard Taubman called *Honey* "bittersweet, with the bitter outweighing the sweet. At its base, however, there is an unfaltering sense of the dignity of life" (October 5, 1960). Helene Keyssar believes the play recognizes "female power, particularly in contests where men attempt to exploit or demean women . . ."[1] Although *A Taste of Honey* was not roundly lauded by critics (one wrote that "Delaney . . . exhibits more generalized feeling for humanity in the aggregate than penetration of characterization individually"[2]), the New York production won a Drama Critics Circle Award. The film adaptation, written by Delaney and Tony Richardson, who also directed, won the British Film Academy Award for Best Picture.

Delaney's only other work written for the stage was *The Lion in Love*, an account of three generations of a disturbed and unhappy family. There is an ever-present contradiction that runs through the play like a mantra: at last you've arrived, one thinks; you know what you want. But when the time comes for it, one is unable to recognize or acknowledge it. The characters in *Lion* are unable to transcend the misery of their lives: "Nothing passes. Everything stays with you. Everything makes its mark," says Jesse, the grandfather. *Lion* also exposes the unfortunate truths about women's reliance on men. "Some women will have any sort of a man rather than no man at all," muses Nell, a prostitute.

Lion did not fare well with critics or audiences, and since then Delaney has focused on writing for film and television, where she has received positive accolades. The feature film *Charlie Bubbles* won a Writers' Guild Award, and *Dance with a Stranger* landed the Prix Populaire from the 1985 Cannes International Film Festival. Delaney's short stories and nonfiction have appeared in the *New York Times* and *Cosmopolitan* magazine, among others. She has adapted a couple of her television plays for stage, and has also directed for television.

Despite Delaney's depiction of women as economically dependent and male-responsive, Claude Schumacher, espousing her off-beat feminism, says, "Nevertheless, the very act of representing such lives, of celebrating the strength and endurance of these women, of declaring that such things are an appropriate subject to place centrestage, is a proto-feminist gesture."[3]

PLAYS

A Taste of Honey (also screenplay, 1962), 1958; *A Winter House*, 1986; *Dance with a Stranger*, 1985; *The Lion in Love*, 1960; *Love Lessons*, 1987; *The Raging Moon*, 1970; *The White Bus*, 1966

OTHER WORKS

Charlie Bubbles (screenplay), 1968; *Did Your Nanny Come from Bergen?* (teleplay), 1970; *Don't Worry About Matilda* (radio and teleplay, 1983), 1987; *Find Me First* (teleplay), 1981; *The House That Jack Built* (TV series, 1977), 1979; *So Does the Nightingale* (radio), 1980; *St. Martin's Summer* (teleplay), 1974; *Sweetly Sings the Donkey* (short stories), 1963

1. Keyssar.

2. *Variety*, October 12, 1960.

3. Essay by Claude Schumacher in Hawkins-Dady (2).

Jean Devanny
(1894–1962)

Paradise Flow, Jean Devanny's only extant play, depicts the sexual and political liberation of Laurel, a woman who perseveres amidst the corrupt world of the Australian sugar industry, infamous for its favoritism of landowners over migrant workers. The play conveys a strong anti-fascist message, manifested in part by its sympathetic portrayal of the workers.

The politicized theme of *Paradise Flow* complements the real-life activities of Devanny. Born and raised in New Zealand, she married a miner at the age of seventeen. Although she was aware of the injustices shouldered by men like her husband, it was not until she emigrated to Australia in 1929 and became an active member of the Communist Party that Devanny mobilized fully. She spoke on the party's behalf throughout eastern Australia and helped create several writers' groups in Sydney and Melbourne in the 1930s and 40s, including the influential Writers' League. Her involvement in the 1935 sugar strike at Innisfall, an event instigated by the hunger strike of her French contemporary Simone Weil, provided the basis of her 1936 nonfiction work *Sugar Heaven*. Devanny's affiliation with the Communist Party was not without its troubles: At one point she was asked to leave due to her alleged involvement in a sex scandal. Eventually, she was reinstated.

Although Devanny wrote prolifically during her life, most of her novels, short stories, political speeches, articles, stage plays, and screenplays have been lost. However, scholars such as Carole Ferrier, who discovered the manuscript of *Paradise Flow*, continue in their efforts to uncover Devanny's work.

PLAYS

Paradise Flow, 1938?

OTHER WORKS

The Butcher Shop (repr. 1981), 1926; *Cindie: A Chronicle of the Canefields* (repr. 1986), 1949; *Paradise Flow*, 1938; *Sugar Heaven* (repr. 1982), 1936

WORKS ABOUT

Ferrier, Carole, ed., *Point of Departure* [autobio.] (Manchester, N.H.: University of Queensland Press, 1986).

Rosalyn Drexler
(NOVEMBER 25, 1926–)

WOMAN. You want it because it's mine. . . . And you think that I belong to you too, and that's why you want me. You want me and my art reproduction. You want my art reproduction and my entire reproduction system. You hate both my systems. The HOW TO LIVE FOREVER System and the HOW TO LIVE HARMONIOUSLY AS A WOMAN system.

—from *Skywriting*

Rosalyn Drexler's Bronx childhood was filled with Marx Brothers movies (she saw them all—her father's cousin was married to Chico) and the free vaudeville skits that followed so many films in the 1930s. Not surprisingly, her own creative work has been influenced by both. As a young girl, Drexler considered herself an outsider who found solace in writing. For some time she habitually transcribed her parents' arguments; she then presented the "court record"[1] to them, which they promptly ripped up. Drexler attributes to this experience her understanding that "writing has an effect and is disposable."[2]

She opted for the school of real-life experience over a traditional education. After marrying Sherman Drexler, a painter and professor at the City University of New York, she assumed the pseudonym Rosa Carol, the Mexican Spitfire, and toured as a lady wrestler, an experience she later recounted in her semiautobiographical novel *To Smithereens*. Her musical play *Delicate Feelings* also makes

use of her wrestling escapades through the characters of two lady mud wrestlers.

After Drexler had written for fifteen years with little recognition, her first play, *Home Movies*, opened at the Judson Poets' Theater in Greenwich Village. With the support of Ellen Stewart of Café La MaMa and the help of actor Orson Bean, *Home Movies* moved to the Provincetown Playhouse, where it won a 1964 Obie for most distinguished off-Broadway play.

Home Movies exemplifies the unorthodox women who defy stereotypes so familiar in Drexler's work; for example, Vivienne, the outrageous, indecent maiden spinster, and the pusillanimous Sister Thalia, a nun who pins a platinum-blonde wig beneath her wimple. The play's "zany cabal of women"[3] presents "a grotesque fantasy of domestic life," as Guatam Dasgupta, editor of New York's *Performing Arts Journal*, put it. He praised "Drexler's anarchic use of dramatic material and her satiric pen—emphasizing puns, language and word games, and a shrewd Dadaist manipulation of meaning . . . [*Home Movies*] established her reputation as a distinct voice in the contemporary American theater."[4]

Since the mid-1960s Drexler has written more than thirty-five plays and novels. She writes speedily and does not labor over her work. Among her more notable plays are *The Writer's Opera*, for which she won an Obie in 1979; *She Who Was He*, a feminist retelling of an Egyptian legend; *Starburn*, "an interplanetary, camp, bisexual, new-wave, pornographic, S&M nostalgic musical"[5]; and the 1985 Obie-winning *Transients Welcome*, three one-act plays that, according to Jack Kroll, "constitute a triple meditation on the polluting presence of the artist. The artist pollutes reality, but reality pollutes the artist; it's a reciprocal corruption that crystallizes the flawed diamonds of consciousness."[6]

Like many of her fellow women playwrights, such as MARIA IRENE FORNES, ADRIENNE KENNEDY, MEGAN TERRY, JULIE BOVASSO, and ROCHELLE OWENS, with whom she founded the Women's Theater Council in 1972, Drexler continually addresses women's issues in her work. The feminist theater historian Helen Keyssar notes an important distinction: "Drexler, like Owens, attacks the treatment of women as objects and property, but whereas Owens's and Bovasso's women are often as remote and dissembling as are their male characters, Drexler's female characters are more frequently engaging models of a newly released strength or whimsical mouthpieces of women's wit."[7] Drexler herself has written of her (male and female) characters:

. . . none is in lifelike relation to the others; none has a history or a future or a place to go after the play is over. They have all been invented only in order to rush madly around, armed to the teeth with language and also with the capacity to be quick-change artists, con men and false prophets, wolves in sheep's clothing and the reverse, so that they might do nothing else than establish an atmosphere of freedom . . . they make up new worlds of farce whose highly serious intention, as in all true examples of the genre, is to liberate us from the way things are said to be.[8]

Drexler has also served on creative writing faculties throughout the United States. Her 1966 short story "Dear" (which she adapted for the stage in 1983) won the Paris Review Fiction Prize in 1966. She has received both Rockefeller (1965) and Guggenheim (1970–71) grants, and was a MacDowell Fellow in 1965. She wrote Lily Tomlin's 1974 TV special "The Lily Show," for which she won an Emmy. Under the pseudonym Julia Sorel, Drexler has novelized several motion pictures, including *Rocky* and *See How She Runs*. In addition to writing, painting, and sculpting, Drexler includes singing among her skills. She has performed with the jazz group Écoutez at New York's S.n.a.f.u. Finally, Drexler's life is the subject of the 1975 documentary *Who Does She Think She Is?*

Jack Kroll's remarks about *Transients Welcome* might be applied to the whole of Drexler's ouevre: "Out of these dances, dirges, and drolleries . . . Drexler makes high and sagacious comedy. She is a tough-minded poet and a total theatrician."[9]

PLAYS

The Bed Was Full, 1972; *Dear*, 1983; *Delicate Feelings*, 1984; *The Flood*, 1982; *Graven Image*, 1980; *Green River Murders*, 1986; *The Heart That Eats Itself*, 1988; *Home Movies*, 1964; *Hot Buttered Roll*, 1966; *The Ice Queen*, 1965; *The Investigation*, 1966; *Invitation*, 1971; *The Line of Least Existence*, 1968; *The Mandrake*, 1983; *Message from Garcia*, 1971; *She Who Was He*, 1973; *Skywriting*, 1968; *Softly, and Consider the Nearness*, music by Al Carmine, 1973; *Starburn*, music by Michael Meadows, 1983; *Transients Welcome* (inc. *Room 17C*, *Lobby*, and *Utopia Parkway*), 1985; *Travesty Parade*, 1974; *The Tree Artist*, 1981; *Vulgar Lives*, 1979; *Was I Good?*, 1971; *The Writer's Opera*, 1979

NOVELS

Alex: Portrait of a Teenage Prostitute, 1977; *Bad Guy*, 1982; *The Cosmopolitan Girl*, 1974; *I am the Beautiful Stranger*, 1965; *One or Another*, 1970; *PD MAR*, 1976; *Starburn*, 1977; *To Smithereens*, 1972

WORKS ABOUT

Gilman, Richard, intro. *The Line of Least Existence and Other Plays* (collec.), 1967; Drexler, Rosalyn, *Rosalyn*

Drexler (autobio.), 1986; *Who Does She Think She Is?* (film bio.), 1975

1. Quoted in eassy by Carolyn Karis in Robinson.
2. *New York Times*, February 27, 1975.
3. Gilman, Richard, *The Line of Least Existence and Other Plays* (New York: Random House, 1967).
4. Essay by Guatam Dasgupta in Hochman.
5. Review by Eileen Blumenthal, *The Village Voice*, March 8, 1983.
6. Preface to *Transients Welcome* by Jack Kroll.
7. Keyssar.
8. Op. cit., Gilman.
9. Op. cit., *Transients*.

Maureen Duffy
(OCTOBER 21, 1933–   )

ADA. Bastard men! Get a man she says. I'll get him right where I want him.

—from *Rites*

Although Maureen Duffy is recognized primarily as a novelist, her lesser-known stage dramas are sophisticated, intelligent works. She frequently borrows from Greek myths for her plays' construction. The farcical *Rites*, first performed in 1969 by the experimental program at London's National Theatre, remodels the myth of the Bacchae in order to illustrate the religious-like rituals that occur in women's washrooms: "purging, washing up, combing, making-up."[1] The play "attempts to move women and men too, away from easy slogans and self-righteous separatism, while simultaneously achieving a respect for communities of women and their need to escape victimization."[2] *Solo* also takes place in a lavatory; its central character is a man who reflects upon his mirrored image. *Olde Tyme* uses the tale of the castration of Uranus to spark a story about a maniacal television tycoon who controls his employees under a cruel thumb.

Not all Duffy's plays are conceived from Greek and Roman mythology. *The Silk Room* follows the rise and fall of a popular musical group and *A Nightingale in Bloomsbury Square* journeys into the complex mind of Virginia Woolf.

Frank Marcus asserts that Duffy's plays are not "easy . . . [They are] densely written, pitched between fantasy and realism, and have allegorical undertones." Like her poetry, Duffy's plays demonstrate her preference for high theatrics, making use of song, dance, and masked actors. Marcus calls Duffy "a writer of fierce originality and imaginative depth . . ."[3]

Born in Worthing, Sussex, Duffy received her B. A. in English with honors at King's College in London. A social and literary activist, she confounded the Writers Action Group in 1972 and served as vice president of Beauty Without Cruelty. She has also been the fiction editor of *Critical Quarterly* (1987) and edited several books on APHRA BEHN, among others. In 1962 Duffy received the City of London Festival Playwright's Prize and, in 1985, was made a Fellow of the Royal Society of Literature.

PLAYS

A Nightingale in Bloomsbury Square, 1973; *Josie* (teleplay), 1961; *The Lay-Off*, 1962; *Olde Tyme*, 1970; *Only Goodnight* (radio play), 1981; *Rites*, 1969; *The Silk Room*, 1966; *Solo*, 1970

NOVELS AND OTHER WORKS (SELECTED)

Actaeon (verse), 1973; *Capital*, 1975; *Change*, 1987; *Collected Poems*, 1985; *The Erotic World of Faery*, 1972; *Gor Saga*, 1981; *Illuminations*, 1991; *Inherit the Earth: A Social History*, 1980; *Love Child*, 1971; *Lyrics for the Dog Hour* (verse), 1968; *Men and Beasts: An Animal Rights Handbook*, 1984; *The Passionate Shepherdess: Aphra Behn 1640–1689*, 1977; *The Single Eye*, 1964; *That's How it Was*, 1962

1. Keyssar.
2. Ibid.
3. Essay by Frank Marcus in Berney (2).

Daphne du Maurier
(MAY 13, 1907–APRIL 19, 1989)

MRS. DANVERS. Why don't you go? Why don't you leave Manderley? He doesn't need you. He's got his memories. He doesn't love you. He wants to be alone again, with her. You've nothing to stay for. You've nothing to live for, really, have you? (*Pointing to the sea, several stories below.*) Look down there. It's easy, isn't it? Why don't you, why don't you . . . Go on, go on, don't be afraid . . .

—from *Rebecca*

Before Alfred Hitchcock shocked audiences with shower curtains, he got his feet wet adapting Daphne du Maurier novels for the big screen. The modern gothic sensibilities of *Rebecca* and *Jamaica Inn* aptly primed the master of suspense for his later films.

Du Maurier inherited her literary genes from her grandfather, the artist and writer George du Maurier, and her love for drama from her actor parents, Sir Gerald du Maurier (who was also a successful manager) and Muriel Beaumont. The middle child of three girls, du Maurier enjoyed a privileged childhood. Her first flush of success arrived with the publication of some of her short stories when she was but twenty-one. A few years later she married Sir Frederick Arthur Montague Browning, a Lieutenant-General in the Royal Armed Forces, in 1932.

Rebecca, perhaps du Maurier's best-known novel and winner of the National Book Award, was published in 1938; her popular stage adaptation premiered at the Queens Theatre in London on April 5, 1940. *Rebecca's* heroine is the unnamed, shy second wife of the handsome sophisticate Maxim de Winter. When he takes her home to his imposing country estate, Manderley, she is confronted by the omnipresence of Maxim's dead first wife, Rebecca, and her sinister housekeeper, Mrs. Danvers, whose obsession with the memory and possessions of her deceased mistress terrify the timid heroine.

Despite the success *Rebecca* enjoyed on stage, du Maurier wrote few other plays; instead, she concentrated on novels, several of which have been adapted for film. In addition to *Rebecca* and *Jamaica Inn*, there are screen versions of *My Cousin Rachel* (featuring Richard Burton in his American debut), *Frenchman's Creek*, *Hungry Hill*, *Don't Look Now*, and Hitchcock's interpretive variation of her short story "The Birds."

Du Maurier also wrote biographies of the Brontës and of Sir Francis Bacon. In 1969 she was made a Dame of the Order of the British Empire. Whether writing for stage or print, du Maurier's sophisticated style of storytelling offers an often spellbinding psychological exploration of complicated human emotion.

PLAYS

Rebecca (novel, 1938; screenplay), 1940; *September Tide*, 1948; *The Years Between*, 1945

NOVELS (SELECTED)

The Apple Tree (short stories), 1952; *Don't Look Now* (also film, 1973), 1970; *Frenchman's Creek* (also film), 1941; *The Glassblowers*, 1963; *Happy Christmas*, 1940; *Hungry Hill* (also film), 1943; *I'll Never Be Young Again*, 1932; *Jamaica Inn* (also film), 1936; *The King's General*, 1946; *The Loving Spirit*, 1931; *Mary Anne*, 1954; *My Cousin Rachel* (also film, 1952), 1951; *The Parasites*, 1949; *The Progress of Julius*, 1933; *Queen's April*, 1940; *The Scapegoat*, 1975

OTHER WORKS

The du Mauriers (history of her family), 1937; *Gerald: a Portrait* (bio. of her father), 1935; *Growing Pains* (autobio.), 1977; *Myself When Young: The Shaping of a Writer*, 1977; *The Rebecca Notebook and Other Memories*, 1981

Andrea Dunbar
(MAY 22, 1961–1991)

GIRL. It's not that I don't like you. I just want to be alone.
SAM. How long for? How long do you need?
GIRL. It could be a week, it could be a month, I don't know, it could be longer. I just couldn't say at this time.
SAM. But why do you need so long?
GIRL. I need that time. I gotta have it. And I'm going to get it at all costs.

—from *The Arbor*, Act II, Scene 8

Although she wrote only three plays during her short life, Andrea Dunbar's work shed new light on the difficult lives of British working-class women, using her home turf of the Bradford area near Yorkshire as her setting. Actress, writer, and director Carole Hayman alleges, "Her plays, not so much slices as hacksaw chunks, expose rough life where family violence is the norm, drinking and fighting the main entertainments, and you're the odd one out if you haven't been sexually abused by the time you are twelve."[1]

Her first play, *The Arbor*, chronicles the experiences of a pregnant teenager. Dunbar portrays the girl's bleak home life with her abusive father and ineffectual mother. When the girl is sent to a home for unmarried mothers, her inability to connect emotionally to the authorities there illustrates the extent of her psychological damage, and reveals the void that separates those who have and have not. Dunbar was fifteen years old when she wrote *The Arbor*, which was first performed at the Royal Court Theatre in 1981; the play won her the George Devine Award.

Dunbar's other works delve into similarly difficult territory. The ménage à trois of *Rita, Sue, and Bob Too* betrays the relentless hunger for sex, booze, and violence among the powerless and unemployed. *Shirley* depicts a mother and daughter, each struggling to contain her uncontrolled fury in order to find some peaceful territory in their relationship. Hayman observes that Dunbar's women "rise to challenge the terms of their existence and express their anarchy. [They are] a band of bloodied but unbowed women whose raw existence is supported, not by the men in their lives, but by the offer of survival techniques from other women . . ."[2]

Before her untimely death at age thirty, Dunbar bore three children and saw all of her work produced, as well as a quirky film version of *Rita, Sue, and Bob Too*.

PLAYS

The Arbor, 1980; *Rita, Sue, and Bob Too* (also film, 1988), 1982; *Shirley*, 1986

1. Essay by Carole Hayman in Berney (2).
2. Ibid.

Nell Dunn
(1936–   )

JOSIE. He made me wild last night, we was having it and I was really getting into it and enjoying it, when he's come. "Hold up!" I says, "What about me?" Well, after that I made him plate me for an hour till I come, every time he lifts his head I push it back down—I wouldn't even let him up to breathe . . . I can feel it from the bottom of my toes to the top of my skull. It's as if something pealed right through my body . . . I hadn't come like that for months. It did me the world of good.

—from *Steaming*, Scene 1

Even though the London born, convent-educated playwright Nell Dunn hails from a secure, middle-class background, her literary works have consistently focused on the experiences of women from lower social status who exist "without the safety net of money or education."[1] She spent the first half of her adult life raising three sons from her 1956 marriage to writer Jeremy Sandford, which did not last, and penning several novels and stories. Then, in 1981, her controversial drama, *Steaming*, exploded on the London theater scene, and Dunn's career as a playwright took off.

Steaming features six women who meet regularly for conversation and escape at a Turkish steam bath. Together they compose a cross section of the British social structure. Nancy and Jane find the bathhouse a perfect haven for their lapsed friendship, which was fractured by class structure after their marriages. Mrs. Meadow and her strange daughter, Dawn, retreat, albeit briefly, from their penurious existence. All are entertained by the foul-mouthed Josie, a lower-class woman who loves to brag and shock her cohorts with tales of her sexual exploits and fantasies. Yet the play pivots around Violet, the bathhouse's custodian, who acts as a catalyst for the other characters' self-growth when her announcement that the baths may close due to a lack of public funding galvanizes the group. Critical response to *Steaming* varied greatly. Frank Rich of the *New York Times* wrote that it was "sharp, pointed, and witty."[2] But *Village Voice* critic Jan Hoffman remarked that, while she admired a play that focused on female bonding, the nudity seemed exploitative: "What I do find offensive about *Steaming* is its mush-headed assumption that feminism can triumph over class lines at the drop of a towel."[3] Ultimately, Dunn won over her detractors. *Steaming* was awarded the coveted Susan Smith Blackburn Prize, the Evening Standard Award, and the Society of West End Theatre Award.

I Want wraps itself around a sixty-year love affair that began between a young Liverpudlian scholar and a proper, convent-educated girl who share a love of poetry, their passion for one another, and little else. The inevitable separation of their classes is an obstacle they manage to surmount with a constant flow of letters and postcards and occasional trysts. While critic John Conner called it "a love story of great depth,"[4] Nicholas de Jongh found it pretentious and tiresome.[5]

One of Dunn's more recent works, *The Little Heroine* (1988), delves into a somewhat different territory: parenthood and drug addiction. After suffering through a painful divorce and receiving word that her thirteen-year-old son has been diagnosed with diabetes, Imogen, the play's protagonist, gravitates toward heroin. In the end, it is Tom, the son, who helps his mother relocate her sense of self.

In addition to writing prolifically, Dunn, an active grandmother, has also worked as a literary editor.

PLAYS

Every Breath You Take (teleplay), 1988; *I Want* (also novel, 1972), w/Adrian Henri, 1983; *The Little Heroine*, 1988; *Steaming*, 1981; *Variety Night* (w/others), 1982

OTHER WORKS

Every Breath You Take (teleplay), 1988; *Freddy Gets Married* (for children), 1969; *Grandmothers* (interviews), 1991; *The Incurable* (novel), 1971; *Living Like I Do*, ed. (a.k.a. *Different Drummers*), 1977; *The Only Child* (novel), 1978; *Talking to Women* (interviews), 1965; *Up the Junction* (short stories; also teleplay, 1965), 1963

NOVELS

The Incurable, 1971; *The Only Child: A Simple Story of Heaven and Hell*, 1978; *Poor Cow* (also film w/Ken Loach, 1967), 1967; *Tear His Head off His Shoulders*, 1974

1. Essay by Clare Colvin in Berney (1).
2. *New York Times*, December 13, 1982, p. C16.
3. *Village Voice*, September 26, 1982, p. 120.
4. *City Limits*, London, November 11, 1986.
5. *The Guardian*, London, November 14, 1986.

Marguerite Duras
(APRIL 4, 1914–1996)

CLAIRE. I am not intelligent enough for the intelligence within me.

—from *The Lovers of Viorne*

From the mid-1940s on, Marguerite Duras created a unique type of fiction, drama, and film that defied categorization. She rejected linear narratives, favoring instead a poetic mosaic composed of memory, landscape, emotion, and character. "Duras undertakes nothing less than to establish a new type of communication between people," wrote theater historian Claire Brandicourt Saint-Léon. "She refuses any complicity with the reader or spectator; she refuses to catalog things, to allow the audience to take anything for granted. Duras seeks instead 'a collective conspiracy' in order to come closer to reality. In the process, a comfortable sense of clear meaning is sacrificed. 'Clarity is a disease of the French,' says Duras. 'They believe in it, it is everywhere!' With complex and subtle narrative techniques, Duras attempts to destroy memory, culture, clarity, to arrive at a *tabula rasa* on which to build. She is moving toward greater sobriety and complexity."[1]

Not coincidentally, Duras's work reflects both Eastern and Western influences. She was born Marguerite Donnadieu in Giadinh, Indochina (now Saigon, Vietnam), where she lived for eighteen years. Her father died when she was four years old, and her mother, distracted by the needs of her four young children, allegedly forgot to send Marguerite to school for two years. Duras claims this period of her life as the closest she has come to "complete happiness."[2]

In 1932 Duras moved to Paris to study at the Sorbonne, where she earned degrees in both law and political science. At the time she completed her university studies, France was heating up with anticipation of World War II. Duras took a secretarial post with the Ministry of Colonial Affairs, joined the Communist Party, and reportedly aided the French Resistance. Just as she became disillusioned with communism for "the intrusion of political commitment into literary creation,"[3] her underground activism was discovered, and she was briefly deported to Germany.

Upon returning to France, Duras assumed her pen name (taken from a French village where her family once owned property) and began working as a crime reporter. Soon she turned to writing fiction, finally garnering attention for her 1950 novel *Un barrage contre le Pacifique* (known as both *The Sea Wall* and *Dam Against the Pacific*). After establishing herself as an important writer, Duras broadened her creative scope. Her screenplay for the semiautobiographical *Hiroshima, mon amour*, directed by Alain Resnais, brought her international fame. In 1960 her first play, *Les viaducs de la Siene-et-Oise*, was staged; in 1966 she wrote and directed her first film, an adaptation of her play *La Musica*, a somber tale of a recently divorced couple who, at a chance meeting in a dismal hotel, discover their mutual understanding too late.

Duras dramatized many of her novels, including *Le square* (The Square), a *Godot*-like drama that pits an old live-for-the-moment peddler against a young servant girl who is waiting for something meaningful to happen to her: Their dialogue illustrates a total failure in understanding; *L'amant Anglaise* (The Lovers of Viorne), an intense psychological thriller about a murder in a French village that spins a mesmerizing study of the mysteries of the mind; and Duras's only comic play, *Les eaux et forêt* (The Rivers and the Forest), which challenges the audience's notions about identity, truth, and communication with its barrage of constantly changing, Eugene Ionesco-like characters.

Several of Duras's books and films were awarded prestigious honors: *La femme du Gange,* the film adaptation of her play *India Song,* won the 1973 Prix Jean Cocteau, and *L'amant Anglaise* won the Grand Prix and Académie du Cinema awards. Duras also received the Prix Goncourt (1984) and the Ritz Paris Hemingway Award (1986).

Duras reportedly married twice, first to writer Robert Antelme, then to political philosopher and critic Dionys Moscolo, the father of her only son; however, these liaisons might not have been sanctioned by the laws of the land. Her final years were divided between her apartment in Paris on the Left Bank and her farm house in Heauphle-le-Château, which she shared with writer Yann Andrea. She did not like being categorized; while she was politically committed to individual causes and certainly addressed the problem of feminine identity in many of her works, she did not like being called a feminist and joined no political party after her break with the French communists.

Influenced by modern American literature, particularly the works of Ernest Hemingway and John Steinbeck, some have compared Duras to Harold Pinter and Samuel Beckett. Despite her worldwide recognition, the experimental nature of Duras's work does not always bode well with audiences. While some, such as reviewer Hedy Weiss, believe "[Duras] opens many of the [mind's] shutters that often keep the interior universe in total eclipse"[4]; others find her static approach utterly boring and mystifying.

PLAYS

Abahn-Sabdna David, 1976; *Ah! Ernesto,* 1971; *Aurélia Steiner, Aurélia Steiner, Aurélia Steiner,* 1979; *L'amant Anglaise* (a.k.a., *A Place Without Doors,* 1970, *Lovers of Viorne,* 1971; novel, 1984; screenplay, 1992), 1969; *Le bête dans la jungle* (The Beast in the Jungle), w/James Lord, 1962; *Des journées entières dans les arbres* (Entire Days in the Trees), 1965; *Les eaux et forêts,* 1965; *L'Eden Cinéma,* 1977; *Home,* adapt. from David Storey, 1972; *L'homme assis dans le couloir* (The man seated in the corridor), 1980; *Un homme est venue me voir* (A man came to see me), 1968; *India Song,* 1973; *La maladie de la mort* (The sickness of death), 1983; *Miracle en Alabama,* w/Gérard

Jarlot, 1961; *La musica* (The Music; screenplay, 1966), 1967; *Le navire night,* 1979; *Le square,* 1956 or 1965?; *Suzanna Andler,* 1969; *Les viaducs de la Seine-et-Oise* (The viaducts of Seine-et-Oise, a.k.a. *The Viaduct*), 1960

SCREEN- AND TELEPLAYS (SELECTED)

C'est tout, 1995; *Ce que savait Morgan* (What Morgan Knew), 1974; *Des journées entieres dans les arbres* (short stories, 1954), 1976; *Les enfants,* 1984; *La femme du Gange* (The Ganges Woman), 1973; *Hiroshima, mon amour,* 1959; *L'homme assis dans le couloir,* 1980; *India Song,* 1975; *Nathalie Granger,* 1973; *Nuit noire, Calcutta,* 1964; *Les rideaux blancs* (The White Curtains), 1966; *The Sailor from Gibraltar* (*Le marin de Gibraltar,* novel, 1952), 1967; *10:30 P.M. Summer* (novel, *Dix heures et demie du soir en été,* 1960), 1966; *Un barrage contre le Pacifique* (novel, 1950; a.k.a. Dam Against the Pacific; This Angry Age, screenplay), 1958; *Une aussie longue absence* (A Long Absence, w/Gérard Jarlot, novel), 1961

FICTION (SELECTED)

L'après-midi de Monsieur Andesmas, 1960; *Les impudents,* 1943; *The Malady of Death,* 1986; *Moderato cantabile,* 1958 (also screenplay, 1960); *Les parleuses,* 1974; *Les petits chevaux de Tarquinia* (The Little Horses of Tarquinia, 1960), 1953; *La ravissement de Lol V. Stein,* 1964; *Le square* (The Square, 1959), 1954; *Summer Rain,* 1992; *Le vice-consul* (The Vice-Consul, 1968), 1966; *La vie tranquille,* 1944; *The War: A Memoir,* 1994; *Woman to Woman,* 1987; *Yann Andrea Steiner: A Memoir,* 1993

WORKS ABOUT

Cohen, Susan D., *Women and Discourse in the Fiction of Marguerite Duras: Love, Legends, Language,* 1993; Cranston, Mechthild, *Beyond the Book Marguerite Duras: Infans,* 1996; Duras, Marguerite, *Marguerite Duras,* 1987; Glassman, Deborah N., *Marguerite Duras: Fascinating Vision and Narrative Cure,* 1991; Hill, Leslie, *Marguerite Duras: Apocalyptic Desires,* 1993; Hoffman, Carol, *Forgetting and Marguerite Duras,* 1991; Vircondelet, Alain, *Duras: A biography,* Thomas Buckley, tr., 1994; Williams, James S. *The Erotics of Passage: Pleasure, Politics, and Form in the Later Work of Marguerite Duras,* 1997

1. "Marguerite Duras" by Claire Brandicourt Saint-Léon, in Magill.

2. Moritz, 1985.

3. Ibid.

4. Weiss, Hedy, "Interplay Unpeels Layers of Murder," *Chicago Sun-Times,* October 3, 1990, p. 53.

Bilgesu Erenus
(1943–   )

Turkish playwright Erenus's works focus on ordinary people who yearn for the better things in life, but are trapped by their social status and left stranded in the materialistic world in which they must survive. In *Ortak* (The Partner; 1975), for example, Erenus dramatizes the Walter Mitty-like fantasies of a street vendor who longs to become a partner in the corporate offices that rise above the street where he peddles his wares. Ultimately, the penurious merchant realizes that only his own social class can offer him the sense of community and belonging which he desires.

Considered one of Erenus's best plays, *Ikili oyun* (Twosome Play; 1977) portrays a married couple taking a long-awaited vacation. They camp in the country and play intellectual games to pass the time; the games reveal the underpinnings of many social and economic problems in Turkey.

Educated at the Institute of Journalism of Istanbul University, Erenus began her career as a radio scriptwriter and producer.

PLAYS

El kapisi (Slaving for Foreigners), 1972; *Ikili oyun* (Twosome Play), 1977; *Nereye Payidar?* (Where to, Payidar?), 1976; *Ortak* (The Partner), 1975; *Qasidah* (Kaside), 1979

Michèle Fabien
(FL. 1970)

JOCASTA. One does not gaze upon one's mother when she is a woman. One does not gaze upon a woman when she is one's mother.

—from *Jocasta*, Scene 5

Born in Genk and educated at the University of Liège, where she received a doctorate in philosophy and literature, Fabien has been the dramaturg of the Ensemble Théâtral Mobile since 1974. She has adapted works by Henrik Ibsen, MARGUERITE DURAS, and Christa Wolf for the French stage. She has also translated Pier Paolo Pasolini's *Affabulazione* and published many scholarly articles on theater. Her first play, *Notre Sade*, received the Prix Triennal de Littérature Dramatique in 1987.

In *Jocasta*, Fabien returns to ancient Thebes to give us the unique angle of Jocasta's vision of her tragic destiny. We hear the mother and wife of Oedipus speak in horror and anguish as she vividly recalls her relationship with her son. At the same time familiar and original, the recounting of this ancient tale as seen from the mother's point of view is full of pulsating sexuality and horror. All along Jocasta's imminent death hovers over each of the play's five scenes. She wants to die, yet she is so full of life, one would like to take her away where she can rest and be safe.

PLAYS

Claire Lacombe, 1989; *Jocasta* (Richard Miller, tr.), 1981; *Notre Sade*, 1978; *Plautus, Titus Maccius*, 1992; *Sara Z.*, 1982; *Tausk*, 1985

Abla Farhoud
(1945–)

AMIRA. In the village, there was a woman who could take anything . . . poverty, misery, anything. She'd raised about ten kids. She took everything as it came, never complained. She didn't even mind being beaten. She just smiled. But one day, a day like any other when her husband was about to beat her, she snuck into the kitchen and grabbed a butcher knife. She looked her husband straight in the eye and said, "No, not one more time, not ever again."

—from *The Girls from the Five and Ten*

Abla Farhoud's *The Girls from the Five and Ten* depicts the unhappy lives of two Lebanese émigré sisters, Amira and Kaokab, who are virtually imprisoned in their father's Montreal, Canada, convenience store. Although their family lives comfortably, the girls are expected to work incessantly for their father, until they marry and work incessantly for their husbands. *Five and Ten* reveals the sexism ingrained in the family's culture: The working sisters are overlooked by their father, who focuses his attentions on his only son. The extreme cruelty Amira and Kaokab suffer provokes the girls to act violently: They burn the shop, a decision that results in a deadly consequence.

Farhoud's own family emigrated from a small Lebanese village to Canada in 1951. Her penchant for the theater brought her to the stage when she was seventeen. She returned to Lebanon in 1965, but left four years later to study theater at the University of Paris VIII. In France Farhoud worked with director Jorge Lavelli.

Farhoud reemerged in Quebec in the early 1970s. After her two children were born, she earned an M.F.A. in theater arts at the University of Quebec in Montreal. Currently Farhoud teaches and directs at the University of Montreal.

PLAYS

La camisole rouge, 199?; *Game of Patience* (Jill MacDougal, tr.), n.d.; *The Girls from the Five and Ten* (Jill MacDougall tr.), 1986; *Quand j'étais grande* (Jill MacDougall, tr.), 1983

Edna Ferber
(AUGUST 15, 1885–APRIL 16, 1968)

KITTY (a social climber). I was reading a book the other day . . . It's all about civilization or something. A nutty kind of a book. Do you know that the guy said that machinery is going to take the place of every profession?
CARLOTTA (a former stage star). Oh my dear. That's something you need never worry about.

—from *Dinner at Eight*

Edna Ferber claims literature as the stalwart pillar of her childhood. Ferber's diet of one book a day nourished her in her early years while her family moved in and out of sundry Midwestern towns, where they sometimes suffered anti-Semitic treatment, and during her adolescence, when her Hungarian immigrant father went blind and her mother assumed responsibility for her parents' shop. Her mother, a strong-willed woman born and raised in Milwaukee, was one of four women who were major influences in Ferber's growth, along with social reformers Jane Addams, Ida Tarbell, and Lillian Adler. Her maternal grandfather exerted his influence as well; he enjoyed family theatrics and encouraged the pastime so much that Ferber acted in school plays and went to see shows whenever she could. Her father died when she was in her early twenties. When the time came for Ferber to choose a career, her years of consuming the works of George Eliot, Charles Dickens, and Mark Twain had made their impact: she opted for the world of letters.

Initially she found employment as the first female reporter for the *Appleton Daily Crescent*, but was ousted by a new city editor who insisted on replacing her with a man. She joined the staff of the *Milwaukee Journal*, writing police reports and celebrity interviews. Ferber might have had a long, illustrious career as a journalist, but an illness forced her to return home in 1909, and she discovered her talent for writing fiction.

Soon Ferber transformed her previous practice of reading a book a day into publishing a book a year. In 1915 she collaborated with George V. Hobart on her first play, *Our Mrs. McChesney*, a stage adaptation of her book *Emma McChesney and Co*. However, Ferber did not gain serious recognition as a playwright until she began collaborating with George S. Kaufman in the mid-1920s. The two began their partnership with *Minick*, based on one of her short stories. In 1932 Ferber and Kaufman's *Dinner at Eight* became a favorite with audiences.

The play centers around a flighty, self-absorbed socialite who decides to give a formal dinner party for an aristocratic British couple. She obsesses over the details of the fete, preoccupied with her social image rather than the travails of her exhausted husband, who suffers from a weak heart and potential financial ruin. Ferber and Kaufman followed *Dinner at Eight* with *Stage Door* (1936), one of the flashiest, quickest-paced comedies of the decade. *Stage Door* focuses on a diverse group of young actresses who live in a New York boardinghouse. Their dreams of success are rendered with thrilling, heartbreaking, and comic aplomb while the women interact with, among other characters, a ridiculously regal old actress who coaches them and a producer with a roving eye. It was successfully adapted to a film, in which Katharine Hepburn took on the role Margaret Sullavan had portrayed on Broadway. Impressions of Hepburn speaking the line, "The calla lilies are in bloom again," which is spoken in the play-within-the-play, have been rampant for years.

The popular *The Royal Family* (also made into a successful film) told the story of a Barrymore-like theatrical family torn by the conflict between show business tradition and "normal" private life. As with most of the Ferber/Kaufman plays, she provided the basis for plot and character, while he supplied the dialogue and stage craft.

Throughout her collaboration with Kaufman, Ferber continued to publish novels and stories, many of which became successful films, most notably *Giant* (1952), *Show Boat* (1926), and *So Big* (1925), which won her the Pulitzer Prize for fiction. Like the works of her contemporaries ANITA LOOS, ZOË AKINS, and MAE WEST, Edna Ferber's early plays were produced at a time when women playwrights on the American stage were an uncommon phenomenon. She never married and, with one exception, never wrote alone, but always in collaboration with men. She was eighty-three when she died of cancer.

PLAYS

Bravo!, w/George S. Kaufman, 1948; *Dinner at Eight* (also film, 1933), w/G. S. K., 1932; *The Eldest*, 1924; *The Land Is Bright*, w/G. S. K., 1941; *Minick* (also film), w/ G. S. K., 1924; *Our Mrs. McChesney*, w/George V. Hobart, 1905; *The Royal Family* (also film, 1930), w/ G. S. K., 1927; *$1200 a Year*, w/Newman Levy, 1920; *Stage Door* (also film, 1937), w/G. S. K., 1936

OTHER WORKS (SELECTED)

Buttered Side Down, 1912; *Cimarron* (also film, 1931, 1961), 1930; *Come and Get It* (also film, 1936), n.d.;

Emma McChesney and Co., 1915; *Fanny Herself* (also film, 1921); *Giant* (also film, 1956), 1952; *Gigolo* (short stories; also film, 1926), n.d.; *Ice Palace* (also film, 1960), 1958; *Mother Knows Best* (also film, 1928), n.d.; *Personality Plus*, 1914; *Roast Beef Medium*, 1913; *Saratoga Trunk* (also film, 1945; staged as musical *Saratoga*, 1959), 1941; *Show Boat* (also films, 1929, 1936, 1951; adapted for stage, 1926), 1926; *So Big* (also films, 1925, 1932, 1953; adapted for stage, 1924), 1924

WORKS ABOUT

Gilbert, Julie Goldsmith, *Ferber, A Biography*, 1978

Dorothy Fields
(JULY 15, 1905–MARCH 28, 1974)

SISSY (singing). Obviously, love is an old established track.
Ten million suckers walk the plank.
If you land on your tail
Every time that you fall
There must be a reason for it all.
Love is the reason for it all.

—from *A Tree Grows in Brooklyn*

Dorothy Fields
COURTESY OF THE BILLY ROSE THEATRE COLLECTION

Dorothy Fields's father, Lewis Maurice Schoenfeld, better known as comic Lew Fields of vaudeville's Weber and Fields, cautioned his children against a life in show business. A second-generation Polish immigrant with little formal education, he encouraged his kids to set their sights on more "respectable" careers. Fortunately for audiences everywhere, three of the four Fields children ignored their father's warnings and pursued their dreams of lives in the theater. Dorothy's brothers, Joseph and Herbert, wrote plays, and she, after a brief stint as a poet, established herself as a gifted lyricist and librettist.

While working for the Mills Music Company in the mid-1920s, Fields met composer Jimmy McHugh. Their eight-year collaboration started when they began creating material for performers at Harlem's renowned Cotton Club. Soon they were generating such hits as "Diga-Diga-Doo" and "I Can't Give You Anything But Love." In 1930 Fields's song lyrics for the Broadway production of *The International Revue*, "Exactly Like You" and "On the Sunny Side of the Street," sung by Gertrude Lawrence and Harry Richman, furthered her reputation.

After Fields and her first husband, J. J. Weiner, divorced in 1932, she relocated to Hollywood, where she and McHugh focused their considerable talents on screen musicals. Together they produced memorable songs for forgettable films, notably "Don't Blame Me," "I Feel a Song Comin' On," and "I'm in the Mood for Love." Fields also collaborated with Max Stein and Jerome Kern, with whom she wrote "The Way You Look Tonight" for the film *Swing Time*; it won her an Oscar in 1936 for Best Song.

She returned to New York in the late 1930s, married dress manufacturer, Eli Lahm with whom she had two children, and began two other important partnerships. The first, with Arthur Schwartz, produced material for *Stars in Your Eyes* (score, 1939), *A Tree Grows in Brooklyn* (lyrics, 1951), and *By the Beautiful Sea* (libretto and lyrics, 1954). The second, with her brother Herbert, resulted in the libretto for the beloved musical *Annie Get Your Gun*, for which Irving Berlin wrote the music. The sister-brother team of Fields and Fields eventually created librettos for eight musicals.

Fields's work suggests she took a special interest in the stories of courageous young women who often persevered in spite of their unfortunate childhoods and circumstances, as evidenced by *Annie Get Your Gun, Redhead, A Tree Grows in Brooklyn,* and *Sweet Charity*, adapted from the 1957 film *Nights of Cabiria*, Fellini's bittersweet tale of the proverbial prostitute with a heart of gold: The musical, later made into a film, featured the hit songs "Big Spender" and "If They Could See Me Now." Fields was expert at "delineating character in lyric form," as Dwight B. Bowers has put it.[1] Her ability to use everyday speech set to music, juxtaposed in such a way as to make it captivating and memorable, is what catapulted her to fame's door.

Her husband died in 1958, and Fields never married again. When she died from a heart attack, just shy of her seventieth birthday, she left a number of unfinished projects. Ultimately she wrote musical scores for thirteen Broadway shows, more than 500 songs for film and TV, and a number of libretti and screenplays. She was the first female lyricist to receive on Oscar (1936), an Antoinette Perry Award (1959), and membership in the Songwriters Hall of Fame (1971). In the film *Stage Door Canteen* (1943), Fields appears as herself.

PLAYS

Annie Get Your Gun, w/Herbert Fields (libretto; music & lyrics by Irving Berlin; book by Betty Smith and George Abbott; also film, 1950), 1946; *Arms and the Girl*, w/Morton Gould (colibrettist & lyricist), 1950; *Blackbirds of 1928*, with Jimmy McHugh, 1927; *By the Beautiful Sea*, w/A. S. (libretto & lyrics), 1954; *Hello, Daddy*, w/H. F., 1928; *The International Revue* (lyrics), 1930; *Let's Face It!*, w/H. F. (libretto; film, 1943), 1941; *Mexican Hayride*, w/ H. F. (libretto; film, 1948), 1944; *Redhead*, w/Albert Hague (libretto & lyrics), 1959; *Roberta*, w/Jerome Kern (lyrics for screenplay), 1935; *Seesaw*, w/Cy Coleman (lyrics), 1973; *Something for the Boys*, w/H. F. (libretto), 1943; *Stars in Your Eyes*, w/A. S. (score), 1939; *Sweet Charity*, w/ C. C. (book & lyrics; film, 1969), 1966; *A Tree Grows in Brooklyn*, w/Arthur Schwartz (lyrics), 1951; *Up in Central Park*, w/Sigmund Romberg (libretto & lyrics; film, 1948), 1945; *The Vanderbilt Revue* (lyrics), 1930

FILMS (SELECTED)

Dance, Fools, Dance (song composer, librettist), 1931; *Dancing Lady* (song composer, librettist), 1933; *Every Night at Eight* (song composer, librettist) 1951; *The Farmer Takes a Wife* (song composer, librettist), 1953; *Father Takes a Wife* (coscreenwriter), 1941; *Hooray for Love* (song composer, librettist), 1935; *The Joy of Living*, w/Jerome Kern (lyrics & coauthor of screenplay), 1936; *Lovely to Look At* (song composer, librettist), 1952; *Meet the Baron* (song composer, librettist), 1933; *One Night in the Tropics* (song composer, librettist), 1940; *Swing Time*, w/Jerome Kern (song composer, librettist), 1936; *Texas Carnival* (song composer, librettist), 1951; *When You're in Love* (song composer, librettist), 1937

1. Essay by Dwight B. Bowers in Robinson.

Anne Kingsmill Finch
(1661–1720)

INTRODUCTORY VERSE. Alas! a woman that attempts the pen,
Such an intruder on the rights of men,
Such a presumptuous Creature, is esteem'd
The fault, can by no vertue be redeem'd.

—from *Poems*

Anne Finch, under the pen name Ardelia, wrote two of the finer tragedies of her day, according to Nancy Cotton, as well as various odes, fables, songs, and verse. Nevertheless, she often belittled herself for writing at all, so torn was she between the desire to write and the social expectation that she practice only domestic arts. Her inner turmoil took its toll: Along with her constant self-deprecation, she suffered from insomnia, depression, and panic attacks. "A woman's way to charm is not by writing," she wrote in *Miscellany Poems on Several Occasions*.

She married Heneage Finch, a titled army officer (the son of Lord Winchilsea), in the mid-1680s. He was a great supporter of her work and became a noted antiquarian himself. In her poetry collection, Finch describes Heneage as the "much lov'd husband of a happy wife." In 1712 the couple took the title of Count and Countess of Winchilsea.

Both of Finch's plays, though written as closet dramas, are eminently producible. They are well paced, eloquently versed, and respectably characterized: The righteous are never tedious. Her first play, *The Triumphs of Love and Innocence*, depicts "virtuous heroines, the fearful queen and the self-abnegating Marina. These two give the play its tone of elevated sentiment and pathos."[1] Little of her work was published or signed in her lifetime with the exception of her poetry, which was admired by William Wordsworth. She died in 1720.

PLAYS

Aristomenes, or The Royal Shepherd, ca. 1690; *The Triumphs of Love and Innocence*, ca. 1688

OTHER WORKS

Miscellany Poems on Several Occasions, 1713

1. Cotton.

Marieluise Fleißer
(NOVEMBER 23, 1901–FEBRUARY 2, 1974)

ROELLE. I was naked, and you did not give me any clothes. You have poured your scorn over me, and now it stares you in the face.

OLGA. Oh, that we fall every day into a world of viciousness, just as we fell into our bodies, and now we're stuck with them.

—from *Purgatory in Ingolstadt,* Scene 5

The Ingolstadt-born playwright/novelist/short story writer Marieluise Fleiᵝer (pronounced fly'-sir) led two lives: with Brecht and post-Brecht. She met the acclaimed Marxist theatrician/poet while completing her theater studies at the University of Munich. "She succumbed totally to the spell cast by his genius," writes Ralph Ley[1], and the two began a five-year liaison as lovers, confidantes, and collaborators, intermittently from 1924 to 1929.

Fleiᵝer's own work bears important distinctions from Brecht's. "Where Brecht staged class, Fleiᵝer staged gender, and where he demystified labor relations, she demystified emotional/sexual ones."[2] *Fegefeurer in Ingolstadt* (Purgatory in Ingolstadt), Fleiᵝer's first play, demonstrates her political agenda. Neither the pregnant Olga nor the outcast Roelle, a young man, can escape from the social purgatory imposed on them by the Catholic church. The constant drudgery of Olga's life starkly contrasts with the pathos-filled demise of so many literary ingenues. In an article in the *German Quarterly,* Donna Hoffmeister remarks that Fleiᵝer's "determinist melancholy . . . [asks] the largest possible questions about the historical and ongoing damage to women."[3]

Fleiᵝer describes *Fegefeurer* as "a play about the law of the herd and about those forcefully excluded from it." The Catholicism depicted in the play is self-serving, xenophobic, obsessed with its definition of sexual morality, and absent of love. Ralph Ley observes that in light of *Fegefeurer*'s projection of the Church's failure "to respond actively to Christ's summons to love God in and through one's neighbor, Fleiᵝer's play becomes one of the most remarkably prophetic literary documents of the century."[4] Critics received it with high praise.

Brecht's 1929 rendition of Fleiᵝer's *Pioneres in Ingolstadt* (Soldiers in Ingolstadt) caused a permanent rift in their personal and professional relationships. *Pioneres* was highly controversial in its original conception; Brecht injected sensationalized sexual elements and exaggerated antimilitarism into his staging. The production resulted in a huge scandal, which delighted Brecht. Fleiᵝer, however, endured painful personal slander. The city fathers of Ingolstadt blamed her for what they believed was the vilification of her hometown. She became estranged from her family, and was implicated in a legal suit that dragged on for years. Fleiᵝer crumbled. The criticism, notoriety, and exhausting rewrites Brecht incessantly demanded propelled her to an early retirement from the stage.

After the Brecht breakup, Fleiᵝer spiraled further downward. She formed an alliance with a lesser playwright/poet, Hellmuth Draws-Tychsen, who exploited her fame and financial assets until she was no longer useful to him. During the demise of her partnership with Draws-Tychsen, Fleiᵝer attempted suicide. She wrote two ill-received historical dramas, *Tiefseefisch* (Deepseafish), and *Karl Stuart*, a chronicle of the embattled Charles I of England. Finally, in 1935 the Nazis banned the publication and production of her work.

Fleiᵝer, bottomed-out, returned to Ingolstadt and married Joseph Haindl, owner of a tobacco business and the epitome of a philistine patriarch. He ruled Fleiᵝer with an iron thumb, forbidding her to work outside his home and business. Ironically, Frieda Geier, the heroine of Fleiᵝer's only novel, *Mehlreisende Frieda Geier* (Frieda Geier, Traveling Saleswoman), written four years before her marriage, refuses to marry her fiancé because he allows her to work only in his store. Three years into her marriage, Fleiᵝer suffered a nervous breakdown. She spent several months in a sanitarium. After the war ended, the Americans briefly jailed her, accusing her of black-marketing tobacco. Consequently, her husband lost his store, and eventually died from a protracted illness. At last, Fleiᵝer was able to resume her writing. Concentrating primarily on short fiction, she created four stories during her last decade that certainly rivaled her earlier work.

During the 1960s, Fleiᵝer's oeuvre experienced a renaissance, the apex of which was a 1968 collage by filmmaker Rainer Werner Fassbinder based on *Fegefeurer in Ingolstadt*. Three years later her collected works were published. By the time she died in 1974, she was regarded as a peer of Brecht and Horváth. Fleiᵝer's most popular dramatic work, *Der starke Stamm* (Of Sturdy Stock), celebrates the perseverance of the common people. Framed by a funeral and a birth, the play portrays women and men thick in the muck of life, ignoring love for worry of money, and experiencing happy endings only in their daydreams. The characters' interactions reveal Fleiᵝer's prediction: Capitalism will devastate the importance of morality and friendship; all that will matter is who owns how much. Ralph Ley's interpretation of Balbina, *Der starke Stamm*'s main character, applies to Fleiᵝer as well: "[Her] struggle to compete as a woman alone in a universe controlled, if not constructed, by the male of the species, has made her hard, bitter, and tough without destroying her delicious sense of humor or repressing her vitality."[5]

PLAYS

Fegefeurer in Ingolstadt (Purgatory in Ingolstadt, Annie Castledine, tr., 1991), 1924; *Karl Stuart*, 1938–45; *Pioneres in Ingolstadt* (Pioneers in Ingolstadt), 1927; *Der starke Stamm* (Of Sturdy Stock), 1944–45; *Der Tiefseefisch* (Deepseafish), 1929–30

OTHER WORKS

Abenteuer aus dem englischen Garten (short fiction), 1969;
Andorranische Abenteur (nonfiction), 1932; *Avantgarde*
(short fiction), 1963; "Die im Dunkeln" (Those in Darkness; short fiction), 1965; "Ein Pfund Orangen und neun
andere Geschichten der Marieluise Fleißer aus Ingolstadt"
(short fiction), 1929; "Eine ganz gewöhnliche Vorhölle"
(A Very Ordinary Limbo; short fiction), 1972; "Er hätte
besser alles verschlafen" (Better If He Had Slept Through
It All; short fiction), 1963; *Gesammelte Werke*, vols. 2 &
3, Rühle, Günther, ed., 1972; *Mehlreisende Frieda Geier:
Roman von Rauschen, Sporteln, Lieben, und Verkhaufen*
(Frieda Geier, Traveling Saleswoman in Flour: A Novel
About Smoking, Sporting, Loving, and Selling; novel),
1931; "Das Pferd und die Junger" (The Horse and the
Spinster; short fiction), 1952; "Der Rauch" (Smoke; short
fiction), 1964

WORKS ABOUT

Hoffmeister, Donna L., *Theater of Confinement: The Mi-
lieu Plays of Marieluise Fleisser and Franz Xavier Kruetz*,
1983; Kässens, Wend, and Michael Töteberg, *Marieluise
Fleisser*, 1979; McGowan, Maray, *Marieluise Fleisser*,
1987; Tax, Sissi, *Marieluise Fleisser*, 1984

1. Essay by Ralph Ley in Magill.
2. Case (2).
3. Ibid., cited by Case, n.d.
4. Op. cit., Magill.
5. Ibid.

Anne Crawford Flexner
(JUNE 27, 1874–JANUARY 11, 1955)

MRS. WIGGS. The worse Mr. Wiggs would act, the harder I
would pat him on the back. And as for the children, I always
did use compliments on 'em instead of switches.

—from *Mrs. Wiggs of the Cabbage Patch*, Act I

Anne Crawford Flexner was an early advocate of the
women's suffrage movement. "Her life was touched at
many points by the movement . . . She marched in the
New York suffrage parades," wrote her daughter Eleanor,
the respected author of *Century of Struggle* (1959), in its
dedication. Several of Flexner's plays depict the lives of
unconventional women, most notably *The Marriage
Game*, a 1913 comedy in which a single woman, mistakenly invited on a cruise with three couples, shares her insights on marriage. Eleanor proclaims that her mother
"made her mark as a playwright at a time when such an
achievement was still unusual for a woman."[1] The highly

respected American actress/manager Minnie Fiske staged
Flexner's first produced play, *Miranda on the Balcony*, in
1901. Two years later, the playwright's adaptation of the
Alice Hegan Rice novel *Mrs. Wiggs of the Cabbage Patch*
enjoyed a successful run in New York and at other venues.
Despite the stiffness of her plots, writes Susan Krantz,
Flexner was lauded for "her gifts for dialogue, sentiment,
and comedy."[2]

Born Anne Crawford in Georgetown, Kentucky, she
graduated from Vassar College in 1895. Three years later
she married Dr. Abraham Flexner, who became Director
Emeritus of the Institute for Advanced Study in Princeton,
New Jersey.

Her last work, *Aged 26*, portrays the final months in
the life of poet John Keats. In it, Flexner utilized the more
contemporary technique of incorporating Keats's poetic
language into the drama. Although she was granted some
merit for the ambitiousness of the project, the play was
not well received.

Flexner remained a political activist throughout her
life. She helped found the American Dramatists, serving
twice as its president, and was active with the Dramatists
Guild and the Authors League.

PLAYS

Aged 26, 1936; *All Soul's Eve*, 1919; *The Blue Pearl*, 1918;
Bravo! Maria, 1925; *A Lucky Star*, 1909; *A Man's Woman*,
1899; *The Marriage Game*, 1913; *Miranda on the Balcony*,
1901; *Mrs. Wiggs of the Cabbage Patch*, 1903; *Wanted—
An Alibi*, 1917

WORKS ABOUT

Flexner, Abraham, *I Remember: An Autobiography*, 1940;
Flexner, Eleanor, *Century of Struggle*, 1959

1. Flexner, Eleanor. *Century of Struggle*. 1959.
2. Essay by Susan Krantz in Robinson.

Maria Irene Fornés
(MAY 14, 1930–   )

FEFU. Women have to find their natural strength and when
they do find it, it comes forth with bitterness and it's erratic.
. . . Women are restless with each other. They are like live
wires . . . either chattering to keep themselves from making
contact or else, if they don't chatter, they avert their eyes like
Orpheus . . . as if a god once said 'and if they shall recognize
each other, the world will be blown apart . . .'

—from *Fefu and Her Friends*

Attempting to categorize the plays of Maria Irene Fornés is an ultimately fruitless effort. As with the work of CARYL CHURCHILL, each of Fornés's creations is a unique fusion of form and content: Some of her plays use slapstick conventions, some are interactive, some multilingual, musical, vaudevillian, some violent, and some erotic. Tish Dace summarizes what may be the common thread of Fornés's work: "the origin of evil and the site of salvation, the nature of societies, and of the individual soul." A true avant-gardist, "She wishes the audience to see and understand people and their relationships as she does."[1]

Born the youngest of six children in Havana, Cuba, Fornés grew up in an economically poor but culturally rich environment. Her father, Carlos Luis Fornés, spoke perfect English, as did her grandmother, who had attended an exclusive Catholic school in Baltimore, Maryland, and went on to found an English-language school in Cuba. Prior to becoming a family man, Fornés's father had been stationed with the American army in Hawaii. Upon his return from the service, he married Carmen Hismenia Collado, a teacher employed at his mother's school. Although her father's position as a government clerk provided little income, the family home was constantly bustling with books and discussion and the smell of Carlos

Maria Irene Fornés
COURTESY OF THE PLAYWRIGHT, PHOTO BY
KIM ZUMWALT

Luis's fine cooking. All of the Fornés children were encouraged to embrace learning, particularly with respect to the arts; still, Maria Irene attended school only from the third through the sixth grades.

In 1945 Carlos Luis died, and Fornés, along with her mother and a sister, emigrated to the States. American schooling bored her relentlessly, so she found employment in a string of wide-ranging jobs—factory worker, waitress, translator, usher, export clerk, office clerk, textile designer, ceramic painter. By 1950 she had begun studying painting in New York, locating herself around Greenwich Village and the New School for Social Research; she became a naturalized U.S. citizen in 1951. Soon she managed to save enough funds to study under Hans Hoffman at the Provincetown School, after which she pursued her schooling in Europe for three years. In Paris, however, a chance viewing of Samuel Beckett's *Waiting for Godot* quite literally changed her life. Fornés's focus shifted from painting to theater. At a memorial tribute to Beckett, Fornés remarked: "I more than just admire [him]. He had a personal impact on me; he provided me with a new vision . . . I was illuminated by it."[2]

She returned to New York and roomed with Susan Sontag, though neither woman was writing at that time. In the early 1960s Fornés completed her first plays, *Tango Palace* and *The Widow*, the latter of which, originally written in her native Spanish, was produced by the New York Actors Studio in 1961. Within a few short years, her plays, which she started directing herself despite her complete lack of directorial background, were appearing at the Open Theatre, the Judson Poets' Theatre, and La MaMa Experimental Theatre Club.

Even Fornés's earliest works reflect her experimental style. In *The Successful Life of 3* (1965), the lives of three main characters are interlaced so completely, nearly no boundaries exist between them. Regardless of the forms their lives take, they always come together again, like water molecules forever linked. According to John MacNicholas, the play sends up "masculine rivalry, financial success, justice, and roles of women [which] all serve to subvert conventional theatrical and ethical values"[3]; the play ends with a song: "Let Me Be Wrong, but also Not Know It." Also in 1965 Fornés staged her musical *Promenade*, which sharply comments on the injustices of life and love through its depiction of the journey of two prisoners, released into the world only to be brought back to jail. *Dr. Kheal* (1968) expertly plays with one of Fornés's favorite themes: "Opposites," Dr. Kheal says, "contradictions compress so that you don't know where one stops and the other begins." He lectures to his unseen class that though we have ideals, we always settle for whatever is easiest and simplest. Dr. Kheal concludes, "We can only do what is possible for us to do. But still it is good to know what the impossible is."

In the early 1970s Fornés became somewhat side-tracked by her work as a founding member of the Women's Theater Council, which she formed along with ROSALYN DREXLER, JULIE BOVASSO, ADRIENNE KENNEDY, ROCHELLE OWENS, and MEGAN TERRY. In 1973 the Council evolved into the New York Theater Strategy, an expanded group of playwrights that included male writers such as John Ford Noonan and Sam Shepard. The group eventually dissolved, but its impetus had lasting results in the discovery and production of scripts by women playwrights, culminating, particularly, with MARSHA NORMAN's Pulitzer prize-winning play *'night, Mother,* produced on Broadway in 1983. The energy Fornés put into the Theater Strategy as president, production manager, and all-purpose secretary helps explain the six-year gap in her own writing.

Fornés returned with a vengeance in 1977, however, with her most famous work, *Fefu and Her Friends,* which featured the unusual device of dividing up the audience and rotating it during the performance from one space in Fefu's home to another. The *L.A. Weekly* called *Fefu* "One of the most powerful plays about the mysteries and shared hallucinations of the female experience." Set in 1935, *Fefu* opens with the gathering of eight well-to-do women, unaffected by the Depression, who assemble at the home of Fefu in order to plan a fund-raiser. Philip, Fefu's husband, is an invisible omnipresence for the audience as well as most of the women: While they converse and interact throughout the day, Philip remains outside, seen only occasionally by some of the characters, but never by the audience. Fornés's message is clear: Women may achieve some freedom of expression inside the home, but in the outside world, they are constantly watched and controlled by men. Yet the playwright acknowledges the deep-rooted complexity of this gender stratification. As Fefu says, "Women are always eager for the men to arrive. When they do, they can put themselves at rest, tranquilized. . . . That's the closest they can be to feeling wholesome. The danger is gone, but the price is the mind and the spirit." At *Fefu*'s close, the women surround the wheelchair-bound figure of Julia, the victim of a fantastic hunting accident in which, although she was not hit by a bullet, she suffered an incapacitating injury. The impression left as the lights fade is, according to Helene Keyssar, "Symbolically at least, and on stage where all things are possible, the woman-as-victim must be killed in her own terms in order to ignite the explosion of a community of women."[4]

Critical response to Fornés's work has been mostly favorable. The *Village Voice*'s Michael Feingold said of her play *Aurora,* "It's as if Fornés had taken an old book of 19th-century illustrations and comically defaced the pictures with pencilled-in mustaches and suchlike distortions. At first one thinks it's all a joke, then voila! The mustaches are shown to be concealing tragic weaknesses in the faces— a different and rather wittier joke, and with some sub-stance to it."[5] On the other hand, *New York Times* critic Clive Barnes called this same piece "pure bunk."[6]

When asked what she wants most in her plays, Fornés responded, "Innocence, tenderness, a sense of humor, a special kind of joy."[7] The winner of more Obies than any other playwright except Sam Shepard and Samuel Beckett, she has also received grants from the Whitney Foundation, the Yale ABC Fellowship in Film Writing, the Rockefeller Foundation, the Centro Mexicano de Escritores, the Guggenheim Foundation, the New York State Council on the Arts, the National Endowment for the Arts, and the American Academy and Institute of Arts and Letters. Her plays have been presented in Amsterdam, London, and Stockholm, and at the Festival of Two Worlds in Spoleto, Italy.

In addition to her work with the Theater Strategy, for many years Fornés was active with International Arts Relations (INTAR), a New York–based Hispanic theater group. She likens her work with theater organizations to that of an army planning strategies to win victories—feminist victories, in her case. Fornés has been a presence to be reckoned with in the theater for more than three decades. Author/critic Phillip Lopate has stated that Fornés "helped clear a way through the claustrophobic landscape of Broadway vapidity and off-Broadway ponderous symbolism, by making theater that was fresh, adventurous, casual, fantastic, perceptive and musical."[8]

PLAYS

Abingdon Square, 1987; *And What of the Night?,* 1988; *The Annunciation,* 1967; *Art,* 1986; *Aurora,* 1972; *Balseros* (libretto; music by Robert Ashley), 1997?; *Blood Wedding* (adapt. of Lorca play), 1981; *Cap-a-Pie,* 1975; *Cold Air* (tr. & adapt. of Virgilio Piñera's *Aire Frío*), 1985; *The Conduct of Life,* 1985; *The Curse of Langston House,* 1972; *The Danube,* 1984; *Dr. Kheal,* 1968; *Drowning* (adapt. of Chekov's *Orchards*), 1985; *Evelyn Brown (A Diary),* 1980; *Eyes on the Harem,* 1979; *Fefu and Her Friends,* 1977; *In Service,* 1978; *Life Is a Dream* (adapt. of Calderón play), 1981; *Lolita in the Garden,* 1977; *Lovers and Keepers,* w/ Tito Puente & Fernando Rivas, 1986; *Molly's Dream,* 1968; *The Mothers* (a.k.a. *Charley*), 1986; *Mud,* 1983; *No Time,* 1985; *The Office,* 1966; *Promenade* (book & lyrics), 1965; *The Red Burning Light. or Mission XQ3,* 1968; *Sarita,* 1984; *The Successful Life of 3,* 1965; *Tango Palace* (a.k.a. *There! You Died*), 1963; *The Trial of Joan of Arc on a Matter of Faith,* 1986; *A Vietnamese Wedding,* 1967; *A Visit,* 1981; *La viuda* (*The Widow,* 1963), 1961

WORKS ABOUT

Kent, Assunta Bartolomucci, "Maria Irene Fornés and Her Critics," *Contributions in Drama and Theatre Studies* 70, (1996)

1. Essay by Tish Dace in Berney (1).

2. Cited in Burke, Sally, *American Feminist Playwrights* (New York: Twayne Pub., 1996), p. 158.

3. MacNicholas.

4. Keyssar.

5. September 19, 1974.

6. September 30, 1974.

7. Op. cit., MacNicholas.

8. Cited in MacNicholas.

Rose Franken
(DECEMBER 28, 1895–JUNE 22, 1988)

CLAUDIA. I can't take it, I won't take it. It isn't right for her to die!

DAVID. Who's running this universe. You or God?

CLAUDIA. There isn't any God.

DAVID. Hey, wait a minute. He's given you a home, a husband, a baby.

CLAUDIA. Nothing, and no one really belongs to anyone.

DAVID. If you've learned that, you've learned a lot, my dearest.

—From *Claudia*, Act III

Rose Franken's ability to finely render characters who reflect "the full complexity and bewilderment of the human condition," as professor emeritus Doris E. Abramson of the University of Massachusetts at Amherst couches it,[1] may have developed from her own childhood observations and experiences. Her parents separated while she was still quite young, and her mother, Hannah Younker Lewin, moved Rose and her three older siblings from the small town near Fort Worth, Texas, where she was born, to her mother's family home in Harlem. She rarely saw her father after that, but lived amidst a large, extended family and was privately educated at the School of Ethical Culture. With her "gift for making the apparently casual internally dramatic," Franken went on to write a variety of successful novels and dramas. She is best known for her *Claudia* series, a sweet comedy about a young woman who marries early and quickly faces a world of adult problems.

Like Claudia, Franken also married young. She wed Sigmund W. A. Franken, an oral surgeon, before she began her studies at Barnard College. Also like Claudia, Franken found herself coping with the unexpected twists of married life: Shortly after their wedding, Sigmund, only seven years older than his young wife, was diagnosed with tuberculosis, and the couple spent their first ten months together in a sanitarium. Despite her husband's ongoing battle with the disease, they had three sons. Franken was fortunate in that her husband encouraged her creative work. In fact, it was Sigmund who suggested she try play writing after the success of her first novel.

In 1932 Franken's first play opened on Broadway. *Another Language* weaves the tale of Stella, the youthful, independently minded aunt of a young male artist. Olauson writes of how the plot intensifies as Stella's nephew falls deeply in love with his aunt as she struggles with her own artistic ambitions amidst the suffocating world of her husband's bourgeois family.[2] *Another Language* enjoyed a warm reception; Franken's husband lived to see it, her first play, open first on Broadway and later in London in 1932: Sadly, on December 17 of that year, Sigmund died.

Needing a change, Franken moved to Hollywood to get a fresh start. There she adapted several of her early short stories into screenplays. In the midst of learning to wheel and deal in the cutthroat world of filmdom, she met William Brown Meloney, a lawyer and writer who helped run the *New York Herald Tribune*'s *This Week* magazine. They fell in love, married, and moved to New York shortly after their marriage in 1937. There Franken's new husband produced her next four plays. *Claudia*, based on Franken's own novel, opened to rave reviews on Broadway in 1941. It was packed with a range of domestic turnabouts: a neighbor's sexual overtures to Claudia, her mother's terminal illness, her own pregnancy. The show ran 722 performances. She later adapted her sequel novel for the stage as well: the plays spawned two popular films (*Claudia* and *Claudia and David*), which featured Dorothy McGuire, recreating her stage role, and Robert Young.

Franken followed the success of *Claudia* by writing and directing *Outrageous Fortune*, in which a dying woman's intelligence and inner strength help her family members resolve their differences. Franken subsequently directed several of her own plays, and worked with some of New York's most talented actors, including McGuire, Maria Ouspenskaya, Mildred Dunnock, and John Beal.

Ten years before her death in 1988, Franken retired from the stage, living alternately in New York City and Tucson, Arizona, where she died. She continued to write until her final days in order "to keep my mind alive," she said.[3]

PLAYS

Another Language, 1931; *Claudia* (also novel, 1939, film, 1943), 1941; *Claudia and David* (also film, 1946), 1940; *Doctors Disagree* (also novel, 1940), 1943; *Fortnight* (unproduced), n.d.; *The Hallams*, 1947; *Mr. Dooley, Jr.*, w/ Jane Lewin (her aunt), 1932; *Outrageous Fortune*, 1943; *Soldier's Wife*, 1944; *The Wing* (unproduced), n.d.

OTHER WORKS

American Bred, 1941; *Of Great Riches*, 1937; *Pattern*, 1925; *Strange Victory*, 1939; *Twice Born*, 1926; *When All Is Said and Done* (autobio.), 1963

1. Essay by Doris E. Abramson in Robinson.

2. Olauson.

3. Op. cit., Robinson.

Ketti Frings
(1915?–FEBRUARY 12, 1981)

EUGENE. If he hates it so much here, why does he stay?
BEN. You stupid little fool, it's like being caught in a photograph. Your face is there, and no matter how hard you try, how are you going to step out of a photograph?

—from *Look Homeward, Angel*, Act I, Scene 1

Though she produced relatively few works for the stage, Ketti Frings's superb stage adaptation of Tom Wolfe's novel *Look Homeward, Angel* thrust her into the limelight. Winner of both the Pulitzer Prize and the New York Drama Critics Circle Award (both 1958), it was the crowning achievement of her career. In the *New York Post* Richard Watts, Jr., claimed, "She captures the letter and the spirit of the Wolfe novel in completely dramatic terms and has given it truth, richness, abounding vitality, laughter, and compassion, and enormous emotional impact."[1]

Frings was born Katherine Hartley in Columbus, Ohio; her traveling salesman father provided his peripatetic family with a variety of domiciles during her growing-up years. The lack of a home base, however, did not keep the young girl from applying herself; she won her first literary prize when she was twelve years old. After a brief tenancy at Principia College in St. Louis, Frings obtained employment as an advertising copywriter in a Newark, New Jersey, department store. She also pursued freelance work as a columnist and radio scriptwriter and, under the pseudonym Anita Kilgore, worked as a ghostwriter for a movie magazine.

While traveling in France to work on a novel, she met her husband, German-born Kurt Frings, a lightweight boxer. They married in 1938 and moved to Mexico, waiting two years before Kurt could migrate to the United States. There they settled in Hollywood, where Kurt became an agent and Ketti began her screen writing career, which included an adaptation of William Inge's *Come Back, Little Sheba*. She also wrote short stories for a variety of popular magazines of the day, such as *Good Housekeeping* and the *Saturday Evening Post*. It was Kurt who nicknamed his wife Ketti. They had two children, but were later divorced.

Frings's first play was produced in 1942, but it was not until *Look Homeward, Angel* that her career as a playwright gained any significance. In his introduction to the published play, originally written for *Playbill*, Edward C. Aswell wrote, "Now, more than nineteen years after [Wolfe's] death, *Look Homeward, Angel* has come to Broadway, thanks to the extraordinary insight and dramatic skill of Ketti Frings. How Tom would have rejoiced in this event! It would have been for him the final consummation. . . . Somehow I cannot think [Wolfe] would have been in the least disturbed by the fact that Ketti Frings has succeeded in doing what he could not do, in adapting for the stage the essence of what he had to say."[2]

PLAYS

Judgment at Nuremberg, 1970; *The Long Dream*, 1960; *Look Homeward, Angel* (musical version, 1978), 1957; *Mr. Genius, My Child*, 1981; *Mr. Sycamore*, 1948; *Walking Happy*, w/Roger Hirshon, 1966

SCREENPLAYS (UNLESS OTHERWISE NOTED)

About Mrs. Leslie, 1954; *The Accused*, 1949; *Come Back, Little Sheba*, 1952; *File on Thelma Jordan*, 1949; *Foxfire*, 1955; *God's Front Porch* (novel), 1944; *Guest in the House*, 1944; *Hold Back the Dawn* (novel), 1942; *The Shrike*, 1955

1. Richard Watts, Jr., *New York Post*, November 29, 1957.

2. Introduction to *Look Homeward, Angel* by Ketti Frings, 1957.

Zona Gale
(AUGUST 26, 1874–DECEMBER 27, 1938)

Zona Gale offers a telling story in her autobiography: As a little girl, she snuck a shell from the landlady's knick-knack shelf. Her action caught the sharp eye of her mother, and Zona glumly returned the shell to its ledge. Her mother never mentioned the incident directly, but for days on end, Zona heard references to "the sacredness of the rights of others."[1]

Gale's Midwestern childhood was steeped in her mother's "fierce driving urge toward goodness" and her father's political pacifism: He remarked once, "Secretary of War. What a comment on our civilization. *Secretary of War*! Why not a Secretary of Peace, if anything?"[2] Both parents influenced her deeply and motivated her lifelong commitment to human rights activism.

By the age of eight, Gale had decided to become a writer. She announced her intentions to Ella Wheeler Wilcox, the well-known writer whom she occasioned to meet while living in Portage, Wisconsin. Years later Gale worked up the courage to send Wilcox a story. "You have talent. Keep writing," responded her mentor. Gale wrote stories throughout her school days, submitting piece after piece for publication, and receiving nothing but rejection notices. Finally, in 1891, just as she began her studies at the University of Wisconsin, *The Aegis*, a literary magazine, awarded Gale second prize for her poem "The Rose." She became an editor at the magazine, and sold her first story before she graduated from college. These early triumphs opened no floodgates, however, and she did not

publish again for quite some time. Nevertheless, the ever-persistent Gale continued to write.

She enrolled in a master's program at the university's Milwaukee location, where she enjoyed the city's theater scene and wrote articles for the *Journal*. Gale achieved

Zona Gale
COURTESY OF UPI/CORBIS-BETTMANN

some success as a reporter: In 1901 she took a position with *Evening World*. Still she encountered only rejection for her fiction. Then, in 1903, Gale made a creative leap. She moved from stories about "castles and princesses"³ into more realistic, personal terrain; *Success* magazine bought her first autobiographical piece. Over the next two years, Gale's work made the transition from romance to realism. She began writing the "Pelleas and Etarre" stories and *Friendship Village*, a collection of the stories. Her first novel, *Romance Island*, was published in 1906.

Gale became an official player in the literary world, although she had not yet begun to produce her most powerful works. She developed friendships with Eva Le Gallienne, Mark Twain, Fannie Hurst, and Jane Addams, and she kept in touch with her college roommate, Anne Scribner. Gale wrote her first play, *Neighbors*, adapted from one of the *Friendship Village* stories, for Milwaukee's Wisconsin Players in 1912. It was not until 1920, with the publication of her novel *Miss Lulu Bett*, that Gale garnered the acclaim she had so long desired. Her 1921 stage adaptation of *Lulu* won the Pulitzer Prize for Drama, cementing her career as a playwright. In his review of the play, Ludwig Lewisohn of the *Nation* wrote, "Now it is not too much to say that no other American dramatist has succeeded in so fully and richly transferring to the stage the exact moral atmosphere of a class, a section, and a period, as Miss Gale."⁴

Lulu incorporates the spiritual and political philosophies Gale inherited from her parents; her approach toward social criticism has often been compared to those of her contemporaries, Sinclair Lewis and Sherwood Anderson. Lulu Bett lives in the home of her sister Ina and brother-in-law Dwight, a spoiled, self-serving couple who treat Lulu like a servant. She tends to her difficult teenage niece Diana and her own perpetually neglected mother until the unexpected love and attention of two men inspire Lulu to take control of her life and rise above her compliant existence.

Riding the success of *Lulu*, Gale became a popular lecturer, and she used her celebrity to advocate politically progressive (with the exception of Prohibition) and humanitarian causes. She continued to write prolifically, penning plays, novels, poems, and nonfiction. Her work always drew upon the "quarry of situations"⁵ she gleaned from her beloved Midwest.

Gale considered her greatest achievement to be *Mister Pitt*, a stage adaptation of her celebrated novel *Birth*. The story of a good-hearted traveling pickle salesman, so socially maladjusted even the lonely spinsters of a small Midwestern town cannot abide him, *Pitt* succeeds "in giving theatrical value to the commonplace language of ordinary people."⁶

In 1928, at the age of fifty-five, Gale embarked on adventures of a wholly different sort. First, she assumed parental responsibility for a young boy, and second, she married Llewellyn Breeze, a man she had idolized in her youth. Gale thoroughly enjoyed her last ten years, which she spent writing and raising her adopted son. She died on December 27, 1938, at the age of sixty-five.

PLAYS

The Clouds, 1932; *Evening Clothes*, 1932; *Faint Perfume*, 1934; *Miss Lulu Bett* (also novel, 1920), 1921; *Mister Pitt* (adapt. from her novel *Birth*, 1918), 1925; *The Neighbors*, 1912; *Uncle Jimmy*, 1921

OTHER WORKS

Borgia, 1929; *Bridal Pond*, 1930; *Christmas*, 1912; *A Daughter of the Morning*, 1917; *Faint Perfume*, 1923; *Frank Miller of Mission Inn* (biography), 1938; *Friendship Village*, 1908; *Heart's Kindred*, 1915; *Light Woman*, 1937; *The Loves of Pelleas and Etarre*, 1907; *Magna*, 1939; *Mothers to Men*, 1911; *Neighbourhood Stories*, 1914; *Old-Fashioned Tales*, 1935; *Papa La Fleur*, 1933; *Peace in Friendship Village*, 1919; *Portage, Wisconsin, and Other Essays*, 1928; *Preface to a Life*, 1926; *Romance Island*, 1906; *The Secret Way* (poems), 1921; *When I Was a Little Girl*, 1913; *Yellow Gentians and Blue*, 1927

BIOGRAPHIES AND CRITICISM

Derleth, August, *Still Small Voice*, 1940

1. Derleth, August, *Still Small Voice* (London, D. Appleton-Century, 1940).

2. Ibid.

3. Ibid.

4. (February 2, 1921). Cited in essay by Felicia Hardison Londre in Robinson.

5. Op. cit., Henry Seidel, *Saturday Review of Literature*, cited in Derleth.

6. Op. cit., Londre.

Mary Gallagher
(JULY 7, 1947–)

MARINA. Well, you can't be afraid all the time, or you won't do anything!

—from *Dog Eat Dog*, Act II, Scene 16

Although Mary Gallagher chooses seemingly diverse subjects to people her plays—an Irish Catholic family, Central American illegal immigrants, suburban yuppies—she consistently attempts to reveal "the moral issues which are raised by human behavior."[1]

Born in Van Nuys, California, and raised in Cleveland, Ohio, Gallagher set her sights on theater from a young age. She earned a B.S. from Bowling Green State University in English and theater, and then found work acting in regional theaters and off-off-Broadway. However, performance did not completely satisfy her, and she began writing plays.

Domestic landscapes frequently appear in Gallagher's dramas. In *Father Dreams* (1978) a traditional Irish Catholic family copes with an institutionalized, manic-depressive patriarch. Her 1983 black comedy *Dog Eat Dog* exposes the self-centeredness and absence of humanity and moral integrity in the lives of Al and Marina Foley and their neighbors, all quintessential American suburbanites.

Occasionally Gallagher tackles more politically charged terrain. *¿De Donde?* reveals the institutionalized corruption within the American immigration system. When a group of Central American refugees are caught illegally entering the United States, they encounter brutal treatment from the border patrol; the INS officer says, "You think we're so tough on them—but they still keep coming! If we coddled 'em like you folks want, every goddamn country south of Texas'd be empty!"

Gallagher's plays have been produced in regional theaters throughout the United States, and in Canada and Ireland. She has received a National Endowment for the Humanities grant (1978) and a Guggenheim fellowship (1983), among others. Her play *Chocolate Cake* won the Heideman Award at the 1981 Festival of New American Plays at the Actors' Theatre of Louisville, and *How to Say Goodbye* won the Susan Blackburn Prize. She has directed for the stage as well, although she asserts that while women playwrights are welcomed, women directors are discouraged. Gallagher is married and, with her husband, is raising two stepdaughters.

PLAYS

Buddies, n.d.; *Chocolate Cake*, 1981; *¿De Donde?*, 1991; *Dog Eat Dog*, 1983; *Father Dreams*, 1978; *Fly Away Home*, 1987; *How to Say Goodbye*, 1987; *Little Bird*, 1984; *Love Minus*, n.d.; *Win/Lose/Draw*, w/Ara Watson, 1983

OTHER WORKS

Quicksilver, n.d.; *Spend It Foolishly*, 1978

1. Hale, Sheila, "Women Do Dramatise," *City Limits*, 1979.

Fatima Gallaire-Bourega
(1944–)

LELLA. When the mad speak of calamity, it's best to listen.

—from *Ah! Vous êtes venus . . .*

As a young woman, Algerian-born Fatima Gallaire-Bourega moved to France to pursue filmmaking. While she worked at the Algiers Cinémathèque, she began writing poems and short stories. Her work was published in journals and newspapers in Algiers, Tunis, and Paris.

Gallaire-Bourega's 1988 play *Ah! Vous êtes venus . . .* (You Have Come Back) illustrates the cultural fracture born by a foreign-raised Muslim woman who attempts to reintegrate into her home country's traditional Islamic society. After living abroad for twenty years, Lella, an Algerian princess, returns home to bury her father. She is embraced by Nounou, her old nurse, but is cautioned by her to beware of the village women. Soon, Lella is accused of heresy: She has married an uncircumcised Frenchman. When Nounou and a group of "outsiders"—an old cripple, a madwoman, and a slave—try to defend Lella's position, they, along with Lella, are killed by the village women.

Gallaire-Bourega utilizes the distinctly Western form of Sophoclean tragedy in her play; she incorporates both oracular prophecies and a Greek chorus. The blending of the Eastern content and Western structure lends itself perfectly to the play's point: A Western-thinking woman can never go back to the oppressiveness of life as a Muslim woman and is naive to think she can.

Other plays by Gallaire-Bourega include *Le fou de Layda*, adapted from the novel by André Miquel and based on an Arab legend, and *Les co-éspouses*, which deals with polygamy. Currently Gallaire-Bourega lives in France and continues to address cross-cultural issues in her writing.

PLAYS

Ah! Vous êtes venus . . . là òu il y a quelques tombes (You Have Come Back, Jill MacDougall, tr.), 1988; *Les co-épouses*, 1989?; *Le fou de Layda*, 1987; *Témoinage contre un homme stérile*, 1987

Griselda Gambaro
(JULY 28, 1928–)

FUNCTIONARY. Art is all that deserves to last—lofty sentiments, things and beings coming to life. You haven't smashed the doll so as to assure that there will be beauty in the world, order. In a word: so the trees can keep growing and putting forth new leaves, so the earth does not become a desolate wasteland.

—from *The Walls*

World-renowned Argentinian playwright Griselda Gambaro submits to no one. Her unique brand of *el grotesco*, the theater of the grotesque, lays bare the terror wielded by violent and repressive political regimes. She has written some of the "most powerful plays of the century, dealing mostly with brutalized individuals, [and] victims of social and political pressures that destroy their dignity and freedom."[1]

Gambaro often focuses her sharp eye on Argentina's turbulent political climate. "This is a schizophrenic country," she has said, "a country that lives two lives. The courteous and generous have their counterpart in the violent and the armed who move among the shadows . . . One never really knows what country one is living in, because the two co-exist . . . Argentina is seismic as well as schizophrenic. From night to day, things can change drastically owing to causes below the surface, behind the screen that's offered up as reality."[2]

Her chief concern as a political writer "has always been violence—its roots, manifestations, and spheres of influence, as well as the ways in which it may be perceived, masked, and denied."[3] Some critics have compared her theatrical ideology to Antonin Artaud's Theater of Cruelty. However, Gambaro remains aware that any graphic depiction of violence, no matter how intentionally subversive, may be construed as a reinforcement or endorsement of it; therefore, she chooses to veil her messages in abstractions and ambiguities of language and movement. She is a self-proclaimed dramatist "of disappearances, obsessed with the 'missing.'"

Some of her earliest plays convey the denial experienced by naive and ignorant citizens. In *Las paredes* (The Walls; 1964), a surreal tale of disappearance, a young man is abducted and taken to a deceptively well-decorated room. Although the room's flourishes begin to dissolve, revealing to him his own disappearance, the man cannot accept the reality of his circumstance: "Sunday I am going to the country," he repeats to himself.

El campo (The Camp; 1967) echoes the theme of *Las paredes*. The play's protagonists appear to be vacationing in the country, but they are clearly imprisoned, subject to a brutality cloaked in gentleness. Gambaro takes full advantage of language in *El campo*, playing with the title's multiple meanings of "countryside," "military camp," and "concentration camp."

Another early work, *Los siameses* (The Siamese Twins; 1965), uses the conceit of conjoined twins to illustrate how totalitarianism threatens to annihilate the very population it controls. The power-hungry Lorenzo explains that both he and Ignacio, his attached brother, cannot survive together; they must be surgically separated. He remarks bluntly, "What happens in operations like these, is that they can't save them both. One of them is ruined. In order to leave one of them in perfect condition, they have to ruin the other. They have to." Inevitably, Lorenzo ruins his brother, manipulating events that result in Ignacio's death. The play demonstrates how "victimization . . . invents difference, and fabricates an enemy 'other' even when that 'other' is identical, even inseparable from itself."[4] Ironically, Lorenzo appears to acknowledge this paradox: "But who is capable of distinguishing between us? I can't. We're the same. That's our tragedy. We're so similar that our actions become confused."

Gambaro's political outspokenness eventually brought about her forced exile from Argentina in 1977. The government banned her work and she emigrated to Spain, living in Barcelona until 1980. At the time of her exile, she smuggled out her prophetic masterpiece, *Información para extranjeros* (Information for Foreigners; 1971), which predicted the rise of government thought police who would kidnap, torture, and murder thousands of Argentineans. The playwright herself forbade anyone to stage *Información*, so fearful was she of repercussions against family members still in Argentina. Intended as a location piece to be produced in a space more akin to a torture chamber than a theater, *Información* offers the audience Guides, unctuous versions of Dante's Virgil, who lead the viewers through narrow, darkened corridors, subjecting them to a variety of violent scenes.

Gambaro returned to her beloved Argentina in the early 1980s after the fall of the junta. However, despite the more subdued political climate, her work has remained fierce and passionate. The title character of her 1986 play *Antígona Furiosa* hauntingly mirrors Gambaro herself. She, like Antígona and her Greek namesake, is intent on burying her dead, her disappeared ones. She renounces the traditional sphere, home and hearth, and refuses to remain silent. Gambaro's Antígona endures, abandoned by her Chorus, who has complied with Creon's order to denounce her. "Let the laws, these vile laws! drag me to a grave that will be my tomb," she cries. "No one will hear my weeping; no one will be aware of my suffering. They will live in the light as though nothing were happening. . . . I will be . . . uncounted among the living and among the dead. I will disappear from the world, alive." *Antígona Furiosa* expounds upon what Gambaro perceives to be society's greatest threats: "passivity in the face of repression, popular compliance with terror."

Since 1963 Gambaro's voice has been heard through plays, fiction, and essays. Her first published work, three novellas entitled *Madrigal en ciudad*, won the Premio del Fondo Nacional de las Artes de la Argentina. Her work has been bestowed with many other honors, including the Premio Emece, the Premio de la Asociación de Teatros, and the Premio de la Revista Teatro XX. Originally Gambaro divided herself between prose and drama, but since the mid-1970s she has concentrated primarily on play writing.

PLAYS

Antígona Furiosa, 1986; *El campo* (The Camp; from her short story), 1967; *Decir sí* (Saying Yes), 1972; *Del sol naciente* (From the Rising Sun), 1983; *El desatino* (The Blunder; from her short story), 1965 (or *El desatio*, 1964); *El despojamiento* (Strip), 1972; *Información para extranjeros* (Information for Foreigners, Diane Taylor, tr.), 1971; *In the Country* (a.k.a. *The Camp*), n.d.; *La malasangre* (Bitter Blood), 1981; *Matrimonio* (Matrimony), 1965; *Nada que ver* (Out of It; from her novel), 1972; *Las paredes* (The Walls; from her short story), 1964; *Real envido* (Royal Gambit), 1980; *Los siameses* (The Siamese Twins), 1965; *Solo un aspecto* (One Aspect Only), 1973; *Sucede lo que pasa* (What Happens Happens), 1976

OTHER WORKS (NOVELS, UNLESS OTHERWISE NOTED)

Conversaciones con chicos (Talks with Kids, essays), 1965; *El desatino* (The Unraveling, short fiction), 1965; *Dios no nos quiere contentos* (God Does Not Wish Us to be Complacent), 1979; *Ganarse la muerte* (Beating Death), 1977; *Lo impenetrable* (The Impenetrable), 1984; *Madrigal en cuidad* (Madrigal in the City, short fiction), 1963; *Nada que ver con otra historia* (Nothing to Do with Another Story), 1972; *Una felicidad con menos pena* (Joy Without Pain), 1967

WORKS ABOUT

Cypress, Sandra Messinger, "The Plays of Griselda Gambaro," in *Dramatists in Revolt: The New Latin American Theatre*, 1976, edited by George W. Woodyard and Leon F. Lyday; Feitlowitz, Marguerite, ed., tr. & intro., *Information for Foreigners: Three Plays by Griselda Gambaro*, 1992

1. Essay by William Knapp Jones and Judith A. Weiss in Hochman.

2. Interview by Feitlowitz in "Two Argentine Writers," *Bomb*, no. 32 (Summer 1990): p. 54. Cited in *Information for Foreigners: Three Plays by Griselda Gambaro*, Marguerite Feitlowitz, ed., tr. (Evanston, Ill: Northwestern University Press, 1992).

3. Ibid., Afterword by Diane Taylor.

4. Essay by Diane Taylor in Hawkins-Dady (1).

5. Op. cit., Feitlowitz.

Barbara Garson
(JULY 7, 1941–)

EGG OF HEAD. Security makes cowards of us all.

—from *MacBird!*, Act 1 Scene 1

One might be hard-pressed to think that the daughter of an office manager and a bookkeeper, who would one day write a treatise on the sweatshop impact of computers in the workplace, might also be the creator of the legendary 1960s play that cast Lyndon and Lady-Bird Johnson as Macbeth and Lady Macbeth, politicizing the off-Broadway stage during the Vietnam War, but—think again.

New York City native Barbara Garson describes nearly all of her work as "comedies in which ordinary people struggle ingeniously to keep daily life secure." She excepts *MacBird*, one of her earliest works, however, calling it "a play about world leaders making daily life insecure."[1] (The published play sold over a million copies.) Even though her subsequent efforts have borne little resemblance to this anti-Vietnam War play, Garson's work has remained steadfastly political in its depiction of the lives of working people.

The struggles of working women, in particular, are featured in several of her plays. *The Co-op (Going Co-op)* on which she collaborated with Fred Gardner (1972) shows how the tenants of a New York City building, mostly women who can't afford to buy their apartments, try to make their homes secure for themselves and their neighbors. *The Department* (1983) presents two female bank employees fighting the impending doom brought on by automatic teller machines. *Security* is a screwball comedy about a single mother who devises an ingenious but deadly social scam in order to survive the collapse of the American dream.

Garson has addressed workplace issues in her prose work, *All the Livelong Day* (1975) and *The Electronic Sweatshop* (1988). She has published essays and stories, and writes reviews for the *New York Times*, the *Los Angeles Times*, the *Washington Post*, and the *Village Voice*, among others. Her children's play *The Dinosaur Door* (1976) won her an Obie Award, and she has received fellowships from the Guggenheim and the National Endowment for the Arts. After earning her B.A. in classical history from the University of California at Berkeley in 1964, she met her lifelong partner, photographer Frank Leonardo. Her daughter is also a playwright.

Regarding the existence of feminist themes in her work, Garson has commented that her plays "are about clever working women trying to keep life *human*. I think that's feminist."

PLAYS

A Winner's Tale, 1974; *The Co-op (Going Co-op)*, w/Fred Gardner, 1972; *The Department*, 1983; *Dinosaur Door*, 1976; *MacBird*, 1967; *Security*, 198?

OTHER WORKS

All the Livelong Day, 1975; *The Electronic Sweatshop: How Computers Are Transforming the Office of the Future into the Factory of the Past*, 1988

1. All citations from correspondence with author (March 9, 1996).

Shirley Gee
(APRIL 25, 1932–   )

MOTHER. There's too much hate in this world. I'll not be part of it. Sometimes that's hard, but how I try to think of it is this. The boys on the streets, the soldiers. With them it's not so much the boredom, it's the tension of that boredom. And nobody wants them, and they feel it. That makes explosions in them, trapped inside them, not allowed to burst. So when they get the chance, when there's a bit of trouble, then they let it out, they're full of spite, smash things, smash people.

—from *Never in My Lifetime*, Act I

"I suppose what I write about is outsiders," says London-based playwright Shirley Gee. "I often write about people whose needs or desires are against the needs and desires of society and they have to be sacrificed sometimes. And I think quite often there are large stamping women who are in the wrong place at the wrong time—and find it very hard to knuckle down . . ."[1] Gee's radio and stage plays feature such "large stampers" as Mary Mallon (otherwise known as Typhoid Mary), female garment-industry worker, and Hannah Snell, an unintentional heroine of the eighteenth century.

Born Shirley Thieman, Gee originally studied acting in London and performed on stage and television until 1965, when she married actor Donald Gee. She devoted the following decade to raising their two sons. Then, in the mid-1970s, she began writing radio dramas and quickly made a name for herself with *Typhoid Mary* (1979), which chronicles the tragic life of the Irish immigrant woman who unknowingly spread the disease around New York City at the turn of the century. The Royal Shakespeare Company asked Gee to adapt the play for the stage. The result, a successful preservation of Gee's unusual narrative style, so pleased the playwright that she followed up with another stage adaptation of one of her radio dramas, *Never in My Lifetime*. *Lifetime* details the violent animosity that exists between the Catholic and Protestant communities of Northern Ireland. Gee uses a distinctly female point of view to tell the tragic love story of an Irish Catholic girl and British Protestant soldier. The plot emphasizes women's fierce struggle to hold their families together amidst the horror and grief of war.

Ask for the Moon, Gee's first effort made originally for the stage, parallels the difficult lives of two generations of female garment-industry workers: Victorian lace makers and modern-day sweatshop employees. It is an unconstrained depiction of the workers' inescapable betrayals of each other as they strive to save their own skins in the grueling, oppressive workhouses. Their stories are skillfully woven together, revealing similar injustices: low pay, unsafe working conditions, and inhumanely long hours. The play was quite well received; a *Sunday London Times* reviewer remarked, "Gee's writing is lyrical but tough: it exudes a compassion which is not bought at the expense of sentimentality or melodrama. This is a warm and haunting play."[2]

Gee's stage play *Warrior* was inspired by the true story of Hannah Snell, a young lady who, in the mid-1700s, assumed a male identity and took to the sea in order to save her shanghaied husband. Hannah's adventures and exploits were described in the 1750 chapbook "The Female Soldier, or the Surprising Life and Adventures of Hannah Snell." Susan Fenichell, director of the play's 1992 production at Seattle's Intiman Playhouse, describes Hannah as "a model for us all: a true warrior who answers decorum with brashness, terror with bravery, and the deafening silence of complicity with full words at full volume. Hannah shows us that perseverance and resilience are fueled by an unswerving sense of personal justice. She allows nothing to stand in her way—not even her own frailties, her own doubts. When, for a time, she is hobbled by a sort of madness, it is her mind that begins to break, not her spirit."[3]

PLAYS

Ask for the Moon (also radio play), 1986; *Never in My Lifetime* (also radio play, 1983), 1984; *Stones* (also radio play), 1974; *Typhoid Mary* (also radio play, 1979), 1983; *Warrior*, 1989

RADIO PLAYS (UNLESS OTHERWISE NOTED)

Against the Wind, 1988; *Bedrock*, 1979; *Flights* (teleplay), 1985; *The Forsyte Chronicles* (adapt. of work by John Galsworthy), 1990; *Long Live the Babe* (teleplay), 1984; *Men on White Horses*, 1981; *Moonshine*, 1977; *Our Regiment*, 1982; *Stones*, 1974; *The Vet's Daughter*, 1976

1. "A Conversation with the Playwright." Program notes from Intiman Playhouse, Vol. 2, no. 5., Seattle, Wash., October 1992.

2. *Sunday London Times* article (September 1986), cited in essay by Frances Gray in Berney (2).

3. Op. cit., Intiman Playhouse, "From the Director."

Pam Gems
(AUGUST 1, 1925–   )

FISH (suicide note). My loves, what are we to do? We won't do as they want anymore, and they hate it. What are we to do?

—from *Dusa, Fish, Stas and Vi*

Cloaked in her carefully woven mystique of femininity, Greta Garbo, in a 1933 film about Sweden's Queen Christina, stares wistfully into the camera as the screen fades to black, conveying to all the grief felt by the controversial seventeenth-century crowned head who purportedly relinquished her throne for the sake of love. Almost forty-five years later, Pam Gems shattered the Hollywood myth with her 1977 drama *Queen Christina*. In the introduction to the play, Gems elaborates:

"The reality is harsher. The real Christina was a dark, plain woman with a crippled shoulder, daughter of a beautiful mother whose health and nervous system had been ruined by yearly pregnancies in the effort to provide a male heir. Since Christina was the only survivor, she was, at her father's instruction, reared as a man, that is to say, educated, and taught all the male necessities, how to ride, fence, shoot, how to lead an army. And then, on her accession, told to marry and breed, that is, to be a woman. By which time, of course, like males of her era, she despised women as weak, hysterical, silly creatures. The confusion seems to have been too stressful. She abdicated and went to Rome, at a time and place of seeming warmth and freedom of thought after the cold, Lutheran north. It is a confusion which seems as apposite as ever."[1]

Gems's Christina ultimately discovers her maternal self, but long after her childbearing years are over. Recognizing the real tragedy of her life, she unilaterally rejects all manifestations of dominant power relationships, whether related to gender or social status.

Like Christina, Gems experienced a revelation later in life, although hers was of an artistic nature. After twenty years of marriage and child-raising, she found herself drawn to play writing. Born in rural England in Bransgore, Dorset, she graduated from Brockenhurst County High School in 1941 and went on to receive her B.A., with honors, in psychology at Manchester University in 1949. That same year she married Keith Gems. Like CARYL CHURCHILL, she penned radio and television plays while raising her two daughters and two sons. In the early 1970s,

with the rise of the women's movement, Gems became involved with politicized "fringe" theater.

One of her earlier works, *Dusa, Fish, Stas and Vi* (1976), draws on the dilemma suffered by those who participate in the traditional leftist practice of separating political work from personal, romantic, and sexual fulfillment. When Fish's politically radical boyfriend forsakes her for a more dependent woman, she begins to fall apart, even as she acknowledges the hypocrisy of her ex-lover's actions. She believed that their relationship had successfully combined political work with personal commitment, and the disillusionment she suffers ultimately leads her to commit suicide. In this way Gems's play presents a difficult conundrum: The personal *is* the political; the personal *cannot* coexist with the political. Helene Keyssar suggests that Fish's suicide "calls attention to the central paradox of the play: removed from the company of men, women can focus fruitfully on women. . . . [It] argues forcefully that recognition of women by women is a crucial step in overcoming oppression. It foresees the next step—re-creation of men's and women's relationships to each other—as more difficult than any change yet attempted."[2]

By the mid-1970s Gems began to focus on historical and mythological revisionism in her work. During this period she wrote *Queen Christina*, as well as *Guinevere* (1976) and *Piaf* (1978); the latter became her first big success. Rather than depicting France's greatest vocalist as a romanticized heroine living a tragic life, Gems chose to portray Edith Piaf as a desperate, promiscuous woman. The play follows her life from her discovery by club owner Louis Leplee to her death as a drug addict, revealing her string of abusive lovers along with the unaffected and indomitable spirit that made her a legend. By realistically characterizing Piaf as the working-class woman she was, complete with working-class values and working-class language, Gems allows the audience to understand the difficult identity problems her stardom brought.

In addition to her original revisionist dramas, Gems adapted several classical works and imbued them with her own feminist sensibilities; for example, *Camille*, the story of another dying heroine, once again famously portrayed on film by Garbo. Reconstructing the old romantic tale, Gems turns the drama into a parable of sorts, showing the universality of one woman's degradation, domination, and abuse by men. Camille and her lover Armand quarrel over a matter of trust; he knows she is keeping something from him. Yet the tale she conceals is too horrible to tell: She was raped by his father and bore a child; now the father has threatened to destroy Armand if she marries him. Camille succumbs to the father's insistence that she write to Armand, informing him that she prefers her former existence as a society whore, and that it is all over between them. When they meet again at the opera, where she is plying her trade, he strikes her. Later, in her room, about to bed a drunken Russian prince, she suffers a massive hemorrhage and dies, reproached and destroyed by a man's need to dominate.

Whether adapting or creating revisionist historical dramas or writing about the contemporary world, Gems has continued to advocate a clear feminist message. In her 1984 work *Loving Women*, she focuses on what men and women want from each other and what the ingredients of a relationship are, with dependence, codependence, and independence complicating matters in a tense and changing world. Frank and Susannah are political activists. But when Frank has a breakdown and is taken in by Crystal, a hairdresser, Susannah lets him have it: "You've never been off the tit. Eleven-plus, scholarship, research fellowship project grant. You're free—white and male. And you've caved in."

Her propensity for historical drama saw light again in her 1997 play *Stanley*, based on the life of the twentieth-century British painter Stanley Spencer. It was produced in the United States at New York's Circle in the Square.

A woman who lives by the words she writes, Pam Gems believes "Art is of necessity. Which is why we need women playwrights just now very badly. We have our own history to create, and to write."[3] As Mary Remnant says, "Gems is at her best when snatching back the truth about women's lives out of the jaws of a male-constructed history . . ."[4]

PLAYS

After Birthday, 1973; *The Amiable Courtship of Miz Venus and Wild Bill*, 1973; *Aunt Mary: Scenes from Provincial Life*, 1982; *Betty's Wonderful Christmas*, 1972; *Camille*, 1984; *The Danton Affair*, 1986; *Dead Fish* (later *Dusa, Fish, Stas and Vi*), 1976; *Deborah's Daughter*, 1995; *Franz into April*, 1977; *Go West, Young Woman*, 1974; *Guinevere*, 1976; *Ladybird, Ladybird*, 1979; *Loving Women*, 1984; *My Warren*, 1973; *Pasionaria*, music by Paul Sand, lyrics by Gems and Sand, 1985; *Piaf*, 1978; *The Project*, 1976; *Queen Christina*, 1977; *Sandra*, 1979; *Stanley*, 1997; *The Treat*, 1982; *Up in Sweden*, 1974

TRANSLATIONS AND ADAPTATIONS

The Blue Angel, novel by Heinrich Mann, 1991; *Camille*, play by Dumas fils, 1984; *The Cherry Orchard*, play by Anton Chekhov, 1984; *The Danton Affair*, work by Stanislawa Przybyszewka, 1986; *A Doll's House*, play by Henrik Ibsen, 1980; *My Name Is Rosa Luxemburg*, tr. from Marianne Auricoste, 1976; *The Rivers and Forests*, tr. from Marguerite Duras, 1976; *Uncle Vanya*, play by Anton

Chekhov, 1979; *Yerma*, play by Frederico Garcia Lorca, 1993

TELEVISION PLAYS

A Builder by Trade, 1961; *We Never Do What They Want*, 1979

NOVELS

Bon Voyage, Mrs. Frampton, 1990; *Mrs. Frampton*, 1989

1. Quoted in introduction to *Queen Christina* in Remnant.
2. Keyssar.
3. Op. cit., Remnant, "Afterword."
4. Op. cit., Remnant.

Alice Gerstenberg
(AUGUST 2, 1885–JULY 28, 1972)

HARRIET. I am what you wish the world to believe you are.
HETTY. You are the part of me that has been trained.
HARRIET. I am your educated self.
HETTY. I am the rushing river; you are the ice over the current.

—from *Overtones*

Born into a pioneering Chicago family, Alice Gerstenberg's inclination toward theater was largely influenced by her mother, Julie Wieshendorff. Alice was educated at the Kirkland School and at Bryn Mawr College. She began her literary career as a novelist, but soon heeded her calling as a dramatist. Her first play, *Captain Joe*, was produced by the Sargent Dramatic School at the Empire Theatre. But it was her second effort, a stage adaptation of Lewis Carroll's *Alice in Wonderland* in 1915, that brought her tremendous early acclaim. Of this "most delicate literary" task, Alexander Dean wrote, "Miss Gerstenberg has performed the feat successfully. She has deleted little that the public misses with regret, and she has resisted the temptation to add anything for which there is no warrant in the master's text."[1]

Although *Alice* was a great critical success, Gerstenberg's most important contribution to American theater is her complex psychological drama *Overtones* (1915 and 1922). *Overtones* illustrates the fractured psyches of two women, Harriet and Margaret, in a manner that had been hitherto unseen on the American stage. Rather than simply presenting the women as singular characters, Gerstenberg divided each woman into her social self and her inner self, rather like the id-self and the ego-self. Sally Burke writes,

"Gerstenberg became the first American to present the dramatization of the subconscious mind on stage; by introducing expressionistic devices to the American stage she added the exploration of psychological realism to the dramatist's arsenal."[2] The impact of *Overtones* affected the work of many playwrights, including SOPHIE TREADWELL and Eugene O'Neill.

Unfortunately, most of Gerstenberg's later plays did not enjoy the success or influence of her earlier works. *When Chicago Was Young* (1932) and *Victory of the Belles* (1943), about the plight of wartime women searching for their husbands, were both harshly criticized. Gerstenberg persevered, however, writing one-act dramas intended for home productions—to be performed by a fireplace, staircase, or bay window. She was a staunch believer in the social power of theater, and felt that these domestic one-acts would encourage communities to establish theaters of their own.

In addition to writing and producing her own work, Gerstenberg helped found the Chicago Junior League Theater for Children in 1921. This endeavor resulted in the establishment of many such children's theaters across the country, several of which mounted Gerstenberg's own *Alice* as their first productions. Also in the early 1920s she founded the Playwrights Theatre of Chicago, which provided a venue for the production of plays by new writers. Gerstenberg was active in numerous community services and organizations, untiringly offering her time and energy throughout her life. She died in 1972 in her beloved Chicago, just one week shy of her eighty-seventh birthday.

Her dramatic works are notable for their greatly humane sense of humor. Gerstenberg could take situations that are basically tragic and depict them comically. A contemporary woman, she cleverly wove modern philosophy and psychology into her works.

PLAYS

A Little World (collection, including *Captain Joe*), n.d.; *Alice in Wonderland* (adapt. of Lewis Carroll's story), 1915; *Comedies All* (incl. *At the Club*, 1925; *Facing Facts*, 1926; *Latchkeys*, 1925; *The Menu*, 1926; *Mere Man*, 1929; *The Opera Matinee*, 1925; *The Puppeteer*, 1926; *Rhythm*, 1926; *The Setback*, 1929; *Upstage*, 1927), 1930; *Find It*, 1927; *Four Plays for Four Women* (incl. *Ever Young*), 1924; *Glee Plays the Game*, 1934; *The Hourglass*, 1955; *The Land of Don't Want To* (adapt. of Lilian Bell's book), 1928; *The Magic of Living*, 1969; *On the Beam*, 1957; *Our Calla*, 1956; *Overtones*, one-act, 1915; three-act, 1922; *The Promise*, n.d.; *The Queen's Christmas*, 1939; *Star Dust*, 1931; *Ten One Act Plays* (incl. *Attuned, Beyond, The Buffer, Fourteen, Hearts, He Said and She Said*, and *The Pot Boiler*), 1921; *Time for Romance*, 1942; *Try Your Number*,

n.d.; *Victory Belles*, w/H. Adrian, 1943; *Water Babies* (adapt. of Charles Kingsley story), 1929; *When Chicago Was Young*, w/Herman Clark, 1932; *Within the Hour*, 1934

OTHER WORKS

The Conscience of Sarah Platt, n.d.; *Unquenched Fire*, n.d.

1. From the preface by Alexander Dean in *Comedies All, Short Plays* by Alice Gerstenberg (New York: Longmans, Green & Co., 1930).

2. Burke, Sally, *American Feminist Playwrights* (New York: Twayne Pub., 1996), p. 36.

P. J. Gibson
(1952?–)

"If I live to be 150, I still won't have enough time to write about all the black women inside of me," says P. J. Gibson.[1] Since the early 1970s, Gibson has persistently portrayed these women's passions and struggles. She favors no specific time period or place; her subject matter includes an epic history of black women from slavery to 1969 (*The Black Woman*); a bold exploration of the obsessive love between a teenage girl and an older man (*Brown Silk and Magenta Sunsets*, 1981); a college women's reunion brought about by one friend's suicide (*Long Time Since Yesterday*, 1985); and the life of a single mother raising her teenage daughter in urban America (*Miss Ann Don't Cry No More*, 1980). Her work has been admired for its "readily recognizable characters."[2]

A production of LORRAINE HANSBERRY's *To Be Young, Gifted, and Black* was an early inspiration for Patricia Joann Gibson, a native of Pittsburgh, Pennsylvania. She wrote her first play, *Shameful in Your Eyes* (1971), before graduating from Keuka College. A staunch supporter of public arts programs, she has penned public service announcements for the U.S. Department of Health, Education, and Welfare, and has served as the creative arts director for the Roxbury Children's Theater in Dorchester, Massachusetts. She earned her M.F.A. from Brandeis University in 1975. Subsequently, Gibson administered arts programs for such institutions as WGBH-TV in Boston and Comprehensive Employment and Training (CETA) Arts Program in New York. More recently she taught at the John Jay College of Criminal Justice, where she has been an assistant professor of English.

Gibson has received many honors, such as a Schubert Fellowship, a National Endowment for the Arts play writing grant, and the 1985 Audelco Award for best play and playwright of the year for *Long Time*.

PLAYS

Ain't Love Grand? (musical), 1980; *The Androgyny*, 1979; *Angel*, 1981; *The Black Woman*, 1972; *Brown Silk and Magenta Sunsets*, 1981; *Clean Sheets Can't Soil*, 1983; *Doing It to Death*, 1977; *Konvergence*, 1973; *Long Time Since Yesterday*, 1985; *Miss Ann Don't Cry No More*, 1980; *My Mark, My Name*, 1981; *The Ninth Story Window* (one-act), 1974; *Private Hells, Sketches in Reality* (trilogy), 1981; *Shameful in Your Eyes*, 1971; *Spida Bug* (one-act), 1975; *The Unveiling of Abigail*, 1981; *Void Passage* (one-act), 1973; *The Zappers and the Shopping Bag Lady* (one-act), 1979

1. Unpublished interview with Wilkerson (September 1985), cited in Wilkerson.

2. Review by Elizabeth Bello in *Show Business*, March 13, 1980.

Natalia Ginzburg
(JULY 14, 1916–OCTOBER 7, 1991)

I haven't managed to become learned about anything, even the things I've loved most in my life: in me they remain scattered images, which admittedly feed my life of memories and feelings, but fail to fill my empty cultural wasteland . . .

—from *He and I*

The political drama of Natalia Ginzburg's life initially appears to contrast with the "seemingly banal details of middle-class life"[1] that pepper her creative work. She came of age in Palermo, Italy, when Mussolini was beginning his reign of terror. As the fifth child of actively anti-fascist Jews, Ginzburg understood firsthand the connection between the personal and the political.

She began writing poetry at the age of ten, and completed several novels while still in her teens. Her work was first published in the avant-garde literary journal *Solaria* in 1934, the same year her father and brother were briefly imprisoned by the Nazis. Later that year, she married Leone Ginzburg, a Russian intellectual and hero of the Resistance. For the release of her first published novel, *La strada che va in cittá* (The Road to the City, 1943), Ginzburg adopted the pseudonym Alessandra Tornimparte in order to obscure her Jewish identity. The book received acclaim, but her writing was interrupted by a personal tragedy: In 1944 her husband died in an Italian jail after having been tortured by the Gestapo. Left alone to raise their daughter Alessandra, Ginzburg did not publish again until several years after the war.

She remarried in 1950, and had two sons with her new husband, Gabriel Boldine, an English literature professor at the University of Rome. Over the next fifteen years Ginzburg produced many novels, including *Tutti e nostri*

iere (A Light for Fools), *Le voci della sera* (Voices in the Evening), and *Lessico famigliare* (Family Sayings), which won the prestigious Premio Strega in 1964. Her fiction's "deceptively simple, antirhetorical, conversational style, and her autobiographical themes . . . soon established her as one of contemporary Italy's preeminent writers and the most popular female novelist of her generation," according to Peter Bondanella of Indiana University's Center for Italian Studies.[2]

Ginzburg did not begin writing plays until she was nearly fifty years old. Nevertheless, her first effort, *L'inserzione* (The Advertisement, 1965) received the Marzotto Prize for European Drama and has been produced in English by London's Old Vic as well as the BBC. *L'inserzione* is a psychological thriller; the main character, Teresa, is a lonely woman disregarded and abandoned by Lorenzo, a man who married her only to spite his mother. Teresa places an ad for a boarder and takes in the independently minded Elena, with whom she becomes obsessed. When Lorenzo returns, he falls in love with Elena and persuades her to flee with him. The murderous finale testifies to the dangers of manipulative, codependent relationships. Another notable drama is *Ti ho sposato per allegria* (I Married You for Happiness, 1965).

Although most of Ginzburg's fiction focuses on the sensitivity, melancholy, and pessimism in human relationships, Anne-Marie O'Healy suggests that her plays introduce somewhat different themes, such as "the disintegration of marriage and the family, as well as the absence of moral responsibility, emotion, memory, and hope in the world of today."[3] While Ginzburg has proclaimed Harold Pinter to be the dramatist who has most influenced her, her style has been widely compared by critics to that of everyone from Anton Chekhov to Albert Camus and Jean-Paul Sartre. Most seem to agree on one aspect, however: Her characters are always depicted with psychological subtlety and poetic beauty.

Ginzburg served in the Italian parliament for a single term in the mid-1980s. She died in 1991.

PLAYS

Dialogo (Dialogue), 1970; *Fragola e panna* (Strawberries and Cream), 1966; *L'inserzione* (The Advertisement, Henry Reed tr.), 1965; *Paese di mare* (Sea Resort), 1968; *La parrucca* (The Wig), 1971; *La porta sbagliata* (The Wrong Door), 1968; *La segretaria* (The Secretary), 1967; *Teresa*, 1970; *Ti ho sposato per allegria* (I Married You for Happiness), 1965

OTHER WORKS (SELECTED)

Caro Michele (No Way), 1973; *La città e la casa* (The City and the House), 1984; *Famiglia*, 1977; *Lessico famigliare*

(Family Sayings), 1963; *Mai devi domandarmi* (Never Must You Ask Me; essays), 1970; *Serena Cruz*, 1990; *La strada che va in città* (The Road to the City), 1943; *Tutti e nostri iere* (A Light for Fools), 1952; *Vita immaginaria* (essays), 1974; *Le voci della sera* (Voices in the Evening), 1961

1. From essay by Peter Bondanella in Hochman.

2. Ibid.

3. *Canadian Journal of Italian Studies*, Spring 1986.

Zinaida Gippius
(NOVEMBER 8, 1869–SEPTEMBER 9, 1945)

The Russian writer Zinaida Nikolayevna Gippius (referred to in some texts as Hippius) was a proponent of mystical Christianity. Her earliest dramatic work, *Skvataya krov* (Sacred Blood; 1901) was a precursor to the folkloric trend in literature and drama that accompanied the pending Neo-Romantic movement. The play portrays the familiar tale of a water sprite who longs to be human, but Gippius offers a Christian twist. It is the story of Jesus Christ that inspires the water sprite's desire to become human, a transformation she can achieve only through demonstrating her true love for Jesus. The test of her love is a great sacrifice: She must murder her dearest friend, a monk. This dramatic fantasy came at a time when the Moscow Art Theater had practically cemented the form of naturalistic theater under the guidance of Stanislavsky. It was not long before criticisms of Stanislavsky's theater began to appear and a "new drama" of symbolism and spiritualism was extolled, according to Harold Segel.[1]

In the early 1900s, Gippius met her husband, Dimitri Merezhkovsky (1865–1941), a fairly well-known Symbolist writer especially noted for his 1887 fairy tale adaptation of Calderón's* *La vida es sueño* (Life Is a Dream). Soon the two were collaborating on dramatic pursuits, beginning with *Makov tsvet* (The Red Poppy; 1912), which they wrote with D. V. Filosofov. (Some speculate, however, that Gippius had previously penned this work herself.) The play explores the repercussions borne by an affluent Russian family after the Revolution of 1905, an event that Gippius and her husband had once supported, but with which they had become disillusioned. *Zelyonoe koltso* (The Green Ring; 1914) focused on a group of young rebels, members of "The Green Ring Society," who were at odds with their elders. Not coincidentally, Mer-

ezhkovsky had formed a Green Lamp Society among his and Gippius's literary friends.

The work of Gippius and Merezhkovsky was abruptly halted with the advent of the Russian Revolution and the rise of the Soviet Union. Like their Latvian contemporaries, ASPĀZIJA and Rainis, the couple was not able to return to their homeland. Gippius and many of her contemporaries found themselves to be considered members of a decadent literary trend, and their work was summarily dismissed. The pair emigrated to Paris, returning to Russia just before the outbreak of World War I. Vehemently anti-Bolshevik, they once again left the "new" country (now the Soviet Union) and returned to Paris in 1920, where the Russian-born Gippius remained until her death. She continued to write novels, short stories, critical and political essays, and plays throughout her life, several of which were bitter, angry works against the Bolsheviks.

PLAYS*

Makov tsvet (The Red Poppy), w/Merezhkovsky & D. V. Filosofov, 1912; *Syvataya krov* (Sacred Blood), 1901; *Zelyonoe koltso* (The Green Ring), 1914

OTHER WORKS

Between Paris and Petersburg: Selected Diaries of Z. G., 1975; *Chortova kukla* (The Devil's Doll), n.d.

1. Segel.

Susan Glaspell
(JULY 1, 1876/82–JULY 27, 1948)

STEPHEN. If you're going to separate from psychoanalysis, there's no reason why I should separate from you!
HENRIETTA. What am I supposed to do with my suppressed desires?
STEPHEN. Mabel, you just keep right on suppressing them!

—from *Suppressed Desires*

Susan Glaspell earned acclaim not only for her literary works, but also for her pioneering contributions to American theater. With her husband George Cram Cook, the Pulitzer Prize-winning playwright helped found the influential Provincetown Players, a leading playhouse in the nation's regional theater movement.

Her late-nineteenth-century childhood in Davenport, Iowa, was unexceptional: She received a public school ed-

---

*Pedro Calderón de la Barca (1600–1681), Spanish dramatist and poet who succeeded Lope de Vega as the leading Spanish playwright of the Golden Age.

---

*Some of Gippius's works have been translated into English by Temira Pachmuss.

Susan Glaspell
COURTESY OF THE BILLY ROSE THEATRE COLLECTION

ucation and spent summers on her aunt's farm. At Drake University, Glaspell began to pursue a career in journalism. She wrote a column for the *Davenport Morning Republican* called "The Weekly Outlook" and, after graduating from Drake in 1899, joined the reporting staff of the *Des Moines News*. In 1901 she decided to commit herself fully to creative writing.

Short stories and sentimental novels comprise Glaspell's first fictional efforts. With the prize money she won for an early short piece, she joined the Monist Society, an organization for progressive thinkers founded by George Cram Cook, the son of one of Davenport's leading families. Cook had stood on the faculties of Stanford University and the University of Iowa, and was a respected editor, journalist, critic, novelist, and poet. His energy and enthusiasm electrified Glaspell, challenging her to push her creative abilities beyond simple fiction. He was equally taken with her, and divorced his second wife to marry Glaspell on April 14, 1913.

The couple relocated to New York City, where they involved themselves with the artistic community of Greenwich Village. Glaspell trained briefly with the Neighborhood Playhouse and in 1915 felt ready to stage her first play, a one-act collaboration with Cook entitled *Suppressed*

Desires, which offered a satirical look at the potential backfiring of psychoanalysis. The play's central character, neurotic Henrietta Brewster, undergoes analysis and soon begins to analyze her husband, her marriage, and basically everything else, until she is utterly immobilized. Finally, she fires her analyst and stays with her husband.

Unfortunately, the Cooks could not find a willing theater to produce the show. When the Washington Square Players rejected it, the couple invited several people to their home for a group reading. Neith Boyce brought along her play *Constancy*, and the evening was such a success, the group decided to mount both plays themselves.

Glaspell, Cook, and their friends had frequently spent summers in Provincetown, Massachusetts. In the summer of 1915 they enlisted Robert Edmond Jones, the stage designer who popularized the "New Stagecraft," to help transform a 25-square-foot Provincetown space into a theater venue. *Suppressed Desires* premiered on a 10-by 12-foot stage at what was dubbed the Wharf Theatre.

The following year the Provincetown Players, as they came to be known, cemented their commitment to noncommercial, experimental theater with a staging of Eugene O'Neill's *Bound East for Cardiff*. Accompanying O'Neill's play was Glaspell's second one-act, *Trifles* (1916), which Helene Keyssar calls a "provocative archetype of that form of drama in which there is a focus on female characters and the particular obstacles these characters encounter *because* they are women."[1] A murder-mystery melodrama, the play weaves the tale of two middle-aged rural women and a young male detective, all attempting to find out who murdered the husband of another local woman, Minnie Wright. The detective employs his "surefire" techniques to solve the crime, dismissing the two women who occupy themselves with useless "trifles": Minnie's preserves and unfinished quilt. As the women figure out that Minnie was the murderer, and that she was possibly justified (note the name *Wright*) due to the abuse and cruelty she suffered under her husband, Glaspell's play reveals the danger of men's arrogance toward women. *Trifles* also shows how isolated women can become from one another: "We live close together and we live far apart," says one of the women.

For seven years the Provincetown Players provided playwrights with a place to experiment freely with their ideas. Glaspell continued to write experimental works for the theater, and in 1921 she produced her own play, *The Verge*, an expressionistic masterpiece that predated O'Neill's *The Hairy Ape* by several months. The play centers on the life of Claire Archer, a woman who yearns to defy conventions and yet surrounds herself with ordinary men (Tom, Dick, and Harry, who are, respectively, lover, friend, and husband). She decided to create a greenhouse "dedicated to producing plants that are not better or prettier, but radically different from previous ones."[2] *The Verge* has been noted as "the strongest example of [Glaspell's] rule breaking, and her most overt treatment of the feminist theme. In it, she not only embraces the concept of women's liberation from encrusted social shackles, but also explores the dangers in making that position (and by implication, any radicalism) absolute."[3]

In 1922 Cook and Glaspell determined to settle in Greece for a time. They had lived there only two years when George died quite suddenly. Glaspell returned to the United States. Her only play during the next six years was *The Comic Artist*, which she coauthored with Norman Häghem Matson, a writer seventeen years younger, with whom she lived for seven years.

Glaspell reemerged as a serious dramatist in 1930 with *Alison's House*, a loose adaptation of Genevieve Taggart's biography of Emily Dickinson. The play portrays a gathering of the surviving members of the family of a deceased poet (Alison) on New Year's Eve, 1899. A key character is Elsa, Alison's niece, a headstrong young woman who has disgraced the family by running off with a married man. In the course of the drama, Elsa discovers that her aunt, a spinster poet, once forsook a lover in order to sustain her loyalty to her art. Glaspell's play exposes the complex choices and sacrifices artists, especially women artists, make in their lives. Ultimately, Elsa recognizes that "it is Alison, not she, who has found [through self-sacrifice] an autonomous definition of her life and ultimately is the more liberated of the two."[4] *Alison's House* opened at Eva Le Gallienne's Civic Repertory Theatre on December 1, 1930, just shy of the centennial anniversary of Dickinson's birth. The play was extremely well received, and won the Pulitzer Prize for Drama in 1931.

After receiving the Pulitzer, Glaspell slowed down somewhat. She did not write any more plays, though she continued to create works of fiction. However, she did not abandon theater altogether. In 1936 she took a position with the Works Projects Administration Federal Theater Project in Chicago, Illinois, and helped mount works by many young playwrights.

Glaspell is widely recognized as a major figure in American theater history, as both an innovator and a writer. "Women seeking to live freely, unfettered by male domination, societal restriction, or personal cowardice, are the most dominant concerns in the six full-length plays that Glaspell wrote," remarks Linda Ben-Avi of Colorado State University at Fort Collins. "These plays focus on a fully developed female heroine. Next to those dominant women, the men with whom they live—husbands, fathers, lovers, are painfully lacking in vigor and intelligence. They are portrayed as incapable of understanding the women and, for the most part, resentful of certain women's superiority and independence."[5]

PLAYS

Alison's House, 1930; *Bernice* (also novel; 1924), 1919; *Chains of Dew*, 1922; *Close the Book*, 1917; *The Comic Artist*, w/Norman Matson, 1927; *The Inheritors*, 1921; *The Outside*, 1917; *The People*, 1917; *Suppressed Desires*, w/George Cram Cook, 1915; *Tickless Time*, w/G. C. C., 1918; *Trifles*, 1916; *The Verge*, 1921; *Woman's Honor*, 1918

OTHER WORKS

Ambrose Holt and Family, 1931; *Brook Evans*, 1928; *Cherished and Shared of Old*, 1940; *Fidelity*, 1915; *The Fugitive's Return*, 1929; *The Glory of the Conquered*, 1909; *Judd Rankin's Daughter* (reissued as *The Prodigal Giver*), 1945; *Lifted Masks* (short stories), 1912; *The Morning Is Near Us*, 1940; *Norma Ashe*, 1943; *The Road to the Temple* (bio. of Cook), 1927; *The Visioning*, 1910

WORKS ABOUT

Ben-Zvi, Linda, ed., *Susan Glaspell: Essays on her Theater and Fiction*, 1995; Makowsky, Veronica A., *Susan Glaspell's Century of American Women: A Critical Interpretation of her Work*, 1993; Papke, Mary E., *Susan Glaspell: A Research and Production Sourcebook*, 1993; Waterman, Arthur E., *Susan Glaspell*, 1966

1. Keyssar.
2. Quoted by Robert K. Sarlós in Hawkins-Dady (1).
3. Ibid.
4. Olauson.
5. Essay by Linda Ben-Zvi in Robinson.

Gertrudis Gómez de Avellaneda
(1814–1873)

According to essayist Judith Weiss, the plays of Cuban-born Spanish national Gertrudis Gómez de Avellaneda were an important part of the transition between the neoclassical period and romanticism. Although historically noted more for her poetry, Gómez's dramatic works, while sometimes viewed as imitative or sentimental, "are clearly excellent studies of human sentiment and the psychology of love, and she explored religious themes with a similar depth."[1]

The daughter of a navy captain, Gómez was born in Puerto Príncipe in Cuba, which was at that time a Spanish colony. Longing for a richer literary life, she moved to Spain in 1853 to study and write. Shortly thereafter, she became renowned for her writings and academic abilities, and was even nominated to the Royal Academy of Spain in 1853. She was rejected, however, most likely due to her sex.

She married Pedro Sabater, also a writer, and an invalid whom she nursed until his death. In 1855 she married again, this time to Colonel Domingo Verdugo, a man with connections to Spanish royalty. After they had been together four years, he was the target of an assassination attempt, so the pair moved to Cuba.

During Gómez's heyday, both Spaniards and Cubans considered her one of their leading writers. For a time she edited the review *El album cubano*. When Verdugo died, Gómez sojourned to the United States for a brief spell before returning to Spain in 1864. Sadly, her fame had faded. Alone and in a state of personal crisis, she died in Spain in 1873.

PLAYS

Alfonso Munio, 1844; *Baltasar* (Balthazar), 1858; *Egilona*, 1945; *Saul*, 1849; *Simpatía y antipatía* (Sympathy and Antipathy), 1855; *Los tres amores* (The Three Loves), 1858

WORKS ABOUT

Gómez de Avellaneda y Arteaga, Gertrudis, *Sab and Autobiography*, tr. and ed. by Nina M. Scott, 1993; Harter, Hugh A., *Gertrudis Gomez de Avellaneda*, 1981; Williams, Edwin Bucher, *The Life and Dramatic Works of Gertrudis Gomez de Avellaneda*, 1924

1. Essay by Judith A. Weiss in Hochman.

Ruth Gordon
COURTESY OF CORBIS-BETTMANN

Ruth Gordon
(OCTOBER 30, 1896–AUGUST 28, 1985)

RUTH. I got anything I want to have; but I'll never have anything at all if trouble makes me go and give up!

—from *Years Ago*

For more than seventy years Ruth Gordon wowed audiences with her unmistakable voice and charm in screen performances as wide-ranging as Dolly Levi in *The Matchmaker* and the demonic Minnie Castevet in *Rosemary's Baby*, for which she won an Academy Award for Best Supporting Actress in 1968; she also won an Emmy for her work on the TV series "Taxi." Unbeknownst to the vast majority of her film and television fans, this vivacious and energetic woman also established herself as a screenwriter and playwright.

Her show biz career began early: She made her stage debut in 1915 as Nibs in *Peter Pan* and was praised for such roles as Nora in *A Doll's House* (1937) and Dolly Levi in the original production of *The Matchmaker* (1954). She made her movie debut as Mary Todd Lincoln in *Abe Lincoln of Illinois* (1940). Her first husband, Gregory Kelly, was her leading man in *Seventeen*, a road show in which she was playing in 1921. Together they opened a theater company in Indianapolis, but Kelly died in 1927. Gordon met Garson Kanin in 1939. Their marriage, which took place three years later, was a lasting one.

Each of Gordon's four plays, as well as her several screenplays, features strong female leads. Her 1946 drama *Years Ago* realistically illustrates the relationship between a pragmatic father (having become unemployed, he tells his wife, "Rest easy . . . I been cast overboard before. It ain't like I was lookin' for a job as vice president; there's always plenty of room at the bottom.") and his aspiring actress daughter, Ruth. In the course of the play, despite several setbacks, Ruth remains undeterred, garnering her father's respect and support. On a different note is the family of Mrs. Lord from *A Very Rich Woman*. Greedy and uncaring, they are interested only in what they will inherit from their wealthy, widowed mother, a generous albeit zany woman played by Gordon herself. The family has the mother committed in order to get their hands on the cash immediately. Only a few of Mrs. Lord's friends and her grown granddaughter, Daphne, remain genuine. The play is fast-paced and very funny, and reminiscent of Lear and his daughters.

Gordon and Kanin coauthored the play *Leading Lady* as well as several screenplays, including the Katharine Hepburn and Spencer Tracy classics *Adam's Rib* (1949) and *Pat and Mike* (1952). Gordon continued to act and write until her death in 1985. Along with her stage and film work, she penned several autobiographies. But she will probably be best remembered for her portrayal of the incorrigible and indomitable Maude in the cult classic film *Harold and Maude* (1972).

PLAYS

Leading Lady, w/Garson Kanin, 1948; *Over Twenty-One*, 1944; *A Very Rich Woman* (also screenplay, *Rosie!*, 1967), 1965; *Years Ago*, 1946

SCREENPLAYS

The Actress, 1953; *Adam's Rib*, 1949; *A Double Life*, 1947; *The Marrying Kind*, 1952; *Pat and Mike*, 1952

AUTOBIOGRAPHIES

Myself Among Others, 1971; *My Side*, 1976; *Ruth Gordon: An Open Book*, 1980

Augusta Gregory
(MARCH 5, 1852–MAY 22, 1932)

It is better to be quarreling than to be lonesome.

—from *The Workhouse Ward*

In *Inishfallen, Fare Thee Well*, the autobiography of Irish writer Sean O'Casey, he describes his beloved friend Augusta Gregory as "a sturdy, stout little figure soberly clad in solemn black, made gay with a touch of something white. . . . Her face was a rugged one, hardy as that of a peasant, curiously lit with an odd dignity, and softened with a careless touch of humour in the bright eyes and the curving wrinkles crowding around the corners of the firm little mouth. She looked like an old, elegant nun of a new order, a blend of the Lord Jesus Christ and of Puck, an order that Ireland had never known before, and wasn't likely to know again for a long time to come." O'Casey was not alone in his affection for Gregory; his esteem for her was shared by some of the greatest writers of the Irish Renaissance, including William Butler Yeats and John Millington Synge, both of whom worked with Gregory to develop the Abbey Theatre in Dublin, a venue that actively advocated an appreciation of Irish literature and drama.

Most of Gregory's prodigious oeuvre was staged at the Abbey.

The twelfth of her parents' sixteen children, Gregory spent her early years in Galway on her family's estate. She was greatly influenced by her Catholic nurse, Mary Sheridan, who mesmerized Augusta with traditional Irish fairy tales and folklore. Sheridan so impressed her shy young ward that years later, Gregory, despite her intense Protestant conviction, could create Catholic peasant characters in plays that "[transposed] the gentleness of Irish saintly legend into religious plays acceptable to Catholic and Protestant alike."[1]

An unexpected trip to the south of France with her mother and ill brother in 1879 resulted in a chance meeting with Sir William Gregory, another Galway resident until then unacquainted with Augusta's family. A charming and distinguished widower who had recently retired from the governorship of Ceylon, Sir William's cultural aptitude fascinated Augusta, then twenty-seven years old. The widower reciprocated her affection, and, not long after returning to Galway, they were married at Sir William's estate, Coole Park. Although more than thirty years separated them, the Gregorys were rarely apart. They traveled widely, engaged themselves with London's intelligentsia, and had one child, Robert, born in 1881.

When Sir William died in 1892, Gregory was only modestly provided for, as the estate and rents of Coole Park would pass to her son when he came of age. She determined to earn money by her pen, and began by editing her husband's memoirs, which prompted her to learn Kiltartan, the Anglo-Irish dialect of western Ireland. Soon she was completely absorbed in the revival of traditional Irish folklore and literary traditions.

In 1897 she met the great lyric poet Yeats. They, with Synge and others, founded the Irish Literary Theater, which opened with Yeats's *The Countess Cathleen*. When the Irish Literary Theater became the Abbey, Gregory assumed the roles of artistic director and financial manager: She conducted rehearsals, wrote letters, read scripts, led the Abbey on American tours, raised money, and, not least of all, wrote nearly forty plays for the company.

Impressed by the works of Molière, whose dramas she regularly translated for the Abbey, Gregory found her niche writing Irish "folk history" plays. She began in 1902 by translating and adapting for the stage old Gaelic sagas inspired by her visits with Irish country folk, such as *Cuchulain of Muirthemne* (1902). "[With its] musical and caressing English which never goes very far from the idiom of the people she knows so well," as Yeats said, Gregory introduced her country's non-Kiltartan-speakers to their linguistic and literary heritage.

Gregory's one-acts have been lauded for their realistic portrayal of peasant life. A favorite theme of hers was the power of language. In *Spreading the News* (1904), she reveals the dangers of gossiping, and in *The Rising of the Moon* (1907) she shows how the right words can persuade even the most stubborn individual to have a change of heart. Her 1908 one-act *The Workhouse Ward* portrays two quarrelsome old men, Mike McInerney and Michael Miskell, confined to a debtors' prison. When McInerney's newly widowed sister instigates his release, he refuses to leave without his cell mate and partner in argument of five years. "I sometimes think the two scolding paupers are a symbol of ourselves in Ireland," wrote Gregory.[2]

Also noteworthy are two of Gregory's full-length plays: *The White Cockade* (1905), a folk-history version of James II's flight from Ireland after the Battle of the Boynce, and *Grania* (1907), a three-person drama that sparked Yeats to remark incredulously, "They must have a great deal to talk about." Gregory replied, "And so they have, for the talk of lovers is inexhaustible, being of themselves and one another."[3]

Gregory worked tirelessly for the Abbey. She fed the poorly paid company with baskets of food brought from Coole Park, and fought for the staging of controversial plays, such as Synge's *Playboy of the Western World* (howled down by Dubliners) and George Bernard Shaw's *Showing up of Blanco Posnet* (threatened with censorship by the Viceroy).

She maintained close friendships with her Abbey colleagues. Her estate at Coole Park was kept open as a retreat for poets and playwrights. Yeats was a regular each summer, and celebrated the surrounding woods, lake, and the house itself with his poems. Of her friendship with Synge, Gregory wrote, "We became friends at once. I said of him in a letter: 'One never has to rearrange one's mind to talk to him.' "[4] She and Sean O'Casey were extraordinarily close. They met shortly after her son, Robert, died in the war, and O'Casey's beloved mother passed on. Not only did Gregory discover him as a playwright, she became for him a substitute mother, and he a substitute son. Of Gregory O'Casey wrote, "In the theatre, among the poets and playwrights, she a better playwright than most of them, she acted the part of a charwoman, but one with a star on her breast."

Gregory's last play, *Dave* (1927), was written when she was seventy-four. Her work was heavily criticized after her death due to her Republican sympathies, as well as her family's reputation as Protestant proselytizers. Even during her lifetime, Augusta Gregory was keenly aware of her critics. She had helped anchor the first state-subsidized theater in the English-speaking world, an accomplishment that did not come without its sacrifices. When a government-appointed official interfered with the Abbey's plans, Gregory remarked, "If we have to choose between subsidy and our freedom, it is our freedom we choose."[5]

PLAYS

Aristotle's Bellows, 1921; *The Bogie Men*, 1912; *The Canavans*, 1906; *Coats*, 1910; *Colman and Guaire*, 1898; *Cuchulain of Muirthemne*, 1902; *Damer's Gold*, 1913; *Dave*, 1927; *The Deliverer*, 1911; *Dervorgilla*, 1907; *The Doctor in Spite of Himself*, 1906; *The Dragon*, 1919; *The Full Moon*, 1910; *The Gaol Gate*, 1906; *The Golden Apple* 1920; *Grania*, 1907; *Hanrahan's Oath*, 1918; *Hyacinth Halvey*, 1906; *The Image*, 1909; *The Jackdaw*, 1907; *The Jester*, 1923; *Kincora*, 1905; *A Losing Game*, 1902; *MacDonough's Wife*, 1912; *The Old Woman Remembers*, 1923; *The Poorhouse*, w/Douglas Hyde, 1903; *The Rising of the Moon*, 1906; *Sancho's Master*, 1927; *Shanwalla*, 1914; *Spreading the New*, 1904; *The Story Brought by Brigit*, 1924; *The Travelling Man*, 1909; *Twenty-Five* (a.k.a. *On the Racecourse*, 1926), 1903; *The White Cockade*, 1905; *The Workhouse Ward*, 1908; *The Wrens*, 1914; *The Unicorn from the Stars*, w/William Butler Yeats, 1902

OTHER WORKS (SELECTED)

Autobiography of Sir William Gregory, ed., 1894; *A Book of Saints and Wonders*, 1907; *A Case for the Return of Hugh Lane's Pictures to Dublin*, 1926; *Coole*, 1931; *Gods and Fighting Men*, 1904; *The Golden Apple* (illus. by Margaret Gregory), 1916; *Hugh Lane's Life and Achievement, with some account of the Dublin Galleries*, 1921; *The Kiltartan History Book*, 1910; *The Kiltartan Molière*, 1910; *The Kiltartan Poetry Book*, 1918; *The Kiltartan Wonder Book* (illus. by M.G.), 1910; *Lady Gregory's Journals*, ed., Lennox Robinson, 1946; *Mr. Gregory's Letter Box*, ed., 1898; *Our Irish Theatre*, 1914; *Poets and Dreamers*, 1903; *Saints and Wonders, Seventy Years: 1852–1922; Being the Autobiography of Lady Gregory*, Colin Smythe, ed., 1974; *Visions and Beliefs in the West of Ireland*, 1920

WORKS ABOUT (SELECTED)

Blunt, Wilfrid Scawen, ed., *Diaries*, 1921; Coxhead, Elizabeth, *Lady Gregory: A Literary Portrait*, rev. ed., 1966; Coxhead, *Lady Gregory: Selected Plays*, 1962; Fay, Gerard, *The Abbey Theatre, Cradle of Genius*, 1957; Gonne, Maud, *A Servant of the Queen*, 1938; Gregory, Dr. Vere H., *The House of Gregory*, 1943; Kohfeldt, M. L., *Lady Gregory, The Woman Behind the Irish Renaissance*, 1985; Mikhail, E. H., ed., *Lady Gregory, Interviews and Recollections*, 1977; Saddlemyer, Ann, *In Defence of Lady Gregory*, 1966

1. Coxhead, Elizabeth, *Lady Gregory, A Literary Portrait* (London: Macmillan, 1961).

2. Notes, *The Workhouse Ward*, cited in the foreword by Sean O'Casey in *Lady Gregory: Selected Plays*, chosen and introduced by Elizabeth Coxhead (London: Putnamn, 1962).

3. Op. cit., notes to *Grania* in *A Literary Portrait*.

4. Op. cit., *Selected Plays*.

5. Op. cit., *A Literary Portrait*.

Jessica Tarahata Hagedorn
(1949–)

NARRATOR. As he often told his friend, the painter Frisquito: "I can no longer tolerate contradiction. This country is full of contradiction. If I stay, I shall go crazy." (*Pause*) Frisquito told Bongbong: "There's nothing wrong with being crazy. Being crazy is good for art. The thing to do is to get comfortable with it."

—from *Tenement Lover*

Philippine-born poet, performance artist, novelist, and playwright Jessica Tarahata Hagedorn creates works that reflect her experience as a woman artist of color in the United States. Having immigrated to San Francisco with her family in the 1960s, she has experienced firsthand the issues that fuel her work: "Otherness, the idea of revolution on many levels, terrorism, dominant culture vs. so-called minority culture. And the idea of home, what homesickness and home mean."[1]

Although her earliest writings consist primarily of poetry, Hagedorn has a strong affinity for theater and performance. She attended the American Conservatory Theater's training program and in the mid-1970s joined a collective of women writers and artists of color, which included NTOZAKE SHANGE and Thulani Davis, both of whom influenced Hagedorn's work. The collective published *Third World Women in the Early 1970s*, a multimedia anthology that combines poetry with the works of other artists in dance, music, and film.

The interplay of different media became the signature style of Hagedorn's later work. She assembled a musical group called the West Coast Gangster Choir (later the Gangster Choir) and began to write "little theatrical moments" to be incorporated between songs. The band was soon a popular act at colleges and universities throughout Northern California.

In 1978 she moved to New York City, leaving behind the rich artistic climate among artists of color in San Francisco. Despite the toughness she encountered in New York, Hagedorn says she "welcomed the change, because I wanted more muscle and less sentimentality in what I wrote."[2] Three years later she staged her first major theatrical production, *Tenement Lover* (1981).

Her theatrical work continues to interweave poetry and music, particularly jazz and R&B. Ping Chong, the internationally noted performance artist, has been an inspiration. Her work has been well received; *Dogeaters*, a novel, was nominated for a 1990 National Book Award.

Regardless of the medium she utilizes, Hagedorn recognizes her common themes: "In all my writing there are always these characters who have a sense of displacement, a sense of being in self-exile, belonging nowhere—or anywhere. I think these themes are the human story. When it comes down to it, it's all about finding shelter, finding your identity."[3]

PLAYS

Holy Food (radio play), 1989; *A Nun's Story* (dance theater), 1988; *Tenement Lover: no palm trees/in new york city*, 1981; *Travels in the Combat Zone* (video recording), 1982

OTHER WORKS

Charlie Chan Is Dead, ed., 1993; *Danger and Beauty*, 1993; *Dangerous Music*, 1975; *Dogeaters*, 1990; *The Gangster of*

Love (novel), 1996; *Pet Food & Tropical Apparitions*, 1981; *Third World Women in the Early 1970s*, n.d.

WORKS ABOUT

Ostriker, Alicia Suskin, *Stealing the Language*, 1986; Piercy, Marge, ed., *Early Ripening: American Women's Poetry Now*, 1987; Rexroth, Kenneth, ed., *Four Young Women*, 1973

1. Berson, Misha, ed. *Between Worlds, Contemporary Asian-American Plays* (New York: Theatre Communications Group, 1990).
2. Ibid.
3. Ibid.

Lorraine Hansberry
(MAY 19, 1930–JANUARY 12, 1965)

LENA. Child, when do you think is the time to love somebody the most; when they done good and made things easy for everybody? Well then you ain't through learning—because that ain't the time at all. It's when he's at his lowest and can't believe in hisself 'cause the world done whipped him so. When you starts measuring somebody, measure him right, child, measure him right. Make sure you done taken into account what hills and valleys he come through before he got to wherever he is.

—from *A Raisin in the Sun*, Act III

Lorraine Hansberry's classic play *A Raisin in the Sun* marked a watershed in black American theater history. According to theater historian Mary Remnant, "The play did its part in helping to fuel the civil rights struggle, and opened up the world of black drama in the USA, stimulating the development of new writing for the theatre as well as creating a new black audience."[1]

Although *Raisin* firmly secured her place in history books, Hansberry had lived in the company and under the influence of important members of the black community throughout her life. Her family's upper-middle-class Chicago home served as a hub of black cultural, political, and economic life. Her uncle, William Leon Hansberry, a regular guest at the home during Lorraine's early years, was a distinguished Africanist at Howard University. Other visitors included Paul Robeson, Duke Ellington, Walter White, Joe Louis, and Jesse Owens. Hansberry's parents were both active community leaders. Her father, Carl, a realtor, involved himself with the NAACP, the Urban League, and various civic and business groups. He once ran for Congress on the Republican ticket.

Hansberry's social consciousness intensified in 1938 when her father moved the family into what had been a "restricted" Chicago neighborhood in order to test the covenants barring blacks. The Hansberrys suffered thrown bricks and smashed windows. Mobs gathered outside their home in protest. Her father continued to battle the racist laws; he sued, lost, appealed, and lost again. Finally the family was evicted from their home. With the backing of the NAACP, Carl Hansberry took the case to the U.S. Supreme Court and won a decision against restrictive covenants, but there was little practical effect for the family. Carl Hansberry died on May 17, 1946, in Mexico, where he had been planning to relocate his family to escape the racism they had suffered in the United States. Lorraine was still in high school at the time.

After studying art, literature, drama, and stage design for three years at the University of Wisconsin, Hansberry moved to New York City in 1950 for, as she put it, "an education of a different kind."[2] She began working for Paul Robeson's radical black monthly publication *Freedom*. In 1952 she attended the Intercontinental Peace Congress in Montevideo, Uruguay, as a substitute for Robeson, whose passport request was denied by the U.S. State Department.

Although Hansberry's interest in and connection to the theater community was evident throughout the early to mid-1950s, she did not complete her first play until later in the decade. Instead, she pursued her studies in the academic arena. In 1953 she attended the Jefferson School for Social Science where, under the tutelage of W. E. B. Du Bois, she focused on African history and culture. She married songwriter and publisher Robert Nemiroff that same year.

In 1957 Hansberry submitted *A Raisin in the Sun* to producers Burt D'Lugoff and Philip Rose. Rose promptly agreed to stage it. He signed on Sidney Poitier to play the male lead and Lloyd Richards, an actor who, with this assignment, would be Broadway's first mainstream black director. (Black directors were active in the early part of the century, when there was a separate black theater scene.) However, not a single Broadway theater agreed to open the play. Rose persevered; he thumbed his nose at Broadway's bigotry and took the show to New Haven, Connecticut, and Philadelphia.

The struggle to produce *Raisin* paid off. Packed houses and rave reviews left Broadway theaters knocking loudly at Rose's door. So in 1959 Hansberry became the first black woman to have a play produced on Broadway. When *Raisin* won the New York Drama Critics Circle Award, she became the first black writer, male or female, to receive it.

Raisin concerns the plight of the Youngers, a black family whose various members are struggling to find their places in society. Upon the death of the family patriarch, the Youngers unexpectedly receive a large sum of money from the insurance company. Lena, the matriarch, intends to use the cash for practical purposes: the purchase of a house, her daughter's education. But her son, Walter Lee

Lorraine Hansberry
COURTESY OF UPI/CORBIS-BETTMANN

(Poitier), wants the money to attain his version of the American dream: a self-owned business—in this case, a liquor store. Hansberry's empathetic and genuine portrayal of Lena and Walter Lee's conflict, along with those of the other family members, Lena's daughter, Beneatha, and Walter Lee's wife, Ruth, have moved audiences around the world for over thirty-five years.

Hansberry herself sees the play as a depiction of what happens to people when they endure "a dream deferred," a direct reference to the Langston Hughes poem "Montage of a Dream Deferred," which is printed with the published version of *Raisin*. The deferred dreams in the drama are both Walter Lee's, who suffers as a black man, and those of the women, whose racial strife is intensified by issues of gender. Indeed, the women of *Raisin* are actually more visible and more vocal than the men. Hansberry persistently calls attention to the direct-speaking, righteous Lena, and to the distinctiveness of Beneatha and Ruth—all of whom are rebuked by Walter Lee. Yet part of *Raisin*'s power is how seamlessly Hansberry connects the characters' struggles. In an interview with Frank Perry, Hansberry said, "It really doesn't matter whether you are talking about the oppressed or the oppressor. An oppressive society will dehumanize and degenerate everyone involved . . . and in certain very poetic and very true ways at the same time it will tend to make if anything the oppressed have more stature . . . because at least they are arbitrarily placed in the situation of overwhelming that which is degenerate . . . in this instance the slave society."[3]

The only other play Hansberry completed during her lifetime is *The Sign in Sidney Brustein's Window* (1964), a brutal, realistic drama about people's most universal conflicts: love and dependence, fear, personal growth, and denial. At one point, Gloria, a prostitute, says, "Things as they are are as they are and have been and will be that way because they got that way because things were as they were in the first place."

When Hansberry died of cancer at the age of thirty-four, she left several unfinished works. One, *Toussaint*, a complex look at the politics of oppression, almost certainly would have been a masterpiece. In it, the character Toussaint says, "We have something in our favor, Biassou. The Europeans will always underestimate us. They will believe again and again that they have come to fight slaves. (*He smiles at Biassou*). They will be fighting free men thinking they are fighting slaves, and again and again—that will be their undoing."

Hansberry's husband, Robert Nemiroff, kept her work in the public eye after her death. He adapted *Les Blancs*, one of the first major plays to address black liberation, in 1970. He also compiled Hansberry's letters, plays, and papers into a collection that was later dramatized as *To Be Young, Gifted and Black*. Her impacts on innumerable young theatrical aspirants, black and white, have been myriad: P. J. GIBSON was inspired to write her first play, *The Black Woman*, after seeing a production of *To Be Young, Gifted and Black*. Tim Bond, former artistic director of Seattle's Group Theatre, testifies, "Lorraine Hansberry's *A Raisin in the Sun* changed my life when I first encountered it as a child. To see a young black child my age in a truthful portrayal of a black family on stage with hundreds of people watching somehow legitimized my existence and gave me permission to dream of becoming whatever I wanted to in this country."[4]

"There is both joy and beauty and illumination and communion between people to be achieved through the dissection of personality," wrote Hansberry. "That's what I want to do. I want to reach a little closer to the world, which is to say people, and see if we can share some illuminations together about each other."[5]

PLAYS

The Arrival of Mr. Todog (playlet), n.d.; *Les Blancs*, 1972; *The Drinking Gourd* (teleplay), 1960; *Master of the Dew* (screenplay based on Jacques Romain's novel), n.d.; *A Raisin in the Sun*, 1958; *The Sign in Sidney Brustein's Window*, 1964; *Toussaint*, (uncompleted work), 1961; *What Use Are Flowers?*, 1972

OTHER WORKS

The Dark and Beautiful Warriors (novel), n.d.; *Raisin* (musical adapt. of play), 1974

WORKS ABOUT

Carter, Steven R., *Hansberry's Drama: Commitment Amid Complexity*, 1991; *Freedomways*, "Lorraine Hansberry: Art of Thunder, Vision of Light," special issue, December 1979; Nemiroff, Robert, *To Be Young, Gifted and Black* (play), 1968

1. Remnant.

2. Carter, Steven R. *Hansberry's Drama: Commitment and Complexity* (Urbana: University of Illinois, 1991).

3. Excerpt from unpublished transcript of interview with Lorraine Hansberry by Frank Perry on "Playwright at Work," educational television program, taped May 21, 1961.

4. Program notes to *A Raisin in the Sun* for The Group, October 21–November 20, 1994, Seattle, Wash.

5. From *To Be Young, Gifted and Black* by Robert Nemiroff (Englewood Cliffs, N.J.: Prentice-Hall, 1969).

Irene Hause
(1950–)

The work of Swedish playwright Irene Hause forthrightly focuses on women's identity, roots, and choices. "[Swedish] theaters are mostly owned by men," writes Hause. "Producers and directors are men. The playwrights are usually men. The world is described from a man's eye. The audience: more women than men. It's hard to break the wall—but it is necessary to let woman's world be told and seen." She continues, "When you are pushed in a corner, you have two possibilities: to give up or to fight."[1] Hause has clearly chosen the latter.

Born in Örebro, Sweden, Hause enrolled at the University of Stockholm after attending Skolcscen (a theater school) and Nyckelviksskolan (an art school). She started as an actress, intermittently working as a teacher, hospital worker, and restaurant employee. Her first play, *A Woman's Blues*, was produced in Stockholm in 1987 at the Pistolteatern. Since then four more of her plays have been presented at various Stockholm venues. She names the noted modernist writer Birgitta Trotzig* as a major influence. Hause currently lives in Stockholm with her son, Tobias.

---

*(1929–) Modernist author of novels and essays that assert the integrity of art and criticize materialism and secularism.

PLAYS

The Ballad of the Stranger, 1989; *Nicole*, 1992; *Räddare*, 1994; *White Shadow*, 1990; *A Woman's Blues*, 1987

1. From correspondence with the author, July 1994.

Eliza Fowler Haywood
(1689/93–FEBRUARY 25, 1756)

Criticks! be dumb to-night—no Skill display;
A dangerous Woman-Poet wrote the Play:
One, who not fears your Fury, tho' prevailing,
More than your Match, in every thing, but Railing.
Give her fair Quarter, and whene'er she tries ye,
Safe in superior Spirit, she defies ye . . .

—from *A Wife to Be Let*, prologue

Known primarily for her abundant romance novels, Eliza Haywood lived a somewhat outrageous life. She began humbly enough as the daughter of a London shopkeeper. In 1710 she married Valentine Haywood, a considerably older clergyman, and five years later they had a son. However, soon after the boy's birth, scandal spoiled the marriage. According to newspapers, Eliza had been spied in the company of a Mr. Andrew Yeatman. Rather than do penance for her affair, she left her husband and child, running away to a life in the theater (according to some reports, her husband left her, and there were two children). Haywood's newly claimed freedom had its shortcomings, however, particularly because she was now a "dishonorable woman" without income or legal protection. Nevertheless, with her sharp, curious mind and her self-educated awareness of the classics and French and English literature, she was determined to succeed.

By the following year, Haywood was performing regularly at Dublin's Smock-Alley Theatre. She enjoyed her acting career, but recognized that play writing presented potentially better financial gains. A popular play offered a writer nearly a year's income.[1] Haywood gave the theater her best shot with *The Fair Captive* (1721). It was a huge flop. She then unsuccessfully attempted to reconcile with her estranged husband.

Discouraged but still purposeful, Haywood turned to writing romantic fiction. Ironically, both she and her husband published separate books in the same year, 1719—his a rather dull theological treatise, hers a well-received romance. Haywood had found her niche; her romance novels brought her fame and fortune. She became the renowned "queen of the scandal-sheet, [and] as popular as Defoe."[2]

Her most loved romances were *The History of Miss Betsey Thoughtless* and *The History of Jemy and Jenny Jessamy*.

Unfortunately her stage dramas did not compare to her prose. But she sallied forth with them, and even acted the lead role in her comedy *A Wife to Be Let* (1723), in which the title character exposes her avaricious husband as a pimp. Her only real theatrical success came with a ballad opera that she, with William Hatchett, adapted from Henry Fielding's novel *Tragedy of Tragedies.*

Other well-known writers of Haywood's day generally did not share the public's affection for her work. Jonathan Swift called her "a stupid, infamous, scribbling woman,"[3] and Alexander Pope trounced her in *The Dunciad* (1728). Some feminist critics, however, have remarked that Haywood's "strength is her narrative techniques. . . . At her best she is highly entertaining, but the serious tone underlying even the lightest romance gives depth to her work. . . . One of her favorite themes [is] the education of women. Her arguments are cogent and pertinent; if they occasionally appear startling in their relevance to the twentieth century, it is perhaps because they are still part of a continuing debate, and her points remain tellingly sharp."[4]

From a contemporary perspective Haywood's greatest achievement may be the creation of *The Female Spectator* (1722–46), the first magazine created by and for women. A serious journal, it dealt with pertinent women's issues, as well as literature, art, and philosophy.

By the late 1720s, after only a decade of writing, Haywood had created thirty-eight works of fiction, several plays, and a number of translations. Nancy Cotton identifies her as "the most prolific woman writer of her time."[5] But in 1730 her literary output came to an abrupt halt. She offered no explanation for this sudden cessation in productivity. Some have speculated that she found a more reliable source of income, or that she could no longer endure the attacks on her character. Whatever the reason, she did not take up her pen again until the 1740s, and then never regained her previous popularity. Haywood died in obscurity "with two new novels ready for the press."[6]

PLAYS

The Fair Captive, 1721; *Frederick, Duke of Brunswick-Lunenburgh,* 1729; *The Opera of Operas, or Tom Thumb the Great,* w/William Hatchett, 1733; *The Secret History of the . . . Court of Carimania,* 1727; *A Wife to Be Let,* 1723

OTHER WORKS

La Belle Assemblee, or The Adventures of Six Days, 2 vols., 1724; *Clementina, or The History of an Italian Lady,* 1768; *The Disguised Prince, or The Beautiful Parisian,* 2 pts., 1728; *Epistles for the Ladies,* 2 vols., 1729; *The Female Spectator,* 4 vols., 1746; *The Fortunate Foundlings,* 1744;

The Fruitless Enquiry, 1767; *The History of Jemy and Jenny Jessamy,* 3 vols., 1753; *The History of Miss Betsey Thoughtless,* 1751; *The Husband,* 1756; *The Life of Madam de Villesache,* 1727; *Love in Excess,* 1719; *Love Letters on All Occasions,* 1730; *Mary, Queen of Scotland,* 1725; *Memoirs of a Certain Island Adjacent to the Kingdom of Utopia,* 2 vols., 1725; *The Mercenary Lover, or The Unfortunate Heiresses,* 1726; *A Present for Women Addicted to Drinking,* 1750; *Reflections on the Various Effects of Love,* 1726; *Secret Histories, Novels, and Poems,* 2 vols., 1724; *The Tea Table,* 1725; *The Unfortunate Princess,* 1741; *The Virtuous Villager, or The Virgin's Victory,* 2 vols., 1742; *The Wife,* 1756; *Works of Mrs. Eliza Haywood,* 4 vols., 1724

WORKS ABOUT

Whicher, George F., *The Life and Romances of Mrs. Eliza Haywood,* 1915

1. Mahl.
2. Morgan.
3. Mahl.
4. Mahl.
5. Cotton.
6. Mahl.

Lillian Hellman
(JUNE 20, 1905–JUNE 30, 1984)

BIRDIE. And then, and then, I saw Mama angry for the first time in my life. . . . She said she was old-fashioned enough not to like people who killed animals they couldn't use, and who made their money charging awful interest to ignorant niggers and cheating them on what they bought. She was very angry, Mama was. I had never seen her face like that. And then suddenly she laughed and said, "Look, I've frightened Birdie out of the hiccoughs." And so she had. They were all gone.
ADDIE. Yeah, they got mighty well-off cheating niggers. Well, there are people who eat the earth and eat all the people on it like in the Bible with the locusts. And other people who stand around and watch them eat it. Sometimes I think it ain't right to stand an' watch them do it.

—from *The Little Foxes,* Act III

The theatrical realm provided Lillian Hellman an ideal conduit for her anger, sardonic wit, smoldering sexuality, and rebellious nature. Her unique weave of wildness and sophistication formed during her childhood, which was spent alternately amid the swelter of New Orleans's Garden District with her father's family, old-time Southerners rooted in the swampy politics of Louisiana, and the cosmopolitan world of her mother's family, the upper-middle-class Newhouses of New York (who served as a model for the Hubbards in *The Little Foxes*). These contrasting environs caused conflict for the young Hellman, who was both disgusted by the materialistic Newhouses and attracted to the luxuries of their lives. Hellman also suffered from conflictive feelings toward her parents. Whereas she was contemptuous of her mother, she idolized her father until she discovered his infidelities. Her most stable childhood relationship existed with her black nurse Sophronia. Her great love for Sophronia suggests why Hellman found it natural and necessary to fill her plays with richly rendered black characters long before the American consciousness was raised in this respect.

Hellman remained in Manhattan after high school, furthering her education at New York and Columbia universities, although she did not graduate from either. She married the writer Arthur Kober in 1925 and began her career as a reader, first in Hollywood, where she read film scenarios at MGM, then back in New York, where she read plays for a theatrical producer. By the time she returned to the East Coast, Hellman was divorced from Kober and focused on finding success as a playwright. While still at MGM, she had met Dashiell Hammett. The chemistry between them was undeniable, and though he was thirteen years older than she, the two remained attached romantically and professionally until his death in 1960.

Hammett prodded Hellman to read a story based on a Scottish criminal trial known as the Great Drumsheugh Case about a child who falsely accuses her teachers of having a lesbian relationship. Inspired, Hellman submitted *The Children's Hour* to her producer-boss in 1934. The play opened on Broadway that same year. Like the original story, *The Children's Hour* centers on the lives of two schoolteachers, Karen and Martha, accused by Mary, a manipulative child, of having an "unnatural relationship." Despite its subject matter, the play is not a lesbian or feminist drama. Like many of Hellman's plays, the key issues of *The Children's Hour* are, as Helene Keyssar suggests, "mendacity and social hypocrisy."[1] In fact, Keyssar indicates that the play is ultimately antifeminist in that it "[supports] implicitly society's unhesitant rejection of lesbianism. . . . The woman who acknowledges her sexual attraction to another woman is rejected by everyone, including the friend she loves, and is filled with such self-loathing that she kills herself. . . . [The play] confirms stereotypical images of women and establishes little affection or respect for female characters."[2]

A controversial yet undeniable hit, *The Children's Hour* was nominated for the Pulitzer Prize for drama. It did not win, however, much to the chagrin of the critical community. (*Men in White* by Sidney Kingsley won.) Many felt the oversight of what was certainly an American classic was a veritable low point for the Pulitzer Prize committee.

The controversy over the prize led critics to establish the Drama Critics Circle Award.

Hellman sealed her reputation for delivering well-crafted melodramas in 1939 with *The Little Foxes*, a harsh tale of a cruel Southern family. As in *The Children's Hour*, none of the women characters in *Foxes* present "a constructive or alternative way of being a woman in American culture."[3] On the other hand, the play offers a variety of believable Southern women, such as the dominating, power-hungry Regina and her aptly named sister-in-law Birdie. Faded as the Old South, Birdie patters about the stage attending to the slightest whims of her husband's family. Although they are secondary roles, the black maid, Addie, and Alexandra, Regina's daughter, show a spirit and integrity not found in the other characters. Alexandra finally wrestles herself from the stranglehold of "the little foxes that destroy the vines while the vineyards flourish."[4] But it is Regina who dominates the play and in whom Hellman created a character so driven, so manipulative, "she has been considered one of the most formidable women characters in the history of American drama."[5]

Although Hellman did not consider herself especially political, she was keenly aware of the international political climate. In 1941, in the midst of World War II, Hellman's

Lillian Hellman
COURTESY OF THE BILLY ROSE THEATRE COLLECTION

first anti-fascism drama opened in New York. *Watch on the Rhine* was one of the first American plays to identify how close the threat of fascism was to U.S. soil. It follows the Muller family, refugees from Nazi Germany, to Washington, D.C., where they are tracked down by a Nazi sympathizer. Caught and threatened with blackmail, Kurt Muller must take desperate measures in order to save himself, his family, and the hope for a better world. *Rhine* hit a nerve with American audiences, jarred awake from their dream of isolationism. The play won Hellman her first New York Drama Critics Circle Award.

Hellman's other two plays of the 1940s reflect her continued interest in public and private matters. *The Searching Wind* (1944) again tackles brutish fascism, and *Another Part of the Forest* (1946) revisits the Hubbard family of *The Little Foxes*. It wasn't until *The Autumn Garden* (1950) that Hellman finally veered from her signature tight, linear drama. Apparently influenced by Anton Chekhov's *The Cherry Orchard, Autumn* centers on what Olauson calls "the universal daydream theme," with its cast of summer guest-house visitors in Louisiana who "believe that the setbacks and compromises of ordinary living will be somehow resolved, and that once present frustrations can be eliminated, they will experience serenity and happiness; but their dreams are revealed as delusions preventing them from living in the past."[6] Harold Clurman, who directed its initial production in 1950, has written of the play's concern with "the dead-end of the middle-class spirit."[7]

Shortly after Hellman wrote *The Autumn Garden*, the political drama of real life interfered with her creative work. Although she had never joined the Communist Party, Hellman had been active with the Progressive Citizens of America, a group formed in 1947 that criticized Truman's aggressiveness and the conduct of the House Un-American Activities Committee (HUAC). In 1952, in the wake of the Alger Hiss conviction and the Rosenberg's death sentence, Hellman was called before HUAC, which was just beginning the hearings that resulted in the Hollywood blacklist. Dashiell Hammett had already appeared in front of HUAC and was jailed for refusing to identify Communist Party members. Hellman declared in her now-famous letter to the Committee, "I cannot and will not cut my conscience to fit this year's fashion."

Although immediately after her interaction with the HUAC Hellman found herself blacklisted along with her colleagues, her work was soon staged again. In 1960 she won her second Drama Critics Circle Award with the psychological play *Toys in the Attic* (1960), about a man who comes home to New Orleans with his childlike bride. Unfortunately, her last play, *My Mother, My Father, and Me*, an adaptation of Burt Blechman's novel *How Much*, failed to impress audiences and critics at its 1963 opening. By the end of the 1960s, Hellman stopped writing for the stage and began working on her memoirs. The first volume, *An Unfinished Woman* (1969), won the National Book Award. Hellman also wrote a great deal for the cinema, but her passion was the stage. (In *The Children's Hour* one of the characters comments, "The cinema is a shallow art. It has no—no—no fourth dimension.") She also wrote the book for the 1957 musical *Candide*, for which Leonard Bernstein composed the music.

Hellman was one of the first internationally known women playwrights. She died in 1984 in Martha's Vineyard. Her will established two funds: one in her name for work that applied to arts and sciences, and the other in Hammett's, intended to support radical political causes. She once wrote: "There are lives that are shut and should stay shut . . ."[8] It is fortunate for the world of theater that Hellman's life, through her work, remained open.

PLAYS

Another Part of the Forest, 1946; *The Autumn Garden*, 1950; *Candide*, 1956; *The Children's Hour*, 1934; *Days to Come*, 1936; *The Lark*, 1955; *The Little Foxes*, 1939; *Montserrat*, 1949; *My Mother, My Father, and Me*, 1963; *The Searching Wind*, 1944; *Toys in the Attic*, 1960; *Watch on the Rhine*, 1941

NONFICTION

Maybe, 1980; *Pentimento*, 1973; *Scoundrel Time*, 1976; *Three*, 1979; *An Unfinished Woman*, 1969

WORKS ABOUT

Falk, Doris V., *Lillian Hellman*, 1978; Feibleman, Peter S., *Lilly*, 1988; Holmin, Lorena Ross, *The Dramatic Works of Lillian Hellman*, 1973; Lederer, Katherine, *Lillian Hellman*, 1979; Towns, Saundra, *Lillian Hellman*, 1989; Turk, Ruth, *Lillian Hellman, Rebel Playwright*, 1995; Wright, William, *Lillian Hellman*, 1986

1. Keyssar.

2. Ibid.

3. Ibid.

4. Euphemia Van Rensselaer Wyatt, "The Drama," *The Catholic World* 148 (April 1939), p. 87.

5. Ibid.

6. Olauson.

7. Quoted in Mel Gussow review of 1975 revival in the *New York Times* (April 23, 1975).

8. Carrie in *Toys in the Attic*, Act III (New York: Random House, 1960).

Beth Henley
(MAY 8, 1952–   )

BABE. He started hating me, 'cause I couldn't laugh at his jokes. I just started finding it impossible to laugh at his jokes the way I used to. And then the sound of his voice got to where it tired me out awful bad to hear it. I'd fall asleep just listening to him at the dinner table.

—from *Crimes of the Heart*, Act I

Beth Henley, born Elizabeth Becker, spent her childhood years in bed, suffering from asthma and reading play after play her mother brought home from the New Stage Theater in Jackson, Mississippi, where Mrs. Becker worked as an amateur actress. Henley was a shy, bright girl who had inherited her mother's love of the theatrical and her attorney father's sharp mind.

A high school internship at the New Stage cemented her decision to pursue a stage career, and she earned her B.F.A. in drama at Southern Methodist University in Dallas, Texas, in 1974. Although she had intended to concentrate on performance, she wrote a one-act comedy during her freshman year that altered her plans. Before she graduated, the theater department gave a full production of *Am I Blue* (1973), a play about two lonely teenagers who meet in the New Orleans French Quarter. The diffident Beth Becker was not quite ready to reveal herself, so she adopted the surname Henley, which she has kept ever since.

After college, Henley worked for the Dallas Minority Repertory Theater, where she acted in plays and taught drama. She lived an actor's life, working a panoply of jobs—waitress, file clerk, department store children's photographer—in order to make ends meet. Eventually she did graduate work at the University of Illinois, Champaign-Urbana, which had awarded her a teaching scholarship.

In the late 1970s, Henley's dream of finding success as an actor landed her in Los Angeles. Frustrated in her search for work, she turned again to play writing. She fashioned a comic drama about three Southern sisters, reunited in their hometown of Hazelhurst, Mississippi. But no one was interested in the play, and it nearly perished in obscurity. Henley's friend and fellow playwright Frederick Bailey saved it from such a fate. He clandestinely submitted the script to the prestigious annual drama competition at the Actors Theater of Louisville, Kentucky, where it was named cowinner. Soon the very theaters that had turned it down were clamoring to produce *Crimes of the Heart*. It opened off-Broadway in 1980, and the following year Henley became the first woman since KETTI FRINGS, in 1958, to win the Pulitzer Prize for drama; the play also won the New York Drama Critics Circle Award.

Beth Henley
COURTESY OF THE BILLY ROSE THEATRE COLLECTION

Crimes of the Heart centers on Babe, the youngest of the sisters, who, because she can no longer stand the sight of her rich and powerful husband or bear the drone of his voice, has shot him in the stomach (causing a nonfatal but nonetheless irksome injury). Her sisters come to stay with her, and the three women share their woes and jealousies and acknowledge their common fear of ending up like their mother, whose loneliness had been so unbearable she hung her cat and herself in the basement. Many critics lauded the play, including the *New York Times*'s Frank Rich, who called it "a pure vein of Southern Gothic humor . . . [Henley's] characters always stick to the unvarnished truth, at any price, never holding back a single gory detail. And the truth—when captured like lightning in a bottle—is far funnier than any invented wisecracks."[1] Jack Kroll of *Newsweek* called *Crimes* a "redneck version" of Anton Chekhov's *The Three Sisters*.[2] However, a comparison with Chekhov is widely off the mark, as Henley's attitude is more optimistic.

In *The Miss Firecracker Contest* (1980), which followed *Crimes*, Henley's optimism shines through again, as when Carnelle says to MacSam, "I just don't know what you can, well, reasonably hope for in life," and MacSam replies, "There's always eternal grace." *The Miss Firecracker Contest* is a whimsical tale about Carnelle Scott, a young woman obsessed with winning Yazoo City's Fourth of July Miss Firecracker Contest. Complicating Carnelle's life are the arrivals of her cousins Elaine Rutledge and Delmount Williams. Elaine, a former Miss Firecracker and Carnelle's idol, cannot choose between the comforts afforded her by her wealthy husband and the dream of an independent life. Elaine's high-strung brother Delmount struggles to cope with his sister's resentment of him, as he was their dead mother's favorite. *Miss Firecracker* was not a huge favorite with theater reviewers. Helen Rose of London's *Time Out* remarked that the characters' "grotesque eccentricities may have a certain quirky charm,[but] prove too ungainly for the hesitant balance of this oddball comedy."[3]

None of Henley's plays have attained the early success of *Crimes of the Heart*. Her third full-length play, *The Wake of Jamey Foster* (1982), was blasted as a recycled *Crimes*. It closed after only twelve performances. A more recent play, *Abundance* (1991), fared no better. An "intimate epic" about mail order brides from the Old West, Robert Brustein wrote that it made "no sense at all," lambasting Henley for having "domesticated a savage episode of American history into a story of broken hearts and damaged hearths, where even the Indian wars are an occasion for discussing 'relationships.'"[4]

Henley continues to charge forward, however, defending her penchant for domestic, female-oriented dramas. "Women's problems are *people's* problems," she once stated. "There are certain subjects I mightn't get into, simply because I don't have the necessary knowledge, but I don't think my being a woman limits my concerns."[5] Most likely, she has not yet reached her prime as a playwright.

PLAYS

Abundance, 1991; *Am I Blue*, 1973; *Crimes of the Heart* (also screenplay, 1986), 1979; *The Debutante Ball*, 1985; *The Lucky Spot* (also screenplay, 1983), 1985; *The Miss Firecracker Contest* (also screenplay, *Miss Cracker*, 1989), 1980; *Revelers*, 1997; *The Wake of Jamey Foster*, 1982

SCREENPLAYS

The Moon Watcher, 1983; *Nobody's Fool*, 1986

OTHER WORKS

Beth Henley, 1992

1. November 5, 1981.

2. Cited in a 1979 article in *City Limits* (London) by Sheila Hale.

3. July 23, 1986.

4. Brustein.

5. Interview in the *New York Times*, October 25, 1981.

Henrietta Maria
(NOVEMBER 25, 1609–AUGUST 31, 1669)

The daughter of Henry IV of France, Henrietta Maria married Charles I of England in 1625. Unfortunately, her Roman Catholicism, extravagance, and alleged intrigues undermined Charles's position, contributing to his ultimate downfall. She fled England in 1644 and did not return until 1660, when her son Charles II was restored to the throne. Eventually she returned to France.

In her first year at her consort's court, the sixteen-year-old queen acted in a pastoral play written and directed by herself. Although the play has been lost and she wrote no others, her love of theater and her belief that women belonged on the stage hastened the acceptance of actresses. Without the freedom to appear on stage and earn apprenticeships in theater, women playwrights would not have proliferated as they did in the years following.

WORKS ABOUT

Bone, Quentin, *Henrietta Maria*, 1972

Mary Sidney Herbert
(1561–1621)

Words from conceit do only rise,
Above conceit her honour flies,
But silence, nought can praise her.

—from *Theanot and Piers in Praise of Astrea*

Noted especially for her exquisite translations of the Psalms, Mary Sidney Herbert, the Countess of Pembroke, was the sister of poet Sir Philip Sidney (1554–86). The publication of *The Tragedy of Antonie*, her translation of the Senecan dramatist Robert Garnier's (ca. 1545–90) *Marc-Antoine*, made her the first woman in England to publish a play, though it was never performed. Written in 1590, *Antonie* "transforms rhymed French alexandrines into pedestrian blank verse."[1] Herbert also created the first documented dramatic verse by a woman to appear in print, *Theanot and Piers in Praise of Astrea*, published in the 1602 anthology *A Poetical Rhapsody*. She wrote it as an entertainment for Queen Elizabeth, the Astrea of the title.

Proficient in French and Italian, with a working knowledge of Latin, Herbert counted herself among a literary circle that included John Donne, Ben Jonson, and Thomas Nashe. She was a likely acquaintance of Shakespeare, too, as the first folio edition of his plays bears a dedication to her sons, William and Philip. For some time she served as editor of the *Arcadia*.

She was born at Tickenhill Palace near Bewedley, Worcestershire, the fifth of seven children. Though she was seven years apart from her brother Philip, they were very close and "shared a love of the arts, particularly poetry."[2] Her father, Sir Henry Sidney, was the godson of Henry VIII and a close childhood companion of Edward VI. He held several official posts during his career: governor of Ireland, Lord President of the Marches of Wales, Knight of the Garter, and Lord Deputy of Ireland. Her mother, Lady Mary Dudley, was the daughter of John Dudley, Duke of Northumberland, Earl of Warwick, and Baron Lisle. The family lived at Ludlow Castle in Penshurst.

In 1575 Herbert was sent for by Queen Elizabeth to serve at court as a lady in waiting, which she did for two years until her marriage at age sixteen to Henry Herbert, Earl of Pembroke. Her wedding to a man nearly 30 years her senior was a political alliance. She was his third wife and bore him four children. Herbert outlived her husband by eighteen years and was buried beside him in 1621.

PLAYS

The Tragedy of Antonie (Robert Garnier, tr.), 1592; *Theanot and Piers in Praise of Astrea*, 1602

OTHER WORKS

Apology, 1595; *The Arcadia*, 1590; *The Countess of Pembroke's Emanuel*, Abraham Fraunce, ed., 1591; *Discourse of Life and Death* (DuPlessis Mornay, tr.), 1592; *The Psalmes of David, Begun by . . . Sir Philip Sidney, Knt., and Finished by . . . the Countess of Pembroke His Sister*, 1823; *Triumph of Death* (unpub.); *Two Poems by the Countess of Pembroke*, Bent Juel-Jensen, ed., 1962

WORKS ABOUT

Bulloch, M. M., *Mary Sidney, Countess of Pembroke, an Elizabethan Historiette*, 1895; Young, Frances B., *Mary Sidney, Countess of Pembroke*, 1912

1. Cotton.
2. Ibid.

Christina Herrström
(AUGUST 23, 1959–)

"I want to entertain," says Christina Herrström. "If there is nothing that moves the audience, [the play] is a failure."[1]

Her strategy: "Seduce the audience. Seduce them and make them think as well."

Herrström was born in Stockholm; her mother was a textile artist, and her father, a mathematician, served as director of Stockholm's department of insurance. Her deep and abiding interest in music led her to study its history, along with ethnic and folk music, at the University of Stockholm. By the early 1980s Herrström had begun writing plays. Her first effort, *Love Me Carefully* (1983), tackles the abortion issue from the divergent perspectives of a young woman and her grandmother.

Feminism, says Herrström, is her "main assignment," although she consistently attempts to reach as wide an audience as possible. Her plays illustrate how "something very like love and care can be a way to keep sons and daughters and growing forces of curiosity and liveliness in control."

Her 1987 play *A Wonderful View* won Stockholm's Royal Theatre Dramateus competition. She received her prize directly from Ingmar Bergman, who seriously encouraged her to continue writing. Since then Herrström has penned several dramas for stage, radio, and television. She lives in Sweden with her husband, actor-director Peter Schildt, and their two children, Johannes and Anna Mathilde.

PLAYS

Damen i handskdioken (The Glove Story; teleplay), 1992; *Didrik* (radio series), 1985; *Ebba* (radio series), 1986; *Ebba and Didrik* (TV miniseries), 1990; *Love Me Carefully*, 1983; *Mirrimo Sirrimo* (A Wonderful View), 1987

1. All playwright's remarks are quoted from correspondence with the author, 1994.

Dorothy Hewett
(MAY 21, 1923–)

Katherine Brisbane wrote that "much of the discomfort [Dorothy Hewett's work] causes stems from her defiant intrusion of the private nature of the poetic experience into the naked public arena of the theatre."[1] With her distinctly suburban political sensibility, Hewett has entertained audiences and readers through her poems, novels, plays, and musicals for much of the twentieth century. Born in Perth, Australia, Hewett first made her name as a poet. At seventeen she published poems in the important Australian journal *Meanjin Papers*, and five years later she won a national poetry competition. This was the first of numerous literary awards.

While Hewett studied at Perth College and the University of Western Australia, her political consciousness was greatly influenced by the Communist Party. She joined in the early 1940s, and became an ardent member. She wrote numerous articles and essays for the party, and her political ideology often found its way into her creative work. One of her earliest and best plays, *This Old Man Comes Rolling Home* (1965), presents a house full of working-class Communists living in a Sydney suburb who grapple with the looming political threat of their party's banishment.

In 1968, for undocumented reasons, Hewett was expelled from the party, an experience that left her "isolated, bereft of her beliefs, and newly aware of her mortality."[2] Her desolation was no doubt intensified by her rocky domestic life. In 1944 she married Lloyd Davies, the first of three domestic partners; they had a son who died. For nine years she lived with Les Flood, with whom she had three sons. Then, in 1960, she married Merv Lilley and bore two daughters. Despite these sometimes devastating changes, Hewett's ideological independence flourished through her work. She used aspects of her own life in *The Chapel Perilous* (1971), a musical and Hewett's most widely performed work. *Chapel* relates the story of Sally Banner, a gifted and rebellious poet. Sally wreaks havoc in her hometown, refusing to bow at the local chapel tower. Instead, in an act of further defiance, she climbs the tower. Sally yearns for some semblance of genuineness and guidance in her life. She takes on several lovers, but becomes disillusioned with her men as she matures. She turns to leftist politics, but suffers a similar emptiness and disenchantment. In the show's surreal climax, Sally stands trial, accused by all whom she has known and loved. Ultimately she attains a self-awareness that frees her to embrace the wiles of her own mind. Hewett scholar Margaret Williams calls *Chapel* "a large-scale, even sprawling, epic work."[3]

Hewett's post-Communist work is enormously diverse. *Joan* (1973), a musical rendering of Joan of Arc's life, presents the French heroine as four archetypes: peasant, soldier, witch, and saint. The rock opera *Catspaw* (1974) follows a dropped-out guitarist as he searches for "the real Australia." Hewett broke new ground with her 1976 play *Golden Oldies*, in which she moved "away from her exploration of isolation towards unifying the elements of life."[4]

The Man from Mukinupin (1979), a commissioned work that followed *Golden Oldies*, suggests the scope of Hewett's creative vision. This musical play weaves together a group of back country Australians in the fictional town of Mukinupin. The show balances entertainment, accessibility, and political relevance as Mukinupin becomes a metaphor for Australia, a nation "emerging from a naive but guilty past into a new state of awareness which embraces both the suppressed Aboriginal culture and the European literary, popular, and mythic inheritance."[5]

Before Hewett's literary career took off, she had been a mill worker. Once she established herself, she taught at several institutions, including her alma mater, the University of Western Australia, and worked as an editor, eventually assuming directorship of Big Smoke Books in 1979.

PLAYS

The Beautiful Miss Portland, 1976; *Bon Bons and Roses for Dolly*, 1972; *Catspaw* (rock opera), 1974; *The Chapel Perilous* (musical), 1971; *Christina's World* (libretto), 1983; *The Fields of Heaven*, 1982; *Golden Oldies*, 1976; *Golden Valley*, 1981; *Joan* (musical), 1973; *The Man from Mukinupin*, 1979; *Mrs. Porter and the Angel*, 1969; *Pandora's Cross*, 1978; *Song of the Seals* (musical), 1983; *The Rising of Peter Marsh*, 1988; *The Tatty Hollow Story*, 1976; *This Old Man Comes Rolling Home*, 1965; *Time Flits Away, Lady*, 1941; *Zoo*, w/Robert Adamson, 1991

OTHER WORKS

The Australians Have a Word for It (short stories), 1964; *Bobbin Up* (novel), 1959; *Collected Poems, 1940–1995*, 1995; *For the First Time* (screenplay, w/others), 1976; *Frost at Midnight* (radio play), 1973; *Greenhouse* (poetry), 1979; *He Used to Notice Such Things*, (radio play), 1974; *Journey Among Women* (screenplay, w/others), 1977; *Peninsula* (poetry), 1994; *The Planter of Malata*, w/Cecil Holmes (screenplay), 1983; *Rapunzel in Suburbia* (poetry), 1975; *Susannah's Dreaming* (radio play), 1980; *The Upside Down Sonnets* (poetry), 1991; *Wild Card* (autobio.), 1990; *Windmill Country* (poetry), 1969

WORKS ABOUT

Bennett, Bruce, ed., *Dorothy Hewett: Selected Critical Essays*, 1995; Williams, Margaret, *Dorothy Hewett: The Feminine as Subversion*, 1992

1. Essay by Katherine Brisbane in Berney (3).

2. Ibid.

3. Williams, Margaret, *Dorothy Hewett: The Feminine as Subversion* (London: Oxford University Press, 1992).

4. Op. cit., Berney (3).

5. Essay by Margaret Williams in Hawkins-Dady (1).

Debbie Horsfield
(FEBRUARY 14, 1955–)

PHIL. Oh, we're all dead ignorant up North, aren't we? I am though, aren't I? It's dead embarrassing. How d'y'admit y've never been wind-surfing—never read Gormenghast—never heard of David Hockney? I've missed out. I'm not a Feminist, Friend-of-the-Earth, Ban-the-Bomber, Real Ale Freak. What am I? I don't know anything. Y'go to school, y'sit exams—nobody tells yer about Jean-Luc Godard or reading the *Guardian*. Football? Oh but you don't actually go? Oh no, not me. Not much. What d'y'do if y'can't stand yoga, despise *The Hobbit*—an' thought that Donizetti was a cheap martini? How can y'be taken seriously if yer favorite film's *The Jungle Book*?

—from *True Dare Kiss*

Red Devils Trilogy (1983), Debbie Horsfield's three-play series about the lives of four young female football fans in northern England, thrilled audiences and critics alike, and set the young playwright firmly on the theatrical map. The trilogy is composed of *True Dare Kiss, Command Promise,* and *Red Devils*, all of which follow the lives of Alice, Nita, Phil, and Beth, a formidable quartet from Salford whose growth and development are chronicled through their love affairs, employment crises, domestic dramas, and steadfast devotion to the Manchester United football team. But Horsfield makes it clear that football is simply a metaphor for her characters: "It's the only choice of diversion to which four potential dole-queue candidates attempt to deflect attention from the barren state of their lives in the North of the late '70s and early '80s. As Beth retorts, when reprimanded for lying in bed till 6 p.m.—'Well there's sod-all else to get up for round here, is there?' "[1] An *Observer* reviewer noted, ". . . the dialogue is a robust mixture of rough, go-getting romanticism and sardonic, whiplash northern humour: Horsfield's view of the world is unsentimental and streetwise."[2]

The Manchester-born Horsfield, herself a devoted Manchester United fan, attended Newcastle University in the mid-1970s, where she earned her B.A. in English literature with honors. Even before she began writing her own plays, she found posts with several British theaters. She worked as an administrative assistant at the Gulbenkian Studio Theatre in Newcastle-upon-Tyne (1978–80) and was then made assistant to the artistic director of London's Royal Shakespeare Company, where she served for three years.

Horsfield's early works mark some similarity to the themes of *Red Devils Trilogy*. One of her first plays, *Out on the Floor* (1981), portrays a group of Northern youngsters who attempt to beat the depression of impending employment lines by escaping into the all-night Wigan Casino. *Away from It All* (1982) follows an ill-matched group of tourists on a package holiday to Benidorm. But it was with *In the Blood* that Horsfield discovered her true voice. She describes the play as "a ragged confrontation between two juvenile girl supporters of Manchester United and an innocent bystander wrongly arrested. . . . [Those girls] were the germ that became *Red Devils*."[3]

In 1989 Horsfield took her working-class women to television with her popular series *Making Out*, about female factory workers getting by in a man's world. Several critics have remarked on the universal appeal of Horsfield's work, although some have qualified their comments with references to Horsfield's gender. To those notices, the playwright responds, "We don't quarrel with a good review—except to ask why it's assumed that a woman can't write a play about football without wielding a sledgehammer and aiming it in the general direction of the male."[4] Lizbeth Goodman writes, "Horsfield has an excellent ability to be inclusive even though she focuses on women's lives (though not necessarily women's issues), to make audiences laugh, to be playful and candid, and to refrain from sinking into sentimentality."[5]

Horsfield received a Thames Television award for the broadcast version of *Red Devils* in 1983, the same year she was appointed writer in residence at the Liverpool Playhouse.

PLAYS

All You Deserve, 1983; *Arrangements* (radio play), 1981; *Away from It All*, 1982; *Command or Promise*, 1983; *Face Value* (teleplay), 1982; *In The Blood*, n.d.; *In Touch*, 1988; *Making Out* (also TV series), 1989; *The Next Four Years*, n.d.; *Out on the Floor* (also teleplay), 1981; *Red Devils*, 1983; *Revelations*, 1985; *Royal Borough*, 1987; *Touch and Go*, 1984; *True Dare Kiss*, 1983

1. Introduction in Wandor (1).
2. Cited in frontispiece of published play, n.d.
3. Op. cit., Wandor.
4. Ibid.
5. Essay by Lizbeth Goodman in Berney (1).

Velina Hasu Houston
(MAY 5, 1957–   )

FUMIKO. Ha. First our women put on dresses, then cut their hair, and smoke like men. . . .
KIHEIDA. You see what your Yankee freedom has done? You live in Kobe, a beautiful city ravaged by Yankee fire bombs, your own parents victims of them. How can you strut about in American clothes as Yankees walk in their ashes?
FUMIKO. (*somberly*). I do not look back, Obisan.

—from *Asa Ga Kimashita*, Scene 3

Velina Hasu Houston believes her works "must give something to the world in which we live; they must recycle our emotions, spirit, and intellect to refuel and improve the world—not destroy it."[1] She grew up in Junction City,

Kansas, the daughter of a Native American–African-American father and a Japanese mother who met during the U.S. occupation of Japan after World War II. Her father, orphaned at the age of twelve, suffered many indignities as a man of color in the U.S. armed forces; this, along with the physical and emotional toll of combat fatigue, sent him to an early death when Velina was eleven. Her mother passed on to her two daughters all the richness of her native culture. She encouraged Houston to write haiku at the age of six. Encouraged by a schoolteacher, Houston penned her first play at thirteen, and has not stopped since. She earned her B.A. at Kansas State University and then ventured to UCLA for a master's degree in theater and play writing.

Despite her prolificacy—Houston once said, "Too many ideas seduce my imagination, and I have to hold them at bay,"—she has endured her own brand of indignities. She was once told by a professor that American audiences would never be interested in her play *Tea* (1987), which is set in postwar Japan, and that she would never become a "real playwright." However, *Tea* has become one of the most produced plays about Asians in America. The drama focuses on four Japanese wives of American servicemen who reunite at the house of another of their contemporaries who has killed herself. The fifth woman's ghost lingers, forcing the living women to face their own cultural and emotional dislocation. The work combines naturalistic theater with Japanese theatrical techniques in its exploration of the immigrant experience. Don Shirley wrote, "Although her play is set in Kansas nearly thirty years ago, Houston's concerns are equally those of Los Angeles in 1991."[2]

Tea is the last in a trilogy that begins with the autobiographical *Asa Ga Kimashita* (1981), about the homecoming of Creed, an Native American–African-American soldier and his Japanese war bride who encounter his family's outrage at his interracial marriage and the bitter truth of the myth of the melting pot. *Asa Ga Kimashita* is followed by *American Dreams* (1984), which is filled with characters who examine their duty to country, culture, family members, and love. It is a far-reaching look at how a person discovers the resources to let go, to move on, and to adapt. As Fusae Shimada, a character based on Houston's grandmother, says in the play: "There is nothing but the present moment—the one we can grasp in our fists and feel."

As of 1993 Houston was teaching play writing and modern dramatic literature at the University of Southern California's School of Theater. She is a cofounder and served as president of the Amerasian League, a nonprofit organization dedicated to the educational awareness of Amerasian culture. She has received numerous awards, grants, and citations, among them a McKnight Foundation Fellowship, two Rockefeller Foundation Fellowships, the Lorraine Hansberry Play Writing Award, and the Susan Smith Blackburn Prize of London.

PLAYS

American Dreams, 1984; *Asa Ga Kimashita* (Morning Has Broken), 1981; *Christmas Cake*, 1992; *The Confusion of Tongues* (one-act), 1991; *Father I Must Have Rice* (one-act), 1987; *Kokoro (True Heart)*, 1994; *The Legend of Bobbi Chicago* (musical), 1985; *Necessities*, 1991; *Petals and Thorns* (one-act), 1982; *Tea*, 1987; *Thirst*, 1986

FILM AND TELEVISION

Hishoku, n.d.; *Journey Home*, n.d.; *Kalito*, n.d.; *Summer Knowledge*, n.d.; *War Brides*, n.d.

OTHER WORKS

But Still Like Air I'll Rise, New Asian American Plays, ed., 1997; *Green Tea Girl in Orange Pekoe Country* (poetry), n.d.; *The Politics of Life, Four Plays by Asian American Women*, ed. and intro., 1993

1. Houston.

2. Don Shirley, "Tea and Empathy," *Los Angeles Times* Calendar, January 29, 1991.

Tina Howe
(NOVEMBER 21, 1937–   )

SANDY. When I looked in the mirror this morning, I saw an old lady. Not old old, just used up.

—from *Birth and After Birth*

"Tina Howe is a marvelously perceptive observer of contemporary mores," wrote Judith E. Barlow, a colleague of Howe's at New York University, "and much of the pleasure one receives from her plays comes from her comic skewering of pretentious amateur art critics, couples moaning orgasmically over the yuppie menu of their dreams, and thoroughly enlightened parents thoroughly unable to cope with their monstrous four year old."[1]

Howe's self-proclaimed "antic vision" sprang from a childhood amidst a family peopled with quirky writers and artists. Growing up in New York and Illinois, Howe's keen eye picked up on the idiosyncrasies of her father, Quincy Howe, a well-known news commentator of the 1940s and '50s, as well as an editor and historian; her mother, Mary Post Howe, a painter and Boston socialite with a penchant for eccentric attire; and her grandfather, Mark Antony

DeWolfe Howe, a poet and Pulitzer Prize–winning biographer. Her aunt, too, was a writer. Howe has said that her efforts to keep from drowning in ignominy in the midst of such a talented, productive family is what led to her particular aesthetic; that, coupled with the delight of attending Marx Brothers films with her "staid New England parents and screaming with laughter with them in the darkness."[2]

She became interested in theater while attending an experimental high school in Illinois, where the family had moved when her father accepted a faculty position at the University of Illinois School of Journalism. Her first one-act was produced at Sarah Lawrence College while she was an undergraduate there. In 1961 Howe married historian and novelist Norman Levi (also spelled *Levy*), with whom she has had two children.

Before receiving recognition as a playwright, Howe taught English and staged her own plays in New York City public schools. Her students were helpful critics, allowing her to identify "what worked and what didn't work."[3] Her 1982 drama *Painting Churches* has been her greatest critical success. *Churches* follows Mags, the artist daughter of

an eccentric elderly couple, who returns to her childhood home to paint her parents' portrait. The family has difficulty mutually appreciating and accepting each other. Fanny, Mags's mother, is a gregarious woman who seems unable to support the talent and uniqueness of either her daughter or her famous poet husband. As Mags paints her parents, she realizes that the portrait reveals as much about herself as it does them. Their common satisfaction with the finished painting reflects their recognition of each other. Howe has acknowledged the similarities *Churches* has to her own life: "I suppose my impulse in writing the play was to make some sort of peace with the rather eccentric parents I had, but the only way I could do it was to remake us all—to alter us, to reinvent us. [But] I feel it is primarily a work of art, not a confession."[4]

Howe often weaves the theme of "the redemptive power of artistic creation"[5] into her contemporary comic dramas. *Museum* (1976), essentially a series of ironic vignettes, explores the relationships between art, artists, and art enthusiasts while hilariously sending up the avant-garde art scene. Her satirical food comedy *The Art of Dining* (1979) introduced audiences to one of her most enduring characters, the writer Elizabeth Barrow Colt, "a genius with a pen but a total failure with a soup spoon."[6]

Howe's family-themed plays convey a consistently witty and compassionate perspective on upper-middle-class American society, with the influences of Eugène Ionesco and Samuel Beckett cutting a clear path. (On an occasion when Howe introduced Ionesco, her idol, as the evening's speaker, she recounted how, during the year she spent in Paris after completing her B.A. at Sarah Lawrence, she happened into La Huchette, a tiny Left Bank theater where *The Bald Soprano* was being performed; watching it, she felt she'd been struck by lightning.) *Birth and After Birth* (1974), featuring the contorted Ozzie-and-Harriet-like Apple family, spoofs compulsive, overly serious parents while diving into the murky waters of emotional and physical family abuse. A group of gentrified folk become entangled with a beach resort lifeguard in *Coastal Disturbances* (1986), "a charming play," as critic Moira Hodgson describes it, "a landscape of the human heart in miniature."[7] *Approaching Zanzibar* (1989) accompanies a family traveling from Hastings, New York, to Taos, New Mexico, to visit their elderly artist aunt before she dies. "But it wasn't the actual journey I was writing about," explains Howe. "It's the internal journey that interests me—how each of [the characters] comes to terms with their own problems, their fears, their mortality . . . It's my hymn to life in the face of despair."[8]

Howe claims not to have been hindered by the problems frequently faced by women in theater. "In our family we didn't define our roles in terms of sex, but in terms of talent," she says. Nevertheless, Barlow points out,

Tina Howe
COURTESY OF THE PLAYWRIGHT, PHOTO BY
CORI WELLS BROWN

"Women artists are her favored protagonists: She writes from a clearly female perspective even if not from a consistently feminist one."[9]

She received an Obie and an Outer Critics Circle Award for *Painting Churches* in 1983, as well as grants from the Guggenheim and Rockefeller foundations and the National Endowment for the Arts. In 1992 she won the American Academy of Arts & Letters Award for Literature. In addition to her writing, Howe alternates with her husband as an adjunct professor of drama at New York University, and manages to find the time to patronize classical music concerts, art museums, and, of course, theater.

PLAYS

Appearances, 1981; *Approaching Zanzibar*, 1989; *The Art of Dining*, 1979; *Birth and After Birth*, w/HONOR MOORE, 1974; *Coastal Disturbances*, 1986; *Columbine String Quartet Tonight!*, 1981; *Museum*, 1976; *The Nest*, 1970; *One Shoe Off*, 1993; *Painting Churches*, 1982; *Pride's Crossing*, 1997

1. Essay by Judith E. Barlow in Berney (2).

2. 1982 interview cited in essay by Beverley Byers-Pevitts in Robinson.

3. Hale, Sheila, "Women Do Dramatise," *City Limits* (London, 1979).

4. Program notes to A Contemporary Theatre production, Seattle, Wash., 1986.

5. Op. cit., Barlow.

6. Ibid.

7. Review for the *Nation*, January 10, 1987.

8. Interview with Patricia O'Haire for the *New York Daily News*, May 7, 1989.

9. Op. cit., Barlow.

Hrotsvitha von Gandersheim
(935?–1000?)

ABRAHAM. It is human to sin, but it is devilish to remain in sin.

—from *Abraham*, Scene 7

IRENA. Better far that my body should suffer outrage than my soul.

—from *Dulcitius*, Scene 12

Hrotsvitha,* née Helena von Rossen, who entered the "free" Benedictine Abbey of Gandersheim as a young

---

*Also spelled *Hroswitha*, *Hrosvit*, and *Roswitha*; pronounced hrohs-veet'-ah fuhn gahn'-durs-hym.

woman, was eventually named poet laureate of the Holy Roman Empire. Her name has been translated as both "loud mouth"[1] and "strong voice."[2] She has been documented as the only dramatist from the Middle Ages—male or female—whose works remain wholly extant from the period in which she wrote. Well-educated and trained in philosophy, Hrotsvitha wrote eight devotional epics in verse and six comedies in prose, all in Latin. In the preface to her collected plays, she states:

"Wherefore I, the strong voice of Gandersheim, have not hesitated to imitate a poet whose works are so widely read, my object being to glorify, within the limits of my poor talent, the laudable chastity of Christian virgins in that selfsame form of composition which has been used to describe the shameless acts of licentious women."[3]

The poet to whom she refers is the Roman dramatist Terence, whose six comedies she essentially reconfigured to suit her moral concerns. Sue-Ellen Case believes Hrotsvitha's plays constitute "a feminist revision of the misogynistic images of women"[4] in Terence's plays. Hrotsvitha's women consistently triumph in that they die with their virginity intact; most modern women might not aspire to a similar goal, but they would appreciate the author's delightful sense of humor: In the preface to her plays Hrotsvitha comments that while "it is generally believed that woman's intelligence is slower," she nonetheless offers her work to the learned as evidence that woman is a "teachable creature"; in *Paphnutius*, Antony exclaims, "What pleasures God sends us, when we resign ourselves to have none!"

All of Hrotsvitha's plays portray the victory of Christian values and female purity over evil. In *Dulcitius*, three young women sworn to chastity endure threats of rape, torture, and murder, yet manage to remain true to their vows. The play ends with their ascension to heaven. Similarly, in *Callimachus*, Drusiana, the heroine, pleads to Christ to help her die so that she may escape the cunning and brutal Callimachus. Her wish is granted, proving "women have the power to petition and succeed." Callimachus actually enters the tomb of Drusiana with the intent of raping her corpse—the ultimate perversion of man's desire for female passivity.

The heroine of Hrotsvitha's most famous play, *Paphnutius*, is the dancer Thais (most likely based on Theodora, the actress-courtesan who married Justine in the sixth century). Thais is exhorted to give up prostitution and reclaim her body as her own—only in this way can she save her immortal soul. She meditates, searching her inner feelings for guidance. Case asserts that this is most certainly "the first image of a woman's internal life to be written by a woman playwright and to survive in the annals of theatre history."[5]

Hrotsvitha's plays forge a unique connection between classical and medieval drama. Although stage dramas were not performed in tenth-century Western Europe, Hrotsvitha's reductionist dialogue, exceptional for the time, suggests that she intended her plays for dramatic production; they may have been staged in her convent. If so, they "marked an auspicious beginning for women's plays: written by a woman playwright and produced by women for an all-woman audience within the context of a female community."[6]

After having been lost for several hundred years, Hrotsvitha's works were rediscovered and produced for European audiences in 1501 by the German poet Conrad Celtes, who hailed Hrotsvitha "the mother of German wit" and a "wonder of women."[7] In 1914, during the suffragette movement in England, *Paphnutius* enjoyed a production staged by Edith Craig (famed stage designer Gordon Craig's forgotten sister) in London, but few other professional stagings have occurred. From the time of Hrotsvitha's writing, 700 years passed before female dramatists would emerge again. But when they did, toward the end of the Renaissance and throughout the Restoration, they flourished.

PLAYS (ALL CA. 935–1000)

Abraham, n.d.; *Callimachus*, n.d.; *Dulcitius*, n.d.; *Gallicanus*, n.d.; *Paphnutius*, n.d.; *The Plays of Roswitha* (H. J. W. Tillyard, tr.), 1926; *The Plays of Roswitha* (CHRISTOPHER ST. JOHN, tr.), 1923

WORKS ABOUT

Butler, Mary Marguerite, *Hrotsvitha: The Theatricality of Her Plays*, 1960

1. Keyssar.

2. Case (1).

3. *The Plays of Roswitha*, Christopher St. John, tr. (London: Chatto and Windus, 1923).

4. Case (1).

5. Ibid.

6. Ibid.

7. Keyssar.

Zora Neale Hurston
(JANUARY 7, 1891–JANUARY 28, 1960)

JOHN. So this is the woman I've been wearing over my heart like a rose for twenty years! She so despises her own skin that she can't believe anyone else could love it!

—from *Color Struck*

Describing her early childhood, Zora Neale Hurston wrote, "I used to climb to the top of one of the huge chinaberry trees which guarded our front gate and look out over the world. The most interesting thing that I saw was the horizon . . . It grew upon me that I ought to walk out to the horizon and see what the end of the world was like."[1] Hurston walked with a vengeance, growing up to become a novelist, essayist, playwright, and anthropologist—all in the name of showing the world the existence and importance of African-American folklore and experience. She was born and raised in Eatonville, Florida, an all-black, incorporated, self-governing town (the nation's first) that, according to biographer Lillian Howard, "fostered and nurtured . . . the unshakable sense of self that was later to inform [her] fiction and govern her life."[2] One of eight children, she was just thirteen years old when her mother died. During the difficult years that followed, Hurston was shuffled between her father and new stepmother and the homes of relatives. She studied at Howard University from 1918–24, although she did not earn a degree until 1928 at Barnard College. She also studied under German-American anthropologist Franz Boas at Columbia University. While at Howard, she met her first husband, Herbert Sheen, whom she married in 1937. Because Hurston's creative life remained her top priority, both her marriages—to Sheen and, later, to Albert Price III—ended in divorce.

Her first short story, "John Redding Goes out to Sea," was published in Howard University's literary magazine, *Stylus*, and it caught the eye of sociologist Charlie S. Johnson. Soon Hurston was in New York City working by his side and continuing to pursue her fiction. Even though most contemporary admirers of Hurston think of her primarily as a novelist and folklorist, some of her earliest works were plays. Her first, the 1926 drama *Color Struck*, tragically and unabashedly examines the self-hatred experienced by a dark-skinned black woman. Self-loathing causes Emma, the central character, to sabotage everything and everyone in her life. Although John loves her deeply, her extreme jealousy of every light-skinned woman who crosses their path finally leads her to push him out. Twenty years later, he resurfaces, still very much in love with Emma, who is now caring for her ill daughter, a light-skinned girl. When Emma finally decides to fetch a doctor, John administers a cool handkerchief to the girl's head. But Emma misinterprets this kind act and accuses him of wrongful intentions. John leaves, realizing that Emma's damaged self will never allow a place for him. As he walks out the door, the doctor enters to tell Emma that she waited too long: Her daughter is dead.

The 1930s and '40s were Hurston's most successful years. She was particularly influential for the writers of the Harlem Renaissance. Hurston's characters' use of dialect, her manner of portraying black culture, and her conservatism often created controversy within the black community. Throughout her career she addressed issues of race and gender, often relating them to the search for freedom. Her best-known novel is *Their Eyes Were Watching God* (1937), in which she tracks a Southern black woman's search, over twenty-five years and three marriages, for her true identity and a community in which she can develop that identity.

In 1936 and 1938 Hurston was the recipient of Guggenheim Fellowships, and she served as the head of the Drama Department at North Carolina College in Durham. From 1941–42, she was a technical advisor at Paramount Pictures. She was a member of the American Folklore Society, the American Anthropological Society, the American Ethnological Society, the New York Academy of Sciences, and the American Association for the Advancement of Science.

Sadly, health problems plagued Hurston in her later years. She died in Fort Pierce, Florida, only 115 miles from her birthplace, impoverished and unrecognized by the literary community. Her writings were rediscovered in the 1970s by a new generation of black writers, notably Alice Walker, who helped bring about the reissue of many of Hurston's works. Other celebrated American authors such as Ralph Ellison and Toni Morrison cite Hurston as a seminal influence on black American culture and literature, noting in particular her fine use of metaphorical language and strong storytelling.

Lillian Howard called Hurston "the most prolific and accomplished black woman writer [of her time] in America. . . . She called attention to herself because she insisted on being herself when blacks were being urged to assimilate in an effort to promote better relations between the races. Hurston, however, saw nothing wrong with being black: 'I do not belong to that sobbing school of Negrohood who hold that nature somehow has given them a lowdown dirty deal.' . . . Her works, then, may be seen as manifestos of selfhood, as affirmations of blackness and the positive sides of black life."[3]

PLAYS

Chic Street Man, 1991; *Color Struck*, 1926; *Fast and Furious* (musical), w/Tim Moore, 1931; *The First One* (one-act), 1927; *From Sun to Sun*, 1932; *Great Day*, 1927; *Mule Bone*, w/Langston Hughes, 1931; *Polk County*, 1944

OTHER WORKS

Collection of Bahamian Folk Songs, compiled w/Wm. Grant Still, 1937; *Dust Tracks on a Dirt Road* (autobio.), 1942; *The Gilded Six-Bit: Love Is Fragile*, 1986; *I love myself when I am laughing, and then again when I am looking mean and impressive*, Alice Walker, ed., 1979; *Jonah's Gourd Vine*, 1934; *Moses, Man of the Mountain*, 1939; *Mules and Men*, 1935; *Seraph on the Suwanee*, 1948; *Spunk* (short stories), 1985; *Tell My Horse: Voodoo and Life in Haiti and Jamaica* (a.k.a. *Voodoo Gods*), 1938; *Their Eyes Were Watching God*, 1937

WORKS ABOUT

Holloway, Karla F. C., *The Character of the Word*, 1987; Howard, Lillie P., *Zora Neale Hurston*, 1980

1. Cited from autobiography *Dust Tracks on a Dirt Road* in essay by Lillie P. Howard in Van Antwerp.

2. Ibid.

3. Ibid.

Elizabeth Inchbald
(1753–1821)

MR TWINEALL. We have now a fashion, in England, of speaking without any words at all.

LADY TREMOR. Pray, sir, how is that?

SIR LUKE TREMOR. Aye, do, Mr Twineall, teach my wife to do without words, and I shall be very much obliged to you; it will be a great accomplishment.

MR TWINEALL. Why, madam, when a gentleman is asked a question which is either troublesome or improper to answer, he does not say he won't answer it, even though he speaks to an inferior; but he says, "Really it appears to me e-e-e-e-e—(*Mutters and shrugs.*)—that is—mo-mo-mo-mo-mo—(*Mutters.*)—if you can see the thing—for my part—te-te-te-te—and that's all I can tell about it at present."

SIR LUKE TREMOR. And you have told nothing.

MR TWINEALL. Nothing upon earth.

LADY TREMOR. But mayn't one guess what you mean?

MR TWINEALL. Oh, yes—perfectly at liberty to guess.

SIR LUKE TREMOR. Well, I'll be shot if I could guess.

—from *Such Things Are*, Act 1, Scene 1

When an eighteen-year-old stage-struck farm girl runs away to the big city, meets a successful actor twice her age, marries him, and, with his influence and protection, goes off to tour the provinces, she thinks she's set for life. But for the headstrong Elizabeth Inchbald, it didn't work out that way. This good Catholic girl from Bury St. Edmonds in Suffolk found that beauty was not enough to make a successful acting career, and marriage was hardly a panacea.

Fortunately for Inchbald, her husband's early death saved her from a life of misery in matrimony. Not espe-cially eager to remarry, and well aware that she would never be more than a second-rate actress, she decided to become a dramatist. While David Garrick dominated the English stage, Inchbald picked up her pen, but continued to tour the provinces for a pittance. She struggled to mount her first play, *The Mogul's Tale*, a sharp comedy about the fad for hot air balloons.[1] Finally she secured a venue at London's Covent Garden Theatre. The play was a great success; Inchbald was on the rise. Gradually she abandoned her acting career and devoted herself to her writing. She created fifteen plays between 1785 and 1794, only one of which, *The Massacre* (1792), was neither staged nor published during her lifetime.

Most of Inchbald's plays are social comedies. She fa-vored domestic dilemmas, often addressing the plight of unsuccessful marriages at a time when divorces were nearly impossible to obtain (the Matrimonial Causes Act did not occur until 1857). Audiences shared her fascination. The popularity of her subject matter, combined with solid con-struction, sparkling dialogue, and highly playable charac-ters (helped, no doubt, by her years on the stage), parlayed Inchbald into one of the more celebrated playwrights of her day, along with Oliver Goldsmith, Richard Sheridan, and HANNAH COWLEY.

Two schools of comedy existed at the time she wrote: the sentimental comedy, a holdover from the earlier part of the century, and the traditional comedy of manners, which was embraced by Goldsmith and Sheridan. Inch-bald's plays straddled the two schools, balancing a more practical sentimentality with the humor and intrigue of the contemporary comedies of manners.

Inchbald's charm and wit made her a favorite among London's intellectual and social elite. Her journal writings illustrate the candor and humor for which she was so admired. "My present apartment is so small," she wrote, "that I am all over black and blue with thumping my body and limbs against my furniture on every side; but then I have not far to walk to reach anything I want, for I can kindle my fire as I lie in bed, and put on my cap as I dine . . ."[2] Her social circle included William Godwin, Mary Wollstonecraft, and Thomas Holcroft. Her only novel, *A Simple Story* (1791), was inspired by her quixotic relationship with John Kemble, whom she met through her friend Sarah Kemble Siddons, the great tragedian. Although Inchbald retained friendships with many of her suitors, her reputation, unlike those of many of her female contemporaries, remained unsullied.

Her good business sense—skillfully marketing her works and investing her profits wisely—enabled her to retire with a comfortable income. She never remarried, telling one admirer that she was "too fond of her own way to make a good wife."[3] But Inchbald's understanding of the male psyche was plainly evident. In *I'll Tell You What* (1785), Lady Euston jibes, "There is as severe a punishment to men of gallantry (as they call themselves) as sword or pistol; laugh at them—that is a ball which cannot miss; and yet kills only their vanity."

PLAYS

Animal Magnetism, 1789; *Appearance Is Against Them,* 1785; *A Case of Conscience,* 1833; *The Clandestine Marriage,* 1766; *Everyone Has His Fault,* 1793; *I'll Tell You What,* 1785; *The Jealous Wife,* 1761; *Lovers' Vows* (adapt. of August von Kotzebue's play), 1798; *The Massacre,* 1792; *The Midnight Hour,* 1787; *The Mogul's Tale,* n.d.; *Such Things Are,* 1787; *The Wedding Day* 1794; *Wives as They Were and Maids as They Are,* 1797

OTHER WORKS

The British Theatre, ed., 25 vols., n.d.; *A Simple Story,* 1791

WORKS ABOUT

Boaden, James, *Memoirs of Mrs. Inchbald,* 2 vols., 1833; Manvell, Roger, intro. and notes, *Selected Comedies,* 1987; Rogers, Katharine M., "Britain's First Woman Drama Critic: Elizabeth Inchbald," in *Curtain Calls: British and American Women and the Theatre, 1660–1820,* 1991.

1. Rogers.
2. Boaden, James, *Memoirs of Mrs. Inchbald,* 2 vols. (London: R. Bentley, 1833).
3. Rogers.

Corinne Jacker
(JUNE 27, 1933–   )

LOIS. I write down significant things about beginnings. See—
I'm trying to get it all straight. All my life it turns out that
I've come in at the middle. Korea, Viet Nam, the energy
crisis. And when I try to talk about it, they say, "You don't
understand. That wasn't when it really began." But when I
ask when the start was, nobody knows.

—from *Harry Outside*, Act I, Scene 1

In Corinne Jacker's 1974 play *Bits and Pieces*, a newly
widowed woman embarks on a highly unusual adventure.
Much to Iris's dismay, her brilliant husband's last request
was to help others by donating every one of his body parts.
"There wasn't anything to bury," says Iris. She decides to
search out the recipients of his bits and pieces, and finds
herself assembling her own life in the process. Critics
praised Jacker's sharp dialogue and "the ease with which
[she] manipulates her complex flashback structure to its
startling conclusion."[1] Michael Feingold called her "em-
phatically a writer to take note of."

Since then Jacker has been provoking and entertaining
audiences as she chronicles the lives of women and men
who struggle to locate themselves in their worlds. Relationships are key elements in her plays. *The Chinese Restaurant Syndrome* (1983) portrays two old, intimate
friends who have been driven apart by their "we look alike,
we act alike" competitiveness. Susan asks Maggie to lunch
for a reconciliation on the very day she will be getting back
the results from a breast cancer biopsy. She recognizes how

much she wants Maggie to be with her when she hears the
news. "We weren't running against each other," she tells
her friend. "We were running against ourselves. In a mirror. Reflections. Shadows."

A different kind of emotional dislocation exists in *Domestic Issues* (1980). Two brothers try to reconcile the consequences of choices they did and did not make in the
past. Steve, the pivotal character, is a 1960s revolutionary
whose decision years before resulted in the accidental
death of his colleagues when a bomb mistakenly deto-
nated. His brother Larry, a successful businessman, fi-
nanced and orchestrated Steve's return to the United
States. But Steve is still lost. "I came back here to be safe,
and it's not safe here either," he says. Larry appears to be
in control of his life, but he suffers internally from having
allowed his father to make decisions for him. The brothers'
wives also suffer, but they are more aware of the commit-
ments they have made. Larry's wife, Sue, admits to how
she takes her scream and shoves it into the garbage disposal, as she puts it. And Ellen, Steve's wife, remains steadfast in her political convictions, willing to take continued
risks: "I just want to make one place in the world shining
and clean and rid of all the garbage."

The Chicago-born Jacker attended Stanford and
Northwestern universities. She married Richard Edward
Jacker, taking his name, but has since divorced. She made
her theatrical debut in 1970 with *The Scientific Method* at
the American Shakespeare Festival in Stratford, Connecticut. Jacker has published nonfiction and poetry in addition to her dramas, and has taught play writing at New
York University (1976–78) and Yale (1979). She has written a great deal for television and received an Emmy citation for her work as story editor on the CBS miniseries

"Benjamin Franklin." She has received several awards, including two Obies.

Identity, place, and relationship are the major themes that run throughout Jacker's plays. In an interview, Jacker said, "It's true that women tend to think of domestic, encapsulated incidents as crucial. We look at the microcosm rather than the macrocosm. . . . Perhaps women find their metaphors in domestic experience because we are still new to the world of action."[2]

PLAYS

After the Season, 1978; *Bits and Pieces*, 1974; *Breakfast, Lunch and Dinner*, 1975; *The Chinese Restaurant Syndrome*, 1983; *Domestic Issues*, 1980; *Harry Outside*, 1975; *In Place*, 1983; *The Jilting of Granny Wetherall* (teleplay), 1980; *Later*, 1978; *My Life*, 1977; *Night Thoughts*, 1973; *Other People's Tables*, 1976; *Seditious Acts*, 1970; *The Scientific Method*, 1970; *Terminal*, 1976; *Travellers*, 1973

1. Michael Feingold, *The Village Voice*, November 14, 1974.
2. Betsko.

Elaine Jackson
(DECEMBER 5, 1929–   )

WOMAN. You see, the color *black* has within itself many colors. It is a very complex color and at the same time simple and delicate. It can be made to appear formidable and mysterious in a dark, unlit cave, or can appear as bright and inviting as the twinkling eyes of a child.

—from *Paper Dolls*

Elaine Jackson's *Paper Dolls* illustrates African-American women's continued battle with traditional Caucasian standards of beauty as manifested in American media. Adopting the motif of a minstrel show, *Paper Dolls* characters M-E and Lizzie perform scenes from their lives, rewriting their histories as they go along. Their tales often blend the seriousness of racial prejudice with comedy—during one particularly funny scene, the women, falsely accused of smuggling dope, throw baking soda at a customs clerk. The play's humor capitalizes on the sibling-like rivalry between the two friends, women who ultimately embrace themselves and each other for who they truly are: strong black women.

Jackson is a graduate of Wayne State University. She has received several awards for her work, including the Rockefeller Award for Playwriting (1978–79), the Langston Hughes Playwriting Award (1979), and the National Endowment for the Arts Award for playwriting (1983).

PLAYS

Afterbirth, 198?; *Cockfight*, 1978; *Madre de Alquiler* (Love Child), 1986; *Paper Dolls*, n.d.; *Toe Jam*, 1971

Ann Jellicoe
(JULY 15, 1927–   )

TOLEN. Intuition is, to some degree, inborn, Colin. One is born with an intuition as to how to get women. But this feeling can be developed with experience and confidence, in certain people, Colin, to some degree. A man can develop the knack. First you must realize that women are not just individuals but types. No, not even types, just women. They want to surrender but they don't want the responsibility of surrendering.

—from *The Knack*

Ann Patricia Jellicoe, an English playwright who first gained attention with her experimental work *The Sport of My Mad Mother* (1956), originally trained as an actress and stage manager, but is best known for her play *The Knack* (1961). Born in Middlesborough, Yorkshire, to Frances Jackson Henderson and John Andrea Jellicoe, she was educated at Polam Hall School in Darlington County, Durham, and at Queen Margaret's School in Castle Howard, York. She studied theater at London's Central School of Speech and Drama from 1944–1947, where she later taught acting; the school awarded her its Elsie Fogerty Prize in 1947.

Jellicoe has directed and produced most of her own plays as well as works by others. From 1947–51, she worked as an actress, stage manager, and director in London and the provinces, during which time she married and then became cofounder/director of the Cockpit Theatre Club (1952–54); its intent was to experiment with the already existing Open Stage. Her first marriage dissolved in 1961, and the year after she married again; with her second husband she had a son and a daughter.

From 1973–74 Jellicoe was literary manager for the English Stage Society (formed in 1956) at the Royal Court Theatre in London. During this time, under the noted director George Devine, she created *The Sport of My Mad Mother*. The society was committed to producing new plays and sought work that called attention to class consciousness; it aimed to dislodge British theater from the stodgy rut it was in during the mid-'50s and transform it into a more "innovative and socially influential activity," according to Helene Keyssar.[1]

In the preface to a 1964 revised edition of the play, Jellicoe calls *Sport* "an anti-intellectual play not only because it is about irrational forces and urges but because one hopes it will reach the audience directly through rhythm, noise, music, and their reaction to basic stimuli." *Sport* relates the adventures of four London teenagers and the three people they stumble across—a retarded teenager, a liberal American, and an Australian, Greta, who, according to Malcolm Page, comes to represent Kali, the Hindu goddess of destruction and creation. Thematically it is a

Ann Jellicoe
COURTESY OF THE PLAYWRIGHT, PHOTO BY
RODGER MAYNE

The character Tolen has "the knack" with women; interestingly, he also has "Nazi characteristics." Nancy claims to have been raped by one of the men, but she never identifies which one. Since she has never been alone with any of them, it is clear to the audience that this is a contrivance on her part. Keyssar says Nancy "has grasped a source of power over both Tolen and Colin . . ."[4] "In performance, this transition from seduction to 'rape', from male domination to female control occurs so rapidly and maniacally that the spectator feels transported to a mad and dizzy world where anything might happen next."[5]

Much like her contemporaries MYRNA LAMB in Britain and MEGAN TERRY in the United States, the director-dramatist attempts "to convey meaning to audiences through sight and sound as well as through words," according to the *McGraw-Hill Encyclopedia of World Drama.*[6]

In recent years, Jellicoe has turned toward the interpretive demands of directing and away from those of writing. ". . . [I]t's a bloody relief not to have to be creative any longer. The impulse to create is linked with the aggressive instinct," she told Carol Dix (*The Guardian*, 1972). In addition to her commercial work, she has written children's plays and translated several theatrical works, including those of Henrik Ibsen and Anton Chekhov.

More recently Jellicoe has pioneered a form of theater she calls "community plays," for which she founded the Colway Theatre Trust in 1980. In England, according to Jellicoe, "community theater" means professional involvement in a new form, not the amateur status it is given in the United States. The Colway Theatre Trust specializes in mounting huge works on location—docudramas of a sort—that call on members of the community to participate. The first of these was *The Reckoning (1978),* about the Monmouth Rebellion of 1685; *The Western Women* (1984) deals with the role women played at the siege of Lyme in the Civil War. Jellicoe has found these works extraordinary and satisfying, noting how they contribute to building a sense of community. "Community plays involve hundreds of people in acting, in helping set up the play, grouped around a small core of professionals who share skills and expertise. A play is specially written and researched by a writer of national standing, the aim being to entertain and celebrate the town. This work is now being taken up and copied all over Britain," she says. At last, in protest of grant cuts, she resigned as Colway's director in 1985.

"Jellicoe's dramas raise contemporary feminist issues, but her vision is finally ahistorical and apolitical. She has perhaps best assessed her own work in saying that what she intends is no more than that the audience begin to use its imagination. But she offers no control or direction for our imaginations and thus makes the personal theatrical but not political."[7]

"search for the roots of arbitrary violence. . . . [A] highly original [work, it] . . . anticipates feminist theater vividly in its embrace of a mythical female figure and the celebration of ritual."[2] The play's unique and defiant use of nonliterary speech rhythms brought Jellicoe tremendous attention.

Perhaps it was her passion for reading biography that led to Jellicoe's creation of *Shelley* (1965), which follows the poet through his Oxford years, his two marriages, to his drowning in Italy. Thematically it attempts to deal with the poet's desire to be good, thwarted by his "blindness to the frailty of human nature," as Jellicoe has put it. *The Giveaway* (1969) is a farce pointed at deception and consumerism: A suburban housewife pretends to be fourteen to win a cornflakes contest. And *The Rising Generation* (1960; originally written for but never performed by the Girl Guides' Association) demonstrated an ardent call to feminism.

The Knack, Jellicoe's best-known play, is "exuberant, liberating, youthful," Page says, and "the staccato, repetitive dialogue skims along like jazz."[3] Nancy, a seventeen-year-old, has wandered into a house shared by three men:

PLAYS

The Bargain, 1979; *Changing Places*, 1992; *Clever Elsie, Smiling Jack, Silent Peter*, 1973; *Flora and the Bandits*, 1976; *Der Freischütz* (trans. of Friedrich Kind libretto, music by Weber), 1964; *The Giveaway*, 1969; *A Good Thing or a Bad Thing*, 1974; *The Knack*, 1961; *The Lady from the Sea* (adapt. of Henrik Ibsen play), 1961; *The Reckoning*, 1978; *The Rising Generation*, 1960; *Rosmersholm* (adapt. of Ibsen play), 1960; *The Seagull* (adapt. of Chekhov play, w/Ariadne Nicolaeff), 1964; *Shelley, or The Idealist*, 1965; *The Sport of My Mad Mother*, 1956; *The Tide*, 1980; *The Western Women* (adapt. of FAY WELDON work, music by Nick Brace), 1984; *You'll Never Guess!*, 1973

OTHER WORKS

Community Plays: How to Put Them On, 1987; *Devon: A Shell Guide*, w/Rodger Mayne, 1975; *Some Unconscious Influences in the Theatre*, 1967

1. Keyssar.
2. Essay by Malcolm Page in Berney (1).
3. Ibid.
4. Op. cit., Keyssar.
5. Op. cit., Page.
6. Hochman.
7. Op. cit., Page.

Georgia Douglas Johnson
(SEPTEMBER 10, 1886–MAY 14, 1966)

Born in the wake of black emancipation, Georgia Douglas Johnson wielded her pen like a sword, laying bare for readers and audiences the truths about the black American experience. Johnson was raised in Atlanta, Georgia, and educated at Atlanta University and the Oberlin Conservatory in Ohio. After teaching school in Atlanta, she married Henry Lincoln Johnson, a prominent lawyer and politician. The couple and their two sons relocated to Washington, D.C., when Henry was appointed Recorder of Deeds by President Taft. Johnson became an active member of the D.C. community, transforming her home into a salon of sorts. Her Saturday evening soirees attracted many important literary and political figures of the Harlem Renaissance, such as Langston Hughes, ZORA NEALE HURSTON, Alain Locke, and W. E. B. Du Bois.

Johnson wrote poetry, often setting her work to music, which she performed at social gatherings. Her poems reflected her fervent political views. In her early twenties she dabbled with writing historical dramas, but after her husband's death in 1925, she set her sights on a more con-

temporary agenda. Indeed, Johnson's plays of the 1920s convey a frank fearlessness in their depiction of racism and the sufferings of indigent people. Her first work of this period, *Blue Blood* (1926), dramatizes a young mulatto couple's shock upon discovering, shortly before their wedding, that they share the same white father, a man who raped their mothers.

One of her most successful plays was the 1927 drama *Plumes*, which Rachel France calls "one of the few plays to be written in this country that proved itself a worthy heir to the 'universals' of folk drama."[1] *Plumes* tells the story of Charity, a young mother who has already lost two children to the ethically questionable medical establishment. When her last child becomes ill, the doctor informs Charity that it will cost fifty dollars for an operation that may not save her daughter. She hedges, and the doctor asks, "Don't you love your child?" She must decide whether to resist the doctor or follow her intuition, spending the few dollars she has managed to save on a fine funeral with "plumes." *Plumes*'s sensitive depiction of how the poor are manipulated by the establishment won Johnson *Opportunity* magazine's First Place Drama Award, which included sixty dollars and publication by Samuel French Publishers.

During the mid-1930s, Johnson's plays began to focus on the outbreak of lynch mobs. In *Safe* (1935) a woman in labor hears the cries of a boy being lynched, which fuels her decision to strangle her own newborn son. *Sunday Morning in the South* (1940) centers on the execution of a young black man falsely accused of raping a white woman. Winona Fletcher wrote, "Johnson's short plays are tightly structured dramas with compressed action. Themes of racial identity and social protest dominate her writing."[2]

Not surprisingly, Johnson faced insurmountable obstacles in finding a commercial venue that would produce her work. Her explosive material in conjunction with her identity as a black woman made for bleak prospects. Nevertheless, through connections at black educational institutions such as Howard University and Morgan State College, she was able to see her works staged. But by the early 1940s, frustrated by the continued difficulty of producing her plays, Johnson gave up play writing and turned exclusively to poetry. Her poetry reflected the transition of blacks in America from the desire for a "raceless" society to the "New Negro Renaissance."

PLAYS

Attacks, n.d.; *Blue Blood*, 1926; *Blue-Eyed Black Boy*, ca. 1935; *Frederick Douglass*, 1913; *Plumes*, 1927; *Safe*, ca. 1935; *The Starting Point*, n.d.; *Sunday Morning in the South*, 1924; *William and Ellen Craft*, 1913

OTHER WORKS

An Autumn Love Cycle (poems), 1928; *Bronze* (poems), 1922; *The Heart of a Woman and Other Poems*, 1918; *Share My World*, 1962

1. France, Rachel, *A Century of Plays by American Women* (New York: Richards Rosen Press, 1979).

2. Essay by Winona L. Fletcher in Robinson.

Maria Jotuni
(1880–1943)

Life is laughable indeed, if one takes it seriously.

—from *The Wife of the Henpecked Man*

Finnish dramatist Maria Jotuni was originally a fiction writer; however, the stories in *Rakkautta*, her first publication in 1908, contained such juicy dialogue that Jotuni's transition to play writing came naturally. Her first work for the stage, *Vanha koti* (The Old Home; 1911), was inspired by Anton Chekhov's *Uncle Vanya*. Schoolfield called it "unabashedly sentimental."[1] Her best pieces are erotic comedies such as *Miehen kylkiluu* (The Rib of Man, 1914), which mocks men beset by conniving or stupid wives. Crowell says her comedies are "crisp, aphoristic, and antisentimental."[2] In *Amerikan morsian* (The Bride from America, 1966), which was not recovered until 1966, Jotuni spins a tale about a self-centered, egotistical shoemaker and his wise, forbearing wife. The tone of her work began to change with *Kultainen vasikka* (The Golden Calf, 1918), a politically charged drama about profiteering in Helsinki during World War I. Soon her plays focused more on protesting war and power than on love and marital relationships. With *Klaus, Louhikon herra* (Klaus, the Lord of Louhikko; 1943), which incorporates folk poetry not unlike Renaissance drama, Jotuni portrays women who surpass men both emotionally and intellectually. Yet Jotuni was essentially a traditionalist who believed that women belonged in the home.

She was born into a prosperous family in Kuopio and studied literature at the University of Helsinki in order to become a teacher, one of the few positions acceptable for women of her day. Marriage interrupted her plans, however. She wed Vijo Tarkianen, a historian and professor of Finnish literature, who provided a secure life that allowed Jotuni to concentrate on her writing.

PLAYS

Amerikan morsian (The Bride from America), 1966; *Klaus, Louhikon herra* (Klaus, the Lord of Louhikko), 1943; *Kultainen vasikka* (The Golden Calf), 1918; *Kurdin prinssi* (The Prince of Kurd), 1932; *Miehen kylkiluu* (The Rib of

Man), 1914; *Olen syyllinen* (I Am Guilty), 1929; *Suhteita* (Relations; also teleplay, 1970) n.d.; *Tohvelisankarin rouva* (The Wife of the Henpecked Man), 1924; *Vanha koti* (The Old Home), 1911

OTHER WORKS

Rakkautta (Love; short stories), 1908

WORKS ABOUT

Niemi, Irmeli, *Maria Jotunin näytelmät*, 1964

1. Essay by G. C. Schoolfield in Hochman.

2. Anderson.

Sor Juana Inés de la Cruz
(NOVEMBER 12, 1651–APRIL 17, 1695)

Critics: in your sight
no woman can win:
keep you out, and she's too tight;
she's too loose if you get in.

—from "A Satirical Romance," Stanza 3, Samuel Beckett, tr.

Sor Juana Inés de la Cruz, born Juana Inés de Asbaje y Ramirez de Santillana, was the first important literary figure of the New World and the most outstanding lyric poet of Mexico's colonial period. Revered in her country to this day, she has been called the Tenth Muse, the Phoenix of Mexico, and the Mexican Nun.

Sor Juana, as she is commonly called, was a true genius. The illegitimate child of a Spanish courtesan and a Creole woman, she spent her early years in San Miguel de Nepantla, just outside Mexico City. At nine she mastered Latin in twenty lessons. By the age of sixteen, already honored for her intellectual gifts, she was regularly reading to the court from her works, taking questions from those in attendance. The young Juana devised mental challenges for herself, threatening to cut off her hair, for example, if she did not achieve a certain scholarly goal. After a failed love affair steered her away from a traditional life of marriage, she entered the convent of San Jeronimo with the intention of dedicating her life to learning, her greatest passion. There she assembled a library of 4,000 volumes, experimented in the sciences and music, and wrote poetry as well as religious and secular plays.

Her one full-length play, *Los empeños de una casa* (The Obligations of a Household, 1680), is considered her most important dramatic work. A typical Golden Age comedy, rumored to include some autobiographical elements, she borrowed the title from Pedro Calderón, one of her major influences, and the plot from Lope de Vega Carpio's *La*

Sor Juana Inés de la Cruz
POSTHUMOUS PAINTING BY JUAN DE MIRANDA

discreta enamorada. She also wrote three *autos sacramentales,* allegorical plays performed with lavish costumes and sets that were meant to educate the public about the mystery of the sacrament of the Eucharist.

The short *loas* that introduce the longer *autos* are particularly fascinating. The loa to *El divino Narciso* (The Divine Narcissus, ca. 1680) portrays two Mexican natives in full tribal costume who perform ritualistic dances and songs to the god of the seeds. Soon a Spanish lady and her escort, Zeal, a captain in the Spanish army, enter the scene. When Zeal's attempt to convert the natives proves unsuccessful, the army attacks, forcing the indigenous people to surrender. An explanation of the Eucharist as a continual sacrifice is offered. Few playwrights had ever utilized indigenous ritual and custom in their work. Sor Juana's appreciation of Mexico's native peoples is evidenced in her poetry, as well. She wrote:

> What magical infusions, brewed
> from herbals of the Indian
> of my own country, spilled their old
> enchantment over all my lines?[1]

Evelyn Uhrhan Irving has commented that "the combination of history, mythology, and religion must have produced a wonderfully exhilarating effect on audiences in [Sor Juana's] day, and it is still capable of engaging readers centuries later."[2] Irving also notes the nun's ex-

traordinary skill in handling Baroque conventions, "infusing her delicate language with feminine vision and sensitivity."[3]

Unfortunately, not everyone appreciated Sor Juana's gifts. One of her most powerful and influential detractors was the Bishop of Puebla. In 1690, under the female pseudonym Sor Filotea, he published a bitter criticism of his adversary, whose *Carta Atenagórica* (Letter Worthy of Athena) he himself had had published! He attacked Sor Juana for not dedicating herself to pursuits more suitable to a nun. Sor Juana responded with her classic *Repuesta a Sor Filotea* (Reply to Sister Filotea) in which she masterfully subverts the Bishop's own language in order to substantiate her defense. Sue-Ellen Case asserts that *La repuesta* remains "one of the most important historical documents in defence of women's intellectual abilities and love of learning."[4] Sor Juana wrote,

> I entered the religious order believing that I was fleeing from myself, but—such misery—I brought with me my worst enemy, my inclination to study . . . which has been so vehement, so overpowering, I do not know whether to consider it a gift or a punishment from Heaven.

Tragically, a nun, no matter how brilliant, could not rival the influence of the Bishop of Puebla. Consequently, Sor Juana was forced to discontinue her studies and relinquish her library, musical instruments, and scientific tools. She died while tending the sick during an epidemic in Mexico City. She was forty-seven.

PLAYS

Amor es más laberinto (Love Is More of a Labyrinth), w/ Juan de Guevara, 1668; *El cetro de José,* 1692; *El divino Narciso* (The Divine Narcissus), ca. 1680; *Los empeños de una casa* (A Household Plagued by Love, 1942), 1680; *El mártir del Sacramento, San Hermenegildo,* 1692

OTHER WORKS

La repuesta, 1691

WORKS ABOUT

Paz, Octavio, *Sor Juana Inés de la Cruz o las trampas de la fé,* 1982; Peden, Margaret Sayers, *A Woman of Genius: The Intellectual Autobiography of Sor Juana Inez de la Cruz,* 1982; Portillo, Estela Trambley, *Sor Juana and Other Plays,* 1983

1. "En reconocimiento a las inimitables plumas de la Europa" (In Acknowledgment of the Praises of European Writers), st. 14. Constance Urdang, tr.

2. Essay by Evelyn Uhrhan Irving in Magill.

3. Ibid.

4. Case (1).

Fay Kanin
(1916?–   )

JUDGE. Now, where were we? Oh, yes, plaintiff and defendent were in bed—talking.

—from *His and Hers*

For Fay Kanin, keeping it all in the family is a way of life. The noted dramatist, producer, and actor is married to Michael Kanin, noted screenwriter and brother of Garson Kanin, the noted playwright-director who is the husband of RUTH GORDON, noted actor and playwright. She grew up in Elmira, New York, where her father, David Mitchell, managed a store, and her mother, Bessie Kaisser Mitchell, reminisced about her premarital days as a vaudevillian. Kanin's writing career began early; while still in high school she wrote for the local paper. She also had an early brush with greatness when she won the New York State Spelling Championship and Franklin D. Roosevelt, then governor of the state of New York, personally presented her with the award. In 1936 her family moved to California, where Kanin completed her bachelor's degree at the University of Southern California (1937).

For Kanin, the California move was a fortuitous one: It planted her smack in the middle of the film industry. After graduation, she worked as a writer and script reader at RKO Studios. She joined the RKO Studio Players, acting in and writing plays for the group. Also at RKO, in 1939, she met Michael Kanin, another studio writer, who allegedly proposed to her on the day they met. They married a year later and had two sons: Joel, who died of a

tumor at age thirteen, and Josh, now a film editor and cinema studies professor.

The advent of World War II offered Kanin the opportunity to write and narrate "The Woman's Angle," a radio series produced for the Office of War Information. She used the program to express her egalitarian views of womanhood while attempting to engage women to support the war effort.

In 1948 she collaborated with her husband on her first play, *Goodbye, My Fancy*. Shirley Booth and Madeleine Carroll starred in the original production, along with Sam Wanamaker, who also directed it: It was a hit. Kanin herself acted the leading role in a production at the Pasadena Playhouse in California some years later. *Fancy* is about a liberal congresswoman and former war correspondent who returns to her alma mater to receive an honorary degree, and hopes to recapture the innocence of her youth. But she discovers that both she and her old cohorts have evolved in such a way that going back to their old selves is impossible. According to Judith Olauson, *Fancy* presented a portrait of "the 'new woman' of the 1940s whose combined intelligence and glamour allowed her to play a nonconventional role. . . . Interwoven with the playwright's intention to represent this central idea were several forthright opinions regarding the values of education, moral integrity, women's rights, and the importance of realistic goals."[1] Kanin herself stipulated that the theme of the play "is that every adult in this world has to tell the truth to the young, if we are to have a world at all." She was inspired to write the drama as a direct result of a visit to her own alma mater in Elmira, New York. "By going back to the Elmira I knew so well I found that you can't go back to your past. You must live with the realities of the present."[2]

Kanin wrote some plays on her own, including a 1959 stage adaptation of the Ryunosuke Akutagawa stories more commonly known to American audiences as Akira Kurosawa's classic film *Rashomon*. Most of her scripts, however, were collaborations with her husband. *His and Hers* (1954) is somewhat reminiscent of RACHEL CROTHERS's theme in *He and She*: the successful husband and wife syndrome, only in this case the pair are playwrights and, though now divorced, still collaborate. The play did not begin to approach that of Crothers's probing and insightful work and enjoyed only a short run on Broadway. The Kanins also penned several well-known films together, including *The Opposite Sex* and *Teacher's Pet*, which starred Clark Gable and Doris Day and garnered two Academy Awards for Kanin, one for Best Original Story and one for Best Screenplay. Kanin has also won three Emmys (1974 and 1979). More recently her book for the stage musical *Grind* (1985) was nominated for a Tony.

Under exclusive contract to the ABC television network in 1978, Kanin helped form the first all-female production company. She was the first woman in twenty years elected president of the Writer's Guild, and she became the second woman (Bette Davis was the first) to serve as president of the Academy of Motion Picture Arts and Sciences. Kanin has continued her involvement in the film community worldwide, serving as a spokeswoman for American films. She has received numerous honors and awards not only for her creative work but for her humanitarian efforts.

Kanin has relished her role as a writer particularly because, unlike other entertainment craftspeople who must rely on the mounting of actual productions, writers "can sit down and generate their own employment and determine their own fate to a great extent by the degree of their disciplines, their guts, and their talents."[3]

PLAYS

The Gay Life, 1961; *Goodbye, My Fancy*, w/Michael Kanin (also film, 1951), 1948; *Grind* (book; music, Larry Grossman; lyrics, Ellen Fitzhugh), 1985; *His and Hers*, w/Michael Kanin, 1954; *Rashomon* (from stories by Ryunosuke Akutagawa; also screenplay, *The Outrage*, 1964), 1959

SCREENPLAYS, ALL W/MICHAEL KANIN

Friendly Fire, 1979; *Heat of Anger* (teleplay), 1972; *Hustling*, 1975; *My Pal Gus*, 1952; *The Opposite Sex*, 1956; *Rhapsody*, 1954; *The Right Approach*, 1961; *The Source*, (teleplay), n.d.; *Sunday Punch*, 1942; *The Swordsman of Siena*, 1962; *Teacher's Pet*, 1958; *Tell Me Where It Hurts* (teleplay), 1974

1. Olauson.
2. Fields, "The Playwright," n.p., quoted in Shafer.
3. Froug, William. "Fay Kanin" in *The Screenwriter Looks at the Screenwriter* (Los Angeles: Silman James Press, 1972).

Katherine of Sutton
(FL. 1363–1376)

Although the eleventh-century German dramatist HROTSVITHA has earned the distinction of being the first recorded woman playwright in Europe, Katherine of Sutton was England's first woman dramatist. However, unlike Hrotsvitha's plays, which have persevered, Katherine's have not. An aristocratic baroness, she was the abbess of Barking nunnery, where she rewrote the Easter "dramatic offices" because, according to Nancy Cotton, "people attending the paschal services were becoming increasingly cool in their devotions."[1] Her adaptations put quite a spin on the traditional liturgical dramas: Nuns, rather than the customary male clerics, portrayed the three Marys in the *visitatio sepulchri*. Katherine of Sutton's presence in the dramatic realm indicates that, while women were not allowed to appear on the medieval stage, they participated in theater nevertheless.

1. Cotton.

Charlotte Keatley
(1960–)

MARGARET. My parents are called, my parents are called. . . . Guilt, and . . . Duty. Wonderful, how they keep the family together. . . .

—from *My Mother Said I Never Should*, Act III, Scene 4

One of the youngest playwrights ever produced on the main stage of the Royal Court Theatre in London, Charlotte Keatley made her theatrical debut by starting her own company, The Royale Ballé. She starred in its first production of her first work, *Dressing for Dinner* (1982), essentially a performance piece that focuses on the female preoccupation with "what to wear." She enjoys shocking audiences, and has gone so far as to stage the dressing of a fish in aspic. Lizbeth Goodman has remarked that throughout the 1980s, Keatley's work evolved from the dark humor and broad strokes of *Dressing for Dinner* "to the more sophisticated balance of humour and drama which is explored in *My Mother Said I Never Should* (1987)."[1]

My Mother presents four generations of working-class women, all very involved with the men in their lives. But, as in CLARE BOOTH LUCE's *The Women* (1936), the men in Keatley's plays are present only through the women's comments and references. The dialogue centers on everyday chores like dusting, folding sheets, packing baby clothes, making tea, washing—activities that construct women's domestic rituals—but often goes farther below the surface, as when Doris tells her daughter, "Your father . . . stopped 'wanting me' many years ago. One didn't divorce, then. I thought if I persisted in loving him . . . I wanted to—to be desired. (*Pause*) The night he died, we embraced. He held my hand; he said he loved me most that night. I believed him . . . Was it worth it, I ask myself? (*Silence*)." Although the characters perceive their roles as women to be quite different from each other, the audience appreciates their "whole ways of being . . ." as Keatley puts it, "which only happen when the men have gone out of the room."[2]

Many feminist critics have lauded Keatley for pushing the women-without-men conceit Luce utilized to a more pertinent, politicized level. In her review of the premiere, Lyn Gardner of *City Limits* wrote that *My Mother* was "the equivalent of breaking the four-minute mile in women's theatre writing . . . Like CARYL CHURCHILL's *Top Girls*, this is a play which will influence the next generation of writers." It won the Manchester *Evening News* Best New Play Award (1987) and was joint winner of the 1987 George Devine Award.

The London-born Keatley was educated at Manchester University, where she earned her B.A. in drama in 1982. She has also served as a theater critic for several publications and, along with her work as a writer, actor, and director, has been a drama teacher and lecturer in play writing and theater skills at various educational institutions.

PLAYS

An Armenian Childhood, w/Pete Brooks and Steve Schill, 1983; *Badger* (teleplay), 1989; *Citizens* (radio series, w/ others), 1989–90; *Dressing for Dinner*, 1982; *The Legend of Padgate*, music by Mark Vibrans, 1986; *My Mother Said I Never Should* (also radioplay, 1989), 1987; *The Singing Ringing Tree*, music by Eroollyn Wallen, 1991; *Underneath the Arndale*, 1982; *Waiting for Martin*, 1987; *You're a Nuisance Aren't You*, 1989

1. Essay by Lizbeth Goodman in Berney (1).
2. Ibid.

Adrienne Kennedy
(SEPTEMBER 13, 1931–)

SARAH. I find it necessary to maintain a stark fortress against recognition of myself.

—from *Funnyhouse of a Negro*

Unique among black playwrights, Adrienne Kennedy uses a surrealistic theatrical approach to address the dilemma of identity in a racist and sexist society. Her plays betray an internal world rife with anguished anxieties and nightmare visions. "The characters are myself," Kennedy has confessed, citing her work as "an outlet for inner psychological confusion and questions stemming from childhood."[1]

Kennedy was born in Pittsburgh, Pennsylvania, and raised in Cleveland, Ohio; her father, Cornell Wallace, worked as executive secretary for the YMCA and her mother, Etta Haugabook Hawkins, taught school. When Kennedy was young, her parents read to her from the works of black writers. She majored in education at Ohio State University, where she encountered great racial strife on campus. She began writing while still in college—novels, stories, and poems. Just after receiving her degree in 1953, she married Joseph Kennedy. They moved to New York City, where she did graduate work at Columbia University, with additional studies at the New School of Social Research, the American Theater Wing, and Circle in the Square. The Kennedys had two sons, Joseph, who became a composer and pianist, and Adam, but the marriage dissolved in 1966.

The Obie-winning *Funnyhouse of a Negro*, Kennedy's earliest success (1962), echoes CARSON MCCULLERS's *Member of the Wedding* in that it deals with the search for identity by examining the inner workings of the central character's mind. But unlike the frank individualism of *Member*'s adolescent Frankie Adams, Sarah, the half-white, half-black writer-student of *Funnyhouse*, is a young woman so lost in a society filled with black and white myths that any clear sense of individuality eludes her. Sarah is seen only through the personas that rule her imagination, characters as disparate as Queen Victoria and Jesus Christ. Her identity crisis seesaws upon a "black is evil, white is good" precipice on which Sarah cannot sustain her balance. *Funnyhouse* ranges stylistically from August Strindberg-like dream sequences to a stark, presentational narrative; the play's title derives from a childhood episode of Kennedy's: Looming above the entrance to a Cleveland amusement park she frequented was a huge, laughing, white-faced figure, which became, for the playwright, a symbol of white America ridiculing and mocking blacks.

The use of layered masks and historical figures in Kennedy's plays conveys the concept of the individual's confused sense of interconnectedness in society. In *The Owl Answers* (1963), Clara Passmore, the illegitimate daughter of a black cook and the richest white man in Georgia, escapes each summer from Savannah to New York, where she casts about on subways, looking for men. On one strange ride the subway doors open to reveal the Tower of London, upon which stand masked historical figures such as Chaucer, Shakespeare, Anne Boleyn, and the Virgin Mary. They peel off their masks only to uncover the visages of other characters, including the heroine's mother and father.

Kennedy cites Tennessee Williams and Edward Albee, with whom she studied at Circle in the Square, as major influences on her work, but her plays (like those of MEGAN TERRY) seem more in the vein of the European avant-garde writers Eugene Ionesco and Jean Genet. Although her work springs from autobiographical material, her use of dreams, images, and symbols transcends the boundaries of linear narrative. The message of *A Lesson in Dead Language* (1964) may be to illustrate the meaning of "the blood that every adolescent girl fears will one day humiliate her,"[2] but the way Kennedy conveys it—by depicting seven girls in white dresses instructed to repeat "I bleed" by a large white dog—pushes the emotional territory beyond the reaches of conventional drama.

A Rat's Mass (1966), an abstract rendering of the relationship between a black brother and sister and their childhood involvement with the girl next door, is staged as a parody Mass. In *A Movie Star Has to Star in Black and White* (1976), the character Clara Passmore, central in *The Owl Answers*, makes a comeback in which people and chapters from her own life coalesce with characters and scenes from Hollywood movies. The white movie stars that populate Clara's mind contrast with the real-life black people who comprise her family. In the same melodramatic tones they use in Hollywood movies, celebrities such as Bette Davis and Montgomery Clift relay the events of Clara's life. Sue-Ellen Case suggests that "the play demonstrates how the absence of black actors and black stories in the culture affects the ability of the black playwright to generate new narratives about her life . . . In Kennedy's plays, the realm of racist oppression is an internal one, but the issues of marginality, invisibility, and assimilation are the same."[3] Earlier echoes of a similar theme, within the matrix of conventional drama, are found in ALICE CHILDRESS's *Florence* (1949).

Kennedy's work has been roundly lauded. In addition to her personally oriented dramas, she has written several plays for young people, including *A Lancashire Lad* (1980), based on the childhood of Charlie Chaplin. She has received three Rockefeller Foundation grants, a Guggenheim fellowship, Creative Artists Public Service and National Endowment for the Arts grants, and has served as a lecturer at Yale and Princeton universities. Kennedy

was the only black founding member of the Women's Theater Council, a network dedicated to the discovery and production of new plays by women; others were MARIA IRENE FORNES, ROSALYN DREXLER, JULIE BOVASSO, ROCHELLE OWENS, and MEGAN TERRY. In 1973, a year after it was formed, the Council evolved into Theater Strategy, a group that included male playwrights such as John Ford Noonan and Sam Shepard.

In their book *Black Theatre U.S.A.* James Hatch and Ted Shine aver that "in a tradition in which the major style has long been realism, Adrienne Kennedy has done what few black playwrights have attempted: used form to project an interior reality and thereby created a rich and demanding theatrical style."[4]

PLAYS (SELECTED)

A Beast's Story, 1966; *Black Children's Day*, 1980; *Boats*, 1969; *An Evening with Dead Essex*, 1973; *Funnyhouse of a Negro*, 1962; *A Lancashire Lad*, 1980; *The Lennon Play: In His Own Write* (w/John Lennon and Victor Spinetti), 1967; *A Lesson in Dead Language*, 1964; *A Movie Star Has to Star in Black and White*, 1976; *Orestes and Electra*, 1980; *The Owl Answers*, 1963; *The Pale Blue Flower*, 1956; *A Rat's Mass*, 1966; *Solo Voyages*, 1985; *Sun: A Poem for Malcolm X Inspired by His Murder*, 1970

OTHER WORKS

The Alexander Plays (essays), 1992; *Deadly Triplets: A Theatre Mystery and Journal*, 1990; *In One Act*, 1988; *People Who Led to My Plays* (memoirs), 1987

1. *The Drama Review,* December 1977, p. 42.

2. Case (1).

3. Ibid.

4. Hatch, James V., and Ted Shine, eds. *Black Theatre U.S.A.* (New York: Free Press, 1974).

Jean Kerr
(JULY 10, 1923–   )

FELICIA. Hope is the feeling you have that the feeling you have isn't permanent.

—from *Finishing Touches*, Act III

Brigid Jean Kerr inherited all of her mother's love for theater, but little of the severity that infused the plays of her mother's second cousin, Eugene O'Neill. Instead, she took her cue from her father's dry Irish wit, clearly evident in such shows as *Mary, Mary* and *Finishing Touches*, and her popular magazine essays. Kerr was raised in Scranton,

Jean Kerr
COURTESY OF THE BILLY ROSE THEATRE COLLECTION

1961 show *Mary, Mary* charmed Broadway audiences, running for 1,572 performances. It was made into a film, as was *King of Hearts* (1954), which became the film *A Certain Smile*, increasing her popularity. *Mary* plays with the traditional boy-meets-loses-and-gets-girl formula: In Kerr's version, boy *divorces* girl, then—stunned when he finds her the object of other men's desire—plots to regain her affections. Of course, he succeeds, but not before his wife teaches him a good lesson: "It was hard to communicate with you. You were always communicating with yourself. The line was busy." John McClain praised the play for its "delightfully ludicrous approach to life's more somber moments."[3]

Kerr has used her expertise with comic timing and device, all couched in domestic charm, to illustrate some of the tougher truths about human nature. The female characters, more often than not, uncover such veracities as "Man is the only animal that learns by being hypocritical. He pretends to be polite and then, eventually, he *becomes* polite."[4]

Although Kerr claims that she is a painfully slow writer, she has managed to create an impressive oeuvre. In addition to the demands of her career and prodigious motherhood, Kerr has played an active role for twenty-five years with the Council of the Dramatists Guild. One of America's funniest women writers, Kerr, with her husband, was affectionately lampooned in Ira Levin's 1960 Broadway comedy *Critic's Choice*.

Pennsylvania, to which her parents had immigrated from Ireland. While stage-managing a production of *Romeo and Juliet* as a student at Marywood College in Scranton, Kerr met her future husband, thirty-three-year-old professor Walter Kerr, who became a noted theater critic and author. Despite their physical differences (Jean stood a prodigious five feet, eleven inches—a full four inches above her husband, and was twenty-three), the couple fell in love and married just two months after Jean earned her degree. They went on to produce six children (including a set of twins) and myriad writings, both jointly and separately. A man ahead of his time, Walter assumed many domestic obligations so that Jean could write; he even typed her manuscripts.

Jean Kerr made her solo Broadway debut in 1948 with *Jenny Kissed Me*, of which critic Louis Kronenberger wrote in *Time*, "Leo G. Carroll [who starred in the piece] brightens up Mrs. Kerr's play in much the same way that flowers brighten a sickroom."[1] Fortunately for audiences, it took Kerr ten years, she has said, to appreciate the "felicity"[2] of the remark; she kept writing. Fifteen years later, her name was practically a household word; her fame was due more to her humorous essays, appearing in periodicals such as the *Saturday Evening Post* and *Harper's* and books such as *Please Don't Eat the Daisies*, than her stage works. Still, her

PLAYS

Finishing Touches, 1973; *Goldilocks* (musical), w/Walter Kerr and Leroy Anderson, 1958; *The Good Fairy* (teleplay), 1955; *Jenny Kissed Me*, 1948; *John Murray Anderson's Almanac*, 1953; *King of Hearts*, w/Eleanor Brooke, 1954; *Lunch Hour*, 1980; *Mary, Mary*, 1961; *Our Hearts Were Young and Gay* (adapt. of book by Cornelia Otis Skinner and Emily Kimbrough), 1966; *Poor Richard*, 1964; *The Song of Bernadette*, w/W.K., 1946; *Touch and Go* (rev. of *Thank You, Just Looking*), w/W.K., 1949

OTHER WORKS

Angels on a Pin (novel), 1982; *The Good Fairy* (adapt. teleplay), 1955; *How I Got to Be Perfect*, 1978; *Penny Candy*, 1970; *Please Don't Eat the Daisies*, n.d.; *The Snake has All the Lines* (also TV series), 1965

1. Moritz, p. 222.

2. Ibid.

3. *Journal-American.* March 9, 1961.

4. Kerr, Jean, *Finishing Touches* (New York, Dramatists Play Service, 1973).

Wendy Kesselman
(FEBRUARY 12, 1940–   )

MADAME DANZARD. You have no idea how lucky we are, Isabelle. The servants I've seen in my day. (*She watches her daughter stuff potatoes into her mouth.*) They eat like birds. Always looking so neat, so perfect. You wouldn't think they were maids at all.

—from *My Sister in This House*, Scene 4

Wendy Kesselman, best known for her children's plays, is also a composer, singer, and author of several books. Born in New York City, she earned her B.A. from Sarah Lawrence College, where she was awarded a Fulbright grant, with which she pursued studies in art history, Greek mythology, and poetry in Paris, France. She worked as a singer, songwriter, and author of works for children; eventually she made the transition to penning children's plays, often using her own stories and songs as the basis for them. She is the recipient of many of the most prestigious awards given to artists in her field, among which are National Endowment for the Arts (1982) and Ford Foundation (1979) grants, the Susan Smith Blackburn Prize (1980), and both Guggenheim (1982) and McKnight (1985) Fellowships.

In her first play, *Becca* (1977), Jonathon's prized possession among his menagerie of animals (all played by adult actors) is his doll Becca, who says "I love you" upon command. However, Becca, supported by the menagerie, eventually rebels against the puppet life, and escapes with her animal coterie to live in the forest. When Becca finally returns to Jonathon at the play's end, she is no longer his doll. *The Butcher's Daughter* (1993) follows the bloody destinies of two young women. In this tale, writes theater professor Tish Dace, "Once more, the world proves pernicious to women of any talent or spirit, so utterly denying them autonomy and equity they cannot survive."[1] *I Love You, I Love You Not* (1982) focuses on the demands of the maturing process and how it can only be achieved well in the presence of nurture and care. *The Juniper Tree, A Tragic Household Tale* (1982) deals with child abuse by adapting a Grimm fairy tale; it is the story of a wicked stepmother who brutally murders her stepson, cooks him in a soup for dinner, and then blames her own daughter for his death. *Maggie Magalita* (1980) is about a Spanish-speaking immigrant adolescent struggling for acceptance among her schoolmates. *Merry-Go-Round* (1981) embodies the themes of independence and ethical behavior in the story of the reunion of a man and woman who grew up together. In what Dace calls Kesselman's masterpiece, *My Sister in This House* (1981), the playwright parallels the working class with the privileged class by juxtaposing two sisters who work as maids for a woman and her daughter.

Winner of the prestigious Susan Smith Blackburn Prize and the 1980 Playbill Award, *Sister*, set in France in the 1930s, portrays the desperation of women without men, considered a serious deprivation in that time and place. When the maids are threatened with expulsion, the threat of life on the streets is too much for them, and they take action. Until the play's dramatic (and bloody) ending, the two pairs of women—the lady of the house and her daughter, and the two sisters who are maids—speak only to each other, never to one another.

Although Kesselman's plays are geared for children, they are appreciated by adults as well, for their themes are rife with the import of strong values and relationships, gender inequities, and conflicts of class, age, and culture. Kesselman's use of animals and fantasy is charming and intriguing. Her music, too, can at times be haunting, as exemplified in the songs "We're Stuck" and "Sometimes, I'm Lonely," from *Becca*.

PLAYS

Becca (also book), 1977; *The Butcher's Daughter*, 1993; *Cinderella in a Mirror*, 1987; *The Griffin and the Minor Cannon*, 1988; *I Love You, I Love You Not*, 1982; *The Juniper Tree, A Tragic Household Tale*, 1982; *Maggie Magalita*, 1980; *Merry-Go-Round*, 1981; *My Sister in This House* (also screenplay, *My Sister, My Sister*, 1996), 1981; *Olympe the Executioner*, n.d.; *A Tale of Two Cities* (adapt. of Dickens novel), 1992

OTHER WORKS

Angelita, 1970; *Emma*, 1980; *Flick*, 1983; *Franz Tovey and the Rare Animals*, 1968; *Joey*, 1972; *Little Salt*, 1975; *Maine Is a Million Miles Away*, 1976; *Sand in My Shoes*, 1993; *Slash: An Alligator's Story*, 1971; *There's a Train Going by My Window*, 1982; *Time for Jody*, 1975

1. Essay by Tish Dace in Berney (2).

Lydia Koidula
(DECEMBER 24, 1843–AUGUST 11, 1886)

The founder of the Estonian Theatre, Lydia Koidula was a pioneer of the dramatic arts in her country. Although she is most renowned for her poetry, Koidula essentially initiated Estonian drama in 1870 with *Saaremaa onupoeg* (The Cousin from Saaremaa; 1872). Koidula was born in Vändra, Estonia; her primary influence and mentor was her father, J. V. Jannsen, a leading Estonian intellectual and nationalist who educated Koidula at home before she went off to study at a girl's school in Pärnu (1854–61).

More than twenty years later she finally took a degree, from the University of Tartu in 1882. While still a schoolgirl, Koidula assisted her father with his work for the journal *Pärnu postimees* (Pärnu Postman) by writing translations and adaptations of German stories. In 1863 Jannsen moved his family to Tartu, where he founded another journal, the *Eesti postimees* (Estonian Postman); his daughter did editorial work for the journal, in addition to writing material for its literary column.

Koidula's first poem was published in 1865, followed a year later by the collection *Vainulilled* (Meadow Flowers). With her second volume of poetry, *Emajoeööbik* (The Nightingale of Mother River), Koidula earned real acclaim. Whereas her first poems were largely derivative of German sentimental poetry, the work in *Emajoeööbik* conveyed a fresh, unique voice. Within a few years she was recognized as one of the most notable and influential poets of the national movement. She gave public poetry readings, organized performances at the musical and theatrical society of Vanemuine, corresponded regularly with Finnish and German writers, and, in 1869, helped develop the first song festival, which has since become a staple of Estonian culture. Alfreds Straumanis calls Koidula a natural singer of the sufferings and hopes of her homeland: "her lyric poetry surpassed that of any of her contemporaries."[1] Many of her poems have been set to music and are regularly sung at song festivals and concerts.

Beginning in 1870 with *Saaremaa onupoeg*, Koidula used her plays to establish a tradition of dramatic literature designed not only to entertain, but to instruct and edify. Several of her plays address the attitudes and prejudices of nineteenth-century Estonian villagers. In *Kosjakased* (The Wooing Birches; 1870), a four-act comedy, a poor-yet-kind-and-pure peasant maiden wins the love of a wealthy young bachelor who then determines to enlighten his village. The 1872 three-act comedy *Säärane mulk ehk sada vakka tangusoola* (Such a Bumpkin, or A Hundred Bushels of Coarse Salt) portrays a farmer who learns that not all scoundrels hail from the same origins, and some can even be found among his friends.

In her brief life Koidula published two volumes of poetry; three collections of stories; five plays, all of which were produced; and three volumes of correspondence. She died in Kronstadt, Russia, in 1846. She was forty-three years old.

PLAYS

Kosjakased (The Wooing Birches), 1870; *Kosjaviinad* (The Match-Making Spirits), 1870; *Ojamölder ja tema minia* (The Miller and His Daughter-in-Law), 1946; *Säärane mulk ehk sada vakka tangusoola* (Such a Bumpkin, or A Hundred Bushels of Coarse Salt), 1872; *Saaremaa onupoeg* (The Cousin From Saaremaa), 1870

OTHER WORKS

Emajoeööbik (The Nightingale of Mother River), 18??; *Vainulilled* (Meadow Flowers), 1886

1. Straumanis.

Clare Kummer
(1888?–APRIL 22, 1948)

Before the 1916 opening of *Good Gracious, Annabelle!*, Clare Kummer's first and most popular stage work, Kummer had already established her reputation as a noted songwriter, with two hit songs to her name: "Dearie" and "Egypt." From 1916 to 1937 Kummer wrote more than twenty plays, although after 1933 she had little success. According to Duskey Lobel, her plays possessed "an abundant and buoyant wit" despite their rather weak plots.[1] Alexander Woollcott, an admirer of hers, asserted—somewhat hyperbolically perhaps—that she was "the only American playwright with a style so recognizable that you could spot her authorship by listening to a single scene."[2]

Kummer was born Clare Rodman Beecher. Her second marriage, to Arthur Henry, lasted a great deal longer than her first, to Frederick Arnold Kummer; however, by the time she wed Henry, her professional name had become known. She and Henry had one daughter, Marjorie, who performed in several of her mother's plays. Marjorie married the noted British-cum-Hollywood character actor Roland Young, for whom Kummer wrote *Rollo's Wild Oat*. After 1933, she wrote several plays, but none did well critically, though several were hits; however *Her Master's Voice* (1933) was well received.

PLAYS

Be Calm, Camilla, 1918; *Bridges*, 1921; *Chinese Love*, 1921; *The Choir Rehearsal*, 1921; *Good Gracious, Annabelle!*, 1916; *Her Master's Voice*, 1933; *The Light of Duxbury*, 1921; *Many Happy Returns*, 1944; *The Mountain Man*, 1921; *The Opera Ball*, w/Sydney Rosenfeld, 1912; *Pomeroy's Past*, 1926; *The Rescuing Angel*, 1917; *The Robbery*, 1921; *Rollo's Wild Oat*, 1920; *Roxie*, 1921; *A Successful Calamity*, 1917; *Three Waltzes*, w/Rowland Leigh, 1937

1. Essay by Duskey Lobel in Robinson.
2. *New York Times*, January 23, 1921.

Myrna Lamb
(AUGUST 3, 1935–)

Let us not be compliant earth to willful seed
Let us cast another god from our true vision
Our true need
LIBERATION LIBERATION LIBERATION

—from *The Mod Donna*

Myrna Lamb's fearless portrayals of contemporary women's psyches and experiences caused the *Village Voice*'s Vivian Gornick to hail the playwright as "the first true artist of the feminist consciousness."[1] Since the late 1960s, much like her contemporaries ANN JELLICOE in Britain and MEGAN TERRY in the United States, Lamb's stylized, nonlinear, multimedia productions have approached issues such as gender identity, abortion, marriage, class struggle, and physical violence through a keenly developed feminist lens.

Lamb's love of theater and performance dates back to her childhood: She penned her first play at the age of eight, shortly after she learned to print the alphabet. Her father, a New Jersey sheriff's officer who moonlighted as a musician, encouraged his young daughter's appreciation of music. From her mother, Lamb garnered an understanding of a working mother's life, a role she herself copied with a teenage marriage, motherhood (she had two daughters; one became a painter, the other an actor), and a slew of jobs that ranged from sales clerk to bookkeeper to bakery clerk.

At the Actor's Mobile Theatre, Lamb began training as an actress with Howard da Silva and others. Later she furthered her studies in writing, theater, and directing at the New School for Social Research and Rutgers University. For several years she had been writing one-act plays, and she finally assembled a series of them under the title *Scyklon Z*, which was staged by the New Feminist Theatre in New York City in 1969. Anselma Dell'Ollio, artistic director of the New Feminist Repertory Theater, claims that audiences sat with "clenched fists, gnawed knuckles, head cocked to catch every word"[2] of these plays that, according to Helene Keyssar, "[assault] marriage, possession, and ownership in all elements of life as activities that facilitate self-destruction."[3] One play of the series is considered a watershed in depicting the new consciousness of women's sexual rights: *But What Have You Done for Me Lately?* features a man who awakens one morning to discover that he is pregnant, and without any reproductive rights or choices.

Lamb's first full-scale production occurred in 1970 with the New York Shakespeare Festival Public Theater's staging of *The Mod Donna, A Space-Age Musical Soap Opera with Breaks for Commercials*, directed by Joseph Papp. Utilizing film, video, and photographs, *The Mod Donna* parodies suburban life, replete with materialistic neighbors, spousal swaps, and bickering. Some critics perceived the show to be a lucid view of modern male-female relationships; others decried it as a puritanical anti-sex lecture. Gornick, a staunch Lamb supporter, argued that the playwright intended to convey "woman's imposed and self-imposed obsession not with sex, but with sexuality, the obsession with her own desirability that powers all her actions, and her rage at having no other means by which to define herself."[4] When it comes to structure, Vivian Patraka says Lamb has created ". . . a new form of serious musical drama that resembles neither Broadway musicals nor traditional opera . . ."[5]

Although her plays have a certain thematic consistency, Lamb has been quick to experiment with different subject matter and theatrical forms. *I Lost a Pair of Gloves Yesterday*, based on the death of Lamb's father, is a long monologue. The Greek myth of Iphigenia is retold wholly through song in *The Sacrifice*. *Olympic Park*'s conceit of a fifteen-year-old's diary realistically renders the working-class world of Newark, New Jersey, during World War II. *Crab Quadrille* incorporates many of Lamb's signature devices to poke fun at '60s liberals with '70s business ethics on the Jersey shore.

Despite Lamb's belief that capitalism perpetuates economic and personal oppression, she has accepted grants and fellowships from the Rockefeller (1972) and Guggenheim (1973) foundations, as well as the National Endowment for the Arts (1974–75), among others.

Like her successor MICHELENE WANDOR, Lamb embraces, as she puts it, "an ultimate revolution . . . the liberation of the female of the species so that the male of the species may be freed forever from supermasculine compulsion and may join his sister in full and glorious humanity."[6]

PLAYS

Apple Pie, music by Nicholas Meyers, 1974; *Crab Quadrille*, music by N. M., 1976; *I Lost A Pair of Gloves Yesterday*, n.d.; *The Mod Donna, A Space-Age Musical Soap Opera with Breaks for Commercials*, music by Susan Hulsman Bingham, 1970; *Olympic Park*, 1978; *The Sacrifice*, music by George Quincy, 1977; *Scyklon Z, A Group of Pieces with a Point* (a series of plays), including *But What Have You Done for Me Lately?, Monogolia, Pas de Deux, The Butcher Shop, The Serving-Girl and the Lady*, and *In the Shadow of the Crematoria*, 1969; *Two Party System*, 1972; *With a Little Help from My Friends*, w/others, 1974; *Yesterday Is Over*, music by N. M., 1980

1. Lamb, Mary, *The Mod Donna and Scyklon Z*, (New York: Pathfinder Press, 1971), p. 139.
2. Gornick, Vivian, and Barbara K. Moran, *Women in Sexist Society*, (New York: A Mentor Book, New American Library, 1971), p. 40.
3. Keyssar.
4. Cited in Olauson.
5. Essay by Vivian M. Patraka in Robinson.
6. Op. cit., Lamb, p. 18.

Else Lasker-Schüler
(FEBRUARY 11, 1869–JANUARY 22, 1945)

MEPHISTO. I was the first to crawl across the plain of the Eternal and made my home in darkness. And God's earthly kingdom died from my serpent's sting.

FAUST. Now I'm really lost, my prince.
MEPHISTO. You're not alone. Billions of people, confused like you, go round in circles and cannot find their way.
FAUST. And the Eternal One, is He still firmly on his throne?
MEPHISTO. I'm not too sure of that. But let me ask you, Doctor Faust, with all due respect, why He created me, the Devil, from slime and scorn to live forever?

—from *IandI*, Act I

Known primarily for her accomplishments as a German Expressionist poet, Else Lasker-Schüler's dramatic works reveal her deep concerns with social injustice and anti-Semitism. Although she showed a talent for writing even as a young girl, her artistic sensibilities flourished only after she separated from her first husband and became involved with a circle of antibourgeois artists. She was greatly influenced by her second husband (though that marriage, too, ended in divorce), the editor of the Expressionist publication *Der Sturm*. Lasker-Schüler was a colorful character among her crowd, often appearing publicly dressed as Joseph, Prince of Thebes, or Princess Tino of Baghdad. Sue-Ellen Case remarks on how she exploited "customs and taboos," flaunting her bisexuality and bohemianism.[1]

Her play *Die Wupper* (The People of Wuppertal; 1909), written seven years after the publication of her first collection of poetry, *Styx*, deals with factory workers, proletarians, and social outcasts in Wuppertal at the turn of the century. It invokes the world of Lasker-Schüler's youth. "The play is a classic of a certain kind of social drama in Germany," writes Case, "staging class conflicts, strikes, and the effect of social conditions on personal relationships."[2] Although *Die Wupper* paved the way for Lasker-Schüler's career as a dramatist, she did not write her next plays until the 1930s. Instead she concentrated on poetry, publishing several volumes of Expressionist lyric poems until the early 1920s.

In 1931, the same year she won the Kleist Prize for Literature, Lasker-Schüler was beaten by Nazi followers. She fled to Switzerland, where she wrote two Jewish-themed plays, *Arthur Aronymus und seine Vater* (A.A. and His Father, 1936), in which she exposes the anti-Semitic, petty bourgeoisie, and *IandI* (as in I and I). *IandI* toys with the classical story of Faust, blending the characters of the doomed doctor and Mephistopheles with figures from the Old Testament and from the Nazi regime, with the Ritz brothers and Max Reinhardt tossed in for good measure. Together this array of fictional and historical characters comprises "a complex pastiche . . . [that] serves to dramatize the historical intersection of fascism, sexism, anti-Semitism, imperialism, and the dynamics of desire."[3] Although the complexity of her plays' subject matter may suggest otherwise, Lasker-Schüler believed strongly in the entertainment value of theatrical works. In a letter to Max Reinhardt she wrote, "Theater is theater! Theater isn't a lecture hall for medicine or any other scientific discipline.

... We do not want to go home from a performance saddened or refined but rather shaken by the joy of sorrow or even pleasure."[4]

Sadly, her life in Switzerland offered little satisfaction. She felt disconnected from the Jewish community there, and eventually emigrated to Palestine. But this change, too, proved unfulfilling. Neither fish nor fowl, she seemed unacceptable to Jews as well as Germans. After a long illness, Lasker-Schüler died in extreme poverty in 1945.

PLAYS

Arthur Aronymus und seine Vater (A.A. and his Father), 1936; *IandI*, Beate Hein Bennett, tr., 1940; *Die Wupper* (The People of Wuppertal), 1909

OTHER WORKS

Styx (poetry), 1902; *Meine Wunder* (My Miracles; poetry), 1911; *Mein Herz* (My Heart; autobio. novel), 1912; *Der Prinz von Theben* (The Prince of Thebes; short stories), 1914; *Der Wunderrabbiner von Barcelona* (The Wonder Rabbi of Barcelona; short stories), 1921

1. Case (2).

2. Ibid.

3. Ibid.

4. "Das Konzert (1920–1932)," a collection of essays and poems appearing in *Gesammelte Werke* (Munich: Kösel Verlag, 1962), vol. 2, nos. 635–38.

Mary Leapor
(1722–1746)

EMILA. Our servile Tongues are taught to cry for Pardon
Ere the weak Senses know the Use of Words:
Our little Souls are tortur'd by Advice;
And moral Lectures stun our Infant Years:
Thro' check'd Desires, Threat'nings, and Restraint
The Virgin runs; but ne'er outgrows her Shackles
They still will fit her, even to hoary Age.

—from *The Unhappy Father*

The daughter of a Northamptonshire gardener, Mary Leapor spent most of her tragically brief life as a servant. Despite her meager finances, she managed to procure and study the works of Pope and Dryden. Her one play, a tragedy, contains a passage that is remarkable considering the time frame in which it was written. In it, she laments the training that turns girls into "unhappy Wives." The work was never performed, though she wished it to be. Leapor died from the measles at age 24.

PLAYS

The Unhappy Father, 1751

OTHER WORKS

Poems on Several Occasions, 2 vols., 1748–51

Doris Lessing
(OCTOBER 22, 1919–)

MARY. If a man marries, he marries a woman, but if a woman marries, she marries a way of life.

—from *Play with a Tiger*

One of the twentieth century's most prolific prose writers, Doris Lessing has also created a dozen works for the stage and small screen. Lessing's plays traverse turf similar to her fiction and nonfiction: political commitment, women's search for identity, the connection between the artist and her work, and the male-female dynamic.

She was born Doris May Taylor in Kermansha, Persia (now Iran), and spent much of her youth in Rhodesia (now Zimbabwe). By the time she was thirty years old she had delivered three children and was twice divorced (the second time from Frank Gottfried Lessing). She moved to London in 1949 after her second marriage dissolved, and found work first as a secretary, then as a member of the *New Reasoner* (later the *New Left Review*) editorial board.

Interestingly, her first play, the well-received *Each His Own Wilderness* (1958), predates by four years her best-known work, the experimental novel *The Golden Notebook*. *Wilderness*'s central character is Myra Bolton, a well-meaning, politically conscious leftist whose public activism juxtaposes the inordinate insensitivity she shows to her son. Lessing's ability to successfully intertwine personal and political themes was praised by British writer-director Ronald Hayman.[1]

Her 1962 drama *Play with a Tiger* was less acclaimed critically, but popular among feminists due to its defiant declaration of women's rights over predatory men. *Tiger* begins in a lush, dense jungle of love where women and men engage and disengage—making love, fighting, struggling for sure footing in the dance of intimacy. Like real people, *Tiger*'s characters are works in progress. Among the inhabitants of this underbrush we find Anna, a writer in her mid-thirties who lives alone in her London flat. Self-sufficient and engaging, she is attracted to men but cannot bring herself to submit to male dominance. Helene Keyssar acknowledges that "*Tiger*'s direct exploration of an adult woman's tensions between her images of herself as 'just a little ordinary girl' who 'wants to be married', and a woman who refuses to manacle herself to a man has a poignant appeal for any contemporary woman struggling with her own ambivalence."[2] Structurally the play moves from a naturalistic to a minimalist construct; apropos, Lessing has called stage realism "the greatest enemy of the theatre . . ."[3]

Lessing has received many awards for her prose, including the Hamburg Shakespeare Prize (1982), as well as honorary doctorates from Princeton University (1989) and the University of Durham (1990). In truth, her dramas appear to have taken a back seat to her other writings, in spite of what Hayman identifies as her "very keen instinct for [igniting] a situation theatrically."[4]

PLAYS

Before the Deluge, 1953; *Between Men* (teleplay), 1967; *Care and Protection* (teleplay), 1966; *Do Not Disturb* (teleplay), 1966; *Each His Own Wilderness*, 1958; *The Grass Is Singing* (teleplay; also novel), 1962; *The Making of the Representative for Planet 8*, libretto, music by Philip Glass (also novel), 1988; *Mr. Dollinger*, 1958; *Play with a Tiger*, 1962; *The Singing Door*, 1973; *The Storm* (adapt. of Aleksandr Ostrovsky play), 1966; *The Truth About Billy Newton*, 1960

FICTION (SELECTED)

Canopus in Argos, 1979; *Children of Violence* (five novels, collectively titled), 1952; *The Diaries of Jane Somers*, 1984; *The Fifth Child*, 1988; *The Four-Gated City*, 1969; *The Golden Notebook*, 1962; *The Good Terrorist*, 1985; *The Habit of Loving*, 1957; *A Man and Two Women* (short stories), 1958; *The Memoirs of a Survivor*, 1975; *A Proper Marriage*, 1952; *The Summer Before the Dark*, 1973

OTHER WORKS (SELECTED)

African Laughter: Four Visits to Zimbabwe, 1992; *Fourteen Poems*, 1959; *Particularly Cats*, 1967; *Prisons We Choose to Live Inside*, 1986

WORKS ABOUT (SELECTED)

Bloom, Harold, ed., *Doris Lessing*, 1986; Brewster, Dorothy, *Doris Lessing*, 1965; Draine, B., *Substance Under Pressure*, 1983; Myles, A., *Doris Lessing*, 1990; Sprague, C., *In Pursuit of Doris Lessing*, 1990; Sprague, *Rereading Doris Lessing*, 1987; Sprague, C., and Tiger, V., *Critical Essays on Doris Lessing*, 1986; Whittaker, R., *Doris Lessing*, 1988

1. Essay by Ronald Hayman in Berney (1).
2. Keyssar.

3. Ibid.
4. Op. cit., Berney (1).

Genny Lim
(1946–)

LI-TAI. They all think like one person. The young girls talk like old women and the old women are ignorant and superstitious. In China you're born old before you can walk. As a woman you're allowed to do only one thing. Please men. I've spent my whole life doing that! You see this body? It's not mine. It belongs to Kahuku Plantation. My skin even smells like burnt cane!

—from *Bitter Cane*, Scene 6

In a conversation with fellow Asian-American playwright VELINA HASU HOUSTON, Genny Lim declared, "Art should engage the mind and spirit. It should mobilize people into social action whenever social change is necessary."[1] All of Lim's work supports this belief. The history of Chinese immigrants is a frequent topic of Lim's. *Paper Angels* (1980) dramatizes the experiences of poor rural Chinese who were confined at Angel Island in the San Francisco Bay area, and *Bitter Cane* (1989) depicts the plight of Chinese laborers recruited to work in Hawaiian sugarcane fields in the 1880s. Lim favors an experimental style that incorporates different media; the poetical *Winter Place* (1988) uses sculpture, music, and performance to become an "epic jazz poem," similar to NTOZAKE SHANGE's "choreopoems" or AISHAH RAHMAN's jazz approach to dialogue.

The youngest of her Chinese parents' seven children, Lim grew up in San Francisco, where she still lives. She studied theater and liberal arts as an undergraduate and graduate student at San Francisco State University. The dearth of works by and about the Asian-American experience, particularly that of women, ultimately motivated her to begin creating works for the theater; she did not write her first play until 1980. Today both her plays and her poems have been abundantly anthologized. Lim's work continues to be widely produced, enlightening and teaching audiences about issues concerning "gender and race . . . two of the biggest issues of our time."[2]

PLAYS

Bitter Cane, 1989; *Daughter of Han* (performance piece), 1983; *Faceless*, 1989; *I Remember Clifford* (performance piece), 1983; *The Magic Brush*, 1990; *Paper Angels* (also teleplay), 1980; *Pigeons* (one-act; adapted to film, *Fei Tien*), 1983; *SenseUs: The Rainbow Anthems*, 1990; *Winter Place* (also collection of poetry, 1989), 1988; *XX*, 1987

OTHER WORKS

The Chinese American Experience, ed., 1984; *Island: Poetry and History of Chinese Immigrants on Angel Island, 1910–1940*, w/Him Mark Lai and Judy Jung, 1980; *The Only Language She Knows* (short-subject feature film), 1987; *Wings for Lai Ho*, 1982

1. Houston.
2. Ibid.

Aldona Liobytė
(FEBRUARY 11, 1915–)

Even though Aldona Liobytė expressed an interest in theater as a child in Vilnius, Latvia, she did not pursue her dramatic leanings until she had completed her studies in Polish language and literature at the University of Vilnius (1932–35) and in Lithuanian language and literature at the University of Kaunas (1935–39). After teaching high school for two years, she joined Vaidilla (The Actor's Theater) in 1941. She spent most of the 1940s employed as an actress there and at the State Drama Theater in Vilnius. In 1949 Liobytė decided to leave acting for the world of letters.

For the next twelve years she worked as an editor in the division for children and youth of the Soviet Lithuanian State Publishing House. Shortly after taking this post, she began her play writing career by collaborating with stage director Kazimiera Kymantaitė on an adaptation of the Petras Cvirka novel *Žemė maitintoja* (The Nourishing Earth). Liobytė and Kymantaitė collaborated on at least two other works: *Paskenduolė* (The Drowned Woman, 1956), an adaptation of the A. Vienuolis novel, and Meisteris ir sūnūs (Masters and Sons, 1969), adapted from another Cvirka novel.

Most of Liobytė's own plays utilize aspects of Lithuanian mythology and folklore. Her work suggests that she was influenced by her countrywoman ASPAZIJA, as her fairy tale dramas similarly incorporate realistic scenes and dialogue as well as poetic rhetoric and folk songs. Alfreds Straumanis writes that Liobytė's work "enters the realm of folklore with ease and familiarity, not like a supercilious tourist who snickers at all that archaica and exotica, but rather resembling a relative visiting an ancestral home."[1] She created several plays and puppet shows for young people, such as *Meškos trobelė* (The Bear's Den, 1956) and *Užburtas karaliūnas* (The Enchanted Princess, 1957).

Liobytė's stories and plays have been translated into Russian, Georgian, and English, and have been staged in theaters and on television. She has translated many children's stories into Lithuanian. In 1975 she was recognized as the Cultural Worker of Soviet Lithuania.

PLAYS

Ant kalnelio jovaras žydėjo (On the Hill the Sycamore Blossomed), 1970; *Devyniabrolė* (Nine Brothers), 1971; *Kupriukas muzikantas* (The Little Hunch-back Musician), 1955; *Kuršiukas* (The Lad from Courland, Egle Juodvalkis, tr.), 1969; *Meisteris ir sūnūs* (Masters and Sons; adapt. of Petras Cvirka novel), w/Kazimiera Kymantaitė, 1965; *Meškos trobelė* (The Bear's Den), 1956; *Paskenduolė* (The Drowned Woman; adapt. of A. Vienuolis novel), w/ K.K., 1956; *Trys negražios karalaitės* (Three Ugly Princesses), 1967; *Užburtas karaliūnas* (The Enchanted Princess), 1957; *Žemė maitintoja* (The Nourishing Earth; adapt. of Petras Cvirka novel), w/K.K., n.d.

1. Straumanis.

Joan Littlewood
(1914–)

"I do not believe in the supremacy of the director, designer, actor, or even of the writer," English theatrician Joan Littlewood once wrote in *Encore*. "It is through collaboration that this knockabout art of theatre survives and kicks."[1] Blurring the line between playwright and director, so that distinguishing between them becomes nearly impossible, may not initially appear to be a great achievement. But upon examining the theatrical life of Joan Littlewood, one cannot deny her startling, innovative contributions to ensemble improvisation. She was an essential creative force not only in her own work, but also in the work of writers such as SHELAGH DELANEY (*A Taste of Honey*), Brendan Behan (*The Quare Fellow*), and Frank Norman (*Fings Ain't Wot They Used T'Be*). While her collaborative approach may now seem almost commonplace, particularly among feminist theater groups, Littlewood pioneered the technique around 1934 when she and her husband, Ewan MacColl (neé Jimmy Miller), founded the Theater of Action in Manchester.

By the time she met MacColl, Littlewood had already established herself as a voice of dissent from the commercial West End approach to theater. She began as an outstanding student at the Royal Academy of Dramatic Art in London, but left to work for the British Broadcasting Corporation (BBC), where she met MacColl, then a folksinger and political dramatist. Eventually the BBC asked her to leave because of her outspoken political opinions. She rooted about for a while, searching for a more radical approach to performance and communication, and finally accepted a position acting with the Rusholme Repertory Theatre in Manchester. She toured in Great Britain, Germany, Norway, and Sweden with original works for eight years. Then, in 1953, she came to London's Theater

Royal, where she worked on productions of the classics and more topical works that MacColl had written. For three years in a row, beginning in 1955, she won the Best Production Award at the Theater of the Nations in Paris.

Over the years Littlewood and MacColl formed other companies: Theatre Union, a left-wing touring group that "became a pioneering example for the fringe companies of the 1960s,"[2] and, in the early 1970s, Theatre Workshop in Stratford. MacColl provided the scripts for their early productions such as *Johnny Noble* and *Uranium 235*, both antiwar vehicles. Littlewood's *Oh, What a Lovely War!*, one of her biggest successes, was produced in 1963. She credits Charles Chilton's radio program, *A Long, Long Trail*, a show that presented songs from the war, as a major inspiration. Although Gwyn Thomas and Ted Allan were commissioned to write the script, their efforts were so eviscerated by the company's collaborative changes, their names were removed from the credits. An early experiment in multimedia on stage, *Lovely War!* portrays Pierrot, the classic figure from commedia dell'arte, clowning his way through contrapuntal projections of the grimness of war. Ronald Hayman writes that in *Lovely War!*, Littlewood "arrived at forms of theatrical expression which no playwright could have evolved while sitting at his [sic] typewriter. The combination of farce and horror was seminal . . ."[3] In 1969 it was adapted for the screen by Richard Attenborough.

Among Littlewood's many awards are the Society of West End Theatre Special Award (1983), the Women of Achievement in the Arts Award, the Arts Council of Great Britain Award (1993), and the Lifetime Achievement Award from the Directors' Guild of Great Britain. Littlewood is a member of the French Academy of Writers. In *The Cambridge Guide to Theatre*, John Elsom states, "Her influence on other British directors and companies has been profound."[4]

PLAYS

Alice in Wonderland (adapt. of Lewis' Carroll novel), 1950; *The Chimes* (adapt. of Charles Dickens novel), 1954; *A Christmas Carol* (adapt. of Charles Dickens novel), 1953; *Cruel Daughters* (adapt. of Honoré de Balzac story), 1954; *The Long Shift*, w/Gerry Raffles, 1951; *Make Me an Offer* (adapt. of Wolf Mankowitz's work), 1959; *Oh, What a Lovely War!* (also film, 1969), 1963; *Treasure Island* (adapt. of Robert Louis Stevenson novel), 1953

OTHER WORKS

Joan's Book, 1994

WORKS ABOUT

Goorney, Howard, *The Theatre Workshop Story*, 1981

Joan Littlewood
COURTESY OF THE PLAYWRIGHT

1. "A Goodbye Note from Joan," *Encore* (Natl. Assoc. of Dramatic and Speech Arts), October 1961.

2. Essay by John Elsom in *The Cambridge Guide to Theatre*, Banham, Martin, ed. (Cambridge: Cambridge University Press, 1988).

3. Essay by Ronald Hayman in Weintraub.

4. Op. cit., Elsom.

Anita Loos
(APRIL 26, 1888–AUGUST 18, 1981)

LORELEI. I really think that American gentlemen are the best after all, because . . . kissing your hand may make you feel very, very good, but a diamond and sapphire bracelet lasts forever.

—from *Gentlemen Prefer Blondes*

Not many writers can boast sharing a credit with William Shakespeare, playing a key role in the careers of Douglas Fairbanks and D. W. Griffith, and penning some of Broadway's most-loved shows, but Anita Loos can. This pioneer of silent-screen subtitles made serious waves in the entertainment industry despite her tiny stature—four feet, eleven inches tall, and ninety pounds.

Born in Sisson, California (now Mt. Shasta), to sometimes-stage producer, sometimes-newspaperman Richard

Beers Loos, Anita experienced an often unstable and stressful childhood. Although she was the second of three children, her younger sister died at the age of eight. Loos grew up performing in her father's sporadic productions and in summer stock shows, but her heart belonged to writing.

How Loos shook loose from her family is the object of some speculation. One story asserts that she ran away with Frank Pallma, Jr., a bandleader, and left him twenty-four hours after the marriage ceremony. Other reports claim that she moved to New York City while still in her teens and began writing regularly for the *Morning Telegraph*. Whichever, in 1912 Loos's career leapt forward when D. W. Griffith used her script for his silent short *The New York Hat*, which starred Mary Pickford and Lionel Barrymore. Thrilled with the intelligence and wit of Loos and her work, Griffith asked her to join him at Biograph Studios as a staff writer in 1914. He paid her fifty dollars a week, plus additional fees for scripts purchased. She wrote over 400 film plays. Within four years Loos was earning 300 dollars per script. Her memorable titles for Griffith's film classic *Intolerance* in 1916 (the same year she and the Bard split the credit for the silent-screen version of *Macbeth*) opened new doors for screenwriters. With director John Emerson, her future husband, she penned the film that made Douglas Fairbanks a star: *His Picture in the Paper* satirized "the up-and-at-'em Fairbanks athleticism, a response to the increasing industrialization and encroaching commercialization of the American landscape."[1]

Armed with the friendship and encouragement of such literary heavyweights as H. L. Mencken and George Jean Nathan, Loos began writing fiction and stage plays. In 1926 she introduced audiences to the fractured grammar and hard-nosed romanticism of Lorelei Lee, bombshell flapper heroine of *Gentlemen Prefer Blondes*. The show became an international sensation and spawned a variety of sequels on stage, in film, and in print; it was translated into fourteen languages (including Chinese) and ran through eighty-five editions. Loos's "little girl from Little Rock" reigns as one of American theater's most endearing gold diggers.

Loos enjoyed fame and a decent income during her tenure in New York, but after being adversely affected by the stock market crash of 1929, she and Emerson succumbed to the lure of big money in Hollywood. They secured contracts with MGM to write screenplays. Sadly Emerson, a manic-depressive, found it increasingly difficult to work, and eventually Loos had to institutionalize him. He died in 1956; Loos then married writer-director Richard Sale.

Despite the renown of her work, Loos never took her profession too seriously: She compared it to doing crossword puzzles and at times openly criticized the entertainment industry. "That our popular art forms [have] become so obsessed with sex has turned the U.S.A. into a nation

Anita Loos
COURTESY OF THE BILLY ROSE THEATRE COLLECTION

of hobbledehoys," she once wrote. "As if grown people don't have more vital concerns, such as taxes, inflation, dirty politics, earning a living, getting an education, or keeping out of jail."[2]

PLAYS

The Amazing Adele, based on French play by Pierre Barrillet and Jean-Pierre Gredy, 1955; *Chêri* (adapt. of Colette's work), 1959; *The Fall of Eve* (also film, 1929), 1925; *Gentlemen Prefer Blondes* (also book, 1926; musical, w/ Joseph Fields, 1949; film musical, 1953), 1926; *Gigi* (adapt. of Colette's work; also film, 1958), 1951; *Gogo Loves You*, 1964; *Happy Birthday*, 1946; *Information Please*, w/John Emerson (also film *Temperamental Wife*, 1919), 1918; *The King's Mare* (adapt. from the French), 1966; *Pair o' Fools*, w/J.E., 1926; *The Social Register* (also film, 1934), w/J.E., 1931; *The Whole Town's Talking* (also film, 1926), 1923

SCREENPLAYS (SELECTED)

Babes in Arms, 1939; *The Branded Woman*, 1920; *Double Trouble*, 1915; *His Picture in the Papers*, 1916; *The Hunchback*, 1914; *I Married an Angel*, 1942; *Intolerance*, 1916;

Macbeth, 1916; *The New York Hat*, 1912; *The Perfect Woman*, 1920; *Riffraff*, 1935; *San Francisco*, 1936; *Saratoga*, 1937; *Susan and God* (based on RACHEL CROTHERS play), 1940; *Woman's Place*, w/J.E., 1921; *The Women* (based on CLARE BOOTHE LUCE play), 1939

OTHER WORKS

A Girl Like I (autobio.), 1966; *A Mouse Is Born* (fiction), 1951; *Breaking Into the Movies* (nonfiction) w/J.E., n.d.; *But Gentlemen Marry Brunettes* (also film, 1955), 1928; *Cast of Thousands* (memoirs), 1977; *Fate Keeps on Happening* (autobio.), 1984; *How to Write Photoplays*, w/J.E., 1921; *Kiss Hollywood Goodbye* (autobio.), 1974; *No Mother to Guide Her* (fiction), 1962; *The Talmadge Girls* (bio.), 1978; *Twice Over Lightly* (nonfiction), w/Helen Hayes, 1972

WORKS ABOUT

Carey, G., *Anita Loos*, 1988

1. Baseline's *The Encyclopedia of Film*, James Pallot, ed. (New York: Perigee Books, c1991).

2. Loos, Anita, *Kiss Hollywood Goodbye*. ch.1 (New York: Viking Press, 1974).

Clare Boothe Luce
(APRIL 10, 1903–OCTOBER 9, 1987)

SECRETARY. I wish I could get a man to foot my bills. I'm sick and tired, cooking my own breakfast, sloshing through the rain at 8 A.M., working like a dog. For what? Independence? A lot of independence you have on a woman's wages. I'd chuck it like that for a decent, or an indecent home.

—from *The Women*

CHRYSTAL. There's a name for you ladies, but it isn't used in high society . . . outside of a kennel.

—from *The Women*

Clare Boothe Luce remains a complex figure in American women's theater history. She penned *The Women*, which provided plump roles for one of the largest all-female casts ever assembled on the Broadway stage; however, critics overwhelmingly view *The Women* as void of any real feminist sensibility (although there are some who champion the play's insights on female bonding). Luce herself said, with characteristic sassiness, "The women who inspired this play deserved to be smacked across the head with a meat axe. And that, I flatter myself, is exactly what I smacked them with." By the time the play was produced in 1936, Luce had tasted both extremes of the economic food chain, which may have informed her cynical outlook on empty-headed, male-obsessed, money-hungry society women.

Her New York City childhood was wrought with the economic and religious difficulties of her mismatched parents' marriage. Luce's father, William Franklin Boothe, was a violinist from old American stock who shocked his parents by marrying Ann Clara Snyder, the Roman Catholic daughter of Bavarian immigrants. The couple could not withstand their families' hostility, and the marriage soon dissolved. Luce's mother assumed responsibility for her daughter and son, taking any available job in order to provide her children with books and education, which she considered essential. When Clare's brother David went to a military academy, Luce accompanied her mother to Paris. With their menial allowance, the two absorbed as much art, opera, music, and theater as possible.

Just after Luce graduated from the Cathedral School of St. Mary's (Episcopal) in Garden City, New York, her mother remarried Albert Elmer Austin, a wealthy physician with influential friends. He took the two women back to Europe in high style. Austin introduced them to such luminaries as Jane Cowl, the Barrymores, and Otis Skinner. When they returned, Clare took a job in publishing, but her professional pursuits were placed on hold when, through her stepfather's connections, she eventually met

Claire Boothe Luce
COURTESY OF THE BILLY ROSE THEATRE COLLECTION

and married George Tuttle Brokaw, a man of means more than twenty years her senior. The union lasted only six years, during which she gave birth to a daughter, Ann Clare.

Luce resumed her aborted career, becoming an editorial assistant at *Vogue*; within five years she had become the managing editor of *Vanity Fair*. She also began writing plays. In the mid-1930s she met publishing magnate Henry R. Luce. They were married in 1935, just one year before her third and most famous play, *The Women*, appeared on Broadway.

A comedy of manners about the upper-crust women of Manhattan, *The Women* has been revived repeatedly. "What gives the play its bite," wrote Michael Billington of *The London Guardian*, "is Mrs. Luce's awareness of economic reality. She leaves you in no doubt that these ladies who lunch are bankrolled by rich husbands and shielded from the grosser realities [by] armies of handmaids . . ."[1] Olauson claims some scenes evoke the "pessimistic satire found in Restoration comedy"; she believes that Luce emphasizes the women's complete reliance on men for their own sense of identity in the materialistic world in which they dwell.[2]

Luce's burgeoning political convictions are evident in *Kiss the Boys Goodbye* (1938), a light-hearted satire about the nationwide search for an actress to play Scarlett O'Hara in the film version of *Gone with the Wind*. Luce turns this tale into a political allegory about the fascism of manners and morals in the American South. However, her 1939 war drama *Margin for Error* conveys Luce's beliefs more forthrightly. The play follows the trials and tribulations of Moe Finkelstein, a Jewish policeman from New York who is assigned to guard a German consul. When Moe risks his own safety for the sake of countless potential victims of Nazi terror, he proves to be more noble, indeed more "Christian," than any other character in the play. The sophisticated plot and brilliant dialogue help make *Margin* an effective treatise on prejudice, hatred, and integrity. After *Margin*, it was another twenty years before Luce wrote another play: *Child of the Morning* (1951), about a Catholic family in Brooklyn whose daughter decides not to follow her family's plans for her life in a convent.

Luce published a perceptive study of contemporary Western Europe in 1940, *Europe in the Spring*, and filed a few wartime reports for *Life* magazine, but she began to turn away from writing and toward politics. In 1943 she successfully ran for Congress on the Connecticut Republican ticket, but her tenure was marked by a series of personal tragedies. Automobile accidents killed her mother in 1939 and, only five years later, her daughter. Perhaps coincidentally, Luce converted to Roman Catholicism during this time. In 1948 her brother perished in a plane wreck.

By the late 1950s, Luce's accomplishments as a politician had surpassed what she had achieved as a writer. President Eisenhower appointed her U.S. ambassador to Italy (1953–57), making her the first American woman ever to hold a major diplomatic post. She was also the first woman to sit on the House Military Affairs Committee.

Luce finally returned to play writing in 1970, three years after the death of her husband. She penned *Slam the Door Softly*, a drama about women's coming of age in the 1970s, inspired by Henrik Ibsen's *A Doll's House*. Her sardonic humor had not waned; among *Slam's* several barbs is a black woman's voice intoning, "There's no human being a man can buy anymore—except a woman." Nora decries, "Know what Freud wrote in his diary when he was 77? 'What do women want? My God, what do they want?' Fifty years this giant brain spends analyzing women. And he still can't find out what they want. So this makes him the world's greatest expert on female psychology?"

After this brief return to the boards, Luce went back to the political arena. In 1983 she moved from Honolulu (where she had resided since Henry's death) to Washington, D.C. Living at the Watergate Complex, she served, unpaid, on President Reagan's Foreign Advisory Board and remained active until her death in 1987. Luce clearly recognized her achievements in life. She once said, "My early disadvantages spurred me on to accept the challenges of life, to look for avenues of expression, to be the best I could be in whatever I tried. Coming as far as I have, I see each day's dawning as a triumph, with the curtain rising on a tremendously exciting show. I love every minute of it."[3]

PLAYS

Abide with Me, 1935; *Child of the Morning*, 1951; *Kiss the Boys Goodbye* (film, 1941), 1938; *Margin for Error* (film, 1943), 1939; *Slam the Door Softly* (a.k.a. *A Doll's House*, 1971), 1970; *The Women* (also film, 1939; film musical, *Opposite Sex*, 1956), 1936

OTHER WORKS

Europe in the Spring, 1940; *Saints for Now*, 1952

WORKS ABOUT

Hatch, Alden, *Ambassador Extraordinary—Clare Boothe Luce*, 1956; Shadegg, Stephen C., *Clare Boothe Luce: A Biography*, 1970; Sheed, Wilfrid, *Clare Boothe Luce*, 1982

1. *The London Guardian*, November 27, 1986.

2. Olauson.

3. Berges, Marshall. "Clare Boothe Luce in Hawaii," *National Retired Teachers Association Journal* (July–August 1979), p. 12.

Sharman MacDonald
(1951–)

MORAG. A woman's body is a clock that runs down very rapidly.

—from *When I Was a Girl . . .*

Glasgow-born Sharman MacDonald was educated at Edinburgh University. She started as an actress, but eventually turned to writing full-time. Married with two children, she has been the Thames television writer in residence at London's Bush Theatre (1984–85) and was the 1984 recipient of the Evening Standard Award.

In *When I Was a Girl, I Used to Scream and Shout* (1984), MacDonald uses flashbacks to depict the relationship between the unmarried, childless Fiona and her mother, Morag, a no-nonsense, down-to-earth matriarch. With astonishing accuracy, MacDonald portrays the sexually repressed, guilt-ridden world of 1950s Scotland in all its concurrent Calvinist guilt and preoccupation with sex. London's *Time Out* applauded MacDonald's "true talent for honest, unaffected wit and an ability to pinpoint the destructive emotional games which both tear relationships apart and bond them inescapably together."[1]

The Brave (1988) might best be described as a political terrorist comedy. The central character, Ferlie, is in Morocco visiting her sister, Susan, a political terrorist gone underground. In self-defense, she murders a Moroccan and must get rid of the body. Two visiting Scots come to her aid; after several thwarted efforts, they manage to bury the body in the desert of a faded movie set, originally built for Samson and Delilah. Though *The Brave* is written with

wit and vitality, theater historian Alan Strachan complains that it is nonetheless "too often . . . arid."[2]

A more recent work is *Borders of Paradise* (1995). All MacDonald's works echo themes wrapped around her Celtic heritage and strapped with the bonds of family relationships and adolescent unravelings. And all, says Strachan, embody "an emotional charge and engaging comedy that mark her as a distinctive voice in the British theatre."[3]

PLAYS

All Things Nice, 1991; *Borders of Paradise*, 1995; *The Brave*, 1988; *Shades*, 1992; *When I Was a Girl, I Used to Scream and Shout*, 1984; *When We Were Women*, 1988; *Wild Flowers* (teleplay), 1990; *The Winter Guest* (also screenplay, 1997), 1993

NOVELS

The Beast, 1986; *Night, Night*, 1988

1. Helen Rose in *Time Out*, December 17, 1986.
2. Essay by Alan Strachan in Weintraub.
3. Ibid.

Karen Malpede
(JUNE 29, 1945–)

MICHEL. Nothing we do sullies us; why is that?

—from *Us*

A playwright, theater historian, educator, and peace activist, Karen Malpede cofounded, with Burl Hash, New Cycle Theater in Brooklyn, where her plays were a mainstay from 1976–84. From 1987–94, her plays premiered at Theater for the New City on New York City's Lower East Side. In 1996 she cofounded Theater Three Collaborative with the actor/producer George Bartenieff (her husband, who has starred in four of her plays) and director/performer Lee Nagrin. When she is not writing or involved in production, she teaches, currently at New York University's Drama Department. In January 1995, she was a guest professor at the Dramatic Academy in Sarajevo. Malpede was born on an army base in Wichita Falls, Texas, and was raised in Evanston and Wilmette, Illinois. Both her mother and maternal grandmother were actors in Chicago, where her mother also had her own radio show. Malpede's twin brother John is a performance artist and founder of the Los Angeles Poverty Department (LAPD) Theater; many of the LAPD Theater's members are or have been homeless. Both Malpede twins create socially conscious theater, perhaps reflecting the humble beginnings of their father's ancestors, Italian peasants. She earned a B.S. with honors at the University of Wisconsin, Madison (1967), and an M.F.A. in theater arts at Columbia University (1971).

"Malpede's theatrical works are lyrical epic dramas," writes Gloria Orenstein of the University of Southern California, "embracing the political and ethical positions of feminism, and pacifism."[1] She has acknowledged being particularly influenced by Greek tragedy, Shakespeare, W. B. Yeats, Henrik Ibsen, and Jean Genet, and, in her formative years, by Bertolt Brecht, Antonin Artaud, and the Living and Open theaters. She is also influenced by prehistory and myth; she wrote *Sappho & Aphrodite* (1984), interweaving Sappho's poetry in her text, and she adapted Christa Wolf's novella *Kassandra* (1993) for the stage.

Malpede's recent work addresses contemporary events. *The Beekeeper's Daughter* (1994) is about a Bosnian refugee's encounter with an eccentric American family. "It is not," as Dr. Steven Weine,* the play's dramaturg, wrote, "about how Bosnia plays in the world outside. It is about us and how the historical events in Bosnia enter into our lives . . ." In Zagreb's daily newspaper *Novosti,* playwright-journalist Sloboden Snajder wrote, "I want to assert unequivocally that this play is one of the most honest representations of our tragedy I have encountered."[2] *The Beekeeper's Daughter* is set on a Mediterranean island where an American poet lives an idyllic and erotic life; all is disrupted when his daughter, a human rights activist, brings

to his utopia Admira Ismic, a Bosnian woman who has been raped and is about to give birth. The play premiered during the war in Bosnia, at the 1994 Dionysia World Festival of Contemporary Drama in Italy.

Going to Iraq (1991) is a dramatization of life on New York City's Lower East Side during the Gulf War. It was staged in 1992, and performed on the radio and in a reading on the anniversary of the war. *Better People* (1990) is "a surreal comedy about genetic engineering—shocking, funny, tight and richly original, has caught the attention of scientists as well as theater-goers, and generated a series of panel discussions, composed of prominent scientists, ecologists and ethicists,"[3] wrote Kris Oser in the *New York Law Journal.*

The End of War (1976), set during the Russian Revolution, revolves around the anarchist hero Nestor Makhno, who considered rape an entitlement of victory. His violence brings about the gradual disenchantment of the two women who have loved him. They find the solace and support they need in each other, as do so many of the women in Malpede's plays.

Set during the utopian and Underground Railroad movements of 1840s America, *Making Peace: A Fantasy* (1979) revolves around the feminist agenda of peace and an end to racism and sexism. The process is observed and analyzed by three angels, the historical characters Mother Ann Lee, the founder of the Shakers; François Charles Fourier, the French utopian socialist; and Mary Wollstonecraft, author of the 1792 feminist classic *A Vindication of the Rights of Women.* "The flowing of blood and of milk, the turning of blood into milk, renewable ecstasies—these are commonplaces of female sexuality. In this play, female sexuality works miracles. The play is a celebration of female sexuality."[4] With the collaboration of composer Roberta Kosse, *Making Peace* has, according to Orenstein, "turned important scenes into oratoria arias."[5]

Set in Ireland and based on the myths of the Celtic goddess Macha and the Greek Demeter and Persephone, *A Monster Has Stolen the Sun* (1981) juxtaposes the ancient pantheistic cycles of paganism with the advent of Christianity.

Malpede has been recognized with a McKnight National Playwright's Fellowship (1994), an Art Matters Fellowship (1990), a Creative Artists Public Service grant for play writing (1982), and a Poets Essayists Novelists writer's grant (1981), as well as many production grants to her theater companies. She lives in Brooklyn with George Bartenieff, and her daughter, Carrie-Sophia Malpede-Hash.

PLAYS

The Baghdad Bunker, 1991; *The Beekeeper's Daughter,* 1993; *Better People,* 1990; *Blue Heaven,* 1992; *The End of*

---

*Dr. Steven Weine is codirector of the Project on Genocide, Psychiatry and Witnessing at the University of Illinois at Chicago.

War, 1987; *Going to Iraq*, 1992; *Kassandra*, 1993; *A Lament for Three Women*, 1974; *Making Peace: A Fantasy*, 1979; *A Monster Has Stolen the Sun*, 1981; *Rebeccah*, 1975; *Sappho & Aphrodite*, 1983; *Underexposed: The Temple of the Fetus* (teleplay), 1993; *Us*, 1987

OTHER WORKS

People's Theater in Amerika, 1972; *Three Works by the Open Theater*, ed. and intro., 1974; *Women in Theatre: Compassion and Hope*, ed. and intro., 1983

1. Essay by Gloria Orenstein in Robinson.

2. Sloboden Snajder, *Novosti*, Spring 1994.

3. Article by Kris Oser, *New York Law Journal*, February 16, 1990.

4. Karen Malpede, *Women in Theatre: Compassion and Hope*, (New York: Drama Book Specialists, 1983), p. 255.

5. Op. cit., Orenstein.

Delariviere Manley
(1667/72–JULY 11, 1724)

ACMAT (a eunuch, speaking to the prince of Homais of his
lady's behavior toward the prince's portrait).
How often have I seen this lovely Venus
Naked, extended, in the gaudy Bed,
Her snowy Breasts all panting with desire,
With gazing, melting Eyes, survey your Form,
And wish in vain, 't had Life to fill her Arms.

—from *The Royal Mischief*

The first British woman to author a best-selling novel, work publicly as a political journalist, and be arrested for her writing, Mary Delariviere Manley loved to break socially imposed rules of conduct. She was perhaps "the most fascinating of the women playwrights of her time," Fidelis Morgan enthuses. "At once an example of decaying gentility and of a sort of swashbuckling feminist . . ."[1] By her mid-teens Manley had experienced scandal firsthand. Her father, soldier-writer-politician Sir Rogers Manley, died in 1888, eight years after the death of his wife. The orphaned Mary (who, incidentally, eschewed her first name) and her siblings were sent to live with her father's nephew, John, who persuaded his fourteen-year-old cousin to marry him. She bore him a son, only to discover her "husband's" deception: He was already married! After a few years, John abandoned Manley and their child in order to reunite with his legal wife.

She found brief refuge in the house of Barbara Villiers, Duchess of Cleveland, who averred that Manley brought her luck at the gaming tables. Villiers, an actress who had performed in KATHERINE FOWLER PHILIPS's *Horace*, had been a mistress of the late King Charles II. However, the Duchess, accusing Manley of seducing her son, dismissed her after six months. Manley gathered her resources and retired to Exeter for two years, where she applied herself to play writing.

Although she claimed that she wrote "for [her] amusement," she more likely recognized that stage plays were her best possible source of income. In Exeter she took up with Sir Thomas Skipwith, then comanager of the Drury Lane Theatre. Shortly thereafter, Manley set out for London, with Skipwith in one hand and two plays in the other. In no time her comedy *The Lost Lover* (1696) was opening at the Drury Lane. The show failed to bring down the house, but her other play, a tragedy entitled *The Royal Mischief*, did. *Mischief*'s (1696) extravagant eroticism[2] (see the opening quotation) fueled its enormous popularity, which brought Manley recognition and remuneration. Some critics, however, chastised her for writing so "uninhibitedly." She defended herself forthrightly, pointing out that John Dryden's *The Double Discovery* used similar language, but was accepted by critics simply because the author was male.

Although Manley did not write prolifically for the theater, after the staging of *Mischief* she often mingled with two other women playwrights of the era, CATHERINE TROTTER and MARY PIX. Trotter introduced Manley to John Tilly, deputy warden of the Fleet prison and a former lover of Trotter's. Manley and Tilly engaged in a shamelessly public affair, which prompted Trotter to sever personal ties with her indiscreet colleague. Manley responded by calling Trotter "the most of a prude in her outward professions, and the least of it in her inward practice."[3] Nevertheless, the three women continued to offer professional support to one another, often contributing laudatory verses for the printed editions of each other's plays. The threesome's visibility actually spawned an anonymously written and mean-spirited spoof, mounted at the Drury Lane: *The Female Wits, or The Triumvirate of Poets at Rehearsal*, penned by the mysterious "Mr. W. M." Manley's caricature, a particularly venomous portrayal, was drawn as fatuous and insensibly conceited.

Between the productions of her first plays and *Almyna*, a 1706 feminist drama, Manley discovered her true literary calling: the political and sexual scandal missive. She initiated her new career with a satire, *The Secret History of Queen Zarah and the Zarazians*, in 1705. Four years later she created the satirical political journal *The Female Tattler*, for which she wrote under the nom de plume "Mrs. Crackenthorpe, a lady that knows everything." The paper's contents were inflammatory enough to land Manley in prison briefly. Later she collaborated with Jonathan Swift on *The Examiner*, taking over as editor when he retired in 1711. Swift admired Manley personally, although he once remarked that her writing appeared as though "she had about two thousand epithets and fine words packed up in a bag, and she pulled them out by handfuls, and strewed them on her paper, where about once in five hundred times they happen to be right."[4]

Manley's last known lover, John Barber, who eventually became Lord Mayor of London, allegedly treated her quite cruelly. Manley was no longer young, and afflicted with dropsy; Barber took on a young mistress while "allowing" the failing writer to remain at his house, where she died in 1724. She is buried at the Church of St. Benet, Paul's Wharf.

Theater historian Nancy Cotton writes that "Manley was even more bold than [APHRA] BEHN in the assertiveness and feminism of her life and works. Having been socially ostracized by the double standard, she proceeded to attack it in her work and flaunt it in her life. . . . She avowed for herself a standard of sexual independence. . . . possible only for the [economically independent] woman."[5] Manley herself possessed a keen awareness of her situation. In her autobiography (which she published under a pseudonym) she wrote,

Her virtues are her own, her vices occasioned by her misfortunes; and yet as I have often heard her say: if she had been a man, she had been without fault. But the charter of that sex being much more confin'd than ours, what is not a crime in men is scandalous and unpardonable in woman, as she herself has very well observ'd in divers places, throughout her own writings.[6]

PLAYS (COMPLETE)

Almyna, or The Arabian Vow, 1706; *The Lost Lover, or The Jealous Husband*, 1696; *Lucius, the First Christian King of Britain*, 1717; *The Royal Mischief*, 1696

OTHER WORKS

The Adventures of Rivella, or The History of the Author of Atalantis . . . (autobio. w/pseudonym Sir Charles Lovemore), 1714; *Bath Intrigues*, 1725; *Court Intrigues*, 1711; *Exeter . . .* , 1725), 1696; *The Lady's Paquet Broke Open*, 1706; *Letters Written by Mary de la Rivière Manley* (reissued as *A Stage-Coach Journey to Memoirs of Europe Towards the Close of the Eighth Century . . .*), 1710; *A Modest Enquiry into the Reasons of the Joy Expressed . . .* , 1714; *The Novels of Mary Delariviere Manley*, Kostle, Patricia, ed., 1971; *The Power of Love*, in seven novels, 1720; *The Secret History of Queen Zarah and the Zarazians . . .* , 2 vols., 1705; *Secret Memoirs and Manners of Several Persons of Quality . . .* , 1711; *A True Narrative of What Passed at the Examination of the Marquis de Guiscard . . .* , 1711; *A True Relation of the Several Facts and Circumstances . . .* , 1711

1. Morgan.

2. Cotton.

3. Birch, Thomas. *The Life of Mrs. Catherine Cockburn*, 2 vols. (London, 1751).

4. Swift, Jonathan, *Journal*, August 22, 1710.

5. Op. cit., Cotton.

6. *The Adventures of Rivella, or The History of the Author of Atalantis . . .* (written under pseudonym Sir Charles Lovemore) (1714); a.k.a., *Memoirs of the Life of Mrs. Marley* (London: E. Curll, 1717).

Emily Mann
(APRIL 12, 1952–)

ANNULLA. If women would only start thinking, we could change the world.

—from *Annulla, An Autobiography*

Emily Mann has described her dramatic collages of historical events, personal reportage, trial transcripts, and newspaper clippings as a "theater of testimony."[1] Born in Boston, Mann was raised in Chicago; her father was a professor of history. Her interest in theater took root while she attended the experimental Chicago Laboratory High School. After earning her B.A. at Radcliffe College, she enrolled in the M.F.A. program in theater at the University of Chicago.

Mann's earliest work exhibits her penchant for the use of oral history and documentation. Her first play, *Annulla, An Autobiography* (1977), dramatizes the experience of her aunt, a Holocaust survivor. While visiting her Aunt Annulla in London, Mann learned that her great-grandfather had been humiliated by the Nazis in front of the members of his community, all of whom were slaughtered afterward. Mann carefully recorded the details of her family's experiences under Nazi persecution. In *Annulla*, the widowed title character attempts to write her life story, but is distracted by the demands of her invalid sister and the burden of memory. Mann's indebtedness to her aunt, who so willingly shared her story, is evidenced by Annulla's coauthorship of the play.

Mann continued her work with real-life drama in the 1980 play *Still Life*, an intense tale of a Vietnam veteran's return to civilian life. As Mark, his wife, and his mistress sit side by side on the stage, unable to face each other in their attempts to communicate, the infinite distances between them become painfully clear to the audience. The play's oblique depiction of political and emotional violence made it a great critical success. *Still Life* won Obies for distinguished play writing, distinguished direction, and best production, as well as acting honors for three original cast members. The play also won the Fringe First Award for best play at the Edinburgh Festival.

In 1984 Mann's courtroom drama *Execution of Justice* premiered. *Execution* relays the "Twinkie defense" trial of Dan White, the disgruntled ex-San Francisco city employee who assassinated Mayor George Moscone and openly gay city supervisor Harvey Milk. The play bluntly exposes the outrageousness of White's acquittal, laying bare the underlying homophobia of the jury that arrived at such an insidious conclusion.

More recently, Mann has turned to collaboration with a diverse group of African-American women writers. In the late 1980s she was approached by NTOZAKE SHANGE and Baikida Carroll to help adapt for the stage Shange's novel *Betsey Brown* (1989), about a young African-American woman's coming of age in St. Louis in the 1950s. Then, in 1994, Mann worked with Sadie and Bessie Delaney, two African-American sisters who spent more than a century living together, in the creation of a stage adaptation of their autobiographical book *Having Our Say*. As with *Annulla*, the drama's subjects share play writing credit.

Mann lives in Rockland County, New York, with her husband, actor/writer Gerry Banman, and their son Nicholas Isaac. Despite the success of her work, Mann remains adamant in her criticism of the New York theater world,

which she perceives as dangerously powerful and narrow-minded. "There is a network of caring people in theater all over the country, and outside this country, who don't care about New York reviews, but rather, care about important voices."[2]

PLAYS

Annulla Allen: Autobiography of a Survivor (rev. as "Annulla Allen, An Autobiography", 1985) 1977; *Betsey Brown* (adapt. of NTOZAKE SHANGE book), w/Shange, music by Baikida Carroll, 1989; *Execution of Justice*, 1984; *Having Our Say*, 1994; *Nights and Days* (adapt. of Pierre Laville work), 1984; *Still Life*, 1980

1. Cited in essay by Duskey Lobel in Berney (2).
2. Betsko.

Emily Mann
COURTESY OF THE PLAYWRIGHT

Eeva-Liisa Manner
(1921–)

LASSI. Women! There isn't anything so bad that they don't soon start to enjoy it. Even if they lived in a barrel of shit they'd start making a home out of it, with everything nice and cozy.

—from *The Snow of May*, Act III

Finland can take pride in Eeva-Liisa Manner, who not only is a superb poet, writer, and playwright, but has also translated into her native tongue such classics as *Romeo and Juliet*, *The Tempest*, and *Woyzeck*.

The play with which she made her theatrical debut, *New Year's Eve* (1965), is considered her best by many. In it, a group of middle-aged intellectuals drink copiously while discussing and revealing themselves. Crowell's calls it an "Albee-like chamber play."[1] *The Snow of May* (1967) centers on the love of a sensitive young girl for an unfeeling male, whose treatment has dealt her a disillusioning blow; *Burnt-Out Ocher* (1969), similar in theme, uses a Freudian approach couched in a poetical framework. *Eros ja Psykhe* is "a delicate love story in free verse, speaking with its metaphors and rhythm rather than with its action."[2]

Manner lives in Tampere, Finland, for part of the year; the rest she spends in Spain. She continues to produce translations, poems, and essays in addition to her play writing.

PLAYS

Eros ja Psykhe (also radio play), 1959; *Poltettu oranssi* (Burnt-Out Ocher), 1969; *Tämä matka* (This Journey; poetry), 1956; *Toukokuun lumi* (The Snow of May), 1967; *Uuden vuoden yö* (New Year's Eve), 1965

OTHER WORKS

Kuolleet vedet (poems), 1977; *Varokaa, voittajat . . .* , 1972

1. Anderson.
2. Ibid.

Dacia Maraini
(1935/6–   )

He talked and talked because he didn't know what to say.

—from *The Holiday*, Chapter 1

A poet, playwright, novelist, feminist, and political activist, Dacia Maraini was born in Italy to Sicilian and English parents. She spent eight years of her childhood in Japan, where her father worked as an anthropologist, and another two years in a German concentration camp. The brutal world of those early years informed her highly charged political works. In 1963 Maraini married Alberto Moravia, neé Pincherle, a man considered one of Italy's greatest fiction writers. Also a playwright, Moravia died in 1990.

Not long after her marriage, Maraini turned to play writing. Her dramatic works, often experimental, deal with themes of gender, politics, and social reform—issues that must have begun to concern Maraini during her harsh childhood. *Centocelle* (1972), set in a small Roman suburb, reflects the impact of Mussolini's rule on the common people; *Don Juan* (1976) revisits that classic from a feminist perspective; *Dialogue* (1978) takes a feminist approach toward prostitution. In 1972 Maraini founded La Maddalena in Rome, a feminist theater devoted to exploring the issues examined in her works.

Her prose works include *Bagheria*, a brief narrative on social life and customs, and *E tu chi eri? Interviste sull'infanzia*, a series of interviews with modern Italian artists.

Peter Bondanella, professor of Italian studies at Indiana University in Bloomington, has said of Maraini that she "is one of the most interesting new talents in Italian drama and aptly reflects its current interest in social reform and experimentalism."[1]

PLAYS

Centocelle: gli anni del fascismo (Centocelle: The Years of Fascism), 1972; *Daonna in guerra*, 1975; *Dialogo di una prostituta con un suo cliente* (Dialogue Between a Prostitute and Her Client), 1978; *Don Juan*, 1976; *La donna perfetta sequito da il cuore di una vergine*, 1976; *Fare teatro: materiali, testi, interviste*, 1974; *Il ricatto a teatro e altre commedie*, 1970

OTHER WORKS

The Age of Malaise (Frances Frenaye, tr.), 1963; *Bagheria* (Dick Kitto and Elspeth Spottiswood, trs.), 1994; *Conversazione con Dacia Maraini*, 1995; *Crudelta all Ariá Aperia*, 1966; *E tu chi eri? Interviste sull'infanzia*, 1973; *The Holiday*, 1962; *Letters to Marina* (D.K. and E.S., trs.), 1987; *Searching for Emma*, 1998; *Un clandestino a bordo*, 1966

WORKS ABOUT

Lorch, Jennifer, *Women in Modern Italian Literature*, 1993; Montini, I., *Parlare con Dacia Maraini*, 1977

1. Essay by Peter Bondanella in Hochman.

María Martínez Sierra
(DECEMBER 28, 1874–JUNE 28, 1974)

For most of her one hundred years, María Martínez Sierra was known primarily as the wife of the renowned Spanish novelist, poet, essayist, and theatrician Gregorio Martínez Sierra. However, before her death, the news surfaced that Maria was Martínez's constant collaborator and, in several instances, the principal author of many of the dramatic works that had been accredited solely to him.[1]

Born in San Millán de la Cogolla, María de la O Lejárraga García grew up in a middle-class Castilian home. Gregorio, too, was raised in a similar household; his family adhered to staunch Catholic beliefs, however, while María's parents questioned traditional dogma. When the two met in 1897, their mutual passion for literature acted as a strong bond; three years later they wed. Seven years older than her husband and secure with employment as a teacher, María supported the shy young Gregorio's creative interests. By 1904 he had published his first novel and founded two literary journals. He began to achieve a modicum of success, and the couple went to Paris and then toured Europe, both in search of stimulation and for health reasons (Gregorio was not constitutionally strong). Upon their return, their first play, *Vida y dulzura* (The Sweetness of Life; 1907), was staged.

The drama focuses on the life of an educated young woman who defies her well-meaning parents to be true to herself. The production not only marked the initiation of Gregorio's reputation as a playwright; it also introduced him to the actress Catalina Bárcena, a woman who forever changed his and María's lives. Bárcena became Gregorio's mistress, performing under his direction the plays that María clandestinely penned. Strangely, all three seemed to thrive creatively under these circumstances. Bárcena received recognition for her performances, and the Sierras churned out play after play. The pair collaborated with other artists, such as composer Manuel de Falla, and wrote novels, poetry, screenplays, and essays. They founded the Eslava Theater in Madrid, where Gregorio directed some of the most avant-garde dramas Spain had seen. He was the first to separate stage and set design from the art of directing.

The Sierras saw more than forty of their plays published and produced in their lifetimes. Their early works evoke modernist sensibilities with respect to temporal abstraction and poetic language; their later dramas depict more realistic settings and situations. In most of the Sierras' plays, the women are intelligent, sensitive, and strong-willed, while the men, according to Richard Keenan, are generally narrow-minded, impetuous, and insecure.[2] However, *La sombra del padre* (Father's Shadow; 1909) portrays Don José, a man who at first appears to be traditional, returning to Spain after seventeen years in Argentina to find his children unruly and his wife too lenient. Full of judgment, he is set to leave once again, this time with their youngest son. But he soon realizes, with his wife's prodding, that his absence has caused the imbalance in the family, and that together they can create the kind of stability the children truly need. Many years later, in *Seamos felices* (Let's Be Happy, 1929), the lead male character is depicted more as his wife's partner and friend than her superior. When financial problems begin to plague the happy young couple, Fernanda, a concert pianist, is offered a tour that will alleviate their fiscal woes. Initially, Emilio's response is predictable: a "no wife of mine is going to work" attitude. But Fernanda, through sheer goodwill and common sense, convinces her husband to recapitulate. Perhaps for the first time, Spanish audiences perceived a taste of egalitarianism in a marriage.

The true turning point in the dramatists' careers came with *El ama de la casa* (The Mistress of the House, 1910): "Beginning with this play," attests Keenan, "his [sic] style would be simple and direct, his female protagonist would be an intelligent, self-sacrificing, and capable woman, sometimes a loving wife, other times a virgin, but always a woman filled with the desire to lose herself in the service of others. His recurring theme would be the idea of maternal love, a love characterized by a willingness to renounce one's own desires in order to serve the needs of those under one's charge."[3] This formula recurred in *Canción de cuna* (The Cradle Song, 1911), which won the Royal Academy's prize for best work of 1911. An order of nuns rears an abandoned girl child, creating a conduit for their suppressed maternal instincts that brings health and balance to each of the sisters in a unique way. One might conjecture that Maria's knowledge of Gregorio's and Catalina's relationship, and the position of forbearance into which it thrust her, was the catalyst for this change in their female characters.

The Sierras' relationship altered permanently when Bárcena bore Gregorio a daughter in 1922. Although María and her husband separated, their strong literary ties kept them bound, as in their early days. Evidently, Gregorio always treated María fairly with respect to paying her royalties from their plays. In the late 1920s María discovered the Socialist and feminist movements. She wrote many essays on women's role in society, and was elected by the Socialist party to the legislature, a post she held until the outbreak of the Civil War in 1936. That year she left Spain for Switzerland, and then moved on to Nice, where she remained until 1950. She then traveled to the United States, in an unsuccessful attempt to sell some of her stories to Walt Disney Studios. Spain's first great woman dramatist remained in the Western hemisphere for the rest of her life, eventually settling in Buenos Aires for the last 20 of her 100 years.

PLAYS

El ama de la casa (The Mistress of the House), 1910; *Amanecer*, 1915; *El amor brujo* (Bewitching Love), music by Manuel de Falla, 1915; *Cada uno y su vida* (To Each his Own), 1919; *Canción de cuna* (*The Cradle Song*, 1917), 1911; *El corazón ciego* (Blind Heart), 1919; *Don Juan de España*, 1921; *El enamorado* (*The Lover*, 1919), 1912; *Las golondrinas* (The Doves), w/José Maria de Usandizaga, 1914; *Hechizo de amor* (*Love Magic*, 1917), 1908; *La hora del diablo* (The Devil's Hour), 1930; *Juventud, divino tesoro* (Youth, Precious Treasure), 1908; *Lirio entre espinas* (*A Lily Among Thorns*, 1923), 1911; *Madame Pepita* (Eng. tr., 1923), 1912; *Madrigal* (Eng. tr., 1931), 1913; *Mamá* (based on Henrik Ibsen's *A Doll's House*, Eng. tr., 1923), 1913; *Margot*, 1914; *Mujer* (Woman), 1925; *La mujer del héroe* (*The Wife of a Famous Man*, 1923), 1914; *Navidad* (Holy Night, 1928), 1916; *El palacio triste* (The Sad Palace), 1911; *La pasión* (Passion), 1914; *Los pastores* (*The Two Shepherds*, 1923), 1913; *El pobrecito Juan* (*Poor John*, 1920), 1912; *Primavera en otoño* (*Autumn Spring*, 1927), 1911; *El reino de Dios* (*The Kingdom of God*, 1923), 1915; *Rosina es frágil* (*Fragile Rosina*), 1918; *Seamos felices* (Let's Be Happy), 1929; *La sombra del padre* (Father's Shadow), 1909; *El sombrero de tres picos* (The Three-Pointed Hat), music by de Falla, 1916; *Sortilegio* (Sorcery), 1930; *Sueño de una noche de agosto* (*The Romantic Young Lady*, 1923), 1918; *Teatro de ensueño* (Dream Theater), 1905; *Triángulo* (*Take Two from One*, 1931), 1930; *Vida y dulzura* (The Sweetness of Life), w/Santiago Rusiñol, 1907

OTHER WORKS
NOVELS

El agua dormida, 1907; *Almas ausentes*, 1900; *El amor catedrático*, 1910; *Aventura*, 1907; *Beata primavera*, 1907;

Flores de escarcha (Frost Flowers), 1900; *Horas de sol,* 1901; *La humilde verdad,* 1904; *Pascua florida,* 1903; *El peregrino ilusionado,* 1908; *Todo es uno y lo mismo,* 1910; *Torre de marfil,* 1908; *Tú eres la paz,* 1906

POETRY

La casa de la primavera (poetry), 1907; *El poema del trabajo* (poetry), 1898

NONFICTION

Cartas a las mujeres de España, 1916; *Diálogos fantásticos* (Fantastic Dialogues), 1899; *Feminismo, feminidad, españolismo,* 1917; *Gregorio y yo* (autobio.), 1953; *Nuevas cartas a las mujeres,* 1932; *Obras completas* (14 vols.), 1920–30; *La selva muda,* 1909; *Un teatro de arte en España,* ed., 1926

WORKS ABOUT

Douglas, Frances, "Gregorio Martínez Sierra" in *Hispania,* V (November 1922), pp. 257–369; O'Connor, Patricia W., *Gregorio and María Martínez Sierra,* 1977

1. O'Connor, Patricia W., *Gregorio and María Martínez Sierra* (Boston: Twayne Publishers, 1977).

2. Essay by Richard Keenan in Magill.

3. Ibid.

Carson McCullers
(FEBRUARY 19, 1917–SEPTEMBER 29, 1967)

FRANKIE. The trouble with me is that for a long time I have been just an "I" person.... All people belong to a "we" except me.... Not to belong to a "we" makes you too lonesome.

—from *The Member of the Wedding*

Carson McCullers is recognized primarily for her fiction; her contribution to American theater, however, is small yet significant. Her 1950 adaptation of her novel *The Member of the Wedding* pushed the traditional conventions of stage drama with its stream-of-consciousness-like depiction of a young girl's coming of age and, as Olauson put it, "heralded a new form of drama."[1] Tennessee Williams, a lifelong friend of McCullers's, encouraged her to write the play. The actual plot of *Member* is simple: Twelve-year-old Frankie Addams, a sensitive, awkward adolescent who lives in a small Southern town, becomes enamored with her brother's impending wedding. She spends her days with Bernice Sadie Brown, the earthy, wise African-American housekeeper who serves as a substitute for Frankie's late mother. The body of the play consists of stories and memories shared by Frankie, Bernice, and

Frankie's young cousin John. Throughout the drama is a strong subtext about racial injustice. The original production of *Member* starred Julie Harris and Ethel Waters, both of whom were lauded for their performances. It ran for more than 500 performances and won the New York Drama Critics Circle Award, among others.

McCullers once remarked that Frankie Addams was the character who most resembled herself as a child. Born Lula Carson Smith in Columbus, Georgia, she led a rather solitary existence, preferring reading and time alone to playing with the neighborhood children. An early bout with rheumatic fever sent her to a sanatorium for some time. When she was thirteen, she announced her decision to drop her first name, and in 1939 when she married James Reeves McCullers, a U.S. Army colonel, took his surname. She briefly studied as a concert pianist at Julliard before entering the Columbia University creative writing program. Her first novel, *The Heart Is a Lonely Hunter,* skyrocketed her to public acclaim; she was only twenty-three at the time of its publication.

Although McCullers had much literary success during her lifetime, her personal life was wrought with health and emotional problems. She constantly struggled with alco-

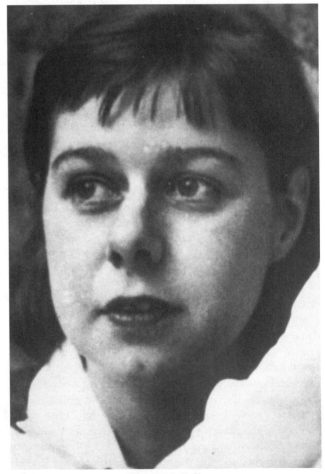

Carson McCullers
COURTESY OF UPI/CORBIS-BETTMANN

holism and depression, and by 1950, she and her husband had divorced and remarried each other twice. Shortly after their final separation, James killed himself in France. Two years later her mother died, leaving her alone (her father had died in 1944). McCullers herself suffered a cerebral hemorrhage in 1967 and died at the age of fifty.

Her only other play, *The Square Root of Wonderful* (1957), also an adaptation from her own novel, did not enjoy the accolades bestowed upon *Member*. A loosely autobiographical work, it focuses on an unsuccessful male writer who tries to dominate a lively woman. Also received unenthusiastically was *F. Jasmine Addams*, a musical version of *Member*, produced at Circle in the Square in New York City in 1971.

McCullers will best be remembered for her sensitive and compassionate renderings of the inner lives of lonely people. She received many awards and scholarships throughout her career, including two Guggenheim Fellowships, and was inducted into the National Institute of Arts and Letters in 1952. As her longtime friend Tennessee Williams wrote in the preface to her novel *The Heart Is a Lonely Hunter*, "She owned the heart and the deep understanding of it, but in addition she had that 'tongue of angels' that gave her power to sing of it, to make of it an anthem."

PLAYS

The Member of the Wedding (novel, 1940; film, 1953), 1950; *The Square Root of Wonderful* (novel, 1958), 1957

NOVELS (SELECTED)

The Ballad of the Sad Café, (stage adapt. by Edward Albee, 1963), 1951; *Clock Without Hands*, 1961; *The Heart Is a Lonely Hunter*, (film, 1967), 1940; *The Mortgaged Heart*, coll., Margarita G. Smith, ed., 1971; *Reflections in a Golden Eye* (film, 1967), 1942; *Sweet as a Pickle and Clean as a Pig*, 1965

WORKS ABOUT

Carr, Virginia Spencer, *The Lonely Hunter: A Biography of Carson McCullers*, 1975; Cook, Richard M., *Carson McCullers*, 1975; Evans, Oliver, *The Ballad of Carson McCullers*, 1966; McDowell, Margaret B., *Carson McCullers*, 1980

1. Olauson.

Eve Merriam
(JULY 19, 1916–   )

MARY JONES. I asked a man in prison once how he happened to be there and he said that he had stolen a pair of shoes. I told him if he had stolen a railroad he would be a United States Senator.

—from *Out of Our Fathers' House*

"It's up to women to shed our old habits, our old self-pity," Eve Merriam has said. "We cannot afford to waste our energies in 'What will men think? How will they respond?' We have to do what is necessary to be done. We have to stop apologizing and stop being cute. We have to become *acute*."[1] The many plays, poetry, and other works Merriam has written reinforce how seriously she meant these words. Since the mid-1940s, she has consistently addressed such issues as the women's movement and civil rights.

Born in Philadelphia, Merriam attended both Cornell University and the University of Pennsylvania, receiving her B.A. from the latter in 1937. She did graduate work at the University of Wisconsin and Columbia University. Her aptitude for words was evident even in her early years when, she claims, while the other children took up sports, she "did [her] ball playing and rope jumping and kidding around with rhyme and with the sound of language."[2] However, Merriam was something of a late bloomer as a playwright. She did not become a prolific playwright and poet until her mid-thirties, after the births of her two children. Merriam sees her late motherhood as a key to the change in her writing habits, believing that the experience showed her the importance of reconciling career and family.

She has held positions in nearly every field that employs writers. After a stint as a copywriter from 1939–42, she wrote radio dramas, documentaries, and dramas in verse for CBS. Also during this time, she produced a weekly radio program on modern poetry for New York City radio station WQXR. She wrote a daily verse column for *PM* magazine in 1945. Between 1946–48 she served as features editor for *Deb* magazine, and as fashion copy editor for *Glamour*. Since 1949 she has worked as a freelance writer.

In the mid-1970s Merriam began to write for the stage when she collaborated with Paula Wagner and Jack Hofsiss on *Out of Our Fathers' House* (1975), an adaptation of Merriam's book *Growing up Female in America*. The play, like Susan Griffin's *Voices* and NTOZAKE SHANGE's *For Colored Girls . . .*, uses the "format of the consciousness-raising group to present a feminist variation of the archetypal journey in search of the self."[3] *Out of Our Fathers' House* derives its text directly from the diaries, journals, and letters of six women, ranging from the great suffragist Elizabeth Cady Stanton to an unrenowned schoolgirl. The play reinforces the message that, regardless of our accomplishments, "the journey out of our fathers' houses is worth taking."[4]

Merriam followed this collaboration by working with musical director Alexandra Ivanoff on *The Club* (1976), a theatrical revue of nineteenth-century American and British misogynist songs and jokes presented in the setting of an Edwardian men's club. The play won a 1977 Obie Award.

Nearly all her original works for the stage deal with women's issues: *At Her Age* (1979) addresses the taboos and indignities associated with aging women in Western society; *And I Ain't Finished Yet* (1982), like *Out of Our Fathers' House*, presents an array of characters that together establish a history—in this case, of African-American women. A former slave girl, comedienne Moms Mabley, and Mississippi freedom fighter Fannie Lou Hamer, among others, share a wide variety of stories and experiences. Although Lynn Thigpin, who played all seven women in the New York production of the play at the Upstage Theatre, was widely praised, some critics accused Merriam of writing a fragmented and incomplete work. *New York Times* critic Frank Rich remarked that its simplicity was more appropriate for "an audience of schoolchildren."[5] Eileen Blumenthal concurred, calling Merriam's play craft "clumsy," but the critic applauded her use of documented sources and traditional songs.

Perhaps in defense of her stage work, Merriam has publicly stated her belief that male critics tend to savage women's plays. Poetry, she has said, is her most rewarding work, but prose pays the bills.[6] Nevertheless, in more than fifty books, plays, and collaborative efforts, Eve Merriam has continued to portray controversial women's issues regardless of genre.

PLAYS

And I Ain't Finished Yet, 1982; *At Her Age*, 1979; *The Classic Question*, 1986; *The Club*, 1976; *Conversation Against Death*, 1977; *Dialogue for Lovers*, 1981; *The Good Life: Lady MacBeth of Westport*, 1979; *Out of Our Fathers' House*, w/Paula Wagner and Jack Hofsiss, 1975; *Plagues for Our Time*, 1983; *Street Dreams, The Inner City Musical* (a.k.a. *Inner City*; adapt. from *The Inner City Mother Goose*), 1970; *Viva Revia*, 1977

OTHER WORKS (SELECTED)

After Nora Slammed the Door, 1964; *American Women in the 1960's*, 1964; *Catch a Little Rhyme*, 1966; *Double Bed: From the Feminine Side*, 1958; *Emma Lazarus, Woman with a Torch*, 1956; *Family Circle*, 1946; *Figleaf; the Business of Being in Fashion*, 1960; *Growing up Female in America*, n.d.; *A Husband's Notes About Her*, 1976; *I Am a Man: Ode to Martin Luther King, Jr.*, 1971; *Montgomery, Alabama*, 1957; *The Nixon Poems*, 1970; *The Real Book About Franklin D. Roosevelt*, 1952; *Tomorrow Morning*, 1953; *The Trouble with Love*, 1960; *The Unfinished Revolution*, 1964

BOOKS AND POEMS FOR YOUNG PEOPLE (SELECTED)

Bam, bam, bam, 1995; *Bam Zam Boom! A Building Book*, 1972; *Blackberry Ink*, 1985; *Fighting Words*, 1989; *Good Night to Annie*, 1980; *It Doesn't Always Have to Rhyme*, 1964; *Male and Female Under 18; Frank Comments*, 1973; *Mommies at Work*, 1961; *The Singing Green*, 1992; *There Is No Rhyme for Silver*, 1962; *Unhurry Harry*, 1978

1. Betsko.
2. Ibid.
3. Essay by Phyllis Mael in Chinoy.
4. Ibid
5. *New York Times*, December 9, 1981.
6. Op. cit., Betsko.

Marlane Meyer
(JANUARY 23, 1951–   )

ETTA. I wish I had a Coke. I saw this science experiment once, where they put this tooth in Coke, and over a period of a few weeks or days . . . or maybe it was just one day, it completely fell apart. Just disappeared.

—from *Etta Jenks*

A native of San Francisco, Marlane Emily Huapala Gomard was raised by her mother, a "painter, designer, writer, astrologer, gambler, and various jobs too numerous . . . zzz," according to the playwright, and her Hawaiian father, a merchant seaman, union official, "roughneck, gambler, and know-it-all." She earned a degree in theater from California State University at Long Beach. Asked to cite her personal and literary influences, Meyer lists everything from Samuel Beckett, David Mamet, and CARYL CHURCHILL to "noir, gothic horror, naked men, the ocean, exercise, nature, and divine revelation."[1]

Her first professional production was *Etta Jenks* in 1976. *Etta* centers on the life of a hopeful actress who falls into the gritty world of pornography and snuff films. Totally contemporary characters toy with themes of intimacy, the value of human life, and redemption, as when Sherman says:

Pornography in its focus on the genital experience creates an ultimately carnal mind that is necessarily death-oriented since the body is always in a progressive state of decay. The earth begins to crawl up inside you . . .

To which Sheri replies, "Ugh," and Etta says, "We're dying anyway, who cares?"

Etta Jenks was coproduced by the Women's Project at the Los Angeles Theatre Center, where Meyer held a playwright's residency (1988), and the Royal Court Theatre in London. It was a finalist for the Susan Smith Blackburn Prize, and received both the Dramalogue Critics Award and the Joseph Kesselring Prize.

Meyer's play *Moe's Lucky Seven* (1990) won the Susan Smith Blackburn Prize. Other grants and awards have included a National Endowment for the Arts Play Writing Fellowship (1990) and the Creative Artists Public Service grant (1989). This veteran of Padua Hills Playwrights' Workshop is a member of the Dramatists Guild, the Writers' Guild of America East, Poets Essayists Novelists, and the New York Playwrights' Lab. She has also taught at the Yale School of Drama. While she has held more than fifty odd jobs during her brief tenure as an adult, Meyer currently supports herself wholly with her writing, much of which is for television. She lives in New York with her friend Mark ("a saint") and "continues to toil happily in obscurity."

PLAYS

Better off Dead, 1993; *Burning Bridges*, w/Riza Abdoh, 1989; *Christmas Cheer*, 1985; *Etta Jenks*, 1986; *Geography of Luck*, 1989; *Kingfish*, 1986; *Lon Shaw*, 1993; *Moe's Lucky Seven*, 1990; *The More I Drive*, 1985; *Relativity*, 1991; *The Spook House*, 1995; *Stick Me, I'm Stuck*, 1985; *Why Things Burn*, 1993

TELEPLAYS

Crime and Punishment, 1992; *Life Stories*, 1990; *Out of the Sixties*, 1990; *Prison Stories*, 1990; *Radio Dreams*, 1990; *Seekers* (TV pilot), 1995; *Sirens* (TV series), 1993

1. All citations from personal correspondence with author, 1994.

Edna St. Vincent Millay
(FEBRUARY 22, 1892–OCTOBER 19, 1950)

COLUMBINE. Why, Pierrot, I can't act.
PIERROT. Can't act? Can't act? La, listen to the woman!
What's that to do with the price of furs?—
You're blonde,
Are you not?—you have no education, have you?—
Can't act! You under-rate yourself, my dear!
COLUMBINE. Yes, I suppose I do.

—from *Aria da Capo*

Edna St. Vincent Millay is famed for her poetry, but her dramatic gems have been largely unseen by audiences. Yet Millay holds an important place in American theater history. She played a key role, along with SUSAN GLASPELL and others, in the establishment of the Provincetown Players, the mother of regional theater in the United States.

Millay, or "Vince," as family and friends called her, grew up with her sisters and mother in Camden, Maine. Cora, her mother, was a nurse who divorced her husband because he was a compulsive gambler. Yet she was determined to bestow on her daughters "all of the luxuries and none of the necessities of life."[1] All of her girls received piano and dance lessons. It was in this world of natural and artistic beauty that Millay penned her best-known poem, "Renascence," which catapulted her to fame at the age of eighteen.

But the young writer refused to be spoiled by her early success. Rather than heading straight to the literary hub in New York City, she accepted a scholarship to attend Vassar College, where she continued her poetry studies and established herself as an actor and playwright. She graduated in 1917, the same year her first collection of verse appeared. *Renascence and Other Poems* was praised for its freshness and vitality.

Joined by her mother and sisters, Millay then moved to New York City's Greenwich Village. Her carefree, bohemian lifestyle in conjunction with her popular lyric poetry made her one of the more visible of the "Village set." She performed regularly with the Provincetown Players, appearing in the SUSAN GLASPELL-George Cram Cook satire *Tickless Time* (1918), among other plays, and acted with other companies, such as New York City's Theatre Guild.

The Provincetown Players produced several of Millay's verse dramas, including *Aria da Capo* (1920) and *Two Slatterns and a King* (1921). The expressionistic staging of *Aria da Capo*, which bookends a pastoral tragedy with a commedia dell'arte farce, points an arrow at the destruction of innocence and simplicity by the politics and nationalism of modern society. The core story is of two young shepherd boys, friends since birth, whose greed for gold (fostered, one must assume, by outside forces) compels them first to build walls between them, then to destroy one another. The prologue and epilogue present Pierrot and Columbine, shallow materialists who pay lip service to their work, their relationship, and humanity (Pierrot brags, "I am a socialist. I love/Humanity; but I hate people," and Columbine cries, "I cannot *live*/Without a macaroon!"). As with many of Millay's poems, the play possessed a cynical tone that was to harden into bitterness with the approach of World War II.

Despite her renown as a writer of serious literature (her technically flawless sonnets exhibit a rare mastery), Millay's primary income came from her satirical Nancy Boyd stories published in *Ainslee's* magazine.

In 1923 Millay married Eugen Boissevain, a Dutch coffee importer twelve years her senior. He assumed all domestic affairs, leaving his wife free to pursue her writing. The two were rarely separated, and though they traveled around the world, they made their home at "Steepletop,"

Edna St. Vincent Millay
COURTESY OF SPRINGER/CORBIS-BETTMANN

PLAYS

Aria da Capo, 1919; *Conversation at Midnight*, 1937; *The King's Henchman*, libretto; opera by Deems Taylor, 1927; *The Lamp and the Bell*, 1921; *Launzi* (adapt. of Ferenc Molnar's play *Heavenly and Earthly Love*), 1923; *The Murder of Lidice*, 1942; *The Princess Marries the Page*, 1917; *Two Slatterns and a King*, 1921; *The Wall of Dominoes*, 1917

POETRY COLLECTIONS

Collected Lyrics, 1943; *Collected Sonnets*, 1941; *Edna St. Vincent Millay: Selected Poems*, the Centenary Edition, 1992; *A Few Figs from Thistles*, 1920; *The Harp Weaver and Other Poems*, 1923; *Letters of Edna St. Vincent Millay*, Macdougall, Allan, ed., 1952; repr. 1972; *Make Bright the Arrows*, 1940; *Renascence and Other Poems*, 1917; *Second April*, 1921

WORKS ABOUT

Atkins, Elizabeth, *Edna St. Vincent Millay and Her Times*, 1936; Brittin, Norman A., *Edna St. Vincent Millay*, 1967; Gould, Jean, *The Poet and Her Book*, 1969; Gray, James, *Edna St. Vincent Millay*, 1967; Gurko, Miriam, *Restless Spirit*, 1962; Shafter, Toby, *Edna St. Vincent Millay: America's Best Loved Poet*, 1957; Sheean, Vincent, *The Indigo Bunting*, 1951

1. Macdougall, Allan, ed., *Letters of Edna St. Vincent Millay* (Camden, Maine: Down East Books, 1952. Reprint 1972).

a farm near Austerlitz, New York. After Boissevain died in 1949, Millay began a downward spiral—drinking too much, overworking, and generally neglecting her health. She died of a heart attack a year later.

Millay's last verse drama, *Conversation at Midnight* (1937), conveys the emotional, political, and spiritual maturity seen in her best poems; however, it did not receive its first staging until more than twenty years after its completion. Interestingly, the play had already experienced one protracted recall: The original manuscript perished in a fire, and Millay had to restructure it from memory. It finally opened in Los Angeles in 1961. After a sixteen-week run, *Conversation* moved to New York City. A dialogue between seven men of diverse social, political, and religious backgrounds, its form is that of a dramatized debate.

A thoroughly modern woman, Millay created a body of work that reflected her concerns with social causes and the relationship between men and women. Her classical scholarship and aptitude with foreign languages, as well as her skill as a pianist, contributed to her distinction as a woman of letters. She won the 1923 Pulitzer Prize for poetry, which cited several of her works. In 1972 "Steepletop" was designated a National Historic Landmark, and in 1974 the 700 acres so beloved by the poet and her husband became home to the Millay Colony for the Arts.

Susan Miller
(APRIL 6, 1944–)

PERRY. There is a moment, like the black holes in space, of complete and irrevocable loss. To allow that moment is to let go of the sides of time, to fall into another place where it is not likely any of your old friends will recognize you again.

—from *Cross Country*

The structures of Susan Miller's plays are serpentine. They wrap around time as though it had no dimension, at the same time giving a whole picture of the lives of her characters, often brilliant women conflicted by issues of power and sexuality, subverting the traditional expectation of drama and storytelling. For example, the central character in *Nasty Rumors and Final Remarks* (1979) is the comatose Raleigh, nearly dead to the "real world," but quite alive to the audience that journeys with her through her memory. A charismatic, egocentric, sexually powerful actress, she not only explores her past—revealing her complex relationships with her male and female lovers, her best friend, and her quite neglected son—but contemplates her impending death.

Miller was born and raised in Philadelphia by Isaac Figlin, a musician and business executive, and Thelma Freifelder, a singer and artist. Educated at Pennsylvania State University, she earned her B.A. in 1965, then promptly married Bruce Miller, an attorney. She taught in the public schools in Carlisle, Pennsylvania, between 1965–68. In 1970 she received her M.A. at Bucknell University. Two years later her son Jeremy was born; four years after that, her marriage ended in divorce.

While her main focus has been creating works for the stage, Miller has also written poetry, film and television scripts, and a novel. Among her many awards and recognitions, she counts an Obie for excellence in play writing for *Nasty Rumors and Final Remarks*, a Rockefeller grant in play writing in 1975, and National Endowment for the Arts Fellowships in 1976 and 1983. She lives in Los Angeles, where she has been playwright in residence at the Mark Taper Forum and has lectured on play writing at the University of California.

"Play writing is a real study in delayed gratification," she once said. "Why do I write plays? Because I'm crazy, that's why."[1]

PLAYS

Arts and Leisure, 1985; *Confessions of a Female Disorder*, 1973; *Cross Country*, 1976; *Daddy and a Commotion of Zebras*, 1970; *Denim Lecture*, 1974; *Flux*, 1975; *For Dear Life*, 1989; *It's Our Town, Too*, 1992; *Nasty Rumors and Final Remarks*, 1979; *No One Is Exactly 23*, 1968; *Silverstein & Co.*, 1972

TELEVISION PLAYS

Home Movie (family series), n.d.; *One for the Money, Two for the Show*, w/Nedra Deen, n.d.; *Visions* (series), n.d.; *A Whale for the Killing*, n.d.

1. Quoted by Sheila Hale in "Women do Dramatise," *City Limit*, London, 1979.

Honor Moore
(OCTOBER 28, 1945–   )

MARGARET. Halfway down the
stairs I stop and put the dishes down,
sit there and remember
as hard as I can where I am, hard as

I can: I am myself, a woman,
nursing a woman who may be dying.
My mother can't feed me any more.

—from *Mourning Pictures*

After graduating cum laude from Radcliffe College in 1967, New York City native Honor Moore studied at the Yale School of Drama. She is perhaps as recognized for her poetry as for her stage works. Regardless of the genre, however, Moore's subject matter often reveals her strong feminist sensibilities. Theater historian Mary Remnant points to Moore's 1974 poem "Polemic #1" as an indication of the author's assertion that women must constantly be aware of the dangers of "M-A-D" (Male Approval Desire), which may cause them "to believe that they must not only produce art which is acceptable to men, but that they must conform to some male standard of excellence (if you're not Shakespeare, you've had it)."[1] In that poem, Moore writes,

M-A-D is the filter through which we're pressed to see ourselves—
If we don't, we won't get published, sold, or exhibited—
I blame none of us for not challenging it
Except not challenging it may drive us mad.

In her first play, *Years*, Moore chronicles the friendship between two women who first meet in high school. One initially aspired to be a conductor, the other a poet. The play is told in scenes, letters, flashbacks, and journal entries. The same technique is applied in *The Terry Project*, written with Victoria Rue, which pieces together the actual writings—journal entries, bits of prose, poetry—of a young woman diagnosed as a schizophrenic. Unlike many stories of mental illness, it is not concerned with the therapeutic experience, but with the patient's view of the world. *Mourning Pictures* (1974) is also episodic, as well as musical; it traces the relationship between a twenty-seven-year-old poet and her fifty-year-old mother, who is dying of cancer. Susan Brady, writing for *Ms.* magazine, called it "a stunning play about the exploration of what a daughter and a mother say to each other and to themselves when the mother is dying."

Moore's poetry has been published in many respected journals, including *American Review, New West*, and *Chrysalis*. She was the recipient of a Creative Artists Public Service award in 1976, and currently resides in Connecticut.

PLAYS

Mourning Pictures, 1974; *The Terry Project*, n.d.; *Years*, n.d.

OTHER WORKS

Leaving and Coming Back (poems), 1981; *Memoir*, 1988; *The New Women's Theatre: Ten Plays by Contemporary American Women*, ed., 1977; *The White Blackbird: A Granddaughter's Life of the Painter Margarett Sargent*, 1996

1. Cited in introduction in Remnant.

Hannah More
(FEBRUARY 2, 1745–SEPTEMBER 7, 1833)

Hannah More distinguished herself by successfully straddling two quite different social realms: She was a favorite among London's erudite literati, particularly the bluestocking circle, and she was a controversial advocate of abolitionism and public education for the poor. Feminist historians Mary Mahl and Helene Koon have remarked that "if in many ways she is a product of her times, it is equally true that often she steps beyond them, demonstrating that a new range of interests and achievements was possible for the properly educated woman."[1] More was born the fourth of five girls in Stapleton, near Bristol; her father, the master of the free school at Fishponds, saw that his daughters all received good early schooling. Hannah excelled academically; by the age of eight, she exhibited gifts in language and mathematics. Her parents actually suffered some concern about her abilities, fearing she might be labeled "unfeminine."

More began writing and publishing in 1762; her first play, *The Search After Happiness*, was completed in 1763. The 1773 Bath production of *The Inflexible Captive*, a translation of Metastasio's *Attilio Regolo*, brought her to the attention of the acclaimed actor-manager David Garrick, with whom she maintained an enduring personal and professional friendship until his death in 1779. Garrick introduced More to the London literary scene and produced two of her plays, *Percy* (1777) and *The Fatal Falsehood* (1779). Among her socially important friends she counted Joshua Reynolds, Elizabeth Montagu, Horace Walpole, and Dr. Samuel Johnson, who once called her "the most powerful versificatrix in the English language."[2]

Yet More was not simply interested in the aesthetics of drama and literature. Her other writings reflect her intense religious and moral interests. An abolitionist, she created a series of moral lessons and tales, *Cheap Repository Tracts* (1799), which flung her into the crossfire of political controversy, as did her and her sisters' efforts to educate the poor. Mary, Elizabeth, and Sarah More had already started "what was to become the best-known girls' school of the eighteenth century. . . . The curriculum, which included Italian and Spanish in addition to the usual French, was considered extremely advanced in an age when most girls'

Hannah More
COURTESY OF THE BILLY ROSE THEATRE COLLECTION

schools offered little more than housekeeping skills."[3] More helped her sisters establish eleven schools in various villages near Bristol, where they taught rudimentary reading, writing, and math skills. Despite the fact that their work with the poor resulted in a lower crime rate and increased literacy, the women were scathingly criticized for their efforts. But More remained active right up to her death; she lived longer than her sisters, even though she had suffered from health problems throughout her life. The author-reformer enjoyed the sobriquet The Laureate of the Bluestockings; some of her writings were published under the pseudonym Will Chip.

PLAYS

The Fatal Falsehood, 1779; *The Inflexible Captive*, 1773; *Percy*, 1777; *Sacred Dramas*, 1782; *The Search After Happiness*, 1763

OTHER WORKS (SELECTED)

Bas Bleu, 1786; *Bible Rhymes*, 1821; *Bishop Bonner's Ghost*, 1789; *Cheap Repository Tracts*, 3 vols., 1799; *Christian Morals*, 1813; *Coelebs in Search of a Wife* (novel), 1808; *Essays on Various Subjects*, 1777; *Florio*, 1786; *Letters of*

Hannah More, 1925; *Letters of Hannah More to Zachary Macaulay, Esq.*, 1860; *The Miscellaneous Works of Hannah More*, 2 vols., 1840; *Moral Sketches*, 1830; *Observations on the Effect of Theatrical Representations with Respect to Religion and Morals*, 1804; *The Pilgrims*, 1830; *Sir Eldred of the Bower and the Bleeding Rock*, 1776; *Strictures on the Modern System of Female Education* (reissued, 1974), 2 vols., 1799; *Thoughts on the Importance of Manners of the Great to General Society*, 1788; *The Twelfth of August, or The Feast of Freedom*, 1819; *Village Politics*, 1792; *The Works of Hannah More in prose and verse* (repr. 11 vols., 1830), 1778

WORKS ABOUT (SELECTED)

Balfour, C. L. A., *A Sketch of Hannah More and her Sisters*, 1854; Buckland, A. J., *The Life of Hannah More*, 1882; Hopkins, Mary Alden, *Hannah More and Her Circle*, 1947; Jones, M. G., *Hannah More*, 1952; Weiss, Harry B., *Hannah More's Cheap Repository Tracts in America*, 1946

1. Mahl.
2. Cited in Mahl.
3. Op. cit., Mahl.

Martha Morton
(OCTOBER 10, 1865?–FEBRUARY 18, 1925)

Hailed as "America's pioneer woman playwright," Martha Morton had fourteen plays professionally produced in New York City between 1888 and 1911.[1] Although Morton's plays may not distinguish themselves in the area of artistic merit, her accomplishments for American woman dramatists informs her importance in the theatrical canon. Morton's unceasing efforts to break through the turn-of-the-century equivalent of the glass ceiling in the theater world was no easy task. Her persistence eventually resulted in the creation of the female-inclusive Society of American Dramatists and Composers.

Morton originally tried to get her work produced in 1884, but found no willing takers due to her sex; finally she used her own funds to mount *Helene*. Using a male pseudonym as a ruse, she submitted her next play to the *New York World*'s play writing competition: It won first prize and was produced at the Madison Square Theatre in 1891. With the success of *Geoffrey Middleton, Gentleman* (1892), Morton gained the support of stage comedians such as William H. Crane and Sol Smith. Though their alliance aided her, she still suffered sexual bias. When Morton began to direct her plays, she was allowed only the credit "supervised by," since it was so scandalous that a

woman should control a production. To some degree Morton acquiesced to these social rules, but after being denied membership in the American Dramatists Club because she was a woman, she fought back by founding the Society of Dramatic Authors in 1907 with a charter membership of thirty women. Soon the male-run ADC relented, and the two organizations merged to become the Society of American Dramatists and Composers, with Morton as vice-president.

Morton was born into a privileged world in New York City; her family members included playwrights John Maddison Morton and Alfred Sutro and novelist-critic Edward Arthur Morton. Her brother Michael also became a playwright and an actor. Morton attended Hunter College (then Normal College), but poor health kept her from completing her studies. She took the obligatory European tour to which so many young men and women of good fortune were privy in her day, then married wealthy importer Hermann Conheim, a leader in the American Zionist movement. She and Hermann kept a huge private library consisting of more than 3,000 volumes. Morton remained a philanthropic advocate of female playwrights throughout her life.

PLAYS

A Bachelor's Romance, 1896; *Brother John*, 1893; *A Fool of Fortune*, 1896; *Geoffrey Middleton, Gentleman*, 1892; *Helene*, 1888; *His Wife's Father*, 1895; *The Merchant*, 1918; *The Senator Keeps House*, 1911; *The Triumph of Love*, 1904

1. Essay by Felicia Hardison Londré in Robinson.

Anna Cora Mowatt
(MARCH 5, 1819–JULY 21, 1870)

TRUEMAN. Fashion is an agreement between certain persons to live without using their souls! To substitute etiquette for virtue—decorum for purity—manners for morals!

—from *Fashion*

The imagination and will of Anna Mowatt knew no boundaries. She managed to reinvent herself countless times and use her pen well in several literary genres. The granddaughter of one of the signers of the Declaration of Independence, she was born in Bordeaux, France, to an American business adventurer who shuffled his family back and forth between the United States and Europe. Anna was the ninth of fourteen children; she and her siblings entertained themselves by mounting amateur theatrical productions, with Anna usually playing the leading lady and writing the adaptations. Clearly possessing more than a passing interest in drama, by the age of ten she had read all of Shakespeare's plays several times.

When she was thirteen, she met James Mowatt, a wealthy twenty-six-year-old New York attorney. Two years later they eloped. Despite the disparity in age and Anna's astonishing youth at the time of their union, the couple enjoyed a long, happy marriage. James showered attention upon his young wife, tutoring her in music, literature, languages, and art. He steadfastly supported and encouraged her creative endeavors throughout his life.

Mowatt embarked on her first serious literary effort with her epic poem *Pelayo, or The Cavern of Cavadonga*, a political romance in five cantos. Her husband published it, but it was spurned by the critics. Undeterred by her lack of success, she applied herself completely to her writing. When doctors advised the couple to live in Paris for a time in order for James to recover from his consumption and Anna from her chronic bronchitis, she worked every day on her first play, *Gulzara, or the Persian Slave* (1841), and attended the theater every night. *Gulzara* never received a professional production, but it was staged by her family upon Mowatt's American homecoming.

Before the opening of her first professional production, *Fashion*, in 1845, Mowatt had managed to earn a reputation as America's leading female elocutionist as well as a writer of poems, novels, and nonfiction. The Park Theatre staging of *Fashion* merely expanded Mowatt's literary repertoire. It ran for an unprecedented twenty nights. Audiences and critics adored this fun, witty comedy that packed a sensible moral: "Don't be led astray by dreams of wealth or deceived by false fashions."[1] Walter J. Meserve asserts, "*Fashion* held something for everyone—moral commentary, a nationalistic theme, a city-versus-country conflict, love episodes, a melodramatic villain, society caricatures, witty epigrams, a country Yankee, an American hero, a Negro servant, patriotic sentiments, a temperance issue, a French count and a French maid, and satire throughout."[2] Edgar Allan Poe, then a critic, called it "the clearest indication of a revival of the American drama."[3]

Mowatt's next and last play, *Armand, the Child of the People*, is a romantic drama in blank verse set in eighteenth-century France. Mowatt acted the role of Blanche, proving herself a gifted actress who instinctually aimed for a naturalistic delivery, rather than the stiff, stylized manner more common in her day. An avid churchgoer (she and James were devotees of Swedenborgianism*), Mowatt brought to acting a current of respectability rarely attained at that time. "She proved that a gentlewoman of taste and breeding could function in the world of the theatre without demeaning herself, thus adding respectability to the profession."[4]

The rest of Mowatt's life occurred with characteristic twists and turns. *Armand* was hailed as a masterpiece in London, and Mowatt and James planned to remain there for a time. But his old infections kept recurring, and his doctors sent him to recuperate in the West Indies. The couple endured yet another financial tragedy when the manager of *Armand*'s theater (among others), William Watts, was arrested and jailed for fraud. The full consequence of Watt's illegal actions became clear when James revealed that most of their money had been invested in Watt's doomed theaters. Mowatt suffered a nervous breakdown and was unable to function for four months.

She soon returned to the road, but her life never regained its previous sheen. On February 15, 1851, authorities notified her of her husband's death. After burying him in London, Mowatt returned to New York, embarking on yet another series of tours. In the mid-1850s she married William Foushee Ritchie, a newspaper editor who fell in love with her during one of her stage appearances. She moved with him to Virginia, where she wrote *The Mimic Life* (1856). She also became deeply involved with a group of women allied to preserve Mount Vernon, the home of George Washington. Together they formed the Mount Vernon Association, the first time a group of women was allowed to band together and purchase property.

Unfortunately, Mowatt's second marriage ended in scandal: She discovered that her husband kept a slave mistress. When her sister fell ill in France, she used the opportunity to escape from Ritchie. She refused to come home until 1862. But soon thereafter she returned to Europe, and never again walked upon American soil. Impoverished and largely forgotten at the time of her death, Anna Mowatt died of tuberculosis at Twickenham on the Thames. She is buried in London beside her beloved James at the Kensal Green Cemetery.

PLAYS

Armand, the Child of the People (a.k.a. *Armand, the Peer and the Peasant*), 1846; *Fashion*, 1845; *Gulzara, or the Persian Slave*, 1841

FICTION

The Clergyman's Wife and Other Sketches, 1868; *Evelyn* (novel), 1845; *Fairy Fingers*, 1863?; *The Fortune Hunter* (novel), 1842?; *The Mimic Life*, 1856; *The Mute Singer*, 1863?; *Pelayo, or The Cavern of Cavadonga* (epic poem), 1836; *Twin Roses*, 1857

---

*A sect founded by Swedish philosopher and religious writer Emanuel Swedenborg (1688–1772), who believed the Bible had spiritual or symbolic meaning, and that there was a correspondence between natural and spiritual things.

NONFICTION

Etiquette of the Toilette, n.d.; *Housekeeping Made Easy*, n.d.; *Management of the Sickroom*, n.d.; *The Memoirs of Madame D'Arblay*, 1844?

WORKS ABOUT

Barnes, Eric Wollencott, *The Lady of Fashion, The Life and the Theatre of Anna Cora Mowatt*, 1954; Mowatt, Anna Cora, *Autobiography of an Actress*, 1854; Mowatt, *Mimic Life, or Before and Behind the Curtain*, 1856

1. Essay by Walter J. Meserve in Hawkins-Dady (1).

2. Ibid.

3. Moses, Montrose J., and John Mason Brown, *The American Theatre as Seen by Its Critics (1752–1934)* (New York: W. W. Norton, 1934).

4. Vaughn, Jack A., *Early American Dramatists from the Beginnings to 1900* (New York: Frederick Ungar, 1981).

Rona Munro
(SEPTEMBER 7, 1959–)

FIONA. I don't know what I'm going to end up looking like. I feel like I'm not born yet.

—from *Piper's Cave*

"I used to resist . . . [the] expectation that I would be concerned with 'women's issues' . . . messy, sticky, biological things, babies and blood and gingerbread with no relevance, interest, or importance in the 'real world,'" says Scottish playwright Rona Munro. "But then I came to think that sticky, biological things actually define what we are and that attempts to evade that realization lead us down the blind alleys where a large part of our culture has taken us."[1]

Munro spent her childhood in Aberdeen, "crawling around woods and cliffs."[2] Her formal theater education did not begin until she was well into her twenties, and her early work reflects her attempts to write "about the weird relationship people have with landscape even now [that] we're nearly all living in towns."[3] Yet, as her writing progressed, she found herself relying, in her own words, more on "oral literature, folk stories, and the real life stories of those I've been lucky enough to befriend, work with, or share with."[4] Her use of Scottish vernacular and cultural themes has led Lizbeth Goodman to call her "one of Scotland's most innovative younger playwrights."[5]

Piper's Cave (1985), one of her best-known works, incorporates issues concerning the natural world and gender politics. She presents a triumvirate of women who individually personify the environment (Helen), the modern world (Jo), and the legendary world (Alisdair, "the piper who walked into the hills and never came out.") Together the three women challenge the audience's preconceptions about the environment, gender, power, sex, and violence. The playwright articulates the questions she wants to raise in an introductory note to *Piper's Cave* in Mary Remnant's anthology: "What happens if women no longer define their sexuality in response to male sexuality? What happens if we acknowledge our own potential for physical strength, for violence, for aggression? What do we do then?"[6] Remnant remarks, "In a play which is noteworthy for the originality of its style and the beauty of its language, Munro overturns those assumptions [of cloying stereotypes, such as the Earth Mother and the Tigress]: she allows that [we] women . . . can choose to change ourselves, to become more truly *ourselves*—whatever that may be—by cooperating and blending with nature rather than fearing, challenging and trying to dominate it as, she suggests, is the male way."[7]

Themes of cultural displacement along with gender issues exist in most of Munro's work. *The Salesman* (1982) reconsiders the myth of Eve and the apple. *Watching Waiters* (1985) deals with a woman escaping from depression in "bedsit land." And the popular *Saturday at the Commodore* (1989), a short, dialect-thick monologue, presents the life of the wry, witty Lena at thirty. Although Munro acknowledges the existence of feminist views in her work, she cautions against adhering to an unwavering feminist agenda: "Plays should show real women, real men and dilemmas that have a reality beyond the narrow confines of anyone's personal obsessions. Power between men and women on a personal level is a much more complicated thing than any sweeping generalizations about the nature of society."[8]

Munro received her M.A. with honors in history at Edinburgh University in 1980. She and her husband Edward Draper have one son, Daniel, born in 1991. A great believer in the theater's ability to bring together communities, Munro has done extensive work since 1985 with youth groups, women's groups, and community theaters, as well as teaching at schools and universities. She has been the writer in residence at the Paines Plough Theater Company and the Hampstead Theater in London. Munro also performs and at one time was a member of the MsFits, a feminist duo. She has received many awards, including the McClaren award for radio (1986), the Susan Smith Blackburn Prize (1991), the Evening Standard Award (1991), and the London Theater Critics Circle Prize (1992).

PLAYS

The Bang and the Whimper, 1982; *The Biggest Party in the World*, 1986; *Bold Girls*, 1990; *The Bus*, 1984; *Dust and Dreams*, 1986; *Fugue*, 1983; *Ghost Story*, 1985; *The Maiden Stone*, 1994; *Off the Road*, 1988; *Piper's Cave*,

1985; *The Salesman*, 1982; *Saturday Night at the Commodore*, 1989; *Touchwood*, 1984; *The Way to Go Home*, 1987; *Winners*, 1987; *Your Turn to Clean the Stairs*, 1992

RADIO PLAYS

Citizens (several episodes), 1988; *The Dirt Under the Carpet* (for Afternoon Theater series), 1988; *Elsie, Elvis, and Eleven* (three half-hour plays), 1990; *Kilbreck* (several episodes), 1983–84; *Three Way Split*, 1992; *Watching Waiters* (for Afternoon Theater series), 1986

TELEVISION PLAYS

Bumping the Odds, 1996; *Casualty* series, "Say It with Flowers" episode, 1990; *Dr. Who* series, 3 segments, 1989;

Hardware, 1983; *Men of the Month*, 1994; *Play On* series, "Biting the Hands" episode, 1989

SCREENPLAYS

Ladybird, Ladybird, 1994

1. Correspondence with the author, 1995.
2. Quoted in notes to *Piper's Cave* in Remnant, vol. 8.
3. Ibid.
4. Op. cit., correspondence.
5. Essay by Lizbeth Goodman in Berney (1).
6. Op. cit., Remnant.
7. Ibid.
8. Op. cit., correspondence.

Anne Nichols
(NOVEMBER 26, 1891/6–SEPTEMBER 15, 1966)

MRS. COHEN. How early it is of late!

—from *Abie's Irish Rose*, Act I

FATHER WHALEN. Shure, we're all trying to get to the same place when we pass on. We're just going by different routes. We can't all go on the same train.

RABBI. And just because you are not riding on my train, why should I say your train won't get there?

—from *Abie's Irish Rose*, Act II

Best known for *Abie's Irish Rose*, which had one of the longest runs in theater history (2,327 consecutive performances), American playwright Anne Nichols was also an actress, director, producer, and scriptwriter. Bitten by the acting bug at the age of sixteen, Nichols ran away from her strict Baptist home to pursue her theatrical dreams. She was on the verge of destitution when she finally got a break: She was cast as a dancer in *The Shepherd Kind*, a biblical spectacle. During the summer stock tour of the production, Nichols began writing sketches. In 1916 she collaborated with Adelaide Matthews on her first full-length play.

Over the following five years, Nichols penned eleven plays before creating *Abie's Irish Rose* in 1922. An interfaith romantic comedy about a Jewish boy and an Irish Catholic girl, much of the play's substance comes from the depiction of the lovers' families, who struggle to cope with the match. *Abie* swiftly became an international classic and was translated into several languages. As author, producer, and licensee of movie rights (which were quickly snatched up), Nichols earned millions of dollars from the play. Unfortunately, the success of *Abie* demanded much of her time, as she worked to protect the show from unethical producers, errant actors, and allegedly plagiaristic rivals: These legal involvements left Nichols little time or energy to devote to new works. Before *Abie's* creation, she had acted in and written scenarios for films in 1911–12. Later, several of her plays were adapted to film. From 1938–42, Nichols had a radio serial, *Dear John*.

Her ten-year marriage to theatrical producer and actor Henry Duffy ended in divorce in 1924; the couple had a son. Nichols converted to Roman Catholicism in her adult years. During the Depression, she lost a substantial portion of her investments. Ill health shrunk her pocketbook further, and in her last year, she went to live at the Actors Fund Home in New Jersey, where she died in 1966. She was working on her autobiography, *Such Is Fame*, at the time.

Despite the fact that the complications induced by *Abie's Irish Rose* prematurely halted Nichols's career, her contributions and legacy to theater still stand. As Laurilyn Harris wrote, "Nichols proved that a woman could operate successfully as a director and theatrical producer in New York City. She disproved George Jean Nathan's contention that women playwrights were somehow 'inferior to their boyfriends.'*[1] She withstood the hostility of critics

---

*Nathan once defeated Nichols in a lawsuit in which she claimed his film *The Cohens and the Kellys* was a plagiarization of *Abie's Irish Rose*. Contending that the theme of young love thwarted by parental bias went back at least as far as Shakespeare's *Romeo and Juliet*, the court decided in Nathan's favor.

and conclusively demonstrated that a well-constructed play would survive without their approval."[2]

PLAYS

Abie's Irish Rose, 1922; *Down Limerick Way*, 1920; *Gilded Cage*, 1920; *The Happy Cavalier*, 1918; *Heart's Desire*, w/ Adelaide Matthews, 1916; *Just Married*, w/A. M. (also film, three versions), 1921; *A Little Bit Old-Fashioned*, 1918; *Longer Letty* (also book), 1919; *The Man from Wicklow*, 1917; *Marry in Haste*, 1921; *Pre-Honeymoon*, 1936; *Springtime in Mayo*, 1919

1. *The Entertainment of a Nation*, 1942, p. 34, quoted in essay by Laurilyn J. Harris in Robinson.

2. Op. cit., Harris.

Marsha Norman
(SEPTEMBER 21, 1947–)

JESSIE. I'm just not having a very good time and I don't have any reason to think it'll get anything but worse.

—from *'night, Mother*

Robert Brustein of *The New Republic* has called Marsha Norman "an authentic universal playwright who speaks to the concerns and experiences of all humankind." Norman grew up in Kentucky, the daughter of an insurance salesman and a fundamentalist Methodist mother. Because her mother felt the neighborhood children were not "good enough" to play with her daughter, Norman's childhood years were lonely. Indoors, she occupied herself with reading books, writing stories, playing the piano, and playing with Bettering, her imaginary companion.

Prior to becoming a playwright, Norman worked at a variety of jobs. She taught gifted children at the Brown School in Louisville, worked at a pediatric burn unit at Atlanta's Grady Memorial Hospital, and, after studying at the Center for Understanding Media in New York, she took a position there as arts administrator. She also served as the director of special projects for the Kentucky Arts Commission from 1972–76, during which time she was married briefly. (She got married again, in 1978, to theatrical producer Dann C. Byck). Jon Jory, artistic director of the Actors Theater of Louisville, advised and encouraged Norman to write.

Her first effort, *Getting Out*, inspired by her work with disturbed children at the Kentucky Central State Hospital, was written in 1977. *Getting Out*, a drama of reintegration, is the story of Arlie, a prostitute, who struggles to lead a straight and honorable life after her recent release from prison. Arlie believes that to properly reemerge in mainstream life, she must strip herself of her past. But she dis-

covers that it is her earlier self, that feisty, full-of-the-devil soul who knew how to defend herself against all odds, who is her greatest ally. In the program notes for a 1981 production at Seattle's A Contemporary Theatre, Norman said, "I was determined [the play] would be truthful about prison . . . they're built for us all in one form or another." *Getting Out* won the 1977 Outer Critics Circle Award and the first annual George Oppenheimer Newsday Playwright Award.

In 1983 *night' Mother* opened to great critical acclaim. The two-character drama centers on the suicidal Jesse and her indigent mother. The play begins with Jesse's announcement that she plans to kill herself at the end of the evening. Her legacy is a set of instructions to her mother detailing how to take care of herself and their apartment. It is a riveting drama; the audience, like the mother, is forced to sit back while the daughter tends to the "last-minute details" before her suicide, which Jesse has rationalized to an unsettling, and almost convincing, degree. *'night Mother* was enormously successful; it won the 1983 Pulitzer Prize for drama, the Susan Smith Blackburn Prize, and an Antoinette Perry Award nomination for best play.

Marsha Norman
COURTESY OF THE PLAYWRIGHT,
PHOTO BY SUSAN JOHANN

Critic Robert J. Forman remarked that Norman's gift for writing about "forgotten people, individuals whose lives seem small, perhaps even mean, but who, faced with some large and overwhelming problem, rise to their own variety of eloquence . . . compares to that of Arthur Miller, though Norman has always avoided the political drama for which Miller is famous."[1] Other plays include *Traveler in the Dark* (1984), which focuses on a brilliant oncological researcher faced with losing a close colleague to the cancer he is trying to cure; *Sarah and Abraham* (1987), which parallels the lives of actors in a regional theater with the biblical characters they are depicting; *Winter Shakers* (1988), a musical about a Kentucky Shaker community; *Circus Valentine* (1979), in which a woman aerialist dares a triple somersault in order to drum up business for a faltering family circus; *The Laundromat* (1978), which is about two women—one recently widowed, the other trapped in a loveless marriage—who meet by chance in a neighborhood laundromat; and *The Pool Hall* (1978), a dialogue between the proprietor and a pool shark.

Norman's awards and honors include numerous grants from such organizations as the National Endowment for the Arts, the Rockefeller Foundation, the American Academy, and the Institute for Arts and Letters. She has also written various works for television and continues to contribute to educational journals and newspapers. Her recent play *The Secret Garden*, a musical adaptation of Frances Hodgson Burnett's classic novel, won her a Tony in 1991.

PLAYS

Circus Valentine, 1979; *Getting Out*, 1977; *The Holdup*, 1980; *'night, Mother* (also teleplay, 1986), 1983; *Sarah and Abraham*, 1987; *The Secret Garden* (musical stage adaptation of Frances Hodgson Burnett novel; book and lyrics), 1989; *Third and Oak* (*The Pool Hall* and *The Laundromat*; also teleplay, 1985), 1978; *Traveler in the Dark*, 1984; *Winter Shakers* (musical), 1988

OTHER WORKS

The Bridge, n.d.; *The Children with Emerald Eyes* (screenplay), n.d.; *The Fortune Teller* (novel), 1987; *In Trouble at Fifteen*, 1980; *It's the Willingness* (teleplay), 1980; *Medicine Woman*, n.d.; *My Shadow* (a.k.a *Face of a Stranger*, teleplay; 1991), screenplay, n.d.; *Thy Neighbor's Wife* (screenplay), n.d.

1. Essay by Robert J. Forman in Magill.

Mary O'Malley
(MARCH 19, 1941-)

MOTHER PETER. Of course nobody ever passed any exam of their own accord. Only prayer will get results. The best thing each one of you can do is to pick out a particular saint and pray to him or her to get you through. Your Confirmation Saint perhaps, or any saint you fancy. But not St. Peter the Apostle, if you wouldn't mind. He's my saint, so he is, and don't any of you go annoying him now.

—from *Once a Catholic*, Act I, Scene 1

British playwright Mary Josephine O'Malley was just seven years old when she started writing plays in her hometown, Bushy-in-Hertfordshire. After penning a number of classroom and backyard productions, she decided she preferred performing to writing. For twenty years she dedicated herself to acting, dancing, and singing, along with marriage, motherhood, and a study of comparative religion. Finally she came full circle; in the early 1970s she returned to her first calling: play writing. Her one-act plays and fringe theater productions eventually led to a residency at the Royal Court Theater.

In 1977 her first full-length play was staged. *Once a Catholic*, a not-unfamiliar tale of school days at a Catholic girls' convent in the 1950s, ran for three years in London. The play's gently satirical approach (for example, all of the students are named "Mary") in depicting the straight-laced and rigid world of the convent in contrast to the rebellious lives of secular youths on the streets fueled its popularity. The *London Tribune*'s Catherine Itzen compared the play to "ceremonial incense . . . one sniff of that

overpowering sweet scent and you're on a spiritual high so orgasmic you can almost see St. Peter at the heavenly gates."[1] Helene Keyssar owns that the play's "primary strategy . . . [is] an unveiling of the oppression and hypocrisy of the Church. Many themes and devices found in feminist drama are apparent . . . but the play is informed by the particular consciousness of Catholic women as Catholics, not of women as women."[2] *Once a Catholic* won O'Malley awards from the *London Evening Standard* and Plays and Players for the most promising new playwright of 1977.

O'Malley's affinity for satire is evident in most of her work, whether she tackles secular institutions, as in the psychiatric ward drama *Look Out . . . Here Comes Trouble* (1978), or religious ones. Her 1986 play *Talk of the Devil* takes another stab at Roman Catholicism, this time aiming to reveal the "mechanical religiosity . . . of the layman and his wife."[3] Critic Eric Shorter felt that the drama, which is peppered with several delightful and salacious visits by the devil (observed by the Virgin Mary), missed its mark, but not without providing a good deal of fun along the way. In addition to her stage work, O'Malley has written fiction and television dramas.

PLAYS

A 'nevolent Society, 1974; *Look Out . . . Here Comes Trouble*, 1978; *Oh If Ever a Man Suffered*, 1975; *Once a Catholic*, 1977; *Superscum*, 1972; *Talk of the Devil*, 1986

OTHER WORKS

A Consideration of Silk (also book), 1990; *On the Shelf* (teleplay), 1984; *Oy Vay Maria* (teleplay), 1977; *Percy and*

Kenneth (teleplay), 1976; *Shall I See You Now?* (teleplay), 1978

1. *Tribune*, 1977.

2. Keyssar.

3. Eric Shorter, *London Daily Telegraph*. October 21, 1986.

Suzanne Osten
(JUNE 20, 1944–   )

In her homeland of Sweden, Suzanne Osten is recognized as much for her dramatic works as for the contributions she has made to the vitality of the Swedish theater community. She was instrumental in the creation of two important theater companies, Fickteatern (Pocket Theater), a traveling performance group that operated from 1967–71, and, since 1975, Unga Klara, the children's theater wing of the Stockholm City Theater, where she is currently artistic director.

Osten targets her theatrical creations for audiences of women, children, and young adults. Music, mime, and movement are often integrated in her productions. According to Birgitta Steene, a professor of Scandinavian Language and Literature at the University of Washington in Seattle, Osten often addresses "the widespread exploitation of women in the sexually 'permissive' Swedish society."[1] *Jösses flickor, befrielsen är nära* (Gee, Girls— Freedom Is Near, 1973), written with Margareta Garpe, blends realism with caricature in its presentation of the fifty-year history of Swedish women's liberation; the play has become a contemporary classic.

Osten has also made her mark as a talented director. She has staged several of the plays of Lars Norén, a man who many Swedes consider a modern-day August Strindberg. While working on the 1982 production of Norén's *Underjordens Leende* (The Smile of Hades), Osten said,

> We at the theater always strive for clarity and always ask for clarification. Lars never gives it to us; instead we get a new way of putting things, which leads to new complications; and this is how his dramas awaken my love for the unbounded. . . . We keep fantasizing about the characters' lies and illusions . . . [Lars] cuts and re-writes. We become like gluttons at a banquet from all the possibilities.[2]

In describing the frustration and camaraderie of mounting an original play, Osten says, "Despair and humor are inseparable."[3]

For her Unga Klara material, Osten has been particularly influenced by the German psychologist-painter Alice Miller's theories of art for children. The company embraces the child's need for art and tragedy, and routinely tackles controversial themes such as divorce, anorexia, and drugs. One of Unga Klara's more recent challenges involved the creation of a theater program for immigrant children. In the spring of 1990 Osten and her company spent three months working with fifty fifteen-year-old students, seventy percent of whom were nonnative Swedes. Together the group spoke thirty-six languages. "For fifteen years we have visited schools and put our ideas to the test, for example our dialogue and our contemporaneity," says Osten. "But [with this group] we felt that we knew nothing about the situation of these young immigrants, nothing about their values: their views on love, the future, justice, humor, Swedes, etc."[4]

In addition to Osten's stage work, she has written and directed a number of award-winning films. *The Guardian Angel* (1990) received the prestigious Felix Award (a sort of European Academy Award) and the French Creteille Film Festival award for best director in 1989.

She has taught seminars and workshops internationally, often focusing on the dramatic portrayal of the childhood experience. She has been the object of several books. More recently she published her first nonfiction work, *Rabén Jogren* (Paper Daddy; 1994), which is about divorce and separation. She is married to actor-director Etienne Glasser, with whom she has a daughter, actor Hanna Hartleb, born in 1965.

PLAYS

Bellman, Blomman och Bruden (Blunder, Bluebell Baby and Birdie), company collaboration, n.d.; *Ett spel om skolan* (A Play About School), 1968; *Ge mej adressen* (Give Me the Address), w/Margareta Garpe, 1972; *Jösses flickor, befrielsen är nära* (Gee, Girls—Freedom Is Near), w/ M.G., 1973; *Kärleksföreställningen* (The Love Performance), w/M.G., 1973; *Lazarilla*, w/Per Lysander, n.d.; *Medeas barn* (Medea's Children), w/P.L., n.d.; *Prins Sorgfri* (Prince Free of Sorrow), w/P.L., n.d.; *Tjejsnack* (Girl Chat), w/M. G., 1971

OTHER WORKS

Bara du och jag (Just You and I; screenplay), 1993; *The Guardian Angel* (screenplay), 1990; *Lethal Film* (screenplay), 1988; *Mama—Our Life Is Now* (screenplay), 1982; *The Mozart Brothers* (screenplay), 1986; *Rabén Jogren* (Paper Daddy; nonfiction), 1994; *Tala, det är så mörkt* (Speak, It's So Dark; screenplay), 1992

1. Essay by Birgitta Steene in Hochman.

2. From "Creating Theatre with Lars Norén," *An Introduction to the Unga Klara Company* (pamphlet produced and published by Unga Klara Company) Stockholm, 1993.

3. Ibid.

4. Op. cit., from "An example of how Unga Klara works," *An Introduction . . .*

Rochelle Owens
(APRIL 2, 1936–   )

CY. I don't want no sow with two feet but with four! Them repeats true things with their grunts not like you human-daughter.

—from *Futz*, Scene 1

Rochelle Owens
COURTESY OF THE PLAYWRIGHT

The shocking 1965 tragicomedy *Futz* brought Rochelle Owens immediate public recognition. Audiences and critics were undone by the play's tale of farmer Cyrus Futz and his erotic relationship with Amanda, his pig, with whom he is in love. Before viewers have resolved their own reaction to this unnatural union, Futz becomes the hostile target of his outraged, self-righteous community as he is blamed for the suddenly violent atmosphere that has consumed it. In jail, he defends himself to the prison warden with a First Amendment-like rationale: "I wasn't near people. They came to me and looked under my trousers all the way up to their dirty hearts! They minded my *own* life." *Futz*, which won 1967 Obies for writing, directing, and acting, bears Owen's signature ability to concurrently appall, entertain, and instruct.

The author of more than a dozen plays to date, Owens "continued to explore perversity, violence and sexuality as responses to the conflict of individual primal impulse with a self-righteous society."[1] *Belch* (1967), a true Theater of Cruelty model, presents a fiendish characterization of corruption and debauchery. *He Wants Shih* (1971) is the story of a Chinese emperor who sheds his own cultural definitions of masculinity and patriarchy to discover the "shih"—the everything—in himself. The Obie winning monologue *Chucky's Hunch* (1981) centers on a failed artist who recites a series of embittered, spiteful letters he has written to his ex-wife. *Emma Instigated Me* (1976) is "a subdued feminist play in a Pirandellian vein as the Author (the playwright herself) mediates between fiction and reality."[2] Keyssar suggests that Owens is what Wallace Stevens once called a "'metaphysician in the dark,' for she leads her audiences through the mysteries of the intangible and through mazes lined with questions that have no certain answers."[3]

Also a poet and an illustrator, she was born Rochelle Bass in Brooklyn, New York, and married George D. Economou, a university professor, on June 17, 1962. She has studied at the University of Montreal, Laval University Quebec, the Herbert Berghof Studios, and the New School for Social Research. Her plays have been featured at festivals in Edinburgh, Avignon, and Berlin, and she has been both widely translated and anthologized. Along with a group of other prominent and experimental female playwrights, Owens was a founding member of the Women's Theater Council, formed in New York City in 1972.

Though the group eventually dissolved, it effected lasting results with the discovery and production of scripts by female playwrights. In addition to her Obies, Owens has received grants from the Rockefeller Foundation (two times), Ford, Guggenheim, and the National Endowment for the Arts, among others, and is a member of the Dramatists Guild; the American Society of Composers, Authors, and Publishers; and Poets, Playwrights, Editors, Essayists and Novelists.

After living in New York City for many years, she moved to Oklahoma, where she and her husband currently reside and teach. In 1988 Owens began a long serial poem entitled "Discourse on Life and Death," a project she has continued to develop.

This pioneer in the experimental off-Broadway theater scene is, as *Newsweek* put it, "a true theater poet." Keyssar has written that "wit and farce are key tools in her craft, but both directors and reviewers have often missed the humor that accompanies the knife in the hands of feminist playwrights. Rochelle Owens's plays are too perplexing to be dismissed as didactic, the common accusation thrust at feminist dramas, but they also demand our tolerance of behavior often considered deviant."[4] Rochelle Owens herself has said, "Any woman . . . who dares to write in areas of human experience which are considered raw or terrifying or investigative . . . is chastised, disciplined, ridiculed."[5]

PLAYS

Belcch, 1967; *Chucky's Hunch,* 1981; *Emma Instigated Me,* 1976; *Futz* (also screenplay, 1969), 1958; *Futz and What Came After,* 1968; *He Wants Shih,* 1971; *Homo,* 1966; *Istanboul,* 1965; *The Karl Marx Play,* w/music by Galt MacDermot, 1971; *Kontraption,* 1970; *The String Game,* 1965; *Who Do You Want, Pierre Vidal?,* 1982; *The Widow and the Colonel,* 1977

OTHER WORKS (POEMS)

A Controversy of Poets, 1965; *I Am the Babe of Joseph Stalin's Daughter: Poems 1961–71,* 1972; *The Joe Chronicles II,* 1977; *The Joe Eighty-Two Creation Poems,* 1974; *Not Be Essence That Cannot Be,* 1961; *Poems from Joe's Garage,* 1973; *Salt and Core,* n.d.

1. Essay by Frances Bzowski in Banham.
2. Essay by Gautam Dasgupta in Hochman.
3. Keyssar.
4. Ibid.
5. "Five Important Playwrights Talk About Theatre Without Compromise and Sexism," *Mademoiselle* 75 (August 1972), p. 289.

Louise Page
(MARCH 7, 1955–   )

LEONARD. You expect everything in you to shrivel [when you get old]. All the hate and the longing. The lust. You don't expect to have them any more. But there isn't much else so you have them all the more. I could kill now. If I had the strength. . . . That's not what you expect.

—From *Salonika*

"I've only had about two days in my life when I've had any doubt that I could write plays," says British dramatist Louise Page. "On those two days I could have thrown myself off the nearest bridge. I write plays because I want to say things. Writing is the most magical thing I know."[1] Page's desire to write dates back to her early childhood. By age fourteen she was penning Shakespearean-influenced pieces and "vast novels set in Victorian times . . . remarkable only in their length."[2] Then she saw her first play, John McGrath's *Events While Guarding the Bofors Gun*, a historical drama about Salonika, which Germans called the world's largest internment camp. Page was "profoundly affected," and decided to devote herself to play writing. She earned her B.A. in drama and theater arts from the University of Birmingham in 1976, and did graduate work in theater studies at the University of Wales in Cardiff.

Since the mid-1970s, Page has explored the coexistence of honesty and hypocrisy through her numerous plays. Her subject matter runs the gamut of human experience: An ambitious young male journalist exploits and distorts a woman's tragic story to promote his own career in *Want-*

Ad (1977); *Tissue* (1978) portrays a mastectomy patient who is more terrified by the possibility of becoming unattractive than the possibility of dying.[3] At one point in the play, a character speaks of his wife as having "wrecked her life trying to keep her body whole. I did not ask her to be beautiful but to be there." In 1979 Page wrote two plays that addressed the experience of physical suffering: *Lucy*, which deals with euthanasia, and *Hearing*, about the isolation induced by deafness.

Her 1980 drama *House Wives* ushered in a group of dramas characterized by elderly people who, at times, exhibit a liberal political consciousness unmatched by their children. *House Wives* chronicles a woman's transformation from political conservative to Labour party candidate. During a period when government decisions are made by mostly all-male committees, the main character receives little support from her army major husband or her Tory-aligned mother. Ultimately she garners courage and inspiration from her grandmother, a former suffragist and hunger-striker.

Other works include *Flaws* (1980), which deals with the relative importance of materialism when a family bakery is threatened with bankruptcy and its owners realize they have a far more serious problem on their hands; *Real Estate*, a more conventionally structured play that uses the theme of desire and ambition within the confines of domesticity: when a 38-year-old pregnant woman returns to the long-neglected home of her career-minded mother, we find it is the young "modern" woman who has conventional expectations, while her middle-aged parents have created a very modern, independent lifestyle, indeed—the young woman's father, Dick, not only does the cooking, he even embroiders tapestries.

Page enjoyed her greatest critical success with *Salonika* (1982), which first appeared at the Royal Court Upstairs. Interestingly, *Salonika* was inspired by the same John McGrath play that originally pushed Page into play writing. But rather than creating a similar historical drama, Page explores the effect of the internment on the camp's survivors fifty years later. An eighty-four-year-old woman and her sixty-four-year-old daughter visit the grave of their dead husband/father, joined by the mother's seventy-four-year-old lover, Leonard. Page dashes smug, youthful notions of love and lust among the aged. *Salonika* received the George Devine Award and was hailed for breaking "the confines of naturalistic theatre with absolute conviction, when a long dead soldier literally parts the sands where he has lain buried for half a century."[4]

Page is frequently asked why she chooses to write about women; she retorts, "Why not? Men write about men and no one asks them why."[5] Yet she appreciates that as a woman playwright, she is a member of the more exclusive club. "I didn't see a stage play written by a woman until *Dusa, Fish, Stas and Vi* (PAM GEMS; 1976). I had read *A Taste of Honey* (SHELAGH DELANEY; 1959) and it didn't strike me as strange that it was written by a woman but neither did it strike me as strange that there were so many plays written by men. It never occurred to me that as a woman I couldn't be a playwright. It took me a long time to realise that this was a contrary philosophy to the one with which a lot of women were brought up."[6] Although she identifies herself as a feminist writer, she is wary of extremists on both sides of the issues: "Feminism is about

doing what you want to do to the best of your ability and not being stopped. It's not about being told what to do by feminists."[7]

PLAYS

Adam Was a Gardener, 1991; *Beauty and the Beast*, 1985; *Diplomatic Wives*, 1989; *Falkland Sound/Voces de Malvinas*, 1983; *Flaws*, 1980; *Glasshouse*, 1977; *Goat*, 1986; *Golden Girls*, 1984; *Hawks and Doves*, 1992; *Hearing*, 1979; *House Wives*, 1981; *Like to Live*, 1992; *Lucy*, 1979; *Real Estate*, 1984; *Salonika*, 1982; *Tissue*, 1978; *Want-Ad*, 1977

RADIO PLAYS

Agnus Dei, 1980; *Armistice*, 1983; *Peanuts* (teleplay), 1982; *Saturday, Late September*, 1978

1. Wandor (1), afterword.
2. "Golden Girl," article in *The Stage Guardian*, April 13, 1984.
3. Essay by Elaine Turner in Berney (1).
4. Op. cit., *The Stage Guardian*.
5. Ibid.
6. Op. cit., notes to *Tissue*, Wandor (1).
7. Article in *The Women's Post*, London, n.d.

Vera Fyodorovna Panova
(MARCH 7, 1905–MARCH 6, 1973)

SHEMETOVA. Sometimes, when the accustomed pattern of things is suddenly broken . . . like today's emergency landing . . . as if you were going along and suddenly: Stop! and you look up . . . and it's terrifying—why has this happened to me? But it's only for a moment; no more. You, too, know how it is: you fall asleep, see something terrible, and you make yourself wake up.

—from *It's Been Ages!*, Act III

Born at Rostov-on-Don, Soviet Russian playwright and novelist Vera Fyodorovna Panova began working as a journalist in 1922 when still in her teens. During World War II she served as a newspaper correspondent for a medical unit, an experience that she would later embody in several of her plays. She eventually settled in Leningrad with her husband, an engineer.

Springtime, her first play, revolved around the uprising of rich peasants on the Don. Her plays were called "models of social realism, full of carefully observed psychological detail and homiletic intention."[1] Writing in a naturalistic style similar to that of Maxim Gorky, she concentrated on prose during the 1950s, writing nine novels as well as other

Louise Page
COURTESY OF THE BILLY ROSE THEATRE COLLECTION/
SARAH AINSILE

works. A decade later she returned to drama. Her works address themes of moral responsibility, modern youth, and the family. Several of her plays were adapted for the screen, and between 1947 and 1950 she won three Stalin Prizes.

PLAYS

Devochiki (Girls), 1945; *Kak pozhivaesh, paren?* (How Goes It, Lad?), 1962; *Plennye* (Captives; later, The Snowstorm, 1956), 1942; *Provody belkykh nochey* (Farewell to White Nights), 1961; *Skolko let, skolko zhit!* (It's Been Ages!), 1966; *Springtime,* n.d.; *Sputniki,* n.d.; *Kruzhilikha,* 1969; *Vremena goda,* n.d.; *Sentimentalnyi roman,* 1970

WORKS ABOUT

Buguslavskaya, Z., *Vera Panova,* 1963

1. Essay by Laurence Senelick in Hochman.

Suzan-Lori Parks
(1963–)

BLACK MAN WITH WATERMELON. There is uh Now and there is uh Then. Ssall there is. (I bein in uh Now: uh Now bein in uh Then: I bein, in Now in Then, in I will be. I was be too but thats uh Then thats past. That me that was be is uh me-has-been. Thuh Then that was be is uh has-been-Then too. Thuh me-has-been sits in thuh be-me: we sit on this porch. Same porch. Same me. Thuh Then thats been somehow sits in thuh Then that will be: same Thens. I swing from uh tree. You cut me down and bring me back. Home. Here. I fly over thuh yard. I fly over thuh yard in all over. Them thens stays fixed. Fixed Thens, Thuh Thems stays fixed too. Thuh Thems that come and take me and thuh Thems that greet me and then them Thems that send me back here. Home. Stays fixed, Them do.

—from *The Death of the Last Black Man . . .*

In Suzan-Lori Parks's Obie-winning play *The Death of the Last Black Man in the Whole World* (1990), she explores America's prejudice toward African-Americans through the portrayal of stereotypical black characters created by the white man: Black Woman with Fried Drumstick, Black Man with Watermelon, and Lots of Grease and Lots of Pork. The story is basically a chase—of a black man who has been chased all his *lives* until he is strung up and lynched, at which point there is divine intervention. Parks describes it as a historical dreamscape of death and non-religious resurrection. Like most of her work, the language in *Last Black Man* is poetic and celebrates Black English; it is at times mesmerizing in its rhythms. Critic Linda Ben-Zvi has compared Parks's experimentation with language

to that of Samuel Beckett and James Joyce, remarking that her characters are "fixed in place by an imposed language that defines them but is not their own . . . they seek to get out from under the weight of words."[1]

Much of Parks's works demonstrate her interest in the nightmare of African-American history and memory. In her 1989 play *Imperceptible Mutabilities in the Third Kingdom,* she reveals, again according to Ben-Zvi, a "composite picture of African-American experience, starting with contemporary time, moving backward to a mythic retelling of the black forced journey from Africa and concluding with two 'family plays' depicting the terrible results of such displacement and estrangement from both language and self."[2] *Mutabilities* is accompanied by slides and photographs; Parks has described the play as African-American history in the shadow of the photographic image.

Parks's work challenges audiences with respect to both form and content. In *Pickling* (1989), a woman remembers the past through the things she has saved: lots of bric-a-brac in formaldehyde. *Betting on the Dust Commander* (1990) is a play about circularity, domestic harmony, and horse racing. In *Devotees in the Garden of Love* (1991), a young woman and her mother wait in a hilltop garden for the end of a war, which they watch on TV. *The America Play* (1991) is a journey in which mother and son search for their husband/father, who has been missing for years. A champion of Abraham Lincoln, the man has left a trail that leads to the unearthing of piles of historical wonders. "He is simultaneously everywhere and of course nowhere to be found," according to Parks.

Her most recent work, *Venus (1996),* which premiered at the Yale Repertory Theatre in March 1996, stems from the real life of Saartjee Baartman, "the Hottentot Venus," an African woman whose "Great Heathen Buttocks" made her a favorite sideshow character of early-nineteenth-century Europeans. Parks manipulates the Baartman story with her unique brand of language and characters, notably The Brother, then The Mother Showman, and finally The Grade School Chum, all played by the same actor, and The Negro Resurrectionist, whose announcement of each scene is accompanied by "historical documentation."

She graduated Phi Beta Kappa with a B.A. from Mt. Holyoke College in 1985, and has studied at the Drama Studio in London. The recipient of National Endowment for the Arts and Rockefeller Foundation grants, Parks has been a guest lecturer and writer in residence at several academic institutions throughout the country.

Parks has acknowledged herself as a "playwright-resurrectionist," a writer who welcomes the opportunity to challenge and play with history: "When I did *The America Play . . .* people said, 'Did it really happen?' and I could say, 'Yeah, it happens every night.' That's as real as anything else. That's why theater's interesting to me. Because you can insert it into real life and sort of make history."[3]

PLAYS

The America Play, 1991; *Betting on the Dust Commander*, 1990; *The Death of the Last Black Man in the Whole World*, 1990; *Devotees in the Garden of Love*, 1991; *Girl 6* (also screenplay, dir. by Spike Lee), 1996; *Greeks*, 1990; *Imperceptible Mutabilities in the Third Kingdom*, 1989; *Pickling*, 1989; *The Sinner's Place*, 1984; *Venus*, 1996

OTHER WORKS

Alive from Off Center (video play), 1991; *Anemone Me* (screenplay), 1990; *Locomotive* (radio play), 1991; *Poetry Spots* (video play), 1989; *The Third Kingdom* (radio play), 1990

1. Essay by Linda Ben-Zvi in Berney (2).

2. Ibid.

3. Interview w/playwright by Tom Sellar in *Theatre Forum* (Summer/Fall 1996), p. 38.

Josephine Preston Peabody
(MAY 30, 1874–DECEMBER 4, 1922)

Josephine Preston Peabody's early childhood in Brooklyn, New York, was filled with the rewards of having parents who were avid theatergoers and keen supporters of arts education. They spent many evenings at home acting out scenes from plays. But her life changed in 1882 with the death of her younger sister, followed by the death of her father, a merchant. Without adequate resources, her mother, Susan Josephine Morrill Peabody, sent Peabody and her remaining sister to live with their grandmother in Dorchester, Massachusetts.

Perhaps as a way of articulating her sudden isolation and alienation, Peabody began writing poetry. By the time she was fourteen, she had already published seven poems in magazines, such as *The Woman's Journal*. Poor health prevented her from finishing secondary school, but a scholarship later enabled her to attend Radcliffe College for two years. There she added prose and drama to her repertoire, and became an activist for women's suffrage and pacifism.

Peabody's first plays were published in the early 1900s, although she did not see her work produced until the 1905 staging of *Marlowe*. Shortly thereafter she married Lionel S. Marks, a mechanical engineering professor at Harvard University. The couple had two children, Allison and Lionel, and bestowed upon them all the richness of Peabody's own early years. Her greatest success as a playwright came with her 1909 drama *The Piper*, about the Pied Piper of Hamelin. It won the $1,500 Stratford-on-Avon Shakespeare Memorial Prize after premiering at the Stratford

Memorial Theater in England. Upon hearing that she had won this award, Peabody wrote in her diary, ". . . this delicious unhoped-for thing that people (and papers) take it as an honor for the country, and a Banner for the cause of womankind. Oh—oh—I wanted to be something or other for these in some manner, some day!" *The Piper* went on to open in New York City and was eventually translated into French, Danish, Swedish, and Russian.

Peabody was always willing to explore new subjects; her later works include *The Wolf of Gubbio* (1913), about St. Francis of Assisi, and *Portraits of Mrs. W* (1922), about one of the godmothers of modern-day feminism, Mary Wollstonecraft, and her husband, the political philosopher William Godwin.

PLAYS

The Chameleon, 1917; *Fortune and Men's Eyes*, 1900; *Marlowe*, 1901; *Pan*, 1904; *Portraits of Mrs. W*, 1922; *The Piper*, 1909; *The Wings*, 1907; *The Wolf of Gubbio*, 1913

POETRY

The Book of the Little Past, 1912; *The Collected Poems of Josephine Preston*, 1927; *Harvest Moon*, 1916; *The Singing Man*, 1911; *The Singing Leaves*, 1903

WORKS ABOUT

Baker, Christina Hopkinson, ed., *The Diary and Letters of Josephine Preston Peabody*, 1925

Lyudmila Petrushevskaya
(MAY 26, 1938–   )

YURA. . . . the family no longer exists. There is just the female tribe with their young ones, and lone males.

—from *The Stairwell*

Lyudmila Petrushevskaya, called "the feminist Chekhov," writes plays that are funny, unpredictable, and sad, revealing the stark, bleak world of Soviet Russia. The government found her dramas to be so subversive, the first staging of her work did not occur until 1975, even though she had begun writing plays in 1963; none of her plays were published until 1988. Even though her work was silenced for so long a period, Patrick Miles comments that she "is the most original and provocative talent of the Russian new wave."[1]

While the theme of the degeneration of life in the Soviet Union fueled the controversy surrounding Petrushevskaya's work, her blunt feminism intensified it. Miles remarks, "Nearly all the male characters in her plays are idle, devoid of self-respect, completely faithless; they are fornicators, drunkards, and cowards."[2] (English-language audiences, Miles points out, have great difficulty comprehending the lack of vituperation revealed in her gritty world.) It is the women and children, she suggests, who contain the hope of survival. In spite of this, hers is no simple feminism. Several of Petrushevskaya's plays show mothers who treat their daughters roughly, but indulge their sons, thereby encouraging the cycle of detrimental male behavior. Yet the children "are symbols of hope amid the depiction of gloom and confusion . . . [they] can create a better life by liberating themselves from the oppressive love of their mothers."[3] She claims to have been deeply influenced by Siberian dramatist Aleksandr Vampilov,* and Miles alludes to a "hint of Dostoevsky" not only in her plays themselves but in the way audiences experience them.

Kvartira Kolombiny (Columbine's Apartment; 1985), written prior to the era of *glasnost*, provides "bleak visions of the prospect for life under the social and moral conditions of contemporary Russia . . ." attests Anthony J. Vanchu. "It portrays a society that fosters the breakdown of identity."[4] Petrushevskaya's most popular drama is perhaps *Tri devshki v golubom* (Three Girls in Blue; 1983), which enjoys at least two English translations. It centers on the dilemmas of three young, single mothers who, with their children and an elderly relative, attempt to work out their differences in a dilapidated dacha they have rented for the summer. Featured are the playwright's familiar ingredients: the "interminable search in the USSR for living space, edible food, effective medical care, and a viable wage."[5] Yet somehow these women manage their difficulties. In response to one's comment, "All men are brothers," Ira, one of the mothers, replies, "Not all—some are sisters!"

In 1979, Yuri Norstein's full-length animated film of Petrushevskaya's scenario *The Tale of Tales*, received six international awards and in 1984 was nominated by an international jury of film critics as the best animated feature ever made.[6]

In addition to her plays, Petrushevskaya is a prolific writer of short stories. Though the journal *Novyi Mir* rejected the short stories she sent in 1969, its editor at the time, Tvardovsky, commented, "Withhold publication, but don't lose track of the author." Petrushevskaya's first story was published in 1972 in the literary journal *Avrora*.

Petrushevskaya was born in Moscow and raised in an orphanage in Ufa in the Urals; her childhood was one of wartime poverty. She was educated at Moscow University,

where she later served on the faculty. From 1962–71 she worked alternately as a nurse and a journalist. In the early 1970s Petrushevskaya was a member of Alexi Arbuzov's playwrights' workshop; he once said of her that she "scared him out of his wits."[7]

In A. Smelyansky's introduction of her works in English, he wrote, "In the course of the past decade there has been no more complex and clearly expressed talent in our theater. Her piercing vision, and interpretation of the commonplace as an unexplored area of Soviet reality, her understanding of so-called "simple people" as they truly are, formed by their history, her precise writer's ear, tuned to contemporary speech, the ways in which people actually speak and communicate—all these things have made Lyudmila Petrushevskaya's plays immensely attractive to the theater . . ."[8]

PLAYS

Andante, 1988; *Bystro khorosho ne byvaet, ili Chemodan chepukhi* (Things Don't Get Better Quickly, or The Suitcase of Nonsense), 1978; *Cinzano* (collection: Cinzano (1987); Smirnova's Birthday, n.d.; Music Lessons (1983); Three Girls in Blue (1986); The Stairwell (1983); Love (1979); Nets and Snares (1974); The Execution, n.d.; The Meeting, n.d.; A Glass of Water (1983); Isolation Box. Stephen Mulrine, intro. & tr.), 1991; *Dva okoshka* (Two Windows), 1975; *Four* (collection: Love (1979); Come into the Kitchen (1979); Nets and Traps (1974); The Violin, 1984; *Krokhmal E Chernaya koshka v "temnoi komnate,"* 1990; *Krokhmal E Razmyshlenya u razbitogo koryta*, 1990; *Ia za shvetsyu* (I'm for Sweden), 1988; *Novye Robinzony; Khronika XX veka* (The New Robinsons: Chronicle of the 20th Century), 1989; *Ozelenenie* (Making It Green), 1980; *Pesni XX veka* (Songs of the 20th Century; collection: Urokoi muzyka [Music Lessons]), 1983; *Kvartira Kolombiny* (Columbine's Apartment), 1985; *Monlogi* (Monologues), 1988; *Temnaya komnata* (The Dark Room, cycle of short plays), 1988; *Pesy* (Plays; collection: Uroki muzyki [Music Lessons]), n.d.; *Lestnichnaya kletka* (The Staircase), 1983; *Tri devshki v golubom* (Three Girls in Blue), 1983; *Vse ne kak u lyudei* (Different from People), 1979

OTHER WORKS

Bessmertnaya lyubov (Undying Love), 1988; *Immortal Love* (short stories, Sally Laird, tr.), 1995; *Svoi krug*, 1990; *Taina doma: povesti i rasskazy*, 1995; *The Time—Night* (novel), 1994

WORKS ABOUT

Mulrine, Stephen, intro. and tr., *Cinzano*, 1991; Smith, M. T., "In Cinzano veritas: The Plays of Liudmila Pe-

---

*(1937–72). His works have been compared with those of Nikolai Gogol and Anton Chekhov, and he has been called the greatest playwright of his generation.

trushevskaia" in *Recent Polish and Soviet Theatre and Drama*, J. A. Phillips, ed., 1985

1. Essay by Patrick Miles in Hawkins-Dady (2).

2. Ibid.

3. Maya Johnson, "Women and Children First," *Canadian Slavonic Papers* 34, no. 1–2 (March-June 1992), p. 97.

4. Anthony J. Vanchu, "Petrushevskaya . . . ," *World Literature Today* 67, no. 1 (Winter 1993), p. 107.

5. Op. cit., Miles.

6. Cited in *Cinzano: Eleven Plays*, Steve Mulrine, intro. and tr. (London: Nick Hern Books, 1991).

7. Op. cit., Miles.

8. Ibid.

Katherine Fowler Philips
(JANUARY 1, 1631–JUNE 22, 1664)

Although she is remembered for her poetry, Katherine Philips was the first woman to have a play professionally produced on the London stage. She spent her early years in the parish of St. Mary Woolchurch, proving herself a bright, precocious child. At the age of eight, Philips was sent to Miss Salmon's school for girls, where she studied foreign languages.

Her merchant father's early death precipitated a series of life changes for the young woman. Her widowed mother married Richard Hector Philips, a Welsh baronet, and the family moved to Wales. There, seventeen-year-old Katherine made the acquaintance of James Philips, a son of Richard's from a previous marriage. Even though James was thirty-seven years older than she, the couple married in 1648.

James's gentrified position allowed a comfortable life, leaving Philips free to pursue writing; however, the two were not without their conflicts. Despite her strong opposition to her husband's politics—he was a staunch Parliamentarian and prominent Cromwellian, she a Royalist—Philips was forced into Presbyterianism. Later, after the Commonwealth's demise, she gladly rejoined the Church of England.

In 1651 Philips formed the Society of Friendship, a women's club. Her poetry celebrated her platonic relationships with women friends, whom she addressed with sobriquets. Philips herself took the name "Orinda" and was often called "the matchless Orinda." Her friend Mary Aubrey, the object of some of her best poems, was known as "Rosania." Philips's relationship with Aubrey, while not likely physical, was quite intense. When Aubrey married William Montague, the dejected Philips, feeling thoroughly betrayed, replaced her old friend with Anne Owen,

"Lucasia." When Anne Owen married, Katherine actually accompanied her on the honeymoon.

To complement her poetic writings, Philips embarked on a translation of Pierre Corneille's play *Pompee*. She had not expected to see her translation staged, but a twist of fate resulted in a full production, which she saw on her trip with Anne Owen and Owen's new spouse. Roger Boyle, Earl of Orrery and a minor playwright, found himself with a copy of Philips's play after running into the writer's husband in Dublin. Boyle encouraged her to add songs to the work. She did, and he produced the show at the newly built Theatre Royal in Smock Alley, Dublin, in 1663. *Pompey* was enormously popular—it featured a hit song (written by Philips), and its initial publication of 500 copies sold out quickly.

To fully appreciate Philips's importance in theater history, the contemporary audience must consider that in her day, translations were looked upon as equal to original works. As Nancy Cotton states, "While we think of Katherine Philips's translation of Corneille's *Pompee*, her contemporaries spoke to Mrs. Philips's *Pompey*."[1]

Soon after the advent of *Pompey*, Philips set to translating Corneille's *Horace*. But before she could finish it, she was struck by smallpox and died at the age of thirty-two. Sir John Denham completed the play, with musical interludes added by John Lacy, a comedian of the day. When it was presented at court in 1668, Katherine Philips was given full credit for the script. It was later produced at the Theatre Royal by the King's Company (1669).

Philips's death generated myriad commemorative verses and tributes to "the matchless Orinda." Unlike so many of her day, she was a purist in translation, opposed to trifling with the original author's intent or structure. Her work essentially paved the way for APHRA BEHN.

PLAYS (COMPLETE)

Horace, tr. from Corneille, 1669; *Pompey*, tr. from Corneille, 1663

OTHER WORKS

Collected Words, 1664, 1667, 1669, 1678; *The Crooked Six-Pence* (attr.), 1743; *Letters from Orinda to Poliarchus*, 1705; 2d ed., 1720; *The Orinda Booklets*, Tutin, J. R., ed., 1903.; *Poems by the Incomparable Mrs K. P.*, 1664; *Poems . . . to Which Is Added Corneille's 'Pompée' & 'Horace'*, 1667; *Selected Poems*, Guiney, L. I., ed., 2 vols. 1904–05

WORKS ABOUT

Souers, Philip Webster, *The Matchless Orinda*, 1931

1. Cotton.

Mary Griffith Pix
(1666–1709/20?)

MRS RICH. . . . I quarrel daily with my destiny, that I was not at first a woman of quality . . . I had rather be the beggarliest countess in the town, than the widow of the richest banker in Europe.

—from *The Beau Defeated*, Act I, Scene 1

Mary Pix, conjoined with CATHERINE TROTTER and DELARIVIERE MANLEY, was one of the more celebrated women playwrights of her day. She found herself lampooned along with her two colleagues in the anonymously written *The Female Wits*, although Pix's character was satirized much less harshly than her friends, perhaps because she so "strenuously protested her modesty and humility,"[1] as Nancy Cotton put it.

Pix's career as a dramatist began relatively late in life. She was thirty years old in 1696 when her first two plays were staged: *The Spanish Wives*, a comedy, and *Ibrahim, the Thirteenth Emperor of the Turks*, a tragedy that premiered at the Drury Lane Theatre. Her first novel was published that same year. In the dedication to *The Spanish Wives*, Pix wrote that she had had an "Inclination to Poetry" since childhood. But until 1696, she appeared to be completely content as a wife and mother.

Born Mary Griffith, she married George Pix in 1684, just two years after the death of her father, the rector of a Buckingham parish and master of the Royal Latin School (a free institution). George, twenty-four when they married, was a merchant tailor in London. He took his new wife to live on a beautiful estate in Kent that he had inherited from his father. Upon the death of their first son just after his June 1689 baptism, the couple moved to London. Two years later their son William was born, and Pix became a working mother, juggling child raising and her writing career.

Pix's strongest works are her comedies, which offer intriguing plots and lively heroines. Yet, despite the strong feminist leanings her works suggest, she was not above having a laugh at the expense of both sexes. For *The Beau Defeated* (1700) Pix created Mrs. Rich, an insipid snob who, her large fortune aside, yearns to be titled. She and her companion, Lady La Bassett, have both set their sights on one Sir John Roverhead, who entertains the ladies' attentions while simultaneously flirting with Mrs. Rich's niece. When Roverhead gives both auntie and niece the same love verses, he seems destined for big trouble. But when La Bassett discovers the deed, shocked to find that the cad had claimed authorship for *her* letters to him, she challenges Mrs. Rich to a duel.

Deceptive men were no strangers to Pix. In the late 1690s she and her friend, playwright William Congreve,

brought plagiarism charges against George Powell, an actor-playwright who played the lead in Pix's *Ibrahim*. The work in question was Powell's *The Imposture Defeated*, which was staged by the Drury Lane, the same theater that had previously rejected Pix's *The Deceiver Deceived* (1665). In her prologue to *Deceiver* she admonished, "Deceiver Deceived, and Imposture cheated! . . . 'Tis t'other house best shows the sleight of hand . . . /Our authoress, like true woman, showed her play/To some, who, like true wits, stole't half away."

Pix remained active as a dramatist until 1706, when her last play, *The Adventures in Madrid*, was published. She died around 1709, according to an advertisement for the production of *The Busybody*, written by Pix's close friend SUSAN CENTLIVRE. Yet other records show her last year as 1720. If the latter is accurate, she was inactive during her last decade.

PLAYS

The Adventures in Madrid, 1706; *The Beau Defeated, or The Lucky Younger Brother*, 1700; *The Conquest of Spain*, 1705; *The Czar of Muscovy*, 1701; *The Deceiver Deceived*, 1698; *The Different Widows, or Intrigue à la Mode*, 1703; *The Double Distress*, 1701; *The False Friend, or The Fate of Disobedience*, 1699; *Ibrahim, the Thirteenth Emperor of the Turks*, 1696; *The Innocent Mistress*, 1697; *Queen Catherine, or The Ruins of Love*, 1698; *The Spanish Wives*, 1696

OTHER WORKS

Alas! When Charming Sylvia's Son, 1697; *The Inhuman Cardinal, or Innocence Betrayed*, 1696; *To the Right Hon. the Earl of Kent . . . This Poem*, 1700; *Violenta, or The Rewards of Virtue*, 1704

WORKS ABOUT

Steeves, Edna L., ed., *Plays*, 1982

1. Cotton.

Sharon Pollock
(APRIL 19, 1936–)

SITTING BULL. In the beginning . . . was given . . . to everyone a cup . . . A cup of clay. And from this cup we drink our life. We all dip in the water, but the cups are different . . . My cup is broken. It has passed away.

—from *Walsh*, Act II

Sharon Chalmers Pollock did not start her artistic career as a dramatist, but as an actress in New Brunswick, Canada. But after graduating from the University of New Brunswick, touring with Prairie Players of Calgary, and mothering six children, her talents as a playwright emerged. Since the early 1970s, she has written more than twenty plays, in addition to several radio dramas and teleplays.

Much of Pollock's works have been inspired by real-life occurrences. "[A play] is a theatrical impression of an historical event seen through the optique of the stage and the mind of the playwright," wrote Pollock.[1] *Walsh* (1973), an early work, finds Mayor John Walsh of the Northwest Mounted Police caught in the middle of the conflict between the Canadian government and the Native American nations in 1876. Despite his militaristic stance, Walsh finds himself sympathetic to the plight of the Native Americans; yet his actions do not reveal his sympathy. Pollack returned to Canadian history in *The Komagata Maru Incident* (1976) in a more contemporary setting that investigates the government's refusal to allow a boatload of East Indian refugees to enter the country.

Blood Relations, however, was the work that truly put Pollack on the theatrical map. The play, produced in 1976, depicts the infamous Lizzie Borden murder case of 1892, which found Borden guilty of brutally murdering her parents. But *Blood Relations* is no mere suspense drama. Pollack uses Borden's life as a scaffold from which she constructs the real issues at hand: the politics of justice, and the nature of storytelling, myth, and memory. The play utilizes a series of flashbacks: Borden, along with the audience, watches as her lover/friend reenacts scenes from the accused's life. Ultimately, the play is not interested in passing judgment on Borden—the question of whether she actually committed the murders remains unanswered. Critic and playwright MICHELENE WANDOR wrote that *Blood Relations* "creates a continually shifting perspective in such matters of guilt, responsibility, sexual repression, and desire, which are shown as ambiguous matters, dependent to some extent on the point of view of the watcher versus the watched."[2] The "watching" audience members must wade through their own prejudices and sensibilities in their effort to indict Borden. Pollock has acknowledged that *Blood Relations* is her most personal work. During her marriage to an extremely violent man, she found herself "devising, quite literally, murderous schemes to rid me of him."[3] And so she came to Lizzie Borden, discovering her own darkness within the world of the alleged murderer. *Blood Relations* received Canada's first Governor General's Award for drama in 1981.

Several years later, Pollock returned to her own personal territory with *Doc* (1986), a semiautobiographical piece that searches out the playwright's "feminine memories of family." Brian Brennan, writing in the *Calgary Herald,* called it her "finest work yet. . . . She has made a strong personal statement with universal implications."

Pollock has also written many children's plays: *The Happy Prince* and *The Star-Child* are adaptations of Oscar Wilde short stories. Her work has been produced in Canada, Great Britain, the United States, and Australia. She has enjoyed extensive experience as an instructor, advisor, and director of theater departments at various institutions, such as the Playwrights' Colony; the Canada Council Advisory Arts Panel, where she has served as chairwoman; and the National Arts Centre and Alberta Theatre Projects where she was playwright in residence. Among the awards garnered by this Calgary resident are the Canada Council Senior Arts Grant (1984) and the Alberta Literary Foundation Award (1987).

PLAYS

A Compulsory Option, 1970; *And Out Goes You?,* 1975; *Blood Relations* (a.k.a. *My Name Is Lisbeth,* 1976), 1980; *Chautauqua Spelt E-N-E-R-G-Y,* 1979; *Doc,* 1986; *Fair Liberty's Call,* 1994; *Generations,* 1980; *The Great Drag Race, or Smoked, Choked and Croaked,* n.d.; *The Happy Prince* (adapt. of Oscar Wilde short story), 1974; *The Komagata Maru Incident,* 1976; *A Lesson in Swizzlery,* 1974; *Mail vs. Female,* 1979; *New Canadians,* 1973; *One Tiger to a Hill,* 1980; *The Rose and the Nightingale* (adapt. of Oscar Wilde short story), 1974; *Superstition Throu' the Ages,* 1973; *The Star-Child* (adapt. of Oscar Wilde short story), 1974; *Walsh* (also radio play), 1973; *Whiskey Six,* 1983; *The Wreck of the National Line Car,* 1978; *Wudjesay?* (also teleplay), 1974

RADIO PLAYS AND TELEPLAYS

The B Triple P Plan (radio), n.d.; *Generation* (radio), 1978; *In the Beginning Was* (radio), n.d.; *In Memory Of* (radio), n.d.; *Intensive Care* (radio), 1983; *Mary Beth Goes to Calgary* (radio), n.d.; *Mrs. Yale and Jennifer* (radio; eight episodes), n.d.; *One Tiger to a Hill* (radio), 1985; *Portrait of a Pig* (television), 1973; *Split Seconds in the Death Of* (radio), 1971; *Sweet Land of Liberty* (radio), 1979; *31 for 2* (radio), 1971; *Waiting* (radio), n.d.; *We to the Gods* (radio), 1971; *Whiskey Sex Cadenza* (radio), 1983

1. Pollock, Sharon, Introduction to *The Komagata Maru Incident* (Toronto: Playwrights Coop, 1978).

2. Wandor (1).

3. Ibid.

Aishah Rahman
(1950?–)

GIRL. It's only in the head of a musician that I begin to understand. Only a musician can make sense for me. Only a musician knows how to connect shoes with cardboard to cover holes to P.S. 184 on 116th Street and Lenox Avenue to the red taste of watermelon and mocking white smiles to Anthony's smiles and smell of Florida Water to late night loneliness and . . . this . . . [her unborn baby].

—from *Unfinished Women* . . .

African-American playwright Aishah Rahman defines heroism as the ability "to be able to love in spite of all the soul-crushing experiences that define black life in America."[1] She cites the early 1970s police killing of ten-year-old Clifford Glover in her native New York City as the event that ignited her passion for writing. Pregnant at the time with her daughter Yoruba, Rahman investigated the case herself, ultimately concluding that the boy's family was "voiceless. And I had to give voice to them."[2]

Rahman labels her works "polydramas" with a "jazz aesthetic": They are not unlike NTOZAKE SHANGE'S choreopoems. One of Rahman's best-known plays, *Unfinished Women Cry in No Man's Land While a Bird Dies in a Gilded Cage* (1984), which Margaret Wilkerson called an "underground classic,"[3] constructs a sophisticated dialectical narrative fused by jazz. In one setting, the Hide-A-Wee Home for Unwed Mothers, several pregnant teenagers struggle with the decision of whether to keep their babies or give them up for adoption. In the other, jazz musician Charlie "Bird" Parker, dying, haunted by

drugs and lost dreams, is confined to the boudoir of his lover, Pasha. Both strands reveal a dialogue imbued with the language of hope and despair, and of innocence exploited and lost. A pregnant girl says, "One day we will not have to be afraid of our dreams." Bird says, "My pain is not unbearable. In none of my secret places inside of me have I condemned myself." Rahman binds the two seemingly disparate scenarios together with Parker's music. In the end both settings merge and all the characters come together, symphonically speaking, repeating their lines, creating a jazz ensemble of language.

The Mojo and the Sayso (1988), a family drama, also exemplifies the incorporation of Rahman's "jazz aesthetic." In her introductory notes she explains that *Mojo* "is not conceived or written in a naturalistic mode. Therefore, the directing style should serve the absurdity, fantasy, and magical mayhem that are intrinsic to the script. The monologues in the play are conceived as jazz solos. In each monologue the actor's speech is conceived as a riff on a specific instrument (the director is free to choose which instrument), and both body movements and speech are rooted in classical jazz rhythms."

Rahman dislikes the distinctions—such as gender, culture, or sexual orientation—used by society to differentiate between groups of writers. "Such categories are only literary apartheid that marginalizes specific groups of writers. They are false commercial distinctions that have nothing to do with the quality of writing. There are only two kinds of writing. Good and bad."[4]

She is the cofounder of the Blackberry Production Company and a professor in Brown University's graduate creative writing program. Among the awards she has received are fellowships from the Rockefeller Foundation and the New York Foundation for the Arts, both in 1988. Rahman also writes regularly for television.

PLAYS

Another Woman, 1983; *The Lady and the Tramp,* n.d.; *Lady Day: A Musical Tragedy,* n.d.; *The Mojo and the Sayso,* 1988; *Sweet Stuff* (radio play), 1987; *The Tale of Madame Zora,* n.d.; *Transcendental Blues,* n.d.; *Unfinished Women Cry in No Man's Land While a Bird Dies in a Gilded Cage,* 1984

1. Mahone.
2. Ibid.
3. Wilkerson.
4. Op. cit., Mahone.

Franca Rame
(193?–)

PROLOGUE. Beautiful, no? Man elevated his member to his image and likeness. It is him, his thing, his power . . . the power assoluto! If we think a little, the world does not revolve around the United States . . . or Russia: The world revolves around the Grand Phallsa! The real tiger, not the paper one, is what it is! Notwithstanding its modest proportions . . .

—from *Orgasmo Adulto Escapes from the Zoo*

Franca Rame, along with her internationally known playwright husband Dario Fo, created a body of theatrical work that advocated and supported a forthrightly leftist agenda. Together the couple has been provoking audiences and governments since the late 1950s, braving criticism, imprisonment, and bodily injury for their efforts.

When questioned about her theatrical education, Rame replies that she studied at a unique Italian school for dramatic arts: her family's band of strolling players, the last and most important group of its kind. With parents, brothers, aunts, uncles, and cousins, Rame performed a repertory of eighteenth-century plays that incorporated adaptations, scenic techniques, inventions, and acting styles inspired by the puppet theater of one of northern Italy's most important theatricians, Pio Rame, Franca's grandfather. She made her stage debut when she was eight days old.

Rame left the family company in her late teens in order to garner some experience with other performance groups. While working in a show, she met Dario Fo, who was just beginning to build his reputation as an author/actor. The two found themselves aligned not only creatively but romantically. They married in 1954, and within five years founded their first company, La Compagnia Dario Fo–

Franca Rame, which enjoyed great popularity and commercial success for nine years. Their increased commitment to radical politics led them to dissolve La Compagnia in 1968 and to form Nuovo Scena, a cooperative theatrical organization allied with the Italian Communist party. But after two years, Rame and Fo seceded from Nuovo Scena, disillusioned with political factionalism within the company. They decided to devise yet another group, Il Collectivo Teatrale La Comune, an independent, self-supporting theater collective that offered the couple more creative control, but was still linked to leftist causes. Fo and Rame literally suffered for their work: In the early 1970s Fo was arrested and indicted, and, as a result of her involvement with Red Aid, a group that collected funds and comforts for Italian political prisoners, Rame was kidnapped from her Milan home by a fascist gang who beat her and left her bleeding in the street.

Although Fo initially did most of the writing for Il Collectivo, often adapting the old farces and comedies performed by the Rame family, Rame collaborated with her husband in 1977 on *It's All Church* and *Home and Bed.* They continued working on scripts, many of which ad-

Franca Rame
COURTESY OF UPI/CORBIS-BETTMANN

dress women's issues, and have frequently performed their work together. Rame also began to create her own material, establishing herself as a powerful, politicized feminist in a society tightly restricted by the Catholic church and institutionalized sexism.

Her best-known work in English is the one-woman monologue series *Female Parts* (1981), which Estelle Parsons translated, adapted, and performed under the title *Orgasmo Adulto Escapes from the Zoo* (1983; there is another English translation of an adaptation by Olwen Wymark, 1981).

According to Sue-Ellen Case,

> The play problematises the personal-political relationship between married Marxists, underlining the exploitation of the wife in the domestic sphere. Rame dramatises male sexual irresponsibility as an exploitation of women that parallels the capitalist exploitation of workers. The humour relies on the male leftist's inability to perceive the connection between a sexual, personal exploitation and the economic variety."[1]

In one of the tales, "Waking Up," the Wife tells the audience, " 'Listen Luigi,' I said, 'You get mad about how nobody pays you for your traveling time but what about me? Do I get paid for all the working and slaving I do at home? No I do not. And believe you me everything I do here is for the multinational, oh yes! . . . We recondition you, regenerate you . . . reproduce you! And all for free!' "

Rame attacks her own political roots in *La Madre* (1983), a fictional account of a mother who discovers that her son has joined the Red Brigades. The play illustrates the tragic impasse reached by the Italian far-left movement in the early 1980s. The mother says, "I went to see the corpse of one of those young policemen murdered by my son's comrades. Yes, I went to the funeral parlor. Because it's too easy to complain about things if you don't see them at first-hand."

Rame and Fo's historical drama *Ulrike Meinhof* sympathetically depicts the life and death of the female leader of, depending on one's political position, the Red Army Faction or the Baader-Meinhof Gang. The play suggests that government assassins were responsible for her alleged suicide (she was found hanged in her jail cell), although it also reminds audiences that Meinhof had advocated terrorism, stating at her trial that engaging in "an 'armed battle' to free society was legal." *Coming Home* (1988) is, in the opinion of critic Julius Novick, "a typical Fo-Rame piece, the comic tale of an ordinary woman trying to do the best she can for herself amid the old-fashioned sexism and the modern mechanization of contemporary Italian life [that possesses a] . . . Chaucerian gusto . . ."[2] Fo-Rame works of the late '80s and early '90s have continued to address issues concerning social power and control. In 1997 Fo received the Nobel Prize for Literature.

PLAYS

Accidental Death of an Anarchist, w/Dario Fo, 1974; *Coming Home* (one-act), w/D.F., 1988?; *Female Parts: One-Woman Plays*, w/D.F. (adapt. by Olwen Wymark, Margaret La Kunzle and Stuart Hood, trs., 1981; a.k.a. *Orgasmo Adulto Escapes from the Zoo*, adapt., tr., and performed by Estelle Parsons, 1983), 1981; *Home and Bed*, w/D.F., 1977; *It's All Church*, w/D.F., 1977; *Madre* (The Mother), 1983; *One Was Nude and One Wore Tails*, w/ D.F., 1985; *An Ordinary Day* (a.k.a. *A Day Like Any Other*), w/D.F., Stuart Hood, and Joe Farrell, tr., 1990; *Ulrike Meinhof* (one act), w/D.F, 1988?; *We Can't Pay, Won't Pay*, w/D.F, 1974; *A Woman Alone & Other Plays* (20 monologues), w/D.F., n.d.

OTHER WORKS

Canzonissima, w/Dario Fo (television series), 1962; *Dario Fo & Franca Rame: Workshops at Riverside Studios*, 1983

1. Case (1).

2. *Village Voice Review* by Julius Novick, January 17, 1989.

Ludmila Razumovskaya
(1948–   )

Ludmila Razumovskaya's drama *Dear Yelena Sergeyevna* deals with how many of today's young people live in a world absent of any strong moral or ethical foundation, so pressured are they to succeed in society. The play points a finger at the youths' parents, whose very lack of action or authority reveals their complicity. A teacher is approached on her birthday by four students, purportedly to offer her their congratulations. They have a hidden agenda, however. They want their grades raised so they can qualify for university. In the Soviet Union at that time, not qualifying automatically consigned young men to the army—a miserable fate. They bribe, cajole, flatter, and finally torture their instructor in a very taut psychological drama.

Born in Riga, the capital of Lithuania, Razumovskaya decided to be an actress at the age of three and wrote her first play at thirteen. When she was refused admission by the Acting Conservatory, she took up theater science, first in Leningrad, then in Moscow. In 1976 she began writing professionally for the stage. She joined a playwrights' workshop run by author Ignati Dvoresky in Leningrad in 1978. Although *Dear Yelena Sergeyevna* was her first work to be staged, it was the sixth play she had written. Banned from repertory by the Brezhnev regime, it was reinstated after Gorbachev's rise, and is now performed throughout Moscow and Germany. It was also filmed by director Eldar

Riasonov. Her plays are collected in *Garden Without Earth*.

PLAYS

Captive, n.d.; *Dear Yelena Sergeyevna* (Zoltan Schmidt and Roger Downey, trs.), 1980; *Garden Without Earth* (collection), n.d.; *Under One Roof*, n.d.; *Your Sister*, n.d.

Gerline Reinshagen
(1926–   )

BUBLITZ. What is it
That's taking hold of me now
Hanging around my neck like a stone
Like a millstone, pulling, pulling
Like I don't know what.

—from *Ironheart*, Part One, 3

Gerline Reinshagen's *Ironheart* (1981) portrays the hierarchy of class and power in the workplace, carefully delineating "the psychological and sexual effects that wage and promotional inequities have upon women."[1] While dealing with women in ordinary, clerical jobs, Reinshagen's play is no ordinary drama; she is not interested in a realistic representation. Instead she pushes the possibilities of language itself—its lyricism, syntax, meaning—so that, in the end, the play's reality, though not the "real world," makes her point far more powerfully than if she had opted for a more "true to life" depiction. Reinshagen's skill and effectiveness with this kind of theater have made her the most prominent contemporary German female playwright today. "Drama," asserts Reinshagen, "is only a revolt if it moves away from this [true to life] reality, if it forces people to think differently. I don't want to repeat the pragmatic way of life on stage."[2]

Trained as a pharmacist before turning to a career in writing, she began by penning radio plays and children's stories, and by 1956 she was working as a professional, self-supporting writer. According to Sue-Ellen Case, "Her plays chronicle the lives of German women from the Nazi era to the present. [Her works] investigate a wide variety of experiences—from illness, to the experience of fascism, to ecological concerns after Chernobyl."[3] Her trilogy, composed of *Sunday's Children* (1976), *Spring Festival* (1980), and *Dance, Marie!* (1987), examines, respectively, the lives of German women from the Nazi era, similar women during post-World War II reconstruction through the 1950s, and finally, an aging bourgeois couple in the 1980s.

At the core of many of Reinshagen's works are women, according to Case, who reach for something beyond the confines of their physical/material worlds: the protagonist of *Heaven and Earth* who chooses death by disconnecting herself from her life support systems, or the girl who sustains her inner self by relying on her imagination amidst the horrors of Nazi nihilism in *Sunday's Children*.

Reinshagen, the recipient of three major literary prizes, continues to challenge her own and her audience's concepts of theater and language. She has called for "a different dramaturgy. . . . When photography was invented, painters reacted very subjectively with impressionism and expressionism. In contrast, in this country, [theater] people try to excel the suspense on television, often even the special effects. The discrepancy between imagination and reality, the persistent pursuit of the inner image, and the failure of the original concept—for all this I would like to find a form."[4]

PLAYS

Die Clownin (The Female Clown), 1985; *Doppelkopf* (Two-Headed), 1968; *Eisenherz* (Ironheart, Sue-Ellen Case and Arlene A. Teraoka, trs.), 1981; *Die Feuerblume* (The Fire Flower), 1988; *Frühlingsfest* (Spring Festival), 2d part of trilogy, 1980; *Himmel und Erde* (Heaven and Earth; teleplay, 1976), 1974; *Leben und Tod der Marilyn Monroe* (The Life and Death of Marilyn Monroe), 1971; *Sonntagskinder*, (Sunday's Children; film, 1981) 1st part of trilogy, 1976; *Tanz, Marie!* (Dance, Marie!), 3rd part of trilogy, 1987

1. Case (1).
2. Interview by Anke Roeder in Case (2).
3. Ibid.
4. Op. cit., Roeder.

Beah Richards
(1925/8?–   )

Born in Vicksburg, Mississippi, Richards is best known for her acting work in dozens of plays, films, and television shows. Her role in the film *Guess Who's Coming to Dinner* (1967) won her a nomination for the Academy Award for best supporting actress. Most admirers who recognize her face, however, are unaware of Richards's role as a playwright. She has written only two plays, *A Black Woman Speaks* (1950), created expressly for Women for Peace in Chicago, and the full-length *One Is a Crowd* (completed in 1951, but not produced until 1970); however, her initiative in creating the first one-woman show by an African-American and her courage in speaking out, both on stage and off, about the experience of being black and female in America mark her as an important theater innovator and pioneer.

Emmy winner *A Black Woman Speaks* is a long poetic monologue in which a black woman addresses white women and confronts them with their role in the oppression of black people. In contrast with the confrontational one-act is the full-length *One Is a Crowd*, which follows a nightclub singer on her quest for revenge against the white father of her half brother. While the play embodies humor, its social sense demands the emancipation of the black woman—both from male domination and from whites.

Richards was educated at Dillard University in New Orleans before she went on to study for three years at the San Diego Community Theater. From California she relocated to New York City, and made her Broadway debut in the 1956 drama *Take a Giant Step*—playing the grandmother, despite her youth. Three years later she made her film debut in the same role. She has been honored with a Tony for best dramatic actress for *The Amen Corner* (1965) and an Emmy for outstanding guest performer in a comedy or drama series for *Frank's Place* (1988). Richards was inducted into the Black Filmmakers Hall of Fame in 1974. She is an active member of the Congress of Racial Equality and the NAACP.

PLAYS

A Black Woman Speaks, 1950; *One Is a Crowd*, 1970

OTHER WORKS

A Black Woman Speaks and Other Poems, 1964

Anne Ridler
(JULY 30, 1912–)

CRANMER. I am too old to learn, Ralph.
MORICE and THIRLBY. My lord Archbishop!
CRANMER. A scholar, you know, is a wingless creature
More tortoise than bird.
MARGARET. But with a bird's domain: that domain of your prayers.
I have often lost you there: I could bear to lose you now
To that place. It does not touch our ground,
But hangs between heaven and our despair of heaven,
Close and calm as a mountain on a clear day
And just as unreachable.

—from *The Trial of Thomas Cranmer*, Sc. 1

Before finding success as a poet, playwright, and librettist, Anne Ridler labored at the publishing house of Faber &

Faber where, for some time, she worked as a secretary for T. S. Eliot. Born in Rugby, Warwickshire, Anne Barbara Bradby was educated at King's College in London. Her main residence has been in Oxford. She and her husband Vivian Ridler married in 1938 and had two sons and two daughters.

Ridler's several dramatic works, all written in blank verse, are based on folktales and historical events. *Henry Bly* (1947), for example, which exemplifies salvation through the work of a miracle worker first thought to be a simpleton, is taken from the Grimm Brothers' "Brother Lustig." *The Trial of Thomas Cranmer* (1956) depicts the sixteenth-century religious reformer's rise as archbishop of Canterbury under Henry VIII and his eventual execution under the Roman Catholic Mary I. Ridler has commented, "It is a great advantage for a dramatist to know the cast and place he [sic] is writing for, the audience he is addressing. . . . Only rarely have I had this opportunity, and this is perhaps why *Thomas Cranmer*, commissioned for performance in the church where Cranmer was tried, has been judged my best play."[1]

Religiosity is frequently a theme in Ridler's plays. In 1946 she wrote a modern-day nativity play, *The Shadow Factory*. The drama is set in a Metropolis-like factory where workers churn out products each day. The company director likes to think of himself as benevolent, and he commissions a mural as an exemplary act, but the chosen artist uses the work to reveal the Orwellian shadow beneath which the employees slave.

Most recently Ridler's forays into the theatrical realm have been via librettos that she has translated. These "singing versions," as she fancies them, stem from the texts of Monteverdi, Cavalli, Handel, and Mozart, as well as the more contemporary Elizabeth Maconchy and Robert Sherlaw Johnson. Christopher Smith praises her "rare combination of verbal and musical sensitivity [that has] set high standards in this very testing art form."[2]

Best known for her poetry, Ridler avoids "grand phrases and extravagant imagery. Instead she prefers a sober style, rarely enlivened by metaphor and spiced with just occasional dry wit. She knows the power of monosyllables and has enough confidence in the power of her verse to avoid gross effects."[3] In addition to exploring religiosity, Ridler's poems celebrate human experience, notably marriage and motherhood. Ironically, her work has occasionally been compared to that of T. S. Eliot, the man for whom she once typed.

PLAYS

Agrippina, (tr. of Grimani libretto), music by Handel, 1982; *Cain*, 1943; *La Calisto*, (tr. of Faustini libretto), music by Cavalli, 1984; *The Coronation of Poppea*, (tr. of Busenello libretto), music by Monteverdi, 1992; *Così fan Tutte* (also teleplay), (tr. of da Ponte libretto), music by Mozart, 1988; *The Departure*, music by Elizabeth Maconchy, 1961; *Don Giovanni*, (tr. of da Ponte libretto), music by Mozart, 1990; *Eritrea*, (tr. of Faustini libretto), music by Cavalli, 1975; *Henry Bly*, 1947; *The Jesse Tree*, music by Elizabeth Maconchy, 1970; *The King of the Golden River*, music by Maconchy, 1975; *The Lambton Worm*, music by Robert Sherlaw Johnson, 1978; *The Marriage of Figaro*, (tr. of da Ponte libretto), music by Mozart, 1991; *The Mask, and The Missing Bridegroom*, 1951; *Orfeo*, (tr. of Striggio libretto), music by Monteverdi, 1975; *Orontea*, (tr. of Cicognini libretto), music by Cesti, n.d.; *The Return of Ulysses*, (tr. of Badoaro libretto), music by Monteverdi, 1978; *Rosinda*, (tr. of Faustini libretto), music by Cavalli, 1975; *The Shadow Factory*, 1946; *The Trial of Thomas Cranmer*, music by Bryan Kelly, 1956; *Who Is My Neighbour?*, 1961

VERSE

Dies Natalist, 1980; *A Dream Observed and Other Poems*, 1941; *The Golden Bird and Other Poems*, 1951; *Italian Prospect*, 1976; *A Matter of Life and Death*, 1959; *New and Selected Poems*, 1988; *The Nine Bright Shiners*, 1943; *Poems*, 1939; *Selected Poems*, 1961; *Some Time After and Other Poems*, 1972; *Ten Poems*, w/E. J. Scovell, 1984

OTHER WORKS

A Victorian Family Postbag, 1988; *Olive Willis and Downe House: An Adventure in Education*, 1967; *Profitable Wonders: Aspects of Thomas Traherne*, w/A. M. Allchin and Julia Smith, 1989

1. Quoted by Christopher Smith in Berney (1).
2. Op. cit., Smith.
3. Ibid.

crime-solving heroine who ultimately had to be rescued from the villain by a male detective. Rinehart's literary output was enormous: She averaged a book a year for more than forty years. By the time of her death, her books had sold more than ten million copies in regular editions and had been translated into thirteen languages!

In 1920 Rinehart and playwright James Avery Hopwood coauthored *The Bat*, a play based on her book *The Circular Staircase*; the play enjoyed a long run and was revised in 1953. The duo collaborated on three more plays, and Rinehart wrote several on her own.

She and her husband, Stanley Marshall Rinehart, had three sons: one, Alan, followed his mother's footsteps and became a writer. The other two formed the book publishing firm known today as Rinehart & Co. Mary was a director of the company, as well as one of its most productive authors. In addition to her mysteries, she wrote the popular "Tish" stories, about a funny, self-reliant single woman. Her first two books, *The Circular Staircase* and *The Man in Lower Ten*, were still in print forty years after their original publication.

Rinehart died in her New York City apartment of a heart ailment at the age of eighty-two.

PLAYS

The Avenger, 1909; *The Bat*, w/Avery Hopwood, 1920; *The Breaking Point*, 1921; *Cheer Up*, 1912; *The Double Life*, 1906; *Seven Days*, w/A. H., 1931; *Spanish Love*, w/A. H., 1920; *A Thief in the Night*, w/A. H., 1920

OTHER WORKS (SELECTED)

The After House, n.d.; *The Album*, 1933; *The Amazing Interlude*, 1918; *The Best of Tish*, 1955; *The Circular Staircase*, 1908; *Episode of the Wandering Knife*, n.d.; *K*, 1915; *The Man in Lower Ten*, 1909; *My Story* (autobio.), 1931 (rev. 1948); *The State Versus Elinor Norton*, 1934; *Swimming Pool*, 1951

May Roberts Rinehart
(AUGUST 12, 1876–SEPTEMBER 22, 1958)

LIZZIE. I've stood by you through thick and thin—I stood by you when you were a Vegetarian—I stood by you when you were a Theosophist—and I seen you through Socialism, Fletcherism and Rheumatism—but when it comes to carrying on with ghosts—

—from *The Bat*, Scene 1

Pittsburgh-born Mary Roberts Rinehart was best known for her mystery stories, which featured an intelligent,

---

Erika Ritter
(1948–)

NICK. You people with "pure motives." You make me nervous.
CHARLIE. Oh, I'm not so pure . . .
NICK. I don't get it. . . . If I can do you a favour, why not? What is it, you've got your life in ledger columns? "Business." "Romance."
CHARLIE. That's right. Just don't mix me in with business, that's all. This town is one giant office. Casting done in bars. Contracts ratified on waterbeds. People sucking up to power

because it might rub off. Those macrobiotic people had it all wrong. Around here, you are *who* you eat.

—from *The Automatic Pilot*, Act I, Scene 3

Like many of Erika Ritter's quirky heroines, Charlie, the stand-up comedienne protagonist of *The Automatic Pilot* (1978), uses sharp verbal repartee to shield herself from the twisted arrows of love and life in the "indecisive age," as the author puts it, of the late twentieth century. Ritter's women struggle with their world's weird rules for sex, sentimentality, art, and folly. Eva, the would-be actress at the center of *A Visitor from Charleston* (1975), escapes from her dull life as a new divorcee by repeatedly viewing *Gone with the Wind*, until her reverie is interrupted by a pushy cosmetics salesman. The memories Eva relives during the protracted sales pitch illustrate Ritter's familiar themes of the conflicts faced by women with artistic and romantic aspirations.

Although her female characters are engaging and often forthright, Ritter "never takes a straight feminist direction. She refuses just to blame 'patriarchal' society, and insists that many women (like Charlie) are their own worst enemies."[1] For example, in *Murder at McQueen* (1986) three women, each a decade apart in age, share their attachment to Rex, a male chauvinist talk-show host. The eldest of the three opens the McQueen Club as a place to nurse her own broken heart. But despite the members' desire to support each other, the women fail in their efforts. When the youngest of the trio, Norah, looks up Rex with the intention of protecting her friend, she winds up in bed with him.

Ritter has juggled a number of professional positions: professor at Loyola College in Montreal, host of "Dayshift" (a Canadian radio program), and stand-up comedian. After earning a degree in drama from McGill University in Montreal, she went on to obtain a master's degree from the Drama Centre at the University of Toronto in 1970. She has written for radio and television, and her short stories have appeared in publications such as *Saturday Night, Ms.*, and *Chatelaine*. She has received several awards, among them the Chalmers Award in 1980 and the Alliance of Canadian Cinema, Television, and Radio Artists (ACTRA) Award in 1982.

PLAYS

The Automatic Pilot, 1978; *Murder at McQueen*, 1986; *The Passing Scene*, 1982; *The Splits*, 1978; *A Visitor from Charleston*, 1975; *Winter 1671*, 1979

RADIO PLAYS

Dayshift, 1985; *The Girl I Left Behind Me*, n.d.; *Miranda*, 1985; *The Road to Hell*, 1985; *Smith and Wesson*, n.d.

OTHER WORKS

Ritter in Residence, 1987; *Urban Scrawl*, 1984

1. Essay by Dorothy Parker in Berney (1).

Friederike Roth
(1948–   )

SHE. (*Raging*) Until the day I die I will insist absolutely that shared joy is half-joy. That love sings and swings and makes you uncritical and doesn't deal in accounts paid in advance, like a greedy, shriveled-up old woman.

—from *Piano Plays*, Scene 12

Raised in what she considers "a very simple home" in Germany, Friederike Roth says that when she was a child and could not sleep, her father would sit on her bed and read her the poetry of Hölderlin.* To this day, she says, she has "the Hölderlin rhythm in [her] ear."[1] Before Roth began to pursue creative work, she earned her doctorate in philosophy and linguistics, and worked as a university lecturer in anthropology and sociology. She studied with Max Bense at the Institute for Philosophical Theory in Stuttgart, focusing on literature as well as classical philosophy. Yet she found herself wanting to create literary works. She began by writing poetry, then experimented with what she calls "minimal stories" before finally writing plays.

According to Sue-Ellen Case, Roth has always been drawn to writing dialogue: "It's connected with the method of my mind, with the way I hear sentences and store them up."[2] Many of Roth's dramas deal frankly with issues of men and women and power. Her first work for the stage, *Piano Plays* (1980), is a lyrical treatment of gender and culture in modern Germany. The piano in the play is owned by SHE, a singer who cannot play it, and is played by HE. But when HE leaves SHE, he cannot take the piano with him, and she cannot bring herself to sell it. Case interprets the piano to duplicitously signify cultural production and the female body: The man has access to it, and the woman cannot use it without the man. In the play, SHE has no personal style in her singing, but wanders from one style to another, trying to find something that will satisfy her. The allusion to promiscuity is unavoidable. Roth offers no solutions to the "games" she puts forth in her play, but the questions and issues she raises, and the way in which she does so, are provocative

---

*Hölderlin, (Johann Christian) Friedrich (1770–1843), one of the greatest German lyric poets; his work forms a bridge between the classical and romantic schools. His poetry, forgotten for many years, was rediscovered early in the twentieth century.

and delectable. The play's first production in Hamburg, directed by Christof Nel, was, in Roth's estimation, a disaster. The character SHE was vulgarized in her dress and made to strip on stage; the male character exhibited no individuality but a great deal of aggressiveness. Roth had been not present during the play's rehearsals, and was shocked and dismayed by what she considered the ruination of her work.

Journey up the Wartburg (1981), her follow-up to *Piano Plays*, humorously tackles such feminist issues as aging, sexual objectification, and, of course, sexual relationships with men, within the context of the differences between West and East German society. The plot centers on a small group of West German women who decide to take their vacation in East Germany.

Roth is the recipient of multiple literary prizes, and numerous collections of her poetry have been published, as have several radio plays. Roth has also translated into German two plays by Dorothy Parker and the only drama composed by Jane Bowles, *In the Summer House* (1953).

PLAYS

Die einzige Geschichte (The Only Story), 1983; *Das Ganze ein Stük* (The Whole: A Piece), 1986; *Klavierspiele* (Piano Plays, Andra Weddington, tr.), 1980; *Krötenbrunnen* (Toad Wells), 1984; *Ritt auf die Wartburg* (Journey up the Wartburg), 1981

1. Case (2).
2. Ibid.

Susanna Haswell Rowson
(1762–1824)

HENRY. This fellow will do some mischief, with his nonsensical prate.

—from *Slaves in Algiers*, Act III, Scene 1

Even though English-born Susanna Haswell Rowson has been recognized as one of America's first produced women playwrights, her works have essentially disappeared into obscurity. During the first four years of her life, she was raised by a hired nurse in Portsmouth, England. Her widowed father, Lt. William Haswell, had ventured to the New World, where he fought Indians in the "wild West." Finally, remarried and resigned from his post, he sent for his daughter in the fall of 1766. Rowson and her nurse endured a torturous trip, rife with rough waters and cramped quarters. The ship finally sighted Boston Harbor on January 27, 1767, but foundered before it reached dry

land. The girl and her guardian spent three miserable days afloat in a lifeboat until a rescue party saved them.

In America Rowson found herself under the tutelage of James Otis, a friend of her father's and brother to MERCY OTIS WARREN. She proved herself to be a fine pupil and was soon reading the classics in Greek and Latin, along with the plays of Shakespeare and other Elizabethan dramatists. However, Rowson's stay in America ended with the onset of the Revolutionary War. Her father's Tory past impelled their return to England. This trip was a veritable repeat of Rowson's first journey; by the time they reached British soil, most of their possessions had been lost.

Once in London, her father tried unsuccessfully to secure a pension for himself. Rowson, who had taken a position as a governess, decided to intervene. Through her friend the Duchess of Devonshire, she met the Prince Regent (and future King George IV). She struck up a flirtation with him, her first of several indiscretions, and eventually the young man signed Haswell's pension order. Rowson promptly ended the romance.

Shortly thereafter, she married William Rowson, a pudgy, middle-aged trumpeter who played in the Royal Horse Guard's band. She also began to write novels. An early effort, *Charlotte Temple* (1794), became a best-seller in England and America, and remained in print until World War II. Still, by 1792, she and William, who turned out to be an alcoholic and a womanizer, were financially insolvent. They decided to join a troupe of players headed for Thomas Wignell's New Theatre Company in Philadelphia. They rehearsed their first play on the voyage to America (finally, a sound journey).

Rowson became a company favorite. She exhibited a natural aptitude for all things theatrical: acting, story adaptation, and lyric writing. Her flair for musical interludes launched a popular new form; one modern-day critic dubbed her "the mother of that uniquely American art form—the Broadway musical!"[1] Some of her most popular shows were *Slaves of Algiers* (1794), a musical farce, and *The Volunteers* (1795), a song-filled entertainment based on the Whiskey Rebellion.

Rowson retired from the stage in 1797. She opened a Massachusetts school for "young ladies." Her biographer, Dorothy Weil, wrote that "Mrs. Rowson was singularly fitted for the office of a teacher. Her industry and intelligence were great and her knowledge and skill in household economy were almost unparalleled."[2] Within three years her school had acquired the affections of Boston's elite—a remarkable achievement, considering Rowson's dubious past. Her writing at this time took a turn toward scholastics, and her textbooks were used in schools for more than fifty years.

PLAYS

Americans in England, 1797; *The American Tar,* 1796; *The Female Patriot,* 1794; *Slaves of Algiers,* 1794; *The Volunteers,* 1795

OTHER WORKS

Charlotte Temple (repr. 1986), 1794

WORKS ABOUT

Nason, Elias, *A Memoir of Mrs. Susanna Rowson,* 1870; Parker, Patricia L., *Susanna Rowson,* 1981; Weil, Dorothy, *In Defense of Women: Susanna Rowson 1762–1824,* 1976

1. Cotton

2. Weil, Dorothy, *In Defense of Women: Susanna Rowson* (University Park, Penn.: Pennsylvania State University Press, 1976).

S

Françoise Sagan
(JUNE 21, 1935–   )

Françoise Sagan burst on the French literary scene in 1954 at the tender age of nineteen with *Bonjour, tristesse*, a melodramatic, yet mature, portrayal of a disillusioned French bourgeois society. The Sorbonne-educated Sagan, (Sagan is the pseudonym of Françoise Quoirez), has gone on to publish a number of novels that feature aimless individuals often entangled in amoral relationships.

In the early 1960s Sagan began writing works for the stage, often writing in the style of the bourgeois comedy of manners. Thematically, her plays are quite similar to her novels. *Bonheur, impair et passe* (The Quirks of Chance, 1964) depicts a guilt-ridden soldier who is in love with his lame friend's wife. In *Le cheval évanoui* (The Vanishing Horse; 1966), a calculating young man attempts to convince his lover to marry his rich fiancée's brother, but she falls in love with the wealthy father instead.

Sagan has also written short stories, nonfiction, and screenplays. Several of her works have been adapted for film, including *Bonjour, tristesse*, which starred the American actor Jean Seberg.

PLAYS

Bonheur, impair et passe (The Quirks of Chance), 1964; *Château en Suède* (Castle in Sweden), 1960; *Le cheval évanoui* (The Vanishing Horse), 1966; *L'écharde* (The Splinter), 1966; *L'excès contraire* (Opposite Extremes), 1987; *La robe mauve de Valentine* (The Purple Dress of Valentine), 1963; *Un piano dans l'herbe* (A Piano on the Lawn), 1970; *Les violons parfois* (Violins Sometimes), 1961

NOVELS (SELECTED)

Aimez-vous Brahms? (Goodbye Again), 1959; *Bonjour, tristesse*, 1954; *Un certain sourire* (A Certain Smile), 1956; *La femme fardee* (*The Painted Lady*, 1983), 1981; *A Fleeting Sorrow*, 1995; *Le garde du coeur; roman* (The Heartkeeper), 1968; *Incidental Music* (tr. by C. J. Richards), 1983; *Lost Profile*, 1976; *Povesti*, 1991; *A Reluctant Hero*, 1987; *Salad Days*, 1984; *Sarah Bernhardt: le rire incassable* (Dear Sarah Bernhardt), 1987; *Scars on the Soul*, 1974; *Toxique*, 1964; *With Fondest Regards* (Christine Donougher, tr.), 1985; *Des yeux de soie: nouvelles* (Silken eyes, 1977), 1976

OTHER WORKS

Night Bird: Conversations with Françoise Sagan (David Macey, tr.), 1980

Christopher (Marie) St. John
(188?–OCTOBER 20, 1960)

WINIFRED. The majority of men in this country shouldn't for years have kept alive the foolish superstition that all women are supported by men. For years we have told them it was a delusion, but they could not take our arguments seriously.

—from *How the Vote Was Won*

A specialist in adapting novels for the stage, St. John was also a novelist, translator, and biographer. She contributed weekly articles on theater and music to *Time and Tide* (1920–31). She also translated HROTSVITHA's *Paphnutius*, and edited many of the letters and writings of actress Ellen Terry. Active in the suffragist movement, she and Cicely Hamilton, another early British feminist, constructed *How the Vote Was Won* (1909), a play that was "quickly recognised by American suffragettes as an exceptionally seductive vehicle for their movement and was performed repeatedly in the United States, especially on the West Coast."[1]

A satire, *Vote* revolves around an Englishman, Horace, who initially righteously extolls the virtue of a woman's place (not in the voting booth). As the play progresses, all of his female relatives, apparently yielding to his dogma, decide to leave their jobs and households and move in with him so that he can care for him, as any proper "master" would. By the play's end Horace has become a passionate advocate for women's suffrage. Keyssar says, "The play not only reveals the absurdity of the logical extension of a social configuration in which women are dependent on men but also demonstrates the potential power of women."[2]

St. John is also credited as being the cofounder of the Writers' Franchise League.

PLAYS

The Brothers Karamazov (adapt.), 1913; *The Children's Carnival* (adapt.), 1920; *The Coronation*, 1911; *The Decision*, 1906; *Du Barry* (adapt.), 1905; *Eriksson's Wife*, 1904; *The First Actress*, 1911; *The Good Hope* (adapt.) 1903; *How the Vote was Won*, 1909; *Macrena*, 1912; *On the East Side*, 1908; *Paphnutius* (adapt. from HROTSVITHA), 1914; *The Pot and the Kettle*, w/Cicely Hamilton, 1909; *The Rising Sun* (adapt.), 1919; *The Wilson Trial*, 1909

OTHER WORKS

Ellen Terry and Bernard Shaw (the correspondence), ed., 1931; *Ellen Terry's Memoirs*, coed. w/Edith Craig, 1933; *Four Lectures on Shakespeare by Ellen Terry*, ed., 1932; *Hungerheart* (novel), n.d.; *Medieval Library: Plays of Hrosvita*, tr., n.d.; *Stars of the Stage: Ellen Terry*, 1907; *The Crimson Weed* (novel), n.d.

1. Keyssar.
2. Ibid.

Milcha Sánchez-Scott
(1954/55–)

SARITA. See, what I actually want to be . . . I mean, what I really am is an actress. . . . I'll give you my credits. I was a barrio girl who got raped by a gang in Police Story, a young barrio mother who got raped by a gang in Starsky and Hutch, a barrio wife who got beat up by her husband who was in a

gang in the Rookies. I was even a barrio lesbian who got knifed by an all-girl gang called the Mal-flores . . . that means Bad Flowers. It's been a regular barrio blitz on television lately. If this fad continues, I can look forward to being a barrio grandmother done-in by a gang of old Hispanics called Los Viejitos Diabilitos, the old devils.

—from *Latina*, Act 1, Scene 2

The urban candidness of Milcha Sánchez-Scott's plays obscures her exotic upbringing. She was born in Bali to a Colombian agronomist father and an Indonesian-Chinese-Dutch mother. Her early education occurred near London at a Catholic girls' school. There she learned English and enjoyed a warm relationship with the nuns, with whom she played toy soldier games. The family spent summer and Christmas holidays at their home in Santa Marta. They would journey two hours to attend their church, an ancient building replete with dirt floor, indigenous paintings of the Virgin Mary, and, lodged in the rafters, the saintly offerings of *milagros*—tin, wooden, or clay ornaments that replicated healed body parts. "My early life was sheer fantasy," says Sánchez-Scott. "Eccentricity was so natural that I didn't know it was eccentricity!"[1]

Her life changed radically when her family moved to La Jolla, California, a suburb of San Diego. For the first time she experienced the brutalities of racism. On her first day of public school, while she was waiting for the bus, a group of local boys threw pebbles at her, taunting, "Go to the Mexican bus stop!" Her mother immediately registered her in an Episcopalian girls' school. Although Sánchez-Scott led a privileged life, she remained keenly aware of her position as a Latin American immigrant. One summer she picked fruits and vegetables alongside migrant workers. After graduating from the University of San Diego with a degree in literature, philosophy, and theater, she took a job at a Beverly Hills employment agency for housecleaners. Sánchez-Scott calls it "the best job I ever had. These immigrant women who had their feet on the ground and their eyes on the stars and their hearts full of love, strengthened me. It was like meeting at the river."[2]

Her award-winning play *Latina* (1980) grew out of that experience. *Latina* examines the white community's exploitation of undocumented workers. The drama begins by chronicling the journey of New Girl from her Peruvian mountain village across the barbed-wired American border and into the Felix Sánchez Domestic Agency in Los Angeles. There, New Girl and seven other disparate Latinas relate their stories to each other. The show ends with a raid by "la migra," the Immigration and Naturalization Service, as yet another New Girl wriggles her way under the barbed-wire fence. Although Sánchez-Scott remains sympathetic to her main characters, she pokes fun at some of the women's cultures: "I'm human," boasts an arrogant Cubana, "I have a green card." Stylistically, *Latina* balances realistic dialogue—the women routinely mix Spanish and English—with expressionistic techniques—the fourth wall is broken and mannequins talk and move. The play opened at L.A. Theatre Works and won seven Dramalogue Critics Circle Awards. She followed up *Latina* with *The Cuban Swimmer* (1982), in which a young woman enters an invitational race, only to be victimized by the condescending American media and the pressure of her family.

In 1984 the International Arts Relation (INTAR) invited Sánchez-Scott to join IRENE FORNES's workshop. Broke, she pawned some jewelry and bought a ticket to New York City. The workshop proved particularly favorable for her when a friend incidentally showed her "a picture of relatives of his . . . [The man] was a rooster trainer; [he'd] been in and out of jail on drug charges, robbery. [The woman] was looking up at him like he was heaven on earth."[3] This photograph became the impetus for *Roosters* (1987), a tough drama about the violent world of cockfighting. The macho pride experienced by men who own and train winning cocks serves as a metaphor for a father and son's conflictive relationship. Ultimately the play confronts the temptations of violence for Latinos. "Each of us chooses whether to continue this legacy, this culture of violence," comments Laura Esparza, who directed a 1994 production of the play at The Group in Seattle. "The family in this play is caught between these choices; whether to continue a family and cultural tradition which is violent or transcend it to create a new destiny."[4] *Roosters* also illustrates Sánchez-Scott's great talent for humorously conveying feelings of great longing, as when Chata retells how, when she discovered she had begun to menstruate, her grandmother said to her, " 'Ah! So you're a woman now. Got your own cycle like the moon. Soon you'll want a man. Well this is what you do. When you see the one you want, you roll the tortilla on the inside of your thigh and then you give it to him nice and warm. Be sure you give it to him and nobody else.' Well, I been rolling tortillas on my thighs, on my nalgas, and God only knows where else, but I've been giving my tortillas to the wrong men . . ."

Sánchez-Scott has received many honors, including the Vesta Award, the Le Compte du Noüy Foundation Award, and a First Level Award for American Playwrights from the Rockefeller Foundation. John Kuhn wrote that Sánchez-Scott finds "holes within harsh realities through which stream magical visions, spells, miraculous cures, transformations, and an old religious faith in past and future."[5]

PLAYS

City of Angels (in progress); *The Cuban Swimmer*, 1982; *Dog Lady*, 1984; *El Dorado*, 1990; *Evening Star*, 1988;

Latina, 1980; *Paper Wedding, Roosters*, 1987; *Stone Wedding*, 1989

1. Osborn.

2. Ibid.

3. Ibid.

4. Program notes, *The Group* 3, no. 1 (August/September 1994) Seattle, Wash.

5. Essay by John G. Kuhn in Berney (2).

Dorothy L. Sayers
(JUNE 13, 1893–DECEMBER 17, 1957)

The only sin passion can commit is to be joyless.

—from *Busman's Honeymoon*

Lauded for her masterful Lord Peter Wimsey detective stories and novels, Dorothy Sayers's religious dramas are often unknown to her fans; however, they comprise a significant piece of her life's work. Sayers's theological interests were influenced in part by her beloved father, the Reverend Henry Sayers, headmaster of the Christchurch Cathedral Choir School and a shy, scholarly man. Reverend Sayers encouraged his daughter's intellect from an early age. She began studying Latin at the age of six, and quickly moved on to French and German. At the Godolphin School in Salisbury, which she attended from 1909–11, she was introduced to theatrics and demonstrated her interest by penning a one-act entitled *The Mocking of Christ*, foreshadowing her midlife calling to theological drama. A scholarship to Somerville College at Oxford University afforded her the opportunity to study medieval literature. She completed her studies in 1915, but did not receive her degree until 1920, when Oxford graduated its first class of women. Sayers took first-class honors in her field.

After graduation she worked at a variety of jobs, eventually landing an administrative position at Les Roches School in France. Her year in Europe left its mark on the impressionable Sayers: She drove a motorcycle, read sensational novels, smoked cigarettes, befriended artists and writers, and thoroughly became one of the "new women" who rejected the rigid Victorianism of their childhoods. When she returned to London in the early 1920s, she found employment as a copywriter at Benson's Advertising Agency (the setting for her 1933 novel *Murder Must Advertise*). Over the next ten years, Sayers juggled her day job and her writing pursuits. She suffered at least one romantic misfortune, which resulted in the birth of a son; she relinquished the boy's custody to a cousin. Eventually, at the age of thirty-three, she married Oswald Atherton Fleming, a lover of history, machinery, and photography, and a former war correspondent. The marriage was not fulfilling. Within three years Atherton succumbed fully to alcoholism. Sayers suffered further personal anguish when both of her parents died during the same brief period. Ironically, however, she was by this time enjoying enormous professional success. Readers loved the nobleman-detective Lord Peter Wimsey and devoured his adventures as quickly as Sayers could create them. In 1931 she quit her job at Benson's and devoted herself to writing.

Around this time Sayers, with G. K. Chesterton and others, founded the Detection Club, a group composed of mystery writers, and they published a parody of the detective story in a novel entitled *The Floating Admiral* (1931).

In the mid-1930s Sayers's interest in theater and liturgical drama was reinvigorated. She brought Peter Wimsey to the London stage with *The Busman's Honeymoon* in 1936; it ran for 400 performances and was soon adapted for film. That same year, she penned a popular religious radio play, *He That Should Come*, notable for its characterizations of Jesus Christ, Judas, and Peter, who are portrayed "with histories and psychology and relationships and accents and tastes that make them thoroughly human."[1] Sayers undertook a third dramatic endeavor that year when The Friends of Canterbury Cathedral commissioned her to write a chancel drama (relating to the church building itself). She delivered to them *The Zeal of Thy House*, a drama in verse about William of Sens, the twelfth-century architect who designed and rebuilt the cathedral choir after its destruction by fire, but, before he completed the project, died in a fall from the scaffolding. The Friends were extremely pleased with Sayers's work, and she was soon flooded with requests for religious historical plays.

Before devoting herself completely to liturgical drama, she wrote one last commercial stage play, *Love All* (1940), a sophisticated comedy about a liberated woman who finds success in the theater after being badly treated by her wayward husband. Then, in 1941, she created what some critics consider her greatest achievement. The British Broadcasting Corporation radio drama *The Man Born to Be King* is a cycle play on the life of Jesus Christ that combined Sayers's theological interests and historical knowledge with her fine skills at character development and dialogue. *King* caused some controversy when the author insisted on presenting a humanized Jesus Christ (an illegal action in 1940) and having her characters speak in modern dialect. But Sayers's demands prevailed. Since its original broadcast, the play has been produced all over the world.

Sayers became deeply involved in the many productions of her religious works right up until her last days. Scholar Nancy Tischler identifies Sayers's theological themes as "the reality of evil, the folly of humanistic faith, the wisdom of the creeds and the church fathers, the reality and dramatic power of Jesus Christ."[2] Toward the end of her life, she wrote theological essays and made several scholarly translations, including three volumes of Dante's *Divine Comedy (Hell, Purgatory,* and *Paradise,* the latter uncompleted at the time of her death).

Sayers was a highly unusual woman who gracefully balanced ardent feminist beliefs and great religious conviction along with intelligence, wit, talent, and the self-discipline to put them to good use. Her chancel plays brought Christ to the modern theater. Her translation of Dante created an audience among the reading public. And Lord Peter Wimsey is one of the most memorable detectives in the English language, along with AGATHA CHRISTIE's Miss Marple and Hercule Poirot and Dashiel Hammet's Nick Charles.

PLAYS

Busman's Honeymoon (novel, 1937; film, 1940), 1936; *The Devil to Pay,* 1939; *The Emperor Constantine,* 1951; *He That Should Come* (radio play), 1936; *The Just Vengeance,* 1946; *Love All* (a.k.a. *Cat's Cradle*), 1940; *The Man Born to Be King* (radio series), 1941–42; *The Mocking of Christ,* 1918; *The Zeal of Thy House,* 1937

OTHER WORKS (SELECTED)
FICTION

Clouds of Witness, 1926; *The Five Red Herrings,* 1931; *Gaudy Night,* 1935; *Hangman's Holiday,* 1933; *In the Teeth of the Evidence and Other Stories,* 1939; *Lord Peter Views the Body,* 1928; *Murder Must Advertise,* 1933; *The Nine Tailors,* 1934; *Strong Poison,* 1930; *Unnatural Death* (a.k.a. *The Dawson Pedigree*), 1927; *The Unpleasantness at the Bellona Club,* 1928; *Whose Body?,* 1923

NONFICTION

Are Women Human?, 1971; *Begin Here: A War-Time Essay,* 1940; *Christian Letters to a Post-Christian World,* ed. Roderick Jellema, 1969 (repr., *The Whimsical Christian,* 1978); *Creed or Chaos? and Other Essays in Popular Theology,* 1947; *A Matter of Eternity,* ed. Rosamond Kent Sprague, 1973; *The Mind of the Maker,* 1941; *The Poetry of Search and the Poetry of Statement . . . ,* 1963; *Strong Meat,* 1939; *Unpopular Opinions,* 1946

TRANSLATIONS

The Comedy of Dante Alighieri the Florentine, Canticas I, II, III (III completed by Barbara Reynolds), 1949–62; *Tristan in Brittany . . . by Thomas the Anglo-Norman,* 1929

WORKS ABOUT

Dale, Alzina Stone, *Maker and Craftsman*, 1978; Harmon, Robert B., and Margaret A. Burger, *An Annotated Guide to the Works of Dorothy L. Sayers*. 1978; Hitchman, Janet, *Such a Strange Lady*, 1952; Hone, Ralph E., *Dorothy L. Sayers: A Literary Biography*, 1979; Tischler, Nancy M., *A Pilgrim Soul*, 1980

1. Essay by Nancy Tischler in Weintraub.

2. Ibid.

Ntozake Shange
(OCTOBER 18, 1948–   )

ALL. i found god in myself/& i loved her/i loved her fiercely.

—from *for colored girls who have considered suicide/ when the rainbow is enuf*

"I was always what you call a nice child," Ntozake Shange (pronounced *n-toe-záhky sháwn-gay*) once said. "I did everything nice. I was the nicest and most correct. I did my homework. I was always on time. I never got into fights. People now ask me, 'Where did all this rage come from?' And I just smile and say it's been there all the time, but I was just trying to be nice."[1]

Shange was born Paulette Williams in Trenton, New Jersey. Both of her parents were successful professionals: her father was a prominent surgeon, and her mother a psychiatric social worker and educator. With her two sisters and brother, she enjoyed a childhood filled with an appreciation of literature, art, music, and African-American culture. Most family members displayed musical talent, and at times the Williams children played as a quartet, with Shange on violin and her siblings on cello, flute, and saxophone. Occasionally they were joined by their father on congas. The Williamses developed close relationships with notable African-Americans such as Dizzy Gillespie, Miles Davis, Chuck Berry, and W. E. B. Du Bois, along with lesser-known writers and musicians. Yet, in spite of this culturally rich upbringing, Shange encountered the bitter reality of sexism at a young age. When she voiced her desire to be either a war correspondent or a jazz musician, she was told that those professions were "no good for a woman."[2] In spite of this rebuff (or perhaps because of it), she set out to prove otherwise.

She enrolled at Barnard College in New York, and in 1970 graduated magna cum laude with a degree in American studies. She then moved to the West Coast, where she received an M.A. in American studies from the University of Southern California in 1973. Soon she was swept up in the feminist and African-American renaissance occurring within the arts community in the Los Angeles area.

Ntozake Shange
COURTESY OF UPI/CORBIS-BETTMANN

It was then that Paulette Williams cast off her "slave name," as she put it, and chose to honor her African heritage by assuming the name Ntozake Shange, Zulu for "she who comes with her own things" and "she who walks like a lion." She befriended dancer-choreographer Paula Moss, and the two, along with several other musicians, began to assemble lively theatrical works that combined poetry, music, and dance.

Shange stayed with the project for several years, performing with the collective in bars and cafés in Los Angeles, San Francisco, and New York City. By 1975 the show had a title: *for colored girls who have considered suicide/ when the rainbow is enuf*. Director Ozzie Scott saw the work at Studio Rivbea, a jazz loft in the SoHo district of New York City. He recruited Woodie King, Jr., to help mount the work at the New Federal Theater off-Broadway. Then Joseph Papp staged it at the Public Theater, and in 1976 the show moved to the Booth Theater on Broadway, where it ran for nearly two years.

for colored girls, which has often been called a "choreopoem," uses seven of Shange's poems to dramatize black women's encounters with male classmates, lovers, rapists, and abortionists, among others. The women (one of whom, Lady Yellow, was played by Shange herself) speak, sing, and dance their stories. According to Anne Mills King, the show's thematic base addresses "the thwarting dreams and aspirations for a decent life by forces beyond one's control: war, poverty, and ignorance . . . Thus, the play is a drama of salvation for women who do not receive their full value in society."[3] Even though *for colored girls* received great critical acclaim, winning an Obie (1977) and an Audelco Award (1977) and receiving a Tony nomination for best play (1977), negative remarks arose from both the black and feminist communities. The former complained about the negative portrayals of black men, and the latter about the depiction of female weakness. Unchastened, Shange defended her work: "My job as an artist is to say what I see."[4]

Since the late 1970s, Shange has been creating a body of work as rich in its content as its presentation. Some of her more notable pieces include *a photograph* (1977), an exploration of the problems of "middle-class, professional, and artistic blacks in a complicated urban society"[5]; *boogie woogie landscapes* (1979), which reveals the subconscious of Layla, a young black woman, by commingling the words of an evenly divided male/female Greek chorus with disparate images of, for example, Fidel Castro, rock and roll, and African women. Layla, Arabic for "born at night," dreams of these characters as exemplifications "of her perceptions of herself and her memories . . . To be black and a woman, to be each of these, is to have two distinct mountains to climb."[6] These plays, along with Shange's *spell #7* (1979), were published as a single work, *three pieces*, in 1992. *spell #7* returned to the "choreopoem" format. In it a group of male and female actors perform a minstrel show. But when the curtain falls, the company retreats to a local bar, their stage masks gradually falling away to reveal their true selves. Early on, the magician narrator of *spell #7* tells the actors he is "fixing you up good & colored & you gonna be colored all yr life & you gonna love it/being colored/ all yr life/ colored & love it love it/ bein colored." Later he says, "All things are possible but ain't no colored magician in his right mind gonna make you white." Many critics have lauded Shange's unusual blending of black English with more sophisticated language. Claudia Tate views this stylistic contradiction as the heart of "the youthful spirit, flair . . . and lyricism that carry her plays to startling and radical conclusions."[7]

Shange's oeuvre includes a more recent stage piece, *Betsey Brown* (1989), a musical based on her 1985 autobiographical novel, and original adaptations of several works, including Bertolt Brecht's *Mother Courage and Her Children* (1980) and Richard Wesley's *The Mighty Gents* (1979), which also marked her directorial debut. She has published many essays, novels, and poetry collections, and

her work has appeared in numerous anthologies and journals, such as *Third World Women, Black Scholar*, and *Ms*. She has also taught women's studies and creative writing at Sonoma State College and the University of Houston, among other institutions. Mixed in with these activities have been two failed marriages, an attempted suicide, and the birth of a daughter, Savannah.

Jack Kroll summed up the playwright's approach in *Newsweek* (n.d., ca. 1982), claiming that "Shange's poems aren't war cries. They're outcries filled with a controlled passion against the brutality that blasts the lives of 'colored girls'—a phrase that in her hands vibrates with social irony and poetic beauty. These poems are political in the deepest sense, but there's no dogma, no sentimentality, no grinding of false mythic axes." Of her use of language, Ysef A. Salaam has written, "Shange flashlights colorful language at the audience . . . [She] flings metaphors, similes and word rhythms that sizzle like Betty Carter's scats. . . ."[8]

Reflecting on her accomplishments during an interview with Stella Dong, Shange was reminded of her girlhood aspirations. After acknowledging that she "draws heavily on her experiences and the frustrations of being a black female in America," she said, "I am a war correspondent after all . . . because I'm involved in a war of cultural and esthetic aggression. The front lines aren't always what you think they are."[9]

PLAYS

Betsey Brown (musical), w/EMILY MANN, Baikida Carroll, composer (also novel, 1985), 1989; *Black and White Two Dimensional Planes*, 1979; *Bocas*, 1982; *boogie woogie landscapes*, 1979; *Educating Rita* (film, 1983), (adapt. of Willy Russell novel), 1982; *for colored girls who have considered suicide/when the rainbow is enuf*, 1974; *From Okra to Greens: a Different Kinda Love Story*, 1978; *The Mighty Gents* (adapt. of Richard Wesley's work), 1979; *Mother Courage and Her Children* (adapt. of Bertolt Brecht play), 1980; *Moths*, 1981; *Negress*, 1977; *a photograph: a still life with shadows/a photograph: a study of cruelty* (rev. as *a photograph: a study of lovers in motion*, 1977), 1976; *spell #7: geechee jibara quik magic trance manual for technologically stressed third world people: a theater piece*, 1979; *Three for a fall moon*, 1982; *Three views of mt. fuji*, 1987; *Where the mississippi meets the amazon*, w/Thulani Nkabinde and JESSICA HAGEDORN, 1977

OTHER WORKS

A daughter's geography (poems), 1983; *I live in music* (poems), 1995; *Liliane* (fiction), 1994; *The love space demands: a continuing saga*, 1991; *Melissa & Smith*, 1976; *nappy edges* (poetry), 1978; *Natural Disasters and Other Festive Occasions*, 1979; *Ridin' the moon in Texas: Word*

Paintings (prose & poems), 1987; *Sassafras* (novel), 1976; *Sassafras, Cypress & Indigo* (novel), 1982; *See No Evil* (collection), 1984; *Three pieces*, 1992

1. Interview by Jean Vallely, *Time*, 1976.

2. Interview with Stella Dong in *Publishers Weekly*, May 3, 1985.

3. Essay by Anne Mills King in Magill.

4. Interview by Connie Lauerman in the *Chicago Tribune*, October 21, 1982.

5. Op. cit., Magill.

6. Ibid.

7. "Ntozake Shange" by Claudia Tate in *Black Women Writers at Work* (New York: Continuum, 1983), p. 173.

8. *New York Amsterdam News Review*, July 3, 1982.

9. Op cit., Dong.

Anna Deavere Smith
(SEPTEMBER 18, 1950–)

MRS. YOUNG-SOON HAN (former liquor store owner). At leasteh they got something back, you know. Just let's forget Korean victims or other victims who are destroyed by them. They have fought for their rights over two centuries and I have a lot of sympathy and understanding for them. Because of their effort and sacrificing, other minorities, like Hispanics or Asians, maybe we have to suffer more by mainstream. You know that's why I understand, and then I like to be part of their 'joyment. But . . . That's why I had mixed feeling as soon as I heard the verdict. I wish I could live together with eh Blacks, but after the riots there were too much differences.

—from *Twilight, Los Angeles, 1992*, "Swallowing the Bitterness"

Upon hearing that Anna Deavere Smith had won a Mac-Arthur "genius" grant in 1996, Sharon Ott, then artistic director at Berkeley Repertory Theatre, stated, "Anna is truly a genius. She is pioneering a way of theater that is absolutely unique, she is reinventing what we think of as the proper turf of theater."[1]

Smith burst on the national scene with *Fires in the Mirror* (1992), based on the outbreak of racial violence that tore through Crown Heights, a Brooklyn, New York, neighborhood, in 1991. The events that informed *Fires* began with the death of a black boy who was killed by a car in an orthodox rabbi's motorcade. Believing this death was racially motivated, members of the black community retaliated by slaying a Jewish student. At the time of these occurrences, Smith was already on the road with her unique series of performance pieces based on interviews with ordinary people. Spurred by her conviction that "the mirrors of society do not mirror society,"[2] Smith took to the streets with her tape recorder, determined to give both the blacks and Jews (two Crown Heights communities

whose mutual rage had been simmering for years) their own voice. The resulting performance involves Smith's transformation into twenty-six different victims of the mayhem: men and women, black and Jewish, immigrant and native, city official, activist, common folk. In a foreword to the published play, Cornel West writes that *Fires* "is the most significant artistic exploration of Black-Jewish relations in our time." He goes on to say that the playwright "neither romanticizes nor idealizes Hasidic, Black, or secular Jewish women. Instead, she humanizes the Black-Jewish dialogue . . ."[3] *Fires* was awarded a Special Citation Obie and was a finalist for the 1992 Pulitzer Prize for drama.

She followed her astounding performance in *Fires* with another one-woman tour de force: *Twilight, Los Angeles, 1992*, inspired by the civil insurrection in Los Angeles after the announcement of the verdict in the Rodney King trial. King, a black motorist, had been brutally beaten by a number of white L.A.P.D. officers, but the officers were found "not guilty" by an all-white jury. Smith leaped into action. She conducted 220 interviews with Los Angeles residents of every race and economic class. On stage, Smith employed her "formidable talent for mimicry" to portray, in their own words, Reginald Denny (the white truck driver who was almost beaten to death by black gang members), police chief Daryl Gates, and a Korean store owner, among others. *Twilight*, called "an American masterpiece"[4] by

Anna Deavere Smith
COURTESY OF THE PLAYWRIGHT, PHOTO BY
SUSAN JOHANN

Newsday, is a painful, multifaceted portrait of racial differences.

Smith was born in Baltimore, Maryland; her father was a coffee merchant and her mother an elementary school principal. She was educated at the American Conservatory Theatre in San Francisco, where she received her M.F.A. in 1970. She made her acting debut as The Savage in *Horatio* at American Conservatory Theater in San Francisco in 1974, and her New York City debut as Marie Laveau in *Alma, the Ghost of Spring Street* at La MaMa in 1976. Her first film appearance was in *Soup for One* (1982). She has taught at several institutions, including Carnegie Mellon (1978–79), Yale (1982), New York University (1983–84), the National Theatre Institute (1984–85); currently she teaches at Stanford University. She is the recipient of a Dramalogue Critics Circle Award and a Drama Desk Award, as well as numerous other theater awards and honors.

About her technique, Smith explains, "The spirit of acting is the travel from the self to the other."[5] She has said, "My work is both political and personal. I'm trying to resolve this problem of strangeness and closeness in our world that's getting closer and closer. I'm interested in telling every side of the story."[6]

PLAYS

A Birthday Card and Aunt Julia's Shoes (one-woman), n.d.; *Aye, Aye, Aye, I'm Integrated*, 1984; *Fires in the Mirror: Crown Heights, Brooklyn, and Other Identities*, 1992; *House Arrest*, 1997; *On the Road*, 1983; *Twilight, Los Angeles, 1992*, 1994

1. Quoted in article by Joan Smith, *San Francisco Examiner*, June 16, 1996.

2. Introduction, *Fires in the Mirror* (New York: Anchor, 1993).

3. Op. cit., foreword, *Fires*.

4. *Newsday*, October 1994.

5. Ibid.

6. "The Beauty of Black Art," *Time*, October 10, 1994.

Dodie Smith
(MAY 3, 1896–NOVEMBER 24, 1990)

ROGER. You know, you women with this skinny complex are laying up a wretched old age for yourselves. String, that's what you'll be. Stringy and desiccated.
DOROTHY. Well, that's better than having two double chins and three double stomachs.
ROGER. I have no stomach whatever.
DOROTHY. How inconvenient.

—from *Call It a Day*

Most readers and filmgoers recognize at least one work in Dodie Smith's oeuvre: the children's classic *One Hundred and One Dalmatians*. Yet few lovers of that work realize that Dodie Smith was one of the few successful woman dramatists in the English language during the early part of the twentieth century. "The ability to recreate detail, to capture the nuances of everyday conversation, to recognize humor in the trivialities of middle-class life marks the dramas of Dodie Smith," wrote Martha Hadsel.[1] These qualities allowed Smith's works, whether on stage or in print, to enjoy wide audience appeal.

When her father died just after her birth, Smith's mother, Ella Furber Smith, took her from Lancashire to a suburb of Manchester, where they resided with her grandparents. Grandfather Furber, a theater enthusiast with a firm knowledge of Shakespeare, had reared his own two children to similarly love the theater—as amateurs, both had trounced upon the boards. By the time Smith was seven years old, she was already determined to be a professional actress. She studied acting at the Royal Academy of Dramatic Arts in London (1914–15) but, although she had debuted professionally, chose to focus on play writing instead. In 1923 her first effort, *British Talent*, was mounted at the Three Arts Club.

Smith had to wait another seven years before her next play was produced, but the payoff was worth it: *Autumn Crocus* opened in 1931 at the Lyric Theatre in London to warm critical response. A romantic comedy set in Alpine country, *Autumn Crocus* depicts a group of idiosyncratic tourists, in the midst of whom are a thirty-five-year-old schoolmistress and an innkeeper who manage a romantic interlude. Although Smith enjoyed the show's success, she had no illusions about it. As she wrote in her autobiography, the play's "financial success was in inverse ratio to its reputation as a serious play."

Autumn ushered in a prolific decade for Smith. In 1932 she penned *Service*, which drew upon her earlier experiences as a buyer for the large London department store Heal and Son. In her play the store (called Services), a family-owned business that has a warm relationship with its employees, is threatened with impending bankruptcy. A few years later her nostalgic drama *Touch Wood* opened. Her 1935 play *Call It a Day* was her most financially successful work, and marks the first time Smith signed her own name. Until then, she had used the pseudonym C. L. Anthony. (Indeed, Smith had experimented much earlier with an alias: During her school days she wrote a screenplay entitled *Schoolgirl Rebels* under the name Charles Henry Percy—and sold it.)

Many of Smith's plays enjoyed the addition of music. While some critics have called her works slight, others have likened them to those of Henrik Ibsen, and still others to the works of George S. Kaufman and EDNA FERBER. The works are comfortable and imaginative; her characters are treated with sympathetic humor and tenderness. Witty repartee not unlike that of JEAN KERR can be found throughout Smith's well-crafted plays.

In 1939 Smith finally married her longtime friend and associate Alec Macbeth Beesley. At the time of their wedding they were in the United States to consult on a production of *Dear Octopus*. There they remained for fifteen years, residing, for the most part, in southern California, where Smith worked on films at Paramount Studios. The couple returned to London in 1952, when her play *Letter from Paris* was produced. From the early 1950s until her death in 1990, the playwright turned to prose and wrote several books, many of which were adapted for film, including the classic *One Hundred and One Dalmatians*.

PLAYS

Aldwych, 1954; *Amateur Means Lover*, 1961; *Autumn Crocus* (also film, 1934), 1931; *Bonnet over the Windmill*, 1937; *British Talent*, 1924; *Call It a Day* (also film, 1937), 1935; *Dear Octopus* (also film, 1945), 1938; *Grand*, 1958; *I Capture the Castle* (also novel, 1948), 1954; *Leeds*, 1958; *Letter from Paris* (adapt. from Henry James's "The Reverberator,") 1952; *Lovers and Friends*, 1943; *Queen's*, 1938; *Service* (also film, *Looking Forward*, 1944), 1932; *These People, Those Books*, 1958; *Touch Wood*, 1934

OTHER WORKS

One Hundred and One Dalmatians (also films, 1961, 1996), 1957; *It Ends with Revelations*, 1967; *Look Back with Mixed Feelings* (autobio.), 1978; *Look Back with Love* (autobio.), 1974; *Look Back with Astonishment* (autobio.), 1979; *The Midnight Kittens*, 1978; *The New Moon with the Old*, 1963; *The Starlight Barking*, 1967; *A Tale of Two Families*, 1970; *The Town in Bloom*, 1965

1. Essay by Martha Hadsel in Weintraub.

Zulu Sofola
(JUNE 22, 1935–   )

ULOKO (to Ogoli, his mother). I did not say anything. You have been of no help as far as my marriage is concerned. It was in your presence that Ogwoma was forced from my hands and given away to Adigwu. Did you speak for me? Did you let Ibekwe know that an injustice was being done to you by his action? Did you let anyone know that, for money, the wife whom you had planned for your son was being forced from your hands and being given to someone else? Did you tell them that my life would become nothing if the one I love so much was given away to someone else? Did you?

—from *Wedlock of the Gods*, Act II, Scene 2

Nigerian-born Zulu Sofola was hailed by Olu Obafemi, director of the Modern European Languages program at the University of Ilorin in Nigeria, as "the first published and established female Nigerian dramatist and theater practitioner of English expression."[1] Sofola received her B.A. in English, cum laude, in 1959 from Virginia Union University in Richmond, Virginia. After marrying J. A. Sofola in 1960, with whom she has five children, she earned her Ph.D. in tragic theory (1977) from the University of Ibadan.

Sofola has been writing for the stage since the late 1960s. Like EFUA SUTHERLAND and AMA ATO AIDOO she explores the conflicts between African traditionalism and the influence of Western modernism, particularly as these conflicts impact the patriarchy that so dominates African life. Many of Sofola's plays include elements of magic, folklore, ritual, and myth. According to Obafemi, Sofola's work addresses "the state and status of women in modern society, the individual in contending with Western and indigenous African cultures, and individual and group moralities as influenced and determined by religious persuasions, social and communal ethics, and history."[2]

Indeed these themes are evident even in Sofola's earliest work. Her 1971 drama *Wedlock of the Gods* finds a young couple's love thwarted by the demands of traditional culture: The young woman's parents insist upon choosing their daughter's suitor. The chosen husband, an older man, dies shortly after the marriage, and the lovers reunite before the prescribed mourning period is over. The woman's enraged mother summons her magical powers and destroys her daughter and her sweetheart. More realistically violent is *The Sweet Trap* (1975), in which a defiant wife ultimately apologizes to her abusive husband for her rebellious actions. Sofola writes, "In my plays I have treated the aspects in traditional society where customs and moral precepts set themselves at war against individual citizens."[3]

Since 1989, Sofola has headed the Performing Arts Department at the University of Ilorin. She spent a year as a visiting professor at the State University of New York, Buffalo. She has received numerous awards and recognitions, such as a Ford Foundation Fellowship (1969–72); an Ife International Book Fair award (1987) issued by the University of Ife (now Awolowo) in Nigeria; and a Fulbright Fellowship (1988). Her most recent plays include *The Love of Life* (1992), *The Ivory Tower*, and *A Celebration of Life*.

PLAYS

A Celebration of Life, n.d.; *The Deer and the Hunters Pearl*, 1976; *The Disturbed Peace of Christmas*, 1969; *Eclipso and the Fantasia*, 1990; *The Ivory Tower*, n.d.; *King Emene*, 1975; *Lost Dreams*, 1991; *The Love of Life*, 1992; *Memories in the Moonlight*, 1977; *Old Wines Are Tasty*, 1981; *The Operators*, 1973; *Queen Omu-Ako of Oligbo*, 1989; *The Showers*, 1991; *Song of a Maiden*, 1977; *The Sweet Trap*, 1975; *Wedlock of the Gods*, 1971; *The Wizard of Law*, 1976

1. Essay by Olu Obafemi in Berney (1).
2. Ibid.
3. Ibid.

Bella Spewack
(MARCH 25, 1899–APRIL 17, 1990)

BENSON. You were saying that this is one of the greatest picture scripts ever written.

C. F. Now, just a minute—

LAW. And do you know why? Because it's the same story Larry Toms has been doing for years.

BENSON. We *know* it's good.

LAW. Griffith used it. Lubitsch used it. And Eisenstein's coming around to it.

BENSON. Boy meets girl. Boy loses girl. Boy gets girl.

Bella Spewack
COURTESY OF UPI/CORBIS-BETTMANN

LAW. The great American fairy-tale. Sends the audience back to the relief rolls in a happy frame of mind.

BENSON. And why not?

LAW. The greatest escape formula ever worked out in the history of civilization . . .

C. F. Of course, if you put it that way . . . but, boys, it's hackneyed.

LAW. You mean classic.

C. F. *Hamlet* is a classic—but it isn't hackneyed!

LAW. *Hamlet* isn't hackneyed? Why, I'd be ashamed to use that poison gag. He lifted that right out of the Italians.

—from *Boy Meets Girl*, Scene 4

For three decades Bella Cohen Spewack, a Rumanian-born immigrant, and her husband Samuel generated some of the world's best-loved comedies. Spewack's family emigrated from Bucharest to New York City when she was still an infant. After graduating from Washington Irving High School, she worked as a reporter for local newspapers. While she was on staff at the *New York Call* she met Samuel Spewack (1899–1971), who was reporting for the *New York World*. Samuel was also the son of Russian immigrants. With so much in common, the duo fell in love and were soon wed. Shortly after Bella got a job working as a press agent, she and Samuel began collaborating on works for the stage. They found their métier in the field of comedy, particularly the madcap variety.

Boy Meets Girl (1935) was their first big hit. A screwball spoof of two sharpster screenwriters in Hollywood with sharp dialogue, it ran for 660 performances. It was later made into a film (1938) starring, among others, James Cagney, Pat O'Brien, Ralph Bellamy—and Ronald Reagan. In 1948, Cole Porter did the music on *Kiss Me, Kate*, their adaptation of Shakespeare's *The Taming of the Shrew*. *Kate* is a backstage farce about a married couple playing the leads in the Shakespearean classic whose lives become intertwined with the Bard's plot. The Porter score includes such classics as "So in Love," "Always True to You in My Fashion" and "Brush up Your Shakespeare." It won a Tony, was later adapted for film and has become a true classic of its genre. *My Three Angels* (1953), an adaptation of Albert Husson's *La cuisine des anges*, ran for 344 Broadway performances, and was also made into a popular film. This comedy follows the antics of three convicts who, using their finely honed but dastardly skills, manage to shower kindness on those they consider good; those they consider evil are ingeniously dispatched. *Clear All Wires* (1932) sprang from the Spewacks' experiences as foreign corespondents around 1922. It is the story of a manipulative, globe-trotting journalist who creates as much news as he covers, highlighting his escapades while in Russia; it was later adapted as a Cole Porter musical, *Leave It to Me* (1938). During her time overseas Bella discovered and interviewed the woman who claimed to be Anastasia Romanov, the only surviving member of Russia's ruling family.

Professor Lynda Hart of the University of Pennsylvania writes that the Spewacks' best plays "indicate a skillful handling of a wide range of comedy from farce to light satire and inject a freshness and vitality into the popular entertainment arena of the American theater."[1] Their plays have been widely anthologized and produced.

In addition to their stage work, the Spewacks wrote twenty screenplays, several of which were adaptations of their stage plays. As an interesting aside, during Bella's years as a press agent she initiated the now entrenched Girl Scout cookie sales.

PLAYS

Boy Meets Girl (also film, 1938), 1935; *Clear All Wires* (also film, 1933), 1932; *The Festival*, 1955; *Kiss Me, Kate* (book; also TV adapt., 1959; also film), 1948; *Leave It to Me* (book), 1938; *Miss Swan Expects*, 1939; *My Three Angels* (also TV adapt., 1960; also film), 1953; *Poppa*, 1928; *The Solitaire Man*, 1926; *Spring Song*, 1934; *The War Song*, w/George Jessel, 1928; *Woman Bites Dog*, 1946

SCREENPLAYS (SELECTED)

The Cat and the Fiddle, 1934; *My Favorite Wife*, 1940; *Rendezvous*, 1935; *Should Ladies Behave?*, 1933; *Weekend at the Waldorf*, 1945; *When Ladies Meet*, 1933

1. Essay by Lynda Hart in Robinson.

Gertrude Stein
(FEBRUARY 3, 1874–JULY 27, 1946)

Saint Therese something like that.
Saint Therese something like that.
Saint Therese would and would and would.
Saint Therese something like that.
Saint Therese.
Saint Therese half in doors and half out of doors.
Saint Therese not knowing of other saints.

—from *Four Saints in Three Acts*

The plays and operas of Gertrude Stein reflect her genius for toying with language and the meaning of language. Although few of her stage works have been produced, her ground-breaking experiments in nonreferentiality and nonlinearity, in the realms of both literature and theater, have had a tremendous impact on theater artists such as avant garde directors Robert Wilson and Richard Foreman, and playwrights from Thornton Wilder to SUZAN-LORI PARKS. In fact, her influence has been so great,

UCLA professor Betsy Ryan calls Stein the "least acclaimed major playwright of all time."[1] Stein articulates the underlying motif of her plays in her introduction to *The Autobiography of Alice B. Toklas* when, having made mention of her first play writing efforts, *It Happened a Play* and *Ladies Voices*, she remarks about herself, "Her interest in writing plays continues. She says a landscape is such a natural arrangement for a battlefield or a play that one must write plays."[2] Stein's use of the term "landscape" conveys her unusual approach to theater as a static form. For Stein, the literal play of the language itself fuels the movement of the drama.

Stein originally hails from Allegheny, Pennsylvania, the seventh child of German immigrants. During her early years, the family moved among various European cities, eventually settling on a ten-acre parcel of land in Oakland, California. By the time she was seventeen both her parents had died, and she was sent to live with an aunt in Baltimore. Even though she lacked a high school diploma, the Harvard Annex (which became Radcliffe College) ac-

Gertrude Stein
COURTESY OF UPI/CORBIS-BETTMANN

cepted her as an undergraduate. A brilliant student, she earned her B.A. magna cum laude, then studied briefly at Johns Hopkins Medical School. In 1903 she abruptly withdrew from school—and from American society. Gertrude and her brother Leo left for Europe.

The two settled in Paris, sharing an apartment and maintaining a close relationship, until tensions between the two art enthusiasts erupted following the publication of her first novel, *Q.E.D.*, in 1903. The book's description of a lesbian relationship met with such strong disapproval from Leo, it caused a schism between them into which Alice B. Toklas slipped—and stayed. From that time on, Toklas lived with Stein, becoming her lifelong lover and companion.

It was Paris, in the 1920s; Stein and Toklas's home became a hub for some of the greatest artists and writers of the modern era: Pablo Picasso, Henri Matisse, Ernest Hemingway, and Sherwood Anderson routinely attended the now-legendary salons. Although Stein wrote two of her seminal works in the early 1910s, *Three Lives* and *The Making of Americans*, she did not become renowned until the publication of *The Autobiography of Alice B. Toklas* in 1936 (which resulted in her brief return to the United States which led to her immensely popular account of that tour, titled *Everybody's Autobiography* [1937]). Also in 1936 Stein's most successful opera was staged.

Stein explained her motivation for writing *Four Saints in Three Acts* with characteristic aplomb: "A saint a real saint never does anything, a martyr does something but a really good saint does nothing and so I wanted to have Four Saints that did nothing and I wrote the *Four Saints in Three Acts* and they did nothing and that was everything. Generally speaking anybody is more interesting doing nothing than doing anything."[3] The work marked Stein's first collaboration with composer Virgil Thomson. The two worked together again on *The Mother of Us All* (1947), based on the life of Susan B. Anthony. Thomson revived *Saints*, with Leontyne Price as St. Cecilia, at New York City's American National Theatre and Academy in 1952.

Because Stein's plays are so seldom produced, few are aware today that Stein authored over seventy-six dramas. Her first, *What Happened*, written in 1912, sketches, as Betsy Ryan puts it, "the images, rhythms, and qualities of an evening dinner party without suggesting a story line. Typical of her first period of play writing, it is an attempt to capture the essence of relationships and subtle movements between things without telling what happened, but rather to make a play the essence of what happened."[4] A later revision of this work, the earlier-mentioned *It Happened a Play*, revived in 1964, won an Obie. Her second play writing spurt produced what Stein referred to as her "landscape plays," works that, according to Ryan, "depend

upon relationships and are expressed in the overly spatial terms of a physical landscape."[5]

Stein's plays have been sporadically revived over the past several decades. *In Circles* was staged by Lawrence Kornfeld at the Cherry Lane Theater in New York City in 1967, and *Listen to Me* (1936) was put on by the Judson Poets Theater in 1974. (Of that production, Marc Robinson, writing in the *Village Voice*, posited, "The moments pass fast and loose . . . [The actors] have fun, flying headlong into the rhyming jabs with all the enthusiasm of overstimulated children. They seem to use Stein's repetitions as a dare . . .") More recently Stein's plays and operas seem to have eked back into the public eye. An Ohio theater company called The Gertrude Stein Repertory Theater has successfully revived many of her works. In 1996, Robert Wilson directed a very well-received production of *Four Saints in Three Acts* in Houston; *Saints* was originally produced in 1934 in Hartford, Connecticut, with an all-black cast.

PLAYS

Four Saints in Three Acts (opera), music by Virgil Thomson, pub. 1929, prod. 1934; *Geography and Plays* (coll.), 1922; *In Circles*, music by Al Carmine, n.d.; *It Happened a Play* (rev. as *What Happened*, 1964), 1913; *Ladies Voices*, n.d.; *Last Operas and Plays* (coll.), 1949; *Listen to Me*, music by A. C., n.d.; *Made by Two* (opera), n.d.; *The Mother of Us All* (opera), music by V. T., 1947; *Operas and Plays* (coll.; rev. 1987), 1932; *Yes Is for a Very Young Man*, 1946

OTHER WORKS (SELECTED)
POETRY

Tender Buttons (1941)

NONFICTION

Autobiography of Alice B. Toklas, 1933; *Composition as Explanation* (literary criticism), 1926; *Everybody's Autobiography*, 1937; *The Geographical History of America* (literary criticism), 1936; *How to Write*, 1931; *Lectures in America*, 1935; *Narration*, 1935; *Picasso* (art criticism), 1938; *Wars I Have Seen* (autobio.), 1945

FICTION

The Making of Americans 1906–08, 1925; *Mrs. Reynolds*, 1952; *Quod Erat Demonstrantum* (novel), written in 1903, pub. 1950 under the title *Things as They Are*; *Three Lives 1905–06*, 1909

WORKS ABOUT

Bridgman, Richard, *Gertrude Stein in Pieces*, 1970; Brinnin, John Malcolm, *The Third Rose: Gertrude Stein and Her World*, 1959; Hoffman, Michael J., *The Development of Abstractionism in the Writings of Gertrude Stein*, 1965; Hoffman, *Gertrude Stein*, 1976; Mellow, James, *Charmed Circle: Gertrude Stein and Company*, 1974; Stewart, Allegra, *Gertrude Stein and the Present*, 1967; Sutherland, Donald, *Gertrude Stein*, 1951; repr. 1972; Weinstein, Norman, *Gertrude Stein and the Literature of the Modern Consciousness*, 1970

1. Essay by Betsy Ryan in Robinson.

2. Introduction to *Last Operas and Plays* by Carl Van Vechten (Baltimore: Johns Hopkins University Press, 1949).

3. Ibid.

4. Op. cit., Ryan.

5. Ibid.

Efua Theodora Sutherland
(JUNE 27, 1924–   )

LABARAN. I was impatient at the beginning; in haste. Seeing the raggedness of my people's homes, I was ashamed, even angry. I heard it, screamed: Progress! Development! I wanted it far and everywhere.

But now I have learned that I can roam all I please, and nothing will change. I can talk all I please—who cares? Friends, when you talk to people and see blankness in their faces, you have to give up. In their eyes you can read the sum of their souls and whether or not they understand. From that derives the patience of which I speak.

—from *Foriwa*, Act 1

Efua Theodora Sutherland, born in Ghana in 1924, is considered one of her nation's leading authors and primary advocates for the necessity of theater in her native country. Her efforts brought in government funding, as well as American support, to build Ghana's first professional theater, the Ghana Drama Studio, in 1961.

After her studies at Homerton College in Cambridge and the School of Oriental and African Studies at the University of London, Sutherland returned to Ghana, where she married and had three children. In 1958 she became the founder of Accra, an experimental theater group, which eventually evolved into the Ghana Drama Studio. She also founded the Ghana Society of Writers (now the Writer's Workshop in the Institute of African Studies, University of Ghana, Legion), as well as Kusum Sgoromba, a children's theater group.

However, she is most widely recognized for her plays. In *Edufa*, Sutherland weaves the tale of a successful man so egocentric that he is willing to ask another to die for him. After a diviner informs him the only way to escape his pending death is to find someone willing to take his place, Edufa brazenly asks for volunteers, including his own wife, Ampona. Ampona accepts the sacrifice. ("I declare to earth and sky and water, and all things with which we shall soon be one, that I am slave to your flesh and happy so to be," she avows on accepting this fate.) The play raises many questions: In what ways do women place their lives at the disposal of men? Which has greater value, the material world for which we have so faithfully worked, or the ones who supposedly love us? After choosing a path, does one give up the option of turning back? What do we wish to leave behind in the memories of people who know us? *Edufa* is more or less a counter to Euripides's *Alcestis*, according to Professor Anthony Graham-White of the University of Illinois, with the latter's Admetus figure represented in Sutherland's title character. But the playwright has made a tragedy of the play, changing the focus from the somewhat indulgent Greek version to one concerning the impact of the loss of traditional values on "the educated modern man."[1]

Foriwa, which is written in her native Twi tongue and intended to be performed on the streets of small towns, embodies much of what Sutherland strives for in all of her work: national unity, reform, and cooperation. The play takes place in a very dilapidated street in Kyerefaso where stands the now dilapidated royal house, a bookstore, a shrine, and Labaran's "camp"—a small tent pitched on the foundation of an unfinished brick building. The plot revolves around the story of Labaran, a university graduate and Hausa* from the north, and Foriwa, the Queen-Mother's daughter, who has returned to her homeland after studying to become a teacher. They fall in love and proceed to commandeer the cooperation of Foriwa's mother to endorse progressive changes, which she demonstrates in a traditional ceremony.

Many of Sutherland's plays use folk legends as their bases. *Anansegoro* retells the story of a deer who turns into a beautiful woman and is then betrayed by her lover Ananse, who reveals her secret identity. Ananse appears again in *The Marriage of Anansewa*, portraying the trickster. He broadcasts the availability of his daughter Anansewa, accepts gifts from those pursuing her, and finally fakes her death, thus allowing his coffers to swell.

Graham-White professes, "It is impossible to consider Efua Sutherland's plays apart from her work as a founder

---

*The Hausa are a numerous tribe of African people from the northwestern part of Nigeria and southwestern Niger.

and organizer of theaters and troupes."[2] While the major focus has been children, in her work as both a writer and an organizer of drama organizations, her contribution to Ghana's theater life is such that one has to wonder whether there would be much theater in Ghana at all were it not for Sutherland.

PLAYS

Ananse and the Dwarf Brigade, 1971; *Anansegoro: You Swore an Oath*, 1964; *Edufa*, 1962; *Foriwa*, 1962; *The Marriage of Anansewa* (one-act), n.d.; *Nyamekye*, n.d.; *Odasani* (a Ghanian interpretation of *Everyman*), n.d.; *The Pineapple Child*, n.d.; *Tweedledum and Tweedledee* (adapt. of Lewis Carroll work), n.d.; *Two Rhythm Plays*, n.d.; *Vulture! Vulture!*, 1968

OTHER WORKS

The Original Bob, 1970; *Playtime in Africa* (verse), 1960; *The Roadmakers*, w/Willis E. Bell, 1961; *The Voice in the Forest*, 1983

1. Essay by Anthony Graham-White in Berney (2).
2. Ibid.

Megan Terry
(JULY 22, 1932–   )

CHESTER. My God, the human baby! A few weeks after birth, any other animal can fend for itself. But *you*! A basket case till you're twenty-one.

—from *The Magic Realist*

Megan Terry has become a master at what is often referred to as "transformation theater"—that is, theater in which actors play several characters, sometimes of the opposite gender; settings change from place to place in the flicker of an eye; and time has no particular sequence and may leap whole centuries. Dreamlike, this style of theater affords Terry the latitude to make cogent her concerns about the sociopolitical economics that, she believes, are destructive to the fabric of America. Believing that "all of human wisdom" is "collected within the structure of the theater," Terry has crafted more than fifty plays that "represent a substantial contribution to American drama, both in their innovative forms and in their political and philosophical substance."[1] "In American popular culture terms, however," according to scholar Phyllis Jane Rose, "her tone and sense of social responsibility are rooted in vaudeville, burlesque, evangelism, and stand-up comedy."[2]

Born Marguerite Duffy in Seattle, Washington, Terry was fascinated by the theater as a child. Of her first early excursions to the Seattle Repertory Playhouse she has said, "I went and I looked at the stage and I fell madly in love. I knew I wanted to do that, whatever it was." Grade school and backyard dramatics were a regular part of Terry's early life, but her play world turned dark when her father went off to the war. When he returned, her parents divorced and she went to live with him, though he was not sympathetic to her theatrical endeavors, as was her mother. He called her "Tallulah Blackhead" and "Sarah Heartburn," deriding her aspirations. But he taught her to catch, clean, and cook fish; build outdoor shelters; hunt; gather edible herbs and berries; and build. In the seventh grade Megan wrote, directed, and acted in her first musical. "I remember being on stage and getting that terrific rush in the frontal lobes every time the audience laughed." She was hooked. "Theater is profoundly physically rewarding."[3]

She eventually moved back with her mother, who was running a florist shop where Megan often worked, and they lived with her grandparents. She spent so much time around the Seattle Repertory Theater (it was only three blocks from her home) that Florence and Burton James, who ran the playhouse, could not ignore the girl. As a result, Terry says, "I had a Greek education by the time I was seventeen." The Jameses, who greatly influenced Terry's political beliefs, taught summers at the Banff School of Fine Arts in Alberta, Canada. After Terry's high school graduation in 1950, they arranged for her to go on a theater scholarship to Banff, where she studied acting and directing. When the Seattle Repertory Theater was shut down a year later under pressure by the state-run Un-American Activities Committee, Terry became politicized.

She developed ideas on her concept of theater while acting as technical director of the Edmonton Children's Theater and studying Antonin Artaud's Theater of Cruelty, all the while studying psychology and sociology at both the University of Washington and the University of Alberta in Edmonton, Canada. After she finished her studies in Seattle, to which she had returned when her grand-

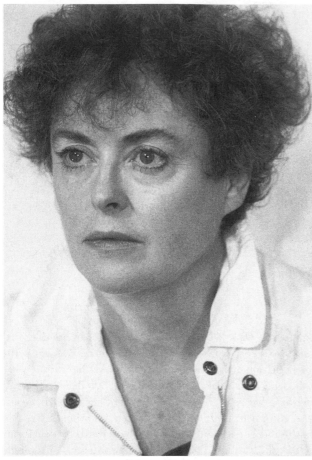

Megan Terry
SELF-PORTRAIT, COURTESY OF THE PLAYWRIGHT

Her gradual shift from realistic plays to transformative ones came about largely through her own impatience. Realism, she decided, took too "bloody long to make a point if you use it as the only style in a play. I needed more ways of talking. I wanted to write a play using realism magically, but also ironically and politically . . ."[4] Her early New York associations undoubtedly influenced this bias, for they included Joseph Chaikin, MARIA IRENE FORNES, and other vital young theater folk who were rejecting the current standards of Broadway's commercial theater and creating what they soon called the Open Theater. It was the 1960s, and the collective theater movement was swelling in both London and New York, where the Open Theater was at its helm. Everyone—actors, directors, designers, and playwrights—collaborated on the making of a play.

Many members of the original Open Theater company, including Terry, were strongly impressed with the theories of both Nola Chilton, whose teaching emphasized the freeing of the individual actor's body and voice through exercises focusing on imagined objects and sensations, and, for Terry particularly, Viola Spolin, the Chicago artist and innovator of "theater games." Terry began to deliberately design her work with sudden changes in mood, time, or character to throw off the audience, creating theater that Bell-Metereau describes as filled with ". . . earthy language, sexual and political content, musical segments, humor, and vaudeville touches [that] all blend to create lively, dynamic experiences for audiences."[5] Terry calls it "a living theater experience."

Terry was a founding member of the influential Women's Theater Council, formed in New York in 1972, along with MARIA IRENE FORNES, ROSALYN DREXLER, JULIE BOVASSO, ADRIENNE KENNEDY, and ROCHELLE OWENS. She worked with many exciting and innovative groups of the day, including off-off-Broadway's La MaMa Experimental Theater Club, the Firehouse Theater in Minneapolis, and several university drama departments. She has also written plays for the National Educational Television network.

Her first play, *Ex-Miss Copper Queen . . .*, which focuses on a one-time beauty queen who has become a pill-popping prostitute, received its initial production in 1963 by the Playwright's Unit Workshop in New York, a group that included the likes of Edward Albee, Richard Barr, and Clinton Wilder. *Viet Rock*, first performed on May 25, 1966, by the Open Theater company at Cafe La MaMa in New York, was the first rock musical, the first controversial stage treatment of the Vietnam War, and perhaps the first documented instance in modern times of actors touching and interacting with audience members within the context of a play. Suddenly, after ten years of plodding along, developing her craft, Terry found herself in the limelight. Three years later *Approaching Simone*, after only five performances at La MaMa Experimental Theater, won

father became seriously ill, she decided to focus on creative dramatics for children. In the meantime, she taught at the Cornish School of Allied Arts and organized the Cornish Players.

Terry became increasingly concerned with children's theater, and disgusted at the patronizing confines of the plays available for youngsters. She began writing frank, improvisational scripts dealing with sex and other forbidden subjects that had kids howling with laughter. However, her certain knowledge of attack by her colleagues for writing so forthrightly for children influenced her to use a pseudonym. Thus Megan (from the Celtic root for Marguerite) Terry (both for terra—the earth—and actress Ellen Terry) was born.

It was not long before Terry had to conclude that academia was not a fertile environment for her propensity toward the bawdy and the burlesque. So in 1956 she headed for New York City. There she wrote in secret for a couple of years, intimidated by her idealistic notion of playwrights being "the pinnacle of civilization," as she put it. She also suffered from "this whole thing of 'women shouldn't be able to do that.' "

the Obie for best play. Terry has received many other honors and awards since, including National Endowment for the Arts, Creative Artists Public Service, and Guggenheim grants.

Approaching Simone explores the life of Simone Weil, the Jewish/Catholic convert and French philosopher who protested the starvation of World War II soldiers at the front by starving herself to death. Reviewing the production in 1972, Jack Kroll wrote, "It is a rare theatrical event for these hysterical and clownish times, a truly serious play, filled with the light, shadow and weight of human life, and the exultant agonies of the ceaseless attempt to create one's humanity."[6] The title role was played by JoAnn Schmidman, who, in the summer of 1968, had founded the Omaha Magic Theater in Nebraska. Terry has always been at her most productive self when in the bosom of a community of artists. That is the only way, she believes, plays can be created that will "bring people together for an entertainment, a celebration, a living theater to cut down the fear and anguish that have got too many people in America by the throat."[7] And so in 1974, after four years of long-distance association with the theater Schmidman had founded, Terry made the leap of faith and moved to Omaha. There she has remained ever since as resident playwright of that tiny, vibrant troupe in the midwest, which is still considered one of America's most innovative theaters.

Following is a brief glimpse of a few of the dozens of works she has crafted: *The Magic Realists* (1966) uses vaudevillian techniques to unfurl the disastrous effects, in Terry's view, of a capitalistic economic power structure on individuals, families, and justice; *Calm Down, Mother* (1965), often hailed as the first truly feminist American drama, explores body image, women's rage, aging: Its underlying theme—anatomy is destiny—confronts the potentialities and limitations of women in society; *Keep Tightly Closed* (1965) parallels a similar track with men. *The People vs. Ranchman* (1967) deals with the celebrity of criminals, both political and otherwise, whereas *Goona Goona* (1979) uses burlesque techniques to expose child and wife abuse. *100,001 Horror Stories* (1976) is based on family histories and folk songs Terry gathered during her long tenure at the Magic Theater. *Home* questions human nature, brutality, cultural influence, and religious values. *American King's English for Queens* (1978), a musical in two acts produced at Omaha Magic Theater in 1978, reveals the sexism abounding in the everyday use of the English language and how that shapes us. *Babes in the Bighouse* (1977), a documentary musical fantasy set in a women's prison, reveals the internal lives of the inmates in songs and stories. Keyssar claims that Terry created "a distinctive dramaturgy" with *Babes*, which utilizes cross-gender casting, much as CARYL CHURCHILL did a few years later. Keyssar asserts that ". . . this led the entire company

to a more rigorous study of women's speech patterns, their physical and emotional behaviors and just how it is to be a woman."[8]

Keyssar affirms, "Although she is a critic of sexism, violence, materialism and social corruption, her work does not call for a radical social revolution as much as it calls attention to the enormous strength she perceives in women, especially in the ability to will transformation."[9] In fact, Terry defines feminist drama as "anything that gives women confidence, shows themselves to themselves, helps them to begin to analyze whether it's a positive or negative image, it's nourishing."[10]

PLAYS (SELECTED)

American King's English for Queens, 1978; *American Wedding Ritual Monitored/Transmitted by the Planet Jupiter* (radio play), 1972; *Approaching Simone,* 1970; *Attempted Rescue on Avenue B: A Beat Fifties Comic Opera,* 1979; *Babes in the Bighouse,* 1977; *Calm Down, Mother,* 1965; *Comings and Goings,* 1966; *Couplings and Groupings,* 1973; *The Dirt Boat* (teleplay), 1955; *Ex-Miss Copper Queen on a Set of Pills,* 1963; *Goona Goona,* 1979; *Home,* n.d.; *Hothouse,* 1974; *In the Gloaming, Oh My Darling,* 1966; *Keep Tightly Closed in a Cool, Dry Place,* 1965; *The Magic Realists,* 1966; *Massachusetts Trust,* 1968; *Megan Terry's Home, or Future Soap* (teleplay; stage, 1974), 1968; *Molly Bailey's Traveling Family Circus: Featuring Scenes from the Life of Mother Jones,* 1981; *Nightwalk,* w/Sam Shepard and Jean-Claude van Itallie, 1973; *100,001 Horror Stories of the Plains,* w/Judith Katz, James Larson, et al., 1976; *One More Little Drinkie* (teleplay), 1969; *The People vs. Ranchman,* 1967; *The Pioneer. and Pro-Game,* 1974; *Sanibel and Captiva* (teleplay), 1968; *Thought,* lyrics only, book by Lamar Alford, 1973; *The Tommy Allen Show,* 1969; *Viet Rock: A Folk War Movie,* music by Marianne de Pury, 1966; *Willa-Willa-Bill's Dope Garden,* 1977

WORKS ABOUT

Pasolli, Robert, *A Book on the Open Theater,* 1970

1. Essay by Rebecca Bell-Metereau in Magill.
2. Essay by Phyllis Jane Rose in Van Antwerp.
3. Cited in Olauson.
4. Cited in Keyssar.
5. Op. cit., Bell-Metereau.
6. "New Baloney," *Newsweek* (November 11, 1968), p. 121.
7. Op. cit., Bell-Metereau, 1968.
8. Op. cit., Keyssar.
9. Ibid.
10. Interview with Megan Terry by Dinah L. Leavitt in Chinoy.

Mia Törnqvist
(JANUARY 16, 1957–)

THE CHILD. Nora Schahrazade is not lonely. You on the other hand could use some company. . . . You have to understand that she can't hold her mother's hand her whole life.

—from *The Dreamed Life of Nora Schahrazade*

Born and raised in Stockholm, where she still lives, Mia Törnqvist earned her B.A. in language and literature at the University of Stockholm. She did her graduate studies in dramaturgy and play writing at the National Academy of Dramatic Arts, earning another degree. Her mother, Gunilla Törnqvist, is a teacher from Trelleborg, and her father, Arne Törnqvist, is a playwright, poet, and art critic from Stockholm. Her partner is Christopher Torch, an artistic director and stage director from Cleveland, Ohio and together they have a child, Joar, born in 1993. Törnqvist currently serves as artistic director of Korsväg, a cultural crossroads program.

Her first play was produced by the Jordciruus theater company in 1989 in Stockholm, and it has appeared in several other venues since then. Törnqvist's themes are existential, frequently making use of biblical formats: *Joseph in the Well* (1991) and *In the Shadow of God* (1993) are about Abraham, Sarah, and Hagar. In both the latter and *Medea* (1990), a monologue that contemporizes the ancient myth, she applies feminist themes that address the powerlessness of women in male societies and "the catastrophic consequences of such power structures."[1] In *Medea*, the central character is an immigrant whose husband leaves her for a Swedish woman. We meet her shortly after her son has drowned, while they were together on the ice and she failed to rescue him. In *Dreamed Life* (1994) we follow the story of a mother and father who, with the guidance of an "angel-child," find their way back to life after losing their newborn. Törnqvist wrote it after losing her own daughter. The play has been very well received, winning both the Government's Prize for best children's performance and the Critic's Prize for best children's play for 1995.

PLAYS

The Dreamed Life of Nora Schahrazade, 1994; *I skuggan av Gud* (In the Shadow of God), 1993; *Josefi brunnen* (Joseph in the Well), 1991; *Kanelbiten* (adapt. from Lars Ahlin work), 1989; *Medea,* a monologue, 1990; *Rom Enkel,* 1991; *Sprángdeg och Tulpaner,* 1990; *There Is a Devil Passing Through the Room,* 1995; *Tre Syslean,* 1990

1. From correspondence with the author, February 29, 1996.

Sue Townsend
(APRIL 2, 1946–)

Friday, January 2nd. BANK HOLIDAY IN SCOTLAND, FULL MOON. I felt rotten today. It's my mother's fault for singing "My Way" at two o'clock in the morning at the top of the stairs. Just my luck to have a mother like her. There is a chance my parents could be alcoholics. Next year I could be in a children's home.

—From *The Secret Diary of Adrian Mole, Aged 13 ¾*

The Secret Diary of Adrian Mole, Aged 13 ¾ (1982) was a runaway international best-seller, as was its sequel *The Growing Pains of Adrian Mole* (1984). These books dealing with adolescent angst catapulted their author to fame; few of her fans realize that Sue Townsend is also a playwright. A self-styled socialist and atheist, Townsend left school and her hometown of Leicester, England, at the age of fifteen. By the time she discovered success as a writer, she had worked as a garage attendant, saleswoman, factory worker, community service assistant, and British Broadcasting Corporation employee. Armed with such diverse experiences, Townsend found a way to bring ordinary people to life in an extraordinary way: through theater.

Some of her earliest plays reveal the unusual lives of a regular folk. In *Womberang* (1979) the free-spirited Rita Onions brings joy and anarchy to the grim waiting room of a gynecology clinic; it is, in the words of *New Society,* "A daydream of mastered fear." *Bazaar and Rummage* (1982) throws together a neurotic do-gooder and a trainee social worker who lure three agoraphobics out of their homes in order to hold a rummage sale. *Groping for Words* (1983; later *Are You Sitting Comfortably?*) shows that ignorance is ultimately the greatest challenge facing working-class students in an adult literacy class. *New Society* writes that in *Groping,* "Townsend examines this terror of social judgement as a means of keeping the working class in its place . . . a powerful play."

She tackles the cross-cultural experience of an Indian immigrant woman in England in *The Great Celestial Cow* (1984). With humor and sensitivity, Townsend portrays Sita, who must sell her beloved cow in India before she and her children can leave for England, where they will join her husband. She keeps her milking buckets with the hope that she will acquire another cow in Leicester. She discovers, however, that England is truly a different world. Faced with prejudice from the British and the traditional restrictions forced upon her by her family, Sita clings to the dream of the cow in order to maintain some semblance of identity. Ultimately *Cow* is a funny, moving, and positive look at the lives of Asian women in England.

Townsend enjoys writing comedy; she sees it as a necessary tool for "people coping with life."[1] She lives in Leicester with her husband, Colin Broadway, and their daughter. Her more recent work includes the 1990 play *Disneyland It Ain't. Adrian Mole* continues to be popular: In addition to its multimedia life (it is a play, a novel, and radio and television series), it enjoys incarnations as an audiocassette and a computer game.

PLAYS

Are You Sitting Comfortably? (a.k.a. *Groping for Words,* 1983) 1986; *Bazaar and Rummage* (adapted for television, 1983) 1982; *Captain Christmas and the Evil Adults,* 1982; *Clients,* 1983; *Dayroom,* 1981; *Disneyland It Ain't,* 1990; *Ear, Nose, and Throat,* 1988; *The Ghost of Daniel Lambert,* 1981; *The Great Celestial Cow,* 1984; *In the Club and Up the Spout,* 1979; *The Secret Diary of Adrian Mole, Aged 13 ¾— The Play* (novel, 1982; radio series, 1982; television series, 1986), 1984; *Ten Tiny Fingers, Nine Tiny Toes,* n.d.; *Womberang,* 1979

OTHER WORKS

The Growing Pains of Adrian Mole (radio series, 1987; television series, 1988), 1984; *Mr. Bevan's Dream,* 1989; *Rebuilding Coventry* (novel), 1988

1. Quoted by Susan Carlson in Berney (1).

Sophie Treadwell
(OCTOBER 3, 1885/90–FEBRUARY 20, 1970)

PRISON BARBER (to Woman). You'll submit my lady, right to the end, you'll submit.

—from *Machinal,* Episode 9

Sophie Treadwell has been called "the first American woman playwright to write the international political play, the experimental (surrealistic) play, the play with a sexually liberated woman, and most importantly, the play with a non-heroic male protagonist. She was unquestionably an agent for change in the content and structure of American drama in the first half of the twentieth century."[1] Born in Stockton, California, to parents of Scottish, Spanish, and English descent, Treadwell took a number of odd jobs in order to work her way through the University of California. Before long, she was writing for campus productions; her first play, *A Man's Own* (1904), hinted at what became a focal point of her life's work: the equality of women.

Upon graduating in 1906, Treadwell worked in Los Angeles as a journalist and teacher while taking bit parts in plays and vaudeville, and continuing to write plays. Her modest acting career had a hand, it seems, from Helen Modjeska, the great Polish actor, whose memoirs Tread-

well was helping to compile. In 1908 she moved to San Francisco to work as a journalist for the *San Francisco Bulletin.* There she met her husband, William O'Connell McGeehan. Soon Treadwell embarked on one of her most distinguished journeys as the first American woman war correspondent. She covered the Mexican Revolution and was the only reporter, worldwide, to get an interview with Pancho Villa in Mexico.

Sympathy, her first professional production, opened in 1915. Shortly thereafter, she wrote *Plumes in the Dust,* a biographical play about Edgar Allan Poe, but it became caught up in a fourteen-year legal battle between Treadwell and John Barrymore and his wife, Michelle Strange, who had also written a play about Poe. Even though the courts eventually sided with Treadwell (*Plumes* was produced in 1936), the stigma of the ordeal clung to her, and her reputation as mannish, temperamental, and aggressive inhibited the production of her plays; in fact, several never saw production.

Her 1928 experimental drama *Machinal,* presently her best-known work, brought her great commercial and critical success. Described by John Gassner as "one of the most unusual plays of the twenties," *Machinal* is an expressionist feminist tragedy. The unnamed characters scurry through a machine-oriented society, surrounded by

Sophie Treadwell
COURTESY OF THE BILLY ROSE THEATRE COLLECTION

unnatural noise and activity, trapped in the prison of the industrialized world. It is tempting to surmise that Treadwell's work influenced the controversial political works of MARUXA VILALTA's *El 9* almost forty years later or GRISELDA GAMBARO's in the 1960s and '70s. In *Machinal* Treadwell focuses on the plight of women in this world, describing the central character as "ready—eager—for life—for love . . . but deadened—squeezed—crushed by the machine-like quality of the life surrounding her."[2] The play's women are forced to submit to a desperate life. Nobody advocates for them: not their ministers, husbands, lovers, not even their mothers. Incidentally, *Machinal* served to launch the career of the dashing, charismatic young man who played the lover in the original cast: Clark Gable. After its successful New York run, the play went to London, Paris, and Moscow, and has since been revived in New York (1960) and at London's National Theatre (1994).

Treadwell managed to combine elements of an avantgarde style (such as the incorporation of film, music, and dance) with socially relevant themes in such plays as *Ladies Leave* (1929), which deals with an adulterous wife (shocking subject matter for the time), and *Lone Valley* (1933), which tells of a young Texas woman who manages a highway chili stand.

After the death of her husband in 1933, frustrated by a dearth of interested producers and bereft at her loss, Treadwell became profoundly depressed. She traveled the world for a year, fighting her way out of despair with a novel, *Hope for a Harvest,* which she later adapted for the stage in 1941. The play is peopled with ordinary, unpretentious folk who struggle with the devastation and turmoil war wreaks on the domestic front.

Her twenty-fifth and final play, *Now He Doesn't Want to Play* (1967), a comedy set in a Mexican boarding house, was mounted at the University of Arizona Theater. It achieved only nominal success. She continued to write at her home in Tucson, Arizona, until her death from cerebrovascular failure in 1970.

PLAYS

Andrew Wells Lady (a.k.a. *Judgment in the Morning*), n.d.; *Constance Darrow,* 1909?; *For Saxophone,* 1934; *Gringo,* 1922; *Harvest* (teleplay, 1954), 1940; *Highway,* 1954; *Hope for a Harvest,* 1941; *Ladies Leave,* 1929; *The Last Border,* n.d.; *Le Grand Prix,* 1907; *Lone Valley,* 1933; *Lonely Lue,* 1923; *Loving Lost,* n.d.; *Machinal,* 1928; *Madame Bluff,* 1918; *A Man's Own,* ca. 1904; *Million-Dollar Gate,* 1930; *Now He Doesn't Want to Play,* 1967; *Oh, Nightingale,* 1925; *Plumes in the Dust,* 1936; *Promised Land,* 1933; *The Right Man,* 1908; *Siren,* 1953; *A String of Pearls,* n.d.; *Sympathy,* 1915

NOVELS

Hope for a Harvest, 1938; *One Fierce Hour and Sweet,* 1959

WORKS ABOUT

Wynn, Nancy E., *Sophie Treadwell: The Career of a 20th-Century American Feminist Playwright,* diss., City University of New York, 1982.

1. Essay by Louise Heck-Rabi in Robinson.
2. Ibid. From a letter dated March 14, 1955, in the Treadwell papers.

Catherine Trotter
(AUGUST 16, 1679–MAY 11, 1749)

LESBIA. Hands, and Seals, and oaths cannot secure
A mind like Man's unfaithful and impure.

—from *Love at a Loss,* epilogue

Catherine Trotter underwent a number of misfortunes during her London girlhood. Her father, Captain David Trotter, died in Scandaroon, Turkey, in 1683 while in service to King Charles II. Her mother's pension lasted only one year before along with the life of the King it ended. Although Trotter then had to live as a poor relation, her intelligence and beauty won her the favor of many. She mastered French and writing skills without any instruction, and received some tutoring in Latin and logic.

By the age of fourteen she had published verses and an impressive autobiographical epistolary novel entitled *Olinda's Adventures.* Lured by the hope of making good money, Trotter determined to find success with stage dramas, which offered successful playwrights a tidy income. Two years after *Olinda,* she penned her first play, an adaptation of APHRA BEHN's novel *Agnes de Castro* (1696). As opposed to the fresh charm of her novel, the drama suffered from stilted plotting and weak blank verse; it fared poorly. She rebounded two years later with *The Fatal Friendship,* a tragedy noted for its "ingenious obsession with money, its advantages, and the problems resulting from the lack of it."[1]

Around this time she, along with her contemporaries DELARIVIERE MANLEY and MARY PIX, was spoofed in the Drury Lane production *The Female Wits,* written by the anonymous Mr. W. M. (possibly a group of actors). Although the three women did not often socialize (Trotter rebuked Manley's friendship, deeming her "indiscreet"), they provided professional support to each other. Unlike Manley and Pix, whose work sometimes resembled bedroom farces, Trotter rarely triumphed commercially; Nancy Cotton remarks that, due to her concern for respectability, she tended toward moral tragedies, which proved unpopular with audiences.[2] However, she had strong feminist leanings. When she was accused of plagiarism by a Lady Mascham in regard to her *A Defence of Mr. Locke's "Essay of Human Understanding"* (the Lady was not able to believe a woman could have penned so academic a reply), Trotter wrote, "Women are as capable of penetrating into the grounds of things and reasoning justly as men are who certainly have no advantage of us but in their opportunities of knowledge . . ."[3] And when she sought her friend William Congreve's approval for her play *The Revolution of Sweden* (1707), Cotton claims, "in spite of his advice, she persisted in making the heroines feminist."[4]

About the time she completed *The Revolution of Sweden*, Trotter married a Mr. Cockburn, a curate of St. Dunstan's on Fleet Street. Her marriage marked the end of her play writing career. Much later in Trotter's life, in a letter of dedication to Alexander Pope, she wrote, "Being married in 1708 I bid adieu to the muses, and so wholly gave myself up to the cares of a family, and the education of my children, that I scarce knew whether there was any such thing as books, plays or poems stirring in Great Britain."[5] No doubt, the needs of three children and the unexpected loss of her husband's post in 1714 (he refused to take the Oath of Abjuration upon the death of Queen Anne) distracted Trotter from creative pursuits. For the following twelve years her husband taught Latin, and the family struggled financially. When Cockburn finally recanted, he received the post of minister of the Episcopalian Church in Aberdeen, and they returned to a life of comfort.

During this time, Trotter had become engrossed in the study of "the most abstruse subjects in morality and metaphysics," according to Cotton.[6] Her essays on these subjects were published in *The History of the Works of the Learned* (1743) and in posthumous essay collections assembled by Thomas Birch. Trotter died in 1749, four months after her husband. Of her work, Birch writes, "Her construction was tight, and her language well disciplined and yet rich." Of the woman herself, he offers that she was a small woman with a lively spirit, modest, even-tempered, generous, kind, and "ready upon all occasions to forgive injuries, and bear them, as well as misfortunes without interrupting her own ease, or that of others, without complaints or reproaches."[7]

PLAYS

Agnes de Castro, 1696; *The Fatal Friendship*, 1698; *Love at a Loss, or Most Votes Carry It* (a.k.a. *The Honourable Deceiver*), 1701; *The Revolution of Sweden*, 1702; *The Unhappy Penitent*, 1701

OTHER WORKS

A Defence of Mr Locke's "Essay of Human Understanding," 1702; *A Discourse Concerning a Guide in Controversies*, 1707; *Notes on Christianity, as Old as Creation*, 1751; *Notions of God*, 1751; *On the Credibility of the Historical Parts of Scripture*, 1751; *On the Infallibility of the Church of Rome*, 1751; *On Moral Virtue and Its Natural Tendency to Happiness*, 1751; *On the Usefulness of Schools and Universities for the Improvement of Mind in Right Remarks on Mr Seed's Sermon on Moral Virtue*, 1751; *Remarks upon an Inquiry into the Origin of Human Appetites and Affections*, 1751; *Remarks upon the Principles and Reasonings of Dr. Rutherford's "Essay on the Nature and Obligations of Virtue,"* 1747; *Remarks upon Some Writers in the Controversy Concerning the Foundation of Moral Duty and Moral Obligations in the History of the Works of the Learned*, 1743; *A Vindication of Mr Locke's Christian Principles from the Injurious Imputations of Dr. Holdsworth*, 1751

WORKS ABOUT

Birch, Thomas, ed., *The Works of Mrs. Catherine Cockburn, Theological, Moral, Dramatic, and Poetical*, 2 vols., 1751

1. Morgan.
2. Cotton.
3. Birch, Thomas. "Account of the Life of the Author." In *The Works of Mrs. Catherine Cockburn, Theological, Moral, Dramatic, and Poetical*, 2 vols. (London: J. & P. Knapton, 1751), p. xlvi.
4. Op. cit., Cotton.
5. Op. cit., Birch.
6. Op. cit., Cotton.
7. Op. cit., Birch.

Marina Tsvetayeva
(SEPTEMBER 26, 1892–AUGUST 31, 1941)

HENRIETTE. God created his marvelous world in a week./A woman is a hundred worlds. With one breath,/How can I become a woman in just one day?/Yesterday a hussar—in spurs and sword./Today, a lace and satin angel./And tomorrow, perhaps, who knows?

—from *An Adventure*

Although the Russian poet and playwright Marina Tsvetayeva wrote at the height of the modernist era, her work aligns itself more with the classical mythology and pagan beliefs of the neoromanticists. All of her plays were written in verse, and while she borrowed liberally from others' works for her dramatic source material, particularly from

Gustav Schwab, Aleksandr Blok, Edmond Rostand, and Giovanni Casanova, her verse has been noted for its originality, directness, and distinctive staccato rhythms. Actually Tsvetayeva preferred that her plays be considered poems with dramatic form.

Tsvetayeva was born in Moscow, where her exposure to the world of art and literature was instigated by her father, a professor at the University of Moscow and the director of a museum. She began writing in her teens, and before she turned twenty wrote a verse translation of Rostand's *L'aiglon* and published her first poetry collection, *The King-Maiden*. Restless at thirty, she left the Soviet Union, roving Europe until she settled in Paris in 1925. There the artist devoted herself to her poetry and embarked on a career as a verse dramatist. In 1939, missing her homeland, Tsvetayeva returned to Moscow.

Her early costume dramas, reminiscent of late-eighteenth-century romantic plays, were quite conservative compared to her poetry at the time. Later her works became more serious: tragedies with classical settings, particularly influenced by Mikhaylovich Vyacheslav and Innokenti Annensky. Tsvetayeva was a nationalist, and much of her work praised the tsar.

Tsvetayeva's versions of classical works often involved subtle but provocative revisions. In her *Theseus* (1924), for example, she departs from the traditional narrative in which the title character abandons Ariadne on Naxos, leaving her instead to Bacchus, who offers her the freedom to ascend to a higher level of existence. Tsvetayeva also made significant changes in her adaptations of Casanova's stories and memoirs. In one of these plays, *An Adventure* (1923), the playwright transforms Henriette, Casanova's mysteri-

ous French lover, from the shy and retiring woman of the traditional legend into a witty, brilliant adventurer: "I am a moonbeam," she says, "free to go wherever I choose." *An Adventure* was Tsvetayeva's final play. It was one of her greatest dramatic successes, along with *Fortuna (1923)*, which is based on the life of Armand Louis de Gontaut Biron, duke of Lauzun, a contemporary of Casanova's.

Sadly the playwright's life came to a tragic end in 1941. Caught in the chaos of World War II, she was exiled to the remote town of Yelabuga. With no friends and no support, consumed by despair, the bereft poet took her life.

PLAYS

Chervonnyi balet, n.d.; *Fedra* (Phaedra), 1927; *Feniks* (Phoenix), 1924; *Fortuna* (Fortune), 1923; *Kamennyi angel*, n.d.; *Konetz Kazanovy* (Casanova's End), 1922; *Metel* (The Snowstorm), 1918; *Priklyuchenie* (An Adventure), 1923; *Tezey* (Theseus; a.k.a. *Ariadna*), 1924

OTHER WORKS (SELECTED)

A Captive Spirit: Selected Prose, 1980; *Art in the Light of Conscience: Eight Essays on Poetry*, 1992; *In the Inmost Hour of the Soul*, 1989; *The King-Maiden* (poetry), 1911; *Krysolov* (The Pied Piper), 1978; *Lebedinyi stan* (The Demesne of the Swans), 1980; *Letters, Summer 1926*, 1985; *Mat i muzyka* (My Mother and Music), 1977; *Moi Pushkin* (My Pushkin), 1977; *Posle Rossii* (After Russia), 1992; *Selected Poems*, 1971; *Selected Poems*, 1994; *Stikhotvoreniia i poemy*, 1980; *Symphony No. 14*, 1986

Maruxa Vilalta
(SEPTEMBER 23, 1932–   )

SEVEN. You're not eating?
NINE. I'm not hungry.
SEVEN. (*Stretching his body*) I'm dying of hunger!
NINE. Dying is going a bit far.
SEVEN. Well, I *am.*
NINE. Don't be so vain. Dying is going too far.

—from *El 9*

An important presence in the Mexican theater scene, Maruxa Vilalta actually emigrated to Mexico at the age of seven, when her family was forced to leave their home country, Spain, during the Spanish Civil War. She earned a degree in Spanish literature at the College of Philosophy and Letters of the National Autonomous University of Mexico in Mexico City, but she did not pursue an academic career. Heeding the call to write her own literature, by 1958 Vilalta had published her first novel, *El castigo* (The Punished Man). By 1960 she had written her first play, an adaptation of her second novel, *Los desorientados* (The Confused).

Most of her work ventures upon the thematic territory she claimed with her 1965 play *El 9* (Number Nine). Like SOPHIE TREADWELL's *Machinal,* *El 9* deals with the social dehumanization brought on by the industrialized world. While, superficially, all appears to be in order—clean cafeterias and work areas, modern conveniences, a compliant bureau—the workers in *El 9* are identified only as numbers. *Nada como el piso 16* (Nothing Like the Sixteenth Floor; 1975), which utilizes a *ménage à trois* to illustrate a world struggling for power, sex, and material goods, ad-dresses similar ideas with the underlying theme of the triumph of sacrifice. The satirical *Historia de él* (The Story of Him; 1978), articulates the playwright's view on the social and political realities of Mexican culture as it follows the progress of its universal protagonist, represented by an anonymous crowd.

Her experimental dramas, filled with alienated, manipulative characters, are perhaps best exemplified in her 1970 work *Esta noche juntos, amándonos tanto* (Together Tonight, Loving Each Other So Much). The poverty-stricken, elderly couple at the center of the play has shut out the contemporary world by covering their windows and locking their doors. They live in the past—gleefully reading aloud from old newspapers stories of yesterday's catastrophes, and living by the complex rules of a cruel game-playing ritual, which Kirsten Nigro suggests is reminiscent of Edward Albee's George and Martha from *Who's Afraid of Virginia Woolf.* But Vilalta offers an even greater tragedy in *Esta noche* when a neighbor dies unnoticed outside the couple's hovel. The play uses multimedia techniques in a style advocated by Brecht's epic theater. Vilalta is the recipient of three Alarcón Prizes from the Mexican Critics Association (Mexico's most prestigious theater award). Her works have been produced internationally and translated into French, Italian, Czech, and Catalan. In 1975 she began directing her own plays, starting with *Nothing Like the Sixteenth Floor,* and has continued doing so in association with the National Autonomous University of Mexico. She is married and has two children.

PLAYS

Cuestión de narices, 1966; *Los desorientados* (also novel, 1958), 1960; *Esta noche juntos, amándonos tanto* (Together

Tonight, Loving Each Other So Much, 1973), 1970; *Historia de él* (The Story of Him, 1980), 1978; *Nada como el piso 16* (Nothing Like the Sixteenth Floor, 1978), 1975; *El 9*, (Number Nine) 1965; *Trio*, 1964; *Pequeña historia de horror (y de amor desenfrenado)* (A Little Tale of Horror [and Unbridled Love], 1986), 1984; *Soliloquio del tiempo* (Soliloquy of Time), n.d.; *La última letra* (The Last Letter), 1964; *Una mujer, dos hombres, y un balazo* (A Woman, Two Men, and a Gunshot, 1984), 1981; *Un día loco* (A Crazy Day), 1969; *Un país feliz*, 1965

FICTION

El castigo (The Punished Man), 1957; *Dos colores para el paisaje* (Two Colors of the Countryside), 1961; *El otro día, la muerte* (Another Day, Death), 1974

1. Essay by Kirsten F. Nigro in Magill.

Paula Vogel
(NOVEMBER 16, 1951–   )

CECIL. Never forget that every single organic being around us strives to increase in numbers; that each lives by a struggle at some period in its life; that heavy destruction inevitably falls either on the young or the old.

—from *And Baby Makes Seven*

"Although clearly writing from a feminist perspective, [Paula] Vogel does not portray her women uncritically or her men unsympathetically," writes Tish Dace.[1] For example, in *Desdemona* (1979), a revision of Shakespeare's *Othello*, the title character gives cause to her husband's rage: She beds almost every man in Cyprus. But, by revealing the unbearable limitation of Desdemona's world, Vogel weaves a tragedy brought about by a patriarchal society.

The works by this Washington, D.C., native vary widely in their subject matter and scope, yet she approaches her plays with great comedic flare and an "antic literacy."[2] She has addressed such diverse topics as pornography and domestic violence in *Hot 'n' Throbbing* (1992); women and poverty in *The Oldest Profession* (1981); and the AIDS epidemic in *The Baltimore Waltz* (1992), in which Anna, a "good girl" schoolteacher, learns she has a fatal illness, ATD—Acquired Toilet Disease. She and her brother decide to travel to Vienna in search of Dr. Todesrocheln, who has supposedly discovered a cure. Despite the humorous take on illness in *Waltz*, the play explores serious issues such as the relationship between loving and dying, sex, sibling dynamics, and the difficulties of separation. The *Village Voice* called the play "spiritually

nourishing."[3] Vogel wrote *Waltz* as a sort of epitaph: Not long before her own brother died of AIDS, they had to cancel a trip to Europe together, and for the playwright, her creation became that unfulfilled journey. The play was well received among critics, such as Michael Feingold, who wrote, "*The Baltimore Waltz* is an airy, funny, endearingly goofball entertainment, magically empowered to treat the harrowing emotions it encloses lightly, yet without trivializing them or diminishing their impact."[4]

Before settling into a career as a playwright, Vogel worked as a secretary, a moving van company packer, a computer processor, and an electronics factory worker. Since 1985 she has been the director of Brown University's graduate play writing program. She was educated at Bryn Mawr College, Catholic University, and Cornell University, and has taught as a visiting guest artist at many universities, including New York University, McGill, University and the University of Alaska in Juneau, as well as a variety of theater institutions such as the Manhattan Theater Club. At one of her alma maters, Cornell University, Ithaca, New York (1977–82), Vogel lectured in women's studies in addition to teaching theater. Among the recognitions she has earned are the American National Theater Academy West Award (1977), the Samuel French Award, National Endowment for the Arts Fellowships (1980, 1981), the MacDowell Colony Fellowship (1981, 1989), and the McKnight Fellowship (1992). She has also worked as artistic director for numerous theaters, among them Theater with Teeth, New York (1982–85) and Theater Eleanor Roosevelt, Providence, Rhode Island, where she has been since 1990.

PLAYS

And Baby Makes Seven, 1986; *Apple-Brown Betty*, 1979; *The Baltimore Waltz*, 1992; *Bertha in Blue*, 1981; *Desdemona*, 1979; *Heirlooms*, 1984; *Hot 'n' Throbbing*, 1992; *How I Learned to Drive*, 1997; *The Last Pat Epstein Show Before the Reruns*, 1979; *Meg*, 1977; *The Oldest Profession*, 1981; *Swan Song of Sir Henry*, 1974

1. Essay by Tish Dace in Berney (2).
2. Frank Rich, *New York Times*, February 2, 1992.
3. *Village Voice*, February 18, 1992.
4. Ibid.

Alena Vostrá
(1938–   )

OFFSIDE. How should I put it? You have to ask yourself the question: are they governing you or are you governing them? This is the only defense. I tell myself: this is a sort of experiment as to what one can endure and what one can make another endure . . . It is all a game. . . . Finally we all shall get it. It is a sort of a merry-go-round.

—from *Eeny Meeny Miney Mo*

Like Jerzy Grotowski's Polish Laboratory Theater, Peter Brooks's Theater of Cruelty Workshop, and Joseph Chaikin's Open Theater, the Cinohern Klub (Drama Club), which Czech playwright and theatrician Alena Vostrá helped found, favored an approach that "relied heavily on physical movement, nonspecific language and sound, and often unusual arrangements of space."[1] In the introductory commentary to her 1966 work *Eeny Meeny Miney Mo*, Vostrá and her husband, the prominent critic Jaraslav Vostry, wrote the following:

> Yes, this is a Drama Club comedy that develops some of its themes and principles in its own way. It was written, so to say, in the theater rather than for a theater that would subsequently adopt it for its own objectives: actually, we have here a comedy to a degree virtually tailor-made for certain actors, not only in the figurative sense of the word but in a literal sense as well: it counts on actors who perform not only with their souls but also with their bodies—it counts on complete actors with their own potential themes, and not on some kind of abstract 'art of acting.' In this sense its production is unthinkable outside the context of the theater in which it premiered.

Eeny, Meeny presents three young men, Offside, Pierrot, and Medica, as examples of modern alienated youth. They are dropouts, without ambition, rancor, or ideology. According to Paul Trensky, Vostrá "succeeds remarkably well in individualizing most of the dramatis personae, whose important traits come through the execution of their games and in their theoretical attitudes toward them . . . The play is filled with comic effects of all kinds, including verbal gags, puns, riddles and nonsense stories, as well as situation comedy of the most exuberant variety."[2]

Trensky calls *On the Knife's Edge* (1968), subtitled "Rêve-Verité," "an unconventionally structured fantasy with symbolic overtones. It is a denser and thematically more complex play, but its dramatic qualities are inferior to those of [*Eeny, Meeny*]." The play, set in a small, decrepit tenement house in Prague, treats audiences to a simultaneous viewing of events taking place in six separate dwellings. Segueing from a realistic to a surrealistic mode, "the old tenement [becomes] a sort of microcosm of a modern, atomized world in which people have ceased to understand each other and lead a sterile, cage-like existence."[3] The central character is Mr. Hrdina, an idealist who tries vainly to find his way in the chaos of specialized knowledge and fragmented interests. Frustrated, he attempts suicide by thrusting a kitchen knife into his head (a sort of intellectual suicide), and the play evolves into a hallucinatory sequence that demonstrates the power of the superficial. Along with her contemporaries Václav Havel, Josef Landovsky, and Josef Topo, Alena Vostrá has written plays that reflect the materialistic, alienated world that surrounded the youth of Czechoslovakia in the 1950s. Rather than creating works of pure absurdity to illustrate this dilemma, Vostrá has chosen to inject grotesque elements into realistic dramas, to correspond with what she believes to be the grotesqueness of reality. She arose out of the fringe theater movement of the 1950s, which dealt almost exclusively with the problems of the young.

PLAYS

Na koho to slovo padne (Eeny Meeny Miney Mo), 1966; *Na ostň nože* (On the Knife's Edge), 1968

1. "Drama and Dramatic Arts" by Paul Trensky. Microsoft Encarta. 1996.
2. Ibid.
3. Ibid.

Jane Wagner
(FEBRUARY 2, 1927/35–)

KATE. I am sick of being the victim of trends I reflect/but
don't even understand.

—from *The Search for Signs. . .*, Part I

Perhaps best known for her 1985 Broadway smash *The
Search for Signs of Intelligent Life in the Universe*, Jane Wagner is also an actor, director, and designer. Born in Norris,
Tennessee, a tiny town about fifteen miles north of Knox-
ville, in 1927, Wagner was educated at the School of Visual Arts in New York City. Before her career in theater,
she was a designer for Kimberly-Clark and Fieldcrest. In
fact, her textile designs have been exhibited at the Brooklyn Museum of Art.

Her collaboration with actor/comedian Lily Tomlin
has reaped success after success. Tomlin, who starred in
the Broadway production of *Search*, was also directed by
Wagner in *Appearing Nightly with Lily Tomlin*. For television, Wagner has directed all the Lily Tomlin specials,
of which she was also chief writer. Among her numerous
awards are the 1969 Peabody Award for *J. T.*, the Writers'
Guild Award and five Emmys for *Lily*, and the New York
Critics Special Award in 1986 for *Search*.

Search is a comedy with a sideways perspective on life
in late-twentieth-century America, as played out through
a series of recurring characters in vignettes tied together
by a bag lady who hears aliens conversing and insists that
she's "got the evidence." Some of the characters include a
wife whose husband does not even notice she has lost the
tip of a finger to their Cuisinart; Agnes, who has the de-
portment of a terrorist, and Paul, who is at once a health
nut and a cokehead. Gloria Steinem called the play "a
work of genius and compassion." Describing the atmosphere of the theater after the performance, Marilyn

Jane Wagner
COURTESY OF THE PLAYWRIGHT

French wrote in the afterword of the published edition, "The roar afterward conveys the feeling one had as one sat there, that people were starving for truth in art, and had finally been fed, and knew it." A *New York Times* review enthused, "Jane Wagner's lines rarely miss a trick." Originally written as a vehicle for Wagner's partner Lily Tomlin, who portrayed all the characters, the play has since enjoyed many venues and has often been performed by two actresses or more.

PLAYS

Appearing Nitely (also teleplay, 1978), 1977; *The Search for Signs of Intelligent Life in the Universe* (also book), 1985

SCREENPLAYS

The Incredible Shrinking Woman, 1981; *Moment by Moment*, 1978

TELEPLAYS

Edith Ann: A Few Pieces of the Puzzle (animated), 1994; *Edith Ann: Homeless Go Home* (animated), 1994; *J. T.* (also book), 1969; *Lily*, 1973, 1974; *Lily for President?* (coauthor), 1982; *Lily: Sold Out*, 1981; *Lily Tomlin*, 1973, 1975; *People*, 1976

BOOKS

Edith Ann: My Life, So Far, 1995

Michelene Wandor
(APRIL 20, 1940–)

ADRIENNE. How can I be serious when I hear my aunt talking of submission to her orders? Could a swallow used to sunshine agree to live with a mole in darkness?

—from *The Wandering Jew*, Part One, Scene 17

London-born Michelene Wandor has been an outspoken and dedicated advocate for female playwrights for more than two decades. She was an original member of the planning committee for the first Women's Theatre Festival, held at the Almost Free Theatre in London in the fall of 1973. Her fervent commitment to the sounding of diverse women's voices and the publication of their plays has led theater historian Helene Keyssar to claim, "More than any single figure, Wandor is responsible for articulating and supporting the interaction of feminism, theater, socialism, and gay liberation in Britain."[1]

A graduate of Cambridge University, she was born to working-class immigrants from the Soviet Union. She earned a B.A. with honors in English from Newham College in Cambridge and an M.A. in sociology in 1975 from the University of Essex in Colchester. She has also studied Renaissance and baroque music at Trinity College of Music in London. Wandor married literary agent Ed Victor in 1963, with whom she had two sons before divorcing twelve years later.

Wandor's well-respected nonfiction works *Understudies* (1981) and *Look Back in Gender* (1987) take intriguing looks at sexual politics in the theater, and the myriad dilemmas women encounter constitute the root of her dramas. The issues addressed in her plays are at once hugely diverse and ultimately similar. She has dealt frankly with women on the verge of retirement (*The Old Wives' Tale*, 1977) and with artificial insemination and parenthood (*Aid Thy Neighbor*, 1978). *The Day After Yesterday* (1972) is about sexual and moral hypocrisy; its plot centers on a "Miss World" contest; *To Die Among Friends* (1974) is five dialogues that focus on inter-and intrasexual politics; *Care and Control* (1977) is about women and child custody; *Floorshow* (1978), in a series of sketches and songs, examines the theme of women and work. She has surrealistically depicted the pressures of motherhood (*Spilt Milk*, 1972), and the lives of prostitutes (*Whores D'Oeuvres*, 1978). She has also adapted and revised a number of classic texts such as Heinrich von Kleist's *Penthesilea*, about the Amazons (1977), and Ernst Toller's *The Blind Goddess* (1981). Her two most commercially successful works are also adaptations: *Aurora Leigh* (1979), about a woman writer, from the Elizabeth Barrett Browning poem, and *The Wandering Jew* (with Mike Alfreds, 1987), about the Jesuits, from the Eugène Sue novel.

This diverse dramatist is no stranger to television, and her adaptation of William Luce's *The Belle of Amherst* won Wandor an Emmy; she also wrote television adaptations of Kate Chopin's *The Story of an Hour* and Radclyffe Hall's *The Well of Loneliness*. Known for her poetry, fiction, and plays, as well as her nonfiction works, Wandor has "earned her a reputation as one of England's most flexible writers . . ."[2] Wandor was a member of the planning committee for the first Women's Theatre Festival, held at the Almost Free Theatre in London in 1973, and she received Arts Council Awards in 1974 and 1983.

An avid anthologizer of works by women, Wandor has edited several editions of Methuen Press's *Plays by Women*. She writes, "Why an anthology of plays by women? If one looks at the contents page of any play anthology, one is already halfway to the answer. . . . Every time a woman writes a play about women, then, she is implicitly challenging the men still at center-stage. She may not be a conscious feminist, she may want to take no part in changing things for other women in the theatrical profession, but she will still in some way be justifying her existence as a woman playwright, and justifying the existence of her subject matter as valid."[3]

PLAYS

Aid Thy Neighbour, 1978; *Aurora Leigh* (adapt. of Eliz. Barrett Browning poem), 1979; *The Blind Goddess* (adapt. of Ernst Toller play), 1981; *Care and Control* (collab. w/ Gay Sweatshop), 1977; *Correspondence*, 1979; *The Day After Yesterday*, 1972; *Floorshow*, 1978; *Friends and Strangers*, 1974; *Future Perfect*, w/Steve Gooch and Paul Thompson, 1980; *Mal de Mèr*, 1972; *The Old Wives' Tale*, 1977; *Penthesilea* (adapt. of Heinrich von Kleist play), 1977; *Scissors*, 1978; *Sink Songs*, w/Dinah Brooke, 1975; *Spilt Milk*, 1972; *To Die Among Friends*, 1974; *The Wandering Jew*, w/Mike Alfreds (adapt. of Eugène Sue novel), 1987; *Wanted*, 1988; *Whores D'Oeuvres*, 1978; *You Too Can Be Ticklish*, 1971

OTHER WORKS

Arky Types (novel), 1987; *The Body Politic*, ed., 1972; *Garden of Eden: Selected Poems*, 1990; *Guests in the Body* (short stories), 1986; *Look Back in Gender*, 1987; *Once a Feminist*, 1990; *On Gender and Writing*, ed., 1983; *Plays by Women*, Vols. 1–4, 1982–85; *Strike While the Iron Is Hot*, ed., 1980; *Touch Papers*, w/Judith Kazantzis and Michèle Roberts, 1982; *Understudies, Theater and Sexual Politics*, 1981; *Upbeat: Poems and Stories*, 1982; *Wandor on Women Writers*, 1988

1. Keyssar.
2. Essay by Lizbeth Goodman in Berney (1).
3. Wandor (1).

Mercy Otis Warren
(SEPTEMBER 25, 1728–OCTOBER 19, 1814)

HATEALL. Then the green Hick'ry, or the willow twig,
Will prove a curse for each rebellious dame
Who dare oppose her lord's superior will.

—from *The Group*, Act II, Scene 3

Greatly influenced by the fervent political beliefs of her brother, the American Revolutionary leader James Otis, Mercy Otis Warren gave herself over completely to the colonial cause and became one of America's first native-born women playwrights. Her clergyman uncle educated his niece alongside her two brothers, one of whom introduced her to the work of philosopher John Locke. She married James Warren, a member of the Massachusetts legislature and fierce advocate of America's independence from England.

Until her mid-forties Warren remained ardently but privately engaged in the issues surrounding the thirteen colonies. Then, in 1769, her husband was brutally attacked by a Tory gang; incapacitated, he was unable to continue his political campaigning. His wife rallied to action, writing hardline revolutionary essays for pamphlets and newspapers. In 1772, at the request of the future commander-in-chief John Adams, Warren composed a play about the Boston Massacre. First published in *The Massachusetts Spy*, a radical newspaper, *The Adulateur* (1773) used a Roman motif: Boston conspirators bore names such as Brutus and Cassius.

The like-minded public received Warren's work enthusiastically, and she proceeded to publish several other political dramas, focusing on key historical events such as the Boston Tea Party in *The Group* (1775), wherein the Tories are all depicted as villainous collaborators with the British. Warren's goal was clear: ". . . to attack the wealthy oligarchies who represented British royal interests against the republican values of the revolution."[1]

An important play of Warren's, in terms of women's theater history, was *The Ladies of Castile* (1790), a depiction of the women of the American Revolution, which was written at the behest of Abigail Adams. At great risk, the heroine, Maria, organizes a group of women to steal valuable relics from the Church in order to replenish the treasury of the revolutionaries. The dialogue reflects the incorrect views Warren considered the male species to have of women:

MARIA. Men rail at weaknesses themselves create
And boldly stigmatize the female mind,
As though kind nature's just impartial hand
Had formed our features in a baser mould.

Unfortunately Warren's dramas were never produced professionally and have been anthologized only on rare occasion, a fate suffered by far too many women playwrights in history.

PLAYS

The Adulateur, 1773; *The Defeat*, 1773; *The Group*, 1775; *The Ladies of Castile*, 1790; *The Sack of Rome*, 1790

OTHER WORKS

History of the Rise, Progress, and Termination of the American Revolution, 3 vols., 1805; *Poems Dramatic and Miscellaneous*, 1790

WORKS ABOUT

Anthony, Katherine S., *First Lady of the Revolution: The Life of Mercy Otis Warren* (repr. 1972), 1958; Delmar, Benjamin Franklin V., ed., *The Poems and Plays*, 1980; Fritz, Jean, *Cast for a Revolution*, 1972; Smith, William Raymond, *History as Argument: Three Patriot Historians of the American Revolution*, 1966

1. Robinson, Alice, "Mercy Warren, Satirist of the Revolution," in Chinoy.

Wendy Wasserstein
(1950–)

GEOFFREY. You don't know what it's like to have absolutely no idea who you are!

—From *The Sisters Rosensweig*

Perhaps America's most-produced living female playwright, Wendy Wasserstein is also one of this country's most professionally recognized. She is the first woman dramatist to have won the Antoinette Perry Award for best play, and she has also been awarded the Susan Smith Blackburn Prize, the New York Critics Circle Award, and the Pulitzer Prize for drama. She is a member of the Dramatists Guild and Playwrights Horizons, for which she serves on the artistic board. For many audiences, Wasserstein's is the voice of American feminism; yet, in spite of the fact that she identifies herself as a feminist, and nearly all of her plays portray women in various phases of life, she has been repeatedly criticized by outspoken feminists for presenting a watered-down, trivialized depiction of contemporary women's experiences.

Wasserstein was born in Brooklyn, New York, to textile manufacturer Morris M. Wasserstein and his wife, Lola. The youngest child in her family, she was named for the heroine in James M. Barrie's *Peter Pan*. Her childhood was peppered with trips to Broadway shows. Wasserstein says, "I always loved the theater. Always. I loved going into rooms and the lights go down and something happens."[1] She attended Mount Holyoke College in South Hadley, Massachusetts, the setting for her play *Uncommon Women and Others* (1975), where she graduated in 1971 with a B.A. in history. While working toward her M.A. in creative writing at City University of New York, her first play, *Any Woman Can't* (1973), was produced. Her works have been staged continually since then. In 1973, Playwrights Horizon mounted her musical *Montpelier Pa-Zazz*. During this same year, she entered the M.F.A. program in play writing at the Yale University School of Drama, from which she graduated in 1976.

Wasserstein wrote *Uncommon Women and Others* (1975) for her Yale thesis. She claims that it was inspired by a daydream in which she saw an all-female curtain call, a sight unseen since the lights darkened on CLARE BOOTHE LUCE's 1937 play *The Women*. In *Uncommon Women*, a group of reunioning Mt. Holyoke graduates toast and reminisce about the loves and follies of their college years. The narrative flashes forward and back, showing the audience how the women have changed since their under-

Wendy Wasserstein
COURTESY OF UPI/CORBIS-BETTMANN

graduate days. The women, particularly in their earlier years, are drawn almost allegorically—each representing a different type of young 1960s woman caught in the wave of the women's movement. The characters include a Germaine Greer fanatic who thrills to taste her own menstrual blood; a catatonic intent on adapting Wittgenstein for film; and a blue-blooded New Englander totally confused by the quick changes occurring in her world. Interestingly, even with this early work Wasserstein was the target of feminist critics. Responding to the differences between the characters as students and as adults, Helene Keyssar wrote, "Six years after their graduation, each of these women is in an utterly predictable situation. The play offers no alternative to or substantial critique of that message, to the contrary, the women are so amusing and banal that other options seem irrelevant."[2] Still, it received tremendous public approval. First produced in 1977 at the Eugene O'Neill National Playwrights Conference in Waterford, Connecticut, it has been revived several times and was telecast for the Public Broadcasting System.

Wasserstein's 1981 play *Isn't It Romantic*, about a working woman struggling to cope with the business of career and romance, opened at the Phoenix Theater to mixed reviews. A revised version opened in 1983 at Playwrights Horizons and ran just short of two years. Also that year, Wasserstein's one-act play *Tender Offer* was presented at New York's Ensemble Studio Theater, and she received a Guggenheim Foundation Fellowship. Wasserstein wrote a variety of material throughout the 1980s, including the musical *Miami* (1986), on which she collaborated with Jack Feldman and Bruce Sussman, and several teleplays such as *The Comedy Zone* (1984) and *Drive, She Said* (1987). In 1986 she wrote *Maggie/Magalita*, which was produced by the Lamb's Theater Company.

The play that won her the Pulitzer Prize for drama was *The Heidi Chronicles* (1989), which follows the life of the title character, an art history professor, through a broad spectrum of episodes that depict key historical events from the 1960s to the 1980s. Again, although the drama addresses a woman's experience, Wasserstein was denounced for conveying what her detractors felt was an essentially antifeminist message. Robert Brustein, who called *Heidi* "the Big Chill of feminism and failed American dreams," believes that the play "seems to suggest that the feminist movement, instead of reforming society, has succeeded largely in introducing women to the ravening competitiveness of the given circumstances, which is to say it has encouraged women to imitate the worst qualities of men."[3] Jill Dolan goes so far as to say that *Heidi* "is a postfeminist mainstream play that distorts the political history of U.S. feminism . . . The play trivializes radical feminist gains, suppresses feminist rage, and acquiesces to the dominant culture's reading of the end of feminism."[4] Wasserstein's supporters, however, argue, as Fred Albert does, that "Wendy Wasserstein has a wry, self-deprecating humor which helps her avoid righteousness without losing her sting. And while her heroine [Heidi] is both more self-conscious and self-aware than the self-deluded types she encounters on her spiritual journey, she is a charter member of her own generation."[5]

One of the playwright's most recent works, *The Sisters Rosensweig*, premiered at New York's Lincoln Center in 1992. Funny and heartwarming, it has a dark side, as well, reflected in its deliberate echoing of Anton Chekhov's *Three Sisters*. However, these sisters are from Brooklyn, not Moscow. They are in London to celebrate the oldest's fifty-fourth birthday—a bittersweet occasion during which their mutual yearnings for identity, completion, and satisfaction become apparent.

Wasserstein herself maintains a positive attitude about the controversy she causes among feminists. She considers the dialogue about her work to be healthy: "What gives me great pleasure is that these women are talking about the play, whether it is politically correct or not—that there is a piece of art about them."[6]

PLAYS

An American Daughter, 1997; *Any Woman Can't*, 1973; *Hard Sell*, 1980; *The Heidi Chronicles*, 1988; *Isn't It Romantic*, 1981; *Maggie/Magalita*, 1986; *Miami* (musical), 1986; *Montpelier Pa-Zazz*, 1974; *Tender Offer*, 1983; *The Sisters Rosensweig*, 1992; *Uncommon Women and Others*, 1975; *When Dinah Shore Ruled the Earth*, w/Christopher Durang, 1975

OTHER WORKS

Bachelor Girls (essays), n.d.; *The Comedy Zone* (television segment), 1984; *Drive, She Said* (teleplay), 1987; *Liz Minelli in Sam Found Out: A Triple Play*, w/Terence McNally, 1988; *Pamela's First Musical*, 1996; *The Sorrows of Gin* (teleplay), 1979

1. Seattle Repertory Theatre program notes, vol. 9, no.1 1989/90.

2. Keyssar.

3. Brustein.

4. Dolan.

5. Op. cit., Seattle Repertory, essay by Fred Albert, "Wendy Wasserstein: Mixing Comedy with Conviction."

6. Op., cit., Seattle Repertory.

Fay Weldon
(SEPTEMBER 22, 1933–   )

WASP. I never thought happiness was a goal worth achieving—cows are happy.
EDWIN. You make jokes when people's hearts are breaking.

—from *After the Prize*

One of Britain's leading writers, Fay Weldon once commented, "I always worked on the basic assumption that the world was peopled by females."[1] Weldon was born in Alvedurah, Worcestershire, in 1933 and raised in New Zealand. Her parents were divorced by the time she was six, and she grew up with her sisters and mother while being schooled by nuns at the local convent school. At fourteen she went to live with her grandmother in England. Weldon considers her mother, also a writer, to have been an exceptional woman who provided her with the moral context that she claims accounts for her own healthy skepticism. Her maternal grandfather and uncle were also writers, and Weldon once remarked, "The ability to respond to words [is] rather like having red hair or blue eyes—[it] tends to run in the family."

Weldon earned an M.A. in economics and psychology from St. Andrews University in Scotland. She then married and, within six months, divorced a man twenty-five years her senior, but not without first conceiving a child; her son Nicholas was born in 1955. A newly single mother, Weldon went to work in the Foreign Office of the Civil Service "shuffling papers that sent spies to an uncertain fate in the East Bloc." In spite of the demands of the working world and motherhood, Weldon found energy to write. She sent out stories and manuscripts and watched her pile of rejection slips grow, but faithfully kept at her creative work. In the 1960s, she worked as a copy editor for several advertising firms. She believes this work afforded her rigorous training, for in advertising, she says, you have to "say a great deal in a few words . . . Apart from the fact that it is mostly lies, it teaches you form." In 1960 she married Ronald Weldon, a former antiques dealer who paints and plays jazz piano. They had three sons: Daniel (1963), who became a filmmaker, Thomas (1970), and Samuel (1977).

Weldon's perseverance paid off: By the mid-1970s she was a well-established novelist and playwright. Her first work written expressly for the stage was the 1969 drama *Permanence*. Since then she has written more than a dozen plays and seventeen novels, all best-sellers. She has also penned eight radio plays for the British Broadcasting Corporation (BBC) and more than fifty teleplays, including a five-part dramatization of Jane Austen's *Pride and Prejudice*.

One of her best-known theatrical works began as a novel, a common progression for Weldon. *The Life and Loves of a She-Devil*, about a woman's obsessive revenge on her unfaithful husband, has also been adapted for the small screen in a lesser-known BBC production, along with the popular Hollywood version, *She-Devil*, starring Meryl Streep and Rosanne Barr. "The film," Weldon once commented, quoting Oscar Wilde, "reminded me of something I once wrote." Indeed, Hollywood managed to utterly water down the wicked bite of the original text.

Weldon's feminism is complex and somewhat cynical, and she has been attacked by critics who have taken issue with what they consider a narrow view of women's options for success. Her 1981 drama *After the Prize* centers on the life of a female particle physicist who has just received the Nobel Prize and her husband, who struggles to cope with his role as "other" to a famous spouse. *Prize* was criticized by Frank Rich, who felt it was too derivative of the classic *Woman of the Year*, calling it an "Alan Ayckbourn farce, minus the humor or feeling or surprise."[2] Clive Barnes reported that, while the play displays "many signs of life and the verisimilitudes of life . . . it trades that life for somewhat lurid fiction."[3] These negative responses by male critics are reminiscent of the response to *He and She*, RACHEL CROTHER's play on the successful wife-husband syndrome, which significantly pre-dated the Hepburn-Tracy *Woman of the Year* film.

The themes of Weldon's books and plays contain sardonic analysis of the often obsessive ways in which men and women cope with the demands of traditional sex roles. "The predicaments of women seem to be universal in

every culture where you have an enormous, aspiring middle class," Weldon postulates. "What I want [is] to illuminate woman's lot. Women must ask themselves: What is it that will give me fulfillment?"

PLAYS

Action Replay (a.k.a. *Love Among Women*), 1978; *After the Prize*, 1981; *A Doll's House* (adapt. of Henrik Ibsen play), 1988; *Friends*, 1975; *The Hole in the Top of the World*, 1987; *I Love My Love*, 1981; *Jane Eyre* (adapt. of Charlotte Brontë novel), 1986; *Moving House*, 1976; *Mr. Director*, 1977; *Permanence*, 1969; *A Small Green Space*, libretto w/ Petula Clark, 1989; *Someone Like You*, 1989; *Tess of the D'Urbervilles* (adapt. of Thomas Hardy novel), 1992; *Woodworm*, 1981; *Words of Advice*, 1974

NOVELS

Affliction (a.k.a. *Trouble*), 1994; *The Cloning of Joanna May*, 1989; *Darcy's Utopia*, 1990; *Down Among the Women*, 1972; *The Fat Woman's Joke*, 1967; *Female Friends*, 1975; *Growing Rich*, 1992; *The Heart of the Country*, 1987; *The Hearts and Lives of Men*, 1987; *Leader of the Band*, 1988; *Letters to Alice on First Reading Jane Austen*, 1984; *The Life and Loves of a She-Devil*, 1984; *Life Force*, 1992; *Little Sisters*, 1977; *Moon over Minneapolis*, 1991; *Polaris and Other Stories*, 1985; *Praxis*, 1978; *The President's Child*, 1982; *Puffball*, 1980; *Rebecca West*, 1985; *Remember Me*, 1976; *The Rules of Life*, 1987; *The Shrapnel Academy*, 1986; *Splitting*, 1995; *Watching Me, Watching You*, 1981; *Words of Advice*, 1977

1. All of Weldon's quotations are from the *Current Biography Yearbook 1990*.

2. *New York Times*, November 24, 1981.

3. *New York Post*, November 24, 1981.

Timberlake Wertenbaker
(1946?–)

PHILLIP. The Greeks believed that it was a citizen's duty to watch a play. It was a kind of work in that it required attention, judgement, patience, all social virtues.
TENCH. And the Greeks were conquered by the more practical Romans, Arthur.
COLLINS. Indeed, the Romans built their bridges but they also spent many centuries wishing they were Greeks.

—from *Our Country's Good*, Act I, Scene 6

The plays of Timberlake Wertenbaker explore a diverse range of cultural, literary, and political territories. She writes gracefully and intelligently, whether she chooses to depict the world of a trendy left-wing couple whose lives take a sudden, dramatic turn when a disability turns their world upside down (*Abel's Sister*, 1985); to rewrite the brutal myth of Philomena as a paradigm adducing that silence breeds violence (*The Love of the Nightingale*, 1989); or to explore the difficult world of an Arab woman who dresses as a man in order to find acceptance and spiritual enlightenment among her people (*New Anatomies*, 1980). Her experimentation with both dramatic form and content has led dramaturg Robert Menna of Seattle to comment that her "archetypal images and symbolic characters guide us away from identifying solely with an individual personality and continually return us to a broader political perspective."[1] Many of the playwright's themes, in fact, wind themselves around issues of identity, displacement, and cultural differences. Perhaps the seeds for her subject matter were planted in her youth.

Although Wertenbaker was born in the United States, her early education was in France, near Basque, where her family had relocated. Charles Wertenbaker, a foreign correspondent for Time-Life, and his third wife, Lael Tucker, were the parents of Lael Louisiana Timberlake, who has been averse to address matters concerning her name, birthplace, or birth date. Before eventually settling in England, Wertenbaker graduated from St. John's College in Annapolis, Maryland in 1966, then went to work as a journalist in New York City, after which she taught French in Greece for a year. In the early 1980s she turned to play writing.

Wertenbaker's first dramatic efforts were spawned in fringe theaters, but by 1984 she was the Thames Television resident writer at the Royal Court Theatre, which has subsequently produced *The Grace of Mary Traverse*, *Our Country's Good*, and *Three Birds Alighting on a Field*. Wertenbaker has used her classical academic background and linguistic abilities to translate plays by Federico García Lorca, Maurice Maeterlinck, and Pierre Carlet de Chamblain de Marivaux, among others. Wertenbaker's plays, frequently revisionist retellings of classical myths and legends, challenge the sexism evidenced by the original texts. In *Inside Out* (1982) she reconstructs the Japanese legend of Komachi by casting an old woman as the lover of a youthful Komachi, portrayed by a young actress; a classical Greek chorus furthers the diversity of form. The chorus states, "They say a woman is a man turned inside out. Most evident in the genitals, his turned out, hers turned in, hers waiting for his, waiting for completion, that's what they say." Later the chorus asks, "What is the anatomy of a woman?;" Li, Komachi's companion, replies, "Not what you imagine through your genitals."

Wertenbaker set her sights on the Western world in *The Grace of Mary Traverse* (1985), which occurs in the late eighteenth century. Grace reveals the title character's personal transformation when she witnesses Lord George Gordon brutally rape another woman. Her subsequent

empowerment animates Mary to leave the oppressive confines of her father's house and embark on a path that will allow her to experience the power of sexual and political corruption. BBC radio drama producer Ned Chaillet writes, "Often the tilt of her writing explores a fluidity between the sexes that is far more revolutionary than any declaration of equality; and she does not hesitate to subvert legend or history in her examinations of human nature."[2]

She received her first Olivier Award and a New York Drama Critics Circle Award for *Our Country's Good*, her 1989 adaptation of Thomas Keneally's novel *The Playmaker*. Set in an Australian prison in 1789, the play centers on a young marine lieutenant intent on staging George Farquhar's Restoration comedy *The Recruiting Officer* for the edification of the prisoners. But the only cast members on hand are the convicts themselves—whores, pickpockets, thieves, and murderers. Initially their language and behavior are base and crude; yet, when called upon to perform, something sublime rises in them. They find within themselves the keys to cooperation, mutual respect, and trust.

Wertenbaker has been honored professionally with numerous awards and recognitions. In addition to her Royal Court Theatre post, she was an Arts Council resident writer for London's Shared Experience Theater Company in 1983. She has been the recipient of the Evening Standard's Most Promising Playwright Award and the All-London Playwrights' Award for *The Third*; after winning the Olivier Award for *Our Country's Good*, she received a second for *Three Birds Alighting on a Field* (1992).

She is known as a dramatist who produces work of merit, substance, and style. Ned Chaillet remarks, "Even in her most explicitly classical plays, Wertenbaker manages to wear her erudition lightly. . . . With her grasp of classical storytelling, her great gift of language and individuality of perception, she is likely to provide some of the most enduring drama of the late 20th century."[3]

PLAYS

Abel's Sister, w/Yvonne Bourcier, 1985; *Breaking Through*, 1980; *Case to Answer*, 1981; *The Grace of Mary Traverse*, 1985; *Home Leave*, 1982; *The House of Bernarda Alba* (adapt. and tr. of Federico García Lorca play), n.d.; *Inside Out*, 1982; *The Love of the Nightingale*, 1989; *Mesphisto* (adapt. and tr. of Ariane Mnouchkine play), 1986; *New Anatomies*, 1980; *Our Country's Good*, 1989; *Second Sentence*, 1980; *The Third*, 1980; *This Is No Place for Tallulah Bankhead*, 1978; *Three Birds Alighting on a Field*, 1992

OTHER WORKS

The Children (screenplay), 1990; *Les disputes* (Pierre Marivaux, tr.), 1989; *Do Not Disturb*, n.d.; *False Admissions* (Pierre Marivaux, tr.), 1989; *Leocadia* (Jean Anouilh, tr.), n.d.; *Pelleas and Melisande* (Maurice Maeterlinck, tr.), n.d.; *Successful Strategies* (Pierre Marivaux, tr.), 1989

1. Intiman Theatre Company program notes, vol. 1, no. 4, October 1991, Seattle, Wash.
2. Essay by Ned Chaillet in Berney (1).
3. Ibid.

Cheryl L. West
(1959–)

> MADEAR. Some folks wear dey scars on de inside . . . you jus wearin' yours on de outside. . . . You show me a woman dat ain't got a scar somewhere an I'll show you a woman dat ain't lived nuttin' but a lie.
>
> —from *Jar the Floor*

In her 1991 play *Jar the Floor*, Cheryl West demonstrates, with great humor and pathos, the misunderstandings and lack of communication that are often passed down from one generation to the next. When four generations of black women (ninety-year-old Madear, sixty-five-year-old Lola, forty-seven-year-old Maydee, and twenty-seven-year-old Vennie) converge on the occasion of Vennie's homecoming, sparks fly, family skeletons rattle, and the similar patterns of these women's lives are revealed. Complicating matters is Vennie's friend Raisa: white, one-breasted, and possibly Vennie's lover. Although she throws these women into a complex emotional situation, West clearly loves her characters. She calls *Jar* a play "about making peace: with one's scars, with one's history, and, of course, with the embodiment of oneself—one's mother."

West's commitment to the lives of African-American families and the communities in which they live is apparent in her work both on and off the stage. She was raised in Chicago by a single mother who worked two jobs in order to support her two daughters. West followed her mother's example as a hard worker. By 1985 she had already earned two master's degrees, one in rehabilitation administration (1980), the other in journalism (1985). She started writing in 1986 while still employed as a social services counselor. While working on her first play (eventually staged at a University of Illinois women's conference), she received an International Rotary Fellowship to study at the Jamaica School of Drama.

Since then West has managed to juggle her life as a dramatist with her life in social services. Indeed the connection between the two is clearly reflected in her creative work. West's plays have tackled miscegenation (*Getting Right Behind Something Like That*, 1986); teenage pregnancy, incest, and drug abuse (*A Mistake & 1/2*, 1988); and interracial relationships (*Puddin' 'n' Pete*, 1993). In *Before It Hits* (1990), which won the coveted Susan Smith Blackburn Prize, she tells the story of a family's struggle

to accept a favorite son's diagnosis of AIDS. Such a frank depiction of a black family's difficulty in dealing with this illness had never been seen on the stage. John Simon of *The New Yorker* commented that the play blasts wide open an aspect of AIDS not touched upon in any form by the media.

In 1994 West ventured into another controversial avenue with *Holiday Heart*, about a homosexual female impersonator who "adopts" his crack-addicted neighbor and her twelve-year-old daughter. But the playwright is not interested in simply covering new turf—*Holiday* reaches far deeper than surface issues. It is a play that attempts to explore the delicate structure of nurturing.

West makes no apologies for her subject matter. She says, "We [blacks] want only positive images of ourselves . . . We have the right to be suspicious of anything that makes us look anything less than pristine, because there have been so many images out there that have been negative and false . . . [but] I'm going to write about—boils, warts and all. . . ."[1]

PLAYS

A Mistake & ½, 1988; *Before It Hits Home*, 1990; *Getting Right Behind Something Like That*, 1986; *Holiday Heart*, 1994; *Jar the Floor*, 1991; *The Other Side of Freedom*, 1987; *Puddin' 'n' Pete*, 1993

1. Quoted in Seattle Repertory Theatre program notes, 1994, Seattle, Wash.

Mae West
(AUGUST 17, 1892?–NOVEMBER 22, 1980)

> You're a fine woman, Lou. One of the finest women that ever walked the streets.
>
> —from *Diamond Lil*

Mae West, America's original sex goddess, made her stage debut in vaudeville at the age of five. It was love at first applause for the inimitable Ms. West, and by the age of thirteen she had dropped out of school to pursue a career in the theater. By her eighteenth birthday she was an eight-year veteran of vaudeville, billed as "Vaudeville's Youngest Headliner," and was married to Frank Wallace, with whom she collaborated on a song-and-dance act. Although the couple stayed together only briefly, West did not divorce Wallace until 1942.

The daughter of a former prize-fighter father and Bavarian-immigrant mother, West grew up in the tough neighborhood of turn-of-the-century Brooklyn. Her exposure to people from all walks of life, along with the fighting spirit she inherited from her father, instilled in her a deep commitment to challenge society's puritanical conventions. Although West is best known as the seductive, drawling, big-bosomed sex icon, many of her greatest admirers are unaware that she created many of the sassy roles which stirred so much attention.

Before West began officially writing her own material, her reputation grew from her outrageous ad libs in shows such as *A la Broadway* and *Hello, Paris*. Her uninhibited sexuality made her an immediate hit. In 1926 West's first original play opened. *Sex*, publicized as having been written by a "Jane Mast," told the story of Margie LaMont, an upper-class debutante who breaks with her ties to high society and sets off on a course of sexual abandon that carries her across the world. Even though newspapers refused to carry advertisements for the play, it ran for forty-one weeks until the Society for the Suppression of Vice forced its premature closure. The *New York Telegraph* (April 28, 1926) said it hit "the speed limit of suggestiveness," and the *New York American* served notice that "a more flaming, palpitating play has not been seen hereabouts for some time." *Sex* was gloriously scandalous, and West was eventually jailed for ten days on an obscenity charge.* Although the court could not convict West based on the script, it justified her incarceration due to her al-

---

*The accompanying photograph was taken at the courthouse during that trial.

Mae West
COURTESY OF CORBIS-BETTMANN

legedly moving "her navel in an obscene way when she danced,"—despite the fact that West was fully clothed throughout the show (as she was in all her appearances).

Of course, a criminal record could do nothing to silence Mae West. Two years later her play *The Pleasure Man*, which centered on a wild party of homosexual carousing, enjoyed a successful New York opening. That same year saw the production of *Diamond Lil*, perhaps West's most recognized play. It takes place in New York's Bowery during the 1890s. Lil, a saloon boss/white slave trader's moll, has a ball toying with the various men who try to seduce her; she finally ends up with a Secret Service agent who busts the boss's ring, to whom she delivers her famous line "Come up 'n' see me some time." Although Lil received some positive reviews (in *The New Yorker*, 1928), a critic wrote there was "a certain flash brashness that reached a climax in the underworld of New York in the 1890's, as few subtler playwrights could have done it."), like many of West's works, it was her performance rather than the play itself that stole the show.

By 1928 West's reputation was known internationally, and she soon launched her successful film career. She began at Paramount Studios with *Night After Night* in 1932, and in 1933 adapted *Diamond Lil* for the big screen. By 1935 West was the highest-paid woman in the United States. Her film career soared; she had four hit shows back-to-back. However, in spite of her enormous popularity, her flamboyance brought her many detractors, some of whom helped implement the ultraconservative Motion Picture Production Code.

The author of sixteen plays and screenplays, as well as several novels and an autobiography, West continued to play her signature roles well into her seventies and eighties in films such as *Sextette* (1978). An authentic American original, she nearly single-handedly opened the locked doors of bedrooms everywhere, flaunting the view for all to see. She appreciated her own cleverness as a punster and uncanny ability to give audiences what they didn't even know they wanted. As she wrote in her autobiography, *Goodness Had Nothing to Do with It*, "It wasn't what I did, but how I did it. It wasn't what I said, but how I said it and how I looked when I did it and said it. I had evolved into a symbol and didn't even know it."[1]

PLAYS

Catherine Was Great, 1944; *Come On Up . . . Ring Twice!* (adapted from Carliss Dale work), 1952; *The Constant Sinner* (also novel, *Babe Gordon*, 1930), 1931; *Diamond Lil* (also screenplay, *She Done Him Wrong*, 1933), 1928; *The Drag*, 1927; *The Pleasure Man* (also novel, 1975), 1928; *Sex*, 1926; *Sextet*, 1961; *The Wicked Age*, 1927

SCREENPLAYS

Belle of the Nineties, 1934; *Every Day's a Holiday*, 1938; *Goin' to Town*, 1935; *Go West, Young Man*, 1936; *I'm No Angel*, 1933; *Klondike Annie*, 1936; *My Little Chickadee*, with W. C. Fields, 1940

WORKS ABOUT

Eells, George, and Stanley Musgrove, *Mae West*, 1982; Juska, Jon, *The Films of Mae West*, 1973; Weintraub, Joseph, *The Wit and Wisdom of Mae West*, 1967; West, Mae, *Goodness Had Nothing to Do with It* (autobio.), 1959

1. West, Mae, *Goodness Had Nothing to Do with It* (Englewood Cliffs, N.J.: Prentice Hall, 1959), p. 43.

Hella Wuolijoki
COURTESY OF UPI/CORBIS-BETTMANN

Hella Wuolijoki
(1886–1954)

Hella Wuolijoki, born Hella Maria Murrik, the daughter of an Estonian lawyer, has been called "a personality of many contradictions and a skillful craftsperson for the stage."[1] This remarkable woman balanced a successful business and play writing career with her fervent political commitment as a socialist. She began writing while still a child, and her first work was published while she was in secondary school. She studied literature and folk poetry at the University of Helsinki. Then, when she was nineteen years old, a general strike swept through Finland, an event that inspired her lifelong advocacy of socialism. Two years later she married the noted socialist Suolo Wuolijoki; the marriage lasted sixteen years.

Wuolijoki turned to play writing early, completing her first play, *The Children of the House*, in 1912. Unfortunately, despite the desire of several theaters to produce the drama, the czarist police forbade any staging whatsoever of this or any play penned by Wuolijoki. Frustrated, for the next twenty years she put her energy into her business ventures, which eventually made her a wealthy woman. She used her financial success to support socialist causes. Her country home became a favorite meeting place of politicians and literati whose sympathies lay with the defeated revolutionaries.

In the mid-1930s Wuolijoki resumed her writing; however, she made two significant changes. First, she decided to write in the dialect of the Finns, rather than the Estonian dialect with which she'd been reared (both countries share linguistic roots in the Finno-Ugric subfamily of the Uralic language); second, she assumed an alias, Juhani Tervapèè. Under this name, during a seventeen-year period, she wrote a five-play cycle about Finnish farm life,

which focused on the changing fate of Niskavuori, a farmhouse in the center of Finland. At the center of the plays is the "monumental, stony figure of the old proprietress, a matriarch keeping the house and family together."[2] Circling this venerable figure are the many women in her family, who represent the changing faces of the Finnish political arena. The last play in the cycle illustrates the new start that was to be made in postwar Finland. All five of the Niskavuori plays, which garnered Wuolijoki considerable popularity, reveal similar themes: "a pronounced admiration for old-fashioned Finnish country people and their values, a mild feminism, and a radical political bias, muted at first but growing all too obvious in the later plays, created by Soviet victory in 1944."[3] Several films have been based on the cycle drama.

The plays of Juhani Tervapèè gained international recognition among socialists throughout the 1930s. When Bertolt Brecht visited Finland in 1940, he sought out the mysterious writer and discovered the truth of her identity. While he lodged at Wuolijoki's home during a protracted stay, the pair collaborated on a new play. *The Master of Great Heikkilè and His Servant Kalle* (1947) plays with traditional expectation by depicting a farmer who, when sober, is the most miserable of men, but when drunk— his more common state—is the quintessence of benevolence. Interestingly, the play is recognized as a collaborative work only in Finland. Elsewhere Brecht receives sole credit. (See MARIELUISE FLEIßER for more on Brecht's tendencies in this area.)

True to her role as a political activist, Wuolijoki was arrested in the early 1940s for harboring a Russian parachutist during Finland's "Continuation War." Charged with treason and condemned to death, Wuolijoki's sentence was eventually reduced to life imprisonment. The sentence was ultimately commuted, but during the two years she was confined in prison walls, she produced four books. Upon her release, she joined the Finnish Communist Party, for which she served in Parliament from 1946–48. She also wrote several radio plays and volumes of memoirs. As an activist, Wuolijoki will be best remembered for her unflinching loyalty; as a playwright, for her clear depiction of character and her keen awareness of social change. "Her realism," it has been written, "is of an agile kind."[4]

PLAYS

Entès nyt, Niskavuori? (What Now, Niskavuori?), 1953; *Hèijynpuoleisiè pikkunèytelmiè* (Half-Malicious Short Plays), 1945; *Iso-Heikkilèn isèntè ja hènen renkinsè Kalle* (The Master of Great Heikkilè and His Servant Kalle; a.k.a. *Mr. Puntila and His Servant Matti*), w/Bertolt Brecht, 1947; *Jurrakon Hulda* (Hulda of Jurrakko), 1937; *Juustina*, 1937; *Kuningas ja hovinarri* (King and Jester), 1946; *Niskavuoren Heta* (Heta of Niskavuori), 1951; *Niskavuoren leipè* (The Bread of Niskavuori), 1939; *Niskavuoren naiset* (The Women of Niskavuori), 1936; *Niskavuoren nuori emèntè* (The Young Mistress of Niskavuori), 1940; *Talulapsed* (The Children of the House), 1912; *Vastamyrkky* (The Antidote), 1939; *Vihreè kulta* (Grccn Gold), 1938

1. Essay by G. C. Schoolfield in Hochman.
2. Anderson.
3. Op. cit., Hochman.
4. Op. cit., Anderson.

Wakako Yamauchi
(OCTOBER 15, 1924–   )

YO. In a war, Obasan, one country wins; the other loses. . . .
We all look the same to them. We lost both ways.

—from *12-1-A,* Act I, Scene 1

Wakako Yamauchi's 1982 work *12-1-A* recounts her experiences in an Arizona internment camp for Japanese-
Americans during World War II. The play's beauty and
poignancy are indicative of the author's ability to create,
as Amy Ling puts it, "moving testaments to human endurance, survival, and strength."[1] California-born Yamauchi was raised in a traditional Japanese household by her
Issei* father and mother, Yasaku Nakamura and Manoko
Machida. She did not learn English until she started elementary school. Her parents first worked as tenant farmers—Japanese-Americans were not yet allowed to own real
estate—in California's Imperial Valley. Later they ran a
hotel for itinerant Japanese farm workers. When World
War II broke out, the family had just opened a boarding
house in Oceanside, a small town near San Diego. Yamauchi was poised to graduate from high school. But in
1941 her family was sent to a Japanese internment camp
in Poston, Arizona.

Her father died there before the end of the war. "It
was a terrible place," Yamauchi has written. "You couldn't
run away from it because you'd die in the desert—*if* you

escaped the bullets from the sentries . . . I felt very bitter
there, and very closed in."[2] Occasionally she managed to
obtain work permits, which took her far away from the
camp to places such as Chicago, where she saw live theater
for the first time in her life.

Upon her family's release from the camp, Wakako settled with her mother and sisters in San Diego. Eventually
she moved to Los Angeles to attend art school. In 1948
she married Chester Yamauchi and, seven years later, gave
birth to her daughter, Joy, who became an editor of the
Asian-American newspaper *Toazi Times.* She and Chester
divorced in 1975.

Yamauchi lived a rather traditional life until the early-
1970s, when she enrolled in a University of California
correspondence course in short story writing. In her fiction
she embraced her cultural heritage, giving voice to a population that had hitherto been silent. Mako, the founder
of the East/West Players of Los Angeles, discovered one of
Yamauchi's stories in an Asian-American journal and
asked the author to adapt it for the stage. *And the Soul
Shall Dance* (1977), a feminist portrayal of Japanese-
American farm workers enveloped by harsh weather and
xenophobia in the Imperial Valley in the 1930s, took
shape. The play illustrates the Japan/America dichotomy
that threatened to fracture family ties: Emiko, a young
mother whose difficult life with her abusive husband leaves
her pining for her lover in Japan, is in conflict with her
daughter, Masako, who wants nothing more than to assimilate into American culture. Yamauchi has said of the
work, "I didn't consciously decide I was going to write the
play from the point of view of the women. But my mother
was a feminist in her time, and she always made me feel
that I was somebody. Japanese men were very chauvinistic,

---

*Issei are first-generation immigrants; Nisei, like Yamauchi, are born of
first-generation Japanese-Americans.

especially in those days, but women had a way of adapting things, of handling the men. That's one of the things I wanted to show, that feeling we had: 'You can step on us, but you haven't got us yet!' "

Since *Soul* brought her to the public's attention, Yamauchi has consistently created simple plays about complex people. She often returns to the rural landscapes of her youth. *The Music Lesson* (1980) focuses on a young widow who, with her three teenage children, struggles to keep her farm viable. She hires a lonely transient laborer who once dreamed of being a concert violinist. He works the fields and gives music lessons to her daughter, a young woman ripe with romantic yearnings. Soon both mother and daughter fall in love with the stranger, and the tense situation ignites the restrained atmosphere of politeness to which the family is accustomed. *The Chairman's Wife* (1990) uses the figure of Madame Mao to explore Yamauchi's preferred themes, only this time we see the political influence of Mao as well as the revolutionary forces in opposition to him, along with Madame Mao's inner struggles and what Houston calls the "incarceration of mind, spirit, and finally body . . ."[3]

Though she may be a late bloomer, Yamauchi has been recognized for her excellence as the recipient of two Rockefeller playwright in residence grants and one award (1977, 1979, 1980), and was singled out by the American Theater Critics Association for the Outstanding Play Award of 1976–77 (*Soul*).

VELINA HASU HOUSTON calls Yamauchi "a trailblazer for Asian-American women writers . . . [Her] work looks at the past and tries to separate the illusion from the reality to find that delicate balance between the sustaining of dreams and coping with reality that allows human beings to survive and endure."[4] As Yo, the central character of *12-1-A*, tells her fellow inmates in the tar-papered barracks of the Poston concentration camp, "What is there to fear? Life? Death? Just roll with the punches."

PLAYS (SELECTED)

And the Soul Shall Dance (also teleplay, 1977; also short story), 1977; *The Chairman's Wife*, 1990; *Gold Watch*, n.d.; *The Memento*, 1984; *The Music Lesson*, 1980; *Not a Through Street*, 1991; *Shirley Temple, Hot-Cha-Cha*, n.d.; *Songs That Made the Hit Parade*, n.d.; *12-1-A*, 1982

OTHER WORKS

Boatmen on Toneh River, n.d.; *The Handkerchief*, n.d.; *In Heaven and Earth*, n.d.; *The Poetry of the Issei*, n.d.; *Sensei*, n.d.; *Songs My Mother Taught Me*, 1994

WORKS ABOUT

Berson, Misha, ed., *Between Worlds, Contemporary Asian-American Plays*, 1990; HOUSTON, VELINA HASU, *The Politics of Life, Four Plays by Asian American Women*, 1993

1. Introduction by Garrett Hongo in *Songs My Mother Taught Me* by Wakako Yamauchi (New York: Feminist Press, 1994).

2. Berson, Misha, ed., *Between Worlds, Contemporary Asian-American Plays* (New York: Theatre Communications Group, 1990).

3. Houston.

4. Ibid.

Susan Yankowitz
(FEBRUARY 20, 1941–   )

BILL. Is she going to be "all there"? I don't know. But during a solar eclipse, the sun is still there, isn't it? And when a star collapses in on itself, isn't that star still there?

—from *Night Sky*, Scene 3

New Jersey native Susan Yankowitz has commented, "My work has been generally informed by the social and political realities which impinge on all our lives; these, to a large extent, influence and shape my plays."[1] Her work addresses a wide array of sociological problems. For example, in *Terminal* (1969) the dead rise to cast judgment upon the living, who are unable to deal with issues of death and dying; *The Ha-Ha Play* (1970) explores how the power of laughter can conquer the stultifying entrapments of enmity; *Boxes* (1972) explores the inhumanity and lack of individuality and community extant in urban environments; and *A Knife in the Heart* (1983) portrays the effect of a mass murderer's actions on a family.

Though her father was an attorney, Yankowitz grew up in a working-class neighborhood. She earned her B.A. at Sarah Lawrence College in 1963, and her M.F.A. at the Yale School of Drama in 1968. She married writer and editor Herbert Leibowitz, in 1977, with whom she has a son, Gabriel. She first came to public attention in 1971 with Joseph Papp's Public Theatre production of her *Slaughterhouse Play*, a dystopian musical set in a white-owned slaughterhouse where black troublemakers are killed, their meat sold as a delicacy to the white community. The message behind Yankowitz's metaphor is undeniable as we learn that the genitalia are the choicest cut: The white power structure literally castrates and emasculates black men. Incorporating both realistic and surrealistic techniques, the play ends with the characters murdering one another.

One of her most recent works, *Night Sky* (1991) focuses on a woman who suffers from aphasia, the loss of the ability to use words. The play was largely inspired by the experiences of her friend and colleague, the notable theater director and innovator Joseph Chaikin, who became aphasic after a massive stroke that occurred as he underwent open heart surgery. In her introduction to the play, Yankowitz wrote, "During a long and arduous recovery, [Chaikin] began to assemble a vocabulary and finally, an original means of expression—a language without conventional syntax, often missing connective words, like prepositions, but nonetheless comprehensible, even poetic—if one listens. *Night Sky* is about listening and language, about inner and outer space, about a medical condition, a family's ordeal, an individual triumph. But most of all, it is about communication."

Yankowitz has been associated with the Open Theater in New York, the Magic Theatre in Omaha, Nebraska (see MEGAN TERRY), and the Women's Project, which first produced *Night Sky*. Her plays have been staged in such diverse locations as London, Paris, Algeria, Israel, and Iran. Also a screenwriter, she has penned several PBS teleplays, including *Sylvia Plath: An Arrow to the Sun, The Prison Game*, and *Milk and Funny*, which centers around the exploits of Velma Vavoom, a closet scientist who has created a formula that transforms nuclear energy into milk.

Yankowitz has taught play writing and dramatic literature at various institutions, and has been playwright in residence at the Academy Theatre, Atlanta; the Provisional Theatre, Los Angeles; and the Magic Theatre, Omaha, Nebraska. Her grants and awards include a National Endowment for the Arts creative writing grant (1972 and 1979); a Rockefeller Foundation grant (1973); a Guggenheim Fellowship (1975); the Vernon Rice Drama Desk Award for the most promising playwright (1969); and others. She is a member of the Dramatists Guild, the Writers Guild of America, and Poets Essayists and Novelists.

Frances Rademacher Anderson has written, "Susan Yankowitz enlivens non-realistic, highly theatrical images of sociological problems with music, dance, pantomime, patterned speech, bold sets and costumes. These devices reinforce her verbal attacks on such contemporary social sins as conformity, alienation, racism, and sexism."[2] She is an instrumental constituent of the avant garde.

PLAYS

Acts of Love, 1973; *Alarms*, 1987; *The America Piece*, 1974; *Baby* (original story; book by Sybille Pearson, music by David Shire, lyrics by Richard Maltby, Jr.), 1983; *Basics*, 1972; *Boxes*, 1972; *The Cage*, 1965; *The Ha-Ha Play*, 1970; *A Knife in the Heart*, 1983; *The Lamb*, 1970; *Night-*

mare, 1967; *Night Sky*, 1991; *Portrait of a Scientist as a Dumb Broad* (also screenplay, 1964), 1974; *Positions*, 1972; *Qui Est Anna Marks?* 1978; *Sideshow*, 1971; *Slaughterhouse Play*, 1971; *Still Life*, 1977; *Tabula Rasa* (inc. *Basics, Up, Positions*, et al.), n.d.; *Terminal*, 1969; *That Old Rock-a-Bye*, 1968; *Transplant*, 1971; *True Romances*, 1977; *Who Done It?*, 1982; *Wooden Nickels*, 1973

OTHER WORKS

The Amnesiac (screenplay), 1980; *An Arrow to the Sun: The Poetry of Sylvia Plath* (teleplay), 1987; *Danny AWOL* (screenplay), 1968; *The Forerunner: Charlotte Perkins Gilman* (teleplay), 1979; *Kali* (radio play), 1969; *The Land of Milk and Funny* (screenplay), 1968; *The Prison Game* (teleplay), 1976; *Rats' Alley* (radio play), 1969; *Silent Witness* (novel; later screenplay, 1979), 1976; *To See the Elephant* (screenplay), 1974

1. Cited in essay by Frances Rademacher Anderson in Berney (1).

2. Ibid.

Rida Johnson Young
(FEBRUARY 28, 1875–MAY 8, 1926)

Against her staid parents' advice (her father was a pillar of his community; her mother, the granddaughter of Hungarian nobles), Rida Johnson left her family's home in Baltimore, Maryland, in 1875 and set off for New York with the hope of having her play about Omar Khayyam produced. Her hopes were soon dashed: The work featured more than 100 characters. But Young was not disillusioned. She made the most of her new locale. Shedding her four-dollars-a-week sales job, she embarked on a somewhat successful acting career (though she herself acknowledged her limitations as an actress). During a tour in the southern United States in 1898, she married fellow actor James Young, Jr., whose father was a senator from Maryland. Rida had written a play, *Lord Byron*, as a vehicle for James, and he managed to have it added to the company's repertory. But neither the play nor the marriage had lasting value; the union shortly soured. After reevaluating her life, Young returned to her original passion: writing song lyrics. Soon she found employment at a music company, where she churned out songs like a mill hand.

Over the following eighteen years, Young collaborated with some of America's most popular composers, including Jerome Kern and Victor Herbert. Additionally she penned more than twenty-six original plays and musical comedies. She once estimated that she wrote more than 500 songs during this period. Some of her more notable pieces are "Mother Machree" from *Barry of Ballymore* (1911), "Sweethearts" from *Maytime* (1917), and "I'm Falling in Love with Someone" and "Ah, Sweet Mystery of Life" from *Naughty Marietta* (1910), as well as "Tramp, Tramp, Tramp," "The Sweet Bye and Bye," and "Live for Today."

Although most of Young's stage works were formulaic, her tunes were lively, her themes romantic, and her plots action-packed. Her most successful play was the 1910 musical *Naughty Marietta*, which is set in old New Orleans and swiftly throws its characters into a whirl of adventure and intrigue. The show features a forbidden romance between the lieutenant governor's son, who is a valiant Indian scout, and a quadroon slave; our hero spurns his former lover when he meets Princess Marietta (naughty because she's run away from France, her homeland). The 1935 film adaptation, which starred Jeanette MacDonald, Nelson Eddy, and Frank Morgan, has been called "an atrocity" that is "beyond kitsch." "Still," writes critic Pauline Kael, "it has a vitality and a mad sort of appeal."[1] Of the original Broadway production, the *New York Evening Journal* said, "A new standard for comic opera has been set on Broadway."[2] It has been revived a number of times,

most recently at the New York City Opera at Lincoln Center in 1978.

Young lived independently, and quite comfortably, for the rest of her life. She continued writing until her final days at her estate in Stamford, Connecticut, and her summer home in Bellhaven, New York.

PLAYS (SELECTED)

Barry of Ballymore, 1911; *The Boys of Company B*, 1907; *Brown of Harvard* (also novel, 1907), 1906; *Captain Kidd, Jr.*, 1916; *Cock o' the Roost*, 1924; *The Dream Girl*, music by Victor Herbert, 1924; *The Front Seat*, 1921; *The Girl and the Pennant*, 1913; *His Little Widows*, 1917; *Lady Luxury*, 1914; *Little Old New York*, 1920; *Lord Byron*, 1898; *Macushla*, 1920; *Maytime*, music by Sigmund Romberg, 1917; *Naughty Marietta*, music by V. H. (also film, 1935), 1910; *Next*, 1911; *The Red Petticoat*, music by Jerome Kern, 1912; *Sometime*, music by Rudolf Friml, 1918

NOVELS

Out of the Night, 1925; *Red Owl*, 1927

1. Pauline Kael review, Microsoft Cinemania, 1996.
2. *New York Evening Journal*, November 9, 1910.

Elina Zālīte
(OCTOBER 19, 1898–JULY 4, 1955)

Elina Zālīte's Latvian translations of classic masterpieces, such as the writings of Aleksandr Pushkin, Mikhail Lermontov, and Aleksis Kivi, are considered her main contribution to Latvian literature; however, she created many original works as well. The daughter of a carpenter, Zālīte was born in Gaujiena, Latvia; her education was interrupted with the onset of World War I. She later graduated from high school in Tartu, Estonia. In 1921 she moved to Riga, where the poet Antons Anstriņš, noting her gifts with language (she had an excellent command of French, German, Estonian, Finnish, and Russian), persuaded her to begin a career as a translator. She also started writing her own poems, which, according to Alfreds Straumanis, "were noted for their romantic attitude and humanity."[1]

In 1928 Zālīte was employed at the Riga Arts Theater, where she translated and adapted prose works for the stage. During her tenure there she began writing original dramas.

Zālīte's plays are predominantly situation comedies, particularly notable for their wry dialogue. One of her earliest works, *Maldu Mildas sapnojums* (Reverie of Wandering Milda; 1931), takes its theme from Latvian poet Plūdonis's assertion that everyone, at least once in life, follows a dream of desire that inevitably leads to disillusionment. Zālīte's drama provides a feminist bent to Plūdonis's belief by locating it in the status of women and the state of marriage. *Svešas asinis* (Strange Blood; 1935) offers another perspective on the state of family values. The wife of a wealthy landowner has kept from her husband the truth about their son: He is not her husband's child. The boy, spoiled by his indulgent parents, grows into a man of lies and deceit. He hates the farm his parents expect him to take over. Finally, when the facts are revealed to all, the son perishes in the farmhouse by his own hand.

Zālīte's stage works were especially popular in Latvia, as well as abroad, from 1927–1953. In addition to writing poems, plays, and translations, she also wrote poetry for children, short stories, and a novel, *Agrā rūsa* (1944). Shortly before her death, Zālīte penned the libretto for a musical comedy, *Zilo ezeru zeme* (The Land of Blue Lakes), which led to her recognition as Cultural Worker of Soviet Latvia in 1954.

PLAYS

Atgūtā dzimtene (A Homeland Recovered), 1948; *Bīstamis vecums* (Critical Age), 1927; *Emīls* (Emile), 1953; *Intermeco* (Intermezzo), 1944; *Lielā gaisma* (The Big Light), 1948; *Maldu Mildas sapnojums* (Reverie of Wandering Milda), 1931; *Mūžīgi vīriškais* (Eternally Virile), 1938; *Pirktā laime* (Purchased Happiness), 1932; *Rudens rozes* (Roses in Autumn), 1939; *Šokolādes princese* (The Chocolate Princess), 1946; *Spēka avots* (A Source of Vigor), 1950; *Svešas asinis* (Strange Blood), 1935; *Tā reiz beidzās kāda dzīve* (A Life Thus Ended Once), 1934; *Vālodzes dziesma* (The Song of a Magpie), 1940; *Vārds sievietēm* (Women's Turn), 1949; *Vissvarīgākais* (The Most Important One), 1953

NOVEL

Agrā rūsa (Early Rust), 1944

1. Straumanis.

Gabriela Zapolska
(MARCH 30, 1857–DECEMBER 17, 1921)

Though she is considered the most outstanding playwright of the naturalist movement in Poland, Gabriela Zapolska originally intended to pursue a career as an actress, inspired by her mother, an opera singer. Born Maria Gabriela Korwin-Piotrowska in Podhajce, Galicia, Austria (now Pidhaytsi, Ukraine), she studied acting at the Théâtre Libre in Paris for several years. Unable to subsist as an actress, Zapolska turned to writing novels and plays, "full of bitterness toward middle-class values, morality, and hypocrisy."[1] Two novels have survived: *Zaszumi las* (The Forest Will Murmur, 1899), a roman à clef about Polish revolutionaries in Paris, and *Sezonowa miłość* (Love in the Season, 1905), about fashionable life among the middle class in the resort town of Zapotane.

Perhaps her own difficult youth, which included a loveless marriage, the death of a child, and years of ill health, influenced her subject matter as much as did the works of Émile Zola, whose ideas had captivated her at the Théâtre Libre. Her plays are peopled with middle-class characters, often women, who endure the zigzags of their lives from "behind the lace curtains of respectability."[2] For example, *Kaśka Kariatyda* (1895) concerns a housemaid, and *Małka Szwarcenkopf* (1897) a poor Jewish shopkeeper. *Miss Maliczewska* (1910) deals with the quandary faced by a young actress who is exploited by manipulative, sexually avaricious males and the prejudices of society.

Zapolska's best known drama is *Moralność pani Dulskiej* (Mrs. Dulska's Morality, 1906), an acrimonious satire about the dominating matriarch of a bourgeois family. In it Zapolska unmasks the narrow, fundamentalist standards of a respectable wife and mother in the community. Over the years, the central character's name has become a synonym for "a narrow-minded, self-righteous hypocrite."[3]

Zapolska was an actress, director, manager, playwright, and novelist; she is credited with introducing the works of Henrik Ibsen to Russia by playing Nora in *A Doll's House* during a guest appearance of the Warsaw Theater in 1883. Zapolska was, in the words of Gerould, "the prototype of the new woman in revolt who enjoyed shocking contemporaries and outraging critics. . . . Because her works are said to be crude and sensational, Zapolska does not enjoy as high a position in Polish literature as she deserves. Her best dramas and comedies are tightly constructed, the characters are drawn with great satirical verve, and the dialogue is lively and biting; on stage, her plays are immensely effective and constant favorites with both actors and audiences. In fact, Zapolska was one of the finest naturalist playwrights in all of Europe and one of the two most important women dramatists of the period (only Lady [AUGUSTA] GREGORY in Ireland is of equal stature)."[4]

PLAYS (SELECTED)

Ich caworo (Four of Them), 1907; *Kaśka Kariatyda*, 1895; *Małaszka*, 1886; *Małka Szwarcenkopf*, 1897; *Moralnošč pani Dulskiej* (Mrs. Dulska's Morality), 1906; *Panna Maliczewska* (Miss Maliczewska), 1910; *Skiz*, 1908; *Tamten* (The Other One), 1898; *Zarewitsch*, 1917

OTHER WORKS (NOVELS)

Kaśka Kariatyda, 189?; *Sezonowa miłość* (Love in the Season), 1905; *Zaszumi las* (The Forest Will Murmur), 1899

1. Essay by Daniel Gerould in Hochman.
2. Ibid.
3. Ibid.
4. Ibid.

Appendix

Supplemental Index

Aldis, Mary Reynolds (1872–1949) Am. poet, artist.

Allen, Jay Presson (1922–) Am. screenwriter. *Plays: Forty Carets* (adapt. of Muriel Spark's *Cactus Flower),* 1969; *The Prime of Miss Jean Brodie,* 1969.

Alvarez, Lynne (1947–) Hisp.-Am. poet, playwright. *Plays: Guittarrón,* 1983: *Hidden Parts,* 1983; *Mundo,* 1982; *The Reincarnation of Jaimie Brown,* 1994; *Thin Air: Tales from a Revolution,* 1979?; tr. *Una doncella para un gorila* by Arrabal, 1986; *The Wonderful Tower of Humbert Lavoignet,* 1985?. *Other Works: The Dreaming Man* (poetry); *Living with Numbers* (poetry). *Awards:* Le Compte du Noüy; NEA Fellowship; CAPS grant in poetry.

Ancelot, Virginia (1792–1875) Fr. novelist, dramatist. Née Chardon. *Relationship:* h. M.A. (author). *Plays: Un mariage raisonnable,* 1835? *Other Works: Gabrielle* (novel), 1840.

Anderson, Jane (1946–) Am. *Plays: The Baby Dance,* 1991; *Food and Shelter,* 1992. *Other Works: A Hard Night's Run,* 1983; *A Good Man,* 1983; *Easy Money the Hard Way,* 1980; *Hello World,* 1983; *The Lucky Break,* 1983; *One Letter Too Many,* 1983; *Run for Your Life,* 1983; *Stay Alive,* 1983.

Angelou, Maya (1928–) Af.-Am. novelist, poet, actor. *Plays: Adjoa Amissah,* 1967; *Ajax,* 1974; *And Still I Rise,* 1976; *Cabaret for Freedom* (musical revue w/Godfrey Cambridge), 1960; *The Clawing Within,* 1966; *The Least of These,* 1966. *TV Plays: Blacks, Blues, Black,* 1968; *Sister, Sister,* 1982. *Screenplays: All Day Long,* 1974; *Georgia, Georgia,* 1972. *Other Works: All God's Children Need Traveling Shoes,* 1986; *Gather Together in My Name,* 1974; *The Heart of a Woman,* 1981; *I Know Why the Caged Bird Sings* (also TV), 1970; *I Shall Not Be Moved,* 1990; *Just Give Me a Cool Drink of Water 'fore I Diiie,* 1971;

Mrs. Flowers: A Moment of Friendship, 1986; *Now Sheba Sings the Song,* 1987; *Oh Pray My Wings Are Gonna Fit Me Well,* 1975; *On the Pulse of Morning* (inaugural poem), 1993; *Shaker, Why Don't You Sing?,* 1983; *Singin' and Swingin' and Gettin' Merry Like Christmas,* 1976.

Araz, Nezihe (1922–) Turkish journalist, dramatist. *Plays: Bozkir Güzellemesi* (A Ballad in Praise of the Steppes), 1974; *Öyle Bir Nevcivan* (He Is Such a Young Fellow), 1979.

Arden, Jane (193?–) Welsh actor, TV personality, screenwriter. *Plays: Conscience and Desire,* 1954; *Dear Liz,* 1954; *A New Communion—for Freaks, Prophets and Witches,* 1971; *The Party,* 1958; *Vagina Rex and the Gas Oven,* 1969. *Screenplays: Anti-Clock,* 1979; *The Logic Game,* 1966; *The Otherside of Underneath,* 1973; *Separation* (as Jane DeWar), 1968; *Vibration,* 1974. *TV Plays: The Thug,* 1959. *Other Works: You Don't Know What You Want, Do You?,* 1978.

Atlan, Liliane (1932–) Fr. *Plays: Mister Fugue or Earth Sick,* 1987.

Bergen, Candice (1946–) Am. actor, writer, photographer. *Relationships:* f. Edgar Bergen (ventriloquist), h. Louis Malle (Fr. film director). *Plays: The Freezer,* 1968. *Other Works: Knock Wood* (autobio.), 1984. *Awards: Emmys,* 1989, 1990, 1992, 1994.

Betsko, Kathleen (1939–) Eng. editor, theater historian. *Plays: Beggar's Choice; Johnny Bull,* 1985; *Stichers and Starlight Talkers. Other Works:* ed., *Interviews with Contemporary Women Playwrights,* w/Rachel Koenig, 1987.

Bonner, Marita (1899–1971) Af.-Am. teacher, journalist. Née Occomy; aka Joseph Marie Andrew.

Plays: Crisis, 1923; Exit, an Illusion, 1923; *Muddled Dream; Opportunity,* 1927 The Pot Maker, 1927; *The Purple Flower,* 1928. *Other Works: Frye Street and Environs: the Collected Works of Marita Bonner,* ed. and intro. by Joyce Flynn and Joyce Occamy Stricklin.

Boucher, Denise (1935–) Can. *Plays: Les fees ont soif* (The Fairies Are Thirsty, tr. by Alan Brown), 1978.

Bowles, Jane Auer (1917–73) Am.-Tangiers novelist, short story writer. *Relationships:* h. Paul Bowles, writer-composer. *Plays: In the Summer House,* 1953; *Other Works: Plain Pleasures,* 1966; *Two Serious Ladies,* 1943.

Brackley, Elizabeth (1623–63) Eng. *Relationships:* s. Jane Cavendish; f. Wm. Cavendish, Duke of Newcastle, patron of playwrights Richard Brome, James Shirley, and Benjamin Jonson; h. Lord Brackley. *Plays: A Pastoral,* 1631; *The Concealed Fansyes,* 1631.

Burnett, Frances Eliza Hodgson (1849–1924) Am. novelist. *Plays: Esmeralda,* 1881. *Other Works: Little Lord Fauntleroy,* 1886; *The Secret Garden,* 1911.

Burrell, Lady Sophia (1750?–1802) Eng. poet. *Relationships:* f. Sir Charles Raymond; h. Sir William (1), Rev. William Clay (2). *Plays: Maximian, 1800; Theodora,* 1800. *Other Works: Comala,* 1794; *Poems,* 1793; *Telemachus; The Thymbriad.*

Cajal, Oana-Maria Hock (1955?–) Rom. literary manager. *Plays: The Almond Seller,* 1991; *Berlin, Berlin,* 1988; *Eastern European Tetralogy,* 1986; *Exchange at Cafe Mimosa,* 1988; *Love in the Shadow of the Umbrella Bamboo,* 1990; *The Man Who Had No Story, A Multicultural Tale,* 1989. *Awards:* NEA Playwriting Fellowship, 1989; Fulbright scholar, 1992–94.

Carson, Jo (1946–) Am. *Plays: A Preacher with a Horse to Ride; Daytrips,* 1989; *Horsepower: An Electric Fable,* w/the Road Company; *Little Chicago,* w/the Road Company; *Pulling My Leg,* 1990; *Stories I Ain't Told Nobody Yet,* 1989; *You Hold Me and I'll Hold You,* 1992. *Other Works: The Great Shaking,* 1994.

Cavendish, Jane (1621–69) Eng. *Relationships:* s. Elizabeth Brackley; f. Wm. Cavendish, Duke of Newcastle; stepm. Margaret Cavendish.

Chalem, Denis (contemp.) Fr. *Plays: A cinquante ans, elle decouvrait la mer* (The Sea Between Us), 1986.

Chartrand, Lina (1948–94) Can. poet, publisher, director, dramaturg, screenwriter, political activist. Cofounder, Company of Sirens (mid-1980s). *Plays: La P'tite Miss Easter Seals,* 1988; *Private Property, Private Parts* and *Switching Channels,* w/Amanda Hale, mid-1980s.

Churchill, Sarah (1914–) Eng. *Plays: Serious Money.*

Cockburn, Alicia (1713–94) Scot. songwriter, poet, society leader.

Cockburn, Catherine (1679–1749) Eng. poet, essayist.

Congdon, Constance S. (1944–) Am. *Plays: Beauty and the Beast,* 1992; *The Bride,* 1980; *Casanova,* 1989; *A Conversation with Georgia O'Keeffe,* 1987; *Fourteen Brilliant Colors,* 1977; *The Gilded Age* (adapt. of Mark Twain novel), 1986; *Gilgamesh,* 1977; *Losing Father's Body, Madeline's Rescue* (adapt. of Ludwig Bemelmans book), 1990; *The Miser* (adapt. of Molière play), 1990; *Mother Goose,* 1990; *Native American,* 1984; *No Mercy,* 1986; *Raggedy Ann and Andy* (adapt. of Johnny Gruelle books), 1987; *Rembrandt Takes a Walk* (adapt. of Mark Strand and Red Grooms book), 1989; *Tales of the Lost Formicans,* 1988; *Time out of Time,* 1990.

Cooper, Elizabeth (fl. 1730s) Eng. anthologist. *Plays: The Nobleman, or The Family Quarrel,* 1736; *The Rival Widows, or Fair Libertine,* 1735. *Other Works: The Muses Library, or A Series of English Poetry, from the Saxons, to the Reign of King Charles II,* 1737.

Cooper, Mary (1946–) Eng. reporter. *Plays: Asking for It,* 1987; *Away with the Fairies,* 1990; *Close to the Bone,* 1987; *Down There,* 1986; *Sacred Ground,* 1990.

Corthron, Kia (contemp.) Af.-Am. *Plays: Cage Rhythm,* 1994; *Come Down Burning,* 1993.

Cresswell, Janet (contemp.) Eng. *Plays: The One-Sided Wall* (w/Niki Johnson).

Cruz, Migdalia (contemp.) Lat. Am. *Plays: Dreams of Home,* 1990; *The Have-Little,* 1991; *Miriam's Flowers,* 1992.

Dangarembga, Tsitsi (195?) Zimbab. writer. *Other Works: Nervous Conditions,* 1988.

Davies, Mary Carolyn (fl. 1920s) Am. poet, songwriter, editor.

De Angelis, April (1960–) Eng. actor. *Plays: Bombshell,* 1989; *Breathless,* 1986; *Crux,* 1990; *Frankenstein,* 1989; *Ironmistress,* 1988; *Me,* 1988; *Visitants,* 1988 (radio); *Women in Law,* 1987.

Delmar, Vina (1905–) Am.

Devlin, Anne (contemp.) Irish **Plays:** *After Easter.* **Other Works:** *Heartlanders: A Community Play . . .,* 1989; *The Long March,* 1986; *Ourselves Alone,* 1985; *The Way-Paver,* 1988; *A Woman Calling,* 1986.

Di Prima, Diane (1934?) Am. poet, writer, editor. **Other Works:** *Memoirs of a Beatnik,* 1988; *Pieces of a Song,* 1990; *Revolutionary Letters, etc., 1966–78,* 1979.

Dizon, Louella (contemp.) Filipina-Am. **Plays:** *The Color Yellow: Memoirs of an Asian-American,* 1990; *Till Voices Wake Us,* 1991.

do Ceu, Violante (1602?–93) Port. nun, musician, poet.

Duffy, Carol Ann (1955–) Scot. **Plays:** *Take My Husband,* 1982. **Other Works:** *Beauty and the Beast,* 1977; *Fifth Last Song,* 1982; *Fleshweathercock,* 1973; *I Wouldn't Thank You for a Valentine: Poems for Young Feminists* (ed.), 1993.

Edmundson, Helen (contemp.) **Plays:** *Anna Karenina; The Clearing; The Mill on the Floss.*

Eisenberg, Deborah (contemp.) Am. **Plays:** *Pastorale,* 1982. **Other Works:** *Air, 24 Hours: Jennifer Bartlett,* 1994; *Stories, So Far . . .,* 1996; *Transactions in a Foreign Currency: Stories,* 1986; *Under the 82nd Airborne,* 1992.

Evaristi, Marcella (1953–) Scot. performer. **Plays:** *Checking Out,* 1984; *Commedia,* 1982; *Dorothy and the Bitch,* 1976; *Hard to Get,* 1980 (also radio, 1981; TV, 1983); *Mouthpieces,* 1980; *The Offski Variations,* 1990; *Scotia's Darlings,* 1978; *Sugar and Spite,* 1978; *Terrestrial Extras,* 1985; *Thank You for Not,* 1982; *Trio for Strings in 3,* 1987; *Visiting Company,* 1988; *The Works,* 1984. **Radio Plays:** *The Hat,* 1988; *The Theory and Practice of Rings,* 1992; *Troilus and Cressida and la-di-da-di-da,* 1992; *Wedding Belles and Green Grasses,* 1983; **TV Plays:** *Eva Set the Balls of Corruption Rolling,* 1982.

Farabough, Laura (195?) Am. stage director, stage designer.

Fengxi, Bai (1932?) Chin. actor.

Field, Rachel Lyman (1905–74) Am. poet.

Fleming, Joan (1908–80) Eng. writer.

Fradonnet, Catherine (1547–87) Fr. poet. **Relationships:** m. Madeleine Fradonnet (poet).

Frank, Florence Kiper (1886?–) Am. poet.

Garro, Elena (1920–) Mex. **Plays:** *Andamos huyendo Lola,* 1980; *La casa junto al rio,* 1983; *La semana de colores,* 1989; *Testimonios sobre Mariana,* 1993; *Un*

hogar sólido (A Solid Home), 1956; *Y Matarazo no llamo—,* 1991. **Other Works:** *Los recuerdos del porvenir* (Recollections of Things to Come), 1963.

Gáspár, Margit (1908–) Hungarian translator. **Plays:** *Hamletnek nincs igaza* (Hamlet Is Wrong), 1962; *Uj Isten Thébában* (New God in Thebes), 1946.

Glancy, Diane (contemp.) Nat. Am. writer. **Plays:** *War Cries: A Collection of Plays,* 1995; *Weebjob,* 1987. **Other Works:** *Asylum in the Grasslands,* 1998; *Claiming Breath,* 1992; *Drystalks of the Moon,* 1981; *Firesticks* (short stories), 1993; *Flutie,* 1998; *Iron Woman* (poems), 1990; *Monkey Secret* (fiction), 1995; *Offering* (poetry and prose), 1988; *One Age in a Dream,* 1986; *The Only Piece of Furniture in the House* (novel), 1996; *Pushing the Bear* (novel), 1996; *Trigger Dance* (short stories), 1990; *The West Pole,* 1997. **Awards:** Lakes and Prairie (1986); Capricorn prize 1988).

Glass, Joanna M. (contemp.) Can.-Am. **Plays:** *Artichoke,* 1979; *Canadian Gothic/American Modern,* 1970?; *The Last Chalice,* 1977; *Play Memory,* 1984; *Santacqua,* 1969; *To Grandmother's House We Go,* 1981. **Other Works:** *Reflections on a Mountain Summer,* 1974; *Woman Wanted,* 1985.

Gore, Catherine (1799–1861) Eng.-Fr. poet, novelist, composer.

Graham, Virginia (1912–) Am. television and radio commentator.

Hemans, Felicia Dorothea (1793–1835) Eng. poet, illustrator, translator, a.k.a. Egeria.

Hogan, Linda (1947–) Am. poet, educator, writer, Indian rights activist.

Hoper, Mrs. (fl. 1740s) Eng. actor. **Plays:** *The Battle of Poictiers, or The English Prince* (unpub.), 1747; *The Cyclopedia* (unpub.), 1748; *Queen Tragedy Restored,* 1749.

Johnson, Niki (contemp.) Eng. actor. **Plays:** *The Carrier Frequency; A Place in Europe; Songs of the Claypeople; The Haunting Tree; In the Eye of a Dead Sheep; The One-Sided Wall* (w/Janet Cresswell).

Kennedy, Margaret (1896–1967) Eng. novelist, playwright. **Relationships:** f. Charles Moore Kennedy; m. Elinor Kennedy; h. David Davies, K. C., judge. **Plays:** *Autumn,* w/Gregory Ratoff, 1937; *Come with Me,* w/Basil Dean, 1928; *The Constant Nymph,* w/B. D. (adapt. from novel; also film), 1924; *Escape Me Never!,* w/B. D., 1934; *Happy with Either,* 1948. **Other Works:** *A Century of Revolution,* 1922; *The Fool of the Family,* 1930; *Forgotten Smile; The Heroes* *of Clone*, Jane Austen, 1950; *The Ladies of Lyndon*, 1923; *Lady Carmichael*; *A Long Time Ago*; *A Long Week-end*; *Mechanized Muse*, 1958; *The Midas Touch*; *Not in the Calendar*, 1964; *The Oracles*; *The Outlaws of Parnassus*, 1960; *Red Sky at Morning*, 1927; *Return I Dare Not*; *Together and Apart*, 1967; *Troy Chimneys*, 1952; *Where Stands a Wingèd Sentry* (autobio.), 1941.

Köksal, Ülker (1931–) Turk. *Plays: Adem'in Kburgasi* (Adam's Rib), 1979; *Besleme* (Child Servant), 1975; *Binbir Çiçek* (Thousand Flowers), 1973; *Ölü Denizde Bir Gemi* (A Boat on the Dead Sea), 1977; *Oyun Bitmedi* (The Play Is Not Ended), 1978; *Sacide*, 1972; *Yollar Tükendi* (All Roads Come to an End), 1973,

Krauss, Ruth (Ida) (1911–) Am. *Plays: Ambiguity 2nd*, 1985; *The Cantilever Rainbow*, 1965; *If I Were Freedom*, 1976; *If Only*, 1969; *Love and the Invention of Punctuation*, 1973; *Small Black Lambs Wandering in the Red Poppies*, 1982; *There's a Little Ambiguity over There Among the Bluebells and Other Theatre Poems*, 1968; *This Breast Gothic*, 1973; *Under Thirteen*, 1976; *Under Twenty*, 1970; *When I Walk I Change the Earth*, 1978. *Other Works: Bears*, 1948; *Big and Little*, 1987; *A Good Man and His Good Wife*, 1944; *A Hole Is to Dig: A First Book of Definitions*, 1952; *How to Make an Earthquake*, 1954; *Little Boat Lighter Than a Cork*, 1976; *The Little King, The Little Queen, The Little Monster, and Other Stories You Can Make up Yourself*, 1966; *Monkey Day*, 1957.

Kveder, Zofka (1878–1926) Slov. First female Slovenian writer. *Plays: Amerikanci* (Americans), 1908.

Laberge, Marie (1950–) Can. dancer, actor, professor, director, theater administrator. *Plays: Au bord de la nuit*, 1983; *Aurélie, ma soeur*, 1988; *Avec l'hiver qui s'en vient*, 1980; *Le banc*, 1981; *Le bourreau*, 1983; *C'était avant la guerre à l'Anse à Gilles*, 1981; *Deux tangos pour toute une vie*, 1984; *Éva et Évelyne*, 1986; *Ils étaient venus pour*, 1981; *Jocelyne Trudel trouvee morte dans ses larmes*, 1983; *L'homme gris*, 1984; *Le Night Cap Bar*, 1987; *On a bien failli d'comprendre*, 1980; *Oublier*, 1987; *Profession: Je l'aime*, 1978; *T'sé veux dire*, 1980. *Other Works: Juillet*, 1989. *Awards:* Governor General's Awards for Drama, 1977, 1982.

Lanfors, Viveca (contemp.) Am.

Lathrop, Mary (1951–) Am. writer. *Plays: The AIDS Circus*, 1991; *A Bris Is Still A Bris*, 1995; *Dreams of Baby*, 1993; *Hell on Wheels*, 1993; *Menstruating*

Waitress from Hell, 1988; *She Always Likes to Travel*, 1992; *The Six Basic Rules*, 1997; *The Urn of Drew*, 1995; *The Visible Horse* (a.k.a. *Undead*), 1996. *Awards:* Susan Smith Blackburn Finalist, 1992; Washington State Arts Commission Playwriting Fellowship, 1993; O'Neill Playwright Fellow, 1996.

Lavery, Bryony (1947–) Eng. *Plays: Bag*, 1979; *The Black Hole of Calcutta*, 1982; *Calamity*, 1984; *Days at Court*, 1968; *The Dragon Wakes*, 1988; *The Drury Lane Ghost*, 1989; *The Family Album*, 1980; *Female Trouble*, 1981; *Flight*, 1991; *Floorshow*, 1978; *Gentlemen Prefer Blondes* (adapt. of Anita Loos novel), 1980; *Getting Through*, 1985; *Grandmother's Footsteps*, 1977; *The Headless Body*, 1987; *Her Aching Heart*, 1990; *Hot Time*, 1984; *I Was Too Young at the Time to Understand Why Mother Was Crying*, 1976; *The Joker*, 1980; *Kitchen Matters*, 1990; *Missing*, 1981; *More Female Trouble*, 1982; *Mummy*, 1987; *Origin of the Species*, 1984; *Over and Out*, 1985; *Peter Pan*, 1991; *Puppet States*, 1988; *Sharing*, 1976; *The Sleeping Beauty*, 1992; *Snakes*, 1977; *Sore Points*, 1986; *Sugar and Spice* 1979; *Twilight of the Gods*, 1982; *Two Marias*, 1989; *Unemployment: An Occupational Hazard?*, 1979; *The Way to Cook a Wolf*, 1993; *Wicked*, 1990; *The Wild Bunch*, 1979; *Witchcraze*, 1985; *Zulu*, 1981. *Radio Plays: Fire the Life-Giver*, 1979; *Laying Ghosts*, 1992; *Let's Get Dressed*, 1982; *Magical Beasts*, 1987. *TV Plays: The Cab Wars*, 1989; *Revolting Women*, 1981; *Rita of the Rovers*, 1989.

Lejeune, Caroline (1897–1973) Eng. film critic.

Leneru, Marie (1875–1940) Fr., deaf and blind, writer.

Lennart, Isobel (1915–71) Am. screenwriter. *Plays: Funny Girl*, 1964.

Lennox, Charlotte (1720–1804) Am.-Eng. poet, possibly first American novelist.

Le Noire, Rosetta Burton (1911–) *Plays: Come Laugh and Cry with Langston Hughes*, 1976; *House Party*, 1971; *Reminiscing with Sissle & Blake*, w/Louis Johnson, 1973; *Soul: Yesterday and Today*, 1970. *Awards:* AUDELCO Award, 1977; Pierre Toussaint Medallion, 1985; New York City's Award of Honor for Arts and Culture, 1986.

Levy, Deborah (1959–) So. Afr.-Eng. *Plays: The B File*, 1992: *Blood Wedding* (adapt. of Federico García Lorca play), 1992; *Call Blue Jane*, 1992; *Clam*, 1985; *Eva and Moses*, 1987; *Heresies*, 1987; *Our Lady*, 1986; *Pax*, 1984, *TV Plays: Celebrating Quietly*, 1988;

Linckin's Bones, 1990; *The Open Mouth*, 1991. **Other Works:** *An Amorous Discourse in the Suburbs of Hell*, 1990; *Beautiful Mutants*, 1987; *Ophelia and the Great Idea*, 1986; *Walks on Water: Five Performance Texts* (ed.), 1992.

Lochhead, Liz (1947–) Eng. **Plays:** *The Big Picture*, 1988; *Blood and Ice* (also radio play, 1990), 1982; *A Bunch of Fives*, w/Tom Leonard and Sean Hardie, 1983; *Dracula* (adapt. of Stoker), *1985; Jock Tamson's Bairns*, w/Gerry Mulgrew, 1990; *Mary Queen of Scots Got Her Head Chopped Off*, 1987; *Now and Then* (screenplay), 1972; *Patter Merchant*, 1989; *The Pie of Damocles* (revue), w/others, 1983; *Quelques fleurs*, 1991; *Silver Service*, 1984; *Sweet Nothings* (teleplay, End of the Line series), 1984; *Tartuffe* (adapt. of Molière), 1985; *Tickly Mince* (revue), w/Tom Leonard and Alisdair Gray, 1982. **Other Works:** *Dreaming Frankenstein, and Collected Poems*, 1984; *The Grimm Sisters*, 1981; *Memo for Spring*, 1972; *True Confessions and New Clichés*, 1985.

Logan, Olive (1839–1909) Am. actress, playwright, journalist, lecturer, feminist. **Relationships:** f. Cornelius Ambrosius Logan. **Plays:** *Evaleen* (a.k.a. *The Felon's Daughter*), 1864; *Newport*, 1879; *Surf*, 1870. **Other Works:** *Apropos of Women and Theatre*, 1869; *Before the Footlights and Behind the Scenes*, 1870; *Get Thee Behind Me, Satan* (novel), 1872; *The Mimic World*, 1871; *Photographs of Paris*, 1866; *They Met by Chance* (novel), 1872. **Works About:** *The Wallet of Time* by William Winter, 1913.

Loranger, Françoise (1913–) Fr.-Can. novelist. **Plays:** *Le chemin du roy*, w/Claude Levac, 1968; *Double jeu* (Double Game), 1969; *Encore cinq minutes* (Another Five Minutes), 1967; *Georges . . . oh! Georges* (teleplay), 1958; *Jour après jour* (Day After Day), 1971; *Un cri qui vient de loin* (A Cry That Comes Far; teleplay), 1956; *Un si bel automne* (Such a Beautiful Autumn), 1971; *Une maison . . . un jour* (A House . . . One Day), 1965. **Other Works:** *Mathieu* (novel), 1949.

Lovell, Marie (1803–77) Eng. actress.

Lyssiotis, Tes (contemp.) Austral. teacher. **Plays:** *Cafe Mistro*, 1986; *Come to Australia They Said*, 1982; *The Forty Lounge Cafe*, 1990; *Hotel Bonegilla*, 1983; *I Go to Australia and Wear a Hat*, 1982; *The Journey*, 1985; *On the Line*, 1984; *The Past Is Here*, 1991; *A White Sports Coat*, 1988; *Zac's Place*, 1991; **Radio Plays:** *A Small Piece of Earth*, 1990.

MacDonald, Ann-Marie (1958–) Can. actress. **Plays:** *Goodnight Desdemona* (*Good Morning Juliet*),

1987. **Other Works:** *I've Heard the Mermaids Singing* (performer), 1987. **Awards:** Governor-General's Award for Drama, 1990.

Maxwell, Florida Scott (1884–?) Am.-Scot. psychologist, suffragist, actor: née Pier. **Other Works:** *The Measure of My Days*, 1968.

May, Elaine (1932–) Am. actress. **Relationships:** f. Jack Berlin; d. Jeannie Berlin, actor. **Plays:** *Adaption*, 1969; *An Evening with Mike Nichols and Elaine May*, 1960; *Mr. Gogol and Mr. Preen*, 1991; *A Matter of Position*, 1962; *Not Enough Rope*, 1962. **Screenplays:** *Heaven Can Wait* (w/Warren Beatty and Buck Henry), 1978; *Ishtar*, 1987; *Micky and Nicky*, 1976; *A New Leaf*, 1970; *Such Good Friends*, 1971 (uncredited); *Tootsie* (w/Larry Gelbart; uncredited), 1982.

McIntyre, Clare (contemp.) Eng. actress. **Plays:** *Better a Live Pompey than a Dead Cyril*, w/Stephanie Nunn, 1980; *I've Been Running*, 1986; *Low Level Panic*, 1988; *My Heart's a Suitcase*, 1990; *The Thickness of Skin*, 1996. **Awards:** Beckett, 1989; Evening Standard, 1990; London Drama Critics, 1990.

McLaughlin, Ellen (1953?–) Am. actor. **Plays:** *Days and Nights Within*, 1985; *Infinity's House*, 1990; *Iphigenia and Other Daughters*, 1995; *A Narrow Bed*, 1985: *Tongue of a Bird*, 1997. **Other Works:** *Hat Tricks* (in-progress). **Awards:** Susan Smith Blackburn award, 1987; NEA, 1990; Actors Theatre of Louisville Great American Play award; Writers Award from Lila Wallace Reader's Fund.

Moberg, Eva (1940–) Swed. journalist. **Plays:** *Hög svansföring*, 1994; *Prylar*, 1987; *Svindlands skönhet* (Dizzying Beauty), 1990.

Moraga, Cherríe (1952–) Chicana poet and "politica." **Plays:** *Giving up the Ghost*, 1984; *Heroes and Saints*, 1994; *Shadow of a Man*, 1992. **Other Works:** *Cuentos: Stories by Latinas*, coed. and contributor, 1983; *The Last Generation: Prose and Poetry*, 1993; *Loving in the War Years*, 1983; *This Bridge Called My Back: Writings by Radical Women of Color*, coed. and contributor, 1981.

Mueller, Lavonne (contemp.) **Plays:** *Breaking the Prairie Wolf Code*, 1986; *Five in the Killing Zone*, *Little Victories*, 1981; *Violent Peace*, 1990; *Warriors From a Long Childhood*. **Other Works:** *Creative Writing: Forms and Techniques*, w/Jerry D. Reynolds, 1990; *Duo!: The Best Scenes for the 90's*, ed. w/John Horvath and Jack Temchin, 1995.

Mumford, Ethel Watts (1878–1940) Am. humorist.

Murray, Judith Sargent (1751–1820) Am. author, feminist, poet.

Nagy, Phyllis (contemp.) *Plays: Butterfly Kiss; Girl Bar*, 1991; *The Strip*.

Neuber, Friederika Carolina (1697–1760) née Carolina Weissenborn.

Njau, Rebeka (1932–) Kenyan educator. *Plays: The Round Chain*, 1963; *The Scar*, 1965. *Other Works: Kenya Women Heroes and Their Mystical Power*, w/Gideon Mulaki, 1984; *Ripples in the Pool* (novel), 1978.

O'Brien, Edna (1932?–) *Plays: A Pagan Place* (also novel, 1970), 1972; *Virginia*, 1980. *Other Works: The Girl with Green Eyes; Three into Two Won't Go*.

Olsson, Hagar (1893–1978) Finn. novelist. *Plays: Det blå undret* (The Blue Wonder), 1931; *Hjärtats pantomim* (The Heart's Pantomine), 1927; *Kärlekens död* (The Death of Love), 1952; *Lumisota* (The Snowball War), 1939; *Rövaren och jungfrun* (The Robber and the Maiden), 1944; *S.O.S.*, 1928. *Other Works: Träsnidaren och döden* (The Woodcarver and Death, Eng. tr., 1965), 1940.

Orczy, Baroness Emmuska (1865–1947) Eng. novelist. *Relationships:* f. Baron Felix Orczy; h. Montagu Barstow. *Other Works: The Adventures of the Scarlet Pimpernel*, 1985; *Beau Brocade*, 1908; *Eldorado*, 1985; *The Elusive Pimpernel: A Romance*, 1984; *The League of the Scarlet Pimpernel*, 1983; *The Legion of Honour*, 1920; *The Man in the Corner* (sound recording), 1993; *Marivosa*, 1930; *Pimpernel and Rosemary*, 1985; *The Scarlet Pimpernel*, w/Felix Orczy, 1905; *The Sin of William Jackson*, 1906; *Sumi No Rojin* (The Old Man in the Corner, tr. into Japanese), 1976; *The Triumph of the Scarlet Pimpernel*, 1984; *The Way of the Scarlet Pimpernel*, 1985.

Ordway, Sally (1939–) Am. *Plays: Allison*, 1970; *The Chinese Caper*, 1973; *Crabs*, 1972; *A Desolate Place Near a Deep Hole*, 1965; *Free! Free! Free!*, 1965; *The Hostess*, 1975; *Ike and Mamie, A Nuclear Romance*, 1985; *The Lay of the Land*, 1971; *Memorial Day*, 1974; *Movie, Movie on the Wall*, 1968; *No More Chattanooga Choo Choo*, 1981; *A Passage Through Bohemia*, 1966; *Playthings; A Pretty Passion*, 1982; *Sex Warfare*, 1974; *Promise Her Anything*, 1980; *S.W.A.K.*, 1978; *There's a Wall Between Us, Darling*, 1966; *Translators*, 1984; *War Party*, 1974.

Osman, Nigar Binti (fl. 1912) Turk. *Plays: Girive*, 1912.

Papadat-Bengescu, Hortensia (1877–1956) Rom. novelist. *Plays: A cazut o stea* (A Star Has Fallen); *Batrinul* (The Old Man), 1921; *Nuvele; Povestiri*, 1980; *Sora mea Ana* (My Sister Anna).

Pemberton, Harriet L. Childe (fl. 1890s) Eng. poet; a.k.a. H. I. C. Pemberton.

Pilkington, Laetitia (1712–50/51) Irish-Eng. poet, printer. *Plays: The Roman Father* (unfinished), 1748; *The Turkish Court, or London Prentice*, 1748. *Other Works: Memoirs*, vols. 1 and 2, 1748; *Memoirs*, vol. 3, 1754.

Przybyszewska, Stanislawa (1901–35) Polish dramatist.

Raif, Ayshe (contemp.) Brit. *Plays: Another Woman*, 1983; *Az Sekerli—An Istanbul Romance* (radio play), 1991; *Café Society*, 1981; *Caving In*, 1989; *Fail/Safe*, 1986; *A Party for Bonzo*, 1985; *Sweet Stuff* (radio play), 1987.

Rayson, Hannie (1957–) Austral. *Plays: Hotel Sorrento*, 1990; *Leave It Till Monday*, 1984; *Mary* 1985; *Please Return to Sender*, 1980; *Room to Move*, 1985; *Sloth* (teleplay), 1992. *Awards:* Australian Writers' Guild awards, 1986, 1990; New South Wales Premier's Literary Award, 1990.

Reid, Christina (1942–) Irish. *Plays: The Belle of Belfast City*, 1989; *Did You Hear the One About the Irishman . . .?*, 1982; *Joyriders*, 1986; *The Last of a Dyin' Race* (also radio play, teleplay), 1986; *Les Misérables* (adapt. of Victor Hugo novel), 1989; *My Name, Shall I Tell You My Name* (also radio play), 1987; *Tea in a China Cup*, 1983. *Radio Plays: Today and Yesterday in Northern Ireland*, 1989; *The Unfortunate Fursey* (adapt. of Mervyn Wall novel), 1989. *Awards:* Ulster Television Drama Award, 1980; Thames Television Playwriting Award, 1983; George Devine Award, 1986.

Renée (1929–) New Zealander; née Renée Gertrude Jones. *Plays: Asking for It*, 1983; *Born to Clean*, 1987; *Breaking Out*, 1982; *Dancing*, 1984; *Form*, 1990; *Groundwork*, 1985; *Jeannie*, 1991; *Missionary Position*, 1991; *Pass It On*, 1986; *Secrets*, 1982; *Setting the Table*, 1982; *Te Pouaka karahe* (The Glass Box), 1992; *Tiggy Touchwood*, 1992; *Touch of the Sun*, 1991; *Wednesday to Come*, 1985; *What Did You Do in the War, Mummy?*, 1982. *Teleplays: Beginnings and Endings, Sheppard Street*, and *Strings*, 1986 (*Open House* series); *Husbands and Wives*, 1985 (*Country G. P..* series). *Other Works: Finding Ruth*, 1987; *Willy Nilly*, 1990.

Requeña, María Asunción (1918–) Chilean dentist. *Plays: Ayayema,* 1964; *Cuento de invierno* (A Winter's Tale; a.k.a. *El criadero de zorros de Magallanes,* Magellan Fox Farm), 1957; *Fuerte Bulnes* (Fort Bulnes), 1953; *Mister Jones llega a las seis* (Mister Jones Arrives at Six o'Clock), 1952; *Pan caliente* (Hot Bread), 1958; *Piel de tigre* (Tiger Skin), 1961; *Un camino mas largo* (A Longer Road), 1959.

Resnik, Muriel (193?–) Am. *Plays: Any Wednesday,* 1964. *Other Works: Life Without Father,* 1956; *Son of Any Wednesday,* 1965.

Robinson, Mary (1758–1800) Eng.-Fr. actress, poet, novelist, teacher.

Roepke, Gabriela (1920–) Chilean educator. Cofounder of El Teatro de Ensayo, Santiago. *Plays: Invitación,* 1954; *Las santas mujeres* (Blessed Women), 1959; *Telaraña* (Cobweb), 1958; *Una mariposa blanca* (White Butterfly), 1957. *Other Works: Conferencia dialogada,* 1968.

Rudet, Jaqueline (contemp.) Eng. *Plays: Basin,* 1985; *God's Second in Command,* 1985; *Money to Live,* 1984.

Sachs, Nelly (1891–1970) Ger.-Swed. *Plays: Eli: A Mystery Play of the Sufferings of Israel,* 1943. *Other Works: O the Chimneys,* 1967; *A Seeker and Other Poems,* 1970. *Works About: Lady Laureates,* Olga S. Opfell, 1978; *On Modern German Literature,* tr. by Mary F. McCarthy and Paul K. Kurz, 1970; *Postwar German Literature,* Peter Demetz, 1971. *Awards:* Peace Prize of German Publishers, 1965; Nobel Prize for literature (shared with S. Y. Agnon), 1966.

Sanchez, Sonia (1935–)Am. née Wilsonia Benita Driver. *Plays: The Bronx Is Next,* 1970; *Dirty Hearts, I'm Black when I'm Singing, I'm Blue when I Ain't,* 1982; *Malcolm/Man Don't Live Here No Mo',* 1979; *Sister Son/Ji,* 1969; *Un Huh, but Do It Free Us,* 1975. *Other Works: Homecoming,* 1969; *homegirls & handgrenades,* 1984; *Ima Talken bout the Nation of Islam,* 1972; *It's a New Day,* 1971; *I've Been a Woman,* 1978; *Liberation Poems,* 1970; *Love Poems,* 1973; *Under a Soprano Sky,* 1987; *We a BaddDDD People,* 1970; *We Be Word Sorcerers; 25 Stories by Black Americans,* 1973; *Wounded in the House of a Friend,* 1995. *Awards:* PEN Writing Award, 1969; National Institute of Arts and Letters grant, 1970; NEA Award, 1978–79; named Honorary Citizen of Atlanta, 1982.

Sandor, Malena (1913–68) Arg. newspaper correspondent; pseud. Maria Janes de Terza. *Plays: An Almost Unbelievable Story,* 1966; *And the Reply Was Given,* 1956; *A Free Woman,* 1938; *I Am the Strongest,* 1943; *I'm Getting a Divorce, Papa,* 1937; *Penelope No Longer Weaves,* 1946. *Awards:* National Culture Prize, 1938; Argentores honoree.

Sarton, May Eleanor (1912–95) Am. poet, novelist. *Other Works: After the Stroke: A Journal,* 1988; *Anger,* 1982; *Bridge of Years,* 1946; *Encounter in April,* 1937; *Faithful Are the Wounds,* 1955; *The Hours by the Sea,* 1977; *Kinds of Love,* 1970; *A Reckoning,* 1978; *The Single Hound,* 1938. *Works About: May Sarton,* Agnes Sibley, 1972; *May Sarton, Woman and Poet,* Constance Hunting, ed., 1982.

Schenkar, Joan M. (1942–) Am. *Plays: Cabin Fever,* 1984; *The Last Hitler, Last Words; The Next Thing; Signs of Life. Awards:* CAPS grant.

Schneider, Barbara (1942–) Ger.-Am. *Plays: Crossings,* 1982; *Details Without a Map,* 1980; *Echo-Location; Flight Lines,* 1982; *Turtles; Verdict on the Shooting of a Police Officer. Awards:* Susan Smith Blackburn Prize, 1980; CAPS Playwriting Fellowship, 1980.

Schwarz-Bart, Simone (Contemp.) Fr. W. Ind. *Plays: Ton beau capitaine* (Your Handsome Captain, Jessica Harris and Catherine Temerson, trs.), 1987. *Other Works: Between Two Worlds,* 1981; *Un plat de porc aux bananes vertes,* w/André Schwarz-Bart, 1967; *Pluie et vent sur telumée-miracle,* 1972; *Ti-jean l'horizon,* 1979.

Shank, Adele Edling (1940–) Am. *Plays: Dry Smoke,* 1981; *Fox & Co.,* 1978; *The Games,* 1963; *The Grass House,* 1983; *Innocence Abroad,* 1983; *The Mayor of Normington,* 1960; *Sand Castles,* 1982; *Stuck: A Freeway Comedy,* 1981; *Sunset/Sunrise,* 1979; *To Those Who Don't Survive,* 1962; *Tumbleweed,* 1985; *War Horses,* 1985; *Winterplay,* 1980. *Awards:* Cowinner, Actors Theatre of Louisville; Rockfeller grant; NEA grant; Drama-Logue Critics Award.

Sheridan, Frances (1724–66) Irish-Eng. poet, novelist. *Relationships:* s. Richard Brinsley.

Sherman, Susan (1939–) Am. poet, editor, educator.

Sisson, Rosemary Anne (contemp.) Eng. *Plays: The Acrobats; Bitter Sanctuary; Fear Came to Supper; A Ghost on Tiptoe,* w/Robert Morley, 1974; *The Queen and the Welshman; Royal Captivity; Splendid Outcasts. Other Works: Bury Love Deep,* 1986; *The Killer of Horseman's Flats,* 1973; *Will In Love* (orig.: *The Stratford Story),* 1977.

Specht, Kerstin (1956–) Ger. actor, film and television director. *Plays: Das glühend männla* (The Little Red-Hot Man, Guntram H. Weber, tr.), 1990; *Lila* (Purple).

Stewart, Ena Lamont (contemp.) Eng. *Plays: Business in Edinburgh; The Heir Ardmally; Men Should Weep,* 1946; *Starched Aprons; Towards Evening; Walkies Time.*

Surface, Mary Hall (195?–) Am. director. *Plays: Most Valuable Player,* 1989; *Prodigy,* 1987; *The Sorcerer's Apprentice,* 1986.

Swados, Elizabeth (1951–) Am. writer, composer, director. *Plays: Agamemnon* (adapt.), 1976; *Dispatches* (adapt. of Michael Herr), 1979; *The Incredible Feeling Show* (also teleplay, screenplay), 1979; *Lullaby of Goodnight* (opera), 1980; *Nightclub Cantata,* 1977; *Runaways,* 1978; *Wonderland in Concert,* 1978 (adapt.). *Awards:* Obie, 1972; Tony nomination, 1978.

Thomas, Joyce Carol (1938–) Am. educator, poet, novelist. *Plays: Ambrosia,* 1978; *Gospel Roots,* 1981; *Look! What a Wonder!,* 1976; *Magnolia,* 1977; *A Song in the Sky,* 1976; *When the Nightingale Sings,* 1991.

Thompson, Judith (1954–) Can. social worker. *Plays: The Crackwalker,* 1980; *Hedda Gabler* (adapt.), 1991; *I Am Yours,* 1987; *Lion in the Streets,* 1991; *The Other Side of the Dark,* 1989; *Pink,* 1989; *White Biting Dog,* 1984. *Awards:* Governor-General's Awards, 1984, 1990; Chalmers Award, 1988; Toronto Arts award, 1990.

Tollet, Elizabeth (1694–1754) Eng. poet.

Tomalin, Claire (contemp.) Eng.? *Plays: The Winter Wife. Other Works: The Invisible Woman: The Story of Nelly Ternan and Charles Dickens,* 1991; *Katherine Mansfield: A Secret Life,* 1988; *Mrs. Jordan's Profession: The Actress and the Prince,* 1995; *Shelley and His World,* 1980.

Trevisan, Anna F. (1905–) Ital.-Am. drama critic.

Turnbull, Margaret (fl. 1920–42) Scot.-Am. scenarist.

Tuthill, Louisa Caroline (1798/99–1879) Am. poet, author.

Vollmer, Lula (1898–1955) Am. writer. *Plays: Dearly Beloved,* 1946; *Dunce Boy, 1925; The Hill Between,* 1938; *In a Nutshell,* 1937; *Jule; Moonshine and Honeysuckle* (also radio play), 1933; *Sentinels,* 1931; *The Shame Woman,* 1923; *Shining Blackness,* 1932; *Sun-Up,* 1923; *Trigger,* 1927; *Troyka* (adapt.

of Imre Fazekas play), 1930. *Radio Plays: Grits and Gravy,* 1930; *The Widow's Son,* 1932.

Voronel, Nina (1933–) Sov. poet, translator.

Weddell, Mrs. (fl. 1730s–40s) Eng. *Plays: The City Farce,* 1737; *Incle and Yarico,* 1742.

West, Jane (1758–1852) Eng. novelist, poet; pseud. Prudentia Homespun.

Wharton, Countess Anne (1632?–85) Eng. novelist, poet, translator. *Plays: Love's Martyr* (unpub.).

Wiseman, Jane (fl. 1701) Eng. servant, tavern keeper. *Plays: Antiochus the Great, or The Fatal Relapse,* 1702.

Wittig, Monique (contemp.) Fr. critic. *Plays: The Constant Journey,* 1984. *Other Works: Across the Acheron,* 1987; *Corps lesbien* (The Lesbian Body), 1975; *Les Guerilleres,* 1969; *Lesbian Peoples: Material for a Dictionary,* w/Sande Seig, 1979; *The Opoponax,* 1966; *The Straight Mind and Other Essays,* 1992.

Wolton, Joan (contemp.) Eng. *Plays: Landscapes,* 1989; *Motherlove.*

Wong, Elizabeth (1958–) Chin. Am. *Plays: Letters to a Student Revolutionary,* 1991.

Wood, Ellen (1813–87) Eng. journalist.

Wood, Victoria (1953–) Eng. comedian. *Plays: Good Fun & Talent. Awards:* Plays and Players, Evening Standard awards for most promising playwright; British Academy Awards for best light entertainment programme, 1986, 1987.

Wymark, Olwen (1932–) Am. lecturer. Née Margaret Buck. *Plays: Best Friends,* 1981; *The Bolting Sisters,* 1974; *Brezhnev's Children,* 1991; *Buried Treasure,* 1983; *The Child,* 1979; *Chinigchinich,* 1973; *The Committee,* 1971; *Daniel's Epic,* w/Daniel Henry, 1972; *Female Parts: One Woman Plays,* 1981; *Find Me,* 1980; *The Gymnasium,* 1967; *Jack and the Giant Killer,* 1972; *Lessons and Lovers,* 1986; *Loved,* 1980; *Lunchtime Concert,* 1966; *Mirror Mirror* (opera), 1992; *Nana* (adapt. of Zola novel), 1987; *Neither Here nor There,* 1971; *Please Shine down on Me,* 1980; *Speak Now,* 1971; *Starters,* 1975; *Stay Where You Are,* 1969; *The Technicians,* 1969; *Three for All,* 1976; *The Twenty-Second Day* (also radio play), 1975; *Watch the Woman,* w/Brian Phelan, 1973; *We Three, and After Nature, Art,* 1977; *The Winners, and Missing Persons,* 1978. *Radio Plays: The Ransom,* 1957; *Vivien the Blockbuster,* 1980; *You Come Too,* 1977. *Teleplays: Not That Kind of People,* 1984; *Oceans Apart,* 1984; *Vermin,* 1974. *Awards:* Zagreb

Drama Festival Prize, 1967; Actors Theatre of Louisville Best New Play Award, 1978.

Yamagina, Rossanna (contemp.) Asian-Am. *Plays: Behind Enemy Lines*, 1982.

York, Y. (contemp.) Asian-Am. storyteller, performer. *Plays: Accidental Friends*, 1996; *Americana '60s in Three Ax; The Beethoven; Gerald's Good Idea; Jeanne Kirkpatrick Raps with a Turkey at the Mudd Club; Life Gap; Love Story/Steak Dinner; Melina's Fish; Picnic!; The Portrait the Wind the Chair*, 1995; *Rain, Some Fish, No Elephants*, 1989; *The Snowflake Avalanche*, 1992. *Awards:* New Dramatists' Joe Calloway Award, 1991.

Youngblood, Shay (contemp.) Af-Am. novelist. *Plays: Shakin' the Mess Outta Misery*, 1994; *Square Blues*, 1993; *Talking Bones*, 1994. *Other Works:*

The Big Mama Stories, 1989; *Soul Kiss* (novel), 1996.

Zeder, Suzan (contemp.) Am. writer, professor. *Plays (Selected): Because You Never Asked Me*, 1984; *The Death and Life of Sherlock Holmes*, 1987; *Doors*, 1981; *In a Room Somewhere*, 1986; *The Miser* (adapt. of Molière play), 1986; *Mother Hicks*, 1983; *Ozma of Oz: A Tale of Time*, 1978; *The Play Called Noah's Flood*, 1972; *Something With Jamie in the Title*, 1975; *Spa!*, 1982; *Step on a Crack*, 1974; *Wiley and the Hairy Man*, 1972; *Wish in One Hand Spit in the Other: A Collection of Plays* (ed. Susan Pearson-Davis), 1990. *Awards:* Children's Theatre Association of America's Charlotte Chorpenning Award for Outstanding Playwright of Plays for Young People, 1978; Distinguished Play Award by the American Association of Theatre for Youth (3 times); Fulbright scholar to England, 1972–73.

BIBLIOGRAPHY

Anderson, Michael John. *Crowell's Handbook of Contemporary Drama.* New York: Crowell, 1971.

Banham, Martin, ed. *The Cambridge Guide to Theatre.* Cambridge: Cambridge University Press, 1992.

Berney, K. A., ed. *Contemporary British Dramatists.* London: St. James Press, 1993. (1)

———. *Contemporary Dramatists.* 5th ed. London: St. James Press, 1993. (2)

———. *Contemporary Women Dramatists.* Detroit: Gale Research, 1994. (3)

Betsko, Kathleen, and Rachel Koenig. *Interviews with Contemporary Women Playwrights.* New York: Beech Tree Books, 1987.

Brisbane, Katherine, ed. *Australia Plays.* London: Nick Hern Books, 1989.

Brustein, Robert. *Reimagining American Theatre.* New York: Hill and Wang, 1991.

Cameron, Alasdair. *Scot-Free, New Scottish Plays.* London: Nick Hern Books, 1990.

Case, Sue-Ellen. *Feminism and Theatre.* New York: Methuen, 1988. (1)

———. ed. *The Divided Home/Land: Contemporary German Women's Plays.* Ann Arbor: University of Michigan Press, 1992. (2)

Charvat, William. *The Profession of Authorship in America 1800–1870,* edited by Matthew Bruccoli, foreword by Howard Mumford Jones. Columbus: Ohio State University Press, 1968.

Chinoy, Helen, and Linda Jenkins, eds. *Women in American Theater.* New York: Crown Publishers, 1981.

Cotton, Nancy. *Women Playwrights in England, c. 1363–1750.* London: Assoc. Univ. Presses, 1980.

Dolan, Jill. *Presence and Desire.* Ann Arbor: University of Michigan Press, 1993.

Feder, Lillian. *The Meridian Handbook of Classical Literature.* New York: New American Library, 1986.

Friedl, Bettina. *On to Victory: Propaganda Plays of the Woman Suffrage Movement.* Boston: Northeastern University Press, 1987.

Grant, David. *The Crack in the Emerald, New Irish Plays.* London: Nick Hern Books, 1990.

Hanna, Gillian. *Monstrous Regiment, A Collective Celebration.* London: Nick Hern Books, 1991.

Hawkins-Dady, Mark, ed. *International Dictionary of Theatre—1: Plays.* Chicago: St. James Press, 1992. (1)

———. *International Dictionary of Theatre—2: Plays.* Chicago: St. James Press, 1994. (2)

Herbert, Ian, ed. *Who's Who in the Theatre.* Vol. 1. Detroit: Gale Research Co., 1981.

Hewitt, Bernard. *Theatre U.S.A. 1668–1957.* New York: McGraw Hill, 1959.

Hochman, Stanley, ed. in chief. *McGraw-Hill Encyclopedia of World Drama.* New York: McGraw-Hill, 1984.

Houston, Velina Hasu. *The Politics of Life, Four Plays by Asian American Women.* Philadelphia: Temple University Press, 1993.

Hubbard, Linda S., and Owen O'Donnell, eds. *Contemporary Theatre, Film, and Television.* Vols. 1–12. Detroit: Gale Research, Co., 1984.

Jones, Stephen, and David Erskine Baker. *Biographia Dramatica, or A Companion to the Playhouse.* Vol. 1. London: Longman, Hurst. Repr. 1812.

Keyssar, Helene. *Feminist Theatre, An Introduction to Plays of Contemporary British and American Women.* New York: Grove Press, 1985.

MacNicholas, John, ed. *Twentieth-Century American Dramatists*. Detroit: Gale Research Co., 1981.

Magill, Frank N., ed. *Critical Survey of Drama: Foreign Language Series*. Vols. 1–5. Englewood Cliffs, N.J.: Salem Press, 1986.

Mahl, Mary R., and Helene Koon. *The Female Spectator: English Women Writers Before 1800*. Bloomington: Indiana University Press, 1977.

Mahone, Sydné. *Moon Marked and Touched by Sun*. New York: TCG, 1994.

Mapp, Edward, ed. *Directory of Blacks in the Performing Arts*. Metuchen, N.J.: Scarecrow Press, 1990.

McGillick, Paul. *International Dictionary of Theatre Playwrights*. Vol. 1.

Merriam-Webster's Encyclopedia of Literature. Springfield: Merriam-Webster, 1995.

Miles, Julia, ed. *Playwriting Women, 7 Plays from the Women's Project*. Portsmouth, N.H.: Heinemann, 1993.

Morgan, Fidelis. *The Female Wits*. London: Virago Press Ltd., 1981.

Moritz, Charles, ed. *Current Biography Yearbook*. Various vols. New York: H. W. Wilson Co., 1980–5.

Olauson, Judith. *The American Woman Playwright, A View of Criticism and Characterization*. Troy, NY: Whitston Pub. Co., 1981.

Osborn, M. Elizabeth. *On New Ground, Contemporary Hispanic-American Plays*. New York: TCG, 1987.

Perkins, Kathy A., and Robert Uno. *Contemporary Plays by Women of Color*. London: Routledge, 1996.

Quinn, Arthur Hobson. *A History of the American Drama from the Beginnings to the Civil War*. 2d ed. New York: F. S. Crofts, 1943.

Remnant, Mary. *Plays by Women*. Vol. 8. London: Methuen, 1990.

Robinson, Alice M., Vera Mowry Roberts, and Milly S. Barranger, eds. *Notable Women in the American Theatre*. Westport, Conn.: Greenwood Press, Inc., 1989.

Rogers, Katharine M., ed. *The Meridian Anthology of Restoration and Eighteenth-Century Plays by Women*. New York: Meridian, 1994.

Segel, Harold B. *Twentieth-Century Russian Drama*. New York: Columbia University Press, 1979.

Shafer, Yvonne. *American Women Playwrights, 1900–1950*. New York: Peter Lang Publishing, 1995.

Shipley, Joseph T. *The Crown Guide to the World's Great Plays*. New York: Crown Publishers, Inc., 1984.

Straumanis, Alfreds, ed. *Baltic Drama: A Handbook and Bibliography*. Prospect Heights, Ill.: Waveland Press, 1981.

Sullivan, Victoria, and James V. Hatch. *Plays by and About Women: An Anthology*. New York: Random House, 1973.

Turner, Mary M. *Forgotten Leading Ladies of the American Theatre*. Jefferson, N.C.: McFarland & Co., 1990.

Van Antwerp, Margaret A., ed. *Dictionary of Literary Biography*. Detroit, Mich.: Gale Research Co., 1978.

Wandor, Michelene. *Plays by Women*. Vol. 1. London: Methuen, 1982. (1)

———. *Understudies*. London: New York: Routledge & Kegan Paul, 1986. (2)

Weintraub, Stanley, ed. *Modern British Dramatists, 1900–1945*. Detroit: Gale Research Co., 1982.

Wilkerson, Margaret, ed. and intro. *9 Plays by Black Women*. New York: New American Library, 1986.

INDEX

Boldface page numbers indicate major treatment of a topic.
The letter *f* following a page number denotes an illustration.

A

12-1-A (Yamauchi) 223
100,001 Horror Stories (Terry) 201
A. A. and His Father (Lasker-Schüler) 132
Abbey Theatre (Dublin) 95
Abbott, Berenice 11
Abel's Sister (Wertenbaker) 217
Abie's Irish Rose (Nichols) 159
abolitionism, novels professing 14
Abortive (Churchill) 40
Abramson, Doris E. 79
Absent in the Spring (Christie) 39
absurdist theater 20
Abundance (Henley) 105
Académie du Cinema award 67
Academy Award
    for best original story 124
    for best screenplay 56, 124
    for best song 73
    for best supporting actress 94, 178
    first female lyricist to receive 74
Academy of Motion Picture Arts and Sciences, female
    presidents of 124
Actors Fund Home 159
Actor's Mobile Theater 131
ACTRA. *See* Alliance of Canadian Cinema, Television,
    and Radio Artists

actresses, tarnished reputations of xi
Adams, Abigail 213
Adams, John 213
Adam's Opera (Dane and Addinsell) 55
Adam's Rib (Gordon and Kanin) 95
Addams, Jane 72, 82
Addinsell, Richard 55
Adler, Lillian 72
Adler, Stella 26
The Adulateur (Warren) 213
Advanced Creative Writing Program at Stanford 3
The Adventures in Madrid (Pix) 173
An Adventure (Tsvetayeva) 206
The Advertisement (Ginzburg) 90
The Aegis (literary magazine) 81
African-American dramatists 26–28, 37–39, 44–46, 47–
    48, 89–90, 98–100, 112–113, 118, 120–121, 125–
    126, 145, 169–170, 175–176, 178, 189–191, 191–
    192, 218
    first one woman show by 178–179
African dramatists 3, 83, 193, 197
Aftel, Luis 19
The After Dinner Joke (Churchill) 41
After the Prize (Weldon) 216
Agate, James 12
Ağaoğlu, Adalet **1**
Aged 26 (Flexner) 76
Agnes de Castro (adaptation: Trotter) 204

Agrarusa (Zalite) 227

Aguirre, Isadora **1–2**

"Ah, Sweet Mystery of Life" (Young) 226

Aidoo, (Christina) Ama Ata **2–3**

Aid Thy Neighbor (Wandor) 212

L'Aiglon (adaptation: Dane) 55

L'Aiglon (translation: Tsvetayeva) 206

Ainslee's magazine 151

Akalaitis, JoAnne **3–4**

Akins, Zoë xi, **4–5**

Akutagawa, Ryunosuke 124

Alarcón Prizes 207

Albee, Edward 126, 200

Albert, Fred 215

Alberta Literary Foundation Award 174

Albina (Cowley) 50

Algerian dramatists 83

Alice in Wonderland (adaptation: Gerstenberg) 88

Alice's Adventures in Wonderland (adaptation: Dane and Addinsell) 55

Alison's House (Glaspell) 93

Allan, Ted 136

Allgood, Myralyn 29

Alliance of Canadian Cinema, Television, and Radio Artists (ACTRA) Award 181

All London Playwrights' Award 217

All the Livelong Day (Garson) 85

Almyna (Manley) 143

Amerasian League 109

American Academy of Arts and Letters 11
    grants from 78, 110, 161

American Conservatory Theater 192
    training program 97

American Dramatists Club 76, 155

American Dreams (Houston) 109

American Film Institute grants 47

American King's English for Queens (Terry) 201

American National Theater Academy West Award 208

American Negro Theater, founding of 37

The American Play (Parks) 169

American Theater Association, women's program of 33

American Theater Critics Outstanding Play Award 224

American Theater Wing for War Relief 51

Am I Blue (Henley) 104

Amis, Aphra 13

A Mistake & ½ (West) 218

The Amorous Prince (Behn) 13

Anansegoro (Sutherland) 197

And, Metin 1

Anderson, Frances Rademacher 225

Anderson, Sherwood 196

Andrade, Elba 2

Andrea, Yann 67

And the Soul Shall Dance (Yamauchi) 223

Anna Karenina (adaptation: Dane) 55

Annensky, Innokenti 296

Anne of a Thousand Days (Boland) 18

Annie Get Your Gun (lyrics: Fields) 73

Annulla, An Autobiography (Mann) 144

Another Language (Franken) 79

Another Part of the Forest (Hellman) 102–103

Anowa (Aidoo) 3

Anstriņš, Antons 227

Antelme, Robert 67

Anthony, C. L. 192

Anthony, Susan B. 196

Antígona Furiosa (Gambaro) 84

The Antiphon (Barnes) 11

Antoinette Perry Award xiii, 48
    for best actress 17, 179
    for best adaptation 161
    for best score 194
    first female lyricist to receive 74
    first woman to receive 214
    nomination for 27, 124, 160, 190

The Ants (Churchill) 40

Any Woman Can't (Wasserstein) 214

Appearing Nightly with Lily Tomlin (Wagner) 211

Applause (Comden and Green) 48

Appleton Daily Crescent 72

Appointment with Death (Christie) 39

Approaching Simone (Terry) 200–201

Approaching Zanzibar (Howe) 110

The Arbor (Dunbar) 65

Arbuzov, Alexi 171

Arcadia (periodical) 105

Ardelia 74

Arden, John 57

Arena Theater, founders of 1

Are You Sitting Comfortably? (Townsend) 202

Argentinian dramatists 84

Aria da Capo (Millay) 151

Ariadne **5**

Armand, the Child of the People (Mowatt) 156

arrest, first women to be placed under, for writing 143

Artaud, Antonin 142, 199

Art Matters fellowship 142

The Art of Dining (Howe) 110

The Art of Management (Charke) 34–35

Arts Council of Great Britain Lifetime Achievement Award 136

Asa Ga Kimashita (Houston) 109

Ask for the Moon (Gee) 86

Aspāzija **5–6**, 135

Aspāzija (Aspāzija) 6

Aswell, Edward C. 80

At Her Age (Merriam) 149

Atlanta Tribune 45

Atriebēja (Aspāzija)

Attenborough, Richard 136

At the Borders (Ağaoğlu) 1

At the Foot of the Mountain theatre collective 18

Attilio Regolo (Metastasio) 154

AUDELCO Award 45, 89, 190

Audience Development Committee. *See* AUDELCO

audiences, abuse of female dramatists by xi

Aurora Leigh (adaptation: Wandor) 212

Austin, Jane 216

Australian dramatists 106

Australian Writers Guild Award 60

Authors League 76

autobiographical drama 53

The Autobiography of Alice B. Toklas (Stein) 195–196

The Automatic Pilot (Ritter) 181

Autos sacramentales (de la Cruz) 121

Autumn Crocus (Smith) 192

The Autumn Garden (Hellman) 102–103

avant-garde theater 77, 195

The Avengeress (Aspāzija) 6

Avrora (periodical) 171

Away from It All (Horsfield) 108

B

Baader-Meinhof Gang 177

Baartman, Saartjee 169

Babes in the Bighouse (Terry) 201

The Bacchae ix

Backlash (Faludi) xi

Bagheria (Maraini) 146

Bagnold, Enid **7–9**, 7*f*

Bailey, Frederick 104

Baillie, Joanna **9**, 9*f*

Baizley, Doris **10**

Baker, Elizabeth **10–11**

The Ballygombeen Bequest (D'Arcy) 57

The Baltimore Waltz (Vogel) 208

Banff School of Fine Arts 199

Banman, Gerry 145

The Banshee (Chase) 35

Barber, John 56, 144

Bárcena, Catalina 146–147

Barlow, Judith E. 109, 110

Barnes, Clive 49, 78, 216

Barnes, Djuna **11–12**

Barnes, Howard 36

Barr, Richard 200

Barr, Rosanne 216

Un barrage contre le Pacifique (Duras) 66

Barrymore, John 203

Barrymore, Lionel 137

Barry of Ballymore (Young) 226

Bartenieff, George 142

Bashkirtseff, Marie 11

The Basset Table (Centlivre) 31

The Bat (Rinehart and Hopwood) 180

Baum, Vicki **12**, 12*f*

Bazaar and Rummage (Townsend) 202

BBC. *See* British Broadcasting Corporation

Beal, John 79

Bean, Orson 62

The Bear's Den (Liobytė) 135

The Beau Defeated (Pix) 173

Beaumont, Muriel **64**

Beauty Without Cruelty 63

Becca (Kesselman) 128

Becker, Elizabeth 104

Beckett, Samuel 11, 26, 77, 110, 150

Beecher, Clare Rodman 129

The Beekeeper's Daughter (Malpede) 142

Before It Hits (West) 218

Behan, Brendan 135

Behn, Aphra xi, 5, **13–14, 13*f*,** 64, 172

Belcch (Ownes) 165
Bellamy, Ralph 194
The Belle of Amherst (adaptation: Wandor) 212
The Belle's Stratagem (Cowley) 51
Bell in Campo (Cavendish) 30
Benmussa, Simone **15–16,** 44
Ben-Zvi, Linda 93, 169
Berg, Gertrude **16–17, 16f**
Berghof, Herbert 20
Bergman, Ellen **17**
Bergman, Ingmar 17, 106
Bernardine (Chase) 35
Berney, William 27
Bernstein, Leonard 103
Berry, Chuck 189
Beside Herself (Daniels) 56–57
Best Production Award 136
Betsey Brown (Shange) 145, 190
Better People (Malpede) 142
Betting on the Dust Commander (Parks) 169
Bibesco, Prince Antoine 8
A Bickerstaff's Burying (Centlivre) 32
The Big Haul (Brigadere) 22
Big Smoke Books 107
Billington, Michael 139
A Bill of Divorcement (Dane) 55
Biographica Dramatica (Jones) 9, 22, 23
Biograph Studios 137
Birch, Thomas 204
The Birds (du Maurier) 64
Birth (Gale) 82
Birth and After Birth (Howe) 110
Bits and Pieces (Jacker) 117
Bitter Cane (Lim) 134
Blackberry Production Co., founding of 175
Black Coffee (Christie) 39
Black Filmmakers Hall of Fame 38, 179
Black Nativity (Hughes) 27
Black Scholar (periodical) 190
Black Theater U.S.A. (Hatch and Shine) 126
The Black Woman (Gibson) 89, 99
A Black Woman Speaks (Richards) 26, 53, 178–179
Blechman, Burt 103
The Blind Goddess (adaptation: Wandor) 212
Block, Haskell M. xii
Blood Relations (Pollock) 174

Blue Blood (Johnson) 120
Blues for an Alabama Sky (Cleage) 45
Blumenthal, Eileen 150
Boas, Franz 112
Boesing, Martha Gross **17–18**
Boland, Bridget **18**
A Bold Stroke for a Husband (Cowley) 51
A Bold Stroke for a Wife (Centlivre) 32
Bolt, Carol **19**
Bolton, Whitney xiii
Bonal, Denis **19–20**
Bond, Tim 99
Bondanella, Peter 90, 146
Bonjour, tristesse (Sagan) 185
Boogie woogie landscapes (Shange) 190
Booth, Shirley 123
Boothby, Frances **20**
Borden, Lizzie 174
Borders of Paradise (MacDonald) 141
Boston Massacre 213
Boston Tea Party 213
Bound East for Cardiff (O'Neill) 92
Bovasso, Julie **20–21, 21f**
Bowers, Dwight B. 73
Bowles, Jane 182
Boxes (Yankowitz) 224
Boyce, Neith 92
Boyd, Neva L. 57
Boyle, Roger 172
Boy Meets Girl (Spewack) 194
Brady, Susan 153
The Braille Garden (Cloud) 47
Brand, Hannah **21–22**
The Brave (MacDonald) 141
Brecht, Bertolt 1, 47, 75, 142, 190, 220
Brennan, Brian 174
Brezhnev, Leonid 177
The Bride from America (Jotuni) 121
Brigadere, Anna **22–23**
Brisbane, Katherine 106
British Broadcasting Corporation (BBC) 135, 188, 202, 216
British Film Academy Award for best picture 61
British Talent (Smith) 192
Broadway musicals, purported mother of 182
Brooke, Frances **23**

"Brother Lustig" (Grimm brothers) 179
The Brothers (Collins) 47
Broun, Heywood xiii
Brown Silk and Magenta Sunsets (Gibson) 89
Brustein, Robert 105, 160, 215
Brzeska, Sophie 58
Buffalo Jump (Bolt) 19
Burke, Sally 88
Burney, Frances **23–24**
Burnt-Out Ocher (Manner) 145
Bush Foundation Fellowship 18
The Busie Body (Centlivre) 31–32
The Busman's Honeymoon (Saycrs) 187
The Butcher's Daughter (Kesselman) 128
But What Have You Done for Me Lately? (Lamb) 131
Byck, Dann C. 160
Byrthrite (Daniels) 56
By the Beautiful Sea (lyrics: Fields) 73

C

Cagney, James 194
Cahiers Renaud-Barrault 15
Calderón de la Barca, Pedro 91, 121
Callimachus (von Gandersheim) 111
Call It a Day (Smith) 192
Calm Down, Mother (Terry) 201
Cambridge Guide to Theatre (Martin, ed.) 136
Camille (Akins) 4
Camille (Gems) 87
The Camp (Gambaro) 84
Canada Council grant 60, 174
Canadian dramatists 19, 173–174, 180–181
canon, literary
    and female dramatists xi
    and racism and sexism xii
Canth, Minna **25**
Capote, Truman 11
CAPS. *See* Creative Artists Public Service Award
Captain Joe (Gerstenberg) 88
Care and Control (Wandor) 212
Carol, Rosa 62
Carr, Marina **26**
Carroll, Baikida 145
Carroll, Leo G. 127

Carroll, Lewis 55–56
Carroll, Madeleine 123
Carroll, Vinette **26–28**
Carta Atenagórica (Sor Juana) 121
Cary, Elizabeth Tanfield **28**
Casanova, Giacomo Girolamo 206
Case, Sue-Ellen 37, 44, 111, 122, 132, 177, 178, 181
Case, Susan xi
Castellanos, Rosario **28–29**
Cather, Willa 4, 46
Catspaw (Hewett) 107
Cavendish, Margaret **29–30**
CBS network 149
Čiurlionienė-Kymantaitė, Sofija **43**
Čiurlionienė, M. K. 43
A Celebration of Life (Sofola) 193
Celtes, Conrad 111
censorship
    political 6
    in schools 38
Centlivre, Susanna **30–32, 31***f*
Centocelle (Maraini) 146
Central School of Speech and Drama 118
Centre de Recherche en Études Féminin 44
Centro Mexicano de Escritores grant 78
Century of Struggle (Flexner) 76
A Certain Smile (Kerr) 126
Chaikin, Joseph 200, 225
Chaillet, Ned 217
Chains (Baker) 10
Chains (Cleage) 45
The Chairman's Wife (Yamauchi) 223
The Chalk Garden (Bagnold) 7
Chambers, Jane **32–33**
Chalmers Award 181
The Chapel Perilous (Hewett) 107
Chaplin, Charlie 126
Charke, Charlotte **34–35**
Charles I (king of Great Britain) 75, 105
Charles II (king of Great Britain) 13, 20, 105, 143
Charlie Bubbles (Delaney) 61
Charlotte Temple (Rowson) 182
Chase, Mary **35–36**
    and Pulitzer Prizes for drama xi
Chatellaine (periodical) 181

Chatterton, Thomas 55

Cheap Repository Tracts (More) 154

Chekhov, Anton 103, 121, 170

The Cherry Orchard (Chekhov) 103

Chesterton, G. K. 188

Chiang, Yang **36–37**

Chicago Junior League Theater for Children, founding of (1921) 89

Child of the Morning (Luce) 139

The Children of the House (Wuolijoki) 220

The Children's Hour (Hellman) 102

children's theater 16, 199–201, 202

Childress, Alice **37–39, 37f,** 126

Chilean dramatists 1–2

Chilton, Charles 136

Chilton, Nola 200

Chinese dramatists 36–37

The Chinese Prime Minister (Bagnold) 7

The Chinese Restaurant Syndrome (Jacker) 117

Chip, Will 154

Chocolate Cake (Gallagher) 83

Chong, Ping 97

Chopin, Kate 212

Christie, Agatha **39–40, 39f**

Christ in a Treehouse (Chambers) 33

A Christmas Carol (adaptation; Baizley) 10

chronology, of female dramatists xix–xxviii

Chucky's Hunch (Ownes) 165

church subjugation of women xi

Churchill, Caryl xiv, **40–43, 41f,** 150

Cibber, Colley 34–35

Cibber, Susanna 46

Cinohern Klub, founding of 209

The Circular Staircase (Rinehart) 180

Circus Valentine (Norman) 160

City Limits (Woddis) 56

City of London Festival Playwright's Prize 64

Cixous, Hélène 15, **43–44**

Clarity, James F. 26

Claudia Series (Franken) 79

Cleage, Pearl **44–46**

Clear All Wires (Spewack) 194

Clive, Catherine **46, 46f**

Clive, Kitty 32

Cloud, Darrah **46–47**

The Club (Merriam and Ivanoff) 149–150

Clurman, Harold 20, 103

Coastal Disturbances (Howe) 110

Cockpit (Boland) 18

Cocoons (Ağaoğlu) 1

Collins, Kathleen **47–48**

Colorado Dateline (Chase) 35

Color Struck (Hurston) 112

Columbia University creative writing program 148

Columbine's Apartment (Petrushevskaya) 171

Colway Theatre Trust 119

Comden, Betty **48–49, 48f**

Come Back, Little Sheba (adaptation: Frings) 80

comedy, classic, evolution of xii

The Comedy Zone (Wasserstein) 215

Come of Age (Dane and Addinsell) 55

The Comic Artist (Glaspell) 93

Coming Home (Rame and Fo) 177

Command Promise (Horsfield) 108

commedia dell'arte xii

Commire, Anne **48–49**

Common Garden Variety (Chambers) 33

community plays 119

The Confused (Vilalta) 207

Congreve, William 32, 173, 205

Conner, John 66

Constancy (Boyce) 92

Conversation at Midnight (Millay) 152

Cook, George Cram 91–93, 151

The Co-op (Garson) 85

Corneille, Pierre 172

Cornell, Katherine 55

Cornish School of Allied Arts 200

Cornwall-on-Hudson 11

Cortis, Diane 55

Cotton, Nancy xi, 13, 29, 31, 46, 74, 101, 124, 144, 172, 173, 204–205

Could Nine (Churchill) 42

The Countess Cathleen (Yeats) 95

The Country Wife (Wycherley) 32

The Cousin from Saaremaa (Koidula) 128

Coveney, Michael 56

Cowl, Jane 138

Cowley, Hannah **50–51, 50f**

Crab Quadrille (Lamb) 132

The Crack in the Structure (Ağaoğlu) 1
The Cradle Song (Martínez Sierra and Martínez Sierra) 146
Craig, Edith 112
Crane, William H. 155
Creative Artists Public Service Award 33, 49, 126, 142, 151, 153, 201
Creteille Film Festival award 164
Crimes of the Heart (Henley) 104
Critical Quarterly 64
critics, literary
    and female dramatists x
    and repression of women dramatists xiii
Critic's Choice (Levin) 127
Critic's Prize for best children's play 202
Crothers, Rachel xii, **51–53, 52***f*
Cruz, Sor Juana Inés de la. *See* Juana Inés de la Cruz, Sor
Cryer, David 53
Cryer, Gretchen **53**
Cryer, Jon 53
CT TV Award 33
Cuban dramatists 76–79, 93–94
The Cuban Swimmer (Sánchez-Scott) 186
Cuchulain of Muirthemne (adaptation: Gregory) 95
La cuisine des anges (Husson) 194
culture
    effecting change in, and female dramatists ix
    women's view of ix
Curb, Rosemary 38
Cvirka, Petras 135
Czech dramatists 209

D

Dace, Tish 21, 77, 128, 208
Dam Against the Pacific (Duras) 66
Dance, Marie! (Reinshagen) 178
Dance with a Stranger (Delaney) 61
Dane, Clemence **55–56**
Daniel in Babylon (Baizley) 10
Daniels, Sarah **56–57**
D'Arcy, Margaretta (Ruth) **57–58**
Darkness at Noon (Koestler) 18
Dark of the Moon (Richardson and Berney) 27

Dasgupta, Guatam 62
da Silva, Howard 131
Dave (Gregory) 95–96
Davenport Morning Republican 92
Daviot, Gordon **58**
Davis, Bette 124
Davis, Miles 189
Davys, Mary xii, **58–59**
Day, Doris 124
The Day After Yesterday (Wandor) 212
A Day in Turkey (Cowley) 51
Dead End Kids (Akalaitis) 3–4
Dean, Alexander 88
"Dear" (Drexler) 63
"Dear John" (radio serial) 159
Dear Yelena Sergeyevna (Razumovskaya) 177
The Death of the Last Black Man in the Whole World (Parks) 169
Death on the Nile (Christie) 39, 40
Deb magazine 149
De Bois, W.E.B. 120
¿De Donde? (Gallagher) 83
Deepseafish (Fleier) 75
de Falla, Manuel 147
A Defence of Mr. Locke's "Essay of Human Understanding" (Trotter) 205
De Groen, Alma **59–60, 60***f*
de Jongh, Nicholas 66
Delaney, Shelagh **60–61,** 135
Delicate Feelings (Drexler) 62
Dell'Ollio, Anselma 131
Denham, Sir John 172
The Department (Garson) 85
Der Sterm (periodical) 132
de Santillana, Juana Inés de Asbaje y Ramirez 121
Desdemona (Vogel) 208
Des Moines News 92
Detection Club, formation of 188
Devany, Jean **61–62**
The Devil's Gateway (Daniels) 56
Devine, George 118
Devotees in the Garden of Love (Parks) 169
Dialogue (Maraini) 146
Diamond Lil (West) 219
Dickinson, Emily 93

The Dilemma of a Ghost (Aidoo) 3
Dinesen, Isak 11
Dinner at Eight (Ferber and Kaufman) 72
The Dinosaur Door (Garson) 85
diplomatic post, major, first woman to hold 139
Directors' Guild of Great Britain Lifetime Achievement
    Award 136
La discreta enamorada (de Vega Carpio) 121–122
Divine Comedy (translation: Sayers) 188
The Divine Narcissus (de la Cruz) 121
Dix, Carol 119
D'Lugoff, Burt 98
Doc (Pollock) 174
Dog Eat Dog (Gallagher) 83
Dogeaters (Hagedorn) 97
Dolan, Jill 33, 215
A Doll's House (Ibsen) 139
Dolpelis ministerijoj tarnauja (Čiurlionienė-Kymantaitė)
    43
Domestic Issues (Jacker) 117
Don Carlos (adaptation: Dane) 55
Dong, Stella 190
Don Juan (Maraini) 146
Donnadieu, Marguerite 66
Donne, John 105
Don't Bother Me, I Can't Cope (Carroll and Grant) 27
Don't Look Now (Du Maurier) 64
Dr. Kheal (Fornés) 77
Drama, experimental, first woman to write 203
Drama Critics Circle Award 27, 36, 61, 80, 103, 104,
    148, 214, 217
    first black writer to receive 98
Drama Desk Award 4, 53, 192
Drama League award 47
Dramalogue Critics Circle Award 33, 151, 187,
    192
Drama Studio, London 169
dramatists
    abuse of, by critics and audiences xi
    female 168
        cabals against 13–14
        denigration of ix, xi–xii
        first, in English 28
        first English 124
        first feminist, in Britain 29

first professional 13
first public performance of 20
frustrations of x
role of ix–x
surge in
    1900–20 xii
    during Restoration xi–xii
variety of backgrounds among ix
Dramatists Guild 76, 127
Draws-Tychsen, Hellmuth 75
Dreamed Life (Törnqvist) 202
Dressing for Dinner (Keatley) 124
Drexler, Rosalyn **62–63**
Drive, She Said (Wasserstein) 215
The Drowned Woman (adaptation: Liobyt and
    Kymantait) 135
Drury Lane Theatre 34, 34*f,* 50
Dryden, John 13, 133
Du Bois, W. E. B. 98, 120, 189
Duffy, Henry 159
Duffy, Marguerite 199
Duffy, Maureen **63–64**
Dulcitius (von Gandersheim) 111
du Maurier, Daphne **64**
du Maurier, George 64
du Maurier, Sir Gerald 64
Dunbar, Andrea **65**
The Dunciad (Pope) 101
Dunn, Nell **65–66**
Dunnock, Mildred 79
Duras, Marguerite x, **66–67**
Dusa, Fish, Stas and Vi (Gems) 87
The Dutch Lover (Behn) 13
Dvoresky, Ignati 177
Dylan Bob 10

E

Each His Own Wilderness (Lessing) 133
Ebony Beat Journal 45
Eddy, Nelson 226
Edufa (Sutherland) 197
Edward VI (king of England) 105–106
Edwy and Elgiva (Burney) 24
Eeny Meeny Miney Mo (Vostrá) 209

Eesti postimees (periodical) 129

Effie and Laurie (Berg) 16

Eisenhower, Dwight D. 139

El 9 (Vilalta) 204, 207

El album cubano (review) 94

The Election (Baillie) 9

Eliot, T. S. 11, 179

Elizabeth (queen of England) 105–106

Ellington, Duke 98

Ellison, Ralph 113

Elsie Fogerty Prize 118

Elsom, John 136

Emerson, John 137

Emma Instigated Me (Ownes) 165

Emma McChesney and Co. (Ferber) 72

Emmy Award 27, 63, 94, 124, 211, 212

The Enchanted Princess (Liobytė) 135

The End of War (Malpede) 142

English Women of Letters (Kavanagh) 14

environmental theater 18

Erenus, Bilgesu **69**

Eros ja Psykhe (Manner) 145

Ervine, St. John 55

Eslava Theater, founding of 147

Esparza, Laura 187

ESPN 139

Essence magazine 38, 45

Estonian dramatists 128–129

The Eternal Feminine (Castellanos) 29

Etta Jenks (Meyer) 150–151

E tu chi eri? Interviste sull'infanzia (Maraini) 146

Eugene O'Neill National Playwrights Conference 214

Eugene O'Neill Prize 33

Euripedes ix

Europe in the Spring (Luce) 139

Evelina (Burney) 23

Evening Standard Award 65, 141, 157, 217

Evening World (newspaper) 82

Events While Guarding the Bofors Gun (McGrath) 167, 168

Everybody's Autobiography (Stein) 196

The Examiner (periodical) 143

Execution of Justice (Mann) 144–145

Exit (Ağaoğlu) 1

Ex-Miss Copper Queen (Terry) 200

F

F. Jasmine Addams (McCullers) 148

Faber and Faber (publishers) 179

Fabien, Michéle **71**

Fairbanks, Douglas 136, 137

The Fair Captive (Haywood) 100

Falkland, Lady **28**

Faludi, Susan xi

Familiar Sayings (Ginzburg) 90

Family Portrait (Bonal) 19–20

Farhoud, Abla **71–72**

Fashion (Mowatt) 156

Fassbinder, Rainer Werner 75

The Fatal Falsehood (More) 154

The Fatal Friendship (Trotter) 204

Father Dreams (Gallagher) 83

Father's Shadow (Martínez Sierra and Martínez Sierra) 146

Fatima's Hand (Bergman) 17

Faulkner, William 11, 47

Fefu and Her Friends (Fornés) 77

Feingold, Michael 78, 117, 208

Felix Award 164

female dramatists, chronology of xix–xxviii

Female Parts (Rame) 176

The Female Spectator (periodical) 101

The Female Tattler 791(Manley) 143

The Female Wits, or The Triumvirate of Poets at Rehersal (Mr. W. M.) 46, 143, 173, 204

feminist drama

first American 201

and Pulitzer Prize xi

subject matter of xiii

La femme du Gange (Duras) 67

Fen (Churchill) 40

Feng hsü (Chiang) 36

Fenichell, Susan 86

Ferber, Edna **72–73**

Ferrier, Carole 62

Fieldcrest, Inc. 211

Fielding, Henry 101

Fields, Dorothy **73–74, 73f**
Fields, Lew 73
Finch, Anne Kingsmill **74**
Finishing Touches (Kerr) 126
Finnish dramatists 25, 121, 145–146, 220–221
Fires in the Mirror (Smith) 191
First Level Award for American Playwrights 187
Fisher, Else 17
Fiske, Minnie 76
Fitzgerald, F. Scott 47
Flaws (Page) 167
Fleetwood, Charles 34
Fleißer, Marieluise **75–76**
Fletcher, Winona 120
Flexner, Anne Crawford **73**
The Floating Admiral (Sayers *et al.*) 188
Floorshow (Wandor) 212
Florence (Childress) 37, 126
The Flower Stand (Aguirre) 2
Flyin' West (Cleage) 45
Fo, Dario 176
The Forced Marriage (Behn) 13, 20
for colored girls who have considered suicide/when the rainbow is enuf (Shange *et al.*) 149, 189–190
Ford, Nancy 53
Ford Foundation grant 18, 27, 128, 165, 193
Foreman, Richard 195
Foreman, Robert J. 161
The Forest Will Murmur (Zapolska) 228
Foriwa (Sutherland) 197
Fornés, Maria Irene xiv, **76–79, 77f,** 127, 187, 200
Fortress Besieged (adaptation: Chiang) 36
Fortuna (Tsvetayeva) 206
Fortune (Aspāzija) 6
Le Fou de Layda (adaptation: Gallaire-Bourega) 83
Fourier, François 142
Four Saints in Three Acts (Stein and Thomson) 196
France, Rachel 120
Francis of Assisi, St. 170
Franken, Rose **79–80**
Franklin, Aretha 44
Freedom (periodical) 38, 98
Freedomway (periodical) 38
French, Marilyn 211
French Academy of Writers 136

French dramatists 15, 19–20, 43–44, 66–67, 71, 185
Frenchman's Creek (du Maurier) 64
Frieda Geier, Traveling Saleswoman (Fleier) 75
Friedl, Bettina xii
Friendship Village (Gale) 82
Fringe First Award 144
Frings, Ketti **80**
    and Pulitzer Prizes for drama xi
Fulbright scholarship 3, 193
Fullerton, Lady 28
Funnyhouse of a Negro (Kennedy) 125
Futz (Ownes) 165

G

Gable, Clark 124, 204
Gale, Zona **81–82, 81f**
    and Pulitzer Prizes for drama xi
Gallagher, Mary **82–83**
Gallaire-Bourega, Fatima **83**
Gambaro, Griselda **83–85,** 204
The Gamester (Centlivre) 31
Garbo, Greta 87
Garden Without Earth (Razumovskaya) 177
Gardner, Fred 85
Gardner, Lyn 56, 125
Garnier, Robert 105
Garpe, Margareta 164
Garrick, David 23, 46, 50, 115, 154
Garson, Barbara **85–86**
Gaslight (Boland) 18
Gassner, John xii, 203
Gaudier, Henri 58
gay dramatists 32–33
Gee, Donald 86
Gee, Shirley **86–87**
Gee, Girls—Freedom Is Near (Osten and Garpe) 164
Gems, Pam **87–88**
generation of the 50s 1
Genet, Jean 20, 142
Gentlemen Prefer Blondes (Loos) 137
Geoffrey Middleton, Gentleman (Morton) 155
George Devine Award 125, 168
George Oppenheimer Newsday Playwright Award 160

German dramatists 75–76, 111–112, 132–133, 178, 181–182

Gerould, Daniel 228

Gerstenberg, Alice **88–89**

Getting Out (Norman) 160

Getting Right Behind Something Like That (West) 218

Ghana Drama Studio, founding of 197

Ghanian dramatists 197

de Ghelderode, Michel 20

Giant (Ferber) 72

Gibson, P. J. **89–90,** 99

Gielgud, John 58

Gilbert, Helen 59

Gill, Brendan 21

Gillespie, Dizzy 189

Gilman, Charlotte Perkins xii

Ginzburg, Leone 90

Ginzburg, Natalia **90–91**

Gippius, Zinaida **91**

Girl Scout cookies, origin of 195

The Girls from the Five and Ten (Farhoud) 71

The Giveaway (Jellicoe) 119

Glamour (magazine) 149

Glaspell, Susan xii, **91–93, 92f,** 151
and Pulitzer Prizes for drama xi

Glass ceiling, in production of plays xiii

Glasser, Etienne 164

The Glass Menagerie (Williams) 26

Glavin, Helen 42

Gloria and Esperanza (Bovasso) 20–21

God, Nature, Work (Brigadere) 22

God's Trombones (Johnson, James Weldon) 27

Godwin, William 116, 170

Going Co-op (Garson) 85

Going to Iraq (Malpede) 142

The Golden Calf (Jotuni) 121

Golden Laurel Prize 2

The Golden Notebook (Lessing) 133

Golden Oldies (Hewett) 107

Goldsmith, Oliver 51

Gold Through the Trees (Childress) 37

Gomard, Marlane Emily Huapala 150

Gómez de Avellaneda, Gertrudis **93–94**

Gone with the Wind 139

Goodbye, My Fancy (Kanin and Kanin) 123

Good Gracious, Annabelle! (Kummer) 129

Goodman, Lizbeth 108, 124, 157

Goodness Had Nothing to Do with It (West) 219

Goona Goona (Terry) 201

Gorbachev, Mikhail 177

Gordon, Ruth **94–95, 94f,** 123

Gornick, Vivian 131

A Gotham Election (Centlivre) 32

Government's Prize for best children's performance 202

Governor General 's Award for Drama (Canada) 174

The Grace of Mary Traverse (Wertenbaker) 217

Graham-White, Anthony 197

Grammy awards 48

Grand Hotel (Baum) 12

Grand Prix award 67

Grania (Gregory) 95–96

Grant, Micki 27

The Great Celestial Cow (Townsend) 202

Greatness (Akins) 4

Greek tragedy, as influence 142

Green, Adolph 48–49

Green Card (Akalaitis) 3–4

Green Lamp Society 91

The Green Ring (Caldern and Merezhkovsky) 91

Greer, Germiane 5

Gregory, Augusta **95–96**

Gregory, Lady xii

Gregory, Sir William 95

Griffin, Susan 149

Griffith, D. W. 136–137

Grind (novelization: Kanin) 124

Groping for Words (Townsend) 202

The Group (Warren) 213

The Growing Pains of Adrian Mole (Townsend) 202

Growing up Female in America (Merriam) 149

The Guardian Angel (Osten) 164

guerrilla theater 18

Guess Who's Coming to Dinner (film) 178

Guggenheim Foundation grant 4, 21, 63, 78, 83, 85, 110, 112, 126, 128, 132, 149, 165, 201, 215, 225

Guinevere (Gems) 87

Gulzara, or the Persian Slave (Mowatt) 156

Gunn, Edward M. 36

Gussow, Mel 41
Gwynne, Nell xi

H

Hadsel, Martha 192
Hagedorn, Jessica Tarahata **97–98**
Hagen, Uta 20
The Ha-Ha Play (Yankowitz) 224
Hall, Radclyffe 212
Hallelujah, Baby! (Comden and Green) 48
Hamburg Shakespeare Prize 134
Hamer, Fannie Lou 150
Hamilton, Cicely 186
Hammett, Dashiell 102, 103
Hansberry, Lorraine xiii, 44, 47, 89, **98–100, 99***f*
Hansberry, William Leon 98
The Happy Prince (adaptation: Pollock) 174
Harlem Renaissance 45, 112, 120
Harold and Maude (film, 1972) 95
Harper's Weekly 11
Harris, Frank 8
Harris, Julie 148
Harris, Laurilyn 159
Harris, Thomas 51
Hart, Lynda 195
Hartleb, Hanna 164
Harvey (Chase) 35–36
Hash, Burl 142
Hatch, James 126
Hatchett, William 101
Hause, Irene **100**
Havel, Václav 209
Having Our Say (adaptation: Mann) 145
Hayman, Carole 65
Hayman, Ronald 18, 133, 136
Haywood, Eliza Fowler **100–101**
He and She (Crothers) 52
Hearing (Page) 167
Hearth and Home magazine 7
The Heart Is a Lonely Hunter (McCullers) 148, 149
Hebbel, Friedrich 55
Heideman Award 83
The Heidi Chronicles (Wasserstein) 215
Helen (Morton) 155
Hellman, Lillian xii, **101–103, 102***f*

Hemingway, Ernest 67, 196
Hendrix, Erlene 11
Henley, Beth xiv, **103–105, 104***f*
    and Pulitzer Prizes for drama xi
Henrietta Maria (queen of Great Britain) **105**
Henry Bly (Ridler) 179
Henry IV (king of France) 105
Henry VIII (king of England) 105
Hepburn, Katharine 72, 95
Herbert, Mary Sidney **105–106**
Herbert, Victor 225
Her Master's Voice (Kummer) 129
A Hero Ain't Nothing but a Sandwich (Childress) 38
Herod and Mariamne (adaptation: Dane) 55
The Hero Rises Up (D'Arcy) 57
Herrström, Christina **106**
He That Should Come (Sayers) 187
He Wants Shih (Owens) 165
Hewett, Dorothy **106–107**
higher education, women's inclusion in xii
High School of Music and Art (NYC) 209
High School of Performing Arts (NYC) 26
Hiley, Jim 42
Hippius 91
Hiroshima, mon amour (Duras) 66
His and Hers (Kanin and Kanin) 124
His Picture in the Paper (Loos) 137
Hiss, Alger 103
The History of Jemy and Menny Jessamy (Haywood) 100
The History of Miss Betsey Thoughtless (Haywood) 100
The History of the Works of the Learned (Trotter) 205
Hitchcock, Alfred 64
Hobart, George V. 72
Hodgson, Moira 110
Hoffman, Hans 77
Hoffman, Jan 65
Hoffmeister, Donna 75
Hofsiss, Jack 149
Holcroft, Thomas 116
Holiday Heart (West) 218
Holliday, Judy 48
The Hollow (Christie) 40

Hollywood blacklists 103
Home and Bed (Rame) 176
Home Movies (Drexler) 62
Home (Terry) 201
homosexuality, as theme of drama 44
Hope for a Harvest (Treadwell) 204
Hopwood, James Avery 180
Horace (translation: Philips and Denham) 20, 143, 172
Horsfield, Debbie 107–108
Hospice (Cleage) 45
Hot and Throbbing (Vogel) 208
Houghton, Norris xiii
The House Across the Street (Cloud) 47
House Military Affairs Committee, first female member of 139
House Un-American Activities Committee (HUAC) 103
House Wives (Page) 167
Houston, Velina Hasu xiii, **108–109,** 224
Howard, Lillian 112, 113
Howe, Mark Antony DeWolfe 109
Howe, Mary Post 109
Howe, Quincy 109
Howe, Tina **109–111, 110***f*
How Much (Blechman) 103
How the Vote Was Won (St. John and Hamilton) 186
How to Say Goodbye (Gallagher) 83
Hrotsvitha von Gandersheim xiii, **111–112,**
Hughes, Douglas 36
Hughes, Langston 27, 37, 44, 99, 120
The Humorous Lovers (Cavendish) 30
The Humpbacked He Goat (Čiurlionienė-Kymantaitė) 43
A Hundred Bushels of Coarse Salt (Koidula) 128
Hungry Hill (du Maurier) 64
Huniades (Brand) 21–22
Hurst, Fanny 82
Hurston, Zora Neale **112–113,** 120
Husson, Albert 194

I

I Ain't Finished Yet (Merriam) 149
IandI (Lasker-Schüler) 132
Ibrahim, the Thirteenth Emperor of the Turks (Pix) 173

Ibsen, Henrik 36, 44, 139, 142, 228
Ice Cream (Churchill) 40
Ife International Book Fair award 193
Il Collectivo Teatrale La Comune, founding of 176
I'll Tell You What (Inchbald) 115
I Lost a Pair of Gloves Yesterday (Lamb) 132
I Married You for Happiness (Ginzburg) 90
"I'm Falling in Love with Someone" (Young) 226
I'm Getting My Act Together and Taking It on the Road (Cryer) 53
Imperceptible Mutabilities in the Third Kindgom (Parks) 169
The Imposter Defeated (Powell) 173
Improvisation 135
Inchbald, Elizabeth **115–116**
In Circles (Stein) 196
India Song (Duras) 67
The Inflexible Captive (translation: More) 154
Información para extranjeros (Gambaro) 84
Inge, William 80
In Harsh Winds (Brigadere) 22
Inishfallen, Fare Thee Well (O'Casey) 95
Inside Out (Wertenbaker) 217
Institute for Arts and Letters grant 161
INTAR. *See* International Arts Relations
International Arts Relations (INTAR) 78, 187
International Directory of Theatre, lack of women in xii
In the Blood (Horsfield) 108
In the Shadow of God (Törnqvist) 202
In the Summer House (translation: Roth) 182
"In the Wings of the Theatre of France" (radio series) 15
Intolerance (Loos) 137
Ionesco, Eugène 20, 110
Irish dramatists 26, 57, 58–59, 95
Irish Literary Theater, founding of 95
Irish Renaissance 95
Ironheart (Reinshagen) 178
Irving, Evelyn Uhrhan 122
The Island of the Mighty (D'Arcy) 57
Isn't It Romantic (Wasserstein) 214–215
Istel, John 47
Italian dramatists 90, 146, 176–177
It Happened a Play (Stein) 195–196
It's All Church (Rame) 176

Itzen, Catherine 163
Ivanoff, Alexandra 149
The Ivory Tower (Sofola) 193
I Want (Dunn) 65

J

J. T. (Wagner) 211
Jacker, Corinne **117–118**
Jackson, Elaine **118**
Jamaica Inn (du Maurier) 64
James II (king of Great Britain) 96
James, Florence and Burton 199
Jane Addams Honor Award 38
Jannsen, J. V. 128
Jar the Floor (West) 218
jazz aesthetic 175
"The Jean Jarris Reading" (Cleage) 45
Jellicoe, Ann **118–120, 119***f*
Jenny Kissed Me (Kerr) 126
Joan (Hewett) 107
Jocasta (Fabien) 71
Johnny Noble (MacColl) 136
"John Redding Goes out to Sea" (Hurston) 112
Johnson, Charlie S. 112
Johnson, Georgia Douglas **120–121**
Johnson, Robert Sherlaw 179
Johnson, Samuel (Dr.) 154
Johnsson, Ulrika Wilhelmina 25
Joint Stock Company 41
Jones, Robert Edmond 92
Jones, Stephen 9, 22, 23
Jones, Vanzella 37
Jonson, Ben 105
Jory, Jon 160
Joseph in the Well (Törnqvist) 202
Joseph Kesselring Prize 151
The Joss Adams Show (De Groen) 59
Jotuni, Maria **121**
The Journal (newspaper) 81
Journey up the Wartburg (Roth) 182
Joyce, James 11
Juana Inés de la Cruz, Sor xiii, **121–122, 122***f*
Judith (Castellanos) 29
The Juniper Tree, A Tragic Household Tale (Kesselman) 128

Junkie! (Boesing) 18
Just a Little Simple (adaptation: Childress) 37

K

Kael, Pauline 226
Kanin, Fay **123–124**
Kanin, Garson 123
Kanin, Michael 123
Karis, Carolyn 20, 21
Karl Stuart (Fleißer) 75
Kaška Kariatyda (Zapolska) 228
Kassandra (adaptation: Malpede) 142
Katherine of Sutton xiii, **124**
Kaufman, George S. 72
Kavanagh, Julia 14
Keatley, Charlotte **124–125**
Keenan, Richard 147
Keep Tightly Closed (Terry) 201
Kelly, Gregory 94
Kemble, Charles 32
Kemble, John 116
Keneally, Thomas 217
Kennedy, Adrienne **125–126**
Kern, Jerome 225
Kerr, Jean **126–127, 127***f*
Kerr, Walter 127
Kesselman, Wendy **128**
Keyssar, Helene 37, 61, 62, 78, 87, 92, 102, 118, 119, 131, 133, 163, 165, 201, 212, 214
Khayyam, Omar 225
Kilgore, Anita 80
Kimberly-Clark 211
King, Anne Mills 190
King, Jr., Woodie 189
King Lear (Shakespeare) 26
The King Maiden (Tsvetayeva) 206
King of Hearts (Kerr) 126
Kingsley, Sidney 102
Kiss Me, Kate (Spewack and Porter) 194
Kiss the Boys Goodbye (Luce) 139
Klaus, the Lord of Louhikko (Jotuni) 121
Kleist Prize for Literature 132
The Knack (Jellicoe) 118, 119
A Knife in the Heart (Yankowitz) 224
Kober, Arthur 102

Koestler, Arthur 18
Koidula, Lydia **128–129**
The Komagata Mary Incident (Pollock) 174
Koon, Helene 154
Kornfeld, Lawrence 196
Kosse, Roberta 142
Kovan onnen (Canth) 25
Kroll, Jack xiv, 63, 104, 190, 201
Kronenberger, Louis 127
Kuhn, John 187
Kummer, Clare **129**
Kurosawa, Akira 124
Kymantaitė, Kazimiera 135

L

La Compagnia Dario Fo–Franca Rame, founding of
    176
Lacy, John 172
Ladies Leave (Treadwell) 204
The Ladies of Castile (Warren) 213
Ladies Voices (Stein) 195
Lagerlöff, Selma 17
La Maddalena theater, founding of 146
Lamb, Myrna **131–132**
A Lancashire Lad (Kennedy) 125
The Land of Blue Lakes (Zālīte) 227
Landovsky, Josef 209
Langston Hughes award 38, 118
Langworthy, Douglas 45
Lasker-Schüler, Else **132–133**
Las tres pascualas (Aguirre) 2
Last Summer at Bluefish Cove (Chambers) 33
The Last Sweet Days of Isaac (Cryer and Ford) 53
Late Bus to Mecca (Cleage) 45
A Late Snow (Chambers) 33
Latina (Sánchez-Scott) 186
Latvian dramatists 5–6, 22, 135, 227
"The Laugh of the Medusa" (Cixous) 44
The Laughing Woman (Daviot) 57
The Laundromat (Norman) 160
Laureate of the Bluestockings 154
Lavelli, Jorge 71
Lawrence, Gertrude 52, 73
Leading Lady (Gordon and Kanin) 95
Leapor, Mary **133**

Leave It to Me (Spewack and Porter) 194
Lebanese dramatists 71–72
LeCompte du Noüy Foundation Award 187
Lee, Ann 142
Left Behind in the Streets (Aguirre) 2
Le Galliene, Eva 82
Le médecin malgré lui (Molière) 31
Leonardo, Frank 85
Les Blancs (Hansberry) 99
Lessing, Doris **133–134**
Lessing, Frank Gottfried 133
A Lesson in Dead Language (Kennedy) 125
Let's Be Happy (Martínez Sierra and Martínez Sierra)
    146
Let's Hear It for the Queen (Childress) 37–38
Letter from Paris (Smith) 193
Levi, Norman 110
Levin, Ira 127
Lewis, Victoria Ann 10
Lewis Carroll Shelf Award 38
Lewisohn, Ludwig 82
Ley, Ralph 75
The Life and Loves of a She-Devil (adaptation: Weldon)
    216
Life (magazine) 139
Life Is a Dream (Calderón de la Barca) 91
A Light for Fools (Ginzburg) 90
Light Shining in Buckinghamshire (Churchill) 41
Lim, Genny **134–135**
Lincoln's Inn Fields Theatre 5
Ling, Amy 223
Liobytė, Aldona **135**
The Lion in Love (Delaney) 61
Listen to Me (Stein) 196
Lithuanian dramatists 43, 177–178
The Little Foxes (Hellman) 102
The Little Gray Home in the West (D'Arcy) 57
The Little Heroine (Dunn) 66
Littlewood, Joan xiv, **135–136, 136f**
"Live for Today" (Young) 226
Lloyd Webber, Andrew xiii
Lobel, Duskey 129
Locke, Alain 120
Locke, John 213
Loeb, Philip 16
London Evening Standard award 163

London Has a Garden (Dane) 55
London Theater Critics Circle Prize 157
Londré, Felicia Hardison 4
Lone Valley (Treadwell) 204
Long Time Since Yesterday (Gibson) 89
Look Back in Gender (Wandor) 212
Look Homeward, Angel (adaptation: Frings) 80
Look Out . . . Here Comes Trouble (O'Malley) 163
Loos, Anita **136–138, 137***f*
Loos, Richard Beers 136–137
Lopate, Phillip 78
Lord Byron (Young) 225
Lorraine Hansberry Play Writing Award 109
Los Angeles Poverty Department (LAPD) Theater, founding of 142
Los Angeles Theater Center, Women's Project at 150
The Lost Lover (Manley) 143
Louis, Joe 98
Love All (Sayers) 187
Love in the Season (Zapolska) 228
Love Me Carefully (Herrström) 106
The Love of Life (Sofola) 193
The Love of the Nightingale (Wertenbaker) 217
The Lovers of Viorne (Duras) 67
Love's Contrivance (Centlivre) 31
Lovesick (Churchill) 40
Loving Women (Gems) 88
Luce, Clare Boothe **138–139, 138***f,* 214
Luce, Henry R. 139
Luce, William 212
Lucy (Page) 167

M

Mabley, Moms 150
MacArthur Fellowship "genius" grant 191
Macbeth (adaptation: Loos) 137
MacBird (Garson) 85
MacColl, Ewan 135
MacDonald, Jeanette 226
MacDonald, Sharman **141**
MacDowell Fellowship 63, 208
Machinal (Treadwell) 203–204
Mackintosh, Elizabeth 58
MacNicholas, John 77

Maconchy, Elizabeth 179
Mad Forest (Churchill) 40
La Madre (Rame) 177
Madrigal en ciudad (Gambaro) 84
Maggie Magalita (Kesselman) 128
Maggie/Magalita (Wasserstein) 215
The Magical City (Akins) 4
The Magic Realists (Terry) 201
Mahl, Mary 154
The Mai (Carr) 26
A Majority of One (Spigelgass) 17
The Making of Americans (Stein) 196
Making Out (Horsfield) 108
Making Peace: A fantasy (Malpede) 142
Malpede, Karen **141–143**
Małka Szwarcenkopf (Zapolska) 228
Mamet, David 150
The Man Born to Be King (Sayers) 188187
Manchester Evening News Best New Play Award 125
The Man from Mukinupin (Hewett) 107
The Man in Lower Ten (Rinehart) 180
The Man in the Queue (Daviot) 57
Manley, Delariviere 46, **143–144**
Mann, Emily **144–145, 145***f*
Manner, Eeva-Liisa **145–146**
The Man's Bewitched (Centlivre) 31
A Man's Own (Treadwell) 203
A Man's World (Crothers) 52
Maraini, Dacia **146**
Marc-Antonie (Garnier) 105
Marcelia (Boothby) 20
Marcus, Frank 63
Margin for Error (Luce) 139
Maria (adaptation: Bergman) 17
Marlowe (Peabody) 170
The Marriage of Anansewa (Sutherland) 197
The Marriage Game (Flexner) 76
Martínez Sierra, Gregorio 146–147
Martínez Sierra, María **146–148**
The Marvelous Metropolis (Chambers) 33
Mary, Mary (Kerr) 126
Mary I (queen of England) 179
Marzotto Prize for European Drama 90
The Massachusetts Spy (periodical) 213
The Massacre (Inchbald) 115

Mast, Jane 219

The Master of Great Heikkilè and His Servant Kalle (Wuolijoki and Brecht) 220

Masterpieces (Daniels) 56

Masters and Sons (adaptation: Liobytė and Kymantaitė) 135

Masters of Modern Drama (Block and Shedd) xii

Matisse, Henri 196

Matrimonial Causes Act 115

Matson, Norman Häghem 93

A Matter of Gravity (Bagnold) 7

Matthews, Adelaide 159

Mayor's Award of Art and Culture (New York City) 48

Maytime (Young and Romberg) 226

McCarthyism 16

McClain, John 127

McClaren award for radio 157

McClure's (magazine) 4

McCullers, Carson 125, **148–149, 148f**

McGillick, Paul 59

McGrath, John 167, 168

McGraw-Hill Encyclopedia of World Drama 119

McGuire, Dorothy 79

McHugh, Jimmy 73

McKnight Foundation fellowship 18, 109, 128, 142, 208

McManus, Irene 56

Meadow Flowers (Koidula) 128

Me and Molly (Berg) 17

Medea (Törnqvist) 202

Meiksins, Robert 10

Melody Sisters (Commire) 49

Meloney, William Brown 79

melting pot, myth of 109

The Member of the Wedding (adaptation: McCullers) 148

Mencken, H. L. 137

Men in White (Kingsley) 102

Menna, Robert 217

Merezhkovsky, Dimitri 91

Merriam, Eve **149–150**

Merry-Go-Round (Kesselman) 128

Meserve, Walter J. 156

Metastasio, Pietro 154

Mexican Critics Association, Alarcón Prizes 207

Mexican dramatists 28–29, 207–208

Meydan Sahnesi, founders of 1

Meyer, Marlane **150–151**

MGM Studios 137

Miami (Wasserstein, Feldman, and Sussman) 215

middle class, as force in theater xiii–xiv

The Mighty Gents (adaptation: Shange) 190

Milay, Edna St. Vincent **151–152, 152f**

Miles, Patrick 170

Milk and Funny (Yankowitz) 225

Miller, Alice 164

Miller, Arthur xiii

Miller, Jimmy 135

Miller, Susan **152–153**

Milwaukee Journal 72

The Mimic Life (Mowatt) 156

Minick (Ferber and Kaufman) 72

Minneapolis Children's Theater 16

Miquel, André 83

Miranda on the Balcony (Flexner) 76

Miscellany Poems on Several Occasions (Finch) 74

Miss Ann Don't Cry No More (Gibson) 89

The Miss Firecracker Contest (Henley) 104–105

Miss Lulu Bett (Gale) 82

Miss Maliczewska (Zapolska) 228

Miss Tassey (Baker) 10

The Mistress of the House (Martínez Sierra and Martínez Sierra) 146

The Mocking of Christ (Sayers) 187

The Mod Donna, A Space-Age Musical Soap Opera with Breaks for Commercials (Lamb) 131

Modjeska, Helen 203

Moe's Lucky Seven (Meyer) 150–151

The Mogul's Tale (Inchbald) 115

The Mojo and the Sayso (Rahman) 175

Molière 31, 95

Money (Čiurlionienė-Kymantaitė) 43

Monist Society 92

A Monster Has Stolen the Sun (Malpede) 142

Monstrous Regiment 41

Montagu, Elizabeth 23, 154

Montpelier PaZazz (Wasserstein) 214

The Moondreamers (Bovasso) 20

Moore, George 15

Moore, Honor **153–154**

Moravia, Alberto 146

More, Hannah 50, **154–155, 154f**

Morgan, Fidelis 20, 143

Morgan, Frank 226

Morning Telegraph (newspaper) 137

Morrison, Toni 113

Morton, Martha **155**

Moss, Paula 189

Mother Courage and Her Children (adaptation: Shange) 190

"Mother Machree" (Young) 226

The Mother of Us All (Stein and Thomson) 196

Motion Picture Production Code 219

Mount Vernon Association, formation of 156

Mourning Pictures (Moore) 153

The Mousetrap (Christie) 40

A Movie Star Has to Star in Black and White (Kennedy) 125

Mowatt, Anna Cora 155–156

Mr. Pinn (Gale) 8282

Mrs. California (Baizley) 10

Mrs. Dulska's Morality (Zapolska) 228

Mrs. Wiggs of the Cabbage Patch (adaptation: Flexner) 76

Ms. (magazine) 45, 181, 190

The Mud Angels (Cloud) 47

Muir, Edwin 11

Munro, Rona **157–158**

Murder at McQueen (Ritter) 181

Murder in Mesopotamia (Christie) 39

Murder Must Advertise (Sayers) 187

The Murder of Roger Ackroyd (Christie) 39

Murder on the Orient Express (Christie) 40

Murrik, Hella Maria 220

Murtovarkaus (Canth) 25

Museum (Howe) 110

La Musica (Duras) 66

The Music Lesson (Yamauchi) 223

My Cousin Rachel (Du Maurier) 64

"My Father Has a Son" (Cleage) 45

My Mother, My Father, and Me (adaptation: Hellman) 103

My Mother Said I Never Should (Keatley) 124

My Sister in This House (Kesselman) 128

The Mysterious Affair at Styles (Christie) 39

My Three Angels (Spewack) 194

N

Nagrin, Lee 142

Nancy Boyd stories 151

Nashe, Thomas 105

Nasty Rumors and Final Remarks (Miller) 152, 153

Nathan, George Jean xiii, 137, 159

National Academy of Dramatic Arts 202

National Achievement Award 52

National Book Award 97, 103

nominations for 38

National Education Television Network 200

National Endowment for the Arts grant 4, 18, 45, 47, 78, 85, 89, 110, 118, 126, 128, 132, 151, 153, 161, 165, 201, 208, 225

National Endowment for the Humanities grant 83

National Institute of Arts and Letters 52, 149

National Velvet (Bagnold) 7

Nation's Award for Poetry 6

natural theater 91

Naughty Marietta (Young and V. H.) 226

NEA. *See* National Endowment for the Arts

Neaptide (Daniels) 56

Neighbors (Gale) 82

Nel, Christof 182

Nemiroff, Robert 98, 99

Neo-Romantic movement 91

Never in My Lifetime (Gee) 86

New Anatomies (Wertenbaker) 217

Newberry Medal, nominations for 38

New England School of Dramatic Instruction 51

New Feminist Repertory Theater 131

New Jersey Women's Politican Caucus 33

New Negro Renaissance 120

New Plays for Black Theater (Cleage) 45

New Reasoner (periodical) 133

The Newsboys (Aguirre) 2

New Year's Eve (Manner) 145

New York Call (newspaper) 194

New York Critics Special Award 211

New York Drama Critics Circle Award. *See* Drama Critics Circle Award

New York Foundation for the Arts grant 176

The New York Hat (Griffith) 137

New York State Council on the Arts grant 47, 78

New York Theater Strategy 21, 78

New York World (newspaper) 194
New Zealand dramatists 59, 61–62
Nichols, Anne **159–160**
Nigerian dramatists 193
Night After Night (West) 219
A Nightengale in Bloomsbury Square (Duffy) 63
The Nightingale of Mother River (Koidula) 128
night' Mother (Norman) 160
Night Sky (Yankowitz) 225
Nightwood (Barnes) 11
Nigro, Kirsten 207
Nin, Anaïs 11
Nobel Prize for literature 177
The Non-Stop Connolly Show (D'Arcy) 57
Noonan, John Ford 78
Norén, Lars 164
Norman, Frank 135
Norman, Marsha **160–161, 160***f*
    and Pulitzer Prizes for drama xi
Norstein, Yuri 171
The Northern Heiress (Davys) xii, 59
"Nothin' but a Movie" (Cleage) 45
Nothing Like the Sixteenth Floor (Vilalta) 207
Not Not Not Not Not Enough Oxygen (Churchill) 40–41
Notre Sade (Fabien) 71
The Nourishing Earth (adaptation: Liobytė and Kymantaitė) 135
Novick, Julius 177
Now He Doesn't Want to Play (Treadwell) 204
Now Is the Time for All Good Men (Cryer and Ford) 53
Number 9 (Vilalta) 207
Nuovo Scena, founding of 176

O

Obafemi, Olu 193
Obie Award xiii, 4, 21, 27, 37, 40, 42, 53, 62, 78, 85, 110, 118, 125, 144, 150, 153, 165, 169, 190, 196, 201
    Special Citation 191
The Obligations of a Household (Sor Juana) 121
O'Brien, Edna 15
O'Brien, Pat 194
O'Casey, Sean 95, 96

Off-Broadway Award. *See* Obie Award
Of Sturdy Stock (Fleißer) 75
Oh, What a Lovely War! (Littlewood) 136
O'Healy, Anne-Marie 90
Olauson, Judith 52, 123
The Oldest Profession (Vogel) 208
The Old Home (Jotuni) 121
The Old Maid (Akins) 4
Old Time (Duffy) 63
The Old Wives' Tale (Wandor) 212
Olinda's Adventures (Trotter) 204
Olivier Award 217
Olympic Park (Lamb) 132
Omaha Magic Theater, founding of 201
O'Malley, Mary **163–164**
Once a Catholic (O'Malley) 163
One Hundred and One Dalmatians (Smith) 192
O'Neill, Eugene 92, 126
One Is a Crowd (Richards) 178–179
On the Knife's Edge (Vostrá) 209
One Night Stand (Bolt) 19
On the Town (Comden and Green) 48
On to Victory: Propaganda Plays of the Woman Suffrage Movement (Friedl) xii
Open Theater 200
O Pioneers! (adaptation: Cloud) 46
Opportunity magazine, First Place Drama Award 120
The Opposite Sex (Gordon and Kanin) 124
Order of the British Empire (O.B.E.) 64
Order of the Commander of the British Empire 56
Orenstein, Gloria 142
Orgasmo Adulto Escapes from the Zoo (adaptation: Parsons) 177
Oroonoko, or the History of the Royal Slave (Behn) 14
Ortiz, Miguel 38
Oscar. *See* Academy Award
Oser, Kris 142
Osten, Suzanne **164–166**
Otis, James 213
O'Toole, Finian 26
Ott, Sharon 191
Our Country's Good (adaptation: Wertenbaker) 217
Our Mrs. McChesney (Ferber) 72

Ouspenskaya, Maria 79
Outer Critics Circle Award 53, 110, 160
Out of Our Father's House (adaptation: Merriam, Wagner and Hofsiss) 149
Out on the Floor (Horsfield) 108
Outrageous Fortune (Franken) 79
Overtones (Gerstenberg) 88
Owens, Dave 47
Owens, Jesse 98
Owens, Rochelle **165–166, 165f**
The Owl Answers (Kennedy) 125
Owners (Churchill) 41

P

Paar, Jack 33
Page, Louise **167–168, 168f**
Page, Malcolm 119
Painting Churches (Howe) 110
Pallma, Jr., Frank 137
Panova, Vera Fyodorovna **168–169**
Papa (Akins) 4
Paper Angels (Lim) 134
Paper Daddy (Osten) 164
Paper Dolls (Jackson) 118
Paphnutius (translation: St. John) 185–186
Paphnutius (von Gandersheim) 111
Papp, Joseph 131, 189, 224
Paradise Flow (Devanny) 61
Paramount Pictures 112
Pariah (Strindberg) 17
Paris Review Fiction Prize 63
Parker, Dorothy 182
Parks, Suzan-Lori **169–170,** 195
Pärnu postimees (periodical) 129
Parsons, Estelle 177
The Partner (Erenus) 69
Partnow, Elaine ix
Pat and Mike (Gordon and Kanin) 95
Patraka, Vivian 131
Paul Robeson Award 38
PBS. *See* Public Broadcasting Sytem
Peabody, Josephine Preston **170**
Peabody Award 211
"The Pearl and the Brood of Vipers" (Cleage) 45

Pelayo, or The Cavern of Cavadonga (Mowatt) 156
"Pelleas and Etarre" stories (Gale) 82
Penthesilea (adaptation: Wandor) 212
The People of Wuppertal (Lasker-Schüler) 132
The People vs. Ranchman (Terry) 201
Pepys, Samuel 30
Percy, Charles Henry 192
Percy (More) 154
Permanence (Weldon) 216
Petrushevskaya, Lyudmila **170–172**
Petzold, Roxana 4
Philippine dramatists 97–98
Philips, Katherine Fowler **172**
a photograph (Shange) 190
Ph*reaks (Baizley) 10
Piaf (Gems) 87
Piano Plays (Roth) 181
Picasso, Pablo 196
Pickford, Mary 137
Pickling (Parks) 169
A Picture Perfect Sky (Bonal) 19–20
Pincherle, Alberto 146
A Pinprick of History (D'Arcy) 57
Pinter, Harold 90
The Piper (Peabody) 170
Piper's Cave (Munro) 157
Piscator, Erwin 26
Pix, Mary Griffith 5, 46, 143, **173**
plagerism
     accusations of 50
     and female dramatists xii
The Platonic Lady (Centlivre) 31
Playbill Award 128
Playboy of the Western World (Synge) 95–96
The Playmaker (Keneally) 217
Plays and Players award 163
Plays by Women (Wandor, ed.) 57, 212
Play with a Tiger (Lessing) 133
Playwrights Theatre of Chicago, founding of 89
Please Don't Eat the Daisies (Kerr) 126
The Pleasure Man (West) 219
Plumes in the Dust (Treadwell) 203
Plumes (Johnson) 120
PM (magazine) 149
Pocket Theater, creation of 164

Poe, Edgar Allan 156, 203
A Poetic Rhapsody (anthology, 1602) 105
Poets Essayists Novelists writer's grant 142
Poitier, Sidney 98
Polish dramatists 228
Pollock, Sharon **173–174**
Pompey (translation: Philips) 172
The Pool Hall (Norman) 160
Pope, Alexander 32, 101, 133
Porter, Cole 194
Portia Coughlan (Carr) 26
Portrait of Dora (Cixous and Benmussa) 15, 44
Portraits of Mrs. W. (Peabody) 170
Powell, George 173
Premio de la Asociación de Teatros 84
Premio de la Revista Teatro XX 85
Premio Emece 84
Premio Strega 90
press, abuse of female dramatists by xi
Price, Leontyne 196
Pride and Prejudice (adaptation: Weldon) 216
A Prisoner (Čiurlionien-Kymantaitė) 43
The Prisoner (Boland) 18
The Prison Game (Yankowitz) 225
Prix Goncourt 67
Prix Populaire 61
Production Code. *See* Motion Picture Production Code
production company, first all-female 124
professional life, women's inclusion in xii
Progressive Citizens of America 103
Promenade (Fornés) 77
prostitute, wife as 14
prostitution, cause of xi
Provincctown Players, founding of 91–92, 151
Public Broadcasting System (PBS) 214, 225
Puddin' 'n' Pete (West) 218
Pulitzer Prize 109
    for drama 36, 80, 82, 91, 93, 104, 160, 214
    nomination for 102, 191
    and female dramatists xi–xii
    for fiction 72
    for poetry 152
The Punished Man (Vilalta) 207

Purgatory in Ingolstadt (Fleier) 75
Put Them All Together (Commire) 49

Q

Q.E.D. (Stein) 195
Queen Christina (Gems) 87
The Quintessential Image (Chambers) 33
The Quirks of Chance (Sagan) 185
Quoirez, Françoise 185
The Quotable Woman (Partnow) xiv

R

racism 186
    in America 47
    of American theater 37
    and the canon xii
Rahman, Aishah 134, **175–176**
A Raisin in the Sun (Hansberry) xiii, 98
Rakkautta (Jotuni) 121
Rame, Franca **176–177, 176f**
Rashomon (adaptation: Kanin) 124
A Rat's Mass (Kennedy) 125
Rattigan, Sir Terence 60
Raudup's Widow (Brigadere) 22
Razumovskaya, Ludmila **177–178**
Reagan, Ronald 139, 194
Real Estate (Page) 167
Rebecca (du Maurier) 64
Rebelliousness of women ix
The Reckoning (Jellicoe) 119
Red Devils Trilogy (Horsfield) 108
Red Emma, Queen of the Anarchists (Bolt) 19
Redhead (lyrics: Fields) 73
The Red Poppy (Calderón and Merezhkovsky) 91
The Reformed Coquet (Davys) 59
Regiment of Women (Dane) 55
The Rehersal, or Bays in Petticoats (Clive) 46
Reinhardt, Max 12, 132
Reinshagen, Gerline **178**
Remnant, Mary 57, 88, 98, 153
Renascence and Other Poems (Millay) 151
Reply to Sister Filotea (Sor Juana) 121
Resnais, Alain 66
Restoration

comedy of xii
drama of, and women xi
unruly atmosphere in theaters during xi
Reverie of Wandering Milda (Zālīte) 227
The Revolution of Sweden (Trotter) 204
Reynolds, Joshua 154
Riasonov, Eldar 177–178
The Rib of Man (Jotuni) 121
Rice, Alice Hegan 76
Rich, Frank 47, 65, 104, 150, 216
Richard Bordeaux (Daviot) 57
Richards, Beah 26, 53, **178–179**
Richards, Lloyd 98
Richardson, Howard 27
Richardson, Tony 61
Richman, Harry 73
Ridler, Anne **179–180**
Rinehart, May Roberts **180**
Rinehart and Co. 180
Ripen Our Darkness (Daniels) 56
The Rise of the Goldbergs (Berg) 16
The Rising Generation (Jellicoe) 119
The Rising of the Moon (Gregory) 95
Rita, Sue, and Bob Too (Dunbar) 65
Ritchie, William Foushee 156
Rites (Duffy) 63
Ritter, Erika **180–181**
Ritz Paris Hemingway Award 67
The Rivers and the Forest (Duras) 67
Rivers of China (De Groen) 59
RKO studios 123
The Road to the City (Ginzburg) 90
Robeson, Paul 38, 98
Robinson, Marc 196
Rockefeller Foundation grant 4, 21, 38, 47, 49, 63, 78,
   109, 110, 118, 126, 132, 153, 161, 165, 175–176,
   187, 224, 225
rock musical, first 200
Rocky (novelization: Drexler) 63
Roinilan talossa (Canth) 25
Rollo's Wild Oat (Kummer) 129
Romance Island (Gale) 82
Romanov, Nadja 37
A Room of One's Own (Woolf) 13, 30
Roosters (Sánchez-Scott) 186
Rose, Helen 105

Rose, Philip 98
Rose, Phyllis Jane 199
Rosenberg, Julius and Ethel 103
Rosenthal Award for Poetry 33
Rosina (Brooke) 23
Rossen, Helena von 111
Rostand, Edmond 55, 206
Rostova, Mira 20
Roth, Friederike **181–182**
Rotunda of Illustrious Men, Palace of Fine Arts, Mexico
   City 28
The Rover (Behn) 14
Rowson, Susanna Haswell **182–183**
Royal Academy of Dramatic Arts, London 135,
   192
Royal Academy of Spain 93
   prize winner 147
The Royal Family (Ferber and Kaufman) 72
The Royal Mischief (Manley) 143
Royal Society of Literature 64
Royal Theatre Dramateus winner 106
Rozenberga, Elza 5–6
Rue, Victoria 153
The Runaway (Cowley) 50
Russian dramatists 91, 205
Ryan, Betsy 195, 196

S

Sabater, Pedro 93
Sackville-West, Vita 88
Sacred Blood (Gippius) 91
The Sacrifice (Lamb) 132
Safe (Johnson) 120
Sagan, Françoise **185**
St. John, Christoper (Maire) **185–186**
Saint-Léon, Claire Brandicourt 66
Salaam, Ysef A. 190
Sale, Richard 137
The Salesman (Munro) 157
Salic Law, and drama xi
Salome (Castellanos) 29
Salonika (Page) 167
Samuel French Award 208
Sánchez-Scott, Milcha **186–187**
San Francisco Bulletin 203

Sappho xii
Sappho & Aphrodite (Malpede) 142
Sarah and Abraham (Norman) 160
Sarraute, Nathalie 15
Sartre, Jean-Paul 1
Saturday at the Commodore (Munro) 157
Saturday Evening Post 127
Saturday Night (periodical) 181
Sayers, Dorothy L. 39, **187–189**
Schildt, Peter 106
Schiller, Friedrich von 55
Schmidman, JoAnn 201
Schoolfield, G. C. 25, 121
Schoolgirl Rebels (Smith) 192
School of Visual Arts (NYC) 211
Schubert's Last Serenade (Bovasso) 21
Schumacher, Claude 61
Schwartz, Arthur 73
Schwartz, Donald Ray 17
The Scientific Method (Jacker) 117
Scott, Ozzie 189
Scott, Sir Walter 9
Scottish dramatists 141, 157–158
Screenwriter's Guild Award 48
Scribner, Anne 82
Scyklon Z (Lamb) 131
The Search After Happiness (More) 154
The Search for Signs of Intelligent Life in the Universe (Wagner) 211
The Searching Wind (Hellman) 102–103
The Sea Wall (Duras) 66
Sebba, Anna 8
The Secret Diary of Adrian Mole, Aged 13 ¾ (Townsend) 202
The Secret Garden (Norman) 161
The Secret History of Queen Zarah and the Zarazians (Manley) 143
Security (Garson) 85
See How She Runs (novelization: Drexler) 63
self-knowledge, drama as search for x
The Self Rival (Davys) 59
Selma (Bergman) 17
Series of Plays (Baillie) 9
Serious Money (Churchill) 40
Service (Smith) 192
Sex (West) 219

sexism, and the canon xii
Sextette (West) 219
The Shadow Factory (Ridler) 179
Shakespeare, William xiii, 26, 105, 136, 142
Shallat, Lee 10
Shameful in Your Eyes (Gibson) 89
Shange, Ntozake 44, 53, 134, 145, 149, 175, **189–191,** **189***f*
Shaw, Mary xii
Shay (Commire) 49
Shedd, Robert G. xii
She-Devil (adaptation: Weldon) 216
Shelley (Jellicoe) 119
Shepard, Sam 21, 78
Sheridan, Richard 23, 51
She Ventures and He Wins (Ariadne) 5
She Who Was He (Drexler) 62
Shine, Ted 126
Shirley, Don 109
Shirley (Dunbar) 65
Shorter, Eric 163
Show Boat (Ferber) 72
Showing up of Blanco Posnet (Shaw) 95–96
Shubert Fellowship 89
The Siamese Twins (Gambaro) 84
Siddons, Sarah Kemble 116
Sidney, Sir Philip 105
The Sign in Sidney Brustein's Window (Hansberry) 99
The Silk Room (Duffy) 63
The Silver Veil (Aspzija) 6
Simon, John 218
"Simple Speaks His Mind" (Hughes) 37
A Simple Story (Inchbald) 115
Singin' in the Rain (Comden and Green) 48
Singleton, Mary 23
The Singular Life of Albert Nobbs (adaptation: Benmussa) 15
The Sirens (Cloud) 47
Sir Patient Fancy (Behn) xi–xii, 14
The Sisters Rosensweig (Wasserstein) 215
Six Chapters from a Cadre School (Chiang) 36–37
Skinner, Otis 138
Skipworth, Sir Thomas 143
Slam the Door Softly (Luce) 139
Slaughterhouse Play (Yankowitz) 224

Slaves of Algiers (Rowson) 182

Smelyansky, A. 171

The Smile of Hades (Norén) 164

Smith, Anna Deavere **191–192, 191f**

Smith, Bessie 44

Smith, Christopher 179

Smith, Dodie **192–193**

Smith, Lula Carson 148

Smith, Sol 155

Smock-Alley Theatre 100, 172

Snajder, Sloboden 142

The Snow of May (Manner) 145

So Big (Ferber) 72

Society for the Suppression of Vice 219

Society of American Dramatists and Composers, founding of 155

Society of Dramatic Authors, founding of 155

Society of Friendship, founding of 172

Society of West End Theatre Award 65, 136

Society of Women Journalists 56

Sofola, Zulu **193–194**

Softcops (Churchill) 40

Solaria (literary journal) 90

Soldiers in Ingolstadt (Fleißer) 75

Solo (Duffy) 63

Solomon, Alisa 41

Sondheim, Stephen xiii

Song for Johanna (Boesing) 18

Songwriters Hall of Fame 48

first female to enter 74

Song Written by Itself (Ağaoğlu) 1

The Sons of Dawn (Čiurlionien-Kymantaitė) 43

Sontag, Susan 77

Sorel, Julia 63

Sor Juana. *See* Juana Inés de la Cruz, Sor 121

Soup for One (film) 192

Soviet Lithuanian State Publishing House 135

Spanish dramatists 146–148

The Spanish Wives (Pix) 173

Special Citation Obie Award 191

spell #7 (Shange) 190

Spencer, Stanley 88

Spewack, Bella **194–195, 194f**

Spīdītis (Brigadere) 22

Spigelglass, Leonard 17

Spilt Milk (Wandor) 212

Spolin, Viola 58, 200

The Sport of My Mad Mother (Jellicoe) 118

Spreading the News (Gregory) 95

Spriditis (Brigadere) 22

Spring Festival (Reinshagen) 178

Spring Soil (Chiang) 36

Springtime (Panova) 168

The Square (Duras) 66

The Square Root of Wonderful (McCullers) 148

Stage Door (Ferber and Kaufman) 72

Stage Relief Fund 51

Stalin Prize 169

Stanhoope-Wheatcroft School of Acting 51

Stanislavsky, Konstantin 91

Stanley (Gems) 88

Stanton, Elizabeth Cady 149

Starburn (Drexler) 62

The Star Child (adaptation: Pollock) 174

Stars in Your Eyes (score: Fields) 73

Starting Monday (Commire) 49

Steaming (Dunn) 65

Steene, Birgitta 164

Stein, Gertrude 47, **195–197, 195f**

Steinbeck, John 67

Steinem, Gloria 211

Steptoe, Lydia 11

Stewart, Ellen 62

The Stick Wife (Cloud) 47

Still Life (Mann) 144

The Stone Cage (Brigadere) 22

The Story of an Hour (adaptation: Wandor) 212

The Story of Him (Vilalta) 207

Strange, Michelle 203

Strange Blood (Zālīte) 227

Strasberg, Lee 26

Stratford-on-Avon Shakespeare Memorial Prize 170

Straumanis, Alfreds 22, 129, 135, 227

Streep, Meryl 216

Strindberg, August 17

Strömholm, Christopher 17

Styne, Jules 48

Styx (Lasker-Schüler) 132

A Suburb Named Hope (Aguirre) 2

The Successful Life of 3 (Fornés) 77

Success (magazine) 82

Such a Bumpkin (Koidula) 128

Such Is Fame (Nichols) 159

Sue, Eugène 212

suffrage, women's struggle for, and female dramatists xi–xii

Sugar Heaven (Devanny) 61

Sullavan, Margaret 72

Sunday Morning in the South (Johnson) 120

Sunday's Children (Reinshagen) 178

Suppressed Desires (Glaspell) 92

surrealism 125

Susan and God (Crothers) 52

Susan Smith Blackburn prize 47, 65, 83, 109, 128, 151, 157, 160, 214, 218

Sutherland, Efua Theodora **197–198**

Swedish dramatists 100, 106, 164, 202

"The Sweet Bye and Bye" (Young) 226

Sweet Charity (lyrics: Fields) 73

"Sweethearts" (Young) 226

The Sweetness of Life (Martínez Sierra and Martínez Sierra) 146

The Sweet Trap (Sofola) 193

Swift, Jonathan 32, 58, 101, 143

Sylvia Plath: An Arrow to the Sun (Yankowitz) 225

Sympathy (Treadwell) 203

Syna, Sy 20

Synge, John Millington 95, 96

T

Taft, William Howard 120

Taggart, Genevieve 93

The Tale of Tales (Petrushevskaya) 171

Tales of the Revolution and Other American Fables (Chambers) 33

Talk of the Devil (O'Malley) 163

The Taming of the Shrew (Shakespeare) 194

Tango Palace (Fornés) 77

Tarbell, Ida 72

A Taste of Honey (Delaney) 60–61

Tate, Claudia 190

Taubman, Howard 61

Taylor, Doris May 133

Teacher's Pet (Kanin and Kanin) 124

Tea (Houston) 109

Tears of Rage (Baizley) 10

Television Theater Award 49

The Temptations 44

Tender Offer (Wasserstein) 215

Tenement Lover (Hagedorn) 97

Ten Little Indians (Christie) 40

Terence (Publius Terentius Afer) 111

Terminal (Yankowitz) 224

Terry, Ellen 186

Terry, Megan xiv, **199–201, 200***f*

The Terry Project (Moore and Rue) 153

Tervapèè, Juhani 220

Tey, Josephine 58

Thames Television award 108

Theanot and Piers in Praise of Astrea (Herbert) 105

theater

    as democratic art form xiii

    experience of ix–x

    racism in American 37

    success in, defining xiii

    unruly atmosphere of, during Restoration xi

Theater Hall of Fame 48

Theater of Action, founding of 135

Theater of Cruelty 84, 165, 199

theater of the grotesque 84

Theater Three Collaborative, founding of 142

Theater World Award 48

Theatre Royal Drury Lane 34, 34*f*

Theatre Union 136

Theatre Workshop 136

theatrician, definition of xiv

Their Eyes Were Watching God (Hurston) 112

Theseus (Tsvetayeva) 206

Thieman, Shirley 86

The Third (Wertenbaker) 217

Third World Women (anthology) 190

Third World Women in the Early 1970s (anthology) 97

This Old Man Comes Rolling Home (Hewett) 106–107

This Week (magazine of *New York Herald Tribune*) 79

Thomas, Gwyn 136

Three Birds Alighting on a Field (Wertenbaker) 217

Three Girls in Blue (Petrushevskaya) 171

Three Lives (Stein) 196

three pieces (Shange) 190

The Three of Us (Crothers) 51

Through the Looking Glass (adaptation: Dane and Addinsell) 55

Tickless Time (Glaspell and Cook) 151

Tilly, John 143

Time and Tide (periodical) 185

time line, of female dramatists xix–xxviii

Tischler, Nancy 188

"Tish" stories 180

Tissue (Page) 167

To Be Young, Gifted and Black (Hansberry) 99

To Die Among Friends (Wandor) 212

Together Tonight, Loving Each Other So Much (Vilalta) 207

Toller, Ernst 212

Tolstoy, Leo 25

Tomlin, Lily 63, 211

Tony. *See* Antoinette Perry Award

Top Girls (Churchill) 40

Topo, Josef 209

Torch, Christopher 202

Tornimparte, Alessandra 90

To Smithereens (Drexler) 62

Touch Wood (Smith) 192

Toussaint (Hansberry) 99

Town and Country magazine 4

The Town Before You (Cowley) 50

Townsend, Sue **202–203**

Toys in the Attic (Hellman) 103

Tracy, Spencer 95

The Tragedie of Mariam, the Fair Queen of Jewry (Cary) 29

The Tragedy of Antonie (translation: Herbert) 105

Tragedy of Tragedies (adaptation: Haywood and Hatchett) 101

"Tramp, Tramp, Tramp" (Young) 226

Transformational theater 199

Transients Welcome (Drexler) xiv, 62, 63

Traveler in the Dark (Norman) 160

Treadwell, Sophie **203–204, 203f**

A Treasury of the Theatre (Gassner) xii

A Tree Grows in Brooklyn (lyrics: Fields) 73

Trensky, Paul 209

The Trial of Thomas Cranmer (Ridler) 179

Trifles (Glaspell) 92

The Triumph of Love and Innocence (Finch) 74

Trotter, Catherine 46, 143, **204–205**

Trotzig, Birgitta 100

Trouble in Mind (Childress) 37

True Dare Kiss (Horsfield) 108

Trumpets of the Lord (adaptation: Carroll) 27

Tsvetayeva, Marina **205–206**

Tune, Tommy 42

Tunner, Jo A. 27

Turkish dramatists 1, 69

Turner, Elaine 57

Tuvin, Judy 48

Twain, Mark 82

The Twelve Brothers Turned into Ravens (Čiurlionien-Kymantaitė) 43

Twilight, Los Angeles (Smith) 191

Two Slatterns and a King (Millay) 151

Twosome Play (Erenus) 69

Typhoid Mary (Gee) 86

U

Ulrike Menihof (Rame and Fo) 177

Unattained Goal (Aspzija) 6

Uncle Vanya (Chekhov) 121

Uncommon Women and Others (Wasserstein) 214

Understudies (Wandor) xii, 212

Unfinished Woman Cry in No Man's Land While a Bird Dies in a Gilded Cage (Rahman) 175

An Unfinished Woman (Hellman) 103

Unga Klara (Swedish children's theater) creation of 164

The Unhappy Father (Leapor) 133

Uranium 235 (MacColl) 136

Urban Arts Corps 27

Urtida Kvinnor (Bergman) 17

V

Vacation from Marriage (Dane) 55

Vaidilla 135

Valois dynasty, and Salic law xi

Vampilov, Aleksandr 171

Vanchu, Anthony J. 171

The Vandaleur's Folly (D'Arcy) 57

The Vanishing Horse (Sagan) 185

Vanity Fair (magazine) 139

Variation on a Theme (Rattigan) 60

Vaudeville, as creative influence 62
Vega Carpio, Lope de
Venus (Parks) 169
The Verge (Glaspell) 92–93
Vernon Rice Drama Desk Award 225
A Very Rich Woman (Gordon) 94
Vesta Award 187
The Vestal (Aspāzija) 6
Les viaducs de la Siene-et-Oise (Duras) 66
Victor, Ed 212
Victory of the Belles (Gerstenberg) 89
Vienuolis, A. 135
Viet Rock (Terry) 200
Vilalta, Maruxa 204, **207–208**
Villa, Pancho 203
Village Voice off-Broadway award 20
The Villa's Adornment (Čiurlionien-Kymantaitė
Villiers, Barbara 143
A Vindication of the Rights of Women (Wollstonecraft)
    142
Vinegar Tom (Churchill) 41–42
Violence, plays depicting x
A Visitor from Charleston (Ritter) 181
Vocations (De Groen) 59
Vogel, Paula **208**
Vogue (magazine) 139
Voices (Griffin) 149
Voices in the Evening (Ginzburg) 90
The Volunteers (Rowson) 182
Vostrá, Alena **208–209**
Vostry, Jaraslav 209
Vyacheslav, Mikhaylovich 296

W

Wagner, Jane **211–212, 211***f*
Wagner, Paula 149
The Wake of Jamey Foster (Henley) 105
Walker, Alice 44, 113
Wallace, Frank 218
The Walls (Gambaro) 84
Walpole, Horace 154
Walsh (Pollock) 174
Walt Disney Studios 14
Wanamaker, Sam 123
The Wandering Jew (adaptation: Wandor and Alfreds)
    212

Wandering Patentee (Wilkinson) 21
Wandor, Michelene xii, 174, **212–213**
Want-Ad (Page) 167
Warren, James 213
Warren, Mercy Otis xii, 182, **213–214**
Warrior (Gee) 86
Wasserstein, Wendy xiv, **214–215, 214***f*
Watching Waiters (Munro) 157
Watch on the Rhine (Hellman) 102–103
Waters, Ethel 148
Watts, Jr., Richard 80
Watts, William 156
The Way of the World (Congreve) 32
The Web (Boesing) 18
Wedding Band (Childress) 38
Wedlock of the Gods (Sofola) 193
Weekend at the Waldorf (Baum) 12
Weicheng (adaptation: Chiang) 36
Weil, Dorothy 182
Weil, Simone 61, 201
Weiss, Hedy 67
Weiss, Judith 93
Weldon, Daniel 216
Weldon, Fay **215–216**
The Well of Lonliness (adaptation: Wandor) 212
Wells, H. G. 8
Wertenbaker, Timberlake **216–218**
Wesley, Richard 190
West, Cheryl L. **218**
West, Cornell 191
West, Mae **218–219, 219***f*
The Western Woman (Jellicoe) 119
Westmacott, Mary 39
Westminster Abbey 14
What Happened (Stein) 196
When Chicago Was Young (Gerstenberg) 89
When I Was a Girl, I Used to Scream and Shout (Mac-
    Donald) 141
White, Walter 98
The White Cockade (Gregory) 95–96
The Whitlings (Burney) 23
Whitney Foundation grant 78
Who Does She Think She Is? (documentary) 63
Whores D'Oeuvres (Wandor) 212
Who's the Dupe? (Cowley) 51
Wide World of Wonder (Brigadere) 22

The Widow (Fornés) 77
A Wife to Be Let (Haywood) 101
A Wife Well Manag'd (Centlivre) 32
Wilcox, Ella Wheeler 81
Wild Decembers (Dane) 55
Wilde, Oscar 174
Wilder, Clinton 200
Wilder, Thornton 195
Wilkerson, Margaret 175
Wilkinson, Tate 21
William of Sens 188
Williams, Margaret 107
Williams, Paulette 189
Williams, Tennessee xiii, 26, 44, 126, 148, 149
The Will Rogers Follies (Comden and Green) 48
Will Shakespeare (Dane) 55
Wilson, Lanford 21
Wilson, Robert 195, 196
Wimsey, Lord Peter (fictional character) 187–188
Windswept Blossoms (Chiang) 36
Wine in the Wilderness (Childress) 38
Winter Place (Lim) 134
Winter Shakers (Norman) 160
The Witch (Aspzija) 6
Witness for the Prosecution (Christie) 40
Woddis, Carol 56
Wolf, Christa 142
Wolfe, Tom 80
The Wolf of Gubbio (Peabody) 170
Wollstonecraft, Mary 116, 142, 170
A Woman's Blues (Hause) 100
The Woman's Journal magazine 170
Womberang (Townsend) 202
women *See also* dramatists; female dramatists.
    of color, paucity of dramatic roles for 26
    common element in ix
    education of 29
    first lyricist to receive Oscar 74
    first magazine by and for 101
    first production company composed of 124
    first professional dramatist 13
    first to enter Songwriters Hall of Fame 74
    first to hold major diplomatic post 139
    first to sit on House Military Affairs Committee 139
    first to write experimental drama 203

inclusion of, in Professional life xii
marginalization of xi
silencing of ix, x
in women's plays xii
The Women (Luce) 138
Women of Achievement in the Arts Award 136
Women's Interart Center 33
Women's Project 225
Women's Theater Council 21, 62, 78, 126, 165, 200
Women's Theatre Festival 212
The Wonder (Centlivre) 32, 46
Wonderful Town (Comden and Green) 48
A Wonderful View (Herrström) 106
The Wooing Birches (Koidula) 128
Woolf, Virginia 8, 13, 15, 30, 47, 63
Woollcott, Alexander 129
Wordsworth, William 74
The Workhouse Ward (Gregory) 95–96
Works Projects Administration Federal Theater 93
Writers Action Group 63
Writer's Franchise League 186
Writer's Guild, female presidents of 124
Writers' Guild Award 33, 61, 211
Writers' League 61
The Writer's Opera (Drexler) 62
Wuolijoki, Hella **220–221, 221f**
Wuolijoki, Suolo 220
Wycherley, William 32
Wymark, Olwen 177

Y

Yale ABC Fellowship in Film Writing 78
Yale School of Drama 224
Yamauchi, Joy 223
Yamauchi, Wakako **223–224**
Yankowitz, Susan **224–225**
Years Ago (Gordon) 94
Years (Moore) 153
Yeats, William Butler 95–96, 142
You Have Come Back (Gallaire-Bourega) 83
Young, Rida Johnson xii, **225–226**
Young, Robert 79
Young, Roland 129
Your Arms Too Short to Box with God (Carroll) 27

Z

Zālīte, Elina **227**
Zapolska, Gabriela 228
Zaudētas tiesības (Aspzija) 6

The Zeal of Thy House (Sayers) 187
Zola, Émile 228
Zuck, Virpi 25